The Royal Arch Of Enoch

The Impact of Masonic Ritual, Philosophy, and Symbolism

by

Robert W. Sullivan IV, Esq.

The Royal Arch of Enoch:

THE IMPACT OF MASONIC RITUAL, PHILOSOPHY, AND SYMBOLISM

by Robert W. Sullivan IV, Esq.

Cover illustrations: (Left) Thoth Hermes Mercurius Trismegistus also known as Hermes the Philosopher; (Right) *The Apotheosis of Washington* ca. 1800.

ISBN: 978-0-692-82271-5

First Edition published 2012-2016.

Second Edition published by **DEADWOOD PUBLISHING, LLC.**, 2016.

This book is dedicated to my mother and father;

without their love, support, and sacrifice,

***The Royal Arch of Enoch* would not have been possible.**

Contents

List of Illustrations

Illustrations contained in chapter text:

CHAPTER XI

- Francis Hopkinson's 1778 fifty dollar colonial note.
- Old Gettysburg College Seal featuring Hermes the Philosopher.
- Jacob's Ladder leading to the Pleiades; the Blue Lodge, a point within a circle, and four goddesses.
- Seal or Coat of Arms College Fraternity Theta Delta Chi.
- Coat of Arms or Seal of Sigma Alpha Epsilon College Fraternity.
- Odd Fellow Seal of California Lodge #1.
- Seal of California Odd Fellow Grand Lodge.
- "Three Times Three" created by Masons to communicate the Royal Arch Word.
- Egyptian goddess Seshat (or Seshet).
- Frontispiece of *Le Soleil Mystique*, 1852.

CHAPTER XII

- Erie Canal Ball Ticket
- Mereworth Castle, England.
- Frontispiece of Dr. John Dee's *General and Rare Memorials pertayning to the Perfect Arte of Navigation*, 1576.
- Engraving of *Hortus Palatinus*.
- Photo of Baltimore, Maryland taken from Federal Hill, 1850.
- Engraving of Solomon's Temple being razed from Martin van Heemskerck's *Septem Orbis Miracula*.
- 1727 image of St. Louis Cathedral of New Orleans.

CHAPTER XIII

- Frontispiece of Johann Valentin Andrae's *Mythologiae Christianae sive virtuous et vitiorum vitae humanae imaginum libri tres*,1619.

CHAPTER XIV

- Frontispiece of Simon Greenleaf's *A Brief Inquiry into the Origin and Principles of Freemasonry*, 1820.
- University of Virginia template engraved by Peter Maverick.

- Seal of University of Virginia.
- The L'Enfant template-street plan of the District of Columbia.
- The Emblem of the Order of the Eastern Star.
- The Joseph Ellicott template for Buffalo, New York.
- Egyptian hieroglyph for Sirius.
- The broken pentagram formed by interconnecting streets over the White House.

CHAPTER XV

- Engraving revealing the riddle of the Third Gate to the Kingdom of Shadows, from the movie *The Ninth Gate*, 1999.

PLATES (Separate Images) not included in Chapter Text:

Plates start on page 560

Plate I: The Priestess Card (#2) of the Major Arcana of the Tarot from the Rider-Waite deck.

Plate II: Oil Painting of an Interior of a Viennese Masonic Lodge - likely Crowned Hope (f/k/a True Harmony) - ca. 1790. Oil Painting, *The Seven Liberal Arts* by Cornelis de Vos, 1590. Hermes or Mercury (the Philosopher-Trismegistus) fountain in the Tom Quad, Christ Church, Oxford University.

Plate III: *Moses* by Michelangelo Buonarroti and *The Adoration of the Golden Calf* by Nicholas Poussin.

Plate IV: Mithras fresco.

Plate V: Jesus Christ within the *Vesica Piscis*. Christian Floor Mosaic of Pisces the Fish. Photo of Pope John Paul II. Floor mosaic in the Vatican grottos featuring Jesus Christ as *Sol Invictus*.

Plate VI: *The Last Supper* by Leonardo Da Vinci.

Plate VII: Zodiac wheel mosaic discovered in the Beit Alpha Synagogue.

Plate VIII: The Royal Arch Irish Jewels and the St. Andrew's Lodge Royal Arch degree certificate (The Hurd Plate).

Plate IX: *The Apotheosis of Washington* engraving by J. J. Barralet.

Plate X: Portrait of Elizabethan Magus Dr. John Dee with autograph (insert).

Plate XI: *The Return of the Holy Family from Egypt* by Nicholas Poussin.

Plate XII: Seal of the Society of Jesus.

Plate XIII: The House of Convocation of the Bodleian Library.

Plate XIV: Seal of the Knights Templar and the arms of the Episcopal Church.

Plate XV: *The Peaceful Reign of James I* by Peter Paul Rubens.

Plate XVI: Masonic George Washington portrait by William J. Williams.

Plate XVII: *The Ancient of Days* by William Blake.

Plate XVIII: The Obverse and Reverse Seals of the United States of America.

Plate XIX: George Washington's chair from the Constitutional Convention, Philadelphia, PA, 1787-1789.

Plate XX: NASA Apollo XIII emblem.

Plate XXI: J. J. Ramée's template for Union College of Schenectady, New York, Union College Minerva Seal, Radcliffe Camera of the Bodleian Library of Oxford University, and the Union College Nott Memorial.

Plate XXII: California State Seal.

Plate XXIII: Postcard featuring Flag and State Seal of Texas.

Plate XXIV: The nave vault in Il Gesu, the Mother Church of the Jesuits and exterior of Il Gesu, Rome.

Plate XXV: The Baltimore Basilica; first Basilica west of the Mississipi dedicated to St. Louis (Louis IX) King of France in St. Louis, Missouri seen beneath the triumphal Gateway to the West arch. The Archdiocese of St. Louis was moved to the Cathedral Basilica of St. Louis. The Baltimore-Washington Monument, Trajan's Column located in Rome, Italy. The Washington Monument obelisk in the District of Columbia.

Plate XXVI: Calverton Estate outside old Baltimore City line.

Plate XXVII: Oil painting titled, *St. Louis - Louis IX of France -*

Burying his Plague-Stricken Troops before Tunis A.D. 1270 by Charles de Steuben.

Plate XXVIII: Federal Triangle, Washington D.C.

Plate XXIX: Solon of Apollo, Versailles, France.

Plate XXX: *The Apotheosis of Washington* by Constantino Brumidi beneath the United States Capitol dome, 1865.

PREFACE

"Yes, sirs, the famous festivals of Ceres at Eleusis, of Isis in Egypt, of Minerva at Athens, of Urania amongst the Phoenicians, of Diana in Scythia were connected with ours. In those places, mysteries were celebrated which concealed many vestiges of the ancient religion of Noah and the Patriarchs."

- Andrew Michael "the Chevalier" Ramsay, *Discourse pronounced at the reception ofFreemasons* (a/k/a Ramsay's Oration), 1737.

"Jewish tradition states that God himself taught Moses his true name and its correct pronunciation at the "burning bush." And they believed that Moses, being thus possessed of the "WORD," used it to perform all his miracles, and to confound and overthrow Pharaoh and his hosts."

- Robert Hewitt Brown, *Stellar Theology and Masonic Astronomy*, 1882.

"....We know that many of the faithful studied and practiced both alchemy and astrology. It is also known that the Qabalah of the Hebrews was also studied, even though the motive exoterically seemed to be that it was a valuable tool with which to convert the unhappy Jews to the joys and blessings of Christendom.

The Catholic Church, and also the Church of the Byzantium, has a glorious history of great mystics, of men and women to whom the highest vocation called, the quest for God. There were teachers of mystical meditation and interior prayer in many of the monasteries so that the proper preparation for such a high calling would not be lost. They were of many persuasions, these teachers, and so were the mystics who came out of these institutions. They have left their mark on the Church, despite its apparent antagonism to mysticism as such, due to fear it might challenge the Church's demand for conformity to fixed inherited dogma."

- Israel Regardie, *The Complete Golden Dawn System of Magic*, 1984.

Freemasonry has long been known to historians for its capacity to influence public affairs. Until recently, however, this was thought simply to be a general shaping of society by individuals impressed with its core principles of liberty and equality: the brotherhood of man and the fatherhood of God. Even more recently it has become abundantly clear that the Masonic tapestry of symbolism is rooted in broader currents of ideas within western science and religion neglected by scholars and historians, yet deeply resonant with major events in civilization. Blue Lodge Masonry, its three degrees of Entered Apprentice, Fellow Craft, and Master Mason, is egalitarian, as such it fundamentally opposes concepts like monarchy and ecclesiastical rule; yet the Masonic high degrees of the Scottish and York Rites embrace ideals such as divine kingship and religiosity, a contradiction. It is the argument of this book that among this contradiction, change, or transition of historical precepts the imagery of Masonic symbolism related to the Biblical patriarch Enoch achieves priority. It is this single set of ceremonies codified into the two prevalent forms of the Royal Arch ceremony, one of which bears his name which is itself a reference to *I Enoch*, of exaltation within the *haute* or high degrees of Freemasonry which define templates of the unfolding of symbolism into material culture. The Royal Arch degree is known as the Royal Arch of Enoch or Solomon in the Scottish Rite, and identified as the Royal Arch of Zerubbabel in the York or American Rite to distinguish itself from the former. This was accomplished through architecture and rhetoric and, in specific, the integration of principles relating to solar emblems transferred into a sphere of public order which defined among other things the *American national character*. In essence, this array of emblems and symbols detail the emergence of the image of the sun as a central form of religiousness from the Ancient Mystery tradition through to the application of Copernicus' scientific heliocentricity dating from 1543 into ideals of personal achievement and national character. The core of the Enochian saga is that lost wisdom was preserved in a secret underground vault or crypt related to an angelic-divine vision by the patriarch who did not die a physical death but who was transported directly into heaven by God. Enoch thus became the paragon of supreme Masonic initiation and his achievement was the preservation of all wisdom and knowledge in the face of a comprehensive flood (of Noah) of re-creation. In Masonic texts and ritual the recovery of the Ark of the Covenant was depicted as the means to this objective as it was deposited between two columns or pillars, not Jachin and Boaz. Upon the Ark was inscribed, on a delta, the ineffable name of God from which all learning could be derived. In time the Ark of the Covenant was transformed into a redolent, rising sun by architects such as Joseph-Jacques Ramée (1764-1842, a friend of Thomas Jefferson) the designer of the campus of Union College in Schenectady, New York, the first college established after the American Revolution and the first civilian institution to teach civil engineering-operative masonry in the United States. This college, in many ways, parallels Christ Church, Oxford University because its pedagogy and research heritage is echoed in its similar material fabric. Fraternal orders other than Freemasonry, notably United States college fraternities and sororities, and Odd Fellowship, took up this concept in various ways.

Odd Fellowship is a fraternal system of ceremonial initiations, broadly reflective of Freemasonry, with a Biblical base. It was founded in October 1810, when 27 men came together to form the Independent Order of Odd Fellows, Manchester Unity, England. Its symbols include specific emblems that Freemasonry uses (i.e. the all-seeing eye), but it has no dominant pervasive thread such as the Masonic emphasis on the building of King Solomon's Temple and the search for the Lost Word of a Master Mason necessary to build it. From Odd Fellows introduction in the United States in Baltimore, Maryland in 1819, the local units spread quickly largely because it had, unlike Freemasonry, a unifying Sovereign Grand Lodge with comprehensive authority and laws conducive to rapid growth. It was an augmented conduit for the application of esoteric emblems to practical life; it paid sick and death benefits and developed a women's branch called The Rebekahs designed to attract and hold family loyalty to the fraternity. Because the Sovereign Grand Lodge met annually in various parts of the nations, men who held multiple fraternal affiliation were in regular contact at local, state, and regional levels. Odd Fellow Schuyler Colfax Jr. (1823-1885), was Speaker of the House of Representatives (1863-1869) and 17th Vice President of the United States (1869-1873) linking the presidential leadership of the Abraham Lincoln (1809-1865), Andrew Johnson (1808

-1875) and Ulysses S. Grant (1822-1885) administrations through his ties with various railroad systems including but not limited to the Central Pacific Railroad and the Illinois Central Railroad. Colfax traveled through the American west instituting Odd Fellow Rebekah Lodges (permitting both female and male membership) which he founded in 1851. Colfax moved from New York City to South Bend, Indiana at an early age which put him in touch with Notre Dame University and the missionary activities of the Holy Cross Fathers with uneven results. The Holy See (Vatican, the Episcopal jurisdiction of the Catholic Church in Rome) condemned Odd Fellow membership while prohibiting Catholics from joining the Knights of Pythias and the Sons of Temperance, the latter being the only lodge in which Abraham Lincoln maintained membership, through its ties with the Notre Dame faculty. Odd Fellow rituals celebrated the pristine period of patriarchal imagery linking the anointment of Abraham to a sequence of so-called higher degrees resonant with Freemasonry. After the American Civil War it created a marching quasi-military order termed the Patriarchs Militant the ritual of which featured the Salem priest king Melchizedek, a figure who was symbolically central to *haute* degree Freemasonry through the rituals of the Order of High Priesthood, a ceremony reserved for Past High Priests of Masonic Royal Arch Chapters and in the Holy Royal Arch Knight Templar Priests, a society linked in England to the emergence of the Masonic Knights Templar. Odd Fellow bodies in England and Scotland became in time insurance societies, a feature which remained minor in the United States. American lodges incorporated substantial emphasis on the human skeleton as an emblem of mortality combined with presence of a hermit figure, a thread which appeared originally in the American Masonic Knight Templar ceremony and was later developed by Justus Henry Rathbone (1839-1889), the founder of the Order of the Knights of Pythias. The emblem of Union College in Schenectady, New York, the Roman goddess of wisdom and magic Minerva, found her way there most likely through the Marian-Isis seal of Columbia University (f/k/a King's College, DeWitt Clinton's Alma Mater) and moved westward through the agency of railroad magnate and tycoon Leland Stanford Sr. (1824-1893) from Watervliet, New York into the seals of an Odd Fellow lodge, California Lodge #1, and the seal of the Odd Fellow Grand Lodge of

California and subsequently onto the state seal of California. Stanford was an Odd Fellow, Freemason, and the founder of Stanford University on the San Francisco peninsula. The state seal of California incorporated emblems which also suggest the Masonic high degrees: a laborer digging towards an underground vault or crypt with a pickax and shovel and the word *Eureka, I have found it*, atop the seal referencing the recovery and restoration of the 47th Proposition of Euclid via the correct pronunciation of the Lost Word of a Master Mason. The result is a set of ordering symbolic features which document the subsistence of the Royal Arch of Enoch emblematized from New York State with reference to higher education and railroad technology into the far west as a recurrent and persistent theme. Like Masonry, Odd Fellowship worked a Royal Arch ceremony termed the Royal Arch of Titus (cf. Titus Flavius Caesar Vespasianus Augustus, 39-81 CE).

These orders, Masonry, Odd Fellowship, and college fraternities and sororities, constituted a mass movement which defined important national values and provided a means for leaders to tap into networks and ideational systems of appeal to the national consciousness. Similarly through Freemasonry in particular the resulting ceremonies appeared on the surface to be conventionally religious both in Christianity in the Knights Templar Grand Encampment in the York or American Rite and in Judaism in the Blue or Craft Lodge echoed through the Free Sons of Israel, and *B'nai B'rith* (Sons of the Covenant). However it is clear from numerous sources that various pagan mythologies and components from the mystery religions survived within an envelope of Christian theology and rationality derived from Renaissance and Enlightenment ideas that merged attempting exposure of this mythology. The Roman Catholic Church in general and the Society of Jesus in specific appears to have appropriated these constricts in a Counter-Reformation ruse, began at the Council of Trent in the sixteenth century, to exchange Thomistic[1] (St. Thomas Aquinas) and Augustinian[2]

1 Thomism is the theology of St. Thomas Aquinas who extended the dualistic nature of the philosophy of Aristotle into Christianity: both the practical and the theoretical. Practical philosophy entailed politics and ethos while theoretical philosophy encompassed logic and physics. Aristotle was a disciple of Plato; the latter taught that knowledge and experience is a priori (Latin for 'from what comes before'): knowledge is independent of experience. Aristotle believed knowledge was a posteriori (Latin for 'from what comes later') knowing is based on experience and tangible empirical evidence. Aquinas' writings and theology borrow heavily from the Neo-Platonic works attributed to Dionysus the Areopagite.

2 Augustine of Hippo (354 – 430 CE) saw the Christian Church as the one unifying factor in the face of

(St. Augustine) theologies for a transformed new age eschatology within which the ideas and philosophies of Christian mystic Joachim of Fiore (ca. 1135-1202) whose theology included a *Third Age of the Holy Spirit* within which a universal monarch, a *Novus Dux* to use von Fiore's own terminology, would rule through a new order of spiritual men. In time this *new age* theology became conflated with Egyptian imagery as an unfolding vista of political and religious order under the general umbrella of papal monarchy. This *Third Age* was to be won by the church only after arduous pilgrimage and great tribulation, like the Israelites marching through the wilderness and crossing the Jordan River into the Promised Land. As guides through this crucial stage, von Fiore prophesied the advent of two new orders of spiritual men, one of hermits to agonize for the world on the mountaintop and one a mediating order to lead men on to the new spiritual plane. As interpreted, the former is the Freemasons in the high degree context; the latter is the Jesuits. The result was the survival of political theories notably of Scots-Irish provenance associated with the Jacobite movement within which rulership was intertwined with critical Masonic devices such as Euclid's 47th Proposition, the Pythagorean Theorem, the emblem of a Masonic Lodge Worshipful Master, and the restoration of a lost yet legitimate monarchy. As such, restoration became associated with antediluvian ideas of the survival of an ideal peaceful or irenic age which survived the redemption of Eve in the Old Testament, and made it possible for the initiated citizen to become as a God; in parallel form to Renaissance humanistic-hermetical ideas of the dignity of man, and to know good from evil through the personal, possession, and correct pronunciation of the Name of God, the "Lost Word of a Master Mason," the Tetragrammaton. The remarkable instance that the saga of Enoch in Masonic rituals and texts predates the discovery in the west of the actual the *Book of Enoch*, *I Enoch*, severely underscores the importance of researching this unique element of intellectual Masonic history and its significance for the culture of the new world's new nation, the United States of America.

The importance of the Masonic-Enochic ritual template to 18th century

the disintegrating Roman Empire. He believed that the grace of Christ was indispensable to human freedom; he framed the concept of original sin which influenced medieval theologies and interpretations of Christian millennialism.

Anglo-American policy can be traced to the ways in which industrial progress was allied with cosmological imagery in commercial and industrial development between the two nations. The failure of Jeffersonian policy with regard to England during the Napoleonic era in specific placed the Democratic Party, termed Jeffersonian Democratic Republicans, on the moral side of the French legacy to the new nation and was cemented with the Louisiana Purchase of 1803-1804 and following with the cession of Florida to the United States by Spain. The War of 1812 strained what was left of the natural cultural linkages surviving from the colonial period and put off for many years the interweaving of social relationships and cultural exchanges with the noted exception of James Smithson's (1764-1829) endowment of the Smithsonian Institution. American Anglicans were ham strung by the rejection of fraternal ties by the Anglican Episcopate and its tethering to the Episcopal Church in Scotland after which its polity was organized. The reorganization and reform of the two English and Welsh Grand Lodges in 1813 under the Duke of Sussex, put together the two rival Masonic ritual workings formerly at odds within Britain, the "Antient" (or Ancient) and "Modern." This merger, in effect, placed the Modern heritage in the policy driver's seat and created a bias in England specifically against the proliferation of French higher degree masonry more in sympathy with the emerging American York Rite which was an extension of the Antient system within which the Royal Arch ceremony of exaltation became the paradigm for subsequent Masonic ritual embroidery, which in turn, philosophically and symbolically abandoned English, Modern Craft Blue Lodge Masonry. By contrast English Masonry required that the Royal Arch ethos, echo the official leadership of the English Grand Lodge and its locally designed chapters to work only as a mere adjunct to English craft lodges. The English Grand Master was temperamentally opposed to the *haute* degrees of Freemasonry although being intimately aware of their continental significance and importance. The result was that the high degree culture in the United States developed, as a cognate of English Antient culture, in tandem with the "Catholic" higher degrees and their structure such that national organizations such as the General Grand Chapter of Royal Arch Masons, the Grand Encampment of Knights Templar and the two Supreme Councils of the Ancient and Accepted Scottish Rite (Northern and Southern Jurisdictions) developed rapidly as regular Masonic Grand Lodges remained state by state entities with limited policy responsibility or capacity. In England, there is no prohibition against joining the Scottish Rite; however in the United States the Scottish Rite is officially recognized by state Grand Lodges as an extension of the degrees of Craft Freemasonry. A few Grand Lodges notably those of Massachusetts and New York came to operate overseas lodges and New York and Louisiana in particular came to host lodges working in foreign languages identified with ethnic migration. The initiatic dynamic of the Enoch concept of restored antediluvian wisdom derived from the correct pronunciation of the restored and formerly Lost Word of Master Mason came to appeal to the fissiparous quality of a divided system of state grand lodges and the requirements of a national system of influential senior grades of ritual elements. During the American Civil War the Southern Jurisdiction of the Scottish Rite in specific established lineages globally with other such bodies in Europe notably in France, Ireland, and in England and Wales. This entity emerged as the Mother Supreme Council of the World with Albert Pike (1809-1891) as its Grand Commander. Pike is the author of the voluminous *Morals and Dogma of the Ancient and Accepted Scottish Rite of Freemasonry* published in 1871. Pike's book documents the solar, stellar, and astrological symbolism and iconography transported into high degree Scottish Rite Freemasonry from the Ancient Mystery Religions. Pike's work was heavily influenced, plagiarized verbatim in some parts, by the writings of French Freemason, Platonist, and transcendentalist magician Eliphas Levi (1810-1875).

Thus the Royal Arch of Enoch Masonic ceremony was uniquely suited for reference, both in material culture and in public rhetoric as a device to establish a public ethic of progressive restoration of values perceived to be ancient and conservative yet innovative. The result was the establishment of a public sphere of civic morality well suited to transcend partisan striving. New York Governor DeWitt Clinton was the central engineer of this method of integrating ritual rhetoric with public works notably in the construction of the New York State Erie Canal which opened transatlantic navigation to the interior waterways of the new Republic. In Freemasonry, he was instrumental in the creation of two networks of Masonic higher degrees and orders: the General Grand Chapter of Royal Arch Masons and the Grand Encampment of Knights Templar which carried the individual's path of Masonic initiation into a public pathway of civic leadership. This path can be traced directly to the ordering of emblems on two sides of the Atlantic from 1790 to 1800. One set of emblems from Dublin, Ireland, the Irish Jewels, to Boston, Massachusetts, the Royal Arch degree certificate, the "Hurd Plate" issued by St. Andrew's Lodge. The St. Andrew's Hurd Plate design demonstrates the step by step movement both of the individual and of the United States into mystical solar influenced order with reference to the Pillars of Enoch upon which were inscribed all of ancient antediluvian learning including Euclid's 47th Proposition. The result was an initiative template available for reference by DeWitt Clinton and his circle as a means to carry forward a national Masonic mission following the transformation of George Washington from Revolutionary War hero into the *Masonic Father of the Nation*. This was in turn achieved via the Thomas Smith Webb *Masonic Monitor* elucidated in the further augmentation of Royal Arch emblemature in the Royal Arch of Enoch ritual or ceremony. This ceremony came to be incorporated in the evolution of the Lodge of Perfection in the Scottish Rite. This ceremony was summarized in T. S. Webb's ceremonial (*Monitor* or *Illustrations*) and in addition to the Royal Arch degree certificate, the Hurd Plate, combined a line of ritual based language easily adaptable to executive, legislative, and judicial implementation in the new republic as a bridge between formal governmental operation and the moral universe of the informed citizen. The transformation of Masonic ceremonial, from one set of emblems to another, took place precisely at the pinpoint of the restructuring of Freemasonry in America to accommodate the necessity of a post-Revolutionary building of the new nation including the December 1799 death of George Washington, a close friend of the Clinton family. This pathway also describes important developments in the Jeffersonian epoch of American politics when religiosity was reconstrued in terms of a nonconfessional ordering of mystical and rational values necessary for the establishment of public morality, to take the place of established churches. DeWitt Clinton's system also devolved from this template into craft lodge, Royal Arch Chapter, and Knight Templar Commanderies, duly chartered, which proliferated as the nation moved westward along the frontier. Careful analysis of this system which came later to be termed the York or American Rite reveals the infrastructure of a nuanced network of emergent solar order calibrated carefully to integrate scientific discovery with confessional Christianity. Thereby the Clintonian initiatic pathway resembled Christianity on its surface but delved much more deeply into the principal current of Enlightenment and Renaissance philosophy to interlink heliocentric, hermetical, cabalistic, and Neo-Platonic streams of ideas and philosophies to establish a more compliant approach to the integration of foreign and domestic statecraft to pluralism. The result was a system of symbolic religiousness designed to work hand in glove with the various churches but in effect to make of religious denominations an extension of Masonic lodge activity. This was uniquely true in the borrowing of the symbolism of the Anglican Church in the creation of local Masonic Knight Templar Commanderies which became de facto extensions of Episcopal Church ethos and hierarchy.

It was in specific the integration of mathematically nuanced rationality and mysticism associated with the Greek philosopher Pythagoras combined with the pomp and ceremonial of medieval chivalry that defined Platonian religiosity and provided an altering effect whereby Masonic ritual came to appear publicly as conventional Biblical imagery but in fact pointed to much deeper reservoirs of policy related intellect. The legendary histories of Freemasonry provided troves of dynamic symbolism that were conflated from the material associated with the medieval Gothic Manuscripts and other early Masonic documents which were written to govern guilds of stonemasons and to provide a spiritual and a symbolic link between the process of medieval construction methods and the Catholic Church. These manuscripts became the basis of what became the *Constitutions of the Free-Masons* published in 1723, revised in 1738, documenting the pervasive influence of Geometry; this meant something akin to political theory applied as a science of symbolic craftsmanship which underlay material engineering, construction, and statecraft related to nation building. As such it provided the conceptual means to integrate mysticism with practical politics and statecraft; an alliance which came to be associated with European Masonry as it was co-mingled with the Illuminati occult tradition began on 1 May

1776 by Freemason Adam "Spartacus" Weishaupt (1748-1830). Such a configuration was uniquely suited to the dynamic emblemature of the Royal Arch of Enoch degree ceremonial precisely because it bridged the legends of geometric mysticality with the legend that the medieval Order of Knights Templar who, during the Crusades, allegedly located the Vault of Enoch under the traditional site of King Solomon's Temple itself derived from the Biblical text discussing the threshing floor of Ornan the Jebusite. The identification of geometry was understood this way: as a form of mystical political science with rulership in general and virtuous monarchy in specific that in turn provided masons like DeWitt Clinton to carry forward a policy rhetorical device linking the ideal of Solomonic kingship as a paragon for wise elective leadership after the death of President Washington.

George Washington's symbolic transformation into Enoch was itself depicted in the funeral oration of Jean-Simon Chaudron shortly after Washington's death and the related engraving by J. J. Barralet of the Great Man, the Masonic Godfather of the New Nation, being lifted up in corporeal form by angelic beings into heaven, an allusion to the Biblical record which said that Enoch did not die. The perfection of the initiate as a perfected citizen was presaged in Masonic ritual construed by Clinton and the Clintonians to erect a public sphere through which objectives might be achieved without rancor or partisan division. Local Masonic units became, as a result, strategically emplaced centers of practical and moral support for a fresh vision of the republic distinct from European monarchy and clericalism yet with adroitly concealed references to both of these streams of ideas within the folds of a democratic Masonic Republic: the United States of America, with the District of Columbia, *the City of the Sun,* as its capital city.

INTRODUCTION

"And, no doubt, the Royal Art was brought down to *Egypt* by MITZRAIM, the second Son of *Ham*, after about six Years after the Confusion at *Babel*, and after the *Flood* 160 Years, when he led thither his Colony; (for *Egypt* is *Mitzraim* in *Hebrew*) because we find the River *Nile's* overflowing it Banks, soon caus'd an Improvement in *Geometry*, which consequently brought Masonry much in request: For the ancient noble Cities, with the other magnificent Edifices of that Country, and particularly the *famous* PYRAMIDS, demonstrate the early Taste and Genius of that ancient Kingdom. Nay, one of those *Egyptian* PYRAMIDS is reckon'd the *First* of the *Seven Wonders* of the World, the Account of which, by Historians and Travellers, is almost incredible."
- Dr. James Anderson, *The Constitutions of the Free-Masons,* 1723.

"The Occult Science of the Ancient Magi was concealed under the shadows of the Ancient Mysteries: it was imperfectly revealed or rather disfigured by the Gnostics: it was guessed at under the obscurities that cover the pretend crimes of the Templars; and it is found enveloped in enigmas that seem impenetrable, in the Rites of the Highest Masonry."
- Albert Pike, *Morals and Dogma of the Scottish Rite*, 1871.

"Then again, Pythagoras showed that a right angle can be formed without the contrivances of the artisan. Thus, the result which carpenters reach very laboriously, but scarcely to exactness, with their squares, can be demonstrated to perfection from the reasoning and methods of its teaching."
- Vitruvius, *De Archtectura,* (Book IX, Introduction,VI), ca. 15 BCE.

The *Book of Enoch*, or *I Enoch*, is a Hebrew text left out of the Bible nor is it part of the Hebrew Canon of Scripture. Nevertheless, it was considered Holy Scripture by second and third century Christian church fathers; it became discredited after the Council of Laodicea of 363-364 CE, that restricted church readings to only the canonical books of the Old and New Testaments. The *Book of Enoch* dates from approximately 350 BCE, and details the journey of the Biblical patriarch Enoch as he was lifted into heaven in corporeal form by God at Genesis 5:24. Enoch, the great grandfather of Noah, is imparted celestial and divine secrets by God's Archangels, namely Michael, Uriel, Gabriel, and Raphael, the latter instructs Enoch in Kabbalah. Enoch also learns of a group of fallen or demonic angels known as the Watchers who have displeased God by siring a race of beings known as the Nephilim (Genesis 6:4 and Numbers 13:33) by mating with human women. Further, these 200 fallen angels have taught mankind forbidden knowledge such as the art of warcraft, the making of enchantments, and astrology. Enoch serves as an intermediary between the two angelic groups. "The fallen Angels were also fallen Stars; and the first allusion to a feud among the spiritual powers in early Hebrew Mythology, where Rahab and his confederates are defeated, like the Titans in a battle against the gods, seems to identify the rebellious Spirits as part of the visible Heavens, where the 'high ones on high' are punished or chained, as a signal proof of God's power and justice."[3] The esoteric knowledge and experiences that Enoch gleans from his interaction with the two angelic groups, good and evil, in turn parallels King Solomon's use and control of demons and satanic angels to construct God's first temple as detailed and described in the *Testament of Solomon*; the sorcery King Solomon used to control and disperse these evil beings can be found in a grimiore called *The Lesser Key of Solomon* (a/k/a *Ars Goetia,* a/k/a *Lemegeton*). *Ars Goetia* documents the occult rituals, incantations, and rites that a sorcerer can perform in order to conjure one of seventy-two specific demons. The identities of some of these demons are Vassago, Barbas, Beleth, Zepar, Furfur, Marax, Sabnock, and Ronoue. Each of the seventy-two demons in *Ars Goetia* has a unique sigil as well as a diabolical skill set. *Ars Goetia* aside, *I Enoch* documents that while in

3 Pike, Albert, *Morals and Dogma of the Ancient and Accepted Scottish Rite,* page 510.

heaven Enoch beholds the Hebrew Kabbalah, the *Sephirotic Tree of Life,* as an emanation of the name (or names) of God; God himself: the symbolic source of all knowledge. It is also explained to Enoch that the sun is the premiere luminary and the source of all divine *Light.* According to the Old Testament Enoch does not die a physical death as he was taken by God; however *I Enoch* clearly details what Enoch saw in heaven suggesting he returned to earth at some point to create a record of his vision,

> "And he began his story saying: Enoch a righteous man,
> whose eyes were opened by God, saw the vision of
> the Holy One in heaven, which the angels showed me,
> and I heard everything from them, and I saw and
> understood, but it was not for this generation, but
> for a remote one which is to come."[4]

Thus upon returning to earth, according to Masonic legend and philosophy, Enoch inscribed the heavenly and celestial knowledge he received onto two pillars, including the art of writing with ink and paper, in order to preserve this wisdom in the face of destruction of mankind by way of the deluge of Noah. Enoch concealed these Pillars and the name of God in an underground vault to save this knowledge for future generations in the wake of Noah's destructive flood. This is mentioned in The Constitutions of the Free-Masons of 1723, revised 1738, by Dr. James Anderson. However, the *Book of Enoch* was lost to history from approximately 2-3 CE to 1773 until when copies were discovered in Ethiopia by traveler James Bruce. These copies were unused until the nineteenth century; it was not translated into English until 1821 by Richard Laurence at the Bodleian Library at Oxford University. Despite this it is clear that Masonic High Degree ritual and philosophy, a Masonic theology, developed out of the 1737 Oration of Andrew Michael "the Chevalier" Ramsay. Ramsay, a Roman Catholic convert and member of the Royal Society, claimed in his famous Oration that Masonry descended from the Knights Templar; Ramsay also mentions the Vault of Enoch, its two Pillars upon which was inscribed the knowledge taught to Enoch during his heavenly visitation. One of these higher or

4 *I Enoch*, 1:2

further degrees, developed from Ramsay's Oration, contains elements and ideologies from *I Enoch*; a historical anomaly because *I Enoch* was not known to the world until well after the formulation of the Masonic *haute* degrees. These Enochic components can be found in the high degree ritual known as the Royal Arch; in the Thomas Smith Webb ritual synthesis this is the premier degree in all of Freemasonry. Bernard E. Jones, in his *Freemasons' Book of the Royal Arch* (1957), writes,

> "The legends incorporated in the English, Irish, and Scottish Rites are not the only ones by any means. The many variants cannot be given here (they belong to more certain additional degrees), but reference may be made to a vision of Enoch, father of Methuselah and author of a Biblical book, which is known in a considerable number of versions. A.E. Waite, in a paper read before the Somerset Masters' Lodge in 1921, speaks of 'The Book of Enoch,' said by him to be a series of visions beheld 'by the Prophet when he was in the spirit ... a prototype of Masonic tradition ... especially reflected in the Royal Arch. It is said that God showed Enoch nine vaults in a vision, and that, with the assistance of Methuselah, his son, he proceeded to erect in the bosom of the mountain of Canaan a secret sanctuary, on the plan of which he had beheld, being vaults beneath one another. In the ninth, or undermost, Enoch placed a triangle of purest gold, on which he had inscribed that which was presumably the heart, essence and centre of the Sacred Tradition, the True Name of God.'
>
> Later in the paper the author refers 'to the Royal Arch of Enoch or Knight of the Royal Arch, two titles and two forms, the second being incorporated into the long series of the Scottish Rite.'"[5]

Ramsay's Oration birthed Masonic chivalric high degrees, originally developed in France, known as the Rite of Perfection in 1754. This rite was midwifed into the United States via the West Indies from France and a Rite of Perfection was established in Albany, New York in 1767 under the aegis of Henry A. Francken. This rite served as the template and basis for not only the Scottish Rite (both Southern and Northern Jurisdictions), but also

5 Jones, Bernard E., *Freemasons' Book of the Royal Arch*, page 130.

influenced Thomas Smith Webb's York or American Rite. As the Royal Arch degree developed, not only in France and America but also Great Britain, the theme of the Royal Arch ceremony, some with Enoch, others without, essentially remained the same. That is, in this further or higher degree, the candidate symbolically discovers the treasure of Masonry by beholding the name of God, the Tetragrammaton, on a golden delta placed upon the Ark of the Covenant concealed beneath nine arches in an underground vault. It is from the correct pronunciation of the Tetragrammaton, the Lost Word of a Master Mason that the restoration of all knowledge, inscribed on Enoch's Pillars, is made possible. The knowledge encoded on these Pillars, alluded to in the *Old Charges* collected and assembled by Dr. Desaguliers, Anderson's *Constitutions* of 1723, 1738, and directly referred to in Ramsay's Oration of 1737, is the wisdom imparted to Enoch while in heaven by Archangels and the evil Watchers as described in *I Enoch*. Yet, Freemasonic literature has already documented some of this information as early as the Masonic *Constitutions* of 1723 and elaborated and detailed and propagated further by the Chevalier Ramsay in 1737; thus a historical anomaly or paradox is presented. Masonic ritual parallels Enoch's visions in heaven where he beholds the Kabbalah, its Sephirot, as the source of all Godly knowledge and wisdom as part of the Hebrew Mysteries as stated in *I Enoch*, discovered in Ethiopia by Bruce in 1773, translated into English in1821, *yet incorporated into Masonic Ritual, the Holy Royal Arch, as part of a Rite of Perfection in France circa 1754*. In the United States the Rite of Perfection and the Royal Arch ceremonial was established in Albany, New York, by Henry A. Francken in 1767; this in time became the Scottish Rite founded in 1801 in Charleston, South Carolina. Like the earlier Rite of Perfection (French and Albany, New York equivalent) the Holy Royal Arch was incorporated into the Scottish Rite degrees, the 13th degree, Southern and Northern Jurisdiction, as the Royal Arch of Enoch[6] integrating components of *I Enoch* and thereby presenting a historical, unsolved, and unique mystery as part of intellectual history. The Royal Arch ceremonial is the 7th degree in the York Rite of T.S. Webb and DeWitt Clinton.

6 Known as the Knight of the Ninth Arch in the Scottish Rite, Northern Jurisdiction.

The name of God or the *Word of a Master Mason* is lost in the third degree ritual of Craft Lodge Masonry upon the death of Hiram Abif, the architect of Solomon's Temple. The identification of the ineffable Name of God with the lost and recovered Masonic Word derived from the symbolic and narrative device within Masonic ritual that the building of the Temple of Solomon required the daily confabulation of King Solomon, Hiram King of Tyre, and Hiram Abif to lay designs upon the trestleboard for the diurnal construction of the edifice. The evidence for this device is made explicit in English and other Masonic rituals which have been subjected to exposé now clearly in the scholarly and public domain. Yet, it is the equivalency between this Word which was deemed unpronounceable, lost, after Abif's death became linked with the Ark of the Covenant as further explained in various versions of the Exaltation Ceremony of the Holy Royal Arch degree. As will be seen, the recovery of the Lost Word, symbolically restored in the Royal Arch liturgy, became synonymous and intertwined with the sun, the latter being the most important symbol in all of Freemasonry.

The Royal Arch degree in the United States became a predominant and premiere source of philosophy and ideology that helped define the United States shortly after the Revolution of 1775-1783. Masonic Royal Arch ethos can be found in the architecture, cityscapes, policy formation, material culture, and rhetoric of the United States as the new nation became a beacon of New World democracy, the manifestation of liberty and egalitarianism as embodied in the teachings and philosophies of the Masonic Temple. On that it must be stated that Freemasonry embraces, if not encourages, Deism: the belief, faith in God, a Supreme Being, the Great Architect of the Universe, the Ancient of Days; Masonry is not a religion. Belief in God is faith, the purest, noblest celebration and worship of divinity; beliefs surrounding the personality of Deity are religion. The Founding Fathers of the United States, Washington, Adams, Jefferson, Franklin, Paine, etc., were enlightened deists, not Christians, as commonly thought. Deism implies a kind of practicalism in public affairs and government which first becomes evident in the role of the new educated urban classes of urban England.[7] Whereas the medieval state took a view only to the preservation of order; the Renaissance

7 Ferguson, Arthur B., The Articulate Citizen and the English Renaissance, pages 402-409.

Tudor State, and the State during the deistic era of the 18th Century presumed that educated, affluent elites would be par excellence active and informed citizens. Because deism was the de facto "religion" of the Founding Fathers,[8] we are accustomed to thinking of it as a backdrop for both the American Revolution of 1776, and the French Revolution of 1789. Masonry also incorporates elements of Universalism: in the religious context Universalism claims that religion or religious man is a universal quality; a tenet of the Universalist is the ultimate redemption of evil. Nevertheless religions, such as the Abrahamic Faiths, contain their own unique mysteries. As will be discussed in Chapter III these religious esoteric mysteries or truths were not to be disseminated to the lay practitioner but were reserved for the initiated few. These truths are veiled in symbolic allegory; once these religious symbols are properly interpreted and understood the initiatic will avail himself or herself to a higher Godhead. Although generally not the rule, women were occasionally admitted to the Ancient Mysteries often resulting with great disdain and tragedy. Hypatia of Alexandria (ca. 365-415 CE), the most wise female Pythagorean initiate, Neo-Platonist, teacher of mathematics, philosophy, and astronomy was skinned alive with oyster shells by a Christian mob who then burned her body at the behest of St. Cyril of Alexandria (ca. 376-444). The teachings that religions were astrological, esoteric allegory was the modus operandi of the Ancient Mysteries; again, the secrets imparted only to the initiated few and not to be divulged to the profane: a word popularized by Freemasons such as Albert Pike to describe the ignorant and uninitiated.

To better understand the importance of solar iconography in Masonry, especially in the Craft or Blue Lodge, the first three degrees of Masonry, and the Royal Arch high degree, the nexus between church canon law and the Masonic *Constitutions* of 1723 and 1738; the 1723 edition published in America by Dr. Benjamin Franklin in 1734 (reprint of 1723), must be explored. *The Constitutions of Free-Masons* in turn set the parameters of Masonic Law, which, in the context of the United States, would help define not only masonry but New World American jurisprudence. This is important if one is to understand the high degrees of Masonry, its ideology

8 Commager, Henry Steele, *The Empire of Reason*, p. 43 ff.

or even theology, developed in France derived from Ramsay's Oration. *The Constitutions of Free-Masons* were developed after the formation of the Premiere Grand Lodge of London and Westminster on 24 June 1717, three days after the summer solstice of June 21st. At its foundation, canon law is designed to address the issue of governance of the Church and its members in the absence of the *Parousia*, the second coming of Jesus Christ. Its core premise is that such governance and its polity, or ecclesiology, is necessary in order to advance the end purpose of the Kingdom of God and therefore the entire mission of the Church. As such it reduces the mystical, or more technically the numinous (i.e. supernatural, quasi-mystical rationality) element in faith to codification and process. Further it relates directly to what is perceived to be the private life of the individual and to the collective lives of the Church's members. Freemasonry took up this dynamic as a direct parallel to the Church for specific purposes relative to the institutional administration of a voluntary society and to the moral behavior of its members. From the period of the Henrician Settlement (1535), Anglican canon law developed uniquely as the law of the realm because the parliament of the nation became the chief judicatory of the Church. The Act of Supremacy of 1535 successively framed and defined ecclesiastical law as an extension of common law and statutory process as a moral mission. In the same way that the foundation of the Premier Grand Lodge framed and defined Masonic practice, its *Constitutions*, at the organization and personal level.

An important element of comprehending the Masonic *Constitutions* as canon law relates to the ways in which Claudius Ptolemy, the Egypto-Roman (who wrote in Greek) cosmographer, mathematician, astrologer, and astronomer (Claudius Ptolemy held the earth was the center of the universe) was utilized by Nicolaus Copernicus and others of his contemporaries to create a new heliocentric religion through the reworking of imperial power as a pantheistic suffusion of nature as an expression of Egyptian mythology understood at different levels. Copernicus thought the sun's central position was implied by Hermetic philosophy going back to the time of Moses; Hermes the Philosopher described the sun as the visible and second

God.[9] In the Masonic *Constitutions*, three Ptolemies are conflated with one another: Ptolemy I Soter who established the Ptolemic Dynasty in Egypt after Alexander the Great and founded the Library of Alexandria as the great source of enlightenment, his son Ptolemy Philadelphus the second Ptolemic King of Egypt, and Claudius Ptolemy the Astronomer-Mathematician.[10] This parallels the Renaissance tradition of intertwining Hermes the Philosopher also known as Hermes Mercurius Trismegistus (himself a combination of three gods) with the Biblical patriarch Moses into one persona. Freemasonry took up this idea, a heliocentric theology, at Oxford University in general and Christ Church specifically through Huguenot enthusiasm for modernity rooted in Calvinist ecclesiology and Newtonian Science in the career of Christ Church fellow Dr. John Theophilus Desaguliers (1683-1744) and his English Presbyterian colleague Dr. James Anderson (1679/1680-1739) through the inter-linkage between Masonic Law and traditional legendary history in which Pythagoras, Euclid, the three Ptolemies, and even Charles Martell were deemed forerunners of modern day Freemasons as contained in their *Constitutions of Free-Masonry*. As a result, the great discoveries of the 1540s, including Andreas Vesalius' (1514-1564) work on vascular and circulatory systems, Gerolamo Cardano's (1501-1576) work on algebra, Girolamo Fracastoro's (1478-1553) articulation of germ theory, were published and established at precisely the point Anglican political theory was defined at the Henrician Settlement creating the Church of England with the English Sovereign as its de facto Pope. This political theory would, in time, come to incorporate elements of John Fortesque's (ca. 1394-1476) *De Laudibus Legum Angliae*, first published during the reign of Henry VIII; Archbishop of Canterbury Matthew Parker's (1504-1575) *Thirty-nine Articles of Religion* of 1563 that attempted to reconcile Calvinism with Catholicism; and Richard Hooker's (1554-1600), *Of the Lawes of Ecclesiastical Politie*, which outlined Anglican philosophy published in 1594. As such the capacity to balance the rational with the numinous lay at the heart of Anglicanism and generally can be traced to the

9 Churton, Tobias, *The Invisible History of the Rosicrucians*, page 39.

10 In the *Constitutions of Free-Masons* Dr. James Anderson combines Ptolemy Philadelphus with Ptolemy the Astronomer by stating that Ptolemy Philadelphus was a "great Improver of liberal art and of all useful knowledge" a direct reference to Ptolemy the Astrologer-Geographer-Mathematician and not Philadelphus. See *Constitutions of Free-Masons*, Drs. Anderson and Franklin (1734, reprint of the *Constitutions* of 1723), page 23.

survival of royal political theory in the doctrine of the king's two bodies as a representative of the spiritual and material bodies of Jesus Christ in the doctrine of the incarnation. By the time of Henry VIII this doctrine had been developed in the work of John Fortescue whose work *De Laudibus Legum Angliae* positioned the divine majesty of the king as being enhanced by his conciliar, advised and assisted by council and not ruling by dictatorial whims, activity in governance; thus, *the king never sits so high as when he sits in council*. Such a concept can be traced to the application of the law as both a social and philosophical current rooted in cosmological concepts of harmony and celestial order. This political theory was tested by the Calvinist zeal during the reign of Edward VI, and after setback stemming from the reign of Bloody Mary Tudor, it was institutionalized in the Elizabethan marriage of hermetical, occult, kabbalistic-cabalistic, and Neo-Platonic idealism and symbolism through an alliance between court culture and imperial policy in which learning assumed both empirical and esoteric missiologies. This esoteric policy formulation is clearly echoed in the works of Dr. John Dee, the Virgin Queen's court astrologer. It can also be found in Edmund Spenser's *The Faerie Queene* (the first half published in 1590, the second half published in 1596) where the Church of England is transformed into a Cabalistic Temple. Such events positioned a *new religion* of heliocentric imperial power through enterprise, Lockean political theory and Newtonian physics as *the religion of modernity*. As such Masonic Law became an embryo of world civilization though which a scarce few in the 18th century grasped the enormity of its dynamic and ultimate consequences: the development of a Masonic Republic, the United States of America. The English Glorious Revolution of 1688 made it clear that the new Constitution including its attendant Bill of Rights of 1689[11] must carry law making and its practice beyond efforts of the Tudor Commonwealth to extend the mystique of monarchy into a mere extension of the royal supremacy, however nuanced and modified. This idea, which Fortescue put squarely, was that the king's majesty was enhanced by his

11 The Bill of Rights was passed by Parliament on 16 December 1689. It was a re-statement in statutory form of the Declaration of Right presented by the Convention Parliament to William and Mary in March 1689 (or 1688 by Old Style dating), inviting them to become joint sovereigns of England. It lays down limits on the powers of sovereign and sets out the rights of Parliament and rules for freedom of speech in Parliament, the requirement to regular elections to Parliament and the right to petition the monarch without fear of retribution.

conciliar function and further that medieval notions of chivalry, reworked according to Renaissance ideals, might make up for constitutional stresses through a robust if subtle judicious working of rationality. Taken together, Thomas Elyot's *Boke named the Governour* (1531) and Richard Hooker's *Of the Lawes of Ecclesiastical Politie* pressed this concept to its breaking point. The Puritan mindset in specific was adversely animated by a profound rejection of such subjectivity working within the class system and moved aggressively into Calvinist holy commonwealth making until it played out into extremes rejected wholesale by the nation at the Restoration.

It is likely that Martin Luther's (1483-1546), the initiator of the Protestant Reformation, abiding mistrust of imperial power and his reliance upon local and regional Protestant sovereigns for the governance of the Church along Pauline and Augustinian lines, was that he understood that the inevitable thrust of a Counter-Reformation would equip itself, albeit with halts, starts, and disingenuity; with the power of a new demonology over which, in his poetic term *The Prince of Darkness-Grim*, would rule. The etiology of this rule can indeed be seen in Tridentate (Council of Trent) initiatives to restore papal monarchy as a universal referent through the Catholic alliance with Baroque culture, notably in the aesthetics of the Jesuit Order's doctrine of a new spiritual class of monks dedicated to the eradication of heresy and the triumph through Egyptianate-Christianity of a world spiritual order. The equipage for this maneuver came to include a marriage between the subsequent Masonic vista of a vast global lodge, *a New World Order*, dedicated to a new science and to a solar hegemonic brotherhood within which power was suffused through the diffusion, metaphorically, of *Light* with the endgame resulting in a deistic one world government ruled by an occult theocracy, as articulated by the Bavarian Illuminati (a/k/a the Perfectibilists) of 1776. This idea was to be accomplished by *any means necessary* to use Adam Weishaupt's own terminology. The linkages between Masonic initiatic metaphor enshrined in the codifications of the *Constitutions* of 1723 and 1738 adroitly suited the Jesuit cooption of the millennial theory of Christian mystic Joachim of Fiore whose prophecies included a *Third Age of the Holy Spirit* within which a universal monarch would rule through *two new orders of spiritual men*. Copernican theory provided the means to affect such a layered strategy again notwithstanding papal condemnations of Giordano Bruno and Galileo whose work was deemed to be dangerously premature and undisciplined in terms of the perceived destiny of Catholic eclectic political theology. It is further likely that Wolfgang Amadeus Mozart's (1756-1791) celebration of such a numinous solar age within *Die Zauberflote* (*The Magic Flute*, 1791) did not find favor amongst Freemasons of his day precisely because of its accuracy as a hymn to a new brotherly order of universal harmony which was in reality a fresh articulation of solar autocracy within which political heterogeneity was managed as a means to an end to make democracy and liberty de facto tools of Masonic tyranny at a spiritual and arguable political level. In other words, the celebration and institutionalization of democracy and liberty is the celebration of Masonic absolutism and oligarchy as liberty, democracy, and Craft Lodge Freemasonry have always walked hand in hand. They are inseparable. Alternatively, countries and governments that have suppressed Freemasonry have degraded into backwardness and political idiocy such as Nazi Germany and Communist Russia.

The Platonic (and Neo-Platonic) hierarchies of Elizabethan court life survived at Oxford University and within Freemasonry through solar symbolism of hermetical radiance articulated both by Edmund Spenser and Thomas Elyot in complementary rhetorics of citizenship rooted in imperial glory. This rhetoric found its way into Freemasonry through the revived interest in chivalry among civic leaders and the nobility and eventually became enshrined in the Pre-Raphaelite celebration of Arthurian destiny and the works of Sir Walter Scott derived conceptually from the Irish writer Maria Edgeworth. At Christ Church, Oxford, the mystique of empire was carefully cultivated simultaneously with Newtonianism as two sides of the same coin. Various Viceroys and Governor-Generals were products of the house as were colonial missionaries, clergy and bishops deployed to shape and define the Anglican Communion as a mirror of the British Empire *at prayer*. Similarly, lodges were introduced into a variety of colonial settlements, most fatefully in America, where Freemasonry took on a new definition becoming a strong arm of the American Revolution, more aptly a civil war of two radically similar elites with divergent loyalties, the

Antients versus the Moderns. The American Masonic ethos, in particular, came to view Irish and French Freemasonry, the former a cognate order from Scotland, as a patriotic fraternity devoted to real equality as an elite ideology rooted in patriotic values independent from the Monarchy yet, importantly, bearing its own fruit of civic religiosity in a theological context dominated by rival denominations.

The reworking of pagan mythology together with Isaac Newton's heliocentrism provided lawyers and lawmakers both within the Church of England and without a means to conflate and integrate their view of Christianity *not mysterious* to reference John Toland's phrase, with the new empiricism of John Locke (1632-1704) and his French counterpart, Rene Descartes (1596-1650). This approach inserted mathematics both as a symbol and as a method as an ally of lawmaking by exalting the quantitative and laying groundwork for the alliance between utilitarianism and social justice as it triumphed in the axiom, "the greatest good for the greatest number," of Jeremy Bentham (1748-1832) and later John Stuart Mill (1806 -1873). Indeed, *number* was a convenient means to link social approaches to the application of justice through a new approach to polity which enabled Masonic constitutional process as a de facto ecclesiology within which society was deemed an extension of the lodge through a process of cultural illumination. In England, this process rejected the various continental reworking of English Masonry to fit absolutism which took both Jacobite, absolutist, and Enlightenment views; the formers becoming the seedbed for the rich lore of Masonic *haute* grades ritualizing and in the latter the ideas of French philosophers Voltaire (1694-1778), Montesquieu (1689-1755, not a mason), and Claude Adrien Helvetius (1715-1771). This idiom found realization shortly before the outbreak of the French Revolution in the famed Lodge of the Nine Sisters (Muses) in Paris itself a type of UNESCO of the day. This idiom can also be found in eighteenth century England in the caves belonging to the Monks of Medmenham Abbey, later known as the Hellfire Club: a more esoteric and debauched version of the Royal Society. Founded by Sir Francis Dashwood circa 1749, Medmenham Abbey's members included the Earl of Sandwich, William Hogarth, John Wilkes, and, like the Temple of the Nine Sisters, Dr. Benjamin Franklin can be counted among its ranks. In turn Franklin was involved with a French version of the Hellfire Club, through his contacts in the Nine Sisters Lodge, called the Apollonian Society whose purpose was to unite religion with science. The Apollonian Society celebrated Franklin's eighty-third birthday with the erection of his statue crowned with myrtle and laurel.[12]

*　　*　　*　　*　　*

Both Masonic and Catholic canon law riveted upon a systemic rigidity with an envelope of piety, one confessional and dogmatic the other ideationally liberal in outlook, which developed dual means to reject earlier static models of social changelessness. Their overlap worked in tandem with the self-authenticating mechanistic approaches to solar symbolism which elicited from both revisions which attached Counter-Reformation zeal to Enlightenment philosophy and science in a freshly articulated paganism. This development was fateful for modernity specifically because it invited comparisons between scientific laws and social order without reference to the existential vagaries of human individuals and communities. In Benjamin Franklin's work, for example, there are distinctive parallels between his publication of the first edition of Anderson's *Constitutions of the Free-Masons* in America and the striking equivalency between the theory of electricity suggesting parallels between human activity and the activity of particles. This metaphor has persisted into the atomic age in which physics, chemistry and biology have set the tone for ideals of epistemology rooted in Cartesian and Lochean rationality integrated with logical positivism and behavioristic psychology notably in the work of B.F. Skinner (1904-1990). Thethread of consistency has passed throughlegal developments on corporate organization of industry within which human values have been surrogated by perceived economic necessity. Catholic objections to such developments have, in the main, pivoted as cognates of universal papal monarchy as the foundation and source of liberal moral order. Similarly, Masonic ideals have, for example, been realized in various national revolutions in America, France, Latin America, and Spain and have worked de facto hand in glove

12 Hieronimus, Robert, *Founding Fathers, Secret Societies,* page 56 citing C. Heline, *America's Invisible Guidance,* page 40.

with common principles of natural law in which science and politics merge into autocratic systems within which solar symbolism is a tacit but tangible executive and dynamic principle.

This alliance has been neglected by theoreticians and historians largely because its predecessors were Hellenic and cyclical in their view of history or narrowly apocalyptic in various chiliastic and fatalistic mythologies. Hegelian dialectic and its adverse Kierkegaardian criticism both fall subject to flaws which the prevailing solarisms override in their efficiency and until recently unopposed ownership of the higher morality associated with inevitable progress. Interestingly, various forms of Christian and Islamic fundamentalism have been tricked or allusively lured into extremist and reactive modalities and sometimes absurd intellectual claims which have defeated their own critiques of solar modernity and drive advocates of creedal unbelief to discredit religion in general for effective social and political criticism. In particular, Freemasonry's capacity to midwife symbolism into the public vision of order through private hieraticism midwifed the easements over which mathematics framed a new vocabulary linking ordinary, day to day life to calculus, algebra, geometry and physics. This was maneuvered adroitly by the esoteric merging of science through Masonry in France and America specifically to enmesh with Catholic educational pedagogies whereby together the two systems worked publicly at cross purposes but inchoately and esoterically along parallel and intersecting vector lines of policy and group thought rooted in quantitative ideas of motion intrinsic to perceived cosmic dynamics. The Catholic adherence to reactionary scientific ideas is instructive in this regard largely because punitive efforts against Giordano Bruno, Galileo and later Voltaire and Helvetius appear to have elements of disingenuous duplicity. This suggests that such figures were more accurately loose cannons on the ecclesiastical decks rather than enemy artillery. They could not, given circumstances, be mustered to the movement of post-Tridentine militancy effectively in time to advance an overall mission agenda very much at the core of Roman Catholic apostolacy and therefore must be rejected.

* * * * *

The etiquette of the law was defined both in the United States and in England as the *cultura*; easement within which developed a working imagery of the attorney as a moral agent managing the interstices between statutory applications of legal enactments. This role mirrored the Masonic ideal of initiation as paragon citizenship and augmented the development of the bar as a clerisy between the role of ordained clergy and the role of numinous initiate. The refinement of this latter function can be seen in the devolution of comparative religion as understood in the 17th century from the work of Lord Herbert of Cherbury in *De Veritate* (*The Truth*) in 1624 as it was mirrored in the further work of John Toland, an early pre-Masonic ritualizer and thinker close to the Electress Sophia of Hanover, Mother of George I and daughter of Elizabeth, the Winter Queen of Bohemia, who was Electress Palatine of the Rhine. *De Veritate* was published on the advice of Hugo Grotius the godfather of International Law. Elizabeth was in turn daughter of James I and brother both to Charles I and his elder brother Henry, Prince of Wales whose Court became a center for Renaissance learning prior to his early death. Toland (1670-1722) projected an ethos of moral clerisy into a policy matrix which attempted to dismantle Trinitarian Christianity in favor of a proto-Unitarian ideal of pagan morality with an Egyptian and Druidical mystical core. Toland, who produced a prototype Masonic ritual, *The Pantheisticon*, was linked to Dutch philosopher, proto-Enlightenment thinker, and Bible critic Baruch Spinoza (1632-1677); Toland first introduced the use of Celtic and Druidical lore to Masonic speculation. It was Toland's view that pantheism offered lawmakers a reservoir of universal moral reference which pursued the civil order of society beyond the formal statutory elements of legislation into the fabric of enlightened citizenship. This idiom, a century later, was taken up almost precisely by Thomas Paine (1736-1809) and Thomas De Quincey (1785-1859), both of whom viewed Freemasonry as a vital legacy of Ancient Egyptian and Druidical civil purity transmitted into modernity. Paine authored the pamphlet *Common Sense* (published 1776), which strongly argued for American independence as well as *On the Origin of Free-Masonry* (published 1818) that presented Masonry as the inheritor of the Ancient Mysteries. De Quincey wrote essays on Freemasonry and Rosicrucianism; his most famous work (non-Masonic) being *Confessions of an Opium Eater* published in 1821. Rosicrucianism, in a nutshell, is a form of alchemical-mystical Protestantism that appears to be born out of the works and philosophies of Dr. John Dee. In this historical period, the Toland, Paine, De Quincey and Simon Greenleaf thread pinpoints the relationship between the emergence of the American legal profession at its origins after the War of Independence as operating at two levels, the juristic and rational as well as the numinous and mystical. It was the interplay of these two seemingly opposing perspectives which carved out the mission of Masonic law as a numinous parallel to empirical rationalistic definitions of legal practice within the new nation, as practiced by eminent attorneys such as Greenleaf, DeWitt Clinton, and Ephraim Kirby, a student of Tapping Reeve's (1744-1823) Law School, the United States' first school to offer a comprehensive legal curriculum in Litchfield, Connecticut.

Masonic Law was eminently effective as a device for sociological transformation precisely because it shared with Roman Catholic canon law in important ways with the established ecclesiastical law of England a base foundation in natural theology. In Catholicism this was an integral indeed umbilical cognate of Thomas Aquinas as derived from Aristotelian ideas redefined over and against Platonism in the controversy at the University of Paris in the 1260s between Dominican and Franciscan theories of ministry. Masonry added the Neo-Platonic overlay through which its degree hierarchy of moral and esoteric pedagogy was developed institution yet both systems were able to conceal a thorough-going embrace of heliocentric culture within the folds of what looked like orthodox moral conventionality. To the Catholic, this was a guide of monastic and hagiographic piety enshrouding the identification of papal supremacy and monarchy with Egyptianate solar iconography as a Jesuit apologetical device. To Freemasonry, it was the creation of a proactive Oxonian clerisy which extended an altered view of mechanistic reality to the definition of the modern professions at the birth of the industrial revolution through the application of Newtonian ideas of gravity and optics to a socio-political Enlightenment commonwealth. Because the two systems were contra-distinct and because of Clement VIII's papal bull, *In Eminenti* (1738), Roman Catholicism from there on out condemned and excommunicated masons from its ranks. Nevertheless,

Mozart and his Masonic circle, which included *Magic Flute* librettist Emmanuel Schikaneder, under the aegis of Holy Roman Emperor Joseph II provides critical evidence that Masonic ideas found an intimate appreciation by Catholic literati in Vienna and Paris. This lasted well into the 19th and 20th centuries as Freemasons came to play roles of enlightened liberals as well as duplicitous reactionaries (i.e. the Carbonari[13]) with a democratically nuanced veneer. Jacobites and *Philosophes* in an otherwise unlikely alliance were responsible for this as Catholic nobles and Stuart enthusiasts concocted an amalgam of chivalric restoration high degree Freemasonry which superimposed medievalism over the Biblical and medieval accounts of Masonic ritual origins. Joachim von Fiore's ideas were core central to this maneuver in the identification of Logos theory[14] to apocalyptic as a means to mutate eschatology in to a domesticated theory of unfolding neonatology (the study of spiritual beings and phenomena, especially the interactions between humans and God) into political order through a reworking of comparative religion and mythology as, again, was so lyrically and visually clear in *Die Zauberflote*. As such the equivalency between Jacobite-nuanced Templar myth and the political agenda of the *philosophes* found its purest expression in the ritual and activity of the Rite of Strict Observance: a specific alteration of Freemasonry to accommodate chivalry and political rationality. Originated by the Baron von Hund after his Knight Templar initiation in 1743, the essential premise of the rite was obedience to an *unknown superior*, whom the Baron thought to be Charles Edward Stuart (1720-1788). This feature anticipated the secret organizational structure

13 Carbonarism integrated elements of Illuminism, mysticism, Rosicrucianism, policy oriented Freemasonry, and militant revolutionary ideally as a means to preserve Imperial ideas within the ranks of the French Army and to effect a transformation of the regime along ritualized lines. More importantly, it arrayed against the mounting power of reactive conservatism in Europe, coordinated by Prince Klemens von Metternich (1773-1859), which sought the annihilation of Reformism and Bonapartism in general, and secret societies in specific. The Carbonari incorporated a pragmatic organizational structure which survived into political initiatives for the Second French Empire and the consolidation of Italy, the leaders of both of which borrowed heavily from Masonic and Illuministic ideas of ritual order. In the context of Clinton politics (Chapter VIII), Carbonarism became important as a Pan-European political movement because it took up Masonic ritual features and applied them to revolutionary idealism and action. The Carbonari's energy exhibited the intrinsic points of Masonic ritual ideas to channel political loyalties either 1) to reconcile religion and liberty, or 2) to put them at odds. Anti-Masonry in America in particular prefigured Italian Freemasonry's initial struggle with the papacy on political and religious grounds. As such DeWitt Clinton resembled Count Camillo Bensodi Cavour (1810 - 1861) in their mutual efforts to construct a decisively harmonious sphere within which the authority of religion and the nationalist aspirations of the state might project shared ideals onto a pragmatic world order.

14 Petrus Alphonsi's diagram of the Tetragrammaton as the *Trinity* (cf. Three Ages) heavily influenced von Fiore. See Chapter VIII

of the Illuminati, but more importantly for DeWitt Clinton's usage, it institutionally and ceremonially articulated the concept, originated by the Chevalier Ramsay, that Freemasons were, ancestrally, not simple artisans and commercial stone-builders, but noble aristocrats to whom had been entrusted the welfare of secrets designed to regenerate society. This quality of Templar-related ritual was carried over through the *Cerneau system* into the establishment of the Grand Encampment, later Grand Commandery of Knights Templar of New York, of which Clinton was Grand Master from 1814-1828, which formed the nucleus of the national Grand Encampment of Knights Templar (U.S.A.) of which Clinton was also Grand Master from 1818 until his death in 1828. In Clinton's era the Grand Encampment became the state jurisdictional governing body first for Knights Templar. Subsequently, state bodies were termed Grand Commanderies; local bodies, commanderies, and the National representative governing organization, the Grand Encampment.

The association of Enlightenment values with noble and chivalric Masonic Templary is best seen in the development of the Order of the Red Cross of Babylon, a core Masonic myth dealing with the mission of Zerubbabel from King Cyrus of Babylon to rebuild the second temple at Jerusalem. The order is important because it was the only Masonic *haute* degrees to appear , almost simultaneously, in the three principal centers of Masonic activity in the 18th century, Britain, France, and the United States. The premise of the order, or degree, was that an observant Jew is knighted by a Babylonian monarch to undertake a spiritual mission for the reconstruction of the nation. In T.S. Webb's hands this was applied to the Masonic settlement of the mid-west. Yet in its earliest formulation, in the Royal Order of Scotland, the oldest *haute* grades ceremonial extant which details the Templar survival in Scotland after 1314, it has a clear and distinct association with the vacant throne of the King of Scotland, in whose place a vicar or Provincial Grand Master governs the Order's two degrees: The Rosy Cross and the Heredom (*Harodim*: Hebrew, "elect men") of Kilwinning, an ancient Scottish Masonic centre. The result was that Clinton headed, in New York State, two separate Masonic orders within which were two separate workings of the same ceremonial, which equated the intrinsic Stuart mission of the Templar tradition with a ritual mandate that symbolically identified the expansion of the United States westward with the rebuilding of the Temple of Jerusalem ordered by Cyrus and achieved by Zerubbabel.

The result is that both systems, Craft Masonry and the High Degrees, were able to posit a view of mechanistic oneness as the end point of society which identified de facto heresy with the solar drive to eliminate imperfection through Tridentine Counter-Reformation militancy and high degree Masonic rituality. The Counter-Reformation was begun at the Council of Trent, between 1545 and 1563, at the close of the Thirty Years War. Its purpose consisted of four major elements: 1) Religious Orders, 2) Ecclesiastical Reconfiguration, 3) Spiritual Movements, and 4) Political Dimensions. It was, essentially, a reactionay movement based on the Protestant Reformation of Martin Luther seeking to discourage, infiltrate, and thwart Protestantism at both outward (Baroque art and architecture) and secret levels. It is this thread or nexus between the Masonic High Degrees and the Catholic Revival that has fed so many wrong and confused theories of Illuminati-Masonic rooted conspiracies over the years. The more sober reality, however, is not *dark conspiracy* but a profound and *subterranean alliance* between Catholic magisterium and apologetics and the *cooler, rational mystique of ancient texts*, to provide mythic legitimacy for the principal agenda of modernity: to recreate society along heliocentric lines at a metaphysical and therefore confessional levels through the shift from Pythagoras (ca. 570-ca. 495 BCE), Archimedes of Syracuse (ca. 287 -ca. 212 BCE), and Ptolemy the Astronomer (ca. 90-ca 168 CE), to Nicolaus Copernicus (1743-1543), Johannes Kepler (1571-1630), Galileo Galilei (1564-1642) and Isaac Newton (1643-1727). Since Masonic Law, through the conceptual endpoint of initiation, the Royal Arch restoration of the lost name of God came ultimately to serve a numinous mission of managing access to the ineffable name of God, naming through the symbolism and metaphors of mechanism became a primary method of the Fraternity cultural dynamic. In the United States, through the teaching of military and civil engineering at West Point and Union College, both deeply steeped in Masonic culture (West Point was founded by Freemason and the originator of the Order of the Cincinnati, Henry Knox), the mechanistic idiom was extended through canalization, railroading and telegraphy into the American frontier. Similarly, the same inventions in Britain coupled with the heritage of empire and navigation, the symbolic naming process was extended through the powerful capacities of imperial forces to establish persuasive hegemonies over undeveloped regions.

*   *   *   *   *

With this in mind, chapter one introduces the reader to Masonic symbolism which identifies the sun as the most important symbol or icon in all of Freemasonry. Architecturally, the sun would be defined by Renaissance masters such as Leon Battista Alberti and Andrea Palladio, who based their works on that of Roman architect Vitruvius 80/70 BCE-15 CE). Vitruvian perspective has also been a common Masonic-Renaissance denominator in both art and architecture, a principle developed by Fillippo Brunelleschi (1377-1446), but used in differing ways by Protestants, Roman Catholics, and Freemasons. In Protestant English society, informed by values inherited from the medieval architectural style in the British Isles, this was initially Palladian, and subsequently that of the Gothic revival. In nineteenth century America, the Gothic revival became a significant expression of Anglican political values. Similarly, Baroque, and Rococo architecture reinforced absolutism, and papal monarchy connecting the vision of a Glorious God to a sinful and supplicating world. Vitruvian anthropometrism in English Palladianism in the work of Inigo Jones (1573-1652) and Sir Christopher Wren (1631-1723) preserved an avenue of political symbolism in buildings from the Renaissance notably implicit in the influence of Andrea Palladio (1508-1580). This pragmatic expression was appropriated in the policies of activist intellects, such as diplomatist Sir Joseph Williamson (1633-1701), Secretary of State under Charles II, and Sir George Clarke (1660 -1736), his protégé Nicholas Hawksmoor (1661-1736). Clarke's designs for Worcester College, Oxford established in the same period as the Premier Grand Lodge, 1717, accommodated Benedictine foundations with academic respectability. Clarke was a polymathic Tory scholar and public servant who forged Jacobite links as well as ties to Desaguliers and Christ Church. At

Oxford his energy and taste were felt in all directions encompassing irenic values in a turbulent era. It was Palladio (as well as Alberti) who developed the concept of a domed solar throne room indicative of the triumphal sun god Apollo. This idiom was transported into England by architects such as Inigo Jones and Christopher Wren, the latter a mason, and into America by mason Benjamin Henry Latrobe the godfather of American architecture. In turn this solar iconography would be transformed into material culture and rhetoric by Freemasons and lawyers such DeWitt Clinton, Ephraim Kirby, and Simon Greenleaf who would help define a path of heliocentric rulership and enlightenment for the new nation. This can in turn be found in the *Illustrations of Freemasonry* by American Masonic ritualist Thomas Smith Webb. His *Illustrations* were in turned based upon the *Illustrations of Freemasonry* by William Preston with one distinct difference: the Webb ritual culminated with the Royal Arch ceremony where the initiate was exalted as a divine citizen by beholding the Tetragrammaton often associated with solar symbolism; the Preston ritual ended with the Master Mason degree where the new Freemason was deemed most loyal subject of the monarch.[15] Preston made the Vitruvian architect the moral prototype of the Masonic initiate, as a master of moral design, and/or a client of royal patronage such as Vitruvius served the Emperor Augustus. The purpose of initiation was morally to replicate architecture as servant to the national interest through loyalty to the sovereign. This separated *ascensio* (aristocratic leadership) and *apotheosis* (divine approbation) through the political concept of time in architectural structure as *eschatology*, away from revolutionary, millenarian hands found in the United States and Revolutionary France (both in the eighteenth and nineteenth centuries). Preston also referenced Sir Christopher Wren; patronage as allegiance to a royal sovereign and royal clientage of useful mechanical arts as political process can be seen in the academic designs of George Clarke's prints at Worcester College, Oxford University. Preston regarded Wren as a Grand Master of the Grand Lodge, and like Inigo Jones, his ideas as executive principles in its social organization. Unlike Jones, Preston demonstrated Wren's vision was an effort to remake all of English society. In this he was thwarted, because

15 See Stemper, William H. Jr., *Crafted Links: The Transformation of Masonic Ritual Order, 1772-1802: An Intellectual History of the Preston-Webb synthesis.*

the "citizens" of London could not be persuaded to surrender self-interest for a larger good. This was Preston's coded reference to the lingering hold of Medievalism (cf. Antient ideas) on the public, commercial and the Masonic mind. On the other end of the Masonic spectrum, it is through the Webb philosophy and its related Royal Arch ethos that helped define the American national character. Webb shifted Vitruvianism away from Jones and Wren toward Enochian Biblical ritual texture. He altered Preston's idea that Pythagoras, a model for Masonic initiation, was a precursor of Jones and Wren, and developed Preston's inchoate Enochian Pythagoras into a model of the Mason as Royal Arch priest. Webb's transformation reflected the initiative of Giovanni Pico della Mirandola (1463-1494), to integrate individual dignity with Christian Cabala, to accommodate a broader image of apotheosis. Pico della Mirandola is famed for the events of 1486, when at the age of twenty-three, he proposed to defend 900 theses on philosophy, religion, natural philosophy, and magic against all comers, for which he wrote the famous *Oration on the Dignity of Man*, which has been called the Manifesto of the Renaissance and a key text of Renaissance humanism and of what has been called the *Hermetic Reformation*. This image reconnected hermetical *ascensio* to cabalistic apotheosis by recapitulating a divine spark of Jesus Christ, the Sun-Son of God with humanism. Thus the Masonic initiate, as a symbolic Royal Arch keystone, realized Christhood or became like God. Webb also extended initiatic status into a broader and domestic culture which could include women, such as Martha Washington, as initiatic figures, extending the rule of Enoch to hearth and home, as well as to the corridors of policy and power. The articulation of Webb's template into the material culture of androgynous orders esotericized domestic devices, and regalized the role of women as patriotic, protective seeresses witnessing –and guiding–the divine creation of cosmic order within the home. The ritual sigillism of such societies and orders as the White Shrine of Jerusalem, the Daughters of the American Revolution, Heroines of Jericho, and Royal Neighbors of America, each derived from threads of Webb's system, made countless dwellings and estates miniature replicas of Palladian temples and villas. While explaining solar Masonic symbolism, this author also disposes with the notion that the planet Venus, *Lucifer*, is important in Freemasonry; masonry incorporates astrological symbolism but again this is either most likely referencing the sun or the star Sirius, the latter referred to as the "Blazing Star of Masonry." It was the Ancient Egyptians who adored the stars and constellations as divine icons, if not divinity itself.

Chapter one also details the concept of the Lost Word of a Master Mason, the word of Hiram Abif, lost with his death by the hands of three ruffians while building Solomon's Temple. This word, necessary to build the temple, is recovered in the various Royal Arch high degree ceremonies. Nevertheless, the new mason, upon being raised from his symbolic death in the third or Master Mason degree of the Craft Lodge has a *substitute word* whispered in his ear in low breath. In order to communicate this word the *five points* of fellowship must be formed, a symbolic pentagram, the symbol in Masonry for Sirius correctly detailed by Albert Pike in his book *Morals and Dogma of the Ancient and Accepted Scottish Rite.* Sirius, the brightest or *blazing star* in the nighttime sky was adored as the goddess Isis in the Egyptian Mysteries. Isis secretly possessed the secret name of Amun Re/Ra, the supreme Egyptian solar deity, which she used to procure magic to raise her brother-husband Osiris from the grave. Masonic ritual obviously parallels this where the candidate is raised from the grave with a *substitute word*, communicated by creating five points, a pentagram, forging a nexus to Sirius and Isis and to Hiram Abif as Osiris. Isis upon the death of Osiris became a widow; Freemasons are thereby known as *widow's sons*. This is not conspiratorial nor a stretch; Solomon, the construction of his temple is the basis of the Master Mason degree, adored and worshipped Isis at I Kings 11:5 and II Kings 23:13. Lastly, there are two sets of pillars or columns in masonry: Jachin and Boaz that sit on the portico and Solomon's Temple, and the Pillars of Enoch upon which Enoch inscribed the celestial secrets and knowledge he received while in heaven. These are not the same. The recovery of the Lost Word in the Royal Arch ritual symbolically restores this knowledge as inscribed on Enoch's Pillars. In the Masonic Royal Arch ceremony the means to accomplish this was to find the Ark of the Covenant which was discovered in a hidden underground vault, built by Enoch, by temple builders constructing the second temple (of Zerubbabel) according to the ritual liturgy. It is upon the Ark[16] that rests a golden delta on which

16 Ark of the Covenant in the York Rite, Foundation Stone in the Scottish Rite.

is inscribed the Tetragrammaton. In 1790, in St. Andrews Lodge in Boston, Massachusetts a degree certificate was designed. It was attributed to Royal Arch Mason and lawyer Benjamin Hurd to be awarded to masons exalted into the Holy Royal Arch degree. Unlike the ritual, however, the contents of the Vault of Enoch *were not the Ark of the Covenant*. Instead the degree certificate displayed a *rising sun* emerging from the vault as the symbol for the Tetragrammaton symbolically detailing the solar pathway of initiation for citizens that would ultimately be codified in the York Rite or American Rite ending in the Christian Knight Templary of DeWitt Clinton organized in 1814; St. Andrew's Royal Arch Lodge was the first in the United States to confer the degree of Knight Templar in 1769. It was in this ethos that Masons such as DeWitt Clinton, Simon Greenleaf, and the Livingston family paved the way for the enlightened citizen to use Freemasonry, its *haute* degrees, to inform and create the destiny of the new nation through policy formation and rhetoric as Masonry and the country expanded westward. This ideology and formula was undone by the William Morgan Affair of 1826.

Chapter two explores and explains Masonic ritual, both the Blue Lodge and the high degrees, as developed by T.S. Webb in the United States. This entails the three degrees of craft masonry and the degrees of Mark Master Mason, Virtual Past Master, Most Excellent Master and naturally the Holy Royal Arch. These rituals were born out of the Henry Francken's Rite of Perfection established in Albany, New York in1767. Francken's Rite was the antecedent of what became the Ancient and Accepted Scottish Rite. Webb published his own *Illustrations of Freemasonry* in 1797 detailing his ritual synthesis which was inspired by not only Francken's Rite but also the *Illustrations of Freemasonry* by William Preston (1772); both Preston and Webb's monitors have the exact same name. As stated above Preston's rite concludes with the Master Mason being, symbolically, the most loyal subject of the crown; Webb's ritual culminates with the Holy Royal arch where a *parfait* or supreme initiate became a perfected divine citizen by beholding the Tetragrammaton as detailed in the Royal Arch ceremony. The high degree mason thus became the arbiter and template for perfection, a term much utilized in high grades of Freemasonry wherein the imagery of the *parfait(s)*, or Elu (i.e. Perfect Elu or Elect of the fourteenth degree) was identified with the virtuous and successful Freemason who embodied the qualities of social and economic power. This idiom refined the core values of the Anglican *via media* into the ideal of interfaith irenicism through harmonious toleration with reference to the changing face of a family-orientated monarch dating from the accession of George III, three of whose sons became fervent Freemasons. Learned and scientifically progressive domesticity simultaneously implied and exalted the Sovereign and his family in unique ways which both concealed *and* revealed the imagery of rulership as a democratic entity at one level and as magical and remote at another. In America this concept was reconciled with a solution whereby George Washington symbolically replaced the English monarch as the model for social perfection as Washington came to embody the supreme Masonic initiate: those who sacrifice for the nation are rewarded with perfected citizenship, a concept echoed in the various Royal Arch, Scottish Rite Consistory, and Knight Templar ceremonies.

Chapter three details the sun and the heavens as the source of adoration and worship of the Ancient Mysteries. These Ancient Mysteries and their related symbolisms were plagiarized and anthropomorphized in the Abrahamic Faiths, and transported into Masonry as the preserver of these ancient mysteries. Like the Ancient Mysteries of old Freemasonry contains the ritual element of the dying yet resurrected *solar man*. This process documents the sun as the source of worship adopting different astrological elements and themes within paganism and Abrahamic religions such as Judaism and Christianity based on an astronomical phenomenon known as the Precessions of the Equinoxes. The reconciliation of Greco-Roman philosophy and paganism with Christianity gave rise to a philosophy called *Neo-Platonism* which incorporated *a priori* elements of Platonism, that is we know Deity independently without having to experience it which, of course, opposed Aristotle's view that knowledge was *a posteriori* or based on experience. In the eighteenth century German philosopher Immanuel Kant advocated a blend of rationalist and empiricist theories. According to Kant, *a priori* knowledge is transcendental, or based on the form of all possible experience, while *a posteriori* knowledge is empirical, based on the content of experience.[17] Neo-Platonic thought was revived during the Renaissance while the Precession of the Equinoxes establishes and distinguishes the concept of *solar ages*: a span of approximately 2000 years where the sun retrogrades through a house of the zodiac. The sun moves one degree backwards through each house of the zodiac every 72 years. This gives rise to the Age of Taurus, the Age of Aries, the current yet waning Age of Pisces, and the quickly approaching Age of Aquarius. This phenomena is echoed in the occult prophecies of Joachim von Fiore whose *Third Age of the Holy Spirit* was to be ruled by a spiritual monarch assisted by two orders of monks: secular hermits and spiritual mystics; this Third Age parallels the humanitarian "Masonic" hallmarks of the Age of Aquarius. It will also be made clear that one of the primary sources of the New Testament was in fact the *Book of Enoch*, because various cosmological and astral components from *I Enoch* emerge in the New Testament.

Chapter four explores a historical anomaly: the *Book of Enoch*, while not yet discovered was incorporated in *haute* degree Masonic Royal Arch ceremony coming out of France. Clearly someone in Europe had access to a copy prior to Bruce's discovery of *I Enoch* in Ethiopia. The person was likely the Chevalier Ramsay from whose Oration of 1737 the Masonic high degrees were born. There is other evidence that a copy of *I Enoch* was making its rounds through medieval Europe and Rosicrucian circles. Evidence can be found in a system of Angelic Magic developed by Dr. John Dee and Irish mystic Edward Kelley in the sixteenth century called Enochian Magic, a direct reference to the angelic secrets contained in the *Book of Enoch*. Dee,

> "...was of the most celebrated and remarkable men of the Elizabethan age. Philosopher, mathematician, technologist, antiquarian, teacher and friend of powerful people, Dee was at the centre of some of the major developments of the English Renaissance; in fact, he inspired several of these developments through his writings and his teachings. But Dee was also a magician deeply immersed in the most extreme forms of occultism: he was Elizabethan England's great magus. ....He was one of a line of philosopher magicians that stemmed from Ficino

17 See *Critique of Pure Reason* first published in 1781.

> and Pico Della Mirandola and included, among others, Trithemius, Abbot of Sponheim; Henry Cornelius Agrippa; Paracelsus; Giordano Bruno; Tommaso Campanella; and Dee's successor in England, Robert Fludd. Like Dee, these philosophers lived in a world that was half-magical, half-scientific. Astronomy and Astrology were not yet completely separated, and Tycho Brahe still cast horoscopes, as did Kepler."[18]

Enochian was the language, according to Dee, by which angels communicated. Enochian had its own grammar and syntax and seemingly owes it origin to I Enoch, or does it? Dee and Kelley's Enochian magic may owe its origin to a grimoire (a medieval magical spell book) called the *Heptameron* which was allegedly written by Pietro d'Abano, born ca. 1257 –died 1316. This book details magical rites concerning the conjuring of specific angels. On the other hand, Tobias Churton, author of *The Invisible History of the Rosicrucians*, suggests that Dr. Dee did in fact have access to copy of *I Enoch* and this copy had once belonged to Friar Roger Bacon (1214-1294).[19] The Divine Comedy by Dante Alighieri written between 1308 and 1321 also contains components of *I Enoch*, that is, an initiate being shown a complete vista of the heavens, its secrets, in the afterlife: Inferno, Purgatory, and Paradise. The question then must be asked: was this the same copy that fell in the hands of those that created and cultivated *haute* degree Freemasonry? Whether Dee or Alighieri actually had access to a copy of *I Enoch* is debatable. What is not debatable, nor open to speculation, is that the Royal Arch of Enoch ritual, and its associated philosophy, contains elements of *I Enoch* prior to the book's discovery in the west and its subsequent translation into English.

Chapter five explores the complexities of philosophies that pre-date Masonry yet heavily influenced it. This includes, but not limited to, the hermetic tradition of *Ars Notoria* developed by medieval hermits and philosophers such as cabalist Raymond Lully. *Ars Notoria* or the Art of Memory is a philosophical device wherein architecture incorporates mystic

18 French, Peter, *John Dee: The World of an Elizabethan Magus,* pages 1-2.
19 Churton, Tobias, *The Invisible History of the Rosicrucians*, page 106.

elements and divine proportions to create a symbolic memory temple wherein man, the microcosm, becomes linked to the heavens, the macrocosm, the universe, the stars and the heavens; and as such the divine, spiritual hand that created them. Masonry would in turn incorporate magical and occult memory devices, both within its ritual and in actual operative Masonry (i.e. construction, city planning) as it is the latter would seemingly reflect the hermetic maxim of "as above, so below." Magical memory is the subject of the Renaissance text *Cantus Circaeus*, where the daughter of the sun, Circe, prays to the sun and offers incantations to the Moon, Saturn, Jupiter, and other celestial bodies to be embedded as a memory, ritual device. To Giordano Bruno this magical system represents the memory of the Supreme Magus, a Master Mason, one who can see the unseen as a sublime initiate; it is a direct descendant of Marsilio Ficino's Neo-Platonic interpretations of celestial images but carried to more daring extremes. Also discussed is Baroque-Enochian levitational art and architecture spawned by the Jesuit led Counter-Reformation began at the Council of Trent shortly after the Protestant Reformation. Baroque art symbolically elevates the soul conforming to triumphal Catholic apologetics. The Jesuits organized their order along military lines; they strongly represented the autocratic zeal of the period. Characterized by careful selection, rigorous training, and iron discipline, the Jesuits ensured that the worldliness of the Renaissance reformed Catholic Church had no part in their new order unless it was the promotion of universal Vatican or Papal Monarchy under the umbrella of Joachim von Fiore's Third Age. The Jesuits, like Freemasons, emerged as an Egyptian-styled solar priesthood: the Jesuits served as elites within the magisterium, spiritual mystics who were balanced out by their secular offshoot the hermetical Freemasons (and Rosicrucians). Egyptianism and hermetical occultism was nothing new to the Jesuits; it is clearly reflected in the works of the learned Jesuit Athanasius Kircher (1601/02-1680) who was one of the first to link Christianity as the inheritor of the Egyptian pagan mysteries. The high degrees of Masonry were created, or at least nourished, by the Jesuits at the College of Clermont in Paris as part of the Counter-Reformation; all evidence points in this direction. The placement of the Jesuit Georgetown University within the borders of the Masonic-Royal Arch themed or nuanced District of Columbia is a concrete example of this underground, irenic alliance. The Society of Jesus had their influence and power undercut drastically, destroyed , when Pope Clement XIV suppressed, in 1793, the order for their overt occult-Egyptian enthusiasms and their political intrigues. The Jesuits would reemerge, but like Freemasonry after the William Morgan Affair, the organization was transformed; diminished from its original purpose, a shadow of its former self. In keeping with the Egyptian theme, chapter five concludes discussing the Masonic musings of Martin Clare, one of the first to write a defense of Masonry while tracing its origins to the Mysteries of Egypt.

Chapter six details Masonic ritual both craft lodge and the high degrees, the end purpose of which is to transform the initiate into a supreme magus who can positively affect change in the community. The role of Christ Church, Oxford, the alma mater of Dr. John Theophilus Desaguliers, and its role within Masonry opens the chapter. Masonry embraces deism, and the godfather of "Masonic Deism" was Lord Herbert of Cherbury (1583 -1648), his philosophies incorporated in masonry as well as elements of Zoroastrianism, the religion of ancient Persia. Zoroastrianism predates Judaism and Christianity; it is from Zoroastrianism that the conflict oflight versus dark, angels versus demons, good versus evil originates. This ritual idiom is carried forward in Masonry where the candidate is brought from a state of darkness to light or transformed into a smooth ashlar from a rough ashlar to use Masonry's own lexicon. Biblical patriarchs such as King David and the Salem priest king Melchizedek will also be explored. Melchizedek was the priest-king of Salem cited in Genesis 14:18-20. Melchizedek's significance within the use of Freemasonry by DeWitt Clinton and T. S. Webb related to his dual role as a 1) priest and king; and 2) as the patriarch who anointed Abraham just prior to his covenant with the Lord. Webb borrowed this image from Laurence Dermott's 1756 *Ahiman Rezon*: the Antient Masonic textbook, and applied its use to an Order of High Priesthood conferred upon each presiding officer of a Royal Arch Chapter. It is likely Webb took Melchizedek either directly from the Gothic Constitutions, in the literary style of traditional histories used by James Anderson in his 1723 and 1738 Constitutions, or with the same moralizing principle in mind. In turn Masonry utilizes the Greek mathematician Pythagoras in the role of the supreme Masonic initiate who employs geometry to explain the universe, the macrocosm, and by default divinity. This is paralleled in Wolfgang Amadeus Mozart's Masonic opera, *The Magic Flute*, where the Masonic magus Sarastro uses logic and reason to defeat superstition or religion, represented by the Queen of the Night who in turn personifies the Virgin Mary as Isis corrupted. The power of this ritual idiom, as discussed in chapter five, is derived from Enochian symbolism in policy rhetoric and material culture was underscored through Freemasonry's links with the history of the *Ars Notoria* or the Art of Memory which was encapsulated in the Masonic degree of the Fellow Craft. This degree associated the recapitulation of learning with a symbolic winding staircase thus summarizing symbolically the structure of medieval learning for the initiate. This ritual event stemmed from the architectural ideas of Vitruvius reinterpreted in the Renaissance by Andrea Palladio. It should also be pointed out to the reader that Lord Herbert of Cherbury (1583-1648), envisaged a solar-centric new religion without revelation as a sole Divine source for a world regime, to which notion Guillaume Postel added the premise of the Joachimite concept of a world emperor, a new order of a middle way spiritual intellectual whose mission and temperament articulated contemplative and activistic devotion to Christian mission symbolically positioned along a middle way, between heaven and earth, within the hermetical concept of *ascensio*.

The Jesuit-Joachimite frame of mind, of which Postel's visionary political concepts were a likely caricature, was soon marginalized because of its provocative polemics. It can however be seen best in the course of Ireland's Masonic development, which uniquely integrated mystical and rationalist threads. This integrated druidical, radical-rationalist lore from the career of John Toland, a Spinozist who ruled out any form of providential revelation in the ordering of the world's affairs. This also included a working missionary premise, implicit in the structure of the Royal Arch Irish Jewels or personal badges (bearing Masonic symbols), that the aim of human existence, paragonized in the symbolatry of initiation, was the establishment of a community of perfected individuals. This radicalized hermeticism within Joachimite historical objective lay at the center of the Irish Masonic consciousness. In essence, it retained Protestant objections to Catholic absolutism, yet opted for a revolutionary redefinition of politics along contractual and mythological lines that preserved conceptual space for a supreme, temporal power. The result was an opening for a new entablature of hermetical and cabalistic imagery as serving both secular and religious aims by appearing to affirm spiritual values whilst encoding Osirian, Egyptianate lore through Druidical references.

Chapter seven introduces the reader the Andrew Michael "the Chevalier" Ramsay (1686-1743), from whose Oration of 1737 the high degrees of Masonry were born. His Oration broke with the Desaguliers-Anderson history that Masonry originated from Biblical stonecutters whose skills passed down to medieval stonemasons. Rather Ramsay, while acknowledging Masonry as a construction trade, stated that Freemasonry as a secret society was born out of Medieval Roman Catholic Knight Templars who were in turn influenced by the Ancient Mysteries. The Ramsay ideology not only incorporated his Oration, but also his work *The Voyages of Cyrus* that exalted religions of Zoroastrianism, Mithraism, and the Mysteries of Egypt as the predecessors to the Christian Mysteries. As such the high degrees contain elements of these religions and mysteries which included, but not limited to, the perfection of the soul as it progresses or matriculates through different and further rites and rituals. In Ramsay's *Voyages*, Cyrus the Great is lifted up as a son of Mithras; it is within the Royal Arch ceremony that the Jewish governor Zerubbabel is permitted by Cyrus to return to Jerusalem to construct the second temple. Persian influence of the development of Blue Lodge Masonry is also presented, elements of Sufism appear in Masonic lore, likely stemming from the works of Persian philosopher, astronomer, and mathematician Omar Khayyám (1048-1131). Sadly, in some Masonic literature and publications, Ramsay is written off as an eccentric crank and the perpetrator of occult monkeyshines; this is unfortunate and untrue because he was a member of the Royal Society and recipient of an honorary degree in Civil Law from Oxford University.

* * * * *

DeWitt Clinton is the focus of both chapters eight and nine, who along with Masonic ritualist Thomas Smith Webb developed the York or American Rite culminating with Christian Knight Templar degree. It was Clinton who presided over the General Grand Chapter of Royal Arch Masons as developed in the later eighteenth century in New York, the Masonic Empire State. Clinton was George Washington's successor as de facto Masonic leader of the nation and quickly carried this motif into formal ritual and institutional application in the creation in 1797 of the General Grand Chapter of Royal Arch Masonry and soon thereafter in the creation of the Grand Encampment of Knight Templars, a modern reworking of the idea of a medieval crusading order. DeWitt Clinton utilized Masonic ideas, including specific ritual symbolism from the Royal Arch ceremony of exaltation, to formulate government and organizational policy. This policy formation related to the concept of Royal Arch initiations in the Webb system and established an equivalency between the ritual possession of the Royal Arch Word, the ineffable Name of God (Tetragrammaton), and morally warranted power to rule as a magus or mystically-nuanced sage; and a Solomonic law-giving Greek philosopher. This was a classical mode of public philosophes such as Thomas Jefferson, but it took the use of Freemasonry an important step farther than Jefferson's circle by exchanging the latter's anti-clerical Unitarianism, with hermetically-nuanced initiatic priestly kingship rooted in the Biblical image of Melchizedek. This ritual positioned Clinton as an irenic King of Peace in a manner parallel to Christian revelation but as a surrogation for Biblical salvation. Thus, Clinton established a mystical ritualistic core at the heart of his personal political piety, and made concrete efforts through public office and amateur scholarship to integrate an ideal of the learned Kingly Priest *qua* public philosopher, with lawyerly attention to administrative and legislative detail. Clinton also applied simultaneously the organization of Masonry in New York into a public sphere of non-partisan political influence designed to incorporate leaders into a Masonic republic within the official government structure. An example of this can be found in the construction and dedication of the Erie Canal, itself a symbol of Nilotic flooding, that expanded the frontier westward linking New York to the Mississippi delta. This concept survived and flourished through the history of the United States as fraternalism became a pan-movement of a vast array of Masonic and other orders each of which addressed the same objective of moral rulership in different but parallel ceremonials. Clinton's raw material can be traced through to the St. Andrew's Royal Arch degree certificate, the Hurd Plate of 1790 in Boston, Massachusetts derived from contemporaneous Irish emblems but ordered into a single path of initiation. Clinton's system devolved from this template into high degree lodges: Royal Arch Chapters and Knight Templar Commanderies, duly chartered, locally and nationally united, which proliferated as the nation moved westward along the frontier. Careful analysis of this system which came later to be termed the York or American Rite reveals the infrastructure of a nuance network of emergent solar order calibrated carefully to integrate scientific discovery with confessional Christianity. The autonomous movement of this system became an important element of its popular success as its participants were encouraged to see themselves as successors to the great General George Washington and as miniature fathers of the nation. This autonomy of moral and political purpose was conceived and disseminated in the evolution of semipublic Masonic Monitors derived from the work of English Masonic writers William Preston and Thomas Smith Webb. The role of the Odd Fellows as well as the emergence of the female deity in the Clintonian political ethos will be investigated; the latter originating from the Isis-Marian seal of King's College (n/k/a Columbia University) as well as Minerva's Ladder (interpreted as Jacob's Ladder within the Craft Lodge) within eighteenth century Masonic publications and literature. On ladder symbolism esoteric Freemason Manly P. Hall elucidates:

> "In the Ancient Wisdom it was also declared that the sacred mountains of the world rose in seven steps or stages (as the Meru of the Hindus), and it was from the high place, or seventh step, that offerings were made to the Lord whose name is Blessed. Not only did the holy place rise in seven platforms or levels, but its topmost level was usually erected a triform symbol of the Divine Nature itself. Thus the seven steps, complemented by this threefold figure, became the Mysterious Pythagorean *decad*, or the symbol of the tenfold order of the universe. Jacob's ladder then actually becomes the symbolic mountain or pyramid. Pyramids, wherever found, are symbolic of the axis mountain of the world-the Olympus, Asgard, and Meru of the pagans, and possibly the rock Moriah upon which stood the temple

> at Jerusalem. In his *Pagan Idolatry*, Faber describes the Mithraic ladder used in the initiatory rites of the Persian Mysteries, which he affirms was in reality a pyramid of seven steps, further declaring that on each step was a door. In the ceremonials, the neophyte climbed the pyramid, passing though the seven doors, and then through similar portals descended on the opposite side. This pyramid was symbolic of both the world and the sidereal system. Nearly all great buildings of antiquity were symbolic of the universe, and according to Cicero the conquering Xerxes destroyed the temples of the Greeks, declaring that the entire world was the proper house of God and the Deity was profaned when man prepared for him a house less dignified than his own solar mansion."[20]

Minerva would take concrete form in the seal of Union College of Schenectady, New York. The Masonic millennialism of Salem Town concludes chapter eight, whose treatise expanded the Logos of fourth gospel of St. John to the Royal Arch vista of the United States, its westward expansion after the Louisiana Purchase of 1803-1804.

Masonic involvement in the creation of the United States can be documented from its outset. The Boston Tea Party in December 1773 was organized by St. Andrew's Lodge in Boston; Freemason Paul Revere warned Americans that the "British were coming" during his famous midnight ride of April 1775. Chapter ten investigates the concept of the United States as a Masonic Republic; its Constitution of 1789 which codified liberal enlightenment-Masonic concepts were celebrated while both neutralizing any furor or reactionary devices, that either elevates or degrades, the protection of free speech and the separation of church and state exalted in the first amendment, because to criticize or dissent within the parameters of the United States Constitution is at the same time to exonerate or defend it. As such, non-masons and anti-Masonic agitators can't win because they're in a sense arguing against themselves. This ideology, the separation of church and state, tolerance, is borrowed from the *Constitutions of the Free-Masons*, Article I, 1723, 1738. The U.S. Government, its triple division of government between an executive, legislative, and judicial, comes from

20 Hall, Manly P., *Lectures on Ancient Philosophy*, pages 415-416.

the tripartite division of government of the Blue Lodge. While it can be successfully argued that Freemasonry in the political hands of Federalists like George Washington, Henry Knox, and Alexander Hamilton, provided the means to create an American Aristocracy, perfected by the creation of the Order of the Cincinnati, an elite society reserved for the families and the descendants of Washington's "Masonic" Officer Corps. However, this author goes much deeper and reveals that Masonry, its high degrees, the Royal Arch of Enoch specifically, and Enlightenment values intertwined with the ideal of solar monarchy informed and influenced the policy rhetoric and material culture of the new nation as it expanded westward. This was implemented by Freemasons such as DeWitt Clinton and John James Buckley, the former instrumental in the creation of the General Grand Chapter of Royal Arch Masons and the Grand Encampment of Knights Templar; the latter the originator of the American Collegiate Fraternal System. This was also carried forward by non-Masons such as President Thomas Jefferson who was influenced by Craft Masonry's egalitarian, democratic, and enlightenment values, but was also seemingly moved and affected by the monarchist French high degrees. This is evidenced by the Louisiana Purchase: Jefferson expanded American territory and boundaries more than any other President (before or after) while at the same time being opposed to an American Empire (cf. Alexander Hamilton and the Federalists) and the Royal Arch Masonic clerisy that would influence if not rule the new territory; a contradiction that was embraced by Jeffersonian-Republican DeWitt Clinton. This ideal in turn was opposed by Federalist and sixth President John Quincy Adams who steered the Federalist Party into anti-Masonry stemming from the book *Proofs of a Conspiracy* by James Robison (1739-1805) coupled with the William Morgan Affair and the anti-Illuminati rhetoric of Jedidiah Morse. Masonry survived this assault, aided by Freemason and seventh President Andrew Jackson who refused to give in to anti-Masonry. It was Jackson who defeated anti-Masonic Presidential nominee William Wirt in the election of 1832. Whether pro-Masonry and anti-Masonry one thing is clear: Renaissance-Enlightenment philosophy is exemplified in the *Constitutions of Free-Masons*, "Reason … surveys the Lodge and makes us one;"[21] so too does Freemasonry *survey the United States and makes us one* in both the

21 See *The Constitution of Free-Masons,* lyric from the Treasurer's Song, 1738.

Federalist and Jeffersonian-Republican idioms. Thus, Masonic symbolism would take concrete form in various seals, emblems, vistas, and templates in the United States; Masonry and its high degrees influenced the vistas of Baltimore, Maryland, St. Louis, Missouri, and the Hudson Valley as explained in chapters eleven and twelve. The William Morgan Affair of 1826, while cutting the legs out from beneath Masonic membership, did little if anything to affect the integration of Masonic symbolism in the iconography and landscape of the new nation. These emblems, vistas, designs, and templates reflect Renaissance-cabalistic concepts such as the hermetic maxim of *as above, so below* meaning that important events are timed to coincide with such movements of the sun, the moon, the planets, the zodiac, and other cosmological occurrences in order to link man the microcosm to the celestial heavens, the macrocosm. In turn architectural edifices can be aligned to astrological bodies by way of cornerstone ceremonies, overall design, or various other alignments conforming to Pythagorean notions of universal harmony and astrological-cosmological order.

Webb's American system, echoed in the Mormonism of Freemasons Joseph Smith (1805-1844) and Brigham Young (1801-1877), secularized irenic inaugural leadership within a complex of social institutions and voluntary societies that preserved progressive American civic piety. The difference was that the formers essential dynamic transformed individuals into a new form of educated clerisy, while the latter sought the transformation of individuals into a leaderly high priesthood, successors to Enoch. The first was experimental and pedagogical, the second political and mystical, with pedagogical emanations. In turn, Preston's Joachimite legacy for the professions and executive leadership transmitted to America was the preservation of a classics-orientated clerisy, consistent with the Joachimite Second Age of the Son. Webb identified the fullness of contemplative wisdom with hermetical and Enochic forms of priestly leadership consistent with the New Age of the Holy Spirit syncretic with the coming "Masonic" Aquarian Astrological Age. The Masters of lodges, ritual arbiters of time, and the High Priests of chapters became perduring regal prototypes for leaders of an array of American voluntary societies, and deemed inaugural successors to George Washington.

Public inaugural ritual also discloses the importance of examining the *ascensio* and apotheosis motifs. It underscores that forms of moral education, the one didactic, and the other transformative through mystic inauguration, worked in American society, frequently side by side, as hermetically-nuanced deistic elements to countervail the American tendency to separate Church and State too radically, and to deem pietistical and sentimentalized Christianity as a de facto national religion. As John F. Wilson has correctly stated, it is remarkable American fraternal ritual has merited little scholarship:

> "The American civic piety is given its most direct institutional and organizational expression through… patriotic voluntary societies and lodges. One of the most interesting aspects of this suggestion is the…lack of attention given…to the complex as a whole…[it is]…an extraordinarily pervasive condition of collective life in American society…in creating and sustaining the American social fabric…[for]…Americans [who have]… built up their collective life and finally governed themselves to quite a remarkable degree in this way."[22]

Mormon Temple ritual further disclosed both Joachimite and political inaugural aspects of Webb's method. Both were symbolically rooted in Royal Arch exaltation. A general set of antediluvian symbols equated with collective personal pilgrimage as the recovery of an implicit, primeval millennial order overshadowed any specific civic script. Royal Arch exaltation and Mormon Temple endowment functioned as mystical Melchizedekian inauguration linked to the power to rule with the implicit mystical harmony of the sabbatarian order imprinted within the self. The Joachimite roots of American society can also be traced to the dynamic transformation of George Washington from a patrician, Prestonian figure into the image of an apotheosised Enoch (or Hermes Trismegistus; Enoch was equated to Thoth Hermes Mercurius Trismegistus among Christian Cabalists, see Plate IX) after his death in December 1799. When evangelical Christianity made its most formidable bid to displace Freemasonry as a source of sabbatarian order, this faltered, but disclosed precisely how Trinitarian

22 Wilson, John F., *Public Religion in American Culture,* page 136.

Joachimism became the principal theoretical instrument for a Masonic policy to triumph in the new world. The insertion of a ritual mnemonic, or memory device within ornate local lodges and temples at the crossroads of each American town, village, and city was the victorious perimeter of this strategy. These initiatory neuron-firings enabled millions of hometown Americans to experience a transformation from intellectual darkness to radiant illumination through a graded numinous system of philanthropic merit. Christian revelation and law were cabalistically reworked to delineate a dazzling anamnesis, which at its apex exalted science, the arts, and the professions to the level of a sacral, patriotic priesthood through architectural imagery. Royal Arch cabalism was ritually transferred by Webb to chivalric Freemasonry, notably the Order of the Temple (i.e. Knights Templar). Webb inherited this Templar element from Ireland (including but not limited to the iconography of the Irish Jewels), but preserved and colorfully amplified its foundation as the Knights Templar orders, evident in the Hebrew nature of the principal Grand password, *Maher shalal hash baz* (Isaiah 8:1). The militant chivalric enchiridion equated Christianity with armed spiritual warfare. This demanded priestly possession of the Royal Arch Name of God as a warrant to rule, and the importance of the linkage between cabalistic symbolism and Joachimite historical vision as civil inauguration. The Hebrew Kabbalistic principle meant that Masonic ritual constituted a mystical instrument, which operated in a cosmic area and penetrated through the world…to the depths of the Godhead. In Joachimistic terms, the Masonic parallel was that ritual prefigured, mapped out, and effectuated *a new order of the ages or of the Holy Spirit.*

Masonic Law is the topic of chapter thirteen, Simon Greenleaf, (1783 -1853), and the Semiotics of Charles Sanders Peirce (not a mason) take center stage. Greenleaf was a founding dean of Harvard Law School who wrote a treatise on the history of Freemasonry tracing it to the Druidic and Pythagorean Mysteries. This work was published in 1820. Pierce developed the concept of Semiotics: the interpretation of the meaning of signs as cognates of groups of three, called Triads. Greenleaf's zeal for Pythagorean lore and its impact upon Masonry was nothing new; the Pythagorean Theorem was incorporated in the template of the District of Columbia of 1791 as developed and informed by George Washington, Benjamin Banneker, Pierre Charles L'Enfant, and Daniel Carroll, the subject matter of chapter fourteen. The Pythagorean Theorem or the 47th Proposition of Euclid can been seen in the Federal Triangle formed by the White House, the Washington Monument obelisk, and Capitol. Pennsylvania Avenue forms the hypotenuse of this Pythagorean Triangle; Pennsylvania is the *Keystone State* a direct reference to Royal Arch Masonic symbolism. The Pythagorean Theorem is also the emblem of a Worshipful Master and represents Masonic rulership. The Masonic Federal District would come to incorporate other esoteric themes, such as the hermetic maxim of *as above, so below*, inscribed on the Emerald Tablet of legendary Hellenistic deity Thoth Hermes Mercurius Trismegistus. This philosophy entails the alignment of buildings to celestial bodies in order to draw upon their divine spiritual energies; this is not conspiratorial as even the *Book of Enoch* contained an Astronomical Book. Trismegistus himself is a combination of three gods: Thoth, who in later history of ancient Egypt became heavily associated with the arbitration of godly disputes, the arts of magic, the system of writing, the development of science, and the judgment of the dead; the Greek Hermes, the great messenger of gods, he is also the patron of boundaries and of the travelers who cross them, of shepherds and cowherds, of the cunning of thieves, of orators and wit, of literature and poets, of athletics and sports, of weights and measures, of invention, and of commerce in general; and Mercury is his Roman equivalent. Chapter fifteen concludes *The Royal Arch of Enoch: The Impact of Masonic Ritual, Philosophy, and Symbolism* by examining Enochian and Masonic symbolism in cinema.

* * * * *

Pike wrote, "The true Mason labors for the benefit of those who are to come after him, …"[23] This codex is the product of approximately nineteen years of research began while I was an associate student of St. Catherine's College, Oxford University for the academic year of 1992-1993, my junior year of college. My time at Oxford was spent studying European history and philosophy. Having taken off the academic year of 1993-1994 to

23 Pike, Albert, *Morals and Dogma of the Ancient and Accepted Scottish Rite*, page 312.

work on Capitol Hill, Washington, D.C., my research continued through my senior year at Gettysburg College where I was awarded a B.A. in History in 1995. I returned to Oxford, England during the Michaelmas (Fall) Term of 1995 to study international law and jurisprudence as an associate graduate student at Trinity College. I continued to research symbolism, esoterica, the occult, and Freemasonry independently through 1996 and during my time at Widener University School of Law, Wilmington, Delaware from 1997 to 2000 that resulted in a grant of a Juris Doctorate. It was during my time at law school that I became a Freemason; my Great Grandfather on my father's side, Robert W. Sullivan Sr., was a Mason of Union Lodge #60 of which he was a Past Master (former Worshipful Master). My Grandfather Robert W. Sullivan Jr. was a Freemason, his father-in-law, my Great Grandfather (Grandmother's side) Frederick J. Wheelehan also served as a Worshipful Master of Freedom Lodge #112. I was entered as an Apprentice in January 1997, passed to the degree of Fellowcraft in May 1997, and raised to the sublime degree of Master Mason in September 1997 in Amicable-St. John's Lodge #25 (f/k/a Amicable Lodge #25) Baltimore, Maryland. I became a 32nd degree Master of the Royal Secret of the Scottish Rite, Southern Jurisdiction, Valley of Baltimore, Orient of Maryland in October 1999. Although I am not a member of the York or American Rite, I have researched it exhaustively. The advent of the internet in the late 1990s prompted the actual writing of this book. It began on MySpace[24] in 2005 with the posting of blogs and photo galleries detailing my research while analyzing Masonic symbolisms and their respective impact on material culture. The purpose of this was to generate and gauge interest in this subject matter and the research I had conducted. These blogs and galleries were met with overwhelming praise by other users; questions were either posted or emailed and I gladly answered them. The seed was thus planted, and this book is the oak tree grown by that seed; it took me six years (2005-2011) to write *The Royal Arch of Enoch*. It is my sincere hope that the reader approaches this volume with an open mind as the tome was researched and written with an open mind; all source material in the bibliography was thoroughly investigated and explored. It is also my intent to present new information and not a rehash of exoteric or base Masonic

24 Account deactivated July 2011.

history that seems to dominate recent Masonic literature while, on the other hand, fiction author Dan Brown intertwines Masonic fact with pure Masonic fantasy. Works of the former seem to take the attitude of what I call "trust me Freemasonry," that is the author, because he is Mason, knows better than everyone else when it comes to Masonry, a position that I do not subscribe to. The latter; the books and the movies based upon them: *The Da Vinci Code*, *Angels and Demons*, and now *The Lost Symbol*, entertain rather than enlighten. That being said, the works of Dan Brown and films such as *From Hell*, *National Treasure*, and *National Treasure: Book of Secrets* have spawned new interest in Freemasonry; of this there is little doubt. The onset of 2012 appears to coincide with the renewed interest in this compelling subject matter, the reader and a new generation is now introduced to the world of Masonic ritual, philosophy, symbolism and its respective impact. To this next generation this book hopes to enlighten and inspire. *Sic transit gloria mundi.*

CHAPTER I

MASONIC SYMBOLISM 101

The Sun, the Lost Word and the Blazing Star,
Two Sets of Pillars, and the Ark of the Covenant

"The story of the secret societies can never
be fully reconstructed, but it has been
badly neglected - even avoided, one suspects - because
the evidence that is available repeatedly leads
us into territory equally uncongenial to
modern historians in the East and in the West."
- James H. Billington, *Fire in the
Minds of Men: Origins of the Revolutionary
Faith*, 1980.

The primary subject matter of this book is esoteric Freemasonry. One has to bear in mind that there are essentially two schools of Masonic thought: the factual realistic history of Masonry and that which took a more spiritual esoteric view of the Craft. The chief example of the first is found the works of Robert Freke Gould (1836-1915, author of *History of Freemasonry, Volumes I-III,* revised VI volumes) and in the literature of the premier lodge of Masonic research, *Quatuor Coronati No. 2076* in 1884. Along with Gould, *Quatuor Coronati's* founders include: Charles Warren (of Scotland Yard-Jack the Ripper infamy), W. Harry Reynolds, Adolphus F.A Woodward, Sisson C. Pratt, Wilson James Hughan, Walter Besant, John P. Rylands, and George W. Speth. Examples of the latter can be found in the works of Albert Pike, Robert H. Brown, Albert Churchward, Albert Mackey, and more recently Manly P. Hall and Dame Frances A. Yates. The chief characteristic of the former being hard oriented historical facts, the latter being the orientation of the interior mindset, or spirit, which esoterically informed the creation of those facts.[25] This book follows the tradition-factual documented history

25 Stemper, William H. Jr., *Freemasonry and the Force*, pages 1-2.

while intertwining the esoteric spiritual concepts of Freemasonry that as will be seen, are veiled in symbolic allegory and metaphor. As such, some of the explanations given in this tome are not necessarily traditional; rather this book explains some of the mystical symbolism and philosophies of Masonry, its rituals, and their respective impact upon society, historical facts, especially within the context of the United States. On that note it must be stated that Freemasonry borrows heavily from the ancient Mystery cults and religions, of this there is little doubt. Even the most exoteric mason would admit that Masonry is steeped in mysticism and mystery going far, far beyond Blue Lodge Craft Masonry, the first three degrees. Most of the true mysteries of Freemasonry, both within the Blue Lodge and especially in the "Red" Capitular high or further degrees, are unknown to the modern mason likely due to the fast paced world we live in; the mason is not able to devote six to eight hours every other day to the study of Freemasonry, its symbols, and the true wisdom and treasure trove of knowledge they contain. In the United States this is especially true as Freemasonry was forced to distance itself from many of the esoteric elements of the Craft after the William Morgan Affair of 1826 or face extinction. Morgan had threatened to publish the secrets of Masonry after having been denied membership in a Masonic lodge; or, as some sources claim he was a Mason and had a falling out with the Fraternity of some kind. Morgan it seems at least tricked his way into a Masonic Lodge in upstate New York. Morgan disappeared and by implication Masonry was demonized as a conspiratorial organization; many lodges in the United States were decimated if not wiped out as a result. In America Masonry reinvented itself as a charity organization thereby prolonging its existence. Nevertheless Masonry still contained esoteric wisdom, concealed and encoded in its symbols, emblems and iconography, only it was de-emphasized; seemingly lost or forgotten though not extinguished. Nevertheless, Masonic symbolism would still be incorporated in various seal and designs despite the Morgan debacle. Freemasonry as an inheritor of the Mysteries Schools and Religions was addressed in the book *The Art and Architecture of Freemasonry*, published in 1991, by Professor James Stevens Curl. Curl explains,

> "Mystery-religions are of great antiquity, but in the Masonic context the most interesting are those of Ancient Egypt invented by Isis herself, the Great Goddess, the Magna Mater. The Egyptian cults, Geometry, and even the Great Architect have Masonic connections that cannot be avoided. Rituals included references to secrets that are not seen or heard, but are handed down, and these secrets were presided over by the jackal-headed Anubis who, significantly, taught Isis the way when she was searching for the dismembered Osiris. Isiac mysteries were participated in by certain Roman Emperors, and involved purification, personal piety, and a variety of symbolic journeys, with a trial and degrees. Hadrian is known to have gone through two ceremonies at Eleusis that had Isiac-Egyptian connotations. Enlightenment (*photismos*), initiation as a *mysterion*, and *symbolon* (password) are words that recur in Antiquity. The term *mysterion* signifies the obtaining of esoteric wisdom after some kind of endurance test involving trials, or ordeals, have been passed. Many cults in the Greco-Roman world required initiates to await enlightenment while being kept isolated in darkness, and there were rules concerning silence, patience, and fortitude. The concept of being reborn in the presence of the Great Goddess Isis after a symbolic death was present in the Isiac cults. An initiate, once reborn, would join a sacred band of chosen ones who would be informed of the divine mysteries by being instructed with esoteric knowledge. Mozart's *O heiliges Band der Freundschaft treuer Bruder* perfectly suggests Masonic ideals of fraternity and a 'sacred band', and was written long before he became a Freemason, but such ideas were there, often just beneath the surface, and had never died, such was the strength of survival of the ancient mysteries in one form or another."[26]

This book restores some, not all, of this esoteric wisdom and the Mystery Tradition of Freemasonry by going beneath the surface of history. To begin this journey the following Masonic symbols must now be explored and explained.

---

26 Curl, James Stevens, *The Art and Architecture of Freemasonry*, pages 34 -35.

THE SUN

The most important symbol within Freemasonry is the sun. Thirty-third degree[27] Mason and scholar, Albert Gallatin Mackey, states in his famed Masonic Encyclopedia,

> "Hardly any of the symbols of Masonry are more important in their signification or more extensive in their application than the sun. As the source of material light, it reminds the Mason of that intellectual light of which he is in constant search. But it is especially as the ruler of the day, giving to it a beginning and end, and a regular course of hours, that the sun is presented as a Masonic Symbol. Hence, of the three lesser lights, we are told that one represents or symbolizes the sun, one the moon, and one the Master of the Lodge, because, as the sun rules the day and the moon governs the night, so should the Worshipful Master rule and govern his Lodge with equal regularity and precision. And this is in strict analogy with other Masonic symbolisms. For if the Lodge is a symbol of the world, which is thus governed in its changes of times and seasons by the sun, it is evident that the Master who governs the Lodge, controlling its time of opening and closing, and the work which is it should do, must be symbolized by the sun. The heraldic definition of the sun as a bearing fits most appositely to the symbolism of the sovereignty of the Master. Thus Gwillim says: "The sun is the symbol of sovereignty, the hieroglyphic of royalty; it doth signify absolute authority."
>
> This representation of the sun as a symbol of authority, while it explains the reference to the Master, enables us to amplify its meaning, and apply it to the three sources of authority in the Lodge, and account for the respective positions of the officers wielding this authority. The Master, therefore, in the East is a symbol of the rising sun; the Junior Warden in the South, of the Meridian Sun, and the Senior Warden in the West, of the Setting Sun. So in the mysteries of India, the chief officers were placed in the east, the west, and the south, respectively, to represent Brahma, or the rising; Vishnu, or the setting; and Siva, or the meridian sun. And

27 The highest degree in Scottish Rite Masonry; it is an honorary degree known as Inspector General.

in the Druidical rites, the Arch-Druid, seated in the east, was assisted by two other officers - the one in the west representing the moon, and the other in the south representing the meridian sun.

This triple division of the government of a Lodge by three officers, representatives of the sun in his three manifestations in the east, south, and west, will remind us of similar ideas in the symbolism of antiquity. In the Orphic mysteries, it was taught that the sun generated from an egg, burst forth with power to triplicate himself by his own unassisted energy.

Supreme power always seems to have been associated in the ancient mind with a three-fold division. Thus the sign of authority was indicated by the three-forked lighting of Jove, the trident of Neptune, and the three-headed Cerberus of Pluto. The government of the Universe was divided between these three sons of Saturn. The chaste goddess ruled the earth as Diana, the heavens as Luna, and the infernal regions as Hecate, whence her rites were only performed in a place where three roads met.

The sun is then presented to us in Masonry first as a symbol of light, but then more emphatically as a symbol of sovereign authority.

But, says Wemyss (Symb. Lang.), speaking of Scriptural symbolism, "the sun may be considered an emblem of Divine Truth," because the sun or light, of which it is the source, "is not only manifest in itself, but makes other things; so one truth detects, reveals, and manifests another, as all truths are dependent on, and connected with, each other more or less." And this again is applicable to the Masonic doctrine which makes the Master the symbol of the sun; for as the sun discloses and makes manifest, by the opening of the day, what had been hidden in the darkness of night, so the Master of the Lodge, as analogue of the ancient hierophant or explainer of the mysteries, makes Divine truth manifest in the neophyte, who had been hitherto in intellectual darkness, and reveals the hidden or esoteric lessons of initiation."[28]

28 Mackey, Albert, *Encyclopedia of Freemasonry,* Vol. II, page 736.

The god Apollo (also called Helios),

> "....in astronomical symbolism he is the sun personified, the source of light and fruitfulness, dispensing his influence over all created things. There is, however, no death in his legend, as if the sun of Athens were at its meridian always, as it is in respect of Freemasonry - according to a familiar thesis. There are blots on the escutcheon of his legend, as there are spots on the solar disc; but he overcame Python, the serpent generated from the slime of the Deluge, as one who conquers corruption and inherits eternal youth. He is youth therefore and strength, in commemoration of which he established the Pythian games. He was a builder also, who erected the walls of Troy, or at least assisted therein, and also the fortress of Megara. The Caduceus which raises thedeadandbestowssleep-itsbrotherwasoriginallyhisbutheexchanged it with Mercury for a lyre, because music is the law of life and more than sleep or resurrection. It seems to me therefore that in the world of symbolismApollo isabovethe Mysteries, being he who expoundsthem: he is the spirit which interprets them, form within the veils of the Temple; he is also the spirit which inspires, abiding behind their forms."[29]

Apollo, the son of Jupiter and Leto, is the foremost solar god of the Mediterranean ancient world. Comparatively Apollo was known as Kinich Ahau to the Mayans. Apollo arches his solar chariot across the sky daily bringing light to the world. Apollo starts to drive his chariot in the east, hits meridian in the south at noon, and ends the day by setting in the west. Thus the sun's daily movement creates a dome of the sky. From the northern hemisphere Apollo is at his weakest at the Winter Solstice (December 21-22) as it is the shortest day of the year in the sign of Capricorn. Capricorn is ruled by the planet Saturn whose concomitant is the god Kronos. Both Saturn and Kronos are associated with death as the sun is at its weakest, from the northern hemisphere perspective, under Capricorn. Apollo the sun is at his most powerful on the Summer Solstice (June 20-22) the longest day of the year. At both the vernal and autumnal Equinoxes, March and September 20-22, Apollo rules the day equally with the night. The word, Equinox, means

29 Waite, Arthur Edward, *A New Encyclopedia of Freemasonry*, pp.39-40.

30 These dates slightly fluctuate slightly due to leap years and the Precession of the Equinoxes.

Frontispiece of *The Constitutions of Free-Masons* by Dr. James Anderson, 1723. The scene depicts Grand Master, the Duke of Montague, passing the scroll of the Constitutions to the next Grand Master Philip, Duke of Wharton as Apollo, the sun god, presides triumphantly above.

"equal night" coming from the Latin *aequus* (equal) and *nox* (night). Apollo driving his solar chariot across the sky can be seen on the frontispiece of Dr. James Anderson's *The Constitutions of Free-Masons* published in London in 1723. Anderson's *Constitutions* recounts a legendary history of Masonry going all the way back to Adam in the Garden of Eden. Anderson's *Constitutions* also contain various charges, laws, orders, songs, and regulations of the Masonic fraternity; it was later reprinted by Benjamin Franklin in Philadelphia in 1734. Apollo can be clearly seen beneath an archway in what appears to be a domed area; on the pavement beneath can be seen the Euclid's forty-seventh proposition, also known as the Pythagorean Theorem under which appears the word Eureka or "I have found it." The Pythagorean Theorem, or the use of 3, 4, 5, in constructing right triangles, is the emblem of the Worshipful Master; it represents completeness and is a symbol of social purification because knowledge was the greatest purification and all knowledge to the Pythagoreans came from numbers and mathematics. The 47th Proposition reads that in every right angled triangle the square of the hypotenuse is equal to the sum of the squares on the other two sides. In turn the Pythagoreans believed that divinity was to be found in mathematics, geometry, and through their study divine astronomical-astrological secrets of the universe could be unlocked.

Apollo's concomitant is the Hebrew solar chariot of the *Merkabah* sun god; it is used in Ezekiel 4-26 and describes the throne chariot of God. When Enoch enters the heavens and is told divine occult secrets; he describes the sun an illuministic chariot; "...And first there goes out the great luminary, named the Sun, and his sphere (orbit, disc) is like the sphere (orbit, disc) of heaven and he is quite filled with illuminating and heating fire. The chariot on which he ascends, the wind drives, and the sun goes down from heaven and returns through the north in order to reach the east, and is so guided that he comes to the appropriate door and shines in face of heaven." (see *I Enoch*, (Chapter) 72: (verses) 4-5) The chariot on which the *Merkabah* solar chariot is driven by four living creatures: an ox, a man, a lion, and an eagle. These "living creatures" are astrological symbols. The ox is Taurus the Bull, the man is Aquarius the Water Bearer, the Lion, Leo, and the Eagle is an esoteric reference to Scorpio, as the constellation Aquila the Eagle encompasses modern day Scorpio the Scorpion; Aquila and Scorpio are thus interchangeable. These four signs compromise the fixed signs of the Zodiac and refer to Apollo's (the sun) passage through the middle of the four seasons. Each one of these signs represents one of the four elements: Taurus, an earth sign; Scorpio, a water sign; Leo, a fire sign; and Aquarius an air sign. Each one of these signs contain one of the four great Royal Stars: Regulus in Leo (north), Fomalhaut in Aquarius (south), Antares in Scorpio (west), and Aldebaran in Taurus (east). Above these four fixed signs is *firmament* symbolizing a dome or vault of the sky; "Then I looked, and, behold, in the firmament (which the Jewish Encyclopedia defines as a "vault or expanse of the sky," a *dome*[31]) that was above the head of the cherubims there appeared over them as it were a sapphire stone, as the appearance of the likeness of a throne." (Ezekiel 10:1) The dome represents the sun; the sun rest on a sapphire throne symbolizing the blue sky as a solar vault; many ancient cultures–Egyptians, Chinese, Greeks–considered the sky to be a solid dome that the sun transverses or "sits upon" daily. As will be analyzed in chapter three, these four fixed signs will come to symbolize the four gospels within the *Mysterion* (Christian Mysteries) and form the great celestial cross: created by Leo and its opposite house Aquarius, and Scorpio and its opposite house Taurus –upon which the sun waxes and wanes upon annually by way of the earth's orbit around it. There is also a terrestrial cross formed by the two equinoxes and two solstices created by the earth's orbit around the sun. It is upon these crosses that God's sun is "crossified" or crucified.

31 The New Revised Standard Version Bible uses the word "dome" instead of firmament.

The Biblical *Merkabah* solar chariot of Ezekiel was further studied by students of Hebrew mysticism, namely within movements such as *Ma'aseh Merkabah* in the late Hellenistic period following the destruction of the Temple of Zerubbabel (second Jewish temple) by the Roman Emperor Titus in 70 CE, and Kabbalah. *Ma'aseh Merkabah* is Hebrew for,

> "'Work of Chariot', is one of the oldest branches of Jewish mysticism, which consists of theory and practice based upon the description of the chariot of God in the first chapter of the Book of Ezekiel. Within the system of *Ma'aseh Merkabah* this chariot was believed to be the spiritual world itself, divided into seven heavens and staffed by various wonderful angelic powers. The structure of the chariot was described in handbooks distributed during the heyday of the *Ma'aseh Merkabah*, which lasted from about 300 BCE until the Middle Ages. The several surviving handbooks indicate they were to be used with oral instruction. Many details of the theory mystics were not content to study and meditate on the structure of heaven, but they were equally interested in going there through visionary journeys which are described in detail in various accounts. Practicing *Merkabah* was considered to be both holy and dangerous. In the Talmud it is related that a child was studying the scriptures his teacher's home, and he comprehended the secret meaning of the word clashmal, radiance, suddenly a fire came forth from the clashmal and consumed him. The *Ma'aseh Merkabah* was still practiced in some circles during the first development of the Kabbalah and its practice emerged into the latter. But unlike the *Ma'aseh Merkabah* the Kabbalah relies on meditation to achieve spiritual development rather than ecstatic visionary experiences."[32]

Likewise, Kabbalah is a form of Hebrew mysticism. Hebrew theology was divided into three parts: the law, the soul of the law (Mishnah) and the soul of the soul of the law: Kabbalah. Only the highest initiates among the Hebrews were instructed in the Kabbalah's secret principles. Kabbalah, when intermingled with Qabalah with a "Q," becomes its Hermetic first cousin; Qabalah combines Hebrew Kabbalah with the alchemical, mystical, and occult arts and sciences. On the other hand, Cabala with a

32 Greer, John Michael, *The New Encyclopedia of the Occult*, p. 285.

"C" is the Christian form of Hebrew Kabbalah supplanting Hebrew with Christian mysticism. Cabala is largely a Renaissance phenomenon; all three revolve around the study of its Sephirotic Tree of Life. It is not uncommon to interchange the "K," "C," and "Q" when defining Kabbalah. The foundation of Kabbalah is the *Zohar*; the *Zohar* itself derives from a group of Hebrew texts that includes commentary on the mystical aspects of the Torah, the five books of Moses, the scriptural interpretations as well as material on mysticism, mythical cosmogony, and mystical psychology. The Kabbalah is an oral tradition, allegedly given to Moses on Mount Sinai by God, and transmitted to Aaron and other great Hebrew prophets. The Kabbalah was reputedly conveyed along with the Law (Ten Commandments) and the Talmud. Rabbi and Neo-Platonist Isaac the Blind (ca. 1160-1235) wrote on Kabbalah and was likely the author of the *Book of the Bahir*, an important early text on Kabbalah that circulated throughout medieval France. The twenty-two paths and ten Sephiroth of the Kabbalah as understood by practitioners formulate a mystical system where, according to Isaac the Blind, *Ain Soph* or divine consciousness, found beyond the first Sephirot, Kether, or Crown meaning above consciousness, could be obtained through various meditations and similar practices.[33] The twenty-two paths connecting the ten Sephiroth when added form the number thirty-two which is an esoteric reference to the thirty two paths of wisdom within *Mishnah*: the soul of the law serving as the symbolic basis for the thirty-two degree system of the Ancient and Accepted Scottish Rite of Freemasonry. Add a hidden, unseen Sephirot in the Kabbalah called Da'at (often thought to be the other ten Sephirot united as one) and one has twenty-two paths when

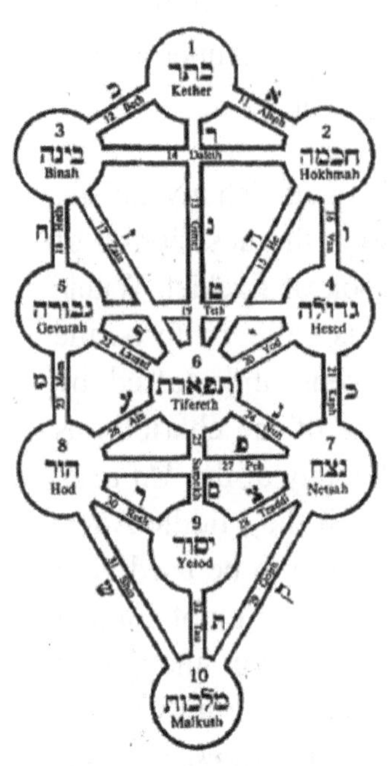

The Kabbalistic Tree of Life-Wisdom with its ten Sephirot, *God through them*, and its twenty-two paths.

33 This is the most common practice of Kabbalah. Other Kabbalists and mystics consider the top three Sephirot - Binah (understanding), Kether (crown), and Hokhmah (wisdom) - representative of the eternal Godhead represented within Christianity as the "Father, Son, and Holy Ghost."

added to the eleven Sephirot becomes thirty-three: an occult reference to the thirty-third and final degree of the Scottish Rite called Inspector General. Kabbalah is a secret doctrine and Kabbalah is often a synonym for the word secret. In turn Christian Cabala interpreted Hebrew Kabbalistic Tetragrammaton, the name of God, as Jesus Christ thus announcing him as the true Messiah. Christian Cabala is a combination of philosophy, theology, astrology, and white magic to achieve communication with angels and through them Deity. Since Cabala proved that the longed for Messiah was Christ Jesus, the use of magic through angelic powers to obtain a higher Godhead was permissible.[34] Cabala heavily influenced Elizabethan magus Dr. John Dee; to Dee and other Renaissance cabalists such as Robert Fludd (Dee's English hermetic-cabalist successor), Marsilio Ficino, Tommaso Campanella, Giovanni Pico della Mirandola, and Giordano Bruno the use of black magic was also permissible. Dr. John Dee served as the inspiration for both Christopher Marlowe's (1564-1593) and Johann Wolfgang Goethe's (1749-1832) Dr. Faustus or Faust; Dee is Shakespeare's Prospero from *The Tempest* published 1610/1611 and Edgar Allan Poe's (1809-1849) Prince Prospero from *The Masque of the Red Death* published in 1842.

Just as the sun is the most important symbol within Masonry, it is also worshipped and adored. Albert Mackey further elucidates,

> "Eusebius says the that the Phoenicians and the Egyptians were the first who ascribed divinity to the sun. But long - very long - before these ancient peoples of the primeval race of Aryans worshipped the solar orb in his various manifestations as the producer of light.
>
> "In the Veda," says a native commentator, "there are only three deities: Surya in heaven, Indra in the sky, and Agni on the earth." But Surya, Indra, Agni are but manifestations of God in the sun, the bright sky, and the fire derived from solar light. In the profoundly poetic ideas of the Vedic hymns we find perpetual allusions to the sun with his life-bestowing rays. Everywhere in the East, amidst its brilliant skies, the sun claimed, as the glorious manifestation of Deity, the adoration of

34 Hancox, Joy, *The Byrom Collection and the Globe Theatre Mystery*, pages 221-222.

> those primitive peoples. The Persians, the Assyrians, the Chaldeans - all worshipped the sun. The Greeks, a more intellectual people, gave a poetic form to the grosser idea, and adored Apollo or Dionysius as the sun-god.
>
> Sun-worship was introduced into the mysteries not as a material idolatry, but as the means of expressing an idea of restoration to life from death, drawn from the daily reappearance in the east of the solar orb after its nightly disappearance in the west. To the sun, too, as the regenerator or reviver of all things, is the Phallic worship, which made a prominent part of the mysteries, to be attributed. From the Mithraic initiations, in which sun-worship played so important a part, the Gnostics derived many of their symbols. These, again, exercised their influence upon the Medieval Freemasons. Thus it is that the sun has become so prominent in the Masonic System; not, of course, as an object or worship, but purely as a symbol, the interpretation of which presents itself in many different ways."[35]

Thirty-third degree Masonic ritualist and philosopher Albert Pike echoes this view in his tome *Morals and Dogma of the Ancient and Accepted Scottish Rite of Freemasonry* published in 1871. Pike concludes,

> "It is not strange that, thousands of years ago, men worshipped the Sun, and that to-day that worship continues among the Parsees. Originally they looked beyond the orb to the invisible God, of whom the Sun's light, seemingly identical with generation and life, was the manifestation and outflowing. Long before the Chaldean shepherds watched it on their plains, it came up regularly, as it now does, in the morning, like a god, and again sank, like a king retiring, in the west, to return again in due time in the same array of majesty. We worship Immutability. It was that steadfast, immutable character of the Sun that men of the Baalbec worshipped. His light-giving and his life-giving powers were secondary attributes. The one grand idea that compelled worship was the characteristic of God which they saw reflected in his light, and fancied they saw in its originality the changelessness of Deity. He had seen thrones crumble, earthquakes

35 Mackey, Albert, *Encyclopedia of Freemasonry Vol. II*, page 737.

> shake the world and hurl down mountains. Beyond Olympus, beyond the Pillars of Hercules, he had gone daily to his abode, and had come daily again in the morning to behold the temples they built to his worship. They personified him as BRAHMA, AMUN, OSIRIS, BEL, ADONIS, MALKARTH, MITHRAS, and APOLLO; and the nations that did so grew old and died. Moss grew on the capitals of the great columns of his temples, and he shone on the moss. Grain by grain the dust of his temples crumbled and fell, and was borne off on the wind, and still he shone on crumbling column and architrave. The roof fell crashing on the pavement, and he shone in on the Holy of Holies with unchanging rays. It was not strange that men worshipped the Sun."[36]

Barring exception (i.e. commercial buildings) domed buildings designate them as temples of the sun both in the ancient and modern world. The Temple of Apollo at Delphi featured a large dome encompassing a circular hall. Italian poet, architect, linguist, philosopher, artist, cryptographer, and Renaissance humanist Leon Battista Alberti's (1404-1472) frequent reference to temples to the sun as domed circulars while temples to Vesta[37] should be like a ball, concepts he picked up from Vitruvius' *De Architectura* (published as *Ten Books on Architecture*), and were discussed in his own work *De Re Aedificatoria (Ten Books of Architecture)* published in 1452 and naturally based on Vitruvius' ten books.[38] Alberti's work in turn influenced Dr. John Dee whose *The Mathematicall Praeface to Elements of Geometrie of Euclid of Megara* (London, 1570) demonstrated how geometry, architecture, and Neo-Platonism integrated both art and science with cosmic harmony with the prototype of the architect as a universal scholar with an irenic mission: the creation of a new world led by a new order of Masonic monks. The differing political function of architectural symbolism in the works of Thomas Smith Webb, presaged by Dr. John Dee, compared with William Preston underscored the vast difference in importance Webb's system attached to iconography, illustrated by Jeremy Cross' (1783-1861) popular, entrepreneurial iconographic interpretation titled *Masonic Chart or Hieroglyphic Monitor* of 1819. In brief, Webb's symbolism became a means to identify Freemasonry with the premise that God, *Deus*, was an architect,

36 Pike, Albert, *Morals and Dogma of the Ancient and Accepted Scottish Rite*, page 77.
37 Virgin goddess of home, family, and hearth in the Roman religion.
38 Curl, James S., *The Art and Architecture of Freemasonry*, page 100.

the Great Architect of the Universe, and that a proper comprehension and useful application of emblems conferred upon Masonic governance a divine quality. Within the New Republic, this concept was greatly empowered and augmented when attached to the core ideal of the enlightened citizen as a wise sage and elected official. There was no formal monarchy, and in theory any Freemason in a position of public trust might assume a mantle of sacred and secret wisdom through a proper comprehension of the Masonic art. Such an identity was, in effect, apologetical propaganda in the face of religious anti-Masonry and fit neatly into Freemasonry's enthusiasm to be perceived as friendly to respectable religion, as laid out in Anderson's *Constitutions*, notably that a Mason could not be a libertine or stupid atheist. William Preston's symbolism to the English nation never had the same populist visual management; after 1813 there was a single United Grand Lodge to manage and restrictively to control such symbolism. In America, however, the proliferation of Webb's approach depended not only upon the political advocacy of men such as DeWitt Clinton, but also upon the commercial dissemination of Jeremy Cross' *Masonic Chart*, midrashed or sacredized in the writings of Dr. Rob Morris (1818-1888, founder of the Eastern Star) and Albert G. Mackey (1807-1881). The result was that Webb's ideas were not only amplified, but illustrated by Jeremy Cross whose own *Masonic Chart* walked hand in hand with the works of Morris, Mackey, and later Albert Pike. T. S. Webb's Masonic ideology, contained in his own *Monitor* and illustrated by Jeremy Cross in 1819, conformed with and was reflected by the profound political resonance of New York Governor and Royal Arch Mason DeWitt Clinton. The implicit mathematically and geometrically nuanced governance dynamic at the core of Webb's ritualized symbolism became, therefore, the premise that the Masonic leader was effectually a form of a sublime enlightened hermit, or god, imitating the divine agency on earth, within political sacral structure what the Great Architect achieved in the creation of the heavens and earth. This fine point, blasphemous to anti-Masons, was surely lost upon the countless politiques in Webb's and DeWitt Clinton's rapidly expanding circles of enthusiastic joiners who deemed Freemasonry, simply, a patriotic sodality associated with the great George Washington. Yet, its subtler elements provided powerful fodder for those who appreciated the uses to which learning might be put to achieve personal ambition, to be part of a new world solar clerisy, and a unitary sense of national mission within, notably, the college fraternity movement.

* * * * *

Domed, circular churches or temples are prevalent throughout history. The Pantheon in Rome has a dome thus making it one of the earliest temples of the sun. Emperor Hadrian visualized himself enthroned directly under the Pantheon's dome, its oculus, as a near-deity symbolizing his solar rulership around which not only the Roman Empire but the universe, the sun, and the heavens obediently revolved. The circular dome form of the church of the Holy Sepulchre in Jerusalem and the circular Knight Templar churches that were modeled after it; the Templar churches were also modeled after the Islamic Dome of the Rock (which was designed after the domed Holy Sepulchre in Jerusalem) was Christianized by the Templars and used by them as their headquarter during the Crusades. The Dome of the Rock was associated with Solomon's Temple, first Jewish Temple completed circa 960 BCE, as well as the Second Temple of Zerubbabel destroyed 70 CE, as it was built upon their ruins along with the Al-Aqsa Mosque. Other domed or circular temples include the great church at Aachen built by Charlemagne, San Stefano Rotondo in Rome, not to mention numerous Renaissance and Baroque designs.[39] The connection between the Dome of the Rock, the church of the Holy Sepulchre, Knight Templar churches in London, and round churches, Cambridge, Ludlow Castle, and the Holy Sepulchre in Northampton are but three examples, must be emphasized because round churches persisted as holy places for Orders and Brotherhoods: Montsalvat in *Parsifal* is one example.[40] Round forms suggest

Frontispiece of Volume II of *Ars Magna Sciendi* (1669) by Athanasius Kircher features the sun as dome symbolism; the sun crossing a heavenly dome, while the nine muses contemplate their respective arts.

39 Ibid.
40 Ibid.

wholeness, completeness, and protection of the outer circumference; they are apposite to Closed Orders or to meeting-places, as is amply demonstrated by the polygonal plans of English Chapter House.[41] The domed Pantheon and the Cathedral at Aachen suggest antique imperial solar design while linking them to the beginning of the Holy Roman Empire.[42] A dome is also a vault of the sky symbolizing the sun as it transverses the sky in the shape of a dome as discussed. Domed churches, cathedrals, or temples designate them as chambers of sun worship; the most clear cut example is St. Peter's Basilica in Rome. It features a dome (projected by Michelangelo, completed between 1585-1590 by Giacomo della Porta with the assistance of Domenico Fontana, the latter being the best engineer of the day) designating it and Vatican City as a temple of sun worship whereApollo (the sun) is worshipped as Jesus Christ (see Chapter III); directly beneath the dome stands Gian Lorenzo Bernini's (1598-1680) *Baldacchino* which originally contained twelve twisted Solomonic columns over the tomb of Saint Peter. The twelve columns symbolize the twelve houses of the Zodiac that aid Apollo on his annual passage; within the Mysterion the twelve houses incarnate as the twelve apostles, to be discussed more in depth in Chapter III. While domed churches designate them as actual temples of sun adoration or worship, the placement of a dome on a library transforms it into a *temple of light*, light meaning learning, knowledge, and wisdom, giving rise to en*light*enment; while the placement of a dome on a governmental building characterizes it as a new age *temple of light*; light defined as new world democracy. "Light is the most appropriate symbol of manifesting spirit because it is the inherent nature of light to radiate,..."[43] The concept of a domed Apollonian solar chamber or divine-kingly throne room (cf. Ezekiel 10:1) was further developed and refined by Renaissance architect Andrea Palladio (1508-1580) in his work *I quattro libri dell'architettura* (*Four Books of Architecture*, 1570), who, like Alberti, was influenced by the Augustinian[44] architect, city planner, writer, and engineer Vitruvius whose architectural designs featured domed buildings, vaults, and triumphal arches. A keystone is a wedge shaped stone inserted at the top of the arch giving it stability and allowing it to stand. A dome is an arch rotated on its axis while

41 Ibid, 100-101.
42 Ibid, 101.
43 Hall, Manly Palmer, *Lectures on Ancient Philosophy*, page 49.
44 Roman Emperor Augustus a/k/a Gaius Julius Caesar Octavianus 63 BCE - 14 CE, not to be confused with Saint Augustine. Vitruvius dedicated his ten books to Augustus.

a vault is a depository for treasure, or an arched structure enclosing a space or chamber resembling a vault.

Finally, an initiate, after being raised to the sublime degree of Master Mason, is told in the third degree lecture to lift his eyes to the sun as "that Bright Morning Star whose rising brings peace and salvation (or tranquility in some lectures) to the faithful and obedient of the human race." The actual bright morning star is the sun, not to be confused with Venus which is correctly known as the "son of the morning" or more accurately the son of the morning star. Venus often rises in the morning hours as a bogus "morning star" appearing in quotations because it is not the true morning star; Venus' faux light is an imposter to the brilliance of the sun's life-giving rays. Adding to the confusion is the fact that Venus was known as the Evening Star to the Greeks. Venus, a negative planet, rises before the dawn as a false morning star, hence its association with Lucifer[45] (from the Latin for light bringer or bearer); or, alternatively the bearer or symbolic bringer[46] of the true light of Masonry: the sun. Even the Roman architect Vitruvius writes in *De Architectura* that Venus (*Veneris stella*) had two names, Vesperugo as the evening star and as Lucifer the morning star. Venus as Lucifer (son of the morning) is confirmed at Isaiah 14:12, "How art thou fallen from heaven, O Lucifer, *son of the morning*! [how] art thou cut down to the ground, which didst weaken the nations!" After rebelling against God, Lucifer, a pretender, establishes his stronghold *northwest* of heaven because in the west the sun sets, dies; while God dwells in the east and south symbolizing the rising, triumphal sun and the sun in the south at highest, most powerful meridian, a polar opposite of Lucifer's northwest haunt.[47] The actual "bright morning star" is the sun which is a *star*, Venus, one is reminded, *is a planet and not a star*. God's sun is the *risen savior* that is *born again* every morning bringing light, life, and salvation to the world. Masons are thus instructed to symbolically travel east, in search of light, because the sun rises in the east as the great source of light. Thus, Venus has no significant role in

45 Lucifer is not to be confused with the concept of the Christian Satan or Devil.
46 Devore, Nicholas, *Encyclopedia of Astrology*, page 247. Venus is occasionally referred to as a "morning star" but only of it appears in quotations denoting that it is not the true morning star. The morning star that the third degree Masonic lecture is referring to is the sun. Venus is appropriately known as the "son of the morning star."
47 Russell, Jeffrey Burton, *Lucifer: The Devil in the Middle Ages*, page 139. See also Isaiah 14:13, "For thou hast said in thine heart, I will ascend into heaven, I will exalt my throne above the stars of God: I will sit also upon the mount of the congregation, *in the sides of the north*:"

Freemasonry; Masons do not adhere to a Luciferian Doctrine.

THE LOST WORD AND THE BLAZING STAR

While the Blue Lodge[48] does not have its own icon for the Lost Word, nevertheless the Lost Word of a Master Mason is an important emblem and has been symbolized. The Lost Word is the Tetragrammaton, the ineffable name of God. God, the Supreme Being, is known within Masonry as the Great Architect of the Universe. It is formed by the Hebrew letters יהוה : *Heh*, *Vav*, *Heh*, *Yodh* (Hebrew reads right to left),Y H V H or Jehovah (reading left to right) which in turn influenced the sacred name of God as IEVE to Christian mystic Joachim von Fiore. In the form of the Pythagorean Tetractys (Jewish Kabbalists were heavily influenced by Greek Philosophy) the Tetragrammaton, its Hebrew version YHVH, has a numeric value of 72: *Yodh* equals 10, *Heh* equals 5, and *Vav* equals 6. The word Yahweh is a modern scholarly convention for the Hebrew יהוה transcribed into the Roman letters as YHWH.

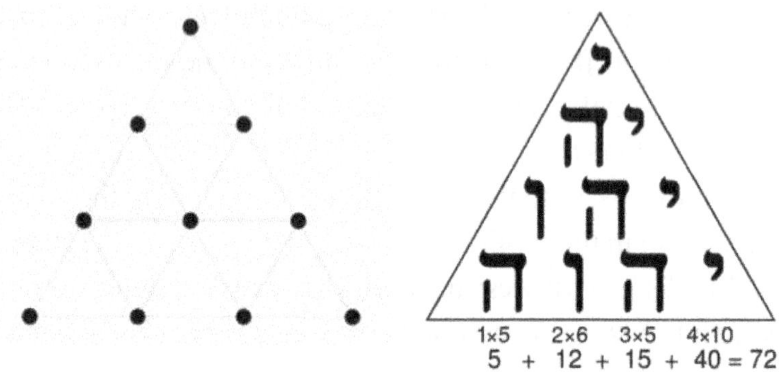

The Pythagorean Tetractys (left) and the Hebrew Tetragrammaton arranged in the Kabbalistic Tetractys (right) formation; the sum of all the letters is 72 according to Gematria, a rabbinic system of assigning an occult, numerical value to each letter of the alphabet.

This value is based upon the *ten*fold arrangement of the Hebrew letters. Philosopher, astrologer, occultist, alchemist, and theologian Heinrich

48 The first three degrees of Freemasonry: Entered Apprentice, Fellowcraft, and Master Mason. It could be argued that the "substitute word" of a Master Mason is symbolized bythe pentagram.

Cornelius Agrippa (1486-1535) referred to this as "the name of Jehovah with ten letters collected" (see *Three Books of Occult Philosophy*, Book II, chapter 13). The number ten in Pythagorean numerology represented divine perfection. Roman architect Vitruvius states,

> "Further, it was from the members of the body that they derived the fundamental ideas of the measure which are obviously necessary in all works, as the finger, palm, foot, and cubit. These they apportioned so as to form the "perfect number," called in Greek (Τέλειον), and as the perfect number the ancients fixed upon ten. For it is from the number of the fingers of the hand that the palm is found, and the foot from the palm. Again, while ten is naturally perfect, as being made up by the fingers of the two palms, Plato also held that this number was perfect because ten is composed of the individual units, called by the Greeks (μονάδες). …"[49]

To Kabbalists the four letters also symbolize the four elements: earth, air, fire, and water. The Hebrews used the word "Adonai" as a substitute for the true name of God. Within Masonry the name or Lost Word has three syllables not four; it is J- B- O-. Symbolically, it is through correct pronunciation of the three syllables Tetragrammaton that all learning (medieval *Trivium* and *Quadrivium*, the seven liberal arts and sciences) is made possible. The word was possessed by the architect of Solomon's Temple, Hiram Abif, as presented in the third degree ritual. It is through possession of the word that Hiram is able to construct the first temple. Upon his murder and before the completion of the Temple the word is forever lost within the Craft Lodge. An initiate, upon being raised to the degree of Master Mason by the strong grip of the Lion's Paw, has a substitute word whispered in his ear; it is not the true name of God. The Masonic substitute word, which is M- H- B-, can only be thereafter transmitted by forming the Five Points of Fellowship: hand to hand, foot to foot, knee to knee, breast to breast, hand to back. In 1842 at the Baltimore Masonic Convention "hand to hand" was replaced with "mouth to ear." The true Word is forever unknown to the Blue Lodge Masons, the word is recovered during the Royal Arch ceremonies: the thirteenth degree in the Scottish Rite and the seventh degree in the York or American Rite. It is the

49 Vitruvius, *The Ten Books on Architecture,* Book III, Chap. i, V.

symbolism of these two latter degrees that takes priority. The word is Logos or God to which reference is given in John I: 1-5,

> "In the beginning was the word (Logos), and was with God, and the word was God; the same was in the beginning with God: all things were made by him, and without him was not any thing made that was made; in him was life, and the life was the light of men: and the light shineth in darkness, and the darkness comprehended it not."

The pagan sage Epictetus held, "The Logos of the philosopher doth promise us peace which God proclaimed through his Logos;" the architect Vitruvius writes, "Let no one think I have erred if I believe in the Logos;" Clement of Alexandria acknowledges "It may be freely granted that the Greeks received some glimmers of the divine Logos;" while early church father Origen (ca. 185-254) described Logos as "the Idea of Ideas;" while Thoth Hermes Mercurius Trismegistus expressed this idea emerging from the Oneness of God like a word of thought.[50] Albert Pike writes that, "The True Word of a Mason is to be found in the concealed and profound meaning of the Ineffable Name of Deity, communicated by God to Moses; and which meaning was long lost by the precautions taken to conceal it. The true pronunciation of that name was in truth a secret, in which, however, was involved the far more profound secret of its meaning. In that meaning is included all the truth than can be known by us, in regard to the nature of God."[51] The word is recovered in the Masonic Royal Arch ceremonies; kabbalistically the expansion or use of Masonic Royal Arch symbolism is the expansion of Logos, the Grand Omnific Royal Arch word, or of God himself.

The Five Points of Fellowship form a pentagram, symbolized within Masonry as the Blazing Star which is the Egyptian Dog-Star Sirius,[52] the

50 Freke, Timothy and Peter Gandy, *The Jesus Mysteries: Was the "Original Jesus" a Pagan God?*, page 83.

51 Pike, Albert, *Morals and Dogma of the Ancient and Accepted Scottish Rite*, page 697.

52 Ibid, pages 486 and 842. Pike contradicts Mackey on this point, Mackey erroneously stating that the Blazing Star is not a pentagram, while Pike both confirms its relation to Sirius symbolized by a pentagram. Mackey likely feared that association between the Blazing Star of Masonry with a pentagram would link it to Venus, symbolized within witchcraft and paganism as a pentagram due to Venus' pentacle orbit. Venus, the bearer of false or inferior light associates itself with Lucifer (Latin for the Light Bringer), hence its importance (and the pentagram) in black magic cults; the planet Venus has no importance within Masonry whatsoever. Mackey, however, does correctly state that the Blazing Star derives from great antiquity.

brightest star in the nighttime sky, appearing in the east as the Eastern Star. Being the brightest star makes Sirius the "Lone Star." The sun aside, the Blazing Star is often called the most important symbol within Masonry. The Blazing Star, Sirius, is symbolized by a five pointed star or pentagram within Masonry. In the ritual of 1735, it is detailed as a part of the furniture of a Lodge, with the explanation that the "Mosaic Pavement is the Ground Floor of the Lodge, the Blazing Star, the Centre, and the Indented Tarsal, the Border round about it!" In the lectures of William Preston (1742-1818), who authored *Illustrations of Freemasonry* published in 1772, states the Blazing Star with the Mosaic Pavement and the Tessellated Border, are called the Ornaments of the Lodge, and explains that:

> "The Blazing Star, or glory in the centre, reminds us of that awful period when the Almighty delivered the two tables of stone, containing the Ten Commandments, to His faithful servant Moses on Mount Sinai, when the rays of his divine glory shone so bright that none could behold it without fear and trembling. It also reminds us of the omnipresence of the Almighty, overshadowing us with His divine love, and dispensing His blessings amongst us; and by its being placed in the centre, it further reminds us, that wherever we may be assembled together, God is in the midst of us, seeing our actions, and observing the secret intents and movements of our hearts."[53]

In the twenty-eighth degree of the Ancient and Accepted Scottish Rite, known as the Knight of the Sun or Prince Adept, the Blazing Star is symbolic of a true Mason, who becomes a "Blazing Star" in his quest for knowledge and truth. In the fourth degree of that same rite, known as Secret Master; the Blazing Star is described as a symbol of light and Divine Providence pointing out the way to truth.[54] To Thomas Smith Webb (1771-1819), who authored his own *Illustrations of Freemasonry* (or *Monitor*) based in part on Preston's work; the Blazing Star was the Star of Bethlehem, while other Masonic authors and thinkers link the Blazing Star to the sun. These symbolisms will be analyzed in a subsequent chapter. The Blazing Star

53 Mackey, Albert, *Encyclopedia of Freemasonry,* Vol. I, page 106.
54 Ibid.

Sirius (or Sothis) was worshipped and adored in the Egyptian Mysteries as the Great Mother Goddess Isis: the Virgin Mother of the solar messiah Horus, she is wife-sister of Osiris, a resurrected sun god, and the daughter of Geb, the Egyptian God of Earth worshipped at Heliopolis the Egyptian City of the Sun. Sirius begins its ascent in the eastern sky coinciding with the summer solstice, Isis weeps for her murdered husband Osiris, her tears turn to rain causing the inundation of the Nile. Isis incarnates as the Virgin Mary within Christianity and is the prototype of many Greco-Roman-Middle Eastern goddesses including but not limited to: Ashtoreth, Minerva, Ceres, Demeter, Astarte, Pallas Athena, Diana, Hecate, and Ishtar. Comparatively Isis is Devaki in India; .....in Carthage Isis was known as Tanit and to the Chinese Ching Mon.[55] Latin prose writer Apuleius (ca. 125-180 CE) in the eleventh book of *The Golden Ass* ascribes this statement to Isis: "Behold, I moved by thy prayers, am present with thee; I, who am nature, the parent of all things, the queen of all the elements, the primordial progeny of the ages, the supreme of Divinities, the sovereign of the spirits of the dead, the first of the celestials, and the uni-form resemblance of Gods and Goddesses. I, who rule by my nod the luminous summits of the heavens, the salubrious breezes of the sea, and the deplorable silences of the realms beneath and whose one divinity the whole orb of earth venerates under a manifold form, by different rites and a variety of appellations. Hence the primogenial Phrygians call me Pessinuntica, the mother of the Gods; the Attic Aborigines, the Cecropian Minerva; the floating Cyprians, Paphian Venus; arrow-bearing Cretans, Diana Dictynna; the three-tongued Sicilians, Stygian Proserpine; and the Eleusinians, the Goddess Ceres. Some also call me Juno, others Bellona, others Hecate, and others Rhamnusia. And those who are illuminated by the incipient rays of that divinity the Sun, when he rises, viz. the Ethiopians, the Arii, and the Egyptians skilled in the ancient learning, worshipping me by ceremonies perfectly appropriate, call me by my true name, Queen Isis."[56] Apuleius was initiated into the mysteries of Isis and Dionysus and was a priest of Asclepius, the Greek god of medicine and healing.

Sirius is the Dog Star because it is part of the constellation Canis Major

55 Busenbark, Ernest, *Symbols, Sex, and the Stars,* page. 46.

56 Quoted in Hall, Manly P. *The Secret Teachings of All Ages,* page 122.

the Great Dog; Sirius heliacally rises in the months of July and August (approximately July 2-4 to August 11, some sources claim July 20 to August 27) making them the dog days of summer.[57] Sirius is one with the sun in early July as the sun passes over Sirius. Masonically, the creation of the Five Points of Fellowship is an esoteric reference to Sirius, Isis, because the five points (symbolic pentagram) are formed in order to communicate in low breath the substitute word of a Master Mason upon being raised from his symbolic death; it is a homage to Isis who in mythology secretly possessed the secret name of God, (cf. Tetragrammaton, the True Word of a Master Mason), Amun Ra or Re, who was worshipped as the supreme solar deity: the spiritual force behind the sun, giving her mastery over the other gods. The secret name of Amun Re/Ra that Isis possessed is unknown. Through possession of this word or name Isis was able to procure magic and resurrect her slain husband Osiris, as Orion risen, in order to conceive her solar child Horus. On the power of names Origen states,

Eliphas Levi's Tetragrammaton *qua* pentagram, which Levi considered to be a symbol of the microcosm, the human being. From *Dogme et Rituel de la Haute Magie*, 1855.

> "There are names which have a natural potency. Such as those which the Sages used among the Egyptians, the Magi of Persia, the Brahmins in India. What is called Magic is not a vain and chimerical act, as the Stoics and Epicureans pretend.
> The names S*abaoth* and *Adonai* were not made for created beings; but they belong to a mysterious theology, which goes back to the Creator. From Him comes the virtue of these names, when they are arranged and pronounced according to the rules."[58]

Even the name *Amun*, among the Egyptians, was a name pronounceable by none save the Priests.[59] Over time, Horus and Amun Re/Ra would

57 Devore, *Encyclopedia of Astrology*, page 128.
58 Quoted in Pike, Albert, *Morals and Dogma of the Ancient and Accepted Scottish Rite*, page 620.
59 Ibid, page 621.

merge into one and the same deity symbolized by a winged solar disk. The relationship of name and essence was analyzed by Neo-Kantian philosopher Ernst Cassirer in *Language and Myth* (1925, English translation 1946 by Susanne K. Langer), which classically outlined the appeal to Egyptian mythology utilized in the creation of a national American civil religion first used by political philosopher Jean Jacques Rousseau (1712-1778) to refer to the religious dimension of polity. Immanuel Kant (1724-1804) who's *Critique of Pure Reason,* first published in 1781, aimed to unite reason with experience and to move beyond what he took to be failures of traditional philosophy and metaphysics. Rousseau's romantic philosophies and political thought heavily influenced both the French and American Revolutions. Cassirer traces symbolic power quintessentially to the ploy used by Isis to secure power over all of the gods by knowing the name of god: Amun Re (Re meaning *Sun* or *King*); the loss of the word is the central theme of the Third Degree ritual and the Masonic Royal Arch ceremony in both the York and Scottish Rite tradition where the word or name of God is recovered. King Solomon, the construction of his Temple provides the basis of the Master Mason degree ritual, "….went after Ashtoreth the goddess of the Zidonians, and after Milcom (or Molech) the abomination of the Ammonites" in I Kings 11:5, and "….high places….Solomon the King of Israel had built for Ashtoreth the abomination of the Zidonians, and for Chemosh the abomination of the Moabites…" in II Kings 23:13. Ashtoreth is Astarte of Sidon, the Mother of the Gods, the Great Mother, with Ascalon the Syrophoenician goddess, with Ishtar the Babylonian and Assyrian goddess, who is of course Isis the Egyptian pancosmic goddess, and who is referred to on inscriptions as Astarte in Delos.[60] King Solomon venerated Isis in one of her many guises, therefore the connection between Solomon, his Temple, the Egyptian-Isian mysteries, and Freemasonry, which celebrates the construction of Solomon's Temple in its rituals, is easy to forge and is not as tenuous as one may initially think.[61] Yet another nexus between Masonry and Isis (as Sirius) is established by way of Masons being known as widow's sons, the original widow's son being Hiram Abif, the architect of Solomon's Temple. Isis became widowed upon the death

60 Curl, James S., *The Art and Architecture of Freemasonry*, page 113.
61 Ibid.

of Osiris by Typhon. As will be analyzed Osiris and Hiram Abif are both metaphoric stand-ins for the sun. One of Masonry's greatest philosophers,[62] Manly Palmer Hall, states "We can apply this analogy to a great modern system of initiation, Freemasonry, which has certainly perpetuated at least the outer form of the ancient rites. Freemasonry as an institution is Isis, the mother of the Mysteries, from whose dark womb the Initiates are born in the mystery of the second or philosophical birth. Thus all adepts, by virtue of their participation in the rites, are figuratively, at least, Sons of Isis. As Isis is the widow, seeking to restore her lord, and to avenge his cruel murder, it follows that all Master Masons or Master Builders, are widow's sons. They are the offspring of the institution widowed by the loss of the living Word, and theirs is the eternal quest–they discover by becoming."[63]

Jachin and Boaz and the Pillars of Enoch

As source of never ending confusion, there are two sets of pillars within Freemasonry; one set is known to all masons, the other set not so much. The first are of course Jachin and Boaz, the two brass pillars that stood at the porch of Solomon's Temple. Jachin is the right hand pillar (or south), Boaz it is the left hand pillar (or north). The word "Jachin" is derived from the Hebrew "*Jah*" from "Jehovah" and "*achin*" or "to establish" while Boaz is compounded from "*B*" or "in," and "*oaz*," "strength; taken together the pillars mean: In strength shall My House be established. Jachin and Boaz were eighteen cubits in height (27 feet) with a circumference of twelve cubits (18 feet); each ornamented with nets and pomegranates. The two pillars represent the active and passive nature of divine energy, the sun and the moon, as the Hebrew year was lunar: the moon established years, months, and weeks; while the sun in whose strength ruled and divided the seasons.[64] They also represent the signs of Cancer in which the summer solstice occurs and Capricorn the house of the winter solstice. Cancer

62 Hall was referred to as one of "Masonry's greatest philosophers" in his obituary in the Scottish Rite Journal after his death in August 1990.
63 Hall, Manly Palmer, *The Lost Keys of Freemasonry,* page 153.
64 Brown, Robert Hewitt, *Stellar Theology and Masonic Astronomy*, page 77; see also I Kings 7:21 and II Chronicles 3:17.

signifies the sun at its strength hence life; Capricorn the sun at its weakest hence death Within the Masonic Lodge, the solstices are known as the appellation of the two Saint Johns.[65] Jachin and Boaz can be seen on the High Priestess card of the Major Arcana of the Tarot (see Plate I).

The other set, the Pillars of Enoch, are not a part of Blue Lodge Masonry but are arguably more significant symbolically especially within the high or further degrees of Masonry. Thomas Smith Webb, in his *Illustrations of Freemasonry* (1797), recounts that Enoch, whose name means the Initiator, had knowledge of the coming Deluge, the Flood of Noah, where God intended to end humanity and start over. Enoch, the great-grandfather of Noah, wishing to preserve all antediluvian knowledge erected an underground temple, built by his son Methuselah who was acquainted with his father's motives,[66] consisting of nine vaults situated perpendicularly beneath each other. The Enochic vault was constructed under Mount Moriah. Within the ninth vault he placed a golden delta (triangle) containing the ineffable name of Deity or the Lost Word of a Master Mason which was sunken into a cube of agate.[67] Tradition holds Enoch, being a man of perfect virtue, received God's name when he walked with him in heaven. This is confirmed in the *Book of Enoch*; Enoch beholds the *Tree of Life* a reference to the Kabbalah, its ten Sephirot, an emanation of the divine attributes of God including his name. Through the pronunciation of this name or word all learning is made possible. Webb recounts the tale that Enoch erected two pillars, one of metal containing all pre-deluge wisdom and knowledge; the other of marble that contained an inscription indicating where the treasure vault, containing both the metal pillar and golden delta, was located a short distance away. Another Masonic legend states that the two Pillars of Enoch contained two sets of information. Upon the first pillar was placed all the knowledge of the arts and sciences, from which the seven liberal arts and sciences and Masonry comes from; the second pillar mathematical wisdom including the 47th Proposition of Euclid. Through the pronunciation of the Lost Word, the knowledge on the two pillars could be restored. This idea is attributed to the 1737 Oration of the Chevalier Ramsay.

65 Hall, Manly Palmer, *The Secret Teachings of All Ages*, pages 307-308.
66 Albert Mackey claims Methuselah was not familiar with his father's motives.
67 Pike, Albert, *Morals and Dogma of the Ancient and Accepted Scottish Rite*, page 209.

According to legend the first pillar was decoded by the sage Thoth Hermes Mercurius Trismegistus (Thrice Greatest), worshipped at the Temple of Thoth at Khemnu known to the Greeks as Hermopolis; while the knowledge on the mathematical pillar was restored by Pythagoras who exclaimed "EUREKA!" or I have found it! The *it* being the 47th Proposition ofEuclid, restored by the correct pronunciation of Tetragrammaton, reintroducing the knowledge thereon inscribed and encoded on the two Pillars. To many Christian writers, including Lactantius (ca. 240-ca. 320) , Augustine of Hippo (354-430), Giordano Bruno (1548-1600), Tommaso Campanella (1568-1639), Marsilio Ficino (1433-1499) and Giovanni Pico della Mirandola (1463-1494), Hermes Mercurius Trismegistus was thought to be a wise pagan prophet who foresaw the coming of Christianity. They believed in a *prisca theologia*, the doctrine that a single, true theology exists, which threads through all religions, and which was given by God to man in antiquity and passed through a series of prophets, which included Zoroaster, Plato, and Dionysius the Areopagite. In order to demonstrate the verity of the *prisca theologia* Christians appropriated the Hermetic teachings for their own purposes. By this account Hermes Trismegistus was either, according to the fathers of the Christian church, a contemporary of Moses or the third in a line of men named Hermes, i.e. Enoch, Noah and the Egyptian priest king who is known to us as Hermes Trismegistus, or *thrice great*. Hermes Trismegistus was not only syncretic of three gods but was also thrice great because he was the greatest priest, philosopher, and king. Hermes Trismegistus (a/k/a Hermes the Philosopher) and Pythagoras can be seen in a painting of the interior of a Viennese Masonic Lodge circa 1790 (see Plate II). The legend of Hermes Trismegistus and Pythagoras restoring this lost antediluvian

The wise Hellenistic deity Thoth Hermes Mercurius Trismegistus a/k/a Hermes the Philosopher, a combination of three ancient gods: Thoth (Egyptian, their Logos) Hermes (Greek) and Mercury (Roman). Engraving from *Historia Deorum Fatidicorum*, 1675.

knowledge comes from one the oldest Masonic manuscripts known; it is the Matthew Cooke Manuscript circa 1450. The Cooke Manuscript incorporates components from the oldest Masonic Manuscript: the Regius Manuscript of 1390. This legend appears again in other Masonic manuscripts such as the Carmick Manuscript of 1727. The Cooke manuscript, along with several others, is part of what is known as the *Old Charges*, a collection of documents that form the legendary history of Masonry as presented in Dr. Andersons *Constitutions* of 1723, revised 1738. The entire Cooke Manuscript is herein presented; it reads as follows:

> "Thanked be God, our glorious Father, the founder and creator of heaven and earth, and of all things that therein are, for that he has vouchsafed, of his glorious Godhead, to make so many things of manifold virtue for the use of mankind. For he made all things to be subject and obedient to man. All things eatable of a wholesome nature he ordained for man's sustenance. And moreover, he hath given to man wit and the knowledge of diverse things and handicrafts, by the which we may labour in this world, in order to therewith get our livelihood and fashion many objects, pleasant in the sight of God, to our own ease and profit. To rehearse all these matters here were too long in the writing or telling, I will therefore refrain ; but I will nevertheless, tell you some; for instance, how and in what manner the Science of Geometry was first invented, and who were the founders both thereof and of several other crafts, as is declared in the Bible, and other histories.
>
> How, and in what manner this worthy Science of Geometry took its rise, I will tell you, as I said before. You must know that there are seven liberal sciences, from which seven all other sciences and crafts in the world sprung; but especially is Geometry the first cause of all the other sciences, whatsoever they be.
>
> These seven sciences are as follows:
>
> The first, which is called the foundation of all science, is grammar, which teacheth to write and speak correctly.
>
> The second is rhetoric, which teaches us to speak elegantly.
>
> The third is dialectic, which teaches us to discern the true from the

false, and it is usually called art or sophistry (logic).

The fourth is arithmetic, which instructs us in the science of numbers, to reckon, and to make accounts.

The fifth is Geometry, which teaches us all about mensuration, measures and weights, of all kinds of handicrafts.

The sixth is music, and that teaches the art of singing by notation for the voice, on the organ, trumpet, and harp, and of all things pertaining thereto.

The seventh is astronomy, which teaches us the course of the sun and of the moon and of the other stars and planets of heaven.

Our intent is to treat chiefly of the first foundation of Geometry and who were the founders thereof. As I said before, there are seven liberal sciences, that is to say, seven sciences or crafts that are free in themselves, the which seven exist only through Geometry. And Geometry may be described as earth-mensuration, for Geometry is derived from geo, which is in Greek "earth," and metrona or a measure. Thus is the word Geometry compounded and signifies the measure of the earth.

Marvel not because I said that all sciences exist only through the science of Geometry. For there is no art or handicraft wrought by man's hands that is not wrought by Geometry which is a chief factor (notabulle cause) thereof. For if a man works with his hands he employs some sort of tool, and there is no instrument of any material in this world which is not formed of some sort of earth (ore) and to earth it will return. And there is no instrument or tool to work with that has not some proportion, more or less. And proportion is measure, and the instrument or tool is earth. And Geometry is earth-mensuration therefore I affirm that all men live by Geometry. For all men here to this world live by the labour of their hands.

Many more proofs could I give you that Geometry is the science by which all reasoning men live, but I refrain at this time because the writing of it were a long process.

And now I will enter further into the matter You must know that among all the crafts followed by man in this world, Masonry has the greatest renown end the largest share of this science of Geometry, as is stated in history, such as the Bible, and the Master of History," and in the Polycronicon a well authenticated (or trustworthy) chronicle, and in the history called Beda De Imagine Mundi, and Isodorus Ethomolegiarum Methodius Episcopus & Martiris. And many others say that Masonry is the chief part of Geometry and so methinks it may well be said, for it was the first founded, as is stated in the Bible, in the first book of Genesis and the fourth chapter. And moreover all the learned authors above cited agree thereto. And some of them affirm it more openly and plainly, precisely as in Genesis in the Bible.

Before Noah's Flood by direct male descent from Adam in the seventh generation, there lived a man called Lamech who had two wives, called Adah and Zillah. By the first wife, Adah, he begat two sons, Jabal and Jubal. The elder son Jabal was the first man that ever discovered geometry and masonry, and he made houses, and is called in the Bible the father of all men who dwell in tents or dwelling houses. And he was Cain's master mason and governor of the works when he built the city of Enoch, which was the first city ever made and was built by Cain, Adam's son, who gave it to his own son Enoch, and give the city the name of his son and called it Enoch, and now it is known as Ephraim. And at that place was the Science of Geometry and Masonry first prosecuted and contrived as a science and as a handicraft. And so we may well say that it is the first cause and foundation of all crafts and sciences. And also this man Jabel was called the father of shepherds. The Master of History says, and Beda De Imagine Mundi and the Polycronicon and many others more say, that he was the first that made partition of lands, in order that every man might know his own land and labour thereon for himself. And also he divided flocks of sheep, that every man might know his own sheep, and so we may say that he was the inventor of that science.

And his brother Jubal or Tubal was the inventor of music and song, as Pythagoras states in Polycronicon, and the same says Isodorous. In his Ethemolegiis in the 6th book he says that he was the first founder of music and song, and of the organ and trumpet; and he discovered that science by the sound of the weights of his brother's, Tubal-Cain's, hammers.

And of a truth, as the Bible says, that is to say, in the fourth Chapter of Genesis, Lamech begat by his other wife Zillah a son and a daughter, and their names Tubal Cain, that was the son, and the daughter was called Naamah. And according to the Policronicon, some men say that she was Noah's wife; but whether this be so or not, we will not affirm.

Ye must know that this son Tubal Cain was the founder of the smith's craft and of other handicrafts dealing with metals, such as iron, brass, gold and silver as some learned writers say; and his sister Naamah discovered the craft of weaving for before her time no cloth was woven, but they span yarn and knit it and made such clothing as they could. And as this woman Naamah invented the craft of weaving it was called woman's-craft.

And these four brethren knew that God would take vengeance for sin, either by fire or water. And they were much concerned how to save the sciences they had discovered, and they took counsel together and exercised all their wits. And they said there were two kinds of stone of such virtue that the one would not burn, called marble, and the other named "Lacerus" would not sink in water. And so they devised to write all the sciences they had found on these two stones, so that if God took vengeance by fire the marble would not burn, and if by water the other would not drown, and they besought their elder brother Jabal to make two pillars of these two stones, that is of marble and of "Lacerus," and to write on the two pillars all the sciences and crafts which they had found and he did so. And therefore we may say that he was the wisest in science, for he first began and carried out their purpose before Noah's flood,

Fortunately knowing of the vengeance that God would send, the brethren knew not whether it would be by fire or water. They knew by a sort of prophecy that God would send one or the other, and therefore they wrote their sciences on the two pillars of stone. And some men say that they wrote on the stones all the seven sciences, but [this I affirm not]. As they had it in mind that a vengeance would come, so it befell that God did send vengeance, and there came such a flood that all the world was drowned and all men died save only eight persons. These were Noah and his wife and his three sons and their wives, of which sons all the world is descended, and they were named in this wise, Shem, Ham and Japhet. And this flood is called Noah's Flood, for he and his children were saved therein. And many years after the flood, according to the chronicle, these two pillars were found, and the chronicle says that a great clerk, Pythagoras, found the one, and Hermes the Philosopher[68] found the other, and they taught the sciences that they found written thereon.

Every chronicle and history and many other writers and the Bible especially relate the building or the tower of Babel; and it is written in the Bible, Genesis, Chap. x how that Ham, Noah's son, begat Nimrod, who grew a mighty man upon the earth and waxed strong, like unto a giant. He was a great king and the beginning of his kingdom was the kingdom of Babilon proper, and Erech and Arend and Calnch and the land of Shinar. And this same Ham began the tower of Babel and taught his workmen the Craft of Masonry and he had with him many masons, more than 40,000, and he loved and cherished them well. And it is written in Polycronicon, and in the Master of History, and in other histories, and beyond this the Bible witnesses in the same 10th chapter, as it is written, that Ashur who was of near kindred to Nimrod went forth from the land of Shinar and built the City of Nineveh and Plateas (*sic*) and many more. For it is written "*Do terra illa*" [&c.]

It is but reasonable that we should plainly say how and in what manner the Charges of the Mason's Craft were first founded, and who first gave it the name of MasonryAnd you must know that it is stated and written in the Polycronicon and in Methothus Episcopus and Martiris that Ashur who was a worthy lord of Shinar, sent to Nimrod the king to send him Masons and workmen of the Craft that they might help him make his city which he was minded to make. And Nimrod sent him 3000 masons. And as they were about to depart and go forth, he called them before him and said to them, "Ye must go to my cousin Ashur to help him build a city, but see to it, that ye be well governed, and I will give you a Charge that shall be to your and my profit.

68 Synonymous for Trismegistus

When you come to that lord, look that you be true to him, even as you would be to me, labour at your Craft honestly, and take a reasonable payment for it such as you may deserve. Love each other as though you were brothers and hold together staunchly. Let him that hath most skill teach his fellow, and be careful that your conduct amongst yourselves and towards your lord may be to my credit, that I may have thanks for sending you and teaching you the Craft." And they received the charge from him, being their lord and master, and went forth to Ashur and built the city of Nineveh in the country of Plateas (*sic*) and other cities also that are called Calah and Rosen, which is a great city between Calah and Nineveh. And in this manner the Craft of Masonry was first instituted and charged as a science.

Elders of Masons before our times had these charges in writing as we have them now in our Charges of the story of Euclid, and as we have seen them written both in Latin and in French. But it is only reasonable that we should tell you how Euclid came to the knowledge of Geometry, as stated in the Bible and in other histories. In the XIIth chapter of Genesis it is told how Abraham came to the land of Canaan and our Lord appeared unto him and said, "I will give this land to thy seed." But a great famine reigned in that land and Abraham took Sarah, his wife, with him and made a journey into Egypt to abide there whilst the famine lasted. And Abraham, so says the chronicle, was as a wise man and a learned. And he knew all the seven sciences and taught the Egyptians the science of Geometry. And this worthy clerk Euclid was his pupil and learned of him. And he first gave it the name of Geometry; although it was practised before his time, it had not acquired the name of Geometry. But it is said by Isodoras in the 5th Book and first Chapter of Ethomolegiarum that Euclid was one of the first founders of Geometry and gave it that name.

For in his time, the river of Egypt which is called the Nile so overflowed the land that no man could dwell therein. Then the worthy clerk Euclid taught them to make great walls and ditches to keep back the water, and by Geometry he measured the land and parcelled it out into sections and caused every man to enclose his own portion with walls and ditches and thus it became a country abounding in all kinds of produce, and of young people and of men and women: so that the youthful population increased so much as to render earning a livelihood difficult. And the lords of the country drew together and took counsel how they might help their children who had no competent livelihood in order to provide for themselves and their children, for they had so many. And at the council amongst them was this worthy Clerk Euclid and when he saw that all of them could devise no remedy in the matter be said to them "Lay your orders upon your sons and I will teach them a science by which they may live as gentlemen, under the condition that they shall be sworn to me to uphold the regulations that I shall lay upon them." And both they and the king of the country and all the lords agreed thereto with one consent.

It is but reasonable that every man should agree to that which tended to profithimself; andsotheytooktheirsonsto Euclidtoberuledbyhimand he taught them the Craft of Masonry and gave it the name of Geometry on account of the parcelling out of the ground which he had taught the people at the time of making the walls and ditches, as aforesaid, to keep out the water. And Isodoris says in Ethomologies that Euclid called the craft Geometry.

And there this worthy clerk Euclid gave it a name and taught it to the lord's sons of that land whom he had as pupils. And he gave them a charge. That they should call each other Fellow and no otherwise, they being all of one craft and of the same gentle birth, lords' sons. And also that the most skillful should be governor of the work and should be called master; and other charges besides, which are written in the Book of Charges. And so they worked for the lords of the land and built cities and towns, castles and temples and lords' palaces.

During the time that the children of Israel dwelt in Egypt they learned the craft of Masonry. And after they were driven out of Egypt they came into the promised land, which is now called Jerusalem, and they occupied that land and the charges were observed there. And [at] the making of Solomon's Temple which King David began, King David loved masons well, and gave them [wages] nearly as they are now. And at the making of the Temple in Solomon's time, as stated in the Bible in the third book of Kings and the fifth chapter, Solomon held four score thousand masons at work. And the son of the king of Tyre was his master mason. And in other chronicles and in old books of masonry, it is said that Solomon confirmed the charges that David his father had given to masons. And Solomon himself taught them their usages differing but slightly from the customs now in use.

And from thence this worthy science was brought into France and into many other regions. At one time there was a worthy king in France called Carolus Secondus, that is to say Charles the Second. And this Charles was elected king of France by the grace of God and also by right of descent. And some men say he was elected by good fortune, which is false as by the chronicles he was of the blood royal. And this same King Charles was a mason before he became king. And after he was king he loved masons and cherished them and gave them charges and usages of his devising, of which some are yet in force in France ; and he ordained that they should have an assembly once a year and come and speak together in order that the masters and follows might regulate all things amiss.

And soon after that came St. Adhabelle into England and he converted St. Alban to Christianity. And St. Alban loved well masons and he was the first to give them charges and customs in England, And he ordained [wages] adequate to pay for their toil.

And after that there was a worthy king in England, called Athelstan, and his youngest son loved well the science of Geometry; and he knew well, as well as the masons themselves, that their handicraft was the practice of the science of Geometry. Therefore he drew to their councils (or took counsel, or lessons, of them) and learned the practical part of that science in addition to his theoretical (or book) knowledge. For of the speculative part he was a master. And he loved well masonry and masons. And he became a mason himself. And he give them charges and usages such as are now customary in England and in other countries. And he ordained that they should have reasonable pay. And he purchased a free patent of the king that they might hold an assembly at what time they thought reasonable and come together to consult. Of the which charges, usages and assembly it is written and taught in our Book of Charges;

wherefore I leave it for the present.

Good men! for this cause and in this way Masonry first arose. It befell, once upon a time, that great lords had so many free begotten children that their possessions were not extensive enough to provide for their future. Therefore they took counsel how to provide for their children and find them all honest livelihood. And they sent for wise masters of the worthy science of Geometry, that through their wisdom they might provide them with some honest living. Then one of them that was called Euclid a most subtle and wise inventor regulated [that science] and art and called it Masonry. And so in this art of his he honestly taught the children of great lords according to the desire of the fathers and the free consent of their children. And having taught them with great care for a certain time they were not all alike capable of exercising the said art, wherefore the said master Euclid ordained that those that surpassed the others in skill should be honoured above the others. And [comman]ded to call the more skillful (*sic*) "master" and for [him] to instruct the less skilful. The which masters were called masters of nobility, of knowledge and skill in that art. Nevertheless they commanded that they that were of less knowledge should not be called servants or subjects, but fellows, on account of the nobility of their gentle blood. In this manner was the aforesaid art begun in the land of Egypt by the aforesaid master Euclid and so it spread from country to country and from kingdom to kingdom. Many years after, in the time of King Athelstan, sometime king of England, by common assent of his Council and other great lords of the land on account of great defects found amongst masons, a certain rule was ordained for them.

Once a year or every three years as might appear needful to the king and great lords of the land and all the community, congregations should be called by the masters from country to country and from province to province of all masters, masons and fellows in the said art. And at such congregations those that are made masters shall be examined in the articles hereafter written and be ransacked whether they be able and skilful in order to serve the lords to their profit and to the honour of the aforesaid art. And moreover they shall be charged to well and truly expend the goods of their lords, as well of the lowest as of the highest ; for those are their lords for the time being of whom they take their pay in recompense of their service and toil.

The first article is this. That every master of this art should be wise, and true to the lord who employs him, expending his goods carefully as he would his own were expended; and not give more pay to any mason than he knows him to have earned, according to the dearth (or scarcity and therefore price) of corn and victuals in the country and this without favouritism, for every man is to be rewarded according to his work.

The Second article is this. That every master of the art shall be warned beforehand to come to his congregation in order that he may duly come, there, unless he may [be] excused for some cause or other. But if he be found [i.e., accused of being] rebellious at such congregation, or at fault in any way to his employer's harm or the reproach of this art, he shall not be excused unless he be in peril of death. And though he be in peril of death, yet must, he give notice of his illness, to the master who is the president of the gathering.

The [third] article is this. That no master take no apprentice for a shorter term than seven years at least, for the reason that such as have been bound a shorter time can not adequately learn their art, nor be able to truly serve their employer and earn the pay that a mason should.

The fourth article is this. That no master shall for any reward take as an apprentice a bondsman born, because his lord to whom he is a bondsman might take him, as he is entitled to, from his art and carry him away with him from out the Lodge, or out of the place he is in. And because his fellows peradventure might help him and take his part, and thence manslaughter might arise; therefore it is forbidden. And there is another reason; because his art was begun by the freely begotten children of great lords, as aforesaid.

The fifth article is this. That no master shall pay more to his apprentice during the time of his apprenticeship, whatever profit he may take thereby, than he well knows him to have deserved of the lord that employs him; and not even quite so much, in order that the lord of the works where he is taught may have some profit by his being taught there.

The sixth article is this. That no master from covetousness or for gain shall accept an apprentice that is unprofitable ; that is, having any maim (or defect) by reason of which he is incapable of doing a mason's proper work.

The seventh article is this. That no master shall knowingly help or cause to be maintained and sustained any common nightwalker robber by which nightwalking they may be rendered incapable of doing a fair day's work and toil: a condition of things by which their fellows might be made wrath.

The eighth article is this. Should it befall that a perfect and skilful mason come and apply for work and find one working who is incompetent and unskilful, the master of the place shall discharge the incompetent and engage the skilful one, to the advantage of the employer.

The ninth article is this. That no master shall supplant another. For it is said in the art of masonry that no man can so well complete a work to the advantage of the lord, begun by another as he who began it intending to end it in accordance with his own plans, or [he] to whom he shows his plans.

These regulations following were made by the lords (employers) and masters of divers provinces and divers congregations of masonry.

[First point] To wit : whosoever desires to become a mason, it behoves him before all things to [love] God and the holy Church and all the Saints ; and his master and follows as his own brothers.

The second point. He must give a fair day's work for his pay.

The third [point]. He shall hele[69] the counsel or his fellows in lodge and in chamber, and wherever masons meet.

The fourth point. He shall be no traitor to the art and do it no harm nor conform to any enactments against the art nor against the members thereof : but he shall maintain it in all honour to the best of his ability.

69 An Old English "Masonic" word meaning to conceal.

The fifth point. When he receives his pay he shall take it without murmuring, as may be arranged at the time by the master; and he shall fulfil (*sic*) the agreement regarding the hours of work and rest, as ordained and set by the master.

The sixth point. In case of disagreement between him and his fellows, he shall unquestioningly obey the master and be silent thereon at the bidding of his master, or of his master's warden in his master's absence, until the next following holiday and shall then settle the matter according to the verdict of his fellows; and not upon a work-day because of the hindrance to the work and to the lord's interests.

The seventh point. He shall not covet the wife nor the daughter of his master or of his fellows unless it be in marriage neither shall he hold concubines, on account of the discord this might create amongst them.

The eighth point. Should it befall him to be his master's warden, he shall be a true mediator between his master and his fellows: and he shall be active in his master's absence to the honour of his master and thc profit of the lord who employs him.

The ninth point. If he be more wise and skilful than his fellow working with him in the Lodge or in any other place, and he perceive that for want of skill, he is about to spoil the stone upon which he is working and can teach him to improve the stone, he shall instruct and help him; so that love may increase the more amongst them and the work of his employer be not lost.

When the master and fellows, being forewarned are come to such congregations, the sheriff of the country or the mayor of the city or alderman of the town in which the congregation is held, shall if need be, be fellow and associate of the master of the congregation, to help him against disobedient members to maintain the rights of the realm.

And at the commencement of the proceedings, new men who have never been charged before are to be charged in this manner. Ye shall never be thieves nor thieves' maintainers, and shall do a fair day's work and toil for your pay that you take of the lord, and shall render true accounts to your fellows in all matters which should be accounted for to them, and love them as yourselves. And ye shall be true to the king of England and to the realm: and that ye keep with all your might and [power] all the aforesaid articles.

After that an enquiry shall be held whether any master or fellow summoned to the meeting, have broken any of the before said articles, which, if they have done, it shall be then and there adjudicated upon.

Therefore be it known; if any master or fellow being forewarned to come to the congregation, be contumacious and appear not ; or having trespassed against any of the aforesaid articles shall be convicted ; he shall forswear his masonry and shall no longer exercise the craft. And if he presume so to do, the sheriff of the country in which he may be found at work shall put him in prison and take all his goods for the use of the king, until his (the king's) grace be granted and showed him.

For this cause chiefly were these congregations ordained; that the lowest as well as the highest might be well and truly served in the aforesaid art throughout all the kingdom of England. Amen, so mote it be."

(end Cooke Manuscript)

The Cooke Manuscript indicates that it was Jabal and Tubal who inscribed and created the two pillars, not Enoch. The concept that it was the Biblical patriarch Enoch who was responsible for the two pillars inscribed with antediluvian heavenly knowledge imparted to Enoch when he walked with God comes from both Masonic ritual and lore transformed into the ceremony known as the Royal Arch of Enoch developed from French sources in the mid-eighteenth century. This legend appears in the *Constitutions of Free-Masons* of 1723, revised 1738 as well as the *Illustrations of Freemasonry* by Thomas Smith Webb, 1797. As will be seen this specific Masonic ceremony contains elements and philosophies found in *I Enoch* (a/k/a *The Book of Enoch*), lost outside of Ethiopia until its discovery by James Bruce while exploring the Nile. Bruce returned to Europe with three copies in 1773. How and by what means contents of *I Enoch* was known within Masonic circles prior to its discovery presents a historical anomaly and is the main theme of this book.

THE ARK OF THE COVENANT

The Ark of the Covenant was constructed by Moses at God's behest at Exodus XXV: 10-22. The Ark contained the broken tablets on which were engraved the Ten Commandments, a golden pot of manna, and Aaron's rod. The Ark was deposited within the Sanctum Sanctorum in King Solomon's Temple upon the Foundation Stone as an object of veneration. The Ark was three feet nine inches long, two feet three inches wide, it was covered with pure gold over which was placed two cherubim with expanded wings. The Ark was lost after the destruction of the first temple circa 586 BCE by the Babylonians; rumors were that it was taken to Babylon as spoils of conquest by King Nebuchadnezzar. However, when Persian emperor Cyrus the Great dispatched the Jewish governor Zerubbabel from Babylon to Jerusalem to build the second temple, the Ark did not accompany Zerubbabel back to Jerusalem. According to the Talmudists five things were missing from the second temple yet present in the first: 1) The Ark of the Covenant, 2) the *Shekinah* or Divine Presence, 3) the Urim and the Thurmmim, 4) the holy fire upon the altar, and 5) the spirit of prophecy. According to Masonic Reverend Salem Town, the Ark was concealed prior to the destruction of Jerusalem and discovered during engineering of the second temple.

Towne was expounding upon the Masonic Royal Arch ceremony where upon the Vault of Enoch was discovered by builders of the second temple; within the vault under nine arches was found the Pillars of Enoch and the Lost Word symbolized by the Ark of the Covenant. The Arch itself symbolizes a rainbow because the rainbow is given as a token of God's covenant with man not to destroy the world by water again from Genesis 8:21-22 and other significant Biblical texts.[70] Within the York or American Rite, namely the cryptic degree of Select Master, the Ark of the Covenant, sometimes referred to as a *Substitute Ark,* had placed upon it the golden delta of Enoch that was inscribed with the name of God, the Tetragrammaton, in a vault under Solomon's Temple by Josiah[71] (c. 649–609 BC) foreseeing the destruction of the Temple by the Babylonians. This knowledge of God, so written there, and of which Masonry has in all ages been the interpreter,

70 Jones, Bernard E., *Freemasons' Book of the Royal Arch*, page 38.
71 King of Judah 641–609 BC.

is the Master Mason's Word.[72] Within Royal Arch symbolism the Ark was a symbol for the name of God, the Lost Word (cf. Logos, Divine Presence, *Shekinah*), now recovered in the Royal Arch degree. As Royal Arch symbolism expanded, the visual iconography of the Ark would change. The Lost Word, depicted upon the Ark of the Covenant deposited between the two Pillars of Enoch, was substituted or interchanged with a vault featuring a rising sun as the symbol of the Lost Word of a Master Mason, Logos, on the St. Andrew's Royal Arch degree certificate (a/k/a the Hurd Plate). How the word of a Master Mason was ultimately lost and recovered within Masonic ritual, both in the Blue Lodge and high degrees, must now be analyzed.

THE ROYAL ARCH AS DEPICTED BY LAURENCE DERMOTT
The illustration is from *The Register of Excellent Masters*; date about 1783.
By courtesy of United Grand Lodge

The Ark of the Covenant in its vault as depicted by Laurence Dermott from *The Register of Excellent Masters* circa 1783. The pentagram suggests both Sirius *qua* Isis who possessed the secret name of Amun Re/Ra necessary to raise Osiris and the five points of fellowship necessary to communicate the substitute word of a Master Mason. The placement of keystone reflects the Excellent Master degree in the Webb system.

72 Pike, Albert, *Morals and Dogma of the Ancient and Accepted Scottish Rite*, page 209.

CHAPTER II

THE BLUE LODGE AND THE HIGH DEGREES

The Hiramic Legend, The Mark Master Mason,
Virtual Past Master, Most Excellent Master,
and the Holy Royal Arch

"And he brought me into the inner court of the LORD'S house, and, behold, at the door of the temple of the LORD, between the porch and the altar, *were* about five and twenty men, with their backs toward the temple of the LORD, and their faces toward the east; and they worshipped the sun toward the east."
- Ezekiel 8:16.

"For the LORD God (is) a sun and shield: the LORD will give grace and glory: no good (thing) will he withhold from them that walk uprightly." - Psalm 84:11.

"Where is there such a combination as this of religious toleration, emotional linkage with the medieval past, emphasis on good works for others, and imaginative attachment to the religion and symbolism of the Egyptians? The only answer I can think of is - in Freemasonry, with its mythical link with the mediaeval masons, its toleration, its philanthropy, and its Egyptian symbolism."
- Frances A. Yates, *Giordano and the Hermetic Tradition*, 1964.

From its official origins, Freemasonry developed in various ways as a means to influence the values of civil society. This ambition arose from within the conviction of its enthusiasts that the values of the body of emblems and symbols were applicable to a broader range of human activity than private local units or lodges. The movement therefore should be understood as a persuasive moral tradition as well as a set of institutions. The transference of specific ritual ideas onto the rhetoric, political events, material culture, connected between sacred artifacts and social relations, through architecture became uniquely positioned in 18th century Europe from specific Renaissance threads of ideas linked to hermeticism, primarily of Dr. John Dee (1527-1608/9), Robert Fludd (1574-1637), and Giordano Bruno (1548-1600); and Cabala, the Renaissance-Christian form of Hebrew Kabbalah (i.eChristian occultism or mysticism), mediated through a system of ceremonies reflective of Neo-Platonism further into the idea of an unfolding new age of universality. Masonic history, legend, and lore can stir argument among both masons and non-Masons. Frances Yates writes,

> "The origin of Freemasonry is one of the most debated, and debatable, subjects in the whole realm of historical enquiry. One has to distinguish between the legendary history of Freemasonry and the problem of when it actually began as an organized institution. According to Masonic legend, Freemasonry is as old as architecture itself. ...."[73]

The legends and lore of early manuscripts, the *Old Charges*, were extracted and conflated in a set of traditional histories characteristically published as introductions to various national editions of Masonic *Constitutions* of John T. Desaguliers and Dr. Anderson and law. The *Old Charges* included, but not limited to, the Lansdowne, Edinburgh-Kilwinning, Sloane, and Harleian Manuscripts and present the Craft as having been stone builders and craftsmen prior to the deluge of Noah having worked on the Tower of Babel. These sagas further described a thread of thought, rooted in core principles of initiation applied to the survival of a producing thread of mathematical order associated with enlightened Monarchy through Geometry. The paragon model for Geometry was derived from ideas of Nilotic flooding in Ancient Egypt (as discussed in Anderson's *Constitutions*); Isis, whose sacred star Sirius heliacally rises in the east coinciding with the inundation of the Nile, was taught geometry by Thoth while within the Egyptian pantheon of gods Thoth's female counterpart Seshat was the Egyptian goddess of geometry, surveying, architecture, mathematics, and astrology. Egyptian Pharaoh Tuthmosis III (ca. 1479-1425 BCE) called her *Sefket-Abwy* or *She of Seven Points*; the Statue of Liberty in New York Harbor was in part inspired by the goddess. Likewise

73 Yates, Francis A., *The Rosicrucian Enlightenment*, page 209.

Euclid, associated and linked with Pythagoras via his 47th Proposition, instructed the Egyptians in geometry;

> "Then came this worthy scholar Euclid and told the King (of Egypt) and the Lords of the Realm and said: 'If you will Give Me your Children to Govern, I will teach them one of the Seven Sceyances whereby they may Live honestly like Gentlemen; but then you Shall Give Me full Power and Commission that I may Rule them After the Manner of the worthey Sceyance Of Geometry or Measondry Requires. Then the King and Council Granted him a Commision Seal'd with their own Seals. Then this worthey Docktor tooke theire Sons and taught them the Sceyance of Geomatrey or Measondry to practice workeing in Stone and all Manner of worthey worke that behoves to the building of Churches, temples, and all manner of buildings, as Monuments and houses.'"[74]

In this Masonic literature and legends such figures, for example Archimedes (ca. 287-212 BCE), Claudius Ptolemy the Astronomer (90-168 CE), and Pythagoras of Samos (570-495 BCE), were deemed supreme initiates, *parfaits*, through whom clusters of ideas were midwifed into society. Masonic law and ideals developed therefore as a secular version of Roman Catholic Canon Law as a means both to regulate the institutions of the movement, as well as a mechanism through values might be exemplified by Masonic thinkers and leaders into policy. In the United States the idea of an unfolding Logos or mystical word of Master Mason came to have unique significance.

This device was derived from two sources: the Gnostic-Docetic Gospel of St. John and the central initiatory search of the neophyte for the Lost Word of Master Mason. Docetism is a heretical belief that Christ's physical body was not real, rather he was a phantom (or angel of some sorts); as such he did not truly suffer on the cross because he was not flesh. As such, the Gospel of St. John was not in accord with the other three (Matthew, Mark, and Luke) and was more in tune with the teachings of Simon Magus. Nevertheless, with the exception of Paul, the *Acts* of the Apostles contain

74 Borneman, Henry S., *Early Freemasonry in Pennsylvania,* page 25, citing the *Old Charges (Tho: Carmick Manuscript,* 1727).

various elements of Docetism. The end result was that Freemasonry and its high degrees came to have a dynamic role in the process of nation building modeled after English Deism of the Blue Lodge yet with a penchant for Catholic ceremony or "pomp and circumstance," especially within the high degrees (minus a real Christ) after the American Revolution. American Revolutionary thinkers such as Thomas Paine (1737-1809), the author of *Common Sense*, argued that Christianity was a form of pagan sun worship[75] –an idea that Paine likely inherited from rationalist English freethinker John Toland (1670-1722) who authored *Christianity not Mysterious* published in 1696. Toland was heavily influenced by John Locke the founder of English Liberalism and British empiricism. Likewise, Jesuit Egyptologist and symbolist Athanasius Kircher traced Christianity as the successor to Egyptian solar paganism. Paine believed that the Druids and Pythagoreans had combined to provide an occult ideological alternative to Christianity.[76]

This process can, in turn, be traced to the amalgamation of Masonic interest in the popularization of the ordered heliocentric ideas of Isaac Newton (1643-1727) and in the set of priestly ideas surrounding the Biblical Ark of the Covenant which in time became the central symbol of Masonry's premier higher degrees ceremony: the Holy Royal Arch. Exaltation or initiation into this degree was the pinnacle of Masonic rank as it developed in various parallel ways in differing Masonic rites or systems of ceremonies. Within this ethos legendary histories and Constitutions described the emergence of restored lost wisdom through the rituals of initiation within which a new concept of solar order was identified with the discovery of the contents of the Ark of the Covenant and the Lost Word. From 1543 renewed emphasis upon scientific solar order within the history of science made such an equivalency more significant as science and religion sought ways to integrate core values of harmonious order within society. The Biblical patriarch Enoch was employed in the Royal Arch to symbolize both the ideal of the paragon initiate and the survival of

75 Paine stated in his "*An Essay on the Origin of Free-Masonry*" that "The Christian religion is a parody on the worship of the Sun, in which they put a man whom they call Christ, in the place of the Sun, and pay him the same adoration which was originally paid to the Sun."

76 Billington, James H., *Fire in the Minds of Men: Origins of the Revolutionary Faith,* page 103.

antediluvian patriarchal order surviving Noah's Flood. Enoch was one of two people in the Bible to have never died; the Prophet Elijah is the other. By implication this device also came to symbolize to critics of Masonry the survival of evil otherwise eradicated by the deluge. The Enochian myth in specific claimed to preserve all of the knowledge of the arts and science as derived from the correct pronunciation of the secret ineffable Name of God. This described the derivation of practical and theoretical knowledge from a mystical reworking of God's name derived from pagan as well as Judaic sources. In time this restoration was emblematically represented in America as an emerging, rising sun in the renderings and designs of city planners and architects such as Pierre Charles L'Enfant (1754-1825), Benjamin Henry Latrobe (1764-1820), Robert Mills (1781-1855), and Joseph-Jacques Ramée (1764-1842). L'Enfant, often considered to be a non-Mason, was at least initiated into the Entered Apprentice degree in Holland Lodge No. 8 in New York in 1789 of which DeWitt Clinton was initiated the following year.[77] L'Enfant was also a member of the Society of the Cincinnati having designed its emblem. The Order or Society of the Cincinnati is historical organization with branches in the United States and France founded in 1783 to preserve the ideals and fellowship of the Revolutionary War officers. Latrobe and Mills were both Masons, Ramée is unconfirmed. To them the implication was clear: the new nation, the United States of America, was a de facto solar ordered mystical republic with an executive, legislative and judicial democracy; yet a state within a state which contained a Masonic clerisy or priesthood that were secretly the mediators and rulers. To begin to understand these concepts the rituals of Freemasonry must be now be explored.

In order to understand the symbolism of the *haute* or high degrees of Masonry, one must first explore the three degrees, the rituals, of Blue Lodge or Craft Masonry. One must bear in mind that there are no real secrets within Craft Lodge Masonry, correctly expressed by Albert Pike in *Morals and Dogma of the Ancient and Accepted Scottish Rite*:

77 d'Esclapon, Pierre F. de Ravel. *The Masonic Career of Major Pierre Charles L'Enfant.* The Scottish Rite Journal of Freemasonry, Southern Jurisdiction, Vol. CXIX Number 2, pages 10-12.

> "The Blue Degrees are but the outer court or portico of the Temple. Part of the symbols are displayed there to the Initiate, but he is intentionally misled by false interpretations. It is not intended that he shall understand them; but it is intended that he shall imagine he understands them. Their true explication is reserved for the Adepts, the Princes of Masonry. The whole body of the Royal and Sacerdotal Art was hidden so carefully, centuries since, in the High Degrees, as that it is even yet impossible to solve so many of the enigmas which they contain. It is well enough for the mass of those called Masons, to imagine that all is contained in the Blue Degrees; and whoso attempts to undeceive them will labor in vain, and without any true reward violate his obligations as an Adept. Masonry is the veritable Sphinx, buried to the head in The sands heaped around it by the ages."[78]

Pike further explains,

> "If you have been disappointed in the first three Degrees, *as you have received them*, and if it has seemed to you that the performance has not come up to the promise, that the lessons of morality are not new, and the scientific instruction is but rudimentary, and the symbols are imperfectly explained, remember that the ceremonies and lessons of those Degrees have been for ages more and more accommodating themselves, by curtailment and sinking into commonplace, too often limited memory and capacity if the Master and Instructor, and to the intellect and needs of the pupil and Initiate; that they have come to use from an age when symbols were used, not to *reveal* but to *conceal*; when the commonest learning was confined to a select few, and the simplest principles of morality seemed newly discovered truths; and that these antique and simple Degrees now stand like the broken columns of a roof-less Druidic temple, in their rude and mutilated greatness; in many parts, also, corrupted by time, and disfigured by modern additions and absurd interpretations. They are but the entrance to the great Masonic Temple, the triple columns of the portico."[79]

78 Pike, Albert, *Morals and Dogma of the Ancient and Accepted Scottish Rite*, page 819.
79 Ibid, page 106.

Nevertheless, without entry into the Blue Lodge one is lacking the proper foundation and instruction to receive wisdom of the high degrees of Masonry. The high degrees are really further degrees meaning they further the education of the mason just as college or university furthers the education of the high school student. This author will not reveal any of the essential secrets of the Blue Lodge, defined by Dr. Oliver in his *Dictionary of Symbolic Masonry* of consisting of nothing more than the grips, signs, passwords, and tokens essential for the preservation of the society from inroads of imposter; while Albert G. Mackey reiterates that American writers are acting on the admission that the only real *aporrheta* (essential secrets) of Freemasonry are the modes of recognition and the peculiar and distinctive ceremonies of the Masonic Order, and to these that it is claimed that reference may be publicly made for the purpose of scientific investigation.[80] This author does not believe he has violated any of the oaths taken within the Masonic fraternity nor harmed Masonry in any way with the writing and publishing of this book.

The first degree of Craft Masonry, the Entered Apprentice, introduces the neophyte to the mysteries of Freemasonry. He is taught morality through Masonry's various symbols. The second degree, Fellowcraft, is an explanatory degree that teaches further moral instruction. It is with the Fellowcraft degree that the candidate is brought into the Middle Chamber of Solomon's Temple via a winding staircase in order to receive a Fellowcraft's wage and the jewel of a Fellowcraft. The candidate is charged to study the seven liberal arts, especially geometry, it being a divine and moral nature as it demonstrates the important truths of morality. The third degree, Master Mason, is an occult (or hidden) degree as it contains symbolic allegory explored in the next chapter. During the third degree ritual the initiate portrays Hiram Abif, the legendary architect of Solomon's Temple. Hiram is mentioned at Kings I: 7-14, "He (was) a widow's son of the tribe of Naphtali, and his father (was) a man of Tyre, a worker in brass: and he was filled with wisdom, and understanding, and cunning to work all works in brass. And he came to King Solomon, and wrought all his work." After King David conquered Jerusalem circa 1004

80 Brown, Robert H., *Stellar Theology and Masonic Astronomy*, pages 7-8, citing Oliver.

BCE, he legally purchased the threshing floor of Ornan the Jebusite[81] (known as Araunah the Jebusite at Samuel II: 24:16) for six hundred shekels of gold (50 silver shekels according to the Book of Samuel). The threshing floor was on the summit of Mount Mariah, the site where Solomon's Temple was allegedly built by the Hiram Abif, presently it is the Muslim Dome of the Rock. The Islamic Dome of the Rock was built 689-691 CE; it features a domed rotunda as copied from Christian "solar" churches in this case the domed Holy Sepulchre. From medieval Masonic lore it was told that the *Vesica Piscis,* the Golden Ratio, and the pentagram or pentangle construction methods (or ratios) were utilized to construct Solomon's Temple. The latter was taken from King Solomon's signet ring which was said to contain a pentagram with the name of God, other sources suggest it was a hexagram (a/k/a the Magen David). He used this signet ring, entrusted to him by the Archangel Michael, to control and manipulate demons. The *Vesica Piscis* is the shape of the intersection of two circles with the same radius so the center of each circle lies in the center of the other. The name literally means the "bladder of the fish" duetoitsfish likeshape. Themathematicalratio of the width of the *Vesica Piscis* to its height is the square root of three, or 1.73205081... since if straight lines are drawn connecting the centers of the two circles with each other, with the two points where the circles intersect, two equilateral triangles join along an edge. The ratios 265/153 = 1.7320261... and 1351/780 = 1.7320513... are two of a series of two approximations of this value. Archimedes of Syracuse (ca. 287 - 212 BCE) used these rations as upper and lower bounds: $\frac{1351}{780} > \sqrt{3} > \frac{265}{153}$. One will immediately recognize the number 153, which appears in the Gospel of St. John 21: 1-14

The Magen David. To Eliphas Levi, the hexagram symbolized the planetary influences, and the macrocosm or Godhead.

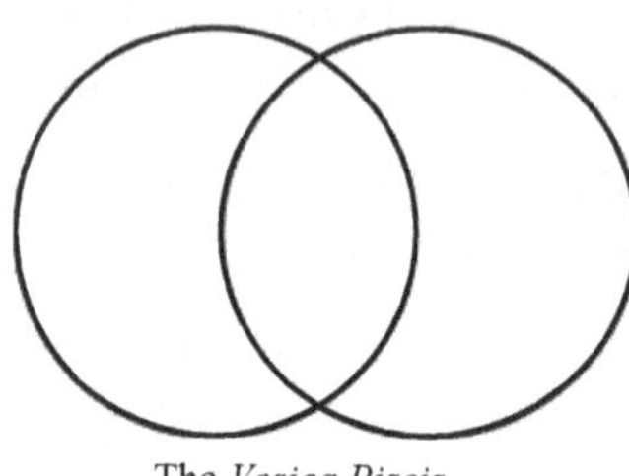

The *Vesica Piscis*

81 The Jebusites were the original inhabitants of Jerusalem until their conquest by King David. Despite being a conquered people King David still honored their property rights.

as the number of fish caught by Jesus in the Draught of the Fish miracle after Jesus' resurrection but prior to his ascension. Jesus' connection to fishand water symbolism will be discussed in the next chapter; Jesus Christ is the "Piscean Fisherman." The *Vesica Piscis* method, along with the Golden Mean or Ratio (1.6180339887, Chapter IV) and the Seal of Solomon, a/k/a the pentagram as developed by architects such as Vitruvius, would be used in medieval cathedral building to symbolically link man the microcosm to the divine heavens or the macrocosm. These latter terms, microcosm, macrocosm, were used by Renaissance cabalist, astrologer, Oxonian, and mathematician Robert Fludd to discuss the circulation of blood in the human body. To Fludd man was influenced by the heavens: the human heart was the sun and the blood like the planets and, by this time, it was known that the planets orbit the sun. Fludd, who announced himself as a disciple of the Rosicrucians in his earliest works, incorporated numerous elements of Ficino, Pico della Mirandola, Dee, and Bruno in his hermetical, magical, occult treatises. Fludd provides a further link between Rosicrucianism, and in turn Freemasonry, to the hermetic-cabalistic magic of the Renaissance. English physician William Harvey (1578-1657) later explained the circulation of blood in more modern and experimental terms, though still referring to the macrocosm-microcosm analogy of Robert Fludd.

Hiram Abif possesses the word of a Master Mason, the Tetragrammaton, which is necessary to construct the Temple; through its possession all knowledge, including geometry, is possible. As Solomon's Temple nears completion three Fellowcrafts conspire to extract the word from Hiram. These three workers are also known as the three ruffians: their names are Jubela, Jubelo, and Jubelum. Per his daily routine, Hiram Abif, at high twelve, enters the nearly finished Holy of Holies, or *Sanctum Sanctorum*, within Solomon's Temple to take refreshment and draw out new architectural designs upon the trestleboard, then offer prayer to deity. Afterwards Grand Master Hiram would retire at the south gate of the outer courts of the Temple. Jubela, the first ruffian, assaults Hiram at the south gate of demanding the word, Hiram refuses, and his throat is slashed. Hiram then approaches the west gate where he is accosted by Jubelo who again demands the word of a Master Mason. Refusing to disclose it to Jubelo, he slashes the left breast of Hiram Abif. Grand Master Hiram, wounded, stumbles to the east gate where he is met by the final assailant Jubelum. Jubelum angrily demands the word; when Hiram Abif refuses to impart the word, Jubelum deals the death blow by striking Hiram Abif across the head with a setting maul. The word of a Master Mason is now forever lost within the Blue Lodge. To Jacobites like the Andrew "the Chevalier" Ramsay Grand Master Hiram Abif symbolized Charles I while the three assassins took form as Oliver Cromwell, Henry Ireton, Hugh Peters and the regicides in general. This concept was likely propagated by Ramsay's fellow Freemason, antiquarian, and devoted monarchist Elias Ashmole (1617-1692). Ashmole, one of the founding fathers of the Royal Society, studied the history of the Order of the Garter created in 1378; he authored the consonant work *The Institutions, Laws, and Ceremonies of the Most Noble Order of the Garter* (1672) dedicated to Charles II, son of martyred Charles I. Ashmole, who some claim was a Rosicrucian, states in his diary he became a Freemason in a lodge at Warrington, England in 1646, well before the creation of the Premier Grand Lodge of England in 1717. Ashmole, who like Fludd, studied mysticism and alchemy, provides a nexus between Rosicrucianism, Freemasonry, and the cabalistic-hermetical occultism of the Renaissance. The Masonic initiate, as Hiram Abif, is dead; the body concealed by the three Fellowcrafts in a grave dug west of Mount Moriah symbolizing the setting sun, or death. At the head of the grave is placed a sprig of acacia in order to conceal the burial spot. The acacia grows in Egypt along the Nile and was once sacred to the sun god Apollo. It is an emblem of solar resurrection and immortality.

Jubelo, Jubela, and Jubelum try to mastermind their escape across the ocean to Ethiopia but the port is closed. King Solomon, confused as to why the workers are not at labor or why there are no plans upon the trestleboard, investigates. He discovers that Hiram Abif is mysteriously missing and calls role. Solomon then discovers that three craftsmen are absent, at which point in time King Solomon is approached by twelve Fellowcrafts. The twelve Fellowcrafts inform Solomon that they, along with Jubelo, Jubela, and Jubelum, had planned to extort Hiram Abif, murder him if necessary, in order to gain the Master Mason's word so they could earn a master's wage. The twelve recant; they now ask Solomon's pardon which is granted with the instruction to divide up into four groups of three and search for the three ruffians. The three ruffians are found, brought before Solomon, plead guilty, and are ordered executed. Solomon then instructs the twelve to search for the remains of Grand Master Hiram, which is located under the acacia sprig. His body is decomposed, but he still wears the jewel of his office around his neck. The jewel is brought to Solomon who identifies it as belonging to Hiram. Solomon orders the twelve Fellowcrafts to return to the grave and raise the body. Solomon laments that the word is now lost. Hiram's body is first attempted to be raised with the grip of an Entered Apprentice, but that fails. Next the grip of a Fellowcraft is tried with no success. Finally the initiate, as Hiram Abif, is resurrected (now known as Adonhiram) from his death upon the third try by the strong grip of the Lion's Paw of the tribe of Judah. The Lion's Paw is an esoteric reference to the constellation Leo the Lion, the sun being at its strongest in the northern hemisphere while in that sign. Leo is the sole house of the sun as it is ruled by it. As Isis was able to raise Osiris from the dead with the true name solar god Amun Re/Ra, the initiate, now a Master Mason, upon his symbolic resurrection has a substitute word whispered in his ear in a low breath; the true word, lost.

The end purpose of Masonic Blue Lodge initiation is the finding of the Master's Word, which, under mythic circumstances, has been forever lost. In the lodge system of degrees, the candidate is a participant in a ceremony in which the loss is re-enacted, the building of Solomon's Temple circa 960-950 BCE; although two other legends, Noah and the Flood and the construction of Tower of Babel, were once in use, or potentially so. The loss then may be seen in in terms of some faculty or element which mankind once had, but no longer possesses. In the Masonic system, the word is (most often) interpreted as the ineffable Name of God, which, as a result of the death of Hiram Abif, is no longer known to man. Jews and Christians have sometimes seen the Hiramic legend as a replication of the Doctrine of the Fall of Eve (and mankind) in the Garden of Eden, thus, symbolically, the recovery of the word places mankind back in the good graces of Deity prior to the Fall, yet with the knowledge that God had tried to deny Adam and Eve. But the loss points more probingly toward something different, if not more profound, understanding of reality than the human impairment or limitation of the Fall; significant as this is to a variety of Western understanding of the nature of man, e.g. St. Paul, Martin Luther, Reinhold Niebuhr, and Sigmund Freud, regardless of religious or psychological point of view. The key to such an understanding is to be found in the syllabic nature of the Mason's Word, as it is recovered in the Third Degree of English speaking Freemasonry: the substitute word. It must be pointed out that which is lost in the Blue Lodge, never found in simple and direct form (as will now be analyzed) even in *haute* degrees which claim to have found that which was lost: the Royal Arch degree in both the York and Scottish Rites are subject to interpretation and suggestion. It remains for the candidate and for the individual Freemason, represented perhaps by future generations in the ritual to uncover that which was lost. In other words, one is left to imagine of what is real rather than reality itself; the penultimate rather than the ultimate. In the Masonic system the word as a symbol for reality is never definitively elucidated. In fact to do so in any final or decisive way would cancel Freemasonry's most distinguished landmark: universality. Even the Knight Templar Order of the Temple, in so far as it is Christian degree in terms of the individual Christian Freemason's confession and commitment, makes the degree not Masonically pure. The universal character of the Word and its lack of theological definition effords Freemasonry its unique, deistic character.[82]

* * * * *

The high degrees develop in France shortly after the revival of Masonry on June 24, 1717 in England. On that date the English Grand Lodge was established. The principles behind the English Grand Lodge were an ideal of tolerance, brotherhood, that combined or fused elements of the Enlightenment and the Scientific Revolution, namely a principle of universal understanding through the application of reason, not superstition. Its Constitutions were written by Dr. James Anderson, published in 1723 (revised 1738) and were based upon the Old Charges. These documents

82 Stemper Jr., William H., *Freemasonry and the Force*, page 11.

were collected by Dr. John Theophilus Desaguliers (1683-1744) who became the Third Grand Master of the English Lodge in 1719. Dr. Desaguliers was educated at Christ Church of Oxford University, was a member of the Royal Society and inventor of the planetarium. Desaguliers assisted Isaac Newton and was instrumental in spreading Newtonianism both within and outside of Masonry. English Lodges conferred the Craft Degrees: Entered Apprentice, Fellowcraft, and Master Mason, called the York Rite so named after York, England, not to be confused with the York Rite or American Rite developed by Thomas Smith Webb. It was through Desaguliers that the concept of solar order and monarch were intertwined. On the *Constitutions of the Free-Masons*, Albert Mackey states "Anderson, we suppose, did the work, while Desaguliers furnished much of the material and thought."[83] However, at some point Lodges in England, Scotland, and Ireland began conferring higher degrees; namely that of the Mark Master Mason and the Holy Royal Arch. The Mark Master is an extension of the Fellowcraft degree while the Royal Arch is an extension of the Master Mason degree. In 1743, the first decisive reference to the Royal Arch degree in Ireland reports of a proceeding at a Lodge at Youghal, County Cork. In 1751 a schism occurred in Masonry. Some Irish Masons formed their own Grand Lodge known as the "Ancients" or Antients which followed the "Old Institutions;" according to the *Ahiman Rezon*, the Constitutions of the Grand Lodge of the Antients authored by Laurence Dermott in 1756 (second edition 1764). Accordingly there were now two classes of Masons in England: the Antients who followed the "Old Institutions," and hence possessed the true esoteric secrets of Masonry; and the Moderns who fell under the name of the Freemasons of England. The Antients held the Royal Arch degree as the most sublime degree, the "root, heart, and marrow," of Freemasonry. The Moderns also embraced the Royal Arch degree but seemed to practice it in conjuncture with the Master Mason degree; the Antients seemed to have fabricated the Royal Arch degree by dividing or cutting it out of the Master Mason degree. One of the Royal Arch's chief advocates was Thomas Dunckerley (1724-1795), the son of the Prince of Wales later King George II. Dunckerley spread Royal Arch masonry all over England; he was a Knight Templar, Grand Master of the Order when the Grand

83 Mackey, Albert, *Encyclopedia of Freemasonry, Vol. I*, page 207.

Conclave was formed in London. Antient Freemasonry spread to the British Colonies in America where it became very popular among the subjects there. Virginia, New York, Pennsylvania, South Carolina and Massachusetts saw the organization of Provincial Grand Lodges; lodges working under them were known as Ancient York Lodges. Modern Lodges were also established in the colonies, namely in New York, Pennsylvania, and New Jersey; Dr. Benjamin Franklin was a Modern Freemason. However, due to their Tory, aristocratic, and loyalist sentiments, Modern Lodges were not as popular in the thirteen colonies and were ultimately extinguished during the American Revolution. In England the schism came to an end when the Antients and Moderns merged in 1813 with the formation of the United Grand Lodge of England which recognized the Craft Degrees and the Most Holy Royal Arch. Within the English tradition the Third Degree Master Mason was considered the most loyal subject of the Crown. At the core of English Freemasonry remained the principle of the equality of law, against which no administrative right might prevail, least of all a sacred precept to crush unruly brethren. The United Grand Lodge of England rejected the Oration of the Chevalier Ramsay and the *haute* degrees that were born out of it.

High Degree Masonry was developed out of the 1737 oration of Andrew Michael "the Chevalier" Ramsay. Ramsay, an English Catholic (convert) Universalist Jacobite living in France, claimed Freemasonry descended from the Crusades and that modern Masonry developed from Knights Templar of Scottish lineage and heredity. This provides a nexus between Catholicism (cf. Knights Templar) and the high degrees first developed in France as the Rite of Perfection. The 1740s saw the rise of Scots Lodges in France; *Scottish* not only because of the Templar link but also because the Stuart monarchy of Scotland: James VI King of Scotland, initiated into the Lodge of Scoon and Perth No. 3 in 1601, became James I (father of Charles I) King of England upon the death of Elizabeth I who died without issue. Ramsay was an ardent Jacobite or supporter of the Stuarts despite the fact the Hanoverians had claimed the throne of England after the death of Queen Anne the last Stuart monarch.[84] Scot's Lodges in France were practicing

84 Queen Anne (1665 – 1714) was the daughter of James II who had been deposed in the Glorious Revolution of 1688 in order to prevent a Roman Catholic Stuart Dynasty. James II, a devout Catholic, fathered a Catholic son James Francis Edward Stuart (the Old Pretender) who would have become King of England superceding his Protestant sister Mary (Mary II of William and Mary).

high degree Masonry; the rituals were diverse but with the same similar theme: the recovery of the Lost Word in an underground vault or crypt by temple builders or by Scottish Knight Templars. 1754 saw the foundation of the Rite of Perfection (a/k/a Rite of Heredom) by Chevalier de Bonneville based on Ramsay's Oration as the Chapter of Clermont referencing the College of Clermont, a Jesuit College, that was working *haute* degree Jesuit-styled or themed Templar degrees apparently left over from when James II, after the Glorious Revolution of 1688, fled to France. James II, a Roman Catholic, had resided at the College of Clermont, founded in 1563, where he remained for some time; he was supported by the Jesuits who manufactured certain degrees and rituals with an occult (or hidden) political intent advancing either their political cause, the Jacobite cause, or both.[85] These Templar degrees or rites were superimposed with Scot's degrees of the 1740s forming the Rite of Perfection of 1754. This is merely one link between Jesuitism and the chivalric high degrees of Masonry as developed in France; it differs philosophically and symbolically from the English York tradition of three degrees of Craft Masonry. *This difference always has to be kept in mind.* It must be pointed out that *Coil's Encyclopedia of Freemasonry* disagrees with the Jesuit link to high degree masonry. *Coil's* (rev. ed. 1996) suggests that the Jesuit College of Clermont and the Masonic Chapter of Clermont are unrelated to each other and the Masonic Chapter is actually named after the Count of Clermont, Louis de Bourbon (1709-1771). *Coil's* in turn is getting this information from Robert Freke Gould's three volume *History of Freemasonry* (1883-1887); Gould is the godfather of factual-exoteric masonry. This seems highly dubious, a stretch, because after being elected perpetual Grand Master in 1743 by sixteen craft lodges in Paris to correct and investigate abuses which had crept in French Masonry, likely originating from the Ramsay Oration and its related ideology, Louis de Bourbon abandoned his supervision of the lodges and investigative duties the following year causing great disorder and chaos among the lodges *yet* still maintaining his Grand Mastership until 1770. Other sources state he quit Masonry altogether in 1744. This being the case, he seems an unlikely and undesirable person to name a set of Masonic high degrees after approximately ten years later. In addition, his biography by Jules Cousin,

85 Mackey, Albert, *Encyclopedia of Freemasonry, Vol. II*, page 730.

Le Comte de Clermont: Sa Cour et Ses Maitresse, published 1867, omits all reference to any of Bourbon's Masonic activity. In their *A History of the Cryptic Rite*, Eugene Hinman, Ray Denslow, and Charles Hunt scoff at the notion that the Chapter of Clermont is named after Bourbon; "May there be a suggestion for us in the fact that ... de Clermont served as Grand Master of French Masonry for *27* years?"[86] On the other hand, the Jesuit-*haute* degree nexus is elucidated by Albert Mackey in his famed Encyclopedia of Masonry. Mackey states:

> "On the 24th of November, 1754 the Chevalier de Bonneville established in Paris a Chapter of the high degrees under this name, which was derived from the Jesuitical Chapter of Clermont. ...They adopted the Templar system, which had been created at Lyons, in 1743, and their Rite consisted at first of six degrees, ...Relics of this attempted system are still to be found in many of the high degrees, and the Chapter of Clermont, subsequently organized in Paris, appears to have had some reference to it. ...Yet it cannot be denied that, while the Jesuits have had no part in the construction of pure Freemasonry, there are reasons for believing that they took an interest in the invention of some degrees and systems which were intended to advance their own interests. But whatever they touched the Institution they left the trail of the serpent. They sought to convert its pure philanthropy and toleration into political intrigue and religious bigotry. Hence it is believed that they had something to do with the invention of those degrees, which were intended to aid the exiled house of Stuart in its efforts to regain the English throne, because they believed that would secure the restoration in England of the Roman Catholic religion. Almost a library of books has been written on both sides of this subject in Germany and in France."[87]

Knowing that the *haute* degree system was born out of the Oration of the Chevalier Ramsay, a Catholic Jacobite, the Jesuit link to the high degree system seems to be the correct one; when viewed within the backdrop of the Counter-Reformation it is the only one that makes sense. An example can be found in the fourteenth degree of the Scottish Rite where the initiate,

---

86 Hinman, Eugene E., Ray V. Denslow and Charles C. Hunt. *A History of the Cryptic Rite, Volumes I.*, page 95-96.
87 Mackey, Albert, *Encyclopedia of Freemasonry*, Vol. I, pages 155-156, 368.

in a Jesuit-esque ritual, makes a Catholic-like vow not to take the Lord's name in vain and swear, or at least try not to. At the very least it appears as though the higher degrees of Masonry were taken and ran with by the Jesuits as part of the Counter-Reformation began at the Council of Trent in 1545; it is unlikely this was Ramsay's intent although this too is debated. In 1758 a body was organized in Paris called the Council of Emperors of East and West. They inherited not only the Clermont Rites and the Scottish lines of Kilwinning and Heredom, but other traditions derived from both Templar and Rosicrucian sources. The Council was composed of men of noble birth, wide knowledge, and high culture from the *ancien regime*; they organized the Rite of Perfection which contained twenty-five degrees, the highest was the Sublime Prince of the Royal Secret. In 1761, the Council granted a patent to Etienne (Stephen) Morin authorizing him to propagate the Rite of Perfection in the West; Morin is known as the founder of the American Scottish Rite.[88] Morin most likely received the twenty-five high degrees from Jean-Baptiste Willermoz (1730-1824) a Freemason and a Martinist (a form of mystical and esoteric Christianity) who aided in the establishment of *haute* degree masonry in France and Germany. Willermoz was the chief archivist of Freemasonry in Lyon. After receiving these new powers, Morin set sail for American and established Rite of Perfection bodies in St. Domingo and Jamaica with the intent of establishing the Rite in America. The Rite of Perfection was developed in Albany, New York by Henry A. Francken which became the core of the Scottish Rite in Charleston, South Carolina in 1801 and influenced the York or American Rite of T. S. Webb and Knight Templary (1814) of DeWitt Clinton.

Drawing upon symbols as a means to harness the living powers of the divine universe seem therefore to underlay various efforts, notably in England to discredit higher degree construction and to subdue popular perceptions linking monarchy and Masonry except through a philanthropically articulated progressive concept embodied in the Constitution of the United Kingdom. Mythic figures such as Apollo, Saturn and Minerva thereby emerged within high degree cultures with specific functions not simply as inspirational motivational emblems but as having an almost autonomous potency to

88 Ibid, Vol. II, page 671.

achieve the direction of human moral activity in specific ways. Masonry appears to have preserved a continuation of this mental state into the early modern period and into an esoteric underbelly to the rational enlightenment in association with rulership. In specific, the goddess Minerva was utilized to protect the avenues of continuity between divine and demonic intelligences as a path between the cosmos and human mental imagery. In this context the idea of a scale of ascent depicting Masonic higher degrees became associated in material culture with a *Ladder of Minerva* depicted in eighteenth century-early 19th century Masonic iconography became interlaced with Jacob's Ladder. In other words, the further one climbed in the high degrees the more esoteric wisdom (cf. Minerva, goddess of wisdom) one obtained. As Frances Yates writes, "By the Ladder of Minerva we rise from the first to the last, collect the external species in the internal sense, order intellectual operations into a whole by art, as in Bruno's extraordinary arts of memory."[89] The Apollonian and saturnine elements of this process should be emphasized in terms of the unique role of solar symbolism and the spiritual psychology which makes it realization possible. The first was typified in the high degree Enochic idiom as the contents of the secret vault, the second as the meditative taciturn state necessary to achieve. Both icons were symbolized in the origins of Masonic emblemature, the first related to *Merkabah* elements of Benjamin Latrobe's dome structure, U.S. Capitol and Baltimore Basilica, as Apollo's throne room; the second in the somber (*qua* Saturn) Chamber of Reflection device within the Clinton Knights Templar initiation ceremony where the initiate reflects upon his own mortality. Thus, as an extension of a reworked theory of kingly polity, external images were psychologically and religiously organized with a comprehensive catholic ethos to order the intellectual operations of statecraft into a manageable policy whole integrating personal experience into collective and institutional behavior. By further implication this imagery was accessible through the policies of the Pythagorean ruler as sovereign as the mediator, with the equipage of a Joachimite militia of spiritual men from the restoration of lost Enochic wisdom.

The parallels between the development of the Constitution of the United

89 Yates, Frances, *The Art of Memory*, page 281.

Kingdom and English Grand Lodge Freemasonry against the French high degrees are tangible and palpable. Nowhere was this more evident than in the period of struggle with Revolutionary France. The French people were thought quite literally to have become mad; drunken with the exuberance of Revolutionary ideas, what author and Librarian of Congress Dr. James H. Billington has termed a *Fire in the Minds of Men.* By contrast, the Glorious Revolution of 1688 had vested the Royal prerogative in a cabinet of ministers who acted on behalf of the Monarch with the expulsion of the Stuarts. It is no doubt that some conspiracists actually saw the Jacobite legitimist threat at work, through wily Jesuit hands, in the Revolution. Although corruption existed, the costs of administration were much less in England than in its continental counterparts. These qualities brought Britain a new Empire, following the loss of the colonies in America, not through imperial design but through the pursuit of commerce and trade. The existence of British Raj India and of the dominion status of Canada indeed could be traced to the mid-century struggle for Empire with the French. It seems to scholars of the Renaissance that Britain's second imperium was realized without a substantial millennial vision. In fact, great theoreticians of the glory of a vast realm within which Reformed, irenic Protestantism fell short of the economic interests which caused the national navy to protect the sinews of commerce. Yet, Freemasonry should also be viewed as a philosophical extension of esoteric values into the civilizing elements of imperial expansion. Great proconsular figures such as the Duke of Connaught (1850-1942) occupied the Grand Mastership late in Victoria's reign, and before him, the Prince of Wales took up this responsibility as part of something appearing to be damage control when the sitting Grand Master became a Roman Catholic and resigned. Earlier still, Army Lodges developed an international network of substantial proportion, as Rudyard Kipling's[90] (1865-1936) novella *The Man Who Would Be King*, 1888, emphasizes. Thus the growth of high degree Masonic culture in England during the period of the struggle with Revolutionary France was profound. In terms of the moral conscience of the nation, the union of Antients and Moderns of 1813-1814 positioned the Craft to participate in this flowering, perhaps best signified by the combination in the person of the Grand Mastership with the Presidency of the Royal Society for the

90 Hope and Perseverance Lodge No. 782 at Lahore Punjab, India on April 5, 1886.

Encouragement of Arts, Manufactures, and Commerce, the environs wherein the aristocracy and the leading merchants met to patronize the midwifery of culture. The seeds of ecumenical Protestantism can be seen within this symbolic exchange through Anglicanism and its *via media* association with the extension of the British Empire through Masonic networks. British Masonic lodges thus became associated with military regiments and imperial institutions, including dominions and vice regalities. The India Act of 1784, in specific, began a long process of subordinating imperial administration to the Crown as did the impeachment of Warren Hastings in 1787. In all, Freemasonry came to reflect the commercial aptitude of England as its symbolism raised up important ideals of the inherent nobility of labor in the service of the nation.

* * * * *

Within the soon-to-be United States (British Colonies at the time), the Royal Arch ritual was first practiced in December 1753 in Fredericksburg Lodge in Virginia (see *Ars Quatuor Coronatorum*, iv., p. 222) where George Washington was initiated into the mysteries of Masonry in this very same Lodge the year before 1752. St. Andrew's Royal Arch Chapter in Boston, Massachusetts, also performed the degree in 1769; the Royal Arch degree certificate (1790) was attributed to Royal Arch Mason Benjamin Hurd, Esquire. In the United States the Royal Arch chapters bestowed four degrees: The Mark Master, Past Master (virtual), Most Excellent Master, and the Royal Arch. These four rituals were developed in the United States by Thomas Smith Webb as outlined in his *Illustrations of Freemasonry* and would come to make up the first four rituals (not counting the three degrees of the Blue Lodge) of the York or American Rite. Webb's *Illustrations* were based on Henry Francken's Rite of Perfection ceremonies developed in Albany, New York in 1767. These four degrees were originally conferred by Royal Arch Chapters using Blue Lodge rooms up to 1797 when in Boston, Massachusetts a convention was held for the purpose of establishing a Grand Chapter of Royal Arch Masons for the Northern States; it leadership was constituted as dais (raised) officers: Thomas Smith Webb was its chairman, he was perhaps the most important

Masonic ritualist in America. The Grand Chapter of the Northern States was established in Hartford, Connecticut January 1798 with Webb as its Grand Scribe; he would become its General Grand King in 1806 with Benjamin Hurd as its General Grand High Priest and Ezra Ames of Albany, New York as its General Grand Scribe. Ames would later go on to become its Grand High Priest. The creation of the Grand Chapter led to the eventual creation of the York or American Rite (cf. DeWitt Clinton; the Clinton-Webb ritual synthesis, Chapter IX); it contains the Capitular Degrees of Mark Master, Past Master (Virtual), Most Excellent Master, and Royal Arch; added was the Cryptic Degrees of Royal Master, Select Master, and Super Excellent Master; and Grand Encampment Knights Templar-Chivalric Degrees of Illustrious Order of the Red Cross (of Babylon in the English Order of the Allied Masonic Degrees), Order of the Knights of Malta, and lastly Knight Templar; the Templar assemblies were organized into encampments and commanderies: the Grand Encampment of the Knight Templars, of which DeWitt Clinton presided, was organized in New York City in 1814 thus making New York State the Masonically nuanced Empire State. As stated above one must be a Christian Master Mason exalted to the Royal Arch degree to become a Knight Templar in the York Rite-American tradition. Thus, the introduction of the French Rite of Perfection into the United States influenced the development of the York or American Rite of Thomas Smith Webb and DeWitt Clinton and the Royal Arch-Lodge of Perfection-High Degree Masonry of the Scottish Rite, Northern and Southern Jurisdiction. In turn the French Rite of Perfection served as the corpus for the Ancient and Accepted Scottish Rite. After arriving in the West Indies, Stephen Morin appointed Henry Andrew Francken as the first Deputy Inspector General; Francken[91] subsequently appointed Moses M. Hayes (1739-1805) of Boston as a Deputy Inspector General for North America. Hayes in turn appointed Isaac De Costa a deputy for South Carolina who in 1783 established the Grand Lodge of Perfection in Charleston. Morin, after establishing Lodges in the West Indies disappears from history. Henry Andrew Francken established a Lodge of Perfection in Albany, New York; the acorn from which the oak of the Scottish Rite would grow upon the east coast. Francken summarized the Rites of Perfection in three

91 Some sources suggest that is was Morin who made the appointment.

manuscripts the most complete being the 1783 *Francken Manuscript*; it was from this that Webb summarized specific ceremonies (Preston's *Illustration's* and Laurence Dermott's *Ahiman Rezon* also provided raw material) and printed them in his own *Illustrations of Masonry* in 1797. Preston English's *Illustrations* (1772) end with the third degree Masonic initiate symbolically being *the most loyal subject of the king*, while Webb's extends the degree system ending not in the third (Master Mason) but the seventh degree of Holy Royal Arch where the exalted initiate becomes a symbolic perfected citizen, a "priest-king" himself by symbolic possession of the Tetragrammaton. This idiom took form in post-Revolutionary war America where the deference and loyalty to the English Monarch, George III, was replaced by the symbolic Masonic father of the new nation, George Washington. Francken was the first to promote high degree masonry within the boundaries of the United States. In 1801, the Supreme Council was founded in Charleston, South Carolina, and contained the twenty-five degrees from the Rite of Perfection, but suddenly, with the organization of the Supreme Council there arose a new Rite, the Scottish Rite, fabricated by the adoption of eight more high degrees making the thirty-third the summit of the Rite, not the twenty-fifth.[92] These extra eight degrees were drawn from Continental sources; most of them previously worked under a Grand Chapter of Prince Masons in Ireland. Thus the Scottish Rite culture can be traced through Etienne Morin, to Henry Andrew Francken. The Scottish Rite Southern Jurisdiction consists of degrees four through fourteen known as the Lodge of Perfection; degrees fifteen through eighteen known as the Chapter of the Rose Croix (i.e. Rosicrucian degrees), degrees nineteen through thirty called the Council of Kadosh; degrees thirty-one through thirty-third, Consistory. The Northern Jurisdiction differs: it consists of degrees four through fourteen as the Lodge of Perfection, degrees fifteen and sixteen as Council of Prince of Jerusalem, degrees seventeen and eighteen as Chapter of Rose Croix, and nineteen through thirty-third as Consistory.

In order to understand the importance and the symbolism of the Royal Arch ceremony, one must first understand the degrees that precede it in the Webb System: Mark Master Mason, Virtual Past Master, and Most

92 Mackey, Albert, *Encyclopedia of Freemasonry,* Vol. II, page 671.

Excellent Master Degrees. The Royal Arch became the thirteenth degree in the Scottish Rite (Royal Arch of Enoch) and the seventh degree in the American Rite of Webb and DeWitt Clinton. The Mark Master Mason, critical within the Clinton-Webb ritual system (Chapter IX), became the fourth degree in the York or American Rite. The Mask Master degree was given in England under the authority of the Grand Lodge of Mark Master starting in 1856; its jurisdiction independent of the United Grand Lodge of England. In the late nineteenth century the quasi-Masonic Victorian secret society known as the Golden Dawn used Mark Mason's Hall to perform their rituals of Isis-Urania. From the beginning, the ceremonies of the Isis -Urania temple were conducted at Mark Masons' Hall in Great Queen Street (now demolished) but members were careful not to embarrass the Masonic authorities, being told that they must not enter Mark Masons Hall by the front door, but go under archway and down passage, entering by a door on the right.[93] The precise contents of the Mark Master Mason degree conferred in the St. Andrew's Lodge in Florida as part of the first American Provincial Grand Lodge detail the selection of a class of workers with the fidelity and skill necessary to construct the Vault of Enoch, notably to insert a cubical white perfect stone within it as its contents. Each worker is invested with a medal with his personal mark and with a solar emblem, a detail differentiating it from Webb's Mark Master ritual and linking directly this ceremony as well as the Royal Arch ritual, as will be seen, to the Joseph-Jacques "J. J." Ramée (1764-1842) Enochian-solar rendering of Union College, the first institution of higher learning in the United States to offer degrees in civil engineering or operative Masonry. Also instrumental to these devices was the emblem of the Chapter penny an emblem of the Mark Master Mason degree within which each Mark Mason inscribed his own personal mark upon a copper penny at his initiation. A penny is the wage of a Mark Master Mason within the degree ceremony. These devices took on a numinous quality and were regarded as amulets of sorts to identify the high rank and Masonic status of the bearer and owner to other members. When such pennies were issued by Mark Lodges, a very few of which continue to exist, named after eminent or successful Masons the prestige was increased. Among these was Girard Mark Lodge No. 214 in Philadelphia, named after

93 Gilbert, R.A., *The Golden Dawn Companion*, page 31.

a noted anti-clerical Freemason and Philanthropist Stephen Girard who fortunes and philanthropies were nationally renowned. The legend of the Mark Master degree can be summarized as follows:

> "A young Craftsman found in the quarries of Tyre a stone of peculiar form and beauty, which was *marked* with a double circle, containing certain mysterious characters that greatly excited his curiosity. He had the ambition to produce this stone to the Inspecting Mark Master as a work of his own. But as it was neither a single nor double cube, nor any other prescribed form, it was rejected notwithstanding the beauty of its execution, and cast forth among the rubbish. The young man then frankly told the Master that the work was not his own, but that he was induced to bring it up on account of its perfect workmanship, which he thought could not be equaled. Some time afterward, when one of the arches in the foundations of the Temple was nearly completed, the keystone was missing. It had been wrought in the quarries by H. A. B. (*Hiram Abiff*) himself, *and was marked with his mark.* Search was made for it in vain, when adventure of the young Fellow Craft was recollected, and among the rubbish the identical stone was found, which completed the work."[94]

The beautiful keystone of Hiram Abif, being neither square nor oblong, is at first rejected because it is unrecognizable, yet it was an object of singular beauty. The keystone, as will be seen in the next chapter, is an esoteric solar symbol. A keystone supports an archway; it binds all the other stones to it, without it an archway cannot stand. Likewise a cornerstone, being the first stone laid when constructing an edifice, symbolically binds the other stones to it as it is the foundation the other stones are built upon. Within the Masonic tradition a cornerstone is laid in the northeast corner symbolizing the sun on the summer solstice as on the morning of June 21 (sun at its highest declination in the northern hemisphere) the sun rises on the north eastern most point on the horizon. A cornerstone, and likewise a keystone, the latter being the stone that the builders reject, denote Masonic solar rulership. A cornerstone, as a solar symbol, becomes esoterically-cabalistically linked to Jesus Christ, the sun

94 Duncan, Malcolm C., *Duncan's Masonic Ritual and Monitor,* page 182, citing *Historical Landmarks* by Rev. G. Oliver, Vol. II, p. 126.

within the Four Gospels. Jesus refers to himself as a cornerstone at Mark 12:10: "Haven't you ever read this Scripture: The stone that the builders rejected has become the cornerstone;" at Luke 20:17: "Then Jesus looked straight at them and asked, 'What then, does this Scripture verse mean: The stone that the builders rejected has become the cornerstone?'" and Matthew 21:42: "Jesus said to them, Have you never read in the Scriptures, The stone that the builders rejected has become the cornerstone. This was the Lord's doing, and it is amazing in our eyes?" Lastly, at Ephesians 2:20: "And are built upon the foundation of the apostles and prophets, Jesus Christ himself being the chief cornerstone;" Thus Jesus is the sun, *God's Sun*, by way of calling himself or being referred to as a "cornerstone." The working tools of this degree are a mallet and chisel, so that each Mark Master Mason can make his own *mark* on his individual work to distinguish it from work that his not his own.

The fifth degree is that of Past Master; it is a virtual degree meaning that it symbolically makes a Freemason that has not governed his lodge a *Virtual* Past Master. This degree follows the Mark Master Mason degree. An actual Past Master is the title bestowed upon a mason who had governed their lodge with equal regularity as a Worshipful Master; once their term as Worshipful Master expires they are now a Past Master. The jewel of a Worshipful Master is a Pythagorean right triangle (ninety degree angle), a symbol of completeness. The jewel of a Past Master is an equilateral triangle (three angels of sixty degrees) symbolizing perfection. The conferring of this degree arises from the following circumstances:

> "Originally, when Chapters of Royal Arch Masonry were under the government of Lodges in which the degree was then always conferred, it was part of the regulations that no one could receive the Royal Arch Degree unless he had previously presided in the Lodge as Master. When the Chapters became independent, the regulation could not be abolished, for that would have been an innovation; the difficultly has, therefore, been obviated, by making every candidate for the degree of Royal Arch a Past Virtual Master before his exaltation.[95]

95 Mackey, Albert, *Encyclopedia of Freemasonry*, Vol. II, page 546.

The Virtual Past Master thus symbolically possesses the jewel of a Past Master, a compasses open to sixty degrees (equilateral triangle), symbolizing the perfected man. This is placed upon a quadrant to emphasize the thirty degrees which he has progressed from the ninety degree right angle of the square to the sixty degree angle of the equilateral triangle, of which the compasses are but the substitute. It is symbolic of his rebirth on the spiritual plane because he has completed the degree work, passed through the chairs (offices) of craft masonry for seven years, analogous of the evolution of the complete man into the perfected man.[96] He has completed his destined course and represents evolved spiritual perfection now ready to be exalted to the Holy Royal Arch.[97] This concept played perfectly with idea of spiritual men "at work from the mountain top" within high degree Freemasonry defining United States ethos and political philosophies. The Holy Royal Arch Degree aptly suited this purpose because the Lost Word, God, or Logos, is symbolically recovered by the Mason. Thus the ideology of secular hermetical order, interpreted as the Freemasons, that moderate and rule the New World was appropriated from the esoteric theologies of Christian mystic Joachim von Fiore whereby two orders of spiritual men or prophets moderate society within an eschatological new Third Age of the Holy Spirit that was to prevail irenically in the New World, the United States. The Third Age follows the first Age of the Father (Old Testament) and second Age of the Son (New Testament); the Third Age of the Holy Spirit would see the defeat of the Antichrist and a rule of universal love. The other order of spiritual men as described by von Fiore is the Society of Jesus as much of their theologies (i.e. Ignatius of Loyola, Athanasius Kircher, Guillaume Postel) contain Joachimite themes. Irenicism is a Christian theology attempting to unify Christian apologetical systems, the use of non-Christian sources, usually pre-Christian philosophy, theology, and paganism, to advance Christianity by using reason, not force.

The sixth degree conferred is that of Most Excellent Master. This degree was invented by Thomas Smith Webb and is indigenous to America. This degree is said to have originated in Temple Chapter in Albany, New York in

96 Steinmetz, George, *The Royal Arch: Its Hidden Meaning*, pages 54-55.
97 Ibid, page 55.

1797. This degree is the sixth within the York (American) Rite. It details the dedication of Solomon's Temple to the Supreme Being with the placement of the keystone into the arch between Jachin and Boaz. George Steinmetz, in his book *The Royal Arch: Its Hidden Meaning*, comments that the Most Excellent Master ritual "…contains no ancient, veiled symbolic meaning. It is modern and was created for a specific purpose. It performs the function for which it was originated. The only symbolism contained therein is that referring to the other degrees, and its import is identical with the meaning in the degree from which taken."[98]

"I am that I am," is the response given by a Freemason when asked if he is a Royal Arch Mason, the premier and supreme degree in the T. S. Webb system when the exalted becomes a *parfait*: a supreme perfected initiate who is now equipped to affect change on a local or global level. "I am that I am," naturally refers to Exodus 3:14 as the response God gave to Moses when he asked him for his sacred name. Kabbalistic tradition teaches that God imparted his name to Moses under the condition that Moses never repeats it. A mason is known to be a Royal Arch Mason by "three times three;" when multiplied equals nine, a reference to the ninth arch under which the sacred Name of Deity is recovered. The Royal Arch degree in the Rite of Perfection was the thirteenth; it is the seventh in the American York Rite and remains the thirteenth in the Ancient and Accepted Scottish Rite alternatively called the Knight of the Ninth Arch in the Northern Jurisdiction of the Scottish Rite. As the degree developed from its early stages some Royal Arch rituals mention Enoch, others do not.[99] The degree was born out of Ramsay's Oration detailing a concealed crypt or vault containing an engraved plate with the Tetragrammaton and two pillars in this vault recorded Enoch's knowledge from his celestial visit as detailed in *I Enoch*. This is, of course, presents a historical anomaly as Enoch's visit and the wisdom he recovered was not known to history. Yet Masonic ritualists, hierophants, and philosophers were already documenting the contents of *I Enoch* by at least 1754, maybe earlier. Elements of *I Enoch* were incorporated into the high or *haute* degree known as the Royal Arch

98 Ibid, pages 58-59.
99 The Royal Arch degree naturally has variances in it from one Masonic body to another as it developed from the Henry A. Francken and Thomas Smith Webb templates.

of *Enoch* which in turn created an esoteric philosophy and theology related to the degree; the Scottish Rite ritual itself bears the name of the Biblical patriarch. The ritual in general details the return of the Jews to Jerusalem to construct the second temple after their seventy year captivity in Babylon. The Zoroastrian-Mithraic Emperor Cyrus the Great dispatches the Jewish governor Zerubbabel, his name means *mouth or seed of Babylon,* to build the second temple circa 538 BCE; he leads a contingent of approximately 42,000 Jews back to the Holy Land. The construction of the Temple of Zerubbabel serves as the template for the Royal Arch ritual. The Temple of Zerubbabel was built on the ruins of Solomon's Temple; the second temple stood until 70 CE when it was razed by the Romans under Emperor Titus.

Masonic scholar and philosopher Albert G. Mackey adds the following regarding Enoch,

> "Of the early history of Enoch, we know nothing. ....The Greek Christians supposed him (Enoch) to have been identical with the first Egyptian Hermes, who dwelt at Sais. They say he was the first to give instruction on the celestial bodies; that he foretold the deluge that was to overwhelm his descendants; and that he built the pyramids, ...The legend goes on to inform us that after Enoch had completed the subterranean temple, fearing that the principles of those arts and sciences (cf. knowledge learned by Enoch from the Watchers and other angelic beings in *I Enoch*) which he had cultivated with so much assiduity would be lost in that general destruction of which he had received a prophetic vision, he erected two pillars - ....On the pillar of brass he engraved the history of creation, the principles of arts and sciences, and the doctrines of Speculative Freemasonry as they were practised in his times;...."[100]

This legend of Enoch learning the arts and sciences comes directly from the *Book of Enoch* which was lost to history, purportedly unknown to those who were creating the Royal Arch degree, and its related mythos as it was being developed in France.

Within the Royal Arch ritual, three weary travelers have come

100 Mackey, Albert, *Encyclopedia of Freemasonry,* Vol. I, pages 244-245.

from Babylon to assist in the rebuilding of the house of the Lord; they must pass through four veils or chambers in order to reach the construction site. After being tested they are allowed passage through to the next; at each veil the travelers are invested with certain passwords and signs that enable them to pass through the next veil. The emblem of the first veil is an eagle, the emblem of the second veil is a man, the third an ox or bull, the fourth a lion. The candidates are given the working tools of a Royal Arch Mason: a pick-ax, shovel, and crowbar, and directed to the northeast corner of the temple to begin work. On the fifth day while clearing debris an ordinary stone is discovered in the ground except that when struck it reverberated with a hollow sound. Upon inspection the stone is the keystone of Hiram Abif; upon closer inspection the keystone contains a trap door leading to a treasure vault. They investigate and discover relics of King Solomon, Hiram King of Tyre, and Hiram Abif. However, when the sun shone through the trap door the sun's brilliance reveals the Enochic name of God, the Lost Word of a Master Mason, on a golden delta atop the Ark of the Covenant placed there by Hiram Abif prior to his death at the hands of the three Fellowcrafts. The temple workers, operative stonemasons, have discovered the legendary Vault of Enoch, thus the Royal Arch Masons become the symbolic preservers of all antediluvian knowledge which God attempted to destroy via the Flood. Anti-Masons would come to characterize Masonry in general as thwarting God's plan by allowing evil or forbidden knowledge to be preserved. The recovery of the Lost Word symbolizes not only the discovery of the Word, but of the symbolic *rebirth* of this Enochic knowledge (antediluvian wisdom) some of which is contained within the *Book of Enoch* as Enoch was told heavenly secrets by a coterie of both Archangels and fallen angels. As such, the device by which the Lost Word was recovered, the keystone, became a symbol of renewal and rebirth. The treasure vault originates with Hiram Abif, who, foreseeing his own death hid the Word of a Master Mason within it. Some legends trace this treasure vault to Solomon who obtained the Name of Deity from Moses, while Irish Royal Arch Temples link the vault to Josiah, King of Judah, who, foreseeing the destruction of Solomon's Temple, built the treasure vault and hid the Ark within it. This theme appears in the Select Master degree in the American Rite where Josiah placed the Ark on the Foundation Stone in the underground vault.

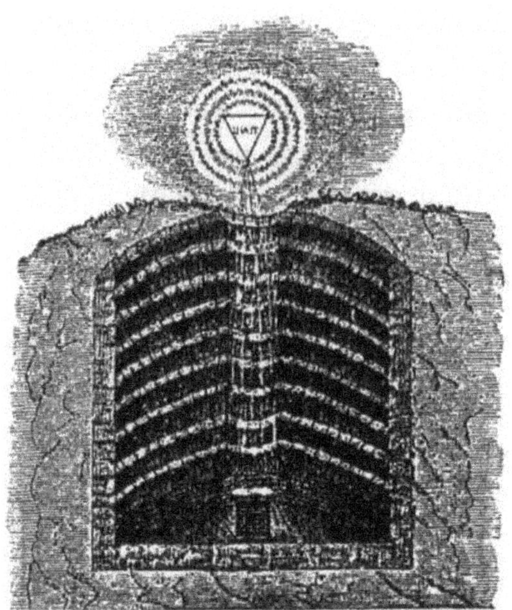

Symbolism of the Select Master degree in the York Rite. It features a sun as the source of divine intellectual light shining down through the nine arches in the vault illuminating the Tetragrammaton on a golden plate. The engraving is from *Cryptic Masonry: A Manual of the Council*, by AlbertMackey, 1867.

The Jesuit styled Scotch Master degree, practiced at the College of Clermont, contained the basic elements of the Royal Arch ceremony with one notable exception: the treasure vault is discovered by Catholic Knight Templars not temple builders. Within the York or American Rite the Delta with the Master Mason's word is atop of the Ark of the Covenant, while in the Scottish Rite the Lost Word is on located within the vault on a cubical Foundation Stone. The Ark of the Covenant originally sat on the Foundation Stone in the Holy of Holies within Solomon's Temple; whether the Foundation Stone in the Scottish Rite degree is supposed to be that Foundation Stone or a substitute of some kind is left to speculation. According to legend, and Albert Pike, the cubical stone that the triangle was affixed to in the secret underground vault was of agate, which as we will see contains solar symbolism. As explained in the previous chapter, the Pillars of Enoch, not mentioned within the actual Royal Arch ritual but alluded to in the Cooke Manuscript and Ramsay's Oration, have been decoded by Pythagoras and Thoth Hermes Mercurius Trismegistus by way of the Grand Omnific Royal Arch Word thus restring all antediluvian knowledge. Nevertheless the two Pillars of Enoch would appear on various Masonic Royal Arch jewelry, documents, and certificates. The Pillars of Enoch are also alluded to in the *Constitutions of Free-Masons* by Drs. Desaguliers and Anderson. It is through the pronunciation of this Royal Arch "Enochic" word that all learning is made possible by restoring the celestial knowledge, obtained by Enoch while in heaven, contained on the two pillars within Masonic legend; the Royal Arch degree is arguably the premier degree in the Lodge of Perfection. Thus pronunciation of the Royal Arch word symbolically makes the pronouncer perfect, a *parfait,* a god-like perfected being. This ideology was summarized by Thomas Smith Webb in his *Illustrations* of how those ancient grand masters were made Royal Arch Knights and thus were admitted to the degree of perfection (cf. Royal Arch),

> "The number of the grand and sublime elected, were at first three, and now consisted of five; and continued so until the temple was completed and dedicated; when King Solomon, as a reward for their faithful services, admitted to this degree the twelve grand masters who had faithfully presided over the 12 tribes; also one other grand master architect. Nine ancient grand masters, eminent for their virtue, were chosen knights of the royal arch, and shortly afterwards were admitted to the sublime degree of perfection. You have been informed in what manner the number of the grand elect was augmented to twenty-seven, which is the cube of three: they consisted of two kings, three knights of the royal arch, twelve commanders of the twelve tribes, nine elected grand masters, and one grand master architect. The lodge is closed by the mysterious number."[101]

Thus the Royal Arch ritual is the climax of the *haute* degrees in the Scottish Rite preparing one for the fourteenth degree of Perfection which follows the Holy Royal Arch; it is called the Perfect Elu in the Southern Jurisdiction and the Grand Elect Mason in the Northern Jurisdiction of the Scottish Rite. The French designate this degree as Grand Scottish Mason of the Sacred Vault of James VI, thereby conferring pronunciation of the *word* with restoration of the Stuart monarchy. The Royal Arch ceremony takes priority because the ritual details the recovery of the word, Logos, or God. This implied a life of ascent (hermetic *ascensio*) and descent through which intercessory moral activity might guide pilgrim-warriors (cf. Knight Templar rhetoric for initiation) to the possession of the Holy Name of God and its implementation. There are of course other degrees within the Scottish and York systems that are salient, but it would be impossible to discuss and analyze them all in the pages of this book. For example, the fifteenth degree of the Scottish Rite, the Knight of the East, or Sword, or Eagle,

101 Webb, Thomas Smith, *Freemason's Monitor or Illustrations of Freemasonry*, pages 288-289.

details events that occur before the Royal Arch degree. This degree depicts Emperor Cyrus the Great granting Zerubbabel permission to return to the Holy Land to build the second temple. Cyrus returns to Zerubbabel some of the treasure of Solomon's Temple that was sacked by Nebuchadnezzar. That notwithstanding, it is from the Royal Arch ceremony that one must turn in order to understand Masonic solar symbolism and its usage, especially in the United States, itself a Masonic Republic with the District of Columbia as Tommaso Campanella's *The City of the Sun*. After one was exalted to the Royal Arch and served as its High Priest, past or present, one could seek membership in an un-numbered *chair* or side degree called the Anointed Order of High Priesthood (Melchizedek) which details Abraham's encounter with Melchizedek after the slaughter of the kings. The candidate participates in a breaking of bread and sharing of wine, assumes an obligation to preside justly over his chapter, and to regard all Companion High Priests as true friends and brothers. He is then solemnly anointed, consecrated and set apart to the Holy Order of High Priesthood. The iconic importance of Melchizedek (The New York Royal Arch Grand High Priest in 1826-1828 was from Salem, New York: Asa Fitch), priest-king of Salem who anointed Abraham at Genesis 14:18-20 before he received God's covenant was instrumental to DeWitt Clinton's political use of Royal Arch idiom in policy templates. This can be seen in the amalgam of Webb's use of Melchizedek's royal political function as a millennial dispenser to Abraham's founding of a nation the activation of the *General Grand Chapter's Constitutions* from the seminal voluntary design articulated in Webb, to that adopted in Middletown, Connecticut January, 1806, the copyright of which was given by resolution to Webb as a national General Grand High Priesthood with Clinton as head. This legislation positioned the ritual core of the Order of the High Priesthood within an involuntary Masonic judicatory which 1) controlled Royal Arch Masonry on a de facto worldwide model basis, and 2) attracted key national policy-law makers identified with Clinton's circle, notably Edward Livingston (1764-1836) Ephraim Kirby (1757-1804); and Joel Poinsett. Each of these officers of the General Grand Chapter were also possessors of the Order of Melchizedek Priesthood, whilst holding, respectively, offices in the Federal Government as Secretary of State; Federal Judge in the Louisiana territory; and Secretary of War. In 1837-38, both Poinsett, who received funds for a Royal Arch Chapter's dispensation in Macon, Georgia, and Livingston once referenced as active participants of an organization over which Clinton presided at his death (1828).

In order to further understand solar symbolism, one must now turn to from whence much of Masonic lore and legend comes: the Ancient Mysteries. The next chapter details how the symbolism of the ancient mystery religions or schools has impacted not only Masonry, but seemingly the development of the Abrahamic faiths as they too contain seemingly eerie symbolic similarities that cannot be dismissed as conspiracy theory or coincidence. As will be seen much of the Abrahamic religions contain numerous elements of astrology, or Astrotheology: that is, the worship of the sun, the moon, the stars, and constellations under the guises of human or divine personalities. At this point I must point out that it is not my intention to offend or upset anyone; one can choose to believe whatever they want. Nevertheless, I will now present evidence and facts, as I have found them, that are no doubt controversial and what can be considered deep, dark, murky waters. It should also be pointed out to the reader that the material presented in the next chapter does not reflect any official religious dogma of the Masonic Institution. Nevertheless, many Masonic scholars have analyzed Astrotheology as contained in the Bible or, alternatively, that the Bible is basically an Astrotheological text. Chief among these supreme and sublime Masonic intellects are Godfrey Higgins (1772-1833), Albert Pike (1809-1891), Manly Palmer Hall (1901-1990), Albert Churchward (1852-1925), and Albert Mackey (1807-1881). This material must be explored with a free and open mind. It must also be acknowledged that Masonry is not exclusive but inclusive: the Christian, Hebrew, Buddhist, Moslem, Hindu, the followers of Confucius or Zoroaster, can come together in the Lodge unified in their shared belief in the one God, the Great Architect, while their individual religious beliefs remain their own. That being said I will now attempt to follow in footsteps of these great Masonic geniuses by showing that the adoration if these heavenly bodies and their subsequent anthropomorphization was at the core of the Ancient Mysteries via an occult or hidden system of symbols, preserved within the Masonic Institution; its rituals, both the Hiramic Legend and the Holy Royal Arch contain numerous astrological references. The heavenly bodies appear to be the objects of the earliest forms of worship; as Tobias Churton correctly states in his work *The Invisible History of the Rosicrucians*,

> "Where there is distance, there is respect. The stars, being far above us, suggest closeness to God, so our ancestors believed. The stars look down on us, we must look up to them. Deduction: the stars were close to God's High Table and deserved worship."[102]

Lastly, the prophecies and eschatology of Christian mystic Joachim von Fiore will be explored; his Third Age of the Holy Spirit, one can easily argue, parallels the coming Aquarian Age based upon the Precession of the Equinoxes, critical within Masonry, will be also be analyzed. Once these concepts are understood, the historical anomaly of how the Royal Arch rituals came to contain elements of *I Enoch* will be explored, and its importance with the development of the high degrees, and its impact upon the policy, rhetoric, and society, especially in the context of the United States.

102 Churton, Tobias, *The Invisible History of the Rosicrucians,* page 13.

CHAPTER III

ESOTERIC MASONRY

The Ancient Mysteries, the Abrahamic Faiths, Astrology, Masonic Ritual Iconography, and Joachim von Fiore

"For from the rising of the sun even unto the going down of the same my name shall be great among the Gentiles; and in every place incense shall be offered unto my name, and a pure offering: for my name shall be great among the heathen, saith the Lord of hosts." - Malachi 1:11.

"Canst thou bind the sweet influences of Pleiades, or loose the bands of Orion?" - Job 38:31

"For as the lightning cometh out of the east, and shineth even unto the west; so shall also the coming of the Son of man be." - Matthew 24:27

"Evidently you have not looked into astrology; I have." - Isaac Newton

"You say we worship the sun, so do you." - Tertullian (early Pagan to Christian convert)

"Observe everything that takes place in the sky, how the lights do not change their orbits, and the luminaries which are in heaven, how they all rise and set in order each in its season (proper time), and do not transgress against their appointed order." - *I Enoch*, 2:1

The Ancient Mysteries were practiced from approximately 6000-4000 BCE in some form (perhaps earlier), to 379-395 CE when Christian Emperor Theodosius I outlawed the Mystery Religions; the Egyptian Serapeum, the Library of Alexandria, and the Temple of Apollo at Delphi were destroyed while Nicene Christianity and Roman Catholicism replaced (or appropriated) the Mysteries and became the official state religion of the Roman Empire. The Mysteries consisted of two primary schools: the Egyptian and the Druidic. From where these traditions come, likely a lost civilization, Atlantis, Lemuria, is left to speculation and open to suggestion. The Mystery Schools contained initiatory rites where select neophytes were disseminated wisdom through a system of degrees; the truths or knowledge imparted was not available to the general populous and great lengths were taken to ensure the wisdom of the Mysteries was sequestered from them. It was through the Mysteries, exoterically called "religion," that mankind was guided, swayed, if not manipulated. Once a candidate was initiated into the greater Mysteries, he could not divulge the knowledge that was imparted to him, usually through allegorical-symbolic metaphor. The Druidic Mysteries dominated the British Isles, while the Mysteries of Egypt were naturally practiced on the banks of the Nile. The philosophical symbolic teachings of both the Druidic and Egyptian Mysteries will now be explored. The Egyptian Mysteries influenced and informed Judaism, the Eleusinian Mysteries, and the Greco-Roman Dionysian-Bacchus cults, all of which predate Christianity. Comparatively, the Persian Mysteries of Mithraism as contained within Zoroastrianism was intertwined with the Egyptian-Greco-Roman Mysteries and ultimately became the *Sol Invictus* cult which in turn became Roman state sanctioned Christianity. These mystery traditions also found their way into Islam seemingly as the worship of the planets, namely Venus. The Mysteries contained two schools: one exoteric open to all, one esoteric known only to the initiated few. The incorporation of the Mysteries into the first state backed non-pagan religion was enough to create the *Mysterion*, the Sacred Mysteries of Christianity, or occult Christianity, within which the true symbolic meanings of Christian religiosity and eschatology were contained. This point was echoed by church father Clement of Alexandria (ca. 150-ca. 215 CE) who stated Christianity had, like the Pagan Mysteries, two schools: one for neophytes and one of secret knowledge transmitted to "a small number, by a succession of masters, and not in writing."[103] Christianity following the Mystery tradition caused the learned church father Origen Adamantius who was a student of Clement of Alexandria to declare:

> "The existence of certain doctrines which are beyond those which are openly taught and do not reach the multitude is not a peculiarity of Christianity only, but is shared by the philosophers. For they had some doctrines which were exoteric and some esoteric."104

Paul the Apostle (of Tarsus, ca. 5-67 CE), in the fourth chapter of his Epistle to the Galatians, speaking of the simplest facts of the Old Testament, asserts they are *an allegory*. Both Origen and Pope Gregory I (a/k/a Gregory the Great) held that the Four Gospels were not to be taken in their literal sense; and Athanasius of Alexandria (ca. 296/298-373, a/k/a Athanasius the Apostolic) admonishes us that "Should we understand sacred writ according to the letter, we should fall into the most enormous blasphemies."[105] In other words, if we take the Bible, or any holy scripture, i.e. the Qur'an, the Vedas literally, we are committing sacrilege and offending God. In this vein it should come as no surprise that each of the Abrahamic faiths contains its own mystery tradition where the true meanings or teachings were concealed in symbolic allegory: the Mysterion within Christianity, Kabbalah within Judaism and Sufism within Islam. The impact of Sufism upon Masonry will be discussed in Chapter VII. Christianity incorporates all the elements of the Pagan Mysteries only with new names assigned: Isis became Mary; Osiris transformed into her husband Joseph; Horus/Mithras/Bacchus/Dionysus/Apollo morphed into Jesus Christ,[106] etc. One must bear in mind that many, if not all, of the *dramatis personae* of both the Old and New Testaments are not real people, but rather are astronomical-astrological or Astrotheological allegories

103 Freke, Timothy and Peter Gandy, *The Jesus Mysteries: Was the "Original Jesus" a Pagan God?*, page 97, citing Clement of Alexandria, *Stromata*, 1.12 and 7.61.
104 Ibid citing Origen, *Contra (Against) Celsus*, 1.7 quoted in Fidler, D. (1993), page 33. *See also* Wallis, R.T. (1992) page 14.
105 Quoted in Pike, Albert, *Morals and Dogma of the Ancient and Accepted Scottish Rite*, page 266.
106 The word "Christ" is a title, not a name. It comes from the Greek *Khristos*, meaning *anointed.*

based upon the sun, the moon, the planets, and their movements through various constellations or relation to the stars or other celestial bodies or arrangements. As will be seen Freemasonry also incorporates elements of these Mysteries as a vessel or preserver of the ancient Mystery Schools. In turn some Masonic historians traced masonry to the Essenes (ca. 2 BCE -1 CE), a mystical Jewish sect allegedly responsible for the creation of the Dead Sea Scrolls. The Essenes incorporated many elements of modern day Masonry such as different levels of initiation and vows of secrecy.

The Mysteries taught that the spirit of man bears the same relationship that God bears to the objective universe; that life was anterior to form and that what is anterior includes all that is posterior to itself.[107] The language of the Mysteries is symbolism and not the written word. A symbol always has more than one interpretation; one is a profane explanation for the masses, the other an esoteric, occult, or hidden meaning known only to the initiated few. The Druidic, like the Egyptian Mysteries, predates Christianity; the teachings of these two traditions were transmitted via esoteric symbolism or allegory. To better comprehend the Druidic and Egyptian Mysteries we again turn to learned masons Albert G. Mackey and Albert Pike. On Druidism, Mackey writes:

> "The Druids were a sacred order of priests who existed in Britain and Gaul, but whose mystical rites were practiced in most perfection in the former country, where the isle of Anglesea was considered the principal seat. (Godfrey) Higgins thinks that they were also found in Germany, but against this opinion we have the positive statement of Caesar.
>
> ...Druidism was divided into three Orders or degrees, which were, beginning with the lowest, the *Bards*, the *Prophets*, and the *Druids*. Higgins thinks that the prophets were the lowest order, but he admits that it is not generally allowed. The constitution of the Order was in many respects like that of the Freemasons. In every country there was an Arch-Druid in whom all authority was placed. In Britain it is said that there were under him three arch-flamens or priests and twenty

107 Hall, Manly P., *The Secret Teachings of All Ages*, page 225.

-five flamens. There was an annual assembly for the administration of justice and the making of laws, and, also four quarterly meetings which took place on the days when the sun reached his equinoctial and solstice points.

The latter two would very nearly correspond at this time with the festivals of St. John the Baptist and St. John the Evangelist. It was not lawful to commit their ceremonies or doctrines to writing, and Caesar says (Bell. Gall., vi., 14) that they used the Greek letters, which was, of course, as a cipher; but Higgins (p. 90) says that one of the Irish Ogum alphabets, which Toland calls secret writing, "was the original, sacred, and secret character of the Druids."

The places of worship, which were also places of initiation, were of various forms: circular, because a circle was an emblem of the universe; an oval, in allusion to the mundane egg, from which, according to the Egyptians, our first parents issued; or serpentine, because the serpent was a symbol of Hu, the druidical Noah; or winged, to represent the motion of the Divine Spirit; or cruciform, because a cross was the emblem of regeneration. Their only covering was the clouded canopy, because they deemed it absurd to confine the Omnipotent beneath a roof; and they were constructed of embankments of earth, and of unhewn stones, unpolluted with a metal tool. Nor was anyone permitted to enter their sacred retreats, unless he bore a chain.

...The doctrines of the Druids were the same as those entertained by Pythagoras. They taught the existence of one Supreme Being; a future state of rewards and punishments; the immorality of the soul, and a metempsychosis; and the object of their mystic rites was to communicate these doctrines in symbolic language, an object and a method common alike to Druidism, to the Ancient Mysteries and to Modern Freemasonry."[108]

Albert Pike also discusses the Druidic Mysteries in *Morals and Dogma*. Pike concisely discloses:

"There was a surprising similarity between the Temples, Priests, doctrines, and worship of the Persian Magi and the British Druids.

108 Mackey, Albert, *Encyclopedia of Freemasonry*, Vol. I, page 221.

The latter did not worship idols in the human shape, because they held that the Divinity, being invisible, ought to be adored without being seen. They asserted the Unity of the Godhead. Their invocations were made to the One All-preserving Power; and they argued that, as this power was not matter, it must necessarily be the Deity; and the secret symbol used to express his name was O.I.W. They believed that the earth had sustained one general destruction by water, and would again be destroyed by fire. They admitted the doctrines of the immortality of the soul, a future state, and a day of judgment, which would be conducted on the principle of man's responsibility. They even retained some idea of redemption of mankind through the death of a Mediator. They retained a tradition of the Deluge, perverted and localized. But, around these fragments of primitive truth they wove a web of idolatry, worshiped two Subordinate Deities under the named of HU and CERIDWEN, male and female (doubtless the same as Osiris Isis), and held the doctrine of transmigration.

.... The Druids, like their Eastern ancestors, paid the most sacred regard to the odd numbers, which traced backwards ended in Unity of Deity, while The even numbers ended in nothing. 3 was particularly reverenced. 19 (7+3+3squared): 30 (7x3+3x3): and 21 (7x3) were numbers observed in the erection of their temples, constantly appearing in their dimension, and the number and distances of huge stones.

They were the sole interpreters of religion. They superintended all sacrifices; for no private person could offer one without their permission. They exercised the power of excommunication; and without their concurrence war could not be declared nor peace made: and they even had the power of inflicting the punishment of death. They professed to possess a knowledge of magic, and practised (*sic*) augury for the public service.

They cultivated many of the liberal sciences, and particularly astronomy, the favorite science of the Orient; in which they attained considerable proficiency. They considered day as the offspring of night, and therefore made their computations by nights instead of days; and we, from them, still use the words fortnight and sen'night. They knew the demission of the heavens into constellations; and finally,

> they practised (*sic*) the strictest morality, having particularly the most sacred regard for the peculiarly Masonic virtue, Truth.[109]

On the Druids, Pike also explains:

> "The main features of the Druidical Mysteries resembled those of the Orient.
>
> The ceremonies commenced with a hymn to the sun. The candidates were arranged in ranks of threes, fives, and sevens, according to their qualifications; and conducted nine times around the Sanctuary, from East to West. The candidate underwent many trials, one of which had direct reference to the legend of Osiris. He was placed in a boat, and sent out to sea alone, having to rely on his own skill and presence of mind to reach the opposite shore in safety. The death of HU was represented in his hearing, with every external mark of sorrow, while he was in utter darkness. He met with many obstacles, had to prove his courage, and expose his life against armed enemies; represented various animals, and at last, attaining the permanent light, he was instructed by the Arch-Druid in regard to the Mysteries, and in morality of the Order, incited to act bravely in war, taught the great truths of the immortality of the soul and future state, solemnly enjoined not to neglect the worship of Deity, nor the practice of rigid morality; and to avoid sloth, contention, and folly."[110]

French Freemason, mystic, and occultist Eliphas Levi states that the Druids lived in abstinence, studied natural sciences, preserved secrets, and admitted new members only after a long probationary period.[111] To be admitted, a candidate had to be from a good family and of high moral character. Before he was instructed in the secret doctrines of the Druids he was bound with a vow of secrecy; afterwards he was taught many things of an occult or hidden nature including the mysteries of the celestial bodies. The Druids had many feast days: the new and full moon and the sixth day of the moon were considered sacred periods. Initiation into the order took place at the

109 Pike, Albert, *Morals and Dogma of the Ancient and Accepted Scottish Rite*, pages 617-619.
110 Ibid, 429-430.
111 Hall, Manly Palmer., *The Secret Teachings of All Ages*, page 45.

equinoxes and solstices; on the dawn on the 25th of December the birth of the sun was celebrated, known as Nollagh, the day (or month) of regeneration, with fires atop their mountains. The Druids had a virgin mother known as Mayence who birthed Hesus or Hu. She was depicted with a child in her arms and both of them were sacred to their Mysteries.

*　　*　　*　　*　　*

Of the Egyptian Mysteries, Albert Mackey provides the following,

> "Egypt has always been considered the birthplace of the mysteries. It was there that the ceremonies of initiation were first established. It was there that the truth was first veiled in allegory, and the dogmas of religion were first imparted under symbolic forms. From Egypt - "the land of the winged globe" - the land of science philosophy, "peerless for stately tombs and magnificent temples - the land whose civilization was old and mature before other nations, since called an empire, had a name" - this system of symbols was disseminated through Greece and Rome and other countries of Europe and Asia, giving origin, through many intermediate steps, to that association which is now represented by the Institution of Freemasonry.
>
> To Egypt, therefore, masons have always looked with peculiar interest as the cradle of that mysterious science of symbolism whose peculiar modes of teaching they alone, of all modern institutions, have preserved to the present day.
>
> The initiation into the Egyptian mysteries was, of all the systems practised by the ancients, the most severe and impressive. The Greeks at Eleusis imitated it to some extent, but they never reached the magnitude of its forms nor the austerity of its discipline. The system had been organized for ages, and the priests, who alone were the hierophants - the explainers of the mysteries, or, as we should call them in the Masonic language, the Masters of the Lodges - were educated almost from childhood for the business in which they were engaged. That "learning of the Egyptians," in which Moses is said to have been so skilled, was all imparted in these mysteries. It was confined to the priests and to the initiates; and the trials of initiation

through which the latter had to pass were so difficult to be endured, that none but those who were stimulated by the most ardent thirst for knowledge dared to undertake them or succeeded in submitting to them.

The priesthood of Egypt constituted a sacred caste, in whom sacerdotal functions were hereditary. They exercised also an important part in the government of the state, and the kings of Egypt were but the first subjects of its priests. They had originally organized, and continued to control, the ceremonies of initiation. Their doctrines were of two kinds - exoteric or public, which were communicated to the multitude, and the esoteric or secret, which were revealed only to a chosen few; and to obtain them it was necessary to pass through an initiation which was characterized by the severest trials of courage and fortitude.

The principal seat of themysteries was at Memphis, inthe neighborhood of the great Pyramid. They were of two kinds, the greater of and the less; the former being the mysteries of Osiris and Serapis, the latter those of Isis. The mysteries of Osiris were celebrated at the autumnal equinox, those of Serapis at the summer solstice, and those of Isis at the vernal equinox.

The candidate was required to exhibit proofs of a blameless life. For some days previous to the commencement of the ceremonies of the initiation, he abstained from all unchaste acts, confined himself to an exceeding light diet, from which animal food was rigorously excluded, and purified himself by repeated ablutions.

Apuleius (*Met.*, lib. xi.), who had been initiated in all of them, thus alludes to cautious reticence, to those of Isis: "The priest, all the profane being removed to a distance, taking hold of me by the hand, brought me into the inner recesses of the sanctuary itself, clothed in a new linen garment. Perhaps, curious reader, you may be eager to know what was then said and done. I would tell you were it lawful for me to tell you; you should know it if it were lawful for you to hear. But both the ears that heard those things and the tongue that told them would reap the evil results of their rashness. Still, however, kept in suspense, as you probably are, with religious longing, I will not torment you with long-protracted anxiety. Hear, therefore, but believe what is truth. *I approached the confines of death*, and, having trod on the threshold of Proserpine, I returned therefrom, being borne through all the elements. At midnight I saw the sun shining with its brilliant light; and I approached the presence of the gods beneath and the gods above, and stood near and worshipped them. Behold, I have related to you things of which, though heard by you, you must necessarily remain ignorant."

The first degree, as we may term it, of Egyptian initiation was that into the mysteries of Isis. What was its peculiar import, we are unable to say. Isis, says Knight, was, among the later Egyptians, the personification of universal nature. To Apuleius she says: "I am nature - the parent of all things, the sovereign of the elements, the primary progeny of time." Plutarch tells us that On the front of the temple of Isis was placed this inscription: "I, Isis, am all that has been, that is, or shall be, and no mortal hath ever unveiled me." Thus we may conjecture that the Isiac mysteries were descriptive of the alternate decaying and renovating powers of nature. Higgins (*Anacal.*, ii, 102), it is true, says that during the mysteries of Isis were celebrated the misfortunes and tragical death of Osiris in a sort of drama; and Apuleius asserts that the initiation into her mysteries is celebrated as bearing a close resemblance to a voluntary death, with a precarious chance of recovery.

...The *Mysteries of Serapis* constituted the second degree of the Egyptian initiation. Of these rites we have but a scanty knowledge. Herodotus is entirely silent concerning them, and Apuleius, calling them "the nocturnal orgies of Serapis, a god of the first rank," only intimates that they followed those of Isis, and were preparatory to the last and greatest initiation. Serapis is said to have been only Osiris while in Hades; and hence the death of Osiris, but leaving the lesson of resurrection for a subsequent initiation. But this is merely a conjecture.

In the mysteries of Osiris, which were the consummation of the Egyptian system, the lesson of death and resurrection was symbolically taught; and the murder of Osiris, the search for the body, its discovery and restoration to life is scenically represented. This legend of initiation was as follows: Osiris, a wise king of Egypt, left the care of his kingdom to his wife Isis, and traveled for three years to communicate to other nations the art of civilization. During his absence, his brother Typhon formed a secret conspiracy to destroy him and usurp his throne. On his return, Osiris was invited by Typhon to an entertainment in the month of November, at which all the conspirators were present. Typhon produced a chest inlaid with gold, and promised to give it to any person present whose body would most exactly fit it. Osiris was tempted to try the experiment; but he had no sooner laid down in the chest, than the lid was closed and nailed down, and the chest thrown into the river Nile. The chest containing the body of Osiris was, after being for a long time tossed about by the waves, finally cast up ay Byblos in Phoenicia, and left at the foot of a tamarisk tree. Isis, overwhelmed with the grief for the loss of her husband, set out on a journey, and traveled the earth in search of the body. After many adventures, she at length discovered the spot whence it had been thrown up by the waves and returned with it in triumph to Egypt. It was then proclaimed, with the most extravagant demonstrations of joy, that Osiris was risen from the dead and had become a god. Such, with the slight variation of details by different writers, are the general outlines of the Osiric legend which was represented in the drama of initiation.

Its resemblance to the Hiramic legend of the Masonic system will be readily seen, and its symbolism will be easily understood. Osiris and Typhon are the representative of the two antagonistic principles - good and evil, light and darkness, life and death.

There is also an astronomical interpretation of the legend which makes Osiris the sun and Typhon the season of winter, which suspends the fecundating and fertilizing powers of the sun or destroys its life, to be restored only by the return of the invigorating spring.

The sufferings and death of Osiris were the great mysteries of the Egyptian religion. His being the abstract idea of the Divine goodness, his manifestation upon earth, his death, his resurrection, and his subsequent office as judge of the dead in a future state, look, says Wilkenson, like the early revelation of a future manifestation of Deity converted into a mythological fable.

Into these mysteries Herodotus, Plutarch, and Pythagoras were initiated, and the former two have given brief accounts of them. But their own knowledge must have been extremely limited, for, as Clement of Alexandria (*Strom.*, v., 7) tells us, the more important secrets were not revealed to even all the priest, but to a select number of them only."[112]

(end of Mackey quote)

Albert Pike, in *Morals and Dogma of the Ancient and Accepted Scottish Rite,* within the chapter presenting the esoteric symbolism of the Prince of the Tabernacle degree, discusses the mysteries of Isis and Osiris. Pike states:

"Whether Egypt originated the legend, or borrowed it from India or Chaldaea, it is now impossible to know. But the Hebrews received the Mysteries from the Egyptians; and of course were familiar with their legend, - known as it was to those Egyptian Initiates, Joseph and Moses. It was the fable (or rather the truth clothed in allegory and figures) of Osiris, the Sun, Source of Light and Principle of Good, and Typhon, the Principle of Darkness and Evil. In all the histories of the Gods and Heros lay couched and hidden astronomical details and the history of the operations of visible Nature; and those in their turn were also symbols of higher and profounder truths. None but rude uncultivated intellects could long consider the Sun and the Stars and the Powers of Nature as Divine, or as fit objects of Human Worship; and they will consider them so while the world lasts; remain ignorant of the great Spiritual Truths of which these are the hieroglyphics and expression.

.....Osiris, said to have been an ancient King of Egypt, was the Sun, and Isis, his wife, the Moon: and his history recounts, in poetic and figurative style, the annual journey of the Great Luminary of Heaven through the different Signs of the Zodiac.

In the absence of Osiris, Typhon, his brother, filled with envy and malice, sought to usurp his throne; but his plans were frustrated by Isis. Then he resolved to kill Osiris. This he did, by persuading him to

112 Mackey, Albert, *Encyclopedia of Freemasonry*, Vol. I., pages 232-233.

enter a coffin or sarcophagus, which he then flung into the Nile. After a long search, Isis found the body, and concealed it in the depths of the forest; but Typhon, finding it there, cut it into fourteen Pieces, and scattered them hither and thither. After tedious search, Isis found the thirteen pieces, the fishes having eaten the other (the privates) , which she replaced with wood, and buried the body at Philae; where a temple of surpassing magnificence was erected in honour of Osiris.

Isis, aided by her son Orus, Horus or Har-oeri, warred against Typhon, slew him, reigned gloriously, and at her death was reunited to her husband, in the same tomb.

.....Horus, who aided in slaying him (Typhon), became God of the Sun, answering to the Grecian Apollo, and Typhon is but the anagram of Python, the great serpent slain by Apollo.

....When Isis first found the body, where it had floated ashore near Byblos, a shrub or erica or tamarisk near it had, by virtue of the body, shot up into a tree around it, and protected it; and by hence our sprig of acacia.

Isis was also aided in her search by Anubis, in the shape of a dog. He was Sirius the Dog-Star,113 the friend and counsellor of Osiris, and the inventor of language, grammar, astronomy, surveying, arithmetic, music, and medical science; the first maker of laws; and who taught the worship of the Gods, and the building of Temples.

In the Mysteries, the nailing up of the body of Osiris in the chest or ark was termed the aphanism, or disappearance [of the Sun at the winter solstice, below the Tropic of Capricorn], and recovery of the different parts of his body by Isis, the Euresis, or finding. The candidate went through a ceremony representing this, in all the Mysteries everywhere. The main facts in the fable were the same in all countries; and the predominant Deities were everywhere a male and a female.

....The mysteries of Osiris, Isis, and Horus, seem to have been the model of all other ceremonies of initiation subsequently established

113 Sirius is sacred to Isis, but associates itself with Anubis the dog headed god because Sirius is part of the constellation Canis Major or the Great Dog, Anubis, within the Egyptian pantheon.

among the different peoples of the world. Those of Atys and Cybele, celebrated in Phrygia; those of Ceres and Proserpine, at Eleusis and Many other places in Greece, but were copies of them. This we learn From Plutarch, Diodorus Siculus, Lactantius, and other writers; and in the absence of direct testimony should necessarily infer it from the similarity of the adventures of these Deities; for the ancients held that Ceres of the Greeks was the same of Isis of the Egyptians; and Dionysus or Bacchus as Osiris."[114]

(end Pike quote)

While Amun Ra/Re was the principal Egyptian solar god, the spiritual omnipotent divine force behind the sun and the generator of heavenly light –the source of all things–the Ruler of Eternity from whence everything came to which all things would return. Other Egyptian deities possess solar attributes; one of these is Osiris (a legendary King of Egypt) who is the sun, Isis (Osiris' legendary wife-sister) is the moon, male and female; while within the Egyptian stellar pantheon Isis' star was Sirius the Dog Star, the brightest star in the nighttime sky, while Osiris was Orion, as Osiris risen, due to its closeness his wife-sister Sirius. Typhon was Scorpio; as Scorpio rose, Orion set signifying the death of Osiris and the temporary victory of Typhon. Greek historian Diodorus Siculus (circa 90-21 BCE) affirms solar and lunar attributes to Osiris and Isis; in his book *The Antiquities of Egypt* where he states:

"Now when the ancient Egyptians, awestruck and wondering, turned their eyes to the heavens, they concluded that two gods, the sun and the moon, were primeval and eternal; and they called the former Osiris, the latter Isis…."[115]

Osiris should be thought of as the material, not spiritual, aspects of the sun which is the beneficent influencer of life and nature on earth. Osiris' mother was Neith: the Great Mother yet Immaculate Holy Virgin; the mysteries of Osiris incorporate solar symbolism. As part of his journey Osiris traverses the twelve sections of the Duat or the night sky. Being a

114 Pike, Albert, *Morals and Dogma of the Ancient and Accepted Scottish Rite*, pages 375-377.
115 Siculus, Diodorus, *The Antiquities of Egypt*, page 14.

sun god had twelve helpers or companions which are of course the twelve houses of the Zodiac.[116] Osiris died, he was ripped into fourteen parts, and was resurrected; just as the sun dies every winter solstice, shortest day of the year, and is resurrected at the vernal equinox, first day of spring-end of winter (death), as such Osiris died and was resurrected. Osiris produced a solar heir, Horus, who was born of Osiris' virgin wife-sister, Isis. Horus was depicted as a winged solar orb whose concomitant was the

The winged solar orb of Amun Re/Ra and Horus; over time Amun Re/Ra was merged with Horus symbolically representing the same spiritual solar force.

Greco-Roman sun god Apollo. Just as Horus defeated Typhon, Apollo in turn slew Python the dragon-serpent who dwelt at Delphi. The Temple of Delphi was built over the cavern where Python's body lay decaying; it was dedicated to Apollo. Fumes rose from the decomposing corpse of Python beneath temple cavern through the cracks and crevasses. These fumes were inhaled by the famed Oracles of Delphi causing them to frenzy and prophesied. Amun Re/Ra, later Horus, the spiritual, not material sun, was also a *risen* deity representing the sun as it rises in the east every morning bringing life, salvation and divine light to the world. In the morning the sun (Amen Ra/Re, Horus) is "born again" as the supreme Holy Father defeating the darkness of the night (Typhon), at high noon at its apex it is a youthful son-sun at full strength, and at evening the sun enters the ghostly underworld beneath the western horizon becoming a Holy Ghost or Spirit; the sun thus has three distinct phases: growth, maturity-strength, and decay. To the Egyptians the sun was a symbol of immorality; it died each night only to be born again in the morning reaching full strength at noon. This is where the concept of the divine trinity of the Father, Son, and Holy Ghost derives from within Christianity, from the Egyptian, as accepted by

116 Bonwick, James, *Egyptian Belief and Modern Thought*, page 152.

Jesuit priest Athanasius Kircher (1602-1680); the word "trinity" does not appear in the Bible. Kircher was a Jesuit honored with the title "master of a hundred arts" who published numerous works on oriental studies, geology, and medicine. Kircher, a hermetist-cabalist, continued the Renaissance tradition of interpreting Egyptian hieroglyphs as symbols containing divine truths; the hieroglyphs on the obelisk of Heliopolis to Kircher contained the forerunners of Christian symbolism including, among other things, the sun or solar disk placed over a "Christian Cross" seemingly *crossified* or crucified. Although one finds frequent reference to both Hebrew Kabbalah –its Sephirot–and Christian Cabala in his works, Kircher condemned the practice of cabalistic magic. He published, among others, *Lingua Aegyptiaca Restituta*, *Obeliscus Aegyptiacus*, *Obeliscus Pamphilius*, *Arithmologia sive De abditis numerorum mysterijs*, *Prodomus coptus sive Aegyptiacus*, *Rituale Ecclesiae Aegyptiacae sive Cophititarum*, *Sphinx Mystagoga*, *sive Diatribe Hieroglyphica*, and *Turris Babel*. These texts were the first real studies of Egyptian hieroglyphs and forged a nexus between the Egyptian religion and Roman culture; the Egyptianizing of Rome itself, in other words. In *Oedipus Aegyptiacus* (1652 -1654), Kircher compared Christianity to the religion and mysticism of Egypt arguing that Christianity's origins were born out of the Egyptian Mysteries; he also believed that Moses and Hermes Trismegistus were one and the same. At the end of *Oedipus Aegyptiacus*, just after the hymn from the *Pimander*

Frontispiece of Athanasius Kircher's *Arithmologia sive De abditis numerorum mysterijs*, 1665, featuring an eye in the triangle inside a cabalistic sun, as God, as the source of knowledge surrounded by nine angels. A cosmological sphere sits below it representing the heavens while two Persian Magi stare in awe. The magi on the right contemplates the 47th Proposition of Euclid - the future emblem of a Masonic Worshipful Master.

with which he concludes, Kircher places a hieroglyph enjoining secrecy and silence concerning these sublime doctrines. And, in effect, in this survival in seventeenth century Jesuitism of the most enthusiastic type of Renaissance religious Hermetism we have something like another of those esoteric channels through which the Hermetic tradition is carried on, which perhaps explains why Mozart could be a Freemason as well as a Catholic.[117] Kircher assisted Gian Bernini in the erection of an Egyptian obelisk in Rome's Piazza Navona near the Fountain of the Four Rivers as a symbolic gesture to Christianity's true occult origins. The symbolism of an obelisk, associated with the spiritual solar energy Amun Ra/Re, was well known to Kircher. Regarding the divine trinity Kircher concluded that the Egyptian solar winged orb represented the Egyptian scarab beetle with its wings spread; it symbolized the beetle rolling it's dung ball from east to west infusing it with it's new seed, life, just as the sun by rising in the east and setting in the west infuses the earth with life and fertility. Kircher also equated the Holy Trinity to occultism as inherited from Egypt and practiced by famed alchemist Paracelsus (1493-1541); the Holy Trinity was fire, water, air, the three elements found on earth but not earth themselves. They were salt, mercury, and sulfur: the Holy Trinity, God, the universal seed of nature. This occult-alchemical philosophy was adopted by Germanic theologian, mystic, and sage Jakob Boehme (1575-1624) who called the Trinity, *The Three Witnesses*, by which the invisible is made known to the visible, tangible universe.

Of the Mysteries of Isis and Osiris was the secrets of Serapis, a specific and particular type of sun deity. Etymologically the word Serapis means "Sol-Apis;" "Sol" meaning sun and "Apis" meaning bull: the solar bull or perhaps "Sor-Apis," the tomb of the bull. Serapis appears to be a combination of Apis, the Egyptian sacred bull worshipped during the Age of Taurus, and Osiris: Osiris-Apis or *Serapis*. It was said t hat Osiris being the sun and a resurrected after-life god assumed the shape of a bull and carried his followers to the afterworld on his back; it was thought that bulls were sacrificed to Osiris. The worship of Serapis occurred in the Serapis, beginning circa 3rd century BCE, at Alexandria, and featured

117 Yates, Frances A., *Giordano Bruno and the Hermetic Tradition*, pages 422-423.

an impressive statue of Serapis; it has been argued that the Christian iconography of Jesus Christ was likely based upon the physical attributes of the Serapis statue. Historian, biographer, and Middle Platonist Plutarch (46-120 CE) gives an account of the statue's origin in his *Isis and Osiris*: "While he was Pharaoh of Egypt, Ptolemy Soter had a strange dream in which he beheld a tremendous statue, which came to life and ordered the Pharaoh to bring it to Alexandria with all possible speed. Ptolemy Soter, not knowing the whereabouts of the statue, was sorely perplexed as to how he could discover it. While the Pharaoh was relating his dream, a great traveler by the name of Sosibius, coming forward, declared that he had seen such an image at Sinope. The Pharaoh immediately dispatched Soteles and Dionysius to negotiate for the removal of the figure to Alexandria. Three years elapsed before the image was finally obtained, the representatives of the Pharaoh finally stealing it and concealing the theft by spreading a story that the statue had come to life and, walking down the street leading from its temple, had boarded the ship prepared for its transportation to Alexandria. Upon its arrival in Egypt, the figure was brought into the presence of two Egyptian Initiates, the Eumolpid Timotheus and Manetho the Sebennite, who immediately pronounced it to be Serapis. The priests then declared that it was equipollent to Pluto. This was a masterly stroke, for in Serapis the Greeks and Egyptians found a deity in common and thus religious unity was consummated between the two nations."[118]

As part of the Egyptian religion was the worship of the solar bull, Apis, which is of course Taurus the Bull, the sun in the house of Taurus circa 4300-2150 BCE The initiate into the Egyptian Mysteries was no doubt instructed in the astronomical phenomena known as the Precession of the Equinoxes. The Precession is based upon the great Solar or Platonic year: that is the sun moves through each house (starting at the vernal equinox from the northern hemisphere perspective) of the zodiac; it remains in that house of the Zodiac approximately 2000-2150 years (due to cusps as the sun does not just leave one house and enter another) and completes the entire cycle about 25,900-26,100 years. It is called a precession because the sun moves in retrograde motion though each house of the zodiac which

118 Quoted in Hall, Manly Palmer, *The Secret Teachings of All Ages*, pages 60-61, see also *Isis and Osiris* by Plutarch.

consists of thirty degrees; it moves one degree backwards every seventy-two years. These seventy-two years were symbolized within Jacob's Ladder as having seventy-two steps, Muslims, of course, receive seventy-two virgins in the heavenly afterlife. In turn, the Kabbalists generate from the Tetragrammaton 72 paths or three-letter combinations; the Jesuit Athanasius Kircher knew, or knew of, 72 languages of the world.[119] The sun's retrograde motion is based upon the earth's wobble as it orbits the

Athanasius Kircher's illustration of the 72 Names of God originating from the Pythagorean -Kabbalistic Tetractys: YHVH, interpreted in Christian Cabala to be the Jesuit I.H.S. Kircher identified the 72 languages of the world all of which, according to Kircher, secretly originated from the Hebrew Tetragrammton. Others interpret the 72 names originating from yet another secret Hebrew Tetragrammaton: *Shem ha-Mephorash* which is, according to Hebrew Kabbalah and Hermetic Qabalah, composed of seventy-two letter groups with each group containing three letters. Each of these letter triplets is the name of an angelic intelligence. The seventy-two demons described in the Lesser Key of Solomon (*Ars Goetia*) is thought to reflect the seventy-two letter-groups composing *Shem ha-Mephorash*. Illustration from Kircher's *Oedipus Aegyptiacus*.

119 Godwin, Joscelyn, *Athanasius Kircher's Theatre of the World*, page 279.

sun; the earth's wobble is why different constellations appear in different places in the night sky. The sun also appears to be in motion in the galaxy likely due to the gravitational pull on it from either Spica within the constellation Virgo or Alcyone within the Pleiades. The Precession of the Equinoxes was officially observed for the first time by Greek astronomer and mathematician Hipparchus (190-120 BCE) in 170 BCE, although it and its influence must have been known to earlier Egyptian astrologers and sabeans, Hebrew Kabbalists, Druidic and Persian mystics as part of their respective mysteries. Hipparchus saw that a specific house of the zodiac lay behind the sun at the vernal equinox and that it slowly moved backward over time, one degree every seventy-two years. The sun thereby moved from one house of the zodiac to the next every 2000 years or so. By his calculation the Piscean Age will end and the Age of Aquarius will begin circa 2040; Aquarius will be behind the sun at the vernal equinox, not Pisces. The 2000 -2160 years the sun remains in a house of the zodiac is called an *age*; *the worship of the sun adopts the personality of the particular house or celestial sign it is in during that 2000 year time frame or "age."* Symbolically, as will be seen, this is of great importance and is one of the great mysteries of the ancients. For the last 2000 years (0–ca. 2012 CE) the sun crossed the equator at the vernal equinox in the constellation Pisces, the Piscean Age; 2000-2160 before that the sun passed through the constellation Aries giving rise to the Arian Age; and 2000-2160 years before that being the age Taurus the Bull; Cain slew his brother Abel, each brother was betrothed to a twin sister; thus the death of Abel symbolically ended the Age of Gemini. Albert Pike describes the reverence the Persians felt for Taurus and the method of astrological symbolism in vogue among them; thus "In Zoroaster's cave of initiation, the Sun and the Planets were represented, overhead, in gems and gold, as was also the Zodiac. The Sun appeared, emerging from the back of Taurus." In the constellation of the Bull are also to be found the *Seven Sisters*, the sacred Pleiades, famous to Freemasonry as the Seven Stars at the upper end of the Sacred Ladder. In ancient Egypt it was during this period, when the vernal equinox was in the sign of Taurus, or the Apis Bull, was adored as the Sun God, who was worshiped through the animal equivalent of the celestial sign which he had impregnated with his presence at the time of its crossing into the Northern Hemisphere. This

Egyptian Ankh

is the meaning of an ancient saying that the celestial Bull "broke the egg of the year with his horns."[120] The primary religious symbol of the Taurean Age was the Ankh. It was the Egyptian symbol of life, the sun; it is the thoracic vertebra of a bull as seen in cross section thus alluding to the Age of Taurus. The Age of Taurus also gave rise to bull cults of the Minoans on the Island of Crete. Murals in the ruined city of Knossos in Crete depict female acrobats entertaining the court by leaping over heads of bulls. In the sacred Indian text Rigveda (composed circa 1700-1100 BCE), the god Surya references a solar bull who shines out through all the sky, while the fire god Agni was likened to a bull with hair on fire. The Age of Taurus was also affected by its opposite house Scorpio, the sign of the occult, death and rebirth, and was a strong influence in Egypt during the Age of Taurus. The Egyptians were thought to be obsessed with death and the occult sciences. Egyptian priests performed special mystical rituals and rites over the mummified bodies of the newly dead to help their spirits navigate the afterlife. Taurus gave way to Aries and then Pisces; starting in approximately 2012 the sun will be in one or two degrees out of Pisces and in the sign of Aquarius thus beginning the humanistic-egalitarian "Masonic" Aquarian Age. Some have argued that Solomon's Temple, the name Solomon when bifurcated: "SOL-OMON" or "Sol/Sun-omon/Moon," and the Sphinx's nose were devices that measured and calculated the Precession of the Equinoxes.

When the Age of Taurus ended, the Age of Aries began. Aries the Ram is a fire sign, Taurus is a fixed earth sign. The Arian Age lasted from approximately 2150 BCE to 0 CE. The most striking example of Arian *fire* or *energy* is that of Alexander the Great, who conquered most of the known world by his early thirties. He left Egypt to his general Ptolemy Soter who founded the Macedonian dynasty of the pharaohs in 323 BCE ending with the suicide of Cleopatra in 30 BCE. The polar influence of Aries'

120 See Manly Palmer Hall's *The Secret Teachings of All Ages*, pages 150-153.

opposite house Libra, the scales of justice, saw the rise of the equality via the democratic ideal in Greece under statesman and lawmaker Solon (638 -558 BCE) as well as formalized justice in both Greece and Rome. As the worship of the sun adopts the personality the house it is in, the religion of Judaism, stemming from both the Egyptian and Zoroastrian, would see incorporation of Arian Age symbolism. It should be pointed out that when an Age ends the worship of the sun under the old sign still continues as Judaism is obviously still with us today despite the Arian Age being over; the sun changing houses by way of the Precession of the Equinoxes does not necessarily extinguish old age religions.

Elements of Zoroastrianism, the religion of ancient Persia, founded circa 7th century BCE, and astrology enter Judaism through the Hebrews seventy year exile in Babylon during the reign of Persian Emperor Cyrus the Great thought by some Hebrews to be the prophesied Messiah. Zoroastrianism was itself an Arian Age *fire religion* and the Babylonians were master astrologers; the science of astrology spread so rapidly among the Israelites, especially the educated classes, during this time as to create Jewish astrological literature based upon the solar calculation of time as opposed to the lunar.[121] The use of the solar calendar as described in *I Enoch*, despite it being left out of the Old Testament, was to coincide with the Jewish religious festivals at the Second Temple. Enoch explained the importance of the sun; it is the source of all mystical illumination, "And this is the first law of the luminaries: the luminary the Sun has its rising in the eastern doors of heaven, and its setting in the western doors of heaven."[122] Enoch then learns the light of the moon is actually generated by the sun, "And Uriel showed me another law: when light is transferred to the moon, and on which side it is transferred to her by the sun."[123] Similarly the practice of Zoroastrianism occurred in fire temples as fire was revered and worshipped amongst them. Accordingly the Old Testament and the story of Moses contain components of Arian fire astrological symbolism. At its offset, Judaism contains astrological symbolism: Abraham sacrifices a ram

121 The lunar calendar divided the year into 12 months representing the 12 houses of the Zodiac each with 29-30 days as there are 29.5-30 days in the lunar cycle.
122 *I Enoch*, 72:2.
123 Ibid, 78:10.

(representing Aries) in the stead of his son Isaac, thus the ram or lamb became a symbol of salvation. The great Judaic patriarch Moses receives the Ten Commandments and the Tetragrammaton from a burning bush as Aries is a fire sign. Pre-Reformation iconography of Moses (see Plate III) depicts him with the ram's horns of Aries representing Moses as the sun in Aries: he is the Judaic law bringer of the Arian Age.[124] The Israelites are led out of Egypt under the protection of a pillar of fire during nightfall (Exodus 13:21-22). Moses (Aries) is angered when Aaron tried to turn the Israelites back worshiping the golden calf, Apis, of Egypt a symbol of the old Age of Taurus. Moses orders the killing of the Israelites who worshiped Aaron's golden calf, Taurus/Apis, at Exodus 32:27. The Tabernacle, the portable temple erected by the Israelites that contained the Ark of the Covenant after their exodus from Egypt, was laid out with the long sides facing north and south, the short sides facing east and west with an entrance to the east showing influence of sun worship. The Jewish Passover is a celebration of the vernal equinox as the sun *passes over* the equator from the southern hemisphere into the northern. Passover starts after the first full moon after the vernal equinox (March 20-22) and was marked by the slaying of the Paschal Lamb and the smearing of lamb's blood upon door posts symbolizing the sun leaving the sign of Pisces and entering Aries. The Shofar (ram's horn) is sounded in synagogue services on Rosh Hashanah and Yom Kippur in homage to Aries. The Hebrews celebrated the autumnal equinox-harvest with the Feast of Tishri, a tradition still continued within the Scottish Rite of Masonry. Notwithstanding, Judaism still incorporates lunar elements within its worship: all Jewish holidays begin after sunset when the sun is below the horizon and the moon is visible. Lunar references can be found in the Old Testament at Isaiah 66:23, "And it shall come to pass, (that) from one new moon to another, and from one Sabbath to another, shall all flesh come to worship before me, saith the Lord." and again at Psalm 89:37 "It shall be established for ever as the moon, and (as) a faithful witness in heaven. Selah." Judaism also contains elements of stellar and planetary adoration too lengthy to discuss here and in need of further research. Zoroastrianism naturally influenced the development

124 Exodus 34: 29-35. From the Hebrew "keren" which literally means "grew horns." Moses' face was also described as "cornuta" ("horned") in the Latin Vulgate translation of Exodus.

of Judaism and later Christianity. The Zoroastrian deity, Ahura Mazda, imparted his commandments to Zoroaster on the Mountain of the Two Holy Communing Ones; Moses gets the commandments from Jehovah atop Mount Sinai. In both traditions God is omnipresent, omniscient, eternal and the creator of the universe and governs it though angels and archangels. Thus Ahura Mazda of Zoroaster and Jehovah of Moses parallel each other; the Zoroastrian Spenta Mainyu is the Christian "Holy Spirit," Ahura Mazda (light) powers are negated by Angra Mainyu or Ahriman (darkness, transformed by Christianity into the concept of Satan) the Zoroastrian devil and his host of demons. Zoroastrian eschatology (end days or end of time) contain elements that would clearly enter Christianity: a perfect kingdom, the coming of a Messiah, the resurrection of the dead and life everlasting.

Mithraism was also an Arian Age solar religion; its antiquity is debated: most date it to Persia being a Mystery tradition within Zoroastrianism and maintained the teachings of Zoroaster only in simpler form; while others date it to the Mediterranean area (via Persian influence) around 0-1 CE emerging at the end of the Arian Age. Plutarch states that Mithraism began to filter in to the Roman Empire circa 70 BCE Pompey's campaign against Cilician pirates exposed Roman soldiers to the religion and it slowly began to grow within the Empire; Persian mystics entered Italy and southern Europe in the first-second century and Mithraism and Christianity were interwoven. Mithras (see Plate IV) symbolically slays the bull ending the Age of Taurus. Mithras was a sun-god born in cave at the winter solstice. His feast were celebrated at that period when the sun started to return northward after the winter solstice. The Roman calendar, published in the time of Constantine, at which period his worship began to gain ground in the Occident, fixed his feast day on the 25th of December. His statues and images were inscribed, *Deo-Soli invicto Mithrae:* to the invincible Sun-God Mithras. To him gold, incense and myrrh were consecrated. "Thee," say Martianus Capella, in his hymn to the Sun, "the dwellers on the Nile adored Serapis, and Memphis worships as Osiris; in the sacred rites of Persia thou are Mithras, in Phrygia, Atys, and Libya bows down to thee as Ammon, and Phoenician Byblos as Adonis; and thus the whole world adores thee under different names."[125] Mithraism, as it supposed, by Zeradusht or Zoroaster, as an initiation into the principles of the religion which he had founded among the ancient Persians, they in time extended into Europe, and lasted so long that traces of them have been found in the fourth century. The mysteries of Mithras "...With their penances and tests of the courage of the candidate for admission, they have maintained by a constant tradition through the secret societies of the Middle Ages and the Rosicrucians down to the modern faint reflex of the latter, the Freemasons."[126] The Mysteries of Mithras were celebrated in a cave and were divided into seven degrees. The aspirant at first underwent purification by water, by fire, and by fasting, after which he was introduced in a cavern representing the world; upon the walls and roofs were inscribed the celestial signs (a/k/a the twelve house of the zodiac). The candidate submitted to baptism, cleansed of his prior transgression representing a spiritual rebirth, and moved through a series of caves instructed in the secrets of Mithras. The candidate at one point was made to impersonate a corpse who was restored to life, resurrected. Commodus (161-192 CE), the Roman Emperor, was initiated into the mysteries of Mithras in Rome and is said to have taken great pleasure in the ceremonies. The Papacy was built upon Mithras and Christianity and contains many parallels to Mithraism; the cave of the Vatican known as the Phrygianum, still situated at the base of the present day Basilica, belonged to Mithras until 376 CE, when a city prefect suppressed the cult of the rival savior and seized the shrine in the name of Christ on the very birthday of the pagan god, December 25th.[127] The highest grade or degree within the Mithraic Mysteries was known as *Pater*; while the title of *Pater Patrum* or *Pontimus Maximus*; "Father of Fathers" or "Pope" was designated for the Grandmaster of the Mithraic Mysteries. Although it was not uncommon for there to be more than one Pater at a time, it is clear that only one *Pater Patrum* presided over the performance of the Mithraic Mysteries as the supreme chief the way a Worshipful Master presides over his Masonic Lodge; the last *Pater Patrum* was the Roman Senator Vettius Agorius Praetextatus (ca. 315-384). The chair of St. Peter in the Vatican is thought to have actually been used by *Pater Patrum* in his duties as master

125 Pike, Albert, *Morals and Dogma of the Ancient and Accepted Scottish Rite*, page 587.
126 Mackey, Albert, *Encyclopedia of Freemasonry*, Vol. II. page 485 citing King, *Gnostics*, page 47.
127 Walker, Barbara, *The Woman's Encyclopedia of Myths and Secrets*, page 155.

of the Mithraic Mysteries in the Phrygianum. The sacred chair of Bar-Jonas was cleaned in 1662 and upon it was discovered a solar symbol: the Twelve Labors of Hercules. Hercules, similar to Mithras, was a metaphoric avatar for the sun known to the Greeks as Haracles. The Twelve Labors represent the twelve houses of the zodiac that the sun moves through annually via earth's orbit; each one presenting its own test for the sun to overcome. For example, Hercules must defeat the Nemean Lion, Leo, and capture the Cretan Bull, Taurus. The similarity between the cult of Mithras and the cult of Christianity, their respective sacerdotalism, upon this issue the *Encyclopedia Britannica* states,

> "The fraternal and democratic spirit of the first communities, and their humble origin; the identification of the object of adoration with light and the sun; the legends of shepherds with their gifts of adoration, the flood, and the ark; the representation in art of the fiery chariot, the drawing of water from the rock; the use of bell and candle, holy water and the communion; the sanctification of Sunday and of the 25th of December; the insistence on moral conduct, the emphasis placed on abstinence and self control; the doctrine of heaven and hell, of primitive revelation, of the mediation of the Logos emanating from the divine, the atoning sacrifice, the constant warfare between good and evil and the final triumph of the formal, the immorality of the soul, the last judgment, the resurrection of the flesh and the fiery destruction of the universe - [these] are some of the resemblances which, whether real or only apparent, enabled Mithraism to prolong its resistance to Christianity." [128]

The name Mithras in Greek, Μιθρας, has a numerical value of 365, the number of days in a solar year, and the decrease of the solar influence in the winter, and its revivification in summer, was made a symbol of the resurrection from death to life.[129] As the sun is in death at the winter solstice (Capricorn-December 21/22) and is at full life at the summer solstice (Cancer-June 21/22); so are the meridians the Tropic of Capricorn and the Tropic of Cancer marked and named on earth to delineate the southern and northern latitudes.

128 Quoted in Hall, Manly Palmer, *The Secret Teachings of All Ages,* page 50.
129 Mackey, Albert, *Encyclopedia of Freemasonry*, Vol. II, pages 486-487.

*　　*　　*　　*　　*

The Dionysian-Bacchus mysteries and those practiced at Eleusis; the emergence of the Roman *Sol Invictus* cult must now be analyzed because they are of great importance. These traditions contain astrological allegory that would filter into Christianity as well as Freemasonry via its rituals. The Mysteries of Dionysus, a solar deity, known as Bacchus to the Romans, Albert Mackey tells us,

> "These mysteries were celebrated throughout Greece and Asia Minor, but principally at Athens, where the years were numbered by them. They were instituted in honor of Bacchus, or as the Greeks called him, Dionysus, and were introduced into Greece from Egypt. In these mysteries the murder of Dionysus by the Titans was commemorated, in which legend he is evidently identified with the Egyptian Osiris, whom was slain by his brother Typhon. The aspirant, intheceremoniesthrough which he passed, represented the murder of the god and his restoration to life, which, says Baron de Sacy (Notes on Sainte-Croix, ii., 86), were the Subject of allegorical cxplanations altogether analogous which were Given to the rape of Proserpine and the murder of Osiris.
>
> The commencement of the mysteries was signalized by the consecration of an egg, in allusion to the mundane egg from which all things were supposed to have sprung. The candidate having been first purified by water, and crowned with a myrtle branch, was introduced into the vestibule, and there clothed in the sacred habiliments. He was then delivered to the conductor, who, after the mystic warning, έχάδ, έχάδ, εοτε, βεβηλοτ, "Depart hence, all ye profane!" exhorted the candidate to exert all his fortitude and courage in the dangers and trials through which he was about to pass. He was then led through a series of dark caverns, a part of theceremonies which Stobaeus calls "a rude and fearful march through night and darkness." During this passage he was terrified by the howling of wild beasts, and other fearful noises; artificial thunder reverberated through the subterranean apartments, and transient flashes of lightning revealed monstrous apparitions to his sight. In this state of darkness and terror he was kept for three days and nights, after which he commenced the aphanism or mystical death of Bacchus. He was now placed on

the pastos or couch, that is, he was confined in a solitary cell, where he could reflect seriously on the nature of the undertaking in which he was engaged. During this time, he was alarmed with the sudden crash of waters, which was intended to represent the deluge. Typhon, searching for Osiris, or Dionysus, for they are identical, discovered the ark in which he had been secreted, and tearing it violently asunder, scattered the limbs of his victims in the waters. The aspirant now heard the lamentations which were instituted for the death of the god. Then commenced the search of Rhea for the remains of Dionysus. The apartments were filled with shrieks and groans; the initiated mingled with their howlings of despair the frantic dances of the Corybantes; everything was a scene of distraction, until, at a signal from the hierophant, the whole drama changed - the mourning was turned to joy; the mangled body was found; and the aspirant was released from his confinement, amid the shouts of Ευρηχαμεν, Ευγςαιρομεν, "We have found it; let us rejoice together." The candidate was now made to descend into the infernal regions, where he beheld the torments of the wicked and the rewards of the virtuous. It was now that he received the lecture explanatory of the Rites, and was invested with the tokens which served the initiated as a means of recognition. He then underwent a lustration, after which he was introduced to a holy place, where he received the name of epopt, and was fully instructed in the doctrine of the mysteries, which consisted in a belief in the existence in one God and a future state of rewards and punishments. These doctrines were inculcated by a variety of significant symbols. After the performance of these ceremonies, the aspirant was dismissed, and the Rites concluded with the pronunciation of the mystic words, Konx Ompax. Sainte-Croix (Myst. Du Pag., ii., 90), says that the murder of Dionysus by the Titans was only an allegory of the physical revolution of the world; but these were in part, in the ancient initiations, significant of life and death and resurrection."[130]

Dionysus-Bacchus cults mirror the mysteries of Osiris in that they were all slain and resurrected representing the sun's death in winter and its rebirth at the vernal equinox. Their bodies were disemboweled and recovered. Pike states "Dionysus is the Sun, that liberator of the elements; and his

130 Mackey, Albert, *Encyclopedia of Freemasonry*, Vol. I, pages 213-214.

spiritual meditation was suggested by the same imagery which made the Zodiac the supposed path of Spirits in their descent and their return."[131] Part of the Dionysian mysteries was that he was the son of the god Zeus; he was often called the twice born being birthed by a mortal woman named Semele after a seven month pregnancy and also birthed from Zeus' thigh. As part of his travels Dionysus rode a pair of donkeys who helped him cross a swamp when he was on his way to Dodona in search of a curse for the madness inflicted upon him by Hera. Hera was a wife of Zeus who became jealous and enraged of learning that Zeus had produced a child with a mortal woman. Dionysus also appears in the Greek tragedy *The Bacchae* by Greek playwright Euripides (480-406 BCE) where Dionysus punishes King Pentheus and his mother Agave for failing to worship him. The played first appeared posthumously at the Theatre of Dionysus in 405 BCE Dionysus was of course the god of the vine, the grape harvest, and was thus able to turn water into wine. His festivals (like those of Bacchus) often occurred in the spring when leaves and grapes reappeared on vines. Many ancient architects belonged to the Dionysian Mysteries, they were known as the Dionysian Artificers. Interestingly the symbol of Dionysus-Bacchus was "IHS" christianized to mean *Iesus Hominum Salvator* (Jesus Savior of Men) is a nexus between Christianity and these mysteries. Other interpretations of "IHS" suggest it means, *In Hac Salus, in this [cross is] salvation*, or the revelation of Emperor Constantine, *In Hoc Signum Vinces, in this sign you will conquer*, which he beheld via a cross in the sky. Within the context of the Society of Jesus, it exoterically refers to the Second Person of the Holy Trinity. Esoterically, "IHS" derives from the Greek IHΣ which has a numerical value of 608, and is emblematic of the sun and constituted the sacred and concealed name of Bacchus.[132] Were early Christians confusing Jesus with Bacchus or Dionysus?

* * * * *

The Mysteries of Eleusis, founded by Eumolpos approximately 1400 BCE, celebrated at Athens in honor of Demeter, Ceres to the Romans, swallowed up the other mystery traditions and incorporated elements of all

131 Pike, Albert, *Morals and Dogma of the Ancient and Accepted Scottish Rite*, page 586.
132 Higgins, Godfrey, *The Celtic Druids*, page 128.

of them. Only candidates who lived pure lives and demonstrated maturity of age were admitted, a *parfait* or perfected initiate. Ceres-Demeter was the creator of the Mysteries, she has been thought to be an earth goddess, but more correctly she is the goddess and protectress of agriculture and corn. These Mysteries center upon her and her daughter Persephone. The initiates into these mysteries were famous throughout Greece for their philosophic concepts and their high standards of morality, as such these mysteries thus spread to Rome and Britain. The Eleusinian mysteries were divided into two classes: the lesser and the greater. The lesser mysteries were celebrated annually in the spring most likely at the vernal equinox. They opened with the candidate standing upon the skins of sacrificed animals; he took an oath not to reveal the sacred and secret truths about to be revealed on pain of death. The ceremony was dedicated to Persephone and it centered on the abduction of the goddess by Pluto (Hades) the lord of the underworld. While Persephone was picking flowers in a meadow the earth opened and the dark lord emerged riding a chariot; he abducted her and despite her struggling and screaming; the goddess was taken to the underworld to become his queen. This ceremony esoterically taught the condition of the unpurified soul invested with an early body, and enveloped in a material nature. The crux of the Eleusinian lesser mysteries were this: man is no wiser in the afterlife than in life if he does rise above his ignorance during his time here, he does not grow or learn from his mistakes this will be carried into the afterlife only to continue to haunt and plague him. If one makes no endeavor to improve himself during their time on earth they will continue to sleep in Hades as they did in life. A parallel to these mysteries can be seen in Freemasonry where initiates are instructed to subdue their passions and improve themselves in Masonry. Just as the Eleusinian mysteries produced great philosophers, so have some of the world's greatest leaders and thinkers been members of the Masonic fraternity.

The greater mysteries of Eleusis were celebrated in the fall likely at the autumnal equinox once every five years. A candidate must have been initiated in the lesser to become a member of the greater, and then not always due to exceedingly high standards. These rites were sacred to Demeter-Ceres and lasted nine days symbolizing the nine spheres through which the human soul descends during the process of assuming terrestrial form. A parallel can be seen in Dante Alighieri's (1265-1321) *Divine Comedy*, where Inferno and Paradise contain nine levels of either punishment or spiritual divine enlightenment; the soul descends or ascends to its particular level based upon its deeds and growth, or lack thereof, in mortal life. These rites focused on Demeter-Ceres and her wanderings to locate her kidnapped daughter Persephone just as within the Egyptian Mysteries, Isis wanders to discover the body of Osiris. Demeter-Ceres locates her daughter in the underworld and appears before Hades-Pluto and pleads with him to allow Persephone to return home. Hades refuses to do so because Persephone has eaten of the sacred fruit, a pomegranate, the fruit of morality. However, Hades is persuaded by Demeter-Ceres to let Persephone live in the upper world for half the year if she returned to Hades for the other six months. Persephone, according to the Greeks, was a solar goddess or heroine; her six months in Hades signified the six months between the autumnal and vernal equinoxes when the sun was in the southern hemisphere (at death –hence she is in Hades, the underworld) and the six months in the upper world represented spring and summer, or the sun in the northern hemisphere. When Persephone left for the underworld the plants and flowers who loved her would die of grief, only to be born again when Persephone returned to life in the spring. The greater mysteries thus incorporated principles of spiritual rebirth and regeneration and revealed to the initiates "not only the simplest but also the most direct and complete method of liberating their higher natures from the bondage of material ignorance. Like Prometheus chained to the top of Mount Caucasus, man's higher nature is chained to his inadequate personality."[133] The occult knowledge imparted in the rituals of Eleusis[134] was kept in strict confidence. By a law of Solon the magistrates met every year at the close of the ceremonies to pass sentence upon any who had transgressed the rules which governed the sacred rites. The discovery of an attempt or disclosure of the esoteric rituals or secrets was punished by death; within Masonry candidates promise not to reveal any of the secrets of the craft under "pain of death." Two Acarnanian youths accidentally entered the temple of Demeter during a performance of the mysteries.

133 Hall, Manly Palmer, *The Secret Teachings of All Ages*, page 71.

134 The Mysteries of Orpheus were likewise similar to the Eleusinian Mysteries.

Asking stupid questions they were immediately detected, removed, and put to death. The rites flourished until Emperor Theodosius I suppressed the mysteries and destroyed all who did not accept the Christian faith; in 396 CE a band of fanatical Christian monks destroyed the temple at Eleusis. Of these mysteries the philosopher, statesmen, and lawyer Marcus Cicero (106-43 BCE), who was initiated into them, said that the Eleusinian Mysteries taught men not only how to live, but also how to die. Cicero was instrumental in making Greek philosophy and education fashionable in Rome. As part of the Greco-Roman mysteries was the worship of the Cabiri: a set of demi-gods responsible for shipbuilding and navigation whose centers of worship were at Samothrace and Thebes.

It was out of the aforementioned mysteries, namely Mithraism, that became the Roman cult of *Sol Invictus*, Unconquered Sun. *Sol Invictus* became the premier sun god within the empire shortly before the adoption of Christianity as the state-wide Roman religion. Christianity was in fact the *Sol Invictus* cult only with a name change. Sol Invictus was strengthened substantially by Emperor Aurelian (214/215-275 CE) who wanted the principle of one god, one empire philosophy to rule his empire, although he did not outlaw other religions or mystery schools. A new temple dedicated to Sol Invictus was built in Rome in 271 CE, by Aurelian who instituted games every four years in the name of *Sol Invictus* beginning in 274 CE. *Sol Invictus* almost disappeared from the empire after Emperor Constantine I (272-337 CE) and the First Council of Nicaea (325 CE) formed the Nicean Creed: the correct beliefs of Christianity and its faith; thus *Sol Invictus* and Mithraism were re-baptized as Christianity. The cult of *Sol Invictus* became state sanctioned Christianity all but overnight eliminating the former while promulgating the latter. The actual god, *Sol Invictus*, was a composite of Apollo, Dionysus-Bacchus, Helios, and Mithras, all sun deities, each of them were *Sol Invictus*! These sun deities were transformed into one solar messiah: Jesus Christ, God's *Sol*-Sun-Son, whom early Christian writer and Bishop of Carthage Cyprian (died 14 September 258) correctly referred to as *Sol Verus*, the *true sun*. Christianity would incorporate numerous components and symbolisms of the pagan mysteries to form a New Age astrological, pagan religion: the worship in the sun in the house of Pisces, from approximately 0/30 CE-2012/2100 CE, based upon the Precession of the Equinoxes. Jesus Christ is a sun in the Piscean Age; he is the Roman Piscean sun god. Emperor Constantine I firmly believed that Jesus Christ and *Sol Invictus* were one and the same or the same aspect of a Superior Divinity. Neo-Platonic thought contended that the religion of the sun represented a bridge between paganism and Christianity. Jesus was often called by the name *Sol Justitiae* and was represented by statutes that were similar to those of Apollo, the principal Greco-Roman sun god. Clement of Alexandria describes Jesus, like Apollo, driving a chariot across the sky; a mosaic of Jesus in a chariot symbolizing Apollo the Sun can be found in the Vatican grottos on the floor near the tomb of Pope Julius I. A large part of the Roman population believed that Christianity was the worship of the sun; the Bishop of Troy openly professed his worship of the sun even during his episcopate.[135] Constantine further designated Sunday in honor of *Sol Invictus* as the day of rest, the day of the sun (*die Solis*), in 321 CE, four years prior to the Council of Nicaea. Sunday would become the holy day within Christianity because Jesus Christ is a metaphoric stand-in for sun hence his day of worship. As such Christian legend holds that the sun (Christ) is obliged to shine for a short time every Sunday so that the Blessed Virgin (cf. Isis) may dry her veil of the tears that she weeps for the dead sun god.[136] Of the adoration of the sun and its links to Christianity, Pope Leo the I (the Great) remarked in 460 CE, "This religion of the Sun is so highly respected that some Christian, before entering the Basilica of St. Peter the Apostle, dedicated to the one true living God, after climbing the steps that lead to the upper entrance hall, turn toward the Sun and bow their heads in honor of the bright star."[137] St. Peter's Basilica (prior to its sixteenth century reconstruction) was situated exactly due east and west so that on the morning of the vernal equinox the doors of the porch of the quadriporticus and the eastern doors of church itself were thrown open at sunrise; as the sun rose its rays penetrated straight through the naïve illuminating the High Altar.[138] Appropriately, Christian basilicas like

135 Grant, Michael, *The Emperor Constantine: The Man and His Time*, page 135.

136 Olcott, William Tyler, *Sun Lore of All Ages,* page264.

137 Pope (and Saint) Leo I (the Great), seventh sermon held on December 25, 460 CE, XXVII - 4. See also Olcott, William Tyler, *Sun Lore of All Ages,* page230.

138 Olcott. William Tyler, *Sun Lore of All Ages,* page 280 citing Keary, C.F., *The Dawn of History.*

St. Clements, St. Stephen Rotundus, and St. Prisca's in Rome sprang up over grottos and caves dedicated to the worship of *Sol Invictus*.[139] Despite the efforts of Neo-Platonic Emperor Julian (331/332-363) the Apostate[140] (a/k/a the Philosopher) to revive *Sol Invictus*–he was a fervent supporter of the Pagan Mysteries–they were gone from history by the fourth-fifth century. However, their language, symbolism, and true meanings and explanations were kept hidden by secret, esoteric groups and mystical societies down through the present age. The Gnostics (*gnosis* means wisdom), who interpret the Christian Mysteries according to pagan symbolism; the Cathers, the Knights Templar, the Jesuits, the Rosicrucians, the Illuminati, and, of course, Freemasonry all preserve these doctrines.

* * * * *

It is clear that the early constructors of the New Testament were familiar with *I Enoch*, its discussion and dialog of the importance of the sun and celestial heavenly secrets as disclosed to Enoch to be distilled and midwifed into society. Enoch was shown the Tree of Life, symbolically the Kabbalah –its ten Sephirot–the Sephirot is the *apple* that Eve symbolically bit to gain knowledge. The Kabbalistic tree is an emanation of the Tetragrammaton, the sacred name of Deity as delivered to Moses on Mount Sinai. Enoch was the seventh son of Adam, the father of Methuselah and the great grandfather of Noah. It was often thought that the New Testament influenced the writing of *I Enoch*; however after the discovery of the Dead Sea Scrolls at Qumran (between 1946-1956) it became clear that *I Enoch* influenced the New Testament and was inexistence long before the creation of Christianity. There are over one hundred comments in the New Testament which find precedence in *I Enoch*. Second-third century church fathers like Clement ofAlexandria, Origen, Irenaeus, and Justin Martyr all accepted *I Enoch* as authentic while Tertullian (ca. 160-ca. 225) called it Holy Scripture. Evidence of the New Testament's use of *I Enoch* can be found at Luke 9:35 within the King James

139 Barbiero, Flavio, *The Secret Society of Moses: The Mosaic Bloodline and a Conspiracy Spanning Three Millennia*, page 161, *citing* Ludovico, Gatto, *Storia di Roman nel Medioevo* [The History of Medieval Rome] (Rome: Newton and Compton, 1999), 23, 32-33.

140 Julian was the grandson of Constantine I and was the last of the Constantinian dynasty; he was raised a Christian but rejected it in favor of paganism hence the he was nicknamed "the Apostate" by the Christian church.

Version describing the transfiguration of Jesus Christ: "And there came a voice out of the cloud, saying, 'This is my beloved Son. Hear him.'" The translator wished to make this verse agree with similar verses in Matthew and Mark. However, Luke's verse in the original Greek reads, "This is my Son, the Elect One (from the Greek, *ho eklelegmenos* (ἐκλελεγμένος), lit., the elect one). Hear him." The Elect One is an important term found fourteen times in the *Book of Enoch*.[141] This cannot be a coincidence; *I Enoch* was indeed known to the creators of the New Testament, with it abundant descriptions of the Elect One who should "sit upon the throne of glory" and the Elect One who should "dwell in the midst of them;" then the great scriptural authenticity is justly accorded to the *Book of Enoch* when the "voice out of the cloud" tells the apostles, "This is my son, the Elect One, …." the one promised in *I Enoch*.[142] Christianity and the New Testament, the story of Christ, would incorporate elements of sun adoration and solar reverence clearly influenced by the *Book of Enoch*. While *I Enoch* clearly bore influence of the gospels that became the New Testament (see next chapter), Christianity itself was not fully canonized for approximately nine hundred to one thousand years after the alleged birth of Christ. Many of the early documents used to create Christianity contain hearsay within hearsay within hearsay and were written long after (100-200 years) the events of the New Testament bringing in to question their authenticity. The learned church father Justin Martyr does not appear to have known of the gospel texts; the names of the four Evangelists Matthew, Mark, Luke, and John do not appear in any of his writings. The earliest canonical texts, the Epistles of Paul of Tarsus, makes no mention of Pilate and the Romans, the holy women, Caiaphas and the Sanhedrin, Herod and Judas, or any person in the gospel account of the Passion; no mention of Christ's supernatural birth nor any of his miracles. Christianity, one can easily argue, was a New Age religion for the Piscean Age (0-2012/2100 BCE) cultivated at the Council of Nicaea where *Sol Invictus* (Unconquered Sun) was transformed into the Christ Jesus, the Sun-Son of God. The New Testamentcontains numerous astrological symbolisms, elements of Doceticism (Christ as a spirit and not a physical person), and vestiges of the Pagan Mysteries. Jesus is the sun

141 Lumpkin, Joseph B., *The Books of Enoch: The Complete Volume Containing: 1 Enoch (the Ethiopic Book of Enoch) 2 Enoch (The Slavonic Secrets of Enoch) 3 Enoch (The Hebrew Book of Enoch)*, page 13.
142 Ibid.

in the house of Pisces, God's Sun for the Piscean Age. If one takes the five Greek words **Ἰησοῦς Χριστός, Θεοῦ Υἱός, Σωτήρ**, which mean Jesus Christ, Son of God, Savior, the initial letters form the Greek word ΙΧΘΥΣ, which means fish, an esoteric reference to Pisces. On this church father Tertullian wrote:

"But we, the Christians, are little fishes after the type of our great Fish (ΙΧΘΥΣ) Jesus Christ, born in the water."[143]

Many Christians observe Friday as the day upon which they shall eat fish and not meat. Christian church art often depicts Jesus Christ within the *Vesica Piscis*, the bladder or measure of the fish (see Plate V). Early Christians often drew fish in the sands or dirt in order to identify each other. Jesus named his apostles Fishers of Men symbolic of the Age of Pisces while the Aramaic word for fish, *nun*, denotes women who have committed themselves to Christian spiritual life. Dante Alighieri's *Divine Comedy* (1308-1321), was written during the height of Piscean Age; while traversing Inferno, Dante must continue his journey with Virgil because, "*Ché i Pesci guizzan su per l'orizzonta…*," or "For quivering are the Fishes on the horizon…" (*Inferno*, Canto XI, 113). Jesus Christ announces that he is the herald of the new astrological age of Pisces at Matthew XXIV: 7-8,

"For nation will make war upon nation, kingdom upon kingdom; there will be famines and earthquakes in many places. With all these things the birth-pangs of the New Age begins."

Jesus calls himself the sun: he makes numerous references to being a "cornerstone that was rejected," the solar symbolism of a cornerstone having been discussed in Chapter II. Jesus is the sun at Revelation 22:16, "I Jesus have sent mine angel to testify unto you these things in the churches. I am the root and the offspring of David, [and] the bright and morning star." Jesus the sun "….cometh with clouds; and every eye shall see him, and they [also] which pierced him: and all kindreds of the earth shall wail because of him. Even so, Amen." Jesus is the morning star, the sun, again not to be confused with Venus, who, "comes in clouds for all eyes to see," at

143 Freke, Timothy and Peter Gandy, *The Jesus Mysteries: Was the "Original Jesus" a Pagan God?*, page 76 citing Eisler, R, *Orpheus the Fisher*, Kessinger Publishing, 1920, page 71.

Revelation 1:7. "Then spake Jesus again unto them, saying, I am the light of the world: he that followeth me shall not walk in darkness, but shall have the light of life." according to John 8:12. There is only one light of the world –*the sun*–who comes in clouds: the sun's rising in the east symbolically defeats the Prince of Darkness or the nighttime sky. Jesus Christ, being a solar allegory or avatar, naturally speaks only in allegory; "All these things spake Jesus unto the multitude in parables; and without a parable spake he not unto them:" at Matthew 13:34. In other words Jesus, being a myth or solar symbol and not a literal personage, by his own admission, can only speak in metaphor or parable: whatever Christ speaks is admittedly a metaphor and not to be taken literally. As such if we take Christ's teachings and his story in the New Testament as literal history we are misinterpreting them according to Christ himself. Therefore one must conclude that the Bible, both Testaments, is an allegory and not literal history as stated by Christ himself. Many early church fathers equated this concept of God's Sun within the doctrine or philosophy of Neo-Platonism. Amongst its chief advocates was Origen, whose name means "son or child of Horus." Origen, who can also be considered a Neo-Pythagorean, was the student of Christian Platonist Clement of Alexander and responsible for coalescence of Christian writings that became the New Testament. Origen understood that Holy Scripture was symbolic allegory, not to be taken as literal history. Neo-Platonism was a philosophy founded by Platonic philosopher Plotinus (ca. 204/5-270 CE) and incorporated a belief in a supreme monotheistic deity, symbolized in Masonry as an all-seeing eye, while trying to the reconcile Christianity, and the Abrahamic Faiths, with Greco-Roman philosophies and paganism. Over time this took on a more extremist view: Christianity was rejected in favor of the Greco-Roman philosophies and pagan religions. This attitude dominated the thought of Neo-Platonists of the Renaissance; Neo-Platonic doctrine also believed that the soul was immortal. Neo-Platonism was mix of Platonism, Egyptian, and Asiatic and Mediterranean Mysteries originating in the Christian Schools in Alexandria, Egypt in the second-third centuries. Christianity in turn was born out of a mix or combination of Neo-Platonic, Hebrew-Egyptian, Zoroastrian, and Pythagorean mysticisms fused with the Mystery School tradition. Neo-Platonic philosophy tries to reconcile paganism and Christianity: that Jesus as the Sun of God was *Logos*, *the word of God, i.e. solar light or wisdom (represented and expounded by solar occult symbolisms)* and that Jesus *spread the word of God as Logos*, but was somewhat lesser, *not God or the Supreme Being himself.* In *Contra Celsus, VI, LXXIX*, Origen attempts this reconciliation between solar paganism and Christianity,

> "And therefore there was no need that there should everywhere exist many bodies, and many spirits like Jesus, in order that the whole world of men might be enlightened to of men might be enlightened by the Word of God. For the one Word was enough, having arisen as the "*Sun of righteousness*," to send forth from Judea, His coming rays into the soul of all who were willing to receive him."[144]

Neo-Platonic philosophy enters the works of Dominican friar, philosopher, theologian, and Saint Thomas Aquinas (ca. 1225-1274) who essentially tried to Catholicize Neo-Platonic thought. *Summa Theologica* (1265-1274) incorporates numerous elements of the works *Celestial Hierarchy*, *Ecclesiastical Hierarchy* and *Divine Names, Mystical Theology* by Dionysius the Areopagite, one of the grandfathers of Neo-Platonism. The philosophies and dogma of Hermes Trismegistus is found almost entire in the writings attributed to Dionysius the Areopagite.[145] During the Renaissance and Enlightenment Neo-Platonism took on more of an extremist-rejectionist view, equating that Christianity (and Judaism and Islam) was sun worship or veiled paganism of one kind or another. Italian philosopher, natural magician, and astrologer Marsilio Ficino (1433-1499) revived Neo-Platonism in the Renaissance; he also translated the *Corpus Hermeticum*, writings ascribed to the sage Thoth Hermes Trismegistus, as well as the works of other Neo-Platonists including Iamblichus (ca. 245-325) and Porphyry of Tyre (ca. 234 -305). Ficino, following guidelines laid out by Gemistus Pletho (ca. 1355 -1452/1454), tried to reconcile Christianity and pagan Platonism. Ficino generally ascribed the title *Pimander* (a/k/a *The Divine Pymander*) to the *Corpus Hermeticum* which also consisted of the text *Asclepius*. Ficino wrote on the parallels between Christianity and sun-worship in his *Book of the Sun*, or *De Sole* published in 1494. In the Preface of *De Sole* Ficino states,

144 Quoted in S, Acharya, *Suns of God: Krishna, Buddha, and Christ Unveiled,* pages 449-450.
145 Pike, Albert, *Morals and Dogma of the Ancient and Accepted Scottish Rite,* page 731.

> "I am daily pursuing a new interpretation of Plato.... Therefore when lately I came to that Platonic mystery where he most exquisitely compares the Sun to God Himself, it seemed right to explain so great a matter somewhat more fully, especially since our Dionysius the Areopagite, the first of the Platonists, whose interpretation I hold in my hands, freely embraces a similar comparison of the Sun to God. Therefore while working for many nights, illumined by this Sun as if it were my lamp, I have thought to cull this choice subject from my great work, and to entrust it to its own compendium, and to send this mystery of the Sun - like the gift of Phoebus - to you. To you also, both as the finest student of Phoebus, the leader of the Muses, and as patron of the Muses, this new complete interpretation of Plato is dedicated, so that meanwhile by this light as if some kind of Moon (just like the Sun to the Moon), you may augur of what nature this whole Platonic opus will be; and if ever you have loved my Plato, or rather yours as he has been for a long time now, henceforth kindled by this light may you love him more ardently, and with your whole mind embrace the beloved."

In Chapter III of *De Sole* entitled "The Sun, the Light-Giver, Lord and Moderator of Heavenly Things," Ficino writes:

> "The Sun, in that it is clearly lord of the sky, rules and moderates all truly celestial things (I shall omit for the present its enormous size which is thought to be 160 times the earth). Firstly, it infuses light into all the stars, whether they have a tiny light of their own (as some people suspect), or no light at all (as very many think). Next, through the twelve signs of the zodiac, it is called living, as Abraham and Haly say, and that sign which the Sun invigorates actually appears to be alive. Moreover, the Sun fills the two adjacent signs with so much potency, that this space on both sides is called by the Arabs the *ductoria* of the Sun - that is the solar field. When planets pass through them, avoiding being burnt up in the meantime, they acquire a marvellous power, especially if the superior planets, finding themselves in this position, rise before the Sun and the inferior ones after the Sun. The sign in which the Sun is exalted, that is Aries, in this way becomes the head of the signs, signifying the head in any living thing. Also, that sign in

> which the Sun is domiciled, that is Leo, is the heart of the signs, and so rules the heart in any living thing. For when the Sun enters Leo, it extinguishes in many regions the epidemic of the Python's poison. Moreover the yearly fortune of the whole world will always depend on the entry of the Sun into Aries, and hence from this the nature of any spring may properly be judged; just as the quality of summer is judged from the ingress of the Sun into Cancer, or that of autumn from its entrance into Libra, and from the coming into Capricorn the quality of winter is discovered; these things are gleaned from the figure of the heavens present at that time. Since time depends on motion, the Sun distinguishes the four seasons of the year through the four cardinal signs. Similarly when the Sun returns by the exact degree and minute to its place in the nativity of any person, his share of fortune is unfolded through the whole year. It happens in this way because the movement of the Sun as the first and chief of the planets is very simple (as Aristotle says), neither falling away from the middle of the Zodiac as the others do, nor retrograding."

Chapter VI of *De Sole* called "The Praises of the Ancients for the Sun, and How the Celestial Powers are all Found in the Sun, and Derive from the Sun," Ficino further explains:

> "For these reasons Orpheus called Apollo the vivifying eye of heaven, and what I am about to say is taken straight from the Hymns of Orpheus: "The Sun is the eternal eye seeing all things, the pre-eminent celestial light, moderating heavenly and worldly things, leading or drawing the harmonious course of the world, the Lord of the world, immortal Jupiter, the eye of the world circling round everywhere, possessing the original imprint in whose image all worldly forms are made. The Moon is pregnant with the stars, the Moon is queen of the stars." These things Orpheus says. In Egypt, on the temples of Minerva, this golden inscription could be read: "I am all those things which are, which will be and which have been. No one has ever turned back my veil. The fruit I have borne is the Sun." Whence it appears that this Sun born of Minerva - that is, of divine intelligence - is both flower and fruit.

The ancient theologians, with Proclus as witness once again, stated that Justice, the queen of all things, proceeds from the middle of the Sun's throne through everything, directing everything, as if the Sun itself could be the moderator of all things. Iamblichus states the opinion of the Egyptians in the following way: Whatever good we have we get from the Sun, that is, either from itself alone, or from another agency as well, in other words either directly from the Sun, or from the Sun through other things. Likewise the Sun is the lord of all elemental virtues. The Moon by virtue of the Sun is the lady of generation. Therefore Albumasar said through the Sun and Moon life is infused into all things. Moses thinks the Sun is lord of celestial things in the day and the Moon, like a nocturnal Sun, at night. They all place the Sun as lord in the midst of the world, although for different reasons. The Chaldaeans put the Sun in the middle of the planets, the Egyptians between two five-fold worlds: the five planets above, the Moon and the four elements below. Indeed they think it is placed by Providence closer to the earth than to the firmament, so that the gross material of the earth and the moisture of the Moon, air and water might be cherished by its fervent spirit and fire. Also, by another theory, the middle place is declared by that prosperity of the planets which requires their disposition to the Sun to be such that Saturn, Jupiter and Mars rise before it and Venus, Mercury and the Moon after it, thereby maintaining the King on the middle path. The others, in proceeding differently, turn out to be weaker. Moreover amongst them those planets are held to be more pre-eminent, which the lord Sun itself ordered to precede it. But let us return to the ancients. The old physicians called the Sun the heart of heaven. Heraclitus called it the fountain of celestial light. Most Platonists located the world soul in the Sun, which, filling the whole sphere of the Sun, poured out through that fiery-like globe just as it poured out spirit-like rays through the heart, and from there through everything, to which it distributed life, feeling and motion universally. For these reasons, perhaps, most astrologers think that just as God alone gave us an intellectual soul so he alone sends it to us under the influence of the Sun; that is, only in the fourth month after conception. But this is something that concerns them. On the other hand there is no doubt that Mercury, which signifies the movement of our mind, moves the least far from the Sun. Saturn, signifying

> the state of the separated mind, departs least from the ecliptic. Moreover Jupiter and Mars the former through Sagittarius and the latter through Aries - are concordant with the Apollonian Lion, and have obtained their respective gifts: Jupiter signifying religious justice, civil laws and prosperity, and Mars magnanimity, fortitude and victory. The Moon, Venus and Mercury are called the companions of the Sun; the Moon because of its frequent conjunction with the Sun, Venus and Mercury because they do not stray beyond the vicinity of the Sun, on account of their advancing in step with it. Hence they have received the rulership of universal generation. Accordingly the Moon, rather humid in conjunction or aspect with the Sun, having absorbed its vital heat, may thereby provide a warming and vital humour to those things to be generated. Moreover in this process of generation Mercury mixes these two parts with the rest in a certain harmonious proportion. Venus applies seemly forms to mixtures of this kind, and adds grace and joy. Thus the Sun has distributed the whole of the light collected in itself through various stars differing amongst themselves in kind, and thus sets in order virtues in every form, with light that can take any form. From which one may clearly conjecture that there are just as many virtues of the Sun as there are stars existing in the heavens."

In Chapter IX, "The Sun is the Image of God. Comparison of the Sun to God," Ficino equates Jesus' resurrection to the sun in Aries; when, after the vernal equinox, life returns to earth after the three months of winter,

> "Having very diligently considered these things, our divine Plato named the Sun the visible son of Goodness itself. He also thought that the Sun was the manifest symbol of God, placed by God himself in this worldly temple so that everyone everywhere could admire it above all else. Plato and Plotinus said that the ancients venerated this Sun as God. The ancient gentile theologians placed all their gods in the Sun, to which Iamblichus, Julian and Macrobius testify. Certainly whoever does not view the Sun in the world as the image and minister of God, has certainly never reflected upon the night, nor looked upon the rising Sun; nor has he thought how extraordinary this is, nor how suddenly those things which were thought to be dead return to life.

Nor has he recognized the gifts of the Sun through which it alone accomplishes that which the surrounding stars cannot. Therefore also consider, together with the Platonists and Dionysius, that Phoebus, the chief intelligence of the Muses, is the visible image of God. Also that Phoebe, that is, the Moon, is the image of Phoebus almost in the same way that he is of God. And as Hipparchus says, she is the mirror of the Sun in that light falling on her from the Sun deflects onto us. It is not appropriate to discuss it at present, but we must not overlook that Platonic comparison which I have described more fully elsewhere.

In the same manner as the Sun generates both eyes and colours, giving the eyes the power by which they may see, and colours the potency by which they are seen, and joining both of them together with a uniting light, so God is thought to be with respect to all meanings and intelligible things. God in fact created the intelligible species of things and intellects, giving them an appropriate natural power. Moreover the Sun daily pours out a universal light through which it excites to mutual action the virtues of both the intelligible and intellectual realms, and joins them together through action. Plato calls this light truth with respect to intelligible things, and knowledge with respect to the mind of man. He thinks moreover that the good that is God, surpasses all these things, just as the Sun is superior to light, eyes and colours. But when Plato says that the Sun prevails over the whole visible realm, doubtless he alludes to an incorporeal Sun above the corporeal one - that is, the divine intellect. Seeing that it really is possible to ascend to the archetypal pattern partly by the taking away of that which is worse and partly by the adding of what is better, take from the Sun - from whom Averroes took gross physical matter - all definite quantity. But leave it with the potency of light, so that there will remain the light itself, cleansed by miraculous power, defined neither by a definite quantity nor by any definite shape, filling with its presence a space immense with respect to the imagination. This pure light exceeds the intelligence just as in itself sunlight surpasses the acuity of the eyes. In this way, in proportion to the strength you receive from the Sun, you will almost seem to have found God, who placed his tabernacle in the Sun. And finally just as nothing is more alien to the divine light than utterly formless matter, so nothing is more different from the light of the Sun than the earth. Therefore since bodies in which the earthly condition prevails are most unsuited to light, they accept no light within. This is not because the light may be powerless to penetrate - for while this light cannot illuminate inside wool or a leaf, it may however penetrate a crystal in a moment, which cannot be easily penetrated by anything else. In this way the divine light also shines in the darkness of the soul but the darkness comprehends it not. Is this not also similar to God, who first sows knowledge of divine things in angelic and blessed minds, and then love? Indeed God kindles a love for us believers here which purifies and converts, before it bestows the intelligence of divine things. Thus the Sun completely fills with light clear and pure natures everywhere, as if they are now, for a moment, heavenly; while those opaque and material natures it first warms and kindles with its light, then refines, and soon illuminates. And sometimes it elevates to the heights through heat and light this matter now made light and accessible. Hence Apollo pierces the dense body of the Python with the stings of his rays, purges it, dissolves it and raises it up. Nor must we forget that in whatever manner we hope that Christ will finally come into his kingdom, resurrecting human bodies from the earth with the splendour of his own body, similarly after the yearly dead winter, we look forward to the Sun's reign in Aries, which will recall to life seeds of things on earth, as if suddenly reviving dead or half-alive animals to life and beauty. Hence Mercurius, as the arms bearer of the Sun, is said to excite those who sleep with his caduceus, and Plato describes an almost similar resurrection in his book on the Kingdom."

Ficino is clear that the sun is not God himself. In Chapter XIII, called "That the Sun is not to be worshipped as the Author of all Things," he concisely distinguishes the physical sun form the spiritual sun:

> "According to Plato, he called the Sun not God himself but the son of God. And I say not the first son of God, but a second, and moreover visible son. For the first son of God is not this visible Sun, but another far superior intellect, namely the first one which only the intellect can contemplate. Therefore Socrates, having been awakened by the celestial Sun, surmised a supercelestial Sun, and he contemplated attentively its majesty, and inspired, would admire the incomprehensible bounty

of the Father. James the Apostle called this Father the father of light; light, I say, more than celestial, in which there is no change or shadow. For he supposes that these supercelestial things are naturally mutable, that the many celestial things are doubtless shadowed in some fashion, and that sub-celestial things are shadowed daily. For which reason every very good thing naturally sown in the mind, every perfect gift beyond natural gifts, does not come down from this Sun and from the mundane stars, but from even higher, from the father of light."

To Ficino and other Renaissance Neo-Platonists such as Giovanni Pico della Mirandola the implication was obvious: Christianity was an adroitly disguised form of sun worship or adoration. Ficino's work came under the watchful eye of the Catholic Church; he had to write an apology for his solar works (*De Sole* and *De Lumine*) entreating Philippo Valori, the Florentine Ambassador to the Pope, to defend him against future accusations of heresy. These solar, theological concepts would be picked up by mathematician, Dominican friar, hermit, and astrologer Giordano Bruno (1548-1600), who argued that Copernican model or template could be applied to each star in the night sky. Bruno thought that each star was a sun with its own planets orbiting around it. Bruno also claimed that the theologies of Egypt such as the worship of Osiris and Isis–Osiris being resurrected, while Isis was the virgin mother of Horus–exerted considerable influence on the development of Christianity. As such Bruno sought a new, reformed Christianity as outlined in *Spaccio della bestia trionfante*. Bruno's hermeticism and philosophy rejected a Christian interpretation of the Hermetic writings in favor of a full blown "Egyptianity:" Egyptian natural religion and Neo-Platonism combined with moral law. On the other hand Ficino's Neo-Platonized magic does not come anywhere near the demonic sorcery of Heinrich Cornelius Agrippa's interpretation on the Hermetic text *Asclepius*. Agrippa knows of black magic, likely practiced by Gnostic magicians and possibly by the Knights Templar, but states in his *Three Books of Occult Philosophy (De Occulta Philosophia)* that mystical prayers and pious mortifications used in a positive way can attract divine angels.[146] During his time in England, Bruno lectured and debated at Oxford University; he was employed as a double agent under the aegis of spymaster

146 Yates, Frances A. *Giordano Bruno and the Hermetic Tradition*, page 133.

Sir Francis Willingham (ca. 1532-1590). Bruno also wrote on the concept of the Art of Memory, *Ars Notoria*: a group of mnemonic techniques that according to Bruno could help reveal ancient Egyptian knowledge enabling man to achieve unity with God. "By engraving in memory the celestial images, archetypal images in the heavens which are shadows near to the ideas in the divine *mens* on which all things below depend, Bruno hopes, ...to achieve this "Egyptian" experience, to become in true gnostic fashion the *Aion* (i.e. god-like), having divine powers within him.[147] By imprinting the figures of the zodiac on the fantasy, "you may gain possession of a figurative art which will assist, not only the memory, but all the powers of the soul in a wonderful way."[148] This would be important within operative Masonry because certain buildings were constructed as memory temples designed to impose memory impressions, ancient wisdom, upon the person's interaction with it. In other words, architecture could convey occult messages embedded within its very construction designed to reveal ancient mystical ideas and ideals derived from the Great Architect of the Universe. Bruno's magic memory system thus represents the memory of a Magus, one who knows the reality beyond the multiplicity of appearances through having conformed his imagination to the archetypical images, and also has powers through this insight. Bruno was burned at the stake in Rome by the Inquisition in 1600 for heresy; Bruno must have cynically smiled when considering that the Inquisition demanding his life ignored the fact that the Vicar of Christ had claimed descent from Osiris through the dubious researches of Annius of Viterbo (1432-1502); while the Apis Bull and other Egyptian deities decorated not only the Missal of Cardinal Pompeo Colonna (1479-1532) but the Borgia apartments in the Vatican as well.[149] Borgia's Vatican apartment also contained an astrological themed mural depicting Hermes Trismegistus with the Twelve Houses of the Zodiac by Pinturicchio (1454-1513). Twenty-three years after Bruno's death saw the publication of Dominican friar, mystic, astrologer, and alleged black magician Tommaso Campanella's Neo-Platonic *The City of Sun*: a utopia

147 Ibid, pages 198-199.
148 Ibid, page 199 citing Bruno, Giordano, *Op. lat.*, II(i), pages 78-79.
149 Curl, James Stevens, *The Art and Architecture of Freemasonry*, page 43.

Thoth Hermes Mercurius Trismegistus with the Twelve Houses of the Zodiac by Pinturicchio, Borgia Apartments, Vatican, Rome, Italy, 1492-1494. Illustration from *Giordano Bruno and the Hermetic Tradition* by Frances A. Yates.

whose inhabitants naturally hold Jesus (the sun) and the twelve Apostles (the zodiac) worthy and great. Campanella's *City* would serve as a template for Washington, D.C., the capital of the New World; the difference being the District of Columbia would contain Masonic astrological and solar symbolisms, not Christian per se.

Jesus Christ's earthly parents, Mary and Joseph, are the constellations Virgo the Virgin and Bootes. Within the Egyptian Mysteries Isis was Sirius, Osiris was Orion. In the Christian Mysterion Jesus, a solar avatar for the Age of Pisces, is birthed by Pisces' opposite house Virgo the Virgin, *Mary*.

During the Piscean Age the influence of Pisces' opposite house Virgo can be clearly seen upon the female and male priest-craft of Christianity who remain celibate virgins. Astrologically, the position of Orion near Sirius would likewise be transformed. Orion-Osiris, the solar father of Horus, would become Joseph the father of the Jesus; Joseph's constellation is the masculine Bootes. The constellation of Bootes, the ploughman of the autumnal harvest, sits in next to Virgo the Virgin, "Mary," just as Sirius-Isis is in close proximity to the constellation Orion as viewed from earth. Virgo the Virgin thus becomes the *Virgin Mary*; Mary as Virgo is the virgin Isis. Christian lore holds there will be three Saturdays a year when the Virgin Mary (Virgo) mourns for the dying sun (Christ); as such God's sun will be "shrouded" in a "burial cloth" of clouds and not shine at all.[150] The Virgin Mary as "Isis plagiarized" can be seen in Wolfgang Amadeus Mozart's Masonic opera *The Magic Flute* (1791) embodied in the Queen of the Night who represents both the Blessed Virgin Mary and the Catholic Church. Within the opera the Queen is referred to in terms of deceit, superstition, and trickery; this represents the Church's Virgin Mary as the usurper of Isis. Mary is the "Queen of the Night" because she has stolen Isis' attributes, the moon and the stars. Within her Egyptian temples, Isis was depicted carrying Horus in her arms, exhibited in her temple, with the inscription "I AM ALL THAT IS, THAT WAS, AND THATSHALLBE;ANDTHEFRUIT

Isis nursing the sun-god Horus. Christian iconography would copy this depicting Mary with the sun god Jesus.

150 Olcott, William Tyler, *Sun Lore of All Ages,* page264.

WHICH I BROUGH FORTH IS THE SUN."[151] King Herod, subservient to the Roman Emperor, is pursuing Mary and Joseph seeking the destruction of the solar messiah. Herod signifies the star Regulus in Leo, the Little King, that forever "follows" Virgo and Bootes; as such Herod symbolically pursues Mary and Joseph. Jesus Christ was born on December 25th after a seven month pregnancy by Mary. The seven month pregnancy is lifted from the Dionysian Mysteries, as Dionysus was removed from the womb of Semele after seven months. Even Christian apologist Justin Martyr had to give this one up conceding in his *Apology, III*:

> "In saying that the Word was born
> for us without sexual union
> as Jesus Christ our teacher,
> we introduce nothing beyond what
> is said of those called
> the Sons of Zeus."

Jesus Christ was born on December 25, the birthday of the sun, when the sun is "born again" annually. In These concepts are taken from both the Mithraic and Dionysian Mysteries. The goddess Hera tricked Semele, the mother of Dionysus, into convincing Zeus, Dionysus' divine father, to reveal his true divine appearance to Semele. Zeus reluctantly agreed; when Semele gazed upon Zeus she was killed instantly as a mortal cannot look upon a god in their true guise. Dionysus' fetus was removed from Semele's womb and transplanted into the thigh of Zeus from whence Dionysus was born seemingly without sexual union. Dionysus was thus "*twice born*" of both Semele and Zeus which is where the concept of God's sun-son being "*born again*" originates. December 25 is the birthday of the sun and is borrowed from Mithraism; Mithras himself being a solar god who's feast day was December 25th.

December 25th is the birthday of the sun because of the winter solstice which occurs on December 21st. The word "solstice" means "sun stands still" deriving from the Latin *sol* (sun) and *sistere* (to stand still); on the 21st of December the sun is at its lowest demarcation in the northern hemisphere. The sun ceases to move northwards for three days,

151 Pike, Albert, *Morals and Dogma of the Ancient and Accepted Scottish Rite*, page 455.

it "stands still" on sundials on December, 22, 23, and 24. On the 25th the sun moves one to two degrees northward hence it is *born* on the 25th of December after having been dead for three days. The birthday of the sun is celebrated on the 25, its resurrection is exalted at the vernal equinox –March 21st/22nd–when the "stone of winter" is rolled away and the sun emerges from its wintery tomb. During the winter solstice the constellation of Virgo the Virgin, as "Mary," rises heliacally with the sun, having the sun in her bosom, hence, within the Christian Mysteries, *the sun of god was born of a virgin* on December 25. Under the reign of Pope Leo I (Leo, Serm. xxi., De Nativ. Dom. p. 148) many Christian Church Fathers said "what rendered the festival (of Christmas) venerable was less the birth of Jesus Christ than the return, and, as they expressed it, the new birth of the sun."[152] The modern day custom of lighting the Christmas tree reflects this,

> "The lighting of the Christmas tree is but the light to guide the Sun-God back to life, and the festival cakes of corn and fruit, made in honor of the Sun in ancient times, and laid on the sacred altars of the Persians as an offering of gratitude to the Lord of Light and Life, find their prototype in the plum pudding that graces the board at our Christmas feasts of rejoicing. Christmas is, therefore, nothing but an old heathen celebration of the winter solstice, the feast of rejoicing that a turning point in the sun's course has been reached, and that the life-giving orb has attained the end of its journey of dwindling hours of daylight, and has started back on a course that brings with it each day an increase of warmth and light."[153]

The birth location of Jesus is Astrotheological: the word "Bethlehem" means "House of Bread" in Hebrew, and is an esoteric reference to Virgo whose sign represents the autumn harvest (August 23-September 23) as symbolized by the sheaf of wheat Virgo clutches as the star Spica in her left hand. Mary as Virgo is confirmed by the date of her feast day and assumption in mid-August. The sun god, having his solar powers increased by way of his annual journey, enters the house of Leo, where he absorbs the celestial Virgin in his fiery course; Virgo disappears in the midst of the luminous rays and the glory of her son around the middle of August. When the sun is in

152 Hall, Manly Palmer, *The Secret Teachings of All Ages*, page 139.
153 Olcott, William Tyler, *Sun Lore of All Ages*, pages 230-231.

a particular constellation, no part of that constellation will be seen except just before sunrise and after sunset, but the opposite house will be visible. Thus the Roman calendar of Columella marks the death and disappearance of Virgo at the period; the sun passes into Virgo on the thirteenth day before the kalends of September. The Greeks fix the assumption of Astraea, the goddess of innocence and purity, who became Virgo, in mid-August. Thus the Catholics affix the Feast of the Assumption in mid-August when the celestial Virgin Mary is united with her solar offspring Jesus.

The birth of Jesus was heralded by three Persian Magi bearing gifts who followed the *eastern star* to locate the birth of god's son-sun. This motif again comes from the Mithriac Mysteries. Just as gold, incense, and myrrh were consecrated to Mithras, so too was gold, frankincense, and myrrh brought by the Persian mystics to the birthplace of Jesus paralleling the birth of Mithras on December 25. The three kings (identified as three by the gifts they present at Matthew 2:11) also refer to the stellar "three kings" or *Drie Konings*, the stars Alnitak, Alnilam, and Mintaka that comprise Orion's Belt. On December 24, they align with the *Eastern Star*, Sirius as Isis the Virgin Mother, the brightest star in the nighttime sky to locate the spot of the sunrise (birth of the sun) on the horizon on December 25, hence Sirius' link to the sun. Sirius aligned with Orion, Isis with Osiris, within the Christian Mysterion would be transformed into the concept of *three kings following the Eastern Star to locate the birth of God's sun-son on December 25*. This alignment is slightly off present day (2012, the initial publication of this book) due to the Precession of the Equinoxes. The life of Jesus contains further astrological allegories and concepts lifted from the Pagan Mysteries. Jesus walks on water; Pisces is a water sign. Jesus transforms water into wine which is borrowed from the mysteries of Dionysus and Bacchus who were the gods of wine and able to perform the same miracle; wine is an important component of the Eucharist. Jesus triumphantly rides a donkey; this too is borrowed from the Dionysian Mysteries. As part on his solar journey Dionysus rode two donkeys in search of a cure from his madness which is a reference to the stars Asellus Borealis: the northern donkey, and Asellus Australis: the southern donkey; these two stars are part of the constellation Cancer. Within the Christian Mysterion they would be transformed into an ass and a colt, the foal of an ass at Matthew 21:5 that the sun (as Jesus, the King) triumphantly rides as God's sun-son is at its strongest (most northern demarcation) in the sign of Cancer, the house in which the summer solstice occurs on June 21/22. Jesus naturally feeds five thousand with two fishes and five loaves of bread in the gospel story. The two fishes are the constellation Pisces; the two celestial fish that that Jesus Christ symbolically embodies, the five loaves of bread refer to Pisces opposite house Virgo, her sheaf of wheat, because Virgo sits five houses away from Pisces. Afterwards "....they took up twelve baskets full of broken pieces.....;" the twelve baskets being the twelve houses of the Zodiac that symbolically divide or "break" the solar calendar into twelve months. In the gospel tale Christ washes feet, and has his feet washed by Mary Magdalene; John 13:10: "Jesus saith to him, He that is washed needeth not save to wash [his] feet, but is clean every whit: and ye are clean, but not all." The sign of Pisces governs the feet.

* * * * *

The most obvious use of the number twelve within the New Testament is the twelve apostles; they are the twelve houses of the Zodiac that assist the sun on its annual travels. The concept of twelve helpers comes from the Old Testament where the division of twelve can be seen in the division of the Israelites into twelve tribes: Jacob's twelve sons or helpers; likewise the Zodiac and its symbolisms was an important element of the Mithraic Mysteries. Regarding the twelve tribes and their specific patriarchs Albert Pike acutely states;

> "There is no more striking proof of the universal adoration paid the stars and constellations, than the arrangement of the Hebrew camp in the Desert, and the allegory in regard to the twelve Tribes of Israel, ascribed in the Hebrew legends to Jacob. The Hebrew camp was a quadrilateral, in sixteen divisions, of which the central four were occupied by images of the four elements. The four divisions at the four angles of the quadrilateral exhibited the four signs that the astrologers called *fixed*, and which they regard as the subject to the influence of the four great Royal Stars, Regulus in Leo, Aldebaran in Taurus, Antares

in Scorpio, and Fomalhaut in the mouth of Pisces, on which falls the water poured out by Aquarius; of which constellations the Scorpion was represented in the Hebrew blazonry by the Celestial Vulture or Eagle, that rises at the same time with it and is its paranatellon. The other signs were arranged on the four faces of the quadrilateral, and in the parallel and interior divisions."[154]

Pike further explains:

"There is an astonishing coincidence between the characteristics assigned by Jacob to his sons, and those signs of the Zodiac, or the planets that have their domicile in those signs.

Reuben is compared to running water, unstable and that cannot excel; and he answers to Aquarius, his ensign being a man. The water poured out by Aquarius flows toward the South Pole, and it is the first of the four Royal Signs, ascending from the Winter Solstice.

The Lion (Leo) is the device of *Judah*; and Jacob compares him to that animal, whose constellation in the Heavens is the domicile of the Sun; the Lion of the Tribe of Judah, by whose grip.....Khūrūm was lifted out of the grave.

Ephraim, on whose ensign appears the Celestial Bull, Jacob compares to the ox. *Dan*, bearing his device a Scorpion, he compares to the Cerastes or horned Serpent, synonymous in astrological language with the vulture or pouncing eagle; and which bird was often substituted on the flag of Dan, in place of the venomous scorpion, as the symbol of Typhon and his malign influences; wherefore the Eagle, as its paranatellon, that is, rising and setting at the same time with it, was naturally used in its stead. Hence the four famous figures in the sacred pictures of the Jews and Christians, and in Royal Arch Masonry, of the Lion, the Ox, the Man, and the Eagle, the four creatures of the Apocalypse, copied there from Ezekiel, in whose reveries and rhapsodies they are seen revolving around blazing Circles.

The Ram, domicile of Mars, chief of the Celestial Soldiery and of the twelve Signs, id the device of *Gad*, whom Jacob characterized as a

154 Pike, Albert, *Morals and Dogma of the Ancient and Accepted Scottish Rite*, page 460.

warrior, chief of his army.

Cancer, in which are the stars termed Aselli, or little asses, is the Device of the flag of *Issachar*, whom Jacob compared to an ass.

Capricorn, of old represented with the tail of a fish, and called by astronomers the Son of Neptune, is the device of *Zebulun,* of whom Jacob says that he dwells on the shore of the sea.

Sagittarius, chasing the Celestial Wolf, is the emblem of *Benjamin,* whom Jacob compares to a hunter: and in that constellation the Romans placed the domicile of Diana the huntress. Virgo, the domicile of Mercury, is borne on the flag of *Naphtali,* whose eloquence and agility Jacob magnifies, both of which are attributes of the Courier of the Gods. And of *Simeon* and *Levi* he speaks as united, as are the two fishes that make the Constellation Pisces, which is their armorial emblem.

Plato, in his Republic, followed the divisions of the Zodiac and the planets. So also did Lycurgus at Sparta, and Cecrops in the Athenian Commonwealth. Chun, the Chinese legislator, divided China into twelve Tcheou, and specially designated twelve mountains. The Etruscans divided themselves into twelve Cantons. Romulus appointed twelve Lictors. There were twelve tribes of Ishmael and twelve disciples of the Hebrew Reformed. The New Jerusalem of the Apocalypse has twelve gates."[155]

Although Pike does not designate Gemini and Libra; Freemason and co-founder of the Hermetic Order of the Golden Dawn S. L. MacGregor Mathers (1854-1918) attributes Libra to the Tribe of *Asher*, Gemini to the Tribe of *Manasseh.* The Four Gospels within Christianity are represented by the four fixed signs of the Zodiac: the symbol for Matthew is the man, Aquarius; the symbol for Mark is the Lion, Leo; the symbol for Luke is the ox, Taurus; and John is represented by the Eagle-Scorpio; the four signs create the great celestial cross the God's sun travels upon annually while also symbolizing the astrological foundations of Christianity. Likewise the breakdown of the Twelve Apostles, the twelve helpers of the sun, and their

155 Ibid, pages 461-462.

respective Zodiacs are as follows:

1. As Aries the Ram is the first house of the Zodiac, so is Peter the first leader of Christianity after Christ. He is fiery, impulsive, yet changeable –he is the *rock* upon which Christ founds his New Church *of the lamb*. Etymologically the name "Peter," comes from the Greek *petra* meaning rock.

2. Taurus the Bull is the dogmatic Simon Zelotes, he who is concerned with property and finance, who rebelled against the payment of taxes. Taurus is admonished by God's Sun: "Render unto Caesar the things that are Caesar's.... ." Economically, it is the sign of Taurus from where the term, "Bull Market," originates.

3. Gemini the Twins is James the Lesser; intelligent but incapable of independent thought. Slow to accept the teachings of the solar messiah, but became an eloquent preacher of the church in Jerusalem and an active evangelist. Astrologically, the city of London, England is aligned to Gemini; its Great Fire of 1666, was predicted by English astrologer William Lilly (1602 - 1681) in 1652. His hieroglyph shows twins, *qua* London, burning. The English monarchy rules from St. James Palace-Court of St. James as an esoteric homage to Gemini.

The Great Fire of London of 1666 showing Gemini-London burning. The print was published in 1652 in William Lilly's book, *Monarchy or No Monarchy in England*.

4. Cancer the Crab is Andrew the homebody who dwells with his brother Simon Peter (a/k/a Peter). His first thought when he discovered the Messiah was to run and

fetch his brother.

5. Leo the Lion is John; as Leo is ruled by the sun so then is John the most inspired and the most beloved of Christ's apostles.

6. Phillip is Virgo: always precise, calculating, enquiring yet practical; the trademarks of Virgo.

7. Libra is Matthew, the even minded tax collector who uses the scales to weigh and collect money.

8. Judas Iscariot is Scorpio the Scorpion the deadly backstabbing traitor who delivers his deadly sting or "kiss" shortly after the autumnal equinox sending the sun of God into death or winter. The "30 Pieces of Silver" that are paid to Judas in return for his betrayal, are an occult reference to the moon and the 30 day lunar cycle.

9. James the Greater is Sagittarius, the wise teacher who along with the other two fire signs, Peter and John, are the most anxious to spread the light of Christ's solar church.

10. Bartholomew-Nathaniel is dependable Capricorn in whom there is no deception.

11. Thaddeus-Jude is Aquarius, the social liberal who sought better living and working conditions and an overall, better, state of being. He interrogates Jesus at the Last Supper as to how Christ would manifest this.

12. Pisces the Fish are Thomas. The two fish represent both the positive and the negative: just as Thomas believes and is courageous one moment (positive), he doubts the next (negative). While believing Christ is the messiah, he is best known for disbelieving the Resurrection; as such he is a "doubting Thomas."

The astral iconography of the Twelve Apostles can best be seen in Leonardo's Da Vinci's painting *The Last Supper* (see Plate VI). During the meal, Christ performs the Eucharist which is borrowed from Judaism; the Salem (peace) priest king Melchizedek performed the first Eucharist of bread and wine at Genesis 14:18. Melchizedek, literally "righteousness is my king," was born of the virgin Sofonim as discussed within the

"Exaltation of Melchizedek," in *II Enoch* (Slavonic Enoch). It is said that the Zadokite priests of Jerusalem were descended from Melchizedek.

The Twelve Apostles are the Zodiac; however, the use of the Zodiac in the New Testament is not exclusive to the apostles. As seen Virgo is not only Philip but the Virgin Mother Mary, so are the three murders of the sun three houses of the Zodiac. They are Libra, Scorpio, and Sagittarius who symbolically kill the sun as it moves through these three signs from the autumnal equinox to the winter solstice when the sun is *dead* or at its lowest demarcation on December 21/22. These three murders of the sun appear to be unique to Christianity and would be incorporated within Freemasonry. The sun begins to enter death when, after the autumnal equinox, it enters the house of Libra (23 September-23 October) symbolized within the Christian Mysterion as Pontius Pilate, the Roman Prefect of Judea who judges the sun upon the scales of justice. The sun is *kissed* by Scorpio's deadly stinger (a scorpion sting resembles a swollen kiss) when it enters Scorpio (23 October-22 November) symbolized by the betrayal of Judas Iscariot. The sun, mortally wounded, is finally killed by the deadly arrow of Sagittarius (22 November-22 December) symbolized by the antagonizing *pointed* questions of Joseph Caiaphas the chief of the Sanhedrin. The idea of a sun god being interrogated comes from Greek tragedy *The Bacchae* where the sun god Dionysus was interrogated by King Pentheus regarding his divinity. Alternatively the Christ the Sun of God is mortally wounded by Sagittarius the Centaur, the Roman *centur*ion Longinus, who pierces Christ's side with a spear (*qua* arrow) at his crucifixion thereby killing him. On his way to his "solar" crucifixion Jesus passes through the fourteen Stations of the Cross which is borrowed from the Egyptian Osirian Mysteries as Osiris was dismembered into fourteen pieces. The fourteen pieces or stations symbolize the maximum amount of annual full moons (each solar year has 12-14 full moons) where the moon fully reflects solar light regardless of the sun god's death or impending demise. The sun is thus symbolically crucified upon the celestial cross formed by the Four Royal stars as discussed, confirmed by the placement of the letters "I.N.R.I" over the head of Jesus on the cross. Exoterically they are the first four letters of the Latin phrase, *Iesus Nazarenus, Rex Iudaeorum*, or "Jesus of Nazareth, King of the Jews." Within the *Mysterion* they are the first letters of the Hebrew words I am or water; Nour, fire; Ruach, spirit or vital air; and Iabeshah, earth; symbolizing the signs Scorpio (water), Leo (fire), Aquarius (air) and Taurus (earth) and their respective Royal Stars that the sun is crossified or crucified upon annually. On the symbolism of the cross, Freemason Albert Pike further explains,

> "The *Cross* has been a sacred symbol from the earliest Antiquity. It is found upon all the enduring monuments of the world, in Egypt, in Assyria, in Hindustan, in Persia, and on the Buddhist towers in Ireland. Buddha was said to have died upon it. The Druids cut an oak into its shape and held it sacred. And built their temples in that form. Pointing to the four quarters of the world, it was the symbol of universal nature. It was on a cruciform tree, that Krishna was said to have expired, pierced with arrows. It was revered in Mexico."[156]

The concept of a crucified sage is likewise borrowed from the death of Pythagoras, who was also put to death via crucifixion. Pythagoras was a great teacher and mathematician who founded his own Mystery School, a select brotherhood or club, where his esoteric teachings and mathematical philosophies were studied and pursued with great zeal. "In his lectures, Pythagoras taught the mathematics, as a medium whereby to prove the existence of God from observation and by means of reason; grammar, rhetoric, and logic, to cultivate and improve that reason, arithmetic, because he conceived that the ultimate benefit of man consisted in the science of numbers, and geometry, music, and astronomy, because he conceived that man is indebted to them for knowledge of what is really good and useful."[157] Interestingly, within Pythagorean numerology, the number 10 was the greatest of all numbers, it was divine, not only because of the tetractys, but because it comprehends all arithmetic and harmonic proportions. Ten is a perfect number relating to age, power, faith, and the power of memory. It was also called unwearied, because, like God, it was

156 Ibid, page 290.
157 Ibid, page 366.

tireless; the Pythagoreans divided the heavenly bodies into ten orders. The sun god thus dies on a cross which is represented by the Roman numeral "X," because the number ten is, itself, a cross.

The birth of the sun is celebrated on December 25th; its resurrection is celebrated at the vernal equinox (March 21/22) when the sun emerges from the three month tomb of winter. Easter is celebrated on the first Sunday –the day of the Sun being the holy day within Christianity–after the first full moon after the vernal equinox. Etymologically the word Easter comes from the word *Eastre* the Anglo-Saxon goddess of light or Spring. The sun begins its ascent into the heights of heaven when it will be at full strength the summer solstice. The mysteries of Dionysus and Bacchus contained springtime celebrations while the Eleusinian Mysteries celebrated the return of Persephone from Hades at the vernal equinox. It can be concluded that Christianity, like the other mysteries, and as will be seen with Freemasonry, contains two schools: one exoteric and one esoteric. Christianity also incorporates the concept of the *dying yet resurrected solar god or man* lifted from the Egyptian and the Greco-Roman mysteries. In truth the entire New Testament is am ingeniously concealed exposition of the secret process of human regeneration told as a solar allegory. The characters of the New Testament are the symbolic personifications of certain processes which take place in the human body when man begins the task of consciously liberating himself from the bondage of ignorance and death.[158] This concept would also be incorporated into Freemasonry whereby, like in the mystery tradition, the candidate undergoes a symbolic voluntary death and is reborn into the *light*. The mystery of this symbolic death is this: when the initiate is reborn he has undergone a symbolic change; a divine spark has been ignited in the candidate as a result of the rituals he has partaken of. What that divine inspiration is can only be known only to the individual person as the true divine light of inspiration differs from one person to the next. As Jesus is the symbolic herald of the new solar age of Pisces, he also foretells the next astrological age. At Luke 22:10, when questioned where the sun (Jesus) will go after the "end days" of Pisces, Jesus states "And he said unto them, Behold, when ye are entered into the city, there shall a

158 Hall, Manly P. *The Secrets Teachings of All Ages*, page 231.

man meet you, bearing a pitcher of water; follow him into the house where he entereth in." The man bearing the pitcher of water is Aquarius, the next house that the sun will entereth in after the age of Pisces thereby beginning the Age of Aquarius. 22:10 is not only a verse but an adroitly concealed date; 2210, when slightly rearranged, is the date 2012 when the sun will be one to two degrees in the sign of Aquarius. Thus the secret of Christian end days or eschatology is the end of Piscean Age and the start of Aquarius, the symbolic return or transference of the sun into *a new age*. This idea is a first cousin to millennialism; the return of Christ the Sun of God, Logos in a new age, a thousand year reign, which is turn a first cousin with von Fiore's Third Age of the Holy Spirit or the new age of Aquarius. In sum:

> "The Jewish and early Christians writers looked on the worship of the sun and the elements with comparative indulgence. Justin Martyr and Clemens of Alexandria admit that God had appointed the stars as legitimate objects of heathen worship, in order to preserve throughout the world some tolerable notions of natural religion. It seemed a middle point between Heathenism and Christianity; and to it certain emblems and ordinances of that faith seemed to relate. The advent of Christ was announced by a Star from the East; and His nativity was celebrated on the shortest day of the Julian Calendar, the day when, in the physical commemorations of Persia and Egypt, Mithras or Osiris was newly found. It was then that the acclamations of the Host Heaven, the unfailing attendants of the Sun, surrounded, as at the spring-dawn of creation, the cradle of His birth-place, and that, in the words of Ignatius, 'a star, with light inexpressible, shone forth in the Heavens, to destroy the power of magic and the bonds of wickedness; for God himself had appeared, in the form of man, for the renewal of eternal life.'"[159]

Was Jesus Christ a real person? The following historians, rhetoricians, philosophers, poets and critics who lived and wrote during or shortly after the time "Jesus Christ" allegedly existed make no mention whatsoever of him, nor the Christian movement in any of their voluminous works:

159 Pike, Albert, *Morals and Dogma of the Ancient and Accepted Scottish Rite*, page 511.

-Aulus Perseus (60 CE)
-Columella (1st century CE)
-Dio Chrysostom (ca. 40 - ca. 112 CE)
-Justus of Tiberius (ca. 80 CE)
-Livy (59 BCE - 17 CE)
-Lucanus (fl. 63 CE)
-Lucius Florus (1st - 2nd century CE)
-Petronius (d. 66 CE)
-Phaedrus (ca. 15 BCE - ca.50 CE)
-Philo Judaeus (20 BCE - 50 CE)
-Phlegon (1st century CE)
-Pliny the Elder (23? - 69 CE)
-Plutarch (ca. 46 - ca. 119 CE)
-Pomponius Mela (40 CE)
-Rufus Curtius (1st century CE)
-Quintilian (ca. 35 - ca. 100 CE)
-Quintus Curtius (1st century CE)
-Seneca (4 BCE? - 65 CE)
-Silius Italicus (ca. 25 - 101 CE)
-Statius Caelicius (1st century CE)
-Theon of Smyrna (ca. 70- ca. 135 CE)
-Valerius Flaccus (1st century CE)
-Valerius Maximus (fl. ca. 20 CE)

In turn, second century philosophers, historians and scientists such Appianus, Favorinus, Arrian, Aulus Gellius, Justinus, Hermogenes, Ptolemy, and Pausanias make no mention of Christ Jesus or of the Christians in general.[160] The Jewish Pharisee and historian Josephus (ca. 37-100 CE) a non-eyewitness to the events of the New Testament was nevertheless the author of the *Antiquities of the Jews*, which seemed to document a historical Jesus. Origen, the chief compiler of the documents that would become the New Testament, in his *Commentary on the Gospel According to Matthew*, (X, XVII) states:

> "And to so great a reputation among the people for righteousness did this James rise, that Flavius Josephus, who wrote the "Antiquities of the Jews" in twenty books, when wishing to exhibit the cause why people suffered so great misfortunes that even the temple was razed to the ground, said, that these things happened to them in accordance with the wrath of God in consequence of the things which they had dared to against the James the brother of Jesus who is called Christ. And the wonderful thing is, that, though he *did not accept Jesus as Christ*, he yet gave testimony that the righteousness of James was so great; and he says that the people thought that they had suffered these things because of James…."[161]

To Origen it was clear: Josephus, while mentioning more than a dozen

160 S,Acharya, *Suns of God: Krishna, Buddha, and Christ Unveiled*, page 378.
161 Quoted in Lundy, John P., *Monumental Christianity: The Art and Symbolism of the Primitive Church*, page 260.

Jesus' in his tome, did not consider any of them to be *the Christ*. So was there a "real Jesus?" There are two likely candidates: 1. Yehoshua Ben-Gamla, a Jewish High Priest (ca. 64 CE) in the Holy Land instrumental in the instruction of the young; he sought educational reform by providing schools in every town for children over five years of age.[162] Ben-Gamla peaceable tried to prevent that fanatical Idumeans from entering Jerusalem during the Zealot Temple Siege (ca. 68 CE). After they had taken control of the city they exacted a brutal torture upon Ben-Gamla ultimately executing him as a traitor. 2. The Neo-Pythagorean philosopher Apollonius of Tyana (ca. 15? -ca. 100? CE) who was often compared to Jesus Christ by Christians in the fourth century. Apollonius was a wise traveler who allegedly performed miracles similar to Jesus. Whether Ben-Gamla or Apollonius of Tyana were of "divine origin" or the basis for the story of Jesus Christ is left to history and to the speculation of the reader. The truth is that the early Christians, the Gnostics,[163] understood the canonical gospels were an allegorical metaphor; a secret passed down through the years by various secret orders and groups to the present day conveyed by the language of symbols, not the written word. One can argue that the Protestant Reformation (1517-1648) of Martin Luther (1483-1546) was an attempt to cleanse Christianity, especially Roman Catholicism, of paganism which, in turn, led to the Catholic *Contrareformatio*, the Counter-Reformation.

While it has been argued that elements of solar adoration are contained in both the religions of Buddhism and Hinduism, it is not the subject matter of *The Royal Arch of Enoch: The Impact of Masonic Symbolism, Ritual, and Philosophy*. Krishna and Buddha, correctly suggested by other researchers, are both solar avatars like Jesus, Apollo, Osiris, Horus, Mithras, etc. It has also been argued that solar elements of both these religions may have influenced the construct of Christianity, the discussion of which is not salient to this book and would increase its length substantially. However, it would be *unfair* not to briefly analyze the mystical aspects of the last of the Abrahamic Faiths, Islam. Mohammed (ca. 570?-632), the Prophet of

162 "But Jesus said, Suffer little children, and forbid them not, to come unto me: for of such is the kingdom of heaven." - Matthew 19:14.

163 Irenaeus tells us the Simonians, one of the earliest sects of the Gnostics, had a Priesthood of the Mysteries. Tertullian states that the Valentinians, the most celebrated of all the Gnostic schools, perverted the Mysteries of Eleusis. See Pike, Albert, *Morals and Dogma of the Ancient and Accepted Scottish Rite*, page 542.

Islam, the desired of all nations, was born in Mecca and died in Medina in the eleventh year after the *Hegira*, the migration of Mohammed and his followers into the city of Medina. In his youth he traveled with his Uncle Abu Taleb and contacted Nestorian Christians who likely instructed the young Mohammed in the mysteries of Christianity which they divided twofold: the divine yet human nature of Christ. In the ninth month of Ramadan, at age forty, was when he received his first revelation from God, *Allah*. In the year 610 while meditating in a cave in Mecca Mohammed was transported to Jerusalem and began his ascent into heaven to receive the Qur'an from the arch-angel Gabriel. His ascent into Heaven in Jerusalem occurred on the Temple Mount; the present day location of the Muslim Dome of the Rock. The Qur'an is the Holy Book of Islam and contains the teachings the Mohammed received from Allah though Gabriel. The Qur'an was dictated to Mohammed over twenty-three years, ending in 632 with the death of Mohammed. The Kaaba is the Holy Place of Islam located in the city of Mecca; its followers must face toward Mecca five times a day at the appointed hours of prayer. To the discerning few it is evident that Mohammed had knowledge of that secret, esoteric doctrine of the Mystery tradition. How he encountered it was either through direct contact with, perhaps, an unknown Mystery School in Arabia, or through Nestorian Christian monks schooled in esoterica. In his cavern on Mount Hira, Mohammed prayed not for new truths, but for old truths to be restated in their original purity and simplicity in order that men might understand again the primitive religion: God's clear revelation to the first patriarchs.[164] The arcana of Islam may yet to be found in the Pagan Mysteries performed at the Kaaba centuries before the birth of the prophet. It is generally admitted that elements of Islam, like Christianity, are the survival of the Pagan Mysteries. For example the feminine principle is repeatedly emphasized in Islamic Symbolism. Friday, the day sacred to Venus,[165] is the Moslem's holy day, green is the color of the prophet, and being symbolic of verdure, is inevitably associated with the World Mother (Isis). Both the Islamic crescent and scimitar may be interpreted to signify with the shape of the moon (*qua* Isis) or Venus. Numerous flags in the Arab world incorporate the color green. Upon the

164 Hall, Manly Palmer, *Lectures on Ancient Philosophy,* page 440.

165 Friday is named after the Scandinavian equivalent to Venus, *Fria* hence the word "Friday." See Brown, Robert H., *Stellar Theology and Masonic Astronomy,* page95.

famous stone of the Caaba, which is kissed by the faithful, can be seen the figure of Venus (or Isis-Ishtar) engraved on it with a crescent. Prior to Islam the Kaaba was an idolatrous temple where Arabians worshipped Al-Uzza, Venus, who the Greeks call Aphrodite. Likewise Mary (as Isis) is the only female mentioned in the Qur'an. As discussed the Muslim Shrine the Dome of the Rock has a dome denoting solar rulership; the base is built on an octagonal ground plan borrowed by the Muslims from Roman precedent. The design is derived from two staggered squares in a central circle forming an octagon denoting Pythagorean and Platonic influence and origin tracing back to the use of sacred geometry in the construction of Greek Temples and the Egyptian Pyramids.[166] The Dome of the Rock incorporates,

> "...a scheme whereby the size of the part is related to every other part in some definite proportion ...a building instead of being a collection of odd notes becomes a harmonious chord in stone, a sort of living crystal... Some of the ratios involved...are fundamentals in time and space, they go right down to the very basis of our nature and of the physical universe in which we live and move."[167]

As there is the Mysterion within Christianity, Kabbalah within Judaism, so too is there Sufism within Islam. Sufism is a mystery tradition that entered Europe by way of either the Knights Templar, or the works of Omar Khayyám, that would influence Masonry's legendary history and ritual.

* * * * *

The institution of Freemasonry tries to preserve these mystery traditions, namely concepts of geometry, its tools as instruments symbolizing morality, originating in Egypt. On this subject Professor James Stevens Curl states,

> "Herodotus identified Hephaestus with Ptah, the Egyptian God of Fire and the Architect of the Universe, and the demi-gods, the Cabiri, as his (Hephaestus-Ptah's) sons who were born in Egypt.

166 Hancox, Joy, *The Byrom Collection and the Globe Theatre Mystery*, pages 156-157.
167 Ibid page 157, quoted in Landay, J.M., *The Dome of the Rock*, New York, 1972, page 71.

Late theology of Antiquity established links between the Great Goddess Isis and Memphis, where the temples of the Cabiri[168] and of Ptah could be found. Isis, as sister consort of Osiris, was also Mother of the God, of the Apis-Bull, and consort of Ptah. Certainly it seems that Isis was therefore linked to Imhotep, known as a son of Ptah, chief Architect to King Zoser, and builder of the pyramid complex at Sakkara. In due course Imhotep, who was a real figure and a real Architect, became the Divine son in the Triad of Memphis, and the subject of worship. Imhotep and Isis had a temple at Epidaurus dedicated to them, which is not surprising, as both were dedicated to medicine and to the occult. Eventually Imhotep achieved precedence over Ptah, and so the Great Architect was none other than Imhotep, Architect and sage, and builder of the Sakkara stepped pyramid: the Master Mason, as Architect, had himself become a God. *This factor seems to have escaped many Masonic commentators, but it goes a long way to explain the importance of Masonic and Egyptian attributes as mystical objects*. The initiates follow the ways of the Cabiri of old, and indeed Isis herself, who searched for Osiris.

...Now it is important to realize that the veneration of Isis, Osiris, Serapis, Ptah, Imhotep, Horus, Harpocrates, and so on was not confined to Egypt, but became widespread in the Greco-Roman world. Isiac legends (or theology) point to an interesting parallel with Freemasonry: the murder of Osiris at the hands of Seth[169] was the great forerunner, but in the rites associated with the Cabiri one of the brothers was killed by other brothers, suggesting the death of Hiram. Apuleius tells us of degrees of trials, of oaths, of secrecy, of passwords, of hidden truths, of passages from darkness to light, and of victory over death in the Isiac mysteries. ...In due course Apuleius translated his initiate to the great Isaeum in the Campus Martius in Rome (one of the greatest of all temples in Rome), where he was admitted to a new degree of Isis and Osiris, who were joined in their mother's womb as brother and sister, as husband and wife, in attributes, and in ritual. Osiris the Resurrected, the Invincible, who was also Ptah/Serapis/

168 Inventors of shipbuilding and navigation who founded the mysteries. One of them was murdered by three others (*qua* Hiram Abif) which was incorporated into their ancient secret rites. Their mysteries were being practiced in the Greco-Roman world in the first century and seemed to be identified with the Egyptian mysteries.

169 Seth or Set, whom Diodorus Siculus associates with the evil Typhon.

Ammon/Horus/Apollo/Dionysus, possessed the All-Seeing Eye.

For the third degree the candidate was guided by Osiris himself, the highest among the greatest, and the greatest among the highest, in a mystical union where two became one and the candidate was alone with the Alone in a sanctuary where serenity, stillness, and silence ruled like gods. So the journey Apuleius indicates was part of the Isiac mystery, and that which the Neo-Platonist writer Plotinus (AD 205-270) connects with an ecstatic elevation of the soul to the divine, could not be revealed, but involved a ritual purification by water, the ducking of the head seven times, a prayer to the Queen of Heaven, Isis, and the donning of different garments or vestments for each of the regions through which the candidate would pass. During the ritual journey the candidate would undergo the *mors voluntaria*, or voluntary death, yet hoped for the rescue and resurrection by Isis."[170]

In the third degree ritual, Hiram Abif represents both the Egyptian architect Imhotep and the dying yet resurrected sun god Osiris. As Imhotep built the Sakkara pyramid, so too was Abif constructing Solomon's Temple –a temple of "Sol," the sun, and "omon," the moon; as such the sun and moon are two of the lesser lights of Masonry. The sun and the moon were further described as two of the grand luminaries of Freemasonry within William Preston's lectures. Solomon's Temple clearly incorporated the adoration of the solar and lunar calendar as the word "temple" derives from the Latin *tempus*, time; the word temple is therefore synonymous with time or year. There are three gates to the temple: one in the east, west, and south representing the rising, setting, and the sun at meridian when it's "the beauty and glory of the day." Within Masonry, like Christianity, there are three murderers of the sun; they are Jebela, Jebelo, and Jebelum and they represent the houses of Libra, Scorpio and Sagittarius. After his death Abif's body is carried westward under the cover of darkness representing the setting, dying sun. Twelve Fellowcrafts go searching for the body paralleling Isis' search for the missing body of Osiris. The twelve Fellowcraft symbolize the zodiac who are looking for their lost sun god. They wish to see if the sun, their symbolic Redeemer, would rise from the

170 Curl, James Stevens, *The Art and Architecture of Freemasonry*, pages 35-36.

The Foundation of the Royal Order of the Free Masons in Palestine A.M. 4037, engraved by D. Lambert in 1789. From Albert Mackey's *Encyclopedia of Freemasonry*. It shows the murder of Hiram Abif by the three ruffians (murderers of the sun), the twelve Fellowcrafts are the twelve houses of the zodiac divided into four groups of three. Overhead the Dog Star Sirius blazes as Isis who possessed the secret name of Amun-Re/Ra that allowed her to perform magic and resurrect Osiris.

dead. Abif's body is found under a sprig of acacia the symbolism of which has been analyzed. Abif's body is resurrected upon the third try; just as the sun is dead for three days after the winter solstice; it is also dead for three months when the sun is resurrected from the tomb of winter at the vernal equinox. Abif is raised by the Lion's Paw of Leo (Leo is ruled by the sun), the candidate has a substitute word (not the True Name of God) whispered in his ear as an homage to the goddess Isis who used the true *word* to procure magic and raise Osiris. Thus the candidate is initiated into the mysteries of Freemasonry, symbolically raised by Isis, borrowed from the Egyptian mystery tradition. The candidate is truly "born again" as he is symbolically the sun (*qua* Hiram Abif-Osiris) raised from the dead; the light of Masonry is now fully illuminated within the newly raised brother. What the brother chooses to do with this new illumination is left to his own recognizance.

The worshipful master rules his lodge; he is seated in the east representing the rising sun. He is the symbolic arch druid of the lodge, its chief governing official. He assists the candidate's conversion from darkness to light; this transformation comes from Zoroastrianism; man has free will to do good, light, while constantly combating the forces of darkness: ignorance, intolerance, and fanaticism. This dualism is highly stressed in Masonic teachings, both within the Blue Lodge and the Higher Degrees. The candidate in Masonry begins in a state of darkness seeking the light of Masonry as a guide to a moral and just life. Masonry is deistic reflected in the Masonic initials for deity, G.A.O.T.U., standing for Great Architect of the Universe. Blue Lodge Masonry includes other elements of the pagan mysteries: within the second degree of Fellowcraft is made reference to the pass grip or handshake (not the real grip) of a Fellowcraft called Shibboleth symbolized by a sheaf of wheat hanging by a water-ford or river. It is an esoteric reference to the Eleusinian-Isiac mysteries and not a battle fought in a cornfield that saw the defeat of forty and two thousand Ephraimites as exoterically explained within the Blue Lodge.[171] As discussed the Eleusinian Mysteries were dedicated to the Greek goddess Demeter, her Roman equivalent Ceres, both mother goddesses of the harvest emblematic of Isis as the supreme mother goddess. Likewise the constellation Virgo the Virgin holds a sheaf of wheat symbolizing the autumnal harvest of Demeter Ceres. In time Demeter-Ceres was fused or synchronized with the goddess Cybele, a Greco-Roman earth goddess. The Syrian word for ear of corn (the battle was allegedly fought in a cornfield) is *sibola,* identical with the word *shibboleth*, which the Ephraimites pronounced *sibboleth* at Judges 12:6 thus identifying them as the enemy. The word shibboleth in Hebrew means both stalk of wheat-corn and torrent of water and is an esoteric reference to Nilotic flooding in Egypt that enriched the soil and brought forth the harvest.

171 The Ephraimites pronounced shibboleth as sibboleth thus preventing their escape across the Jordan River after their defeat at the hands of the Israelites. They could not pronounce the word correctly; they were detected which led to their slaughter. There is no history of this battle outside of the Bible and the works of Josephus; neither account makes any mention of the battle having taken place in a field of corn. Josephus does not even mention the use of the word shibboleth. (*Judges* XII, and *Antiquities of the Jews*, Book V, Chapter VI). See also Brown, Robert H., *Stellar Theology and Masonic Astronomy*, page 73.

The mystical second degree word thereby has a triple hidden meaning: 1) a waterway, the Nile, its flooding emblematic of the rising of Sirius as Isis, 2) the harvest symbolized by a sheaf of wheat, or corn, of Virgo-Demeter-Ceres, and 3) the earth goddess Cybele (*qua* Demeter-Ceres) is almost identical in sound with *sibola* in some dialects.[172] The concept of a secret handshake whether it be within the first, second, third, or higher degrees of Masonry is borrowed from the Mithraic Mysteries; the initiate was admitted into the Mysteries of Mithras by a handshake with *Pater* (*qua* Worshipful Master) just as Sol, the sun, and Mithras *shook hands* thus unifying themselves as one and the same. The Mithraic initiates were thus referred to as *syndexioi*, those *united by the handshake* later incorporated into the mysteries of Freemasonry as a candidate progressed through the degrees by way of a secret handshake. Although Freemasonry can be thought of as a solar brotherhood, *it is not sun worship*. Masonry distinguishes itself from Christianity in that the sun is the symbol for deity (along with the all-seeing eye), while in the latter it is seemingly worshiped as deity. Christianity, especially in its Roman Catholic form, is essentially a form of Masonry. Freemason Godfrey Higgins explains,

> "Every part of Christianity refers back to Abraham, and it is all Freemasonry. Jesus Christ at the table, at the head of the twelve, offering sacrifice of Bread and Wine, is Abraham and Melchizedek over again; such, in fact, it is acknowledged to be by the Romish Church; such is its esoteric religion….."[173]

Lastly, when a Freemason passes away he is immediately raised to the stellar, Celestial Lodge of the heavens representative of Masonry's astrological-mystery tradition.

At last we come to the esoteric solar symbolisms of the Royal Arch degree; briefly described as it is the subject of the remainder of this book. The Persian Emperor Cyrus the Great of the Achaemenid Dynasty thus dispatches the Jewish Governor Zerubbabel and the Hebrews to return to

172 Ibid, pages 72 -74.
173 Higgins, Godfrey, *Anacalypsis: An Attempt to Draw Aside the Veil of the Saitic Isis or an Inquiry into the Origin of Languages, Nations and Religions*, 791.

the Holy Land to construct the Second Temple. This is where the concept of the Whore of Babylon lusting for the Holy City at Revelation XVII: 4-18 originates. The traveler, in order to reach the construction site, must clear through the four veils of the Tabernacle symbolized by the four fixed signs of the zodiac: man, eagle, bull, and lion; Aquarius, Scorpio, Taurus, and Leo. In the lesser mysteries of Egypt the candidate similarly passed through four trials of Air (Aquarius), water (Scorpio), earth (Taurus) and fire (Leo) in order to achieve perfection. The traveler begins his solar journey by symbolically passing through the four fixed sign as borrowed from the Egyptian Mysteries. Similarly in Mozart's *The Magic Flute*, Tamino and Papageno are exposed to the four trials of the Temple. At the construction site the rubble is being cleared in order to build Zerubbabel's Temple, ignorance is symbolically swept away as new knowledge prepares to be restored. As construction begins the keystone of Hiram Abif is discovered in the *northeast* corner; the solar symbolism of which having already been explained. The keystone is a solar astrological symbol representative of the twelve houses of the zodiac.[174] Masonically, a keystone can be formed by any angle that is acute[175] but the proper proportion is an angle of thirty degrees which is one twelfth part of a circle.[176] Astrologically, the zodiac Greek for "circle of animals," is divided into twelve equal parts of thirty degrees each, or thirty days, including cusps of three days, to each part is attributed to one of the twelve houses of the zodiac (see Plate VII).[177] An astrological sign is one twelfth of the circle of the Zodiac, hence for the sun to progress one sign, or thirty degrees, is to be symbolically reborn.[178] Thus thirty degrees astrologically symbolize rebirth because the sun is given new life as it rays enters each new house of the Zodiac per the earth's elliptical orbit around it revealing that a keystone is an esoteric Masonic symbol of a new, spiritual "solar" birth, or en*light*enment. This is confirmed by the revelation that the Keystone of Hiram Abif contains a trap door; when sprung the legendary Vault of Enoch is discovered, the Tetragrammaton, thus allowing the Pillars of Enoch to be decoded revealing lost Antediluvian

174 Steinmetz, George, *The Royal Arch: Its Hidden Meaning*, 69.
175 An angle of less than ninty degrees and greater than zero degrees.
176 Steinmetz, George, *The Royal Arch: Its Hidden Meaning*, pages 67-68.
177 Ibid, 69.
178 Ibid, 54.

knowledge which is now rediscovered or reborn. The imagery of the sun's rays shining into the vault through the keystone equates solar energy and *light* to divine wisdom and Logos. Enoch's years on earth were three hundred and sixty-five (Genesis 5:23), symbolic of the solar calendar. Like the Prophet Elijah Enoch did not die, he was taken into the heavens by God where divine knowledge was revealed to him; this knowledge placed upon his two legendary pillars. Affixed to the Ark of the Covenant is the Tetragrammaton upon a cube of agate; agate is the birthstone of June in which the summer solstice occurs when the sun is exalted at its highest demarcation. The "Royal Arch" itself has astronomical allegory. The great Masonic northern Royal Arch is the arch the sun makes between the vernal and autumnal equinoxes as it passes through Aries, Taurus, Gemini, Cancer, Leo, Virgo, and Libra as depicted in a famed Masonic tracing board. This engraving features the sun and the moon, the blazing star Sirius, and the seven stars of the Pleiades. Beneath the Keystone (Cancer) is the coffin of Hiram Abif which is an esoteric reference to Cancer's opposite house Capricorn when the sun god is in death (lowest demarcation-winter

Masonic tracing board featuring the astronomical Royal Arch the sun creates between the two equinoxes. Cancer is the Keystone because the sun is strongest (cf. summer solstice) while in that house.

solstice). Also apparent are the emblems of the four fixed signs of the zodiac. Likewise the Lost Word is also a solar icon. Each of its three syllables contain solar symbolisms: "Jah" from the Hebrew Jehovah (or Yahweh) who imparts the word to Moses via a fiery burning bush; "Bul" or "Bel" from the Phoenician sun god Ba'al or Baal;[179] "On" from either Osiris or Heliopolis, the latter being the City of the Sun.[180] Over time the Ark of the Covenant and the Lost Word itself would be transformed, both symbolically and architecturally into a *rising sun*, especially in an American context, to be analyzed in the next chapter and throughout this book.

* * * * *

One must always keep in mind that Freemasonry was devised as an immense system for remembering certain moral insights, and for practically inculcating them into their adherents and initiates. Through four strata of ideas: Biblical, medieval, 17th Century (Rosicrucian, alchemical, occult) and Enlightenment, certain basic motifs were perceived, symbolized, encoded in the ceremonial language of the degrees in order that they might, first, be remembered, and at a later point acted upon, existentially, to re create the experience. One can begin to understand the resilience of the Craft if one realizes that it is a living archaeology of at least five centuries of man's perception of the essential unity between man and God in a harmonious universe. This insight is, in turn, related to an understanding of the philosophy of history, and the role of historical understanding in man's ordinary life. In short, men and women live their lives today with tacit and implicit understandings of how the world works. A sense of where one has come from, where one is, and where one is going is central to human maturity and development. In the West these three essential points of reference, past, present, and future have been at center and core of social and political philosophy of religiousness. In politics, a sense of the destiny of a nation, its roles as a unified people, has been crucial to the unfolding of purposeful social and economic life. In religion, for the

179 The identification of Baal as an omnipresent sun god seems to have been abandoned towards the end of the nineteenth century.

180 Genesis 41:45, "And Pharaoh called Joseph's name Zaphnathpaaneah; and he gave him to wife Asenath the daughter of Potipherah priest of On. And Joseph went out over [all] the land of Egypt." The Greeks attribute the "priest of On to priests of Heliopolis. See Steinmetz, George, *The Royal Arch: Its Hidden Meaning*, page 128. Other Masonic authors and thinkers equate "On" as a shorthand name for Osiris the resurrected sun god.

Christian especially, a sense that the Kingdom of God is coming (albeit not as understood from a exoteric perspective) has been pivotal for theological understanding and spiritual insight.[181]

Christianity, indeed, has ordered much of its whole existence around the concept of eschatology: the doctrine of last things or the end days as the end of the Age of Pisces. In the works of St. Paul, and subsequently in St. Augustine, Martin Luther, and others, the Kingdom of God was envisaged as coming after the present world or age. Thus, no one might easily claim to have "God on his side" in particular matter of politics or spirituality and the task of being a good Christian became essentially that of being a good citizen; to adjust and accommodate to the welfare of the whole, corporate body (cf. Romans XIII). By contrast many Christians have seen, somewhat incorrectly, the Kingdom of God as imminent, breaking through at any moment, and to them, established institutions and ideas; and certainly ideas of citizenship have become less crucial. Indeed, the starkest contrast can be found in the New Testament itself, by comparing attitudes toward the state in St. Paul's writings, and those in Revelation for example. They contain different views of history and of human and divine understanding. The truth is that one's life, personal experiences, existence, and state of being impacts their own view, even understanding, of history. Thereby to act on a certain view and to decisively make that view an actual creation of man or woman, in their political and institutional life, may be contrary to divine will, Christian or otherwise.[182]

With this in mind, an important point should be emphasized: Freemasonry came into existence and grew in development because certain men perceived history to be a certain way, and acted upon that perception, and feelings, so as to create the structures of degrees, rituals, constitutions, and landmarks which presently exist. Consequently, as a result, it is possible to act on certain points, elements, and insights available within the whole fabric of the Fraternity and to recreate their sensibility, feeling, and perception; and as a result to continue the process of development of Masonic history.[183] Like Christianity, the concept of eschatology has been

181 Stemper, William H. Jr., *Freemasonry and the Force*, pages 24 - 25.
182 Ibid, page 25.
183 Ibid.

incorporated into Masonry via the author Salem Town; his *A System of Speculative Masonry* (1818) incorporates elements of millennialism: 1000 year Golden Age where Christ will reign for 1000 years; correctly interpreted as the sun entering a new astrological age based upon the Precessions of the Equinoxes. Salem Town's Logos is thus the unfolding of the Royal Arch Word into manifest destiny of the United States. In other words, the United States as a de facto Masonic Lodge itself the embodiment of Logos (Christ –an exoteric Christian Nation) recovered in the Royal Arch ceremony. Town's work links the Royal Arch Word as Logos while incorporating elements of Christian mystic and esoteric Joachim von Fiore's Third Age of the Holy Spirit. Joachim von Fiore–his followers were called Joachimites –prophesied a new Third Age dominated by humanism, irenicism, and universal love, ruled (or moderated) by two orders of spiritual men. The result in America was a potent fusion of religious liberty, nationalism, faith –as it was the truly the new Republic of the *New Order of Ages*. These two orders played out within the Joachimite vista and can be interpreted as the Jesuits:[184] esoterically mystic, exoterically Catholic, who were secretly the moderators if not manipulators of European politics at least until their suppression in 1773; while within the United States the Freemasons would serve as a mediating clerisy as the new country was founded upon Masonic "Catholic" high degree principles and philosophies. The Jesuits and Masons should be thought of in terms of two interlinked solar clerisies in a Joachimite envelope of eschatological new ageism. This is evidenced in the works of the founder of the Society of Jesus, Ignatius of Loyola (1491-1556); his Spiritual Exercises (approved 1548) contain various elements of mysticism and esotericism. Von Fiore's prophesies conform perfectly to the Precession of the Equinoxes: his first Age of the Father, the Old Testament is the old age of Aries while his second Age of the Son is the age of Pisces as Christ is a metaphor for the Son-Sun. Thus one can argue, quite successfully, that von Fiore's Third Age of the Holy Spirit is syncretic of the new Aquarian solar age; its chief signs: humanism and egalitarianism. To von Fiore the New Age was to begin in 1260; however his eschatology and philosophies were carried forward well beyond that time frame and

184 Sometimes thought to be the Dominicans.

into the Renaissance by various religious and hermetic thinkers. It was von Fiore's new age theology that was adroitly adopted by the Jesuits during the Counter-Reformation that resulted in supreme papal monarchy within spiritual men moderate, advocate, or rule. In turn this Jesuit ploy seems to have survived inside the high degrees of Masonry as developed from French-Catholic sources namely within the Royal Arch degree as it is the one degree that links or forges Freemasonry to the concept of symbolic divine monarchy and enlightened, Pythagorean kingship. The Scottish Rite high degrees include the Royal Arch of Enoch (13th) and the Master of the Royal Secret (32nd) suggestive of monarchy and regality. Likewise the United States can be thought of as the country that will midwife the world into this Joachimite new age of the Precession of the Equinoxes, Aquarius. The last one hundred years in the United States have seen women being given the right to vote and the election of an African American President, all heralds of Aquarius. Thus the United States, according to Masonic millennialist Salem Town, was itself Logos, the Royal Arch Word, the first Masonic Republic of the *Novus Ordo Seclorum*. Logos was Christ, the Word of the fourth gospel of St. John, the kabbalistic *Shekinah* or Divine Presence. Thus within a Masonic millennial context the United States as a Masonic Republic would peacefully rule supreme as symbolic *Logos* into and through the next or new age. Interesting Joachim von Fiore appears in Dante Alighieri's *Divine Comedy* in Paradise with St. Thomas Aquinas which is seemingly an anomaly as their theologies and philosophies oppose each other. That notwithstanding the Jesuits too would have their symbolic place in the New World as the high degrees of Masonry were born out of an ideology, propagated by the Chevalier Ramsay, twining republican-democratic Masonic values within an envelope of papal monarchy; as such the premier Jesuit college Georgetown University would sit triumphantly and irenically within the United States Capital, Washington, D.C.

In conclusion, the saga of the Biblical patriarch Enoch is a central in the legacy of Masonic ritual. As seen, he is referenced in the Royal Arch ceremony of the same name also termed the Royal Arch of Solomon and is symbolically incorporated in an important engraving of George Washington as an ideal Masonic initiate and companion of the Society of the Cincinnati by J. J. Barralet in early 1800. Except for the Prophet Elijah, Enoch was deemed never to have died. The *Book of Enoch* (*I Enoch*) and the Slavonic *Book of Enoch* (*II Enoch*, discovered in 1886 by Professor Sokolov in archives of the Belgrade Public Library) were found and translated following the appearance of the Royal Arch (of Solomon-Enoch) ceremonial in the Rite of Perfection first known in America in Albany, New York in 1767 as part of the Rite of Perfection later denominated the Ancient and Accepted Scottish Rite. It is this anomaly which underscores the scholarly significance of Enoch in Western culture notably that Freemasonry as both a moral tradition and as a specific ceremonial of initiation predates the appearance of the complete texts of the pseudepigrapha.[185] For example, Webb's *Illustrations* of 1797 details that Enoch possessed celestial knowledge as imparted to him by angels in *I Enoch* and inscribed upon a single pillar in Webb's monitor. *I Enoch* was not translated into English until *1821*. Webb is no doubt getting this from Ramsay's Oration of 1737. The principal feature of the Masonic degree of Enoch is the preservation and restoration of all knowledge and wisdom as a cognate and derivative of the correct pronunciation of the ineffable Name of God, the Tetragrammaton. This pronunciation enables the candidate to affect, symbolically, the reconstruction of learning and as such became a symbol of the equivalency between secret knowledge and intellectual culture. This, in turn, provided Masonry with the conceptual tools instrumental to the generation of public rhetoric and material culture necessary for the implementation of new ideals of American citizenship, a new age, which were perceived to be remote from the entanglements of Monarchy, the old age.

185 *The Books of Enoch* attributed to Enoch, but not actually written by him.

CHAPTER IV

ENOCH AND THE LOST PROPHET

Enoch, his Books, and Masonic Rites

"Enoch walked with God; then he was no more,
because God took him away."
- Genesis 5:24

"And first the sun goes out and traverses his path
according to the commandment of the Lord of spirits, and
mighty is His name for ever and ever. And after that I saw the
invisible and the visible path of the moon, and
she accomplishes the course of her path in the place by day
and by night-the one holding a position opposite to the
other before the Lord of spirits. And they give thanks and praise
and rest not; but their thanksgiving is for ever and ever."
- *I Enoch*, 41:7

"Even before the sun and the signs were created, before the stars
of heaven were made, His name was named before the Lord
of spirits." - *I Enoch*, 48:3

The historical anomaly by which the Biblical Patriarch Enoch appears in Masonic higher grades prior to the *Book of Enoch's* discovery by explorer James Bruce in Ethiopia will now be analyzed. Before this Genesis 5: 18-24 and Jude (vv 14-15) were in essence the limit of non-Masonic knowledge about Enoch. Jewish legends about Enoch existed which emphasized his kingship over angels, a residency in a secret place, and he was thought to be a spiritual being from whom the Messiah might be birthed. He was associated with the concept of a messianic secret and was thought to have been an intercessor for the Fallen Angels, the Watchers, which invested him with a link to

John Milton's Baroque-styled war in heaven and to the principle of universal salvation . The idiom of universal salvation was in turn carried into orthodox theology (both Protestant and Roman Catholic) by masons like Frederic Dalcho (1770-1836), a founder of the American Scottish Rite in 1801 in Charleston, South Carolina; and by the Chevalier Andrew Michael Ramsay; the former an Anglican priest and the latter the originator of the higher (or further) degrees tradition in French Freemasonry. The *haute* degrees were born out of Ramsay's Oration which served as the basis of the Rite of Perfection, the core of the Scottish Rite foundation in America, containing the thirteenth degree of The Royal Arch of Enoch (or Solomon, Southern Jurisdiction) known as the Knight of the Ninth Arch (Northern Jurisdiction) and the seventh degree within the York or American Rite. The *Book of Enoch* dates from approximately 350 BCE, and consists of five distinct sections:

1. *I Enoch* 1-36: The Book of Watchers
2. *I Enoch* 37-71: The Book of Parables, also called the Similitudes of Enoch
3. *I Enoch* 72-82: The Book of the Heavenly Luminaries,
   also called the Astronomical Book
4. *I Enoch* 83-90: The Dream Visions, also called the Book of Dreams
5. *I Enoch* 91-108: The Epistle of Enoch

I Enoch distinguishes itself from other holy scripture in that it is written in the first person. The *Second Book of Enoch*, *II Enoch*, often called the "Slavonic Enoch" was discovered in 1886 in the archives of the Belgrade Public Library. It contains a section entitled *The Exaltation of Melchizedek* which outlines the priestly succession of Melchizedek as the inheritor of Enoch's secrets. Melchizedek thus fulfills the function of a prophet-priest. There is also *III Enoch*, compiled from fragmentary sources ca. 300-400 CE by Dr. Hugo Odeberg PhD, translated and published in 1928. This latter work documents Enoch becoming an avenging angel called Metatron also known as "the lesser YHWH."

I Enoch documents that Enoch was thought not only to wise, but the keeper of the secrets of judgment, i.e. eschatology, and of the natural order. "And after that I (Enoch) saw all the secrets of heavens, and how the kingdom is divided, and how the actions of men are weighed and balanced." (*I Enoch* 41:1). This quality linked directly to Enochian imagery of pillars (upon which were inscribed heavenly secrets he received from "walking with God") and columns within the European Baroque enthusiasm for levitational exaltation, encouraged by the Roman Catholic Church as part of the Counter-Reformation, in turn associated with the possession of the Tetragrammaton, the ineffable Name of God in Masonic lore and the specific emblems of the Scottish Rite's penultimate, 13th degree within the Lodge of Perfection: the Royal Arch of Enoch or Royal Arch of Solomon. He was also thought to have been exalted like Jesus Christ (the sun) himself, and was given by some sources as the registrar or scribe of the last days of judgment. Enoch was also associated with martyrdom in his resistance to the Antichrist in Revelation XI: 3-12.[186] Enoch sees the end of the world as described in the Book of Revelation; "And I, Enoch, alone saw the vision, the ends of all things: and no man shall see as I have seen."[187] This imagery associated him again with angels and with being lifted to heaven on a cloud, again relevant to the role of martyrdom as it was treated in the sixteenth-eighteenth century in Baroque opulent design. Andrew Michael Ramsay was influenced by the philosophies and theologies of the 2nd -3rd century Neo-Platonist church father Origen[188] who knew of *I Enoch*; the Ethiopic text later found by Scottish traveler James Bruce, considered lost outside of Ethiopia. Bruce returned to Europe with copies of the *Book of Enoch* in 1773 while exploring the Nile; it was not translated into English until 1821 *–54 years after the Royal of Arch of Solomon (Enoch) emerges in Albany, New York, from earlier French sources.*

In *I Enoch*, the patriarch becomes a paragon initiate who is granted a heavenly vision as he is transported to heaven to receive celestial esoteric knowledge that would make him *like god,* the hermetical ideal, after beholding the Tree of Life, an image linked to Kabbalah's Sephirotic Tree

186 Elijah and Enoch are the "two witnesses" granted the power of prophesy at Revelation XI:3 because they are the only two people in the Bible to ascend to heaven without physically dying.
187 *I Enoch* 19:3
188 Despite Sir Walter Raleigh's assertions, who stated in his *History of the World* of 1616 that both Origen and Tertullian had access to a copy of the Astronomy Book as contained within *I Enoch* in the first century. Raleigh references Origen Hom. in Num. 1 supporting this hypothesis though no such statement is found anywhere in extant versions of Origen.

of Life-Wisdom, an emanation of the Tetragrammaton, the name of Deity:

> "Then I said: 'How beautiful is the tree, and how attractive is its look!' Then Raphael the holy angel, who was with me, answered me and said: 'This is the Tree of wisdom, of which your father of old and your mother of old, who were your progenitors, have eaten, and they learned wisdom and their eyes were opened, and they knew that they were naked and they were driven out of the garden.'"
>
> - *I Enoch* 32:6

This historical anomaly can be first seen at cursory glance within the ritual degree of the French Rite of Perfection of 1754, its thirteenth degree, and remained as the thirteenth degree in Francken's Rite of Perfection developed at Albany, New York in 1767. The Royal Arch of Enoch (Solomon) is the thirteenth in the Scottish Rite (Southern Jurisdiction) and is the seventh degree in the York or American Rite of T.S. Webb and DeWitt Clinton. The Royal Arch Masonic ritual parallels *I Enoch*; the ceremony presumes that such knowledge was imparted by beholding the delta within which contained the same power through the Tetragrammaton which furtherd celestial-cosmological knowledge, imparted to Enoch and described in *I Enoch*, was inscribed on Enoch's pillars for revelation and devolution into society by the initiate as an extended metaphor for the material culture arising from the same Tree of Life (Kabbalah) leading toward a solar-astrological-cosmological inspired utopian commonwealth. Kether or Crown, the first Sephirot of the Kabbalah (Tree of Life), is Divine Will to create infinite *Light* (or wisdom) of the Creator by possession of one of the seven[189] *Hebrew names of God "Ehyeh Asher Ehyeh–I am That I am"* (Exodus 3:14) within the Hebrew Mysteries. The Tetragrammaton (YHVH) itself derives from the same verbal root. Thus Enoch acquires God' name from which all light, wisdom derives; within Royal Arch Masonry (cf. Enoch, the ritual's name in the Scottish Rite) possession of God's name imparts exactly the same thing: divine wisdom. It is important, given his own attachment to Freemasonry in Sweden and to the Jacobite cause, that philosopher Emmanuel Swedenborg (1688-1772) named his own work *Arcana Coelestia (The Heavenly Secrets),* published in 1749-1753. The

189 They are: Eloah, Elohim, Adonai, Ehyeh Asher Ehyeh, YHVH, El Shaddai, and Tzevaot.

book does not deny the events of the Bible as real events, but rather describes them as morality lessons for spiritual growth. Swendenborg was a mining engineer, Freemason,[190] theologian, and a Jacobite spy; he provides and important bridge between German Masonic ideology and its relationship to post Kantian thought in America. His theories of angelology parallel Enochian ideas of a third order of inspiration derived through Joachim of Fiore's Third Age of the Holy Spirit and yet integrate mathematically rooted philosophy as a means of comprehending eschatology, the end days. As will be seen in a later chapter, Swedenborg was well known to Charles Peirce's circle and his followers in America; Swedenborg's Church of the New Jerusalem was linked to a specific esoteric-occult Swedenborgian Rite of Freemasonry, originally known as the Rite of the Illuminati, initially developed by Swedenborgian Abbe Pernetty in 1760 in Avignon. The rite was later refined by Marquis de Thome, another Swedenborgian, in 1783.[191]

The movement of the essential elements of the *Book of Enoch* into the framework of the pre-history and paragon iconic myth of Freemasonry's rclationship to the broader world can be traced to the transformation of Enoch into a heavenly king. This king was not only a virtuous and wise Pythagorean ruler; an image that had fateful consequences for Freemasonry's association with Illuminism: the means to the transformation of the world into a perfected Masonic Temple, a one world government or a New World Order, outwardly democratic yet inwardly ruled by an occult theocracy; and with the actual imagery of Pythagoras as the supreme Masonic initiate. The Masonic-Enochic Ritual utilizes the currency of platonic thought, notably that found in Plato's own *Timaeus*, as the medium or method for the achievement of Pythagorean kingship with its array of symbolic effects. *Timaeus*, written circa 360 BCE, is a dialogue detailing the distinction between the physical world and the eternal world; the former changes, the latter never changes and is apprehended by reason. *Timaeus* continues with and explanation of the universe at the hands of a great craftsman *qua* architect. The heavenly bodies move in accord with the design of the

190 According to Freemason Samuel Beswick, author of *The Swedenborg Rite and the Great Masonic Leaders of the Eighteenth Century* (1870) Swendenborg was initiated into Masonry in 1706 in a Scottish Lodge in the town of Lund in Sweden. Quoted in Mackey's *Encyclopedia of Freemasonry, Vol. II.*, page 745.

191 Mackey, Albert, *Encyclopedia of Freemasonry*, Vol. II, page 746.

divine; the universe is composed of four elements: fire, symbolized by a tetrahedron; air symbolized by a octahedron, water is represented by a icosahedron; a cube is earth. *Timaeus* contains the Golden Mean or Ratio:

> "For whenever in any three numbers, whether cube or square, there is a mean, which is to the last term what the first term is to it; and again, when the mean is to the first term as the last term is to the mean - then the mean becoming first and last, and the first and last both becoming means, they will all of them of necessity come to be the same, and having become the same with one another will be all one."[192]

In other words, there is a divinity between numbers, forms, and their proportions, and as such behind Geometry. In mathematics, the Golden Mean or Ratio is perfection represented by the Greek letter *phi*. Two quantities are in the Golden Ratio if the ratio of the sum of the quantities to the larger quantity is equal to the ratio of the larger quantity to the smaller one. The Golden Ratio is an irrational (meaning it cannot be written as a fraction) mathematical constant, approximately 1.6180339887 (square root of 5, halfway to the number 10 representing divinity in the Pythagorean Mysteries, plus 1 divided by 2). One way to get a close approximation of phi is by dividing two consecutive numbers in a simple sequence called the Fibonacci series. Fibonacci numbers follow the pattern 1, 1, 2, 3, 5, 8, 13, 21, 34.... where each number is the sum of the two before it. To Aristotle, philosophically, the Golden Ratio is the desirable middle between two extremes, one of excess and the other of deficiency. *Timaeus* strongly influenced Neo-Platonic cosmology and included 12th century Christian thought especially the Chartres School and its philosophers William of Conches (1090-1154) and Thierry of Chartres (?-1152?). Ancient and Renaissance architects alike, as well as ancient and modern intellects and thinkers, were all fascinated with the Golden Ratio. Chartres Cathedral itself would come to include solar (its tall, solar tower measures 365 feet), lunar, veiled chakras in its stained glass windows, and astronomical symbolisms within its architecture; its floor maze depicts the cosmic pathway of the soul

192 See Plato's *Timaeus*.

after death. The chakras further identify the church and the human body as a temple thus linking the human being and its soul to the macrocosm.

In the context of the Illuminati, the wise Pythagorean ruler was Jesuit trained Freemason and its founder Adam Weishaupt (1748-1830), whose principal book on the Illuminati was entitled *Pythagoras; or Views Over the Secret World and Government Art* (1795). The Illuminati was founded on 1 May 1776, and was modeled after the Jesuit order and dedicated to the ideal of leading mankind into a Rousseauian utopia of moral perfection freed form political and religious authority.[193] This was seemingly to be accomplished by implementing *alchemical and occult powers over both the natural and political processes.* The Illuminati as a secret society disappears from history in the early 1800s[194] although some vestiges seem to remain in some Germanic Masonic lodges; its political methodology, Illuminism, filters into nineteenth century revolutionary groups such as the Carbonari, the "Charcoal Burners" of Europe. It is also been suggested the political illuminism twined with Jacobinism had filtered into the democratic clubs and societies established in late eighteenth-early nineteenth century America. This latter sentiment was echoed in a letter by George Washington dated October 24, 1798. The Illuminati also incorporated elements of Rosicrucianism: a proto-Masonic philosophical hermetical secret movement-society cultivated –according to its manifestos–in late medieval Germany and was dedicated to the restoration of ancient, mystical, alchemical truths for the betterment of mankind. The Rosicrucians legendary founder was Christian Rosenkreutz or *Christian Rose Cross*. The three most important Rosicrucian treatises were the *Fama Fraternitatis Roseae Crucis* (1614), the *Confessio Fraternitatis* (1615), and the *Chymische Hochzeit Christiani Rosencreutz anno 1459* (1616). Frances Yates writes, "[T]here can be no doubt that we should see the movement behind the three Rosicrucian publications as a movement ultimately stemming from Dr. Dee."[195] Rosicrucianism would be midwifed into European society by way of the works of Christian mystic Johann Valentin Andreae (1586-1654) in the seventeenth century. In turn Adam Weishaupt took up the *Confessio Fraternitatis's* idea of a secret order that

193 Billington, James, *Fire in the Minds of Men*, page 94.
194 The Illuminati was outlawed by the Bavarian government in 1785.
195 Yates, Francis, *The Rosicrucian Enlightenment*, page 40.

would overthrow perceived tyrannies as a model for political action.[196] In the following century, 1776, Weishaupt's revolutionary methods were given a pseudognosis of economic theory and aped the communist factions that secularized Joachim von Fiore's three great ages by following Georg Friedrich Hegel's tripartite philosophical scheme of thesis-antithesis-synthesis.[197] According to left-interpreters of Hegel and Ludwig Feuerbach (1804-1872), when the antithesis of capital (rule) and labor (ruled) was resolved in a higher synthesis, revolutionary bliss would result as proletarian selves willingly (or otherwise) surrendered to harmonious collective identity and selfless joy.[198] This could only be achieved by covert means and superior occult insights.

The Illuminist method of the transference of Masonic Lodge symbolism onto the political and material culture linked the origins of European Enlightenment and how it mystically shaped the mission of fraternalism in the United States. This thread carried forward the premise that it was not only the agency of the morally active individual within society who midwifed Masonic ritual values into culture but also an interior dynamism or entelechy[199] of the power of symbolism itself which unfolded a core symmetry and dynamism into the implementation of policy served from ritual emblemature. The core feature of this element of Masonic history in specific can be traced to the pursuit of the Lost Word of Master Mason was a de facto quest for the ultimate ordering of society into universal monarchy prefigured in the wisdom of Solomon, King of Israel. Among these was the association, of course, between stellar arrangement and kingship typified by the association of specific kings (and feminine deities) with particular stars: Isis as Sirius, Osiris as Orion in whose constellation are the Three Kings: the stars Alnitak, Alnilam, and Mintaka which form Orion's Belt. Within Masonry, this took on the redoubled significance of the association of the Blazing Star as a lodge emblem with the formation of the "five points of fellowship," an allusion to the method of imparting the word of a Master

196 Churton, Tobias, *The Invisible History of the Rosicrucians*, page 198.

197 Ibid.

198 Ibid, pages 198-199.

199 In the philosophy of Aristotle, the condition of a thing whose essence is fully realized; actuality. In some philosophical systems, a vital force that directs an organism toward self-fulfillment.

Mason that he receives upon being raised during the Third Degree ritual as discussed. The Word of a Master Mason is a substitute word while the *five points* form a pentagram, the symbol of the Eastern or Blazing Star Sirius, worshiped as Isis, derived in large part from Royal Arch Masonic ritual imagery and polity, in the United States in particular and to the Christian adoration of Christ as King (the Sun) adored by three Zoroastrian Magi. Within the Neo-Platonic, Masonic context, Christ was Logos, the Lost Word, the *Sun of Righteousness,* the *Word of God.* It pre-dates Christianity; Albert Pike states,

> "The WORD was also found in the Phoenician Creed. As in all those of Asia, a WORD OF GOD, written in starry characters, by the planetary Divinities, and communicated by the Demi-Gods, as a profound mystery, to the higher classes of the human race, to be communicated by them to mankind, created the world. The faith of the Phoenicians was an emanation from that ancient worship of the Stars, which in the creed of Zoroaster alone, is connected with a faith in one God. Light and Fire are the most important agents in thc Phoenician faith. There is a race of children of the Light. They adored the Heaven with its Lights, deeming it the Supreme God."[200]

The further investment of the initiate with a crown, and white robes within high degree Masonry can be traced to various rites and ceremonies relative to the Enoch thread in Royal Arch tradition, notably the Melchizedek imagery in the Holy Royal Arch Knights Templar Priesthood, a ceremonial whereby multiple colors devolving from pure white and the kingship of the Priest-King of Salem were taken up by the Royal Arch culture, particularly, in the Order of High Priesthood referenced by Thomas Smith Webb in his re-working of William Preston's 1772 *Illustrations of Masonry* in 1797. Webb's *Illustrations of Masonry* summarized Masonic ritual and served as a means to make local Masonic ritual working consistent as Masonry failed to create a single national governing body except at the higher level of the Royal Arch and Knight Templar degrees and orders. Greek translations of *I Enoch* were published in Oxford, England from 1893 to 1912 which prove the canon for comparing intertestamental Enochian

200 Pike, Albert, *Morals and Dogma of the Ancient and Accepted Scottish Rite*, page 268.

literature with references to him in Masonic literature and ritual. The contents of the Ethiopic *Book of Enoch* contain important elements which underscore its significance within Masonic ritual. These elements include its closeness to the writers of the New Testament; it is beyond question that *I Enoch* influenced the writing of the New Testament. With reference to the Elect One, the Son of Man, and its understanding of things such as angels, the wind, the moon, the sun, and the stars it is beyond question that it influenced the creation of the solar-astronomical New Testament, by first and second century Christians. Like Jesus' teachings, *I Enoch* is replete with mentions of the coming kingdom and other holy themes.[201] Jesus quotes phrases and ideas from Enoch such being the "Son of Man:" Jesus, like Enoch, is the "Son of Man" at Mark 10:45 and is both *the sun* and the "Son of Man" at Matthew 24:27;[202] there are over one hundred comments in the New Testament which find precedence in the *Book of Enoch*.[203] The solar allegory can again be found at *I Enoch* 14:20, "And he who is Great in Glory sat on the Throne, and His raiment shone more brightly than the sun and was whither than any snow;" this is echoed in Matthew 25:31 discussing Jesus, "When the Son of man shall come in his glory, and all the holy angels with him, then shall he sit upon the throne of his glory:." Another example can be found at *I Enoch* 108:12, "And I will bring out in shining light those who have loved My holy name, and I will seat each on the throne of his honor (glory);" this is paralleled in Matthew 19:28, "And Jesus said unto them, Verily I say unto you, That ye which have followed me, in the regeneration when the Son of man shall sit in the throne of his glory, ye also shall sit upon twelve thrones, judging the twelve tribes of Israel." The twelve thrones and twelve tribes are of course the twelve houses of the zodiac. As Enoch represents the sun having lived for three hundred and sixty-five years at Genesis 5:23, so too is Jesus a metaphoric stand-in for the sun: the Son-Sun of God as analyzed in Chapter III. Enoch and Jesus thus parallel and echo each other as solar metaphors. This links the New Testament to *I Enoch* the latter of which documents the sun as the luminary source of godly knowledge; the sun anthropomorphizes into Jesus Christ in the former. This feature became

201 Lumpkin, Joseph B., *The Books of Enoch*, page 12.
202 Verse can be found at beginning of Chapter III.
203 Lumpkin, Joseph B., *The Books of Enoch*, page 12.

significant from 1790 when a new Christian sequence of Masonic degree ceremonies was developed from Anglo-Irish origins, known collectively by the name York Rite. The Dublin ceremonies and jewels contained allusions to Enochic emblems, notably two pillars or columns as a support for a vault within which the Ark of the Covenant was stored. It was upon these Pillars that Enoch inscribed the information he learned while walking with God, from his celestial visitation detailed in *I Enoch.* Although the two different versions of the Royal Arch Ceremony of Exaltation existed, the one in the United States alludes to the story and legend within *I Enoch* as contained within the York Rite (cf. Webb's *Monitor*) which was organized into Chapters, Grand Chapters, and a General Grand Chapter over which Grand Master DeWitt Clinton (1769-1828) came to preside as an extension of his devotion to public service. The original degree certificate of a Royal Arch Mason in the United States; designed and attributed to Royal Arch Mason Benjamin Hurd of St. Andrew's Lodge, Boston, Massachusetts, incorporated imagery of the Christian Knights Templar degree (triangular altar with a skull and crossbones, serpent intertwined upon a cross suggesting Numbers 21:9 and conferring the Brazen Serpent 25th degree in the Scottish Rite Southern Jurisdiction, etc.) as it was reconstructed from medieval legend thus making Enochic allusions nominally Christian, as they were contextually characterized in Thomas Smith Webb's 1797 Masonic textbook, *The Illustrations of Freemasonry*. The earliest written record available in America mentioning the Knights Templar is to befound in the records of St. Andrew's Royal Arch Chapter, called a Royal Arch lodge at that time. On 28 August, 1769, William Davis[204] was Accepted and Accordingly made by receiving the four steps, that of Excellent, Super Excellent, Royal Arch, and Knight Templar anticipating the Mark Master Mason, Virtual Past Master, Most Excellent Master, and Royal Arch degrees of the Webb system. Thus the design of the St. Andrew's Royal Arch Hurd Plate describes the step by step movement both of the individual and of the new nation into mystical solar influenced order, anticipating both the Royal Arch Grand Chapter and the Grand Encampment of Knights Templar of DeWitt Clinton, ruled by the articulate citizen with reference to the pillars

204 Davis owned a chemist shop in Boston, but is perhaps most noted for his efforts at the Battle of Bunker Hill (a/k/a Breed's Hill) in 1775, where Davis reportedly suggested the so-called "barrel defense" in which barrels full of earth and stone were rolled down on the attacking British forces.

of Enoch upon which were inscribed symbolically all of ancient learning and knowledge as well as Euclid 47th Proposition, the Pythagorean theorem. Notably, the St. Andrew's Royal Arch Hurd Plate (1790) features a *rising sun* in place of the Ark of the Covenant or the Foundation Stone upon which it was stored, the symbol of Logos as contained on the Irish Jewels and the symbol for Logos in Webb ritual ceremony (see Plate VIII pages 567, 568). This symbolized new world Egyptian solar order as a seeming departure from old world European Hebrew mysticism: the transformation of Masonic ceremonial, from one set of emblems and icons to another, that coincided precisely at the pinpoint of the restructuring of Freemasonry in America to accommodate the necessity of building the post-Revolutionary nation. As such solar imagery would come to represent Logos, the Tetragrammaton, in the United States: Neoclassical architecture combined with Baroque imagination would be intertwined as a means of expressing triumphant Masonic power and control in the new world, the United States. As such vista of the nation's capital, the District of Columbia, would likewise conform to hermetical, cabalistic, Egyptian, solar, astrological, and esoteric themes.

The identification of discrete Royal Arch-nuanced emblems and jewels in Ireland with the unfolding and proliferation of millennial solar mission of the Hurd York Rite degree certificate implies an important linkage between lodge and Royal Arch Chapter ritual and Illuminism. Illuminism, which has been the subject of important studies, was both a premise and method by which the ideas and concepts of initiatory ceremonies were projected onto, and passed into, the broader society and culture as a means to transform the political order. In the history of ideas it is critical for several reasons, notably as a perceived international conspiracy, and the object of fearful and accusatory reaction in the run-up to the Morgan era of anti-Masonry by opponents of DeWitt Clinton, Thomas Smith Webb's colleague in the application of Masonic agenda to public policy; the so-called Clintonian or Columbian Illuminati. Narrowly speaking it was a tangible and concrete organization and system of Masonic degrees or ceremonies originated by Adam Weishaupt and Xavier von Zwack to prevent the European bourgeoisie from enjoying the full fruit of economic and political freedom, and to circumscribe the power of monarchy. As a symbolic method of projecting the ideas of initiation into material culture, Illuminism also emulated an important Jesuit agenda of supranational Roman Catholic mission to restore the temporal power of the Church consistent with post-Tridentine magisterial theory.

The Irish Jewels, like Webb's system, intended the apex of initiation to be simultaneously past and future time. Iconographically, this principle was represented by the sun, moon, and stars, which in Masonic symbolism, related to the role of the Worshipful Master as one of the great lights in Masonry. Power to rule with cosmic order was significant because it established the sovereign as a millennial-Illuministic figure, invested with institutional authority, and with a spiritual, eschatological dispensation of an evangel which enabled him simultaneously to operate within terrestrial as well as celestial creations. The jewels also anticipate Webb's integration in the 1802 *Monitor* of elective power with initiatic power in such a manner that the Master or Grand Master was not only, as articulated by Anderson and Preston, the magisterial teacher and governor of a representative assembly of craftsmen but also a superior hermetical magus figure. This differentiation is an important key to comprehending the role of the Royal Arch Mason as a mediating intellect, implicit in the Irish Jewels: a mage who is at once an astrological and alchemical initiate and correctly attuned contemplator of nature's mysteries, who might call into being and construct a new world of wonder as an unsurpassable feat of pansophic magic having at once a mystic interior core and a secular and rationalistic exterior political reality. The American high degree system, which can be seen in embryo in Webb's *Monitor* in specific, embroidered ritual order to accommodate absolutism with deep Byzantine resonance which mandated secrecy and secret places within egalitarian constitutional structure in the Scottish Rite. The craft emblems in the jewels as a result indicated a more primitive form of political cosmology than existed in Anderson, or Preston, or then subsequently developed within the French tradition of the *haute* grades, governed by Scottish Rite Supreme Councils, and their related craft entities, the Grand Orients.

The core template for the concept of ideal political order within the Royal Arch emblems exhibited in both the Irish Jewels and the Hurd Plate

(1790) can be traced to the central concept of timeless moral order in the work of Guillaume Postel (1510-1581). Postel articulated Enochian restitution of an unfolding Davidic *Shekhinah* through the medium of a prophetic Isis-like goddess, termed the *Mater Johanna,* through the initiatic interplay of hermetic rationality and kabbalistic symbolism reduced to the relationship between the parts of the human body to grades of cosmic initiation. The central idiom for this reconciliation became sabbatarian order because the kingdom of God on earth, emblematized by the presence of God in the Ark of the Covenant, the central Royal Arch device, joined on the Hebrew Sabbath (Shabbat) with the corporeal elements of the human form (cf. pentagram) to effect the ideal initiatic order. The role of the messianic prophetic goddess of reason was to open the vault wherein the Ark as *Shekinah* (divine presence) was hidden, and to enable the initiate to co-create the unfolding of the kingdom of God into political and social restoration. The *Mater Johanna* achieved Egyptianate and Greek status in subsequent Masonic and related rituals through appeal to Isis and Minerva, the latter a comprehensive symbol within collegiate fraternal emblemature. This function, symbolically, interlinked the healing powers of Hermes, whose emblem was the caduceus which was subsequently celebrated in the ceremonial of American pharmaceutical and medical fraternities, with the role of Johanna, a likely allusion to the Johannine *Logos* taken up into Masonic hagiography, which connected the ideal of the restoration of the Davidic kingdom to *Merkabah* or sun-chariot solar rulership. This construct survived into definitions of Masonic worship or ritual in various ways through the medium of the Jesuit Order, of which Postel was an enthusiastic, if heterodox, prophet-priest. The point at which he deviated from Ignatian ideology, the identification of the whole construct of papal temporal magistracy and rulership, was remedied in the work of fellow Jesuit Athanasius Kircher, who consolidated the Egyptianate, rhetorical emblemature of solar rulership with the role of the Blessed Virgin Mary, as Isis, Minerva, Johanna, etc., as possessing the key to the realization of papal sabbatarian order on earth. Postel was a devoted irenic conciliarist, whose ultimate vision was the imperial rulership of the King of France as Emperor of the East and West, a thread taken up into early French Masonic *haute* grades ritualizing. It was, however, the more heliocentric symbolism which was inserted into the material culture influenced by Royal Arch ideas which triumphed within Masonic polity as it passed into American culture following the death of George Washington through the medium of the Webb ritual system. This core of elements can be seen in Postel's configuration, which documents in embryo a triumph of Enochic vault-centered Hebraism over Hellenic philosophical rationality within the history of ideas. The result was an esoteric underside to multileveled American constitutionalizing in the construction of the new Republic. On the surface, and exterior, was the structure of positivistic and empirical legal construction stemming from the cultural achievement of the Revolution in Constitutional definition at federal, state, and municipal levels, replicated in a variety of professional and volunteer societies. Within this shell unfolded a variety of political forms as symbolically nuanced etiquette codified in rituals.

Postel's contribution to the ideation of political order implicit in the Irish Jewels is understood best in terms of his marginalization of Greek and classical culture in favor of the premise that civilization stemmed from Syriac and Egyptian sources. This meant he read kabbalistic sources as a lens through which to position Egyptianate ideas, in specific, for restoration and recovery through the prophetic mode of the Johannine *Mater Mundi* female prophetess, herself an image of considerable resonance with Isis. Among the three principal sources: *Sepher Yetzirah, Sepher Ha Bahir*, and the *Zohar* which recapitulated the previous two; the first dealt with Nilotic culture through Neo-Platonic concepts of emanation through created hierarchies and relationships corresponding to the mystical interpretation of numbers and letters. This was also an extension of Anderson's (1723) central concept of legendary Nilotic flooding linked to the origin of Masonry, and a code word for the role of implicit solar governance within political order. By the period in which the Webb system gestated into a structured system of national ceremonial, the core of this configuration made it clear that simple classicism, in which the Greeks in specific were celebrated, had given way to a much more elaborate and Hebraically-focused ritual ideology which provided raw material not only for Webb, who adapted William Preston's essential device of a semi-public *Monitor* from Laurence Dermott's Antient coded ritual book, the *Ahiman Rezon*, to regularize catechism and lodge initiation on a vast printed scale, but also the means to insert within the didactic Newtonianism of J. T. Desaguliers a trove of *arcana* deeply rooted in a layered gestalt of sources familiar to Postel and his circle. The structure of the *Zohar* itself, apparently compsed by Kabbalist Moses of Leon (ca.1250–1305) in the late middle ages, lent itself both to a war on ritual rationality as well as it provided, much like John Toland's *Pantheisticon*, a catechetical and dialogical structure designed to create a comprehensive world picture of divine emanations pervading creation, and accessible by means of graded revelations, parallel to Masonic degrees. In this context, Postel's literary presupposition anticipated the Masonic device of esoteric instruction in the essential political order of society, as an extension-in-light from the Tetragrammaton articulated as the Royal Arch word, which Webb appropriated from Antient sources. In American intellectual history, the device conformed to anti-rational threads, and public patriotic piety, within the new Republic in the period between the death of Washington and the presidency of Andrew Jackson, and explains in part the virulent anti-Masonry of John Quincy Adams who would have known that such a populistic approach to morally focused symbolatry threatened both the Federalist premise of an intellectual and economic elite, and post-Puritan evangelical mindsets of the sort articulated by Jedidiah Morse, a friend of John Adams and an early anti-Mason. For this reason it is critical to comprehend that the climate of ideas surrounding the ordering of the Irish Jewels *through* Webb's system relied explicitly on the proliferation of specific emblems to create a successful ritual network put to policy and political purposes by DeWitt Clinton, and others within his circle. It is critical to note also that the deep Hebraicism of Postel's "Masonic," inter alia, not only marginalized Platonic and Aristotelian sources for morality but also discerned through the medium of a female Egyptianate goddess the central core from which Masonic higher degrees, notably the Rite of Strict Observance, came to celebrate ritually idealized irenic religion; such as can be found in Mozart's Masonic career and in *The Magic Flute*. The Hebrew legacy was deemed to encode and unfold Nilotic concepts of emanated deity, notably the identification of solar divinity with the emanating Tetragrammaton, into mystical governance, a premise at the center of Webb's understanding of Masonic rulership.

Postel also eclectically tinkered his Egyptianate core of symbolism into a central device designed to incorporate the ideas of Joachim of Fiore into the spiritually prophetic reign of the Mater Johanna. He wrote a book defending Unitarian Miguel Serveto, burned at the stake in Geneva by John Calvin, and courted orthodox Roman Catholic theologians such as Reginald Pole, the cousin of Queen Mary I of England. The result was a cross-confessional unitary temporal idiom constructed from elements linking the radical Reformation to the roots of post-Tridentine Catholicism in the run-up to the Council of Trent, with an apologetical rhetoric identifying the Third Age of new spiritual men with the restitution of all things. His conciliar bias, specifically, enabled him to construct a dynamic pantheon of deities integrating the *Mater Mundi*, herself an amalgam of Marian, Johannine, and Isian components, with Joachim's Third Age of restitution threaded with Enochic restoration and unfolding cabalistic infusions of emanated divinity within and through the construction of a reformed society. It was his genius, in specific, to provide a means to accommodate papal temporal power as an external template to the radiating solar symbolism implicit in the conciliar dialogue among these elements such that his intaglio might serve, jointly, the aims of post-Tridentine pontifical triumphalism at the core of the Jesuit agenda, with prophetic, solar rule linking Joachim's Third Age with solar-nuanced spirituality and governance. Within Webb's system, all of the above was safely ensconced within the ceremonial concept of the emerging *Shekinah* at the core of Royal Arch exaltation implicit in the Irish Jewels, the Hurd Plate (1790), and Webb's rearticulation of Preston's *Illustrations* in the 1802, amplified Monitor of 1797. To Postel, all of the above was but a self-evident rational mission strategy to win the world for Christ. To lesser minds, and steelier agenda, it also could serve to insert ideas of imperial order within ostensible efforts to establish benign symbolic monarchy and styles of Roman Catholic piety within the folds of Webb and Clintonian policies of democratic process as much feared illuminism in Masonic Knight Templar ceremonials.

In terms of the subsequent history of Freemasonry, the effect of Postel's achievement was to structure a revelatory system within which both the Hebrew religion and Greek philosophy, idealized in the U.S.A. college fraternity system, derived from Masonic ritual order and polity through Union College, Phi Beta Kappa (1776) and local academic lore, were precursors of Christianity. This presumption identified all of material culture with a consummate ideal of Christ as unifying and transforming all traditions and societies into a single spiritual and temporal concept, elevating, in Augustinian and Constantian premises, the City of Man to the City of God deifying the initiate ruler. Its Byzantinity and implicit Caesaro-Papism can be seen in the double-headed eagle in Masonic iconography through the Emperors of the East and West, and in the Clintonian device of equating Masonic rulership with particular public offices and policies. The core of this system was an ideal of world peace which demanded an identity between order and nature, such that disorder and resistance became evil, and politics became the pursuit of right order within the soul, emanating from the supreme rulership of the *Mater Mundi* through a perfected and ideal monarchical order. To anti-Masonry, this became high blasphemy and the sure path of the Antichrist into American culture.

* * * * *

Just as Freemasonry was utilized in the nation building ethos of the United States through the manufacture of material culture and the origin of a clerisy through which to govern the nation, the dynamics of its operation can be seen in other nations and people as a template of order underlying more formal articulations of political policy. The Enoch element of this template can, for example, be traced from efforts to integrate comparative religion, understood as root mythology from the 17th century notably in the works of the originator of English Deism, Lord Herbert of Cherbury. Herbert anticipated John Toland, Thomas Paine, Thomas De Quincey, and Simon Greenleaf in the joining of such mythology with rationality through the integration of solar emblemature largely associated with Egyptian and Druidical ritual through ceremonial, sacrifice, and the administration of law. It was this latter element which "took;" Greenleaf and the others saw Druidical prehistory, accounts of which derived from Julius Caesar's *Commentarii de Bello Gallico* (50s or 40s BCE), as presaging democratic values. Freemasonry's ritual dictum, "Know Thyself," set up a more or less conventional civic psychology within which elites were encouraged to become aware of their own identity as part of the achievement of a type of godhood through hermetical and cabalistic energies applied to the acquisition of degrees of initiation. This involved encounter and interplay with fantasy, provided by the rituals, with the result that policy emerged relevant to nation building.

As American Freemasonry fostered extended Enochic vault symbolism with its rituals, notably such orders the Cryptic Rite of Royal and Select Master(s), now the middle unit of the York Rite, the extenuation of the scientific element of Masonic symbolism became clearer. This not only incorporated Roman Catholic elements of architecture, i.e. solar dome, such as Latrobe incorporated into the Baltimore Basilica but noticeable threads of symbolism linking Catholic piety to American patriotism. The subrogation motif of the Jewish Sabbath for the Christian Seventh Day in specific took on significance as Masonry's imagery of the Solomonic Temple became increasingly spiritualized and utopianized as a national eschatological icon. This was reflected in the construction of an eclectic Royal Arch Word or Tetragrammaton comprised of syllables of both the Jewish God, Jehovah; and two pagan deities, Baal and Osiris (*On* or Heliopolis as analyzed in Chapter III) and the symbolic placement of the Masonic Word in an encrypted vault by the martyred Grand Master Hiram Abif. The implication of this symbolism, extended nationally into a consolidated Rite with multiple local units provided integrity to the Pierre L'Enfant District of Columbia urban design enriching its civil religious meaning to incorporate an implied infrastructure to Washington the man as he was iconically lifted as Enoch into the apotheosis of heaven. The extended metaphor for urban design delineated through L'Enfant's design enabled subsequent designers in a range of towns and villages to replicate the classical and initiatic design from the district throughout the nation. An important further result of L'Enfant's design has been the impact of the cultural apparatus, specifically its extension of principles of spiritual and intellectual advancement along Enochic lines of epistemology into the interior cities of Buffalo, New York, Baltimore, Maryland and St. Louis,

Missouri to be discussed in later chapters

The vision of St. Paul in Romans VIII: 38-39, "(38) For I am persuaded, that neither death, nor life, nor angels, nor principalities, nor powers, nor things present, nor things to come; (39) Nor height, nor depth, nor any other creature, shall be able to separate us from the love of God, which is in Christ Jesus our Lord," is also relevant to this Enochic vista uniquely because his rhetoric addresses the universalistic impulse that nothing can separate the initiate from the love of God, *Deus*, neither height nor depth. This invests Paul, who has an instrumental role in the York Rite Knight of Malta Order, which follows the Cyrus dispensation to build the Second Temple, during the building of which Webb's Royal Arch vault is found, with a Platonic element of universal good as God or Deity. Further, the fragment is instructive for students of the role of Enochian symbolism within Freemasonry because it addresses the capacity of the legend to address the issue of Evil as a matter of individual culpability as well as a collective issue without endorsing apocalyptic propensity to deal en masse. The result is the architectural context for much of the Baroque capacity to deal with the confines of enclosed space with the same symbol addressing the morality associated with the infinite, a core dynamic which relates the Enochic vista to the mission of Illuminism: the conversion of the world and hence the universe into an adept initiatic abode rooted in mathematics, measurement, and Pythagorean Neo-Platonism. In Giordano Bruno's 1591 treatise, *De innumerabilibus, immenso, et infigurabili,* the dynamic of Illuminism was laid out in Enochic terms through Enoch's likely influence on Dante's *Divine Comedy*, in which a heavenly initiate is guided through regions of the spiritual universe: Heaven, Hell, and Purgatory.

The majesty of the *haute* degree Masonic King (cf.. Machiavelli's *Prince*) was envisaged as the direct result of allowing autonomy in politics and economics to dominate the realization of the Enochian-Pythagorean drive wherein successful figures would be Masonically preferred according to how they enhanced the princes aura and potency. The same princely imagery flourished within the Scottish Rite, whose seedbed was established in Albany in 1767 through the Morin-Francken rituals, again effectively summarized by T.S. Webb, but also relied upon. This was in essence a form of Masonically influenced patrimonialism linking and celebrating the Enochic template investing the ruling Enochic-Pythagoras with the mechanism of patronage as long as the end result was the augmentation of the symbolism and power of the solar prince and priest guiding the whole system. In this latter instance it is most likely the stoical elements of Puritanism over against its Calvinist theology which further drove the quintessentially Amphictyonis[205] features of Enochic-Pythagoreanism in the minds of politiques like Clinton, himself a Scots Irish cavalier descendant with lingering Loyalist, Stuart sympathies reinforced by this same element within Knight Templar enthusiasms. His irenic Presbyterianism enabled him to make ecumenical policy decisions in consonance with Joel Pintard, eminent Freemason and founder of Episcopalian General Theological Seminary, to countervail in part John Henry Hobart personal and political opposition to his religious directed public policies.

This symbolism, with its relationship between initiation and kingship, affords the Royal Arch unique status because of its 1799 association with the rising of George Washington as Enoch (see Plate IX) as a supreme initiatic adept into the pantheon of the nation. The engraving by J.J. Barralet features Washington being raised from the grave so that he, like Enoch, could walk with God in corporeal form and uncover the occult secrets of the heavens. Such a transfiguration associated Freemasonry symbolically with a universe of material, largely architectural culture, which envisaged the Baroque imagery as uniquely adapted to the Palladian domes which were regarded as the throne room of the sun god Apollo interlarded with *Merkabah* cabalism as an expression of the domed chamber becoming a throne room for the emergent and radiant sun within which the white robed king-*qua*-initiate was able to achieve Pythagorean initiation and moral monarchy. The English Reformation of the sixteenth century, in specific opened up this potentiality, as the sovereign assumed authority according to Erastian theory as Supreme Governor or State Supremacy of the Church. In turn, the American Presidency utilized Freemasonry, and arguably vice

205 Greek goddess of wine and friendship between nations. The symbolism being that two sides in disagreement should come together for the greater good.

versa, to equate the Presidency with a Washingtonian Grand Mastership of the United States of America.

Thus the *Ma'aseh Merkabah* (work of the solar chariot) imagery of realized Enochic eschatology began to take shape in the minds of architects Joseph-Jacques Ramée, Pierre L'Enfant and Benjamin Henry Latrobe which invested the seer or prophet of a new nation as Pythagorean priest as the executive and driving principle around which to organize the nation. This fit adroitly within the imagery detailed by the Templar themed Hurd Plate because a *Militia Christi* was also envisaged within which a Christian Knight Templar-Paladin ethos as developed merging the Chevalier Ramsay Catholic vista with earlier ideas of Freemasonry's association with Egypt, Rome, and London as a placement for an Erastian civil religion (cf. Thomas Erastus, 1524-1583, a Swiss physician and theologian; an Erastian is one who would see the church placed entirely under the control of the state), at the core of which was an Apollonian throne room as the simultaneously revealing yet concealing icon of the nation. The throne itself was, of course, a solar chariot which transported Enoch to heaven (that also appeared before Ezekiel) as transformed into material culture within Ramée's domed library at Union College of Schenectady New York, and Latrobe's domed Capitol building and Baltimore Basilica. Ecstatic heroes of old merged with the Biblical precedents provided a link, as found particularly in the Prophet Daniel and in Mithraic liturgy from Zoroastrian sources reworked through Masonic piety into ecstatic enthusiasm in an emphatic and detailed design matter linking initiatic ascent to regality of the sun as a metaphor for the burning fire of the chariot bearing the initiate. The point is that patriotic spirit applied to design as a new national civil religion confused whether the vision was that of the individual or the collective such that the design process itself tended to be shared by a lodge magnified into a microcosm of the nation symbolized perhaps best by the three way cooperation of contractor, architect and patron, itself a symbol of the three grand masters necessary preserve the mythology of the Royal Arch as the core idiom for material creation. In this instance Elijah (2 Kings 2:11) functioned as Enoch and Enoch as Pythagoras as sacral perfection was attempted and achieved. Along the same line apocalypse as initiatic vision and or experience of the face of God comes to the dweller of the Enochic city as a reward for rectitude and righteousness. Ezra, who led fifteen hundred Hebrews out of exile in Babylon back to Jerusalem circa 458 BCE, figures significantly in the English Royal Arch, and Enoch, are invested with their vision both as a reward and as a means to mediate the dissemination of moral instruction through government to the nation. Ezra enforced strict observance of the Torah and cleansed the community of mixed marriages. This reward together with the implied punishment of the wicked that they too should see God through initiatic variance but not be empowered to rule remains at the core of the same utopian and millennial vision.

As will be seen, the capacity of Masonic ritual to both reveal and conceal subject matter simultaneously relates the Enochic arched vaulted chamber transformed into a majestic solar dome to the Illuminist strategy of transferring the Pythagorean ideal of measurement to governance through the imagery of the dome. This device which was configured as an Apollonian solar throne room for the elevation of contained space in such a way as to suggest infinity was implicit in the Enochic vista probably first conceived by Giordano Bruno, the pre-Masonic intellect in his work *De innumerabilibus, immenso, et infigurabili.* Bruno, acting on Copernicus' heliocentrism envisaged an infinity of worlds through which the elements of the pre-Masonic world view might be projected to affect a necessary reform in knowledge and to drive home the urgency to develop a micro-cosmogony: a utopian society and urbanscape as a model for the unfolding of Masonic related thought into a reformist policy of extending *the adoration of the Sun and the cosmos*. On Bruno, Professor James S. Curl states:

> "The claims of Giordano Bruno (1548-1600) that the most acceptable theologies had developed in the Egypt of Antiquity and that the cults of Isis have exerted a formative influence on Christianity itself should be clear to all but the most closed of minds: Christianity, with its Saints, emblems, veneration of the BVM (Blessed Virgin Mary), and iconography, owes more, perhaps, to the lands of the Nile than to those of Jordan, at least in the development of its Cults and Arts. The whole of Christendom is permeated with ideas born in Antiquity, with Hermetic notions, and with themes derived from the Greco-Roman-Egyptian Cults. It is hardly surprising that Freemasonry, too,

> has taken on board some of those themes: a vast organization with a code of conduct, a ritual, a system of morality in which allegory and symbol play their parts, with concepts of trials, degrees, initiations, secrecies, and with the ideas of ritual, journeys, death, and rebirth after ordeals, has claims to connections with the mysteries of Greco-Roman-Egyptian Antiquity. The All-Seeing Eye of Ptah, the Isiac mysteries, and the resurrection of Osiris and not very far from the centre of Freemasonry: Ptah's column is not unrelated to Boaz and Boaz's inner meaning, and Ptah was superseded by Imhotep, a real Architect."[206]

Illuminism, the methodology of the Bavarian Illuminati, took up this idiom beginning on 1 May 1776 in various ways, but most particularly in terms of *squaring the circle*, a Masonic idiom for achieving the perfection of society through an occult theocracy. The concept derives from Masonry's two most famous icons: a square and compasses: the *square* and the compasses the latter of which makes a *circle*. This concept derived from FreeMasonic publisher and French Revolutionist Nicholas Bonneville (1760-1828). Bonneville, who was a Freemason member of the Illuminati, believed the Jesuits had introduced High Degree Masonry (the Rite of Perfection) and were responsible for the Knight Templar-Catholic motif found therein. The Knights Templar were, after all, Roman Catholic agents of the Vatican. On "squaring the circle," Dr. James Billington, in his book *Fire in the Minds of Men,* elucidates,

> "But among the pioneers of revolutionary journalism, Nicholas Bonneville was perhaps the most original. He was the first to issue the famous cry of *La Marseillaise*: "*Aux armes citoyens!*" even before it was used to summon the mob to the Bastille. ...Bonneville saw his journal as a "circle of light," whose writers were to transform the world by constituting themselves as "simultaneous a centre of light and body of resistance. They were to be the "legislators of the universe" preparing a "vast plan of universal regeneration," and opposing "those pusillanimous beings whom the indifferent crowd call moderate people." The supreme authority was not to be any elected official, but a "tribune": a modern version of the idealized tribal

206 Curl, James Stevens, *The Art and Architecture of Freemasonry*, page 38.

commander of the uncorrupted early Romans. The revolution to come must be led by a "tribune of the people," a reincarnation Of the special leaders first chosen by the plebeian legions in 494 BCE. To defend them against Roman patricians."[207]

Billington continues,

"The central reality in human life was the transmigration of human souls from one body to another - all moving in cycles like the universe itself. Eighteenth-century Pythagoreans were especially excited by the Illuminist idea of progressive human purification from the lower cycles of animal nature to the heavenly spheres of pure intelligence. The Illuminists' hierarchy of circles - moving inward from "church" to "synod" to the Areopagite center - suggested the concentric circles in the universe itself. The flame at the center of the final, inner circle was assumed to be an image of the inner fire of the universe around which the earth and all planets revolved.

Occultists may not have always believed such images literally, but they did usually feel that some secret inner circle held out the promise of both personal redemption and cosmic understanding. ...

Weishaupt appears to have been the first to use the term "circle" to designate a new type of political organization making both individual moral demands and universal ideological claims. Weishaupt described his recruitment of Illuminists from within Masonic lodges in Munich as 'the progress of the ⊙' in the political area. He introduced italicized variants of the Latin word (*circul*, *circl*) into his German writings to explain politicization of the movement, which he propagated by means of "circulars" and "circulation."

The idea of circles was central to the caricature of Illuminism by Marquis de Luchet no less than to Bonneville's imitation of it. In two key chapters of his expose', Luchet described the "circle" as the key to nine-man cell of conspiracy: the "administrative committee" for an altogether new type of human society in which "each member of the circle belongs equally to all others" and "has broken all the links which attach him to society." The conservative Rosicrucians

207 Billington, James H., *Fire in the Minds of Men: Origins of the Revolutionary Faith*, page 35.

> who dominated the Prussian court after the accession of Frederick William II in 1786, created their own rival conception of a nine-man *Zirkel.* Propagators of the Illuminist ideal variously tried to attack the Rosicrucian "circles of corruption" and/or to incorporate them into their own plans for occult "circulation." ...
>
> Bonneville even before the revolution had traced the Illuminist ideal to Pythagoras, who "brought from the orient his system of true Masonic instruction to illuminate the occident." After the demise of his Effort to "square the social circle" via his organizations of the early 1790s, Bonneville wrote verses of the "numbers of Pythagoras,..."[208]

The same device afforded figures such as New York Governor and Royal Arch Mason DeWitt Clinton the raw material to construct a public sphere within which to build and dedicate the Erie Canal, itself an extension of the imagery of Geometry understood as a Pythagorean approach to the planning of Nilotic flooding as described in theAnderson and Desaguliers legendary Masonic history. The same principle of infinity (*qua* Bruno) relates to the relationship between Masonic ideas to the division between sin understood as personal transgression and evil comprehended as a social ontology.[209] It is the latter that appears to have been linked to the impact of irenicism related to Freemasonry through DeWitt Clinton addresses to the American Bible Society with his Masonic colleague John Pintard (1759-1844). This entity was decisively pluralistic in its mission to denominationalize the United States religious communion and to forge a religiously rooted ethic in New York City which pointed the way toward modern ecumenism and what has been termed the social sources of denominationalism by theologian H. Richard Niebuhr (1894-1962). The result is that the United States almost alone among modern nations developed a non-establishment approach to the moral mission of voluntary collectives leading toward general acts of corporate organization and a literature suited to manage the moral mission of non-individuals within sociology as a scholarly discipline. As the archetypal American voluntarily view society within a national scope, its management of an infinity of worlds dealt masterfully through irenic clerisies and ethics very harshly with institutions and organizations

208 Ibid, pages 102-103.

209 The branch of metaphysics that studies the nature of existence or being as such.

that claimed to be unique, notably Americanized Roman Catholicism and Mormonism; both of which were ultimately domesticated from pristine roots at a populist level and marginalized to fit into a *FreeMasonic* irenic working concept of the Nation's mission.

* * * * *

The difference between Enoch's role, both in the *Book of Enoch* and in the Masonic degree, is that the knowledge imparted to Enoch was evil in the Book of Genesis; but by contrast associated with the presence of God in the *Book of Enoch.* Further, in the *Book of Enoch,* implied in the Masonic degree ceremony, is the solar symbolisms of knowledge as measurement particularly with regard to awareness of how a solar calendar impacts the correct detail for the celebration of Jewish festivals, from which Christian Piscean Sun worship ultimately originated as a new age religion at the Council of Nicaea and codified over the next six hundred years. Within *I Enoch* the sun, along with Kabbalah, represents the source of all illuministic wisdom. It was this element that became associated in the history of ideas linking the restoration of Neo-Platonic Pythagoreanism to the canon of principal elements of wisdom relating to the heliocentric discoveries of Copernicus which, from 1543, positioned the sun as a core initiatic emblem within the Renaissance leading toward its elevation and celebration in the idiom of Baroque material culture. The tradition, again derived and originating from the *Book of Enoch,* that he is to be an agent of judgment, the Son of Man or an agent of wisdom, a recurring theme with Jesus Christ transplanted in the New Testament; "This is the son of Man who hath righteousness, with whom dwells righteousness, and who reveals all the treasures of that which is hidden because the Lord of spirits hath chosen him, and whose lot has preeminence before the Lord of spirits in righteousness and is for ever." (*I Enoch* 46:3). Enoch is the *Son of Man,* "And he (other angel) said to me (Enoch): 'Son of man, you wish to know what is kept secret.'" (*I Enoch* 60:10). This is more evidence that the New Testament plagiarizes the *Book of Enoch* as analyzed. Nevertheless this idea conflated with elements of prophecy (cf. New Testament *Book of Revelation*) which linked Enoch's rulership as a Pythagorean Magus and King with Joachim von Fiore's Third

Age of the Holy Spirit as unfolding Logos into pneumatology.[210] This provided for a further synthesis between and among Enoch as a paragon Masonic initiate, a Grand Master, of specific elements of celestial wisdom, notably astronomy; there is an Enochian Astronomy Book in the text of *I Enoch*, as well as medicine, mathematics, engineering and metallurgy as emanations of the Tetragrammaton from the Tree of Life recorded by Enoch symbolically on his pillars from his celestial visit. These Pillars and the divine knowledge inscribed upon them are alluded in the Masonic Cooke Manuscript and directly referred to in the Masonic *Constitutions* and the *Illustrations of Freemasonry* by T.S. Webb. The above suggests strongly that whoever was the author of the French Rite of Perfection, the ritual of the Royal Arch (of Enoch), had access to a larger fund of ideas shaped by and reflective of the Neo-Platonic incorporation of hermeticism, Kabbalah, occult, and mysticism as it was worked into the Masonic Royal Arch ceremonial in the 18th century. In other words, someone in Europe either had access to a copy of *I Enoch* or at least a text outlining or detailing it prior to its official discovery in the west in 1773 by James Bruce. It is likely, because of his devotion to Universalism, that this was in fact The Chevalier Ramsay, a Lost Prophet, from whose Oration of 1737 the ideology and rituals of the high degrees were constructed. In modern, that is late 18th century fraternalism, the Odd Fellows develop a ritual which celebrates the Samaritans as possessors of such wisdom which contradicts the Genesis account of evil associated with the image of a high priest. This Odd Fellow tread of symbolism deserves further research as related to their own development of a Royal Arch legend. The Enochian element therefore anticipated each principle element which came to characterize Freemasonry's outreach to impact through Pythagorean rooted Neo-Platonism the political and material culture and was celebrated through its unique interior enthusiasm for astronomical and terrestrial measurement a consistency with the legendary and empirical pre-history of the Fraternity.

There is a critical consistency between fraternalism and public policy provided by Enochianism: the refusal, symbolically, to the association of the moral mission of Masonry with any single temple (e.g. an established

210 The doctrine concerning the Holy Spirit; the belief in intermediary spirits between humans and Deity.

Church, Christian or otherwise) in favor of transforming the whole nation into a symbolic millennial temple within which its irenic destiny might be managed and achieved. Thus, the Enochic coming of the Lord to his Masonic Temple became sufficiently generic in that each community came to have an irenic aesthetic achievement made possible, materially, to extend the metaphor to the nation as a Temple dedicated to Enochic Freemasonry. This of course was rooted in the Royal Arch ceremony as practiced by the York Rite and thus alluded directly only to the restoration of the Second Temple of Zerubbabel rebuilt through the efforts of the Emperor Cyrus of Persia, as recounted in Webb's *Order of the Red Cross of Babylon* (1787) with the red cross being the principal symbol of the Knights Templar. Yet the Enochic template held firmly because it was available in summary form in Webb's monitor and because it became commonly available, as for example to Mormon beginnings in New York State, to whom an Order of Enoch[211] became instrumental.

By 1853, the Order of the Red Cross derived from Webb's system became the bridge between the Royal Arch and Templar Masonry established in the premier centre for the dissemination of literary ideas in the American West, Cincinnati, Ohio. This key regional city inherited Clinton's vision of Freemasonry's role in the construction of the Erie Canal and which, in turn; led to the great Western trails through Westport, and Independence, Missouri. The result was the increasing proliferation of Joachimite ideas resonant to the Johannine (Docetic-Gnostic Gospel of St. John) theology of Salem Town in a frontier region imprinted with restorationist millennial and fraternal culture on civic life. The Independent Order of Odd Fellows (1819)–the senior lodge degree of which was 'Truth'–and the Ancient and Accepted Scottish Rite of the Northern Masonic Jurisdiction (1813) paralleled the development of lodges, chapters and consistories with the pursuit of truth as the purpose of ritual initiation.

This ceremonial matrix was set in place at Clinton's premier Royal Arch dedication ceremony for the Erie Canal, conducted 8 October 1823 by

211 The United Order of Enoch within the Mormon Church was one of several 19th century church collectivist programs. Early versions of the Order beginning in 1831 attempted to implement Christian Communism.

Grand High Priest Ezra Ames (1768-1836), an important portrait painter of Clinton and George Washington. The details of this ceremony underscore the importance of ritual language as a conveyor of ultimate Masonic truth at the point it intersected public affairs in the creation of a sacred unitary sphere. This ritual witnessed the creation of an autonomous priestly elite endowed with the philanthropic mission of spreading the eternal evangel to mankind. The implicit premise was that the Canal was rooted in the Name of God as the key to engineering science. It transformed, rhetorically, the plodding labors of workmen into co-artificers of the divine engineering unity making the nation whole,

"Almighty Jehovah,: *Descend now*, and *fill*: This lodge with *thy glory,*:
Our hearts with *good will*! *Preside* at *our meetings,*:
Assist us to *find*: *True pleasure* in *teaching*: *Good will* to *mankind.*"[212]

Ames administratively propagated Mark Masonry and served as Grand Captain General ('third vice-president') of the General Grand Encampment of Knights Templar, USA, and constructed his Masonic designs precisely at the point when Freemasonry, in disarray and decline after the American Revolution, riveted its public image to the fortuitous timing of George Washington's sudden death (December 1799) as a means to reconstruct its public image. Ames was also a friend of Webb's, and a key figure in the dissemination of the Red Cross rituals.

Masonic iconography, which preserved the symbolic importance of cabalistically-nuanced number theory, further proliferated through official and quasi-official certificates, such as that of Benjamin Hurd (1790), and by incorporation of graded Masonic symbolism into ordinary items of everyday life. Their material strata of American craftsmanship demonstrated the influence of Masonic ideas on the ordering of domestic culture, and also constituted a trail to understand the role of degree hierarchy, politics, and eschatology in Masonic ritual. Cornelius Moore's (1806–1883) *Templar Text Book* (1853) was a key to these strata. He refined printing and engraving at a period when Masonic higher degrees, derived from Webb, flourished after

212 Lyrics from T.S. Webb's *Most Excellent Master's Song.*

the success of the Erie Canal, and its concomitant, the western expansion of the railroad. Moore detailed a safe passage from Babylon to the frontier (Jerusalem) with Webb's Red Cross ritual concept.

*　　*　　*　　*　　*

The *Book of Enoch* opened a door to the consideration of Shepherds, both in Masonic and Shepherd Friendly Society ritual, as the equivalent of angels who were either good or bad in terms of their role as angelic guardians of the nation. The Shepherds were a nineteenth fraternal organization along with the Odd Fellows that were deemed a *Friendly Society*: groups that emerged from medieval trade guides to help out its members and protect their families from hunger, illness, and death. The Shepherds drew their rituals from Biblical sources emphasizing pastoral aspects of mutuality that could be exercised for and by lodge members. Masonry developed a further androgynous ceremony late in 1894 termed *The Order of the White Shrine of Jerusalem*, the ritual of which describes the beneficent rulership of the "Watchman of Shepherds." After it became clear, again, during the English Reformation, that a nation's religious settlement impacted not only its domestic tranquility but also its foreign relations Enochic kingship envisaged as an executive principle as metaphor became more critical to the American nation. Uniquely, as Roman Catholic immigration increased in the wake of the Irish famine in the 1840s and religious revivalism dominated sectors of the nation's politics threatening to reintroduce millenarian apocalyptic into the national mission. In this context, Enochianism, as a generic trove for a thematic complex of Pre-Masonic and Masonic imagery, came to be associated first with ceremonial Arminianism, a Dutch religious viewpoint advocating anti-Calvinist emphasis upon Church ceremonial and while promoting Universalism. Universalism is the theology that all people, whatever their particular religion, are loved by God. In the United States Universalist confessionalism developed with reference to Freemason Hosea Ballou (1771-1852), a founder of Tufts University, and with the Masonic clerical leader in South Carolina–Frederic Dalcho–who seems to have had collegial associations with the Huguenot community in Charleston. It can be argued that the Enochic ritual idiom was necessarily both ceremonial and universalistic because Calvinist theology was so divisive in terms of its insistence upon the nation as a uniform, Holy Commonwealth. Implicitly within Masonic Enochianism is the reward of a peaceful individual citizenship was a righteous and wise eldership continuing to serve the nation as *stars among the hosts of heaven.* This in turn relieved the popular anxiety about death and personal judgment between heaven and hell as an extension of generic citizenship as extended Masonic initiation, uniquely as America develop, unlike Great Britain, a multifarious and replete array of little Freemasonries, (i.e. Red Men, Knights of the Golden Eagle, Knights of Pythias), in the founding of Masonic orders frankly imitative of British Masonry, blended with the further array provided by the Ramsay ideology. It is also significant that the wise prosperity tended not only to deny theological judgment as the dominant current in personal eschatology for an irenic Arminian blend of universal religion but that the persistence of the soul came to supplant moral immortality of the initiatic virtuous with Masonry's reliance, through the York Rite through the symbolism of the 1790 Royal Arch Hurd Plate, which made Masonry through the adapting of the Knights Templar ceremony as its apex as a Christian rite. This came to differ substantially from the French Rite of Perfection, within which the Royal Arch of Enoch was inserted, and with the single exception of the Ancient and Accepted Rite in England and Wales, all Scottish Rite bodies make Christian affiliation and conviction optional. The Royal Arch degree within the Rite of Perfection symbolically broke all ties from Christianity. This became the de-emphasis of the Lansdowne Manuscript (1600), one of Masonry's most Gothic, is almost alone in its celebration of the role of Charlemagne's grandfather, Charles Martel (ca. 688 - 741) as the legendary founder of Freemasonry in France, linking as a community the noble and aristocratic foundation of continental Freemasonry, elaborated by Ramsay, as distinctively chivalric and Christian. Charles Martel was regarded as the Savior of Christendom, which to Ramsay would have invited Jacobite embroidery[213] as it was Martel that saved the French nation at the Battle of Tours, October 10, 732 CE, from the Moorish conquest suffered by Spain, precipitating the necessity for the Inquisition. Nostalgia for the unitary concept of Carolingian empire shaped Masonic high degree

213 To Ramsay and the Jacobites, the Old Pretender "James III" would have been the restored protector of Christendom.

ideology, particularly in Germany as the Masonic fantasy emulated the perceptions of a new imperial order incorporating occult elements notably from Rudolf II the Holy Roman Emperor and deistic formulations which made it possible to envisage a new republic along deistic, irenic and secular mystical lines as a Third Joachimite Age of the Holy Spirit (*qua* Aquarius).

In a parallel vein, the Enochic metaphor for citizenship as Masonic initiation found it useful to precipitate Christians thinking about their respective as discrete denominations or communions leading tacitly to the "one among many" approach to religious truth. This achievement within a pluralistic society such as the United States historically made it possible to de-emphasize the apocalyptic idea of the origin and end of evil in history as collective apocalyptic. The *Book of Enoch* traces evil to its individualistic form, that is as the creation of the race of creatures known as Nephilim (Genesis 6: 1-2) by angels known as the Watchers who mated with human females. The Watchers, or fallen angels, include (but not limited to) Samyaza (Shemyazaz), their leader, Araqiel, Rameel, Penemue (who teaches the art of writing with ink and paper) Kokabiel (who teaches astrology), and Shamsiel. Such a race of evil beings, or demons, squared firmly with Ramsay's Zoroastrian theodicy (the issue of evil/darkness) and with the Arminian ceremonial concepts adapted to Universalism which held out for the ultimate salvation of Satan. This further places Enochian theodicy within the Miltonic Baroque *Paradise Lost* (1667) epic with imagery of angelic figures wrestling with demonic figures as a means to manage a broader chiliastic[214] idiom of mass eschatology; in other words the endgame salvation was not the return of Christ but the final redemption of all evil. Masonry, generically, carried the issue of theodicy further by personifying evil in terms of the three ruffians who murder Hiram Abif, the arch Masonic proto-solar martyr, and otherwise tacitly as the privation of Light. Plato also helps this process by placing evil at the lower depths of the *great chain of being*: a moral-metaphysical image cultivated in the Enlightenment specifically which echoed Freemasonry's personification in initiatic terms of evil as privation of good light or positive occultism. Both the Counter-Reformation, began at the Council of Trent between 1545-

214 The theological doctrine of Christ's expected return to reign on earth for 1000 years; millennialism.

1563 and ending with the close of the Thirty Years War in 1648, dealt with evil in terms of diversion from orthodoxy, and its polar opposite Calvinism which dealt only in elitist terms with election and predestination; all else were evil, could not easily accommodate the Watcher element so deeply embedded in Enochic missiology as Freemasonry developed it. It further made evil a matter of esoteric discernment through initiation by implication that only the initiated could determine who or what is evil or not.

Thus Enochianism, as a political ethic within public sphere politics, developed uniquely under the leadership of DeWitt Clinton, New York State Masonic Grand Master, Grand High Priest of Royal Arch Masons, General Grand Master of Royal Arch Masons; from its origin in 1797, he succeeded Ephraim Kirby, a noted American jurist and partial founder of the legal profession in the United States, and Grand Master of Masonic Knights Templar. Clinton assumed a mantle of Enochic inspired leadership both as an irenic Pythagorean Magus, which included pretensions of scholarly learning, forging a bridge between the Masonic universe surrounding Thomas Jefferson (1743-1826) through to Andrew Jackson (1767-1845). Clinton's mindset, it has been argued, was notably Masonic in its aesthetic and encourages the concept, echoing Enoch, that history did not end with the present day but with the realization that the nation's destiny was the critical endpoint of Masonic time. In other words, as Masonic President Franklin D. Roosevelt (1882-1945) later opined, the United States did indeed have a rendezvous with destiny.

CHAPTER V

THE ROOTS OF MASONIC PHILOSOPHY

The Hermetic Tradition, Renaissance Baroque Imagery, *Ars Notoria* (the Art of Memory), Newtonianism, the Jesuits, and the Masonic Egyptology of Martin Clare

"But upon her Demise, King JAMES VI of SCOTLAND succeeding to the Crown of ENGLAND, being a *Mason* King, revived the *English* Lodges; and as he was the *First* King of GREAT BRITAIN, he was also the *First* Prince in the World that recover'd the *Roman* Architecture from the Ruins of *Gothic* Ignorance: For after man dark or illiterate Ages, as soon as all Parts of Learning revived and *Geometry* recover'd its Ground, the polite Nations began to discover the Confusion and Impropriety of the *Gothick* Buildings; and in the Fifteenth and Sixteenth *Centuries* the AUGUSTAN STILE was rais'd from its Rubbish in *Italy*, by BRAMANTE, BARBARO, SANSOVINO, SANGALLO, MICHAEL ANGELO, RAPHAEL URBIN, JULIO ROMANO, SERGLIO LABACO, SCAMOZI, VIGNOLA, and many other bright *Architects*: but above all, by the *Great* PALLADIO, who has not yet been duly imitated in *Italy*, though justly rival'd in *England* by our *great Master-Mason*, INIGO JONES."
- Dr. James Anderson, *The Constitutions of the Free-Masons,* 1723.

"The great mathematical and scientific thinkers of the seventeenth century have at the back of their minds Renaissance traditions of esoteric thinking, of mystical continuity from Hebraic or 'Egyptian' wisdom, of the conflation of Moses with 'Hermes Trismegistus' which fascinated the Renaissance. These traditions survived across the period in secret societies, particularly in Freemasonry."
- Frances A. Yates, *The Rosicrucian Enlightenment*, 1972.

"…God the Father, the supreme Architect, had already built this cosmic home we behold, the most sacred temple of His Godhead, by the laws of His mysterious wisdom." - Giovanni Pico della Mirandola, *Oration on the Dignity of Man,* 1486.

Masonic philosophy and the philosophies that in turn influenced it, as it were, points toward two elements of the Masonic ritual derived from Renaissance currents of ideas available to the authors of the degree ceremony, notably Hermeticism and Cabalism, the Christian version of Kabbalah, the body of Jewish mysticism derived from medieval Spain which assigned to the Torah, the Jewish scripture, an allegorical or hidden meaning as discussed within the *Sefer Yetzirah, Sepher Ha Bahir,* the *Talmud,* and the *Zohar*. By contrast Hermeticism, derived from the Greek interplay of ideas with Egypt, lifted up the mythic image of a figure thought during the Renaissance to be a contemporary of Moses (if not Moses himself), Thoth Hermes Mercurius Trismegistus. Thoth Hermes Trismegistus "authored" treatises describing the transformation of man as a god through the re-emergence of a divine spark seeking union through human striving with the divine nature of creation known as the *Corpus Hermeticum* which dates to the second or third century CE. The *Corpus Hermeticum* broadly fall into two categories: the first is concerned with alchemy, astrology, and magic, the second is more religious and philosophical. The central idea is that man should study his surroundings to gain awareness of his own divine nature.[215] The text detail that a loving God created man in his likeness, but separated Himself from man due to an offense (likely the Garden of Eden); however, buy using his intellect in the spirit of humility he could rediscover the divine spark which he was endowed.[216] Together, the two currents, positioned with a system of a Platonic great chain of being, symbolized the restoration of mankind to its original pre-Flood (antediluvian) order of creation, and promised to restore him to the same. In essence, this dynamic symbolically reversed the Biblical Fall in the Garden of Eden. It followed through with the serpent's promise to Eve in the garden that to eat of the tree of the knowledge of good

215 Hancox, Joy, *The Byrom Collection and the Globe Theatre Mystery,* page 217.
216 Ibid.

and evil meant that 1) Adam and Eve would not die; and 2) they would know what is evil and what was not. Symbolically, within this context, the tree of good and evil was interpreted to be the Hebrew Kabbalistic Sephirotic Tree of Life which detailed the infrastructure of creation by God as it moved from its created state to become a substitute for the same as a divine emanation. Thus what looks like earthly creation is according to this tradition in fact a surrogation of creation as it was intended by God to be. Further, in this tradition, the created world is in fact a substitute for Divine Creation which can be fathomed and explored in its entirety through the application of the spiritual intellect of a magus or initiate (a builder) who is idealized as a philosopher king, such as Enoch, the patriarch after whom the Royal Arch degree was named. The ritualized initiate was also typified as the Greek philosopher Pythagoras. This reintroduction of a Greek pedagogical and philosopher hero as the central paragon initiate sought to obstruct the intrusion of Aristotle (384-322 BCE), through the works of Albertus Magnus (1193/1206-1280) and St. Thomas Aquinas (as "Christianized Platonism"), by secular science and sought to re-divinize philosophy through the use of Neo-Platonism as a means to discover God's intent for a spiritual life. It must be born in mind that the philosophies of Pythagoras greatly influenced Plato. The result of the Council of Florence (1431-1445) was therefore to enrich the mission of Hellenisticism in Renaissance thought with reference to an appreciation for Arabic thinking, which had conveyed classical writings into Western Christian hands, Aristotle and of course Plato himself. It is likely that the core saga of the Royal Arch of Enoch ritual derives from the effort to conceptualize the rediscovery in the West of Greek thinking about the divine re-emergence of the Name of God. This makes more sense because the contents of the Ark of the Covenant rediscovered, as depicted in the story line are replaced by an emergent sun, which carried both Zoroastrian-Mithraic fire imagery and the Egyptian Solar God as Light imagery into a substitution for the Decalogue, or the Ten Commandments. Regardless, the Royal Arch of Enoch became a central metaphor for the mystical concepts, including those of kingship and rulership, as a result of a reworking of the recovery of the contents of the Ark of the Covenant resulting in the placement of various versions of the Royal Arch degree ceremony at the end point of the Masonic search for the restored Lost Word of a Master Mason. Three elements of this policy method appear to relate to the role of the Magus ruler within Freemasonry's high degrees. The first is to represent from antiquity the elements of symbolism deemed to be worthy of revival. The second was to apply specific symbols or images designed to direct the citizen's will politically or ideologically toward their realization. The third was to identify the executive ideas or principles that the Pythagorean Magus ruler should utilize to divine celestial secrets possibly to manage demonic presences through sovereign leadership. The Masonic element of this process appears to have been the insertion of emblems and images within the *Ars Notoria* (the Art of Memory) system current in the Renaissance which figured into various utopian concepts, such as Tommaso Campanella's *The City of the Sun* derived from the medieval philosopher Raymond Lully (1232-1315). Lully, who was bestowed the nickname "Doctor Illuminatus," was Christian cabalist, occultist, astrologer, and philosopher; he sought to unite Roman Catholic, Jew, and Moslem by means of their common, mystical, and scientific beliefs.[217]

The central figure in this tradition was Georgius Gemistus Pletho, a Byzantine participant at the Council of Florence, began in 1431, who foretold the imminent end of conventionally received religions such as Judaism, Christianity, and Islam in favor a new synthesis rooted in an irenic interplay between these Abrahamic faiths. His point is that advancement of the Turkish threat to Constantinople militated for the establishment of a consensus faith which might lead to world peace. Further, Pletho envisaged a concept of imperial expansion transmitted to the Byzantine Emperor of the day (circa 1415) which integrated his irenic vision of integrated faiths with practical elements of applied science, notably navigation, and invention. It was this innovation in political thinking which when filtered into the intellectual universe of the Elizabethan astrologer-magus Dr. John Dee (see Plate X) who was first to coin the term "British Empire" which in turn began the long process of theorizing associated with the match making between the English monarchy and a world vision of economic prosperity and just kingship rooted in the theories of John Fortescue (ca. 1394-1476) and by

217 Curl, James Stevens, *The Art and Architecture of Freemasonry*, page 88.

implication in the Anglican merger with Renaissance thought in Elizabethan court culture signified in the works by Thomas Elyot (1490-1546), Edmund Spenser (1552-1599, author of *The Faerie Queene*) and Richard Hooker (1554-1600). Hooker was Anglican priest and influential theologian who emphasized reason and tolerance, which became the hallmarks of the Church of England and English Masonry beginning in 1717. He is considered the founder of Anglicism along with Thomas Cranmer (1489-1556) and Matthew Parker (1504-1575). In turn the Royal Arch of Enoch mythology, integrating the restoration of divine knowledge, understood as scientific innovation rooted in heliocentrism in science (Newtonianism), and Biblical narrative structure became identified investing the central *Vitruvian Man* figure at least by the date of Michelle Le Blon's (1587-1658) engraving (1615) as a priority icon for the advancement of material civilization.

Masonically nuanced allegorical-hermetical engraving by Michel Le Blon. The sun is triumphantly above; before the sun is a flaming sword representing God defending the Garden of Eden from those seeking forbidden knowledge. On the right and left are the Pillars of Enoch upon which is inscribed celestial knowledge (seven liberal arts and mathematics, Euclid's 47th Proposition) imparted to Enoch. In the center is a square containing a Vitruvian styled figure as a living divine microcosm placed between the Pillars of Enoch upon which godly celestial knowledge was inscribed. Atop the two Pillars are feminine messengers of Deity while on top of the right portico can be seen Hermes-Mercury and Minerva, the virgin goddess of wisdom. Other Masonic images can be seen: the compasses, a sword intertwined with a serpent. Also the flaming sword is being wielded by St. Michael who is about to strike a figure with the tail of a serpent looking into a mirror. St. Michael is about to slay the evil one who learns the truth about himself by looking in the mirror. This recalls the Masonic teaching of "know thyself," a maxim that goes back to ancient Greece and written inside the Temple of Delphi. (See Joy Hancox, *The Byrom Collection and the Globe Theatre Mystery*).

Pletho's thought not only presaged what he thought was the end of religious ideology but also the emergence of the Sun as the central icon for which various mythologies were to afford various names, notably Apollo. After his death Pletho's *Book of Laws* or *Nomoi* was discovered. Compiled during his life, it was an occult mixture of Greco-Paganism, astrology, and Neo-Platonic *daemons*, not demons, as a type of demigod, and concepts relating to the migration of the soul. In the *Corpus Hermeticum* of Hermes Trismegistus, *daemons* functioned as the gatekeepers of the spheres through which souls passed on their way to the highest heaven, the Empyrean. The concept of daemons would influence and inform the Abrahamic faiths development of *demons*. Pletho's conversion of a belief in a restored, true Sun God,[218] basically a return to the Olympian Gods as anathema to orthodox Christians, and presumably Muslims, squarely anticipated the Chevalier Ramsay's 1737 Oration as it related to a new world religion integrating Zoroastrian mythology with Egyptian symbolism as pervaded 17th and 18th century thinking about the high grades, higher as a revision, or more likely a deeper meaning of Masonic degrees implicit and tacit within the Newtonianism held in common faith by the founders of the premier Grand Lodge in England in 1717. In this perspective, Ramsay's own career suggests linkages through Freemasonry whereby he was able through his sense of the irenic moral universe to maintain linkages through Masonic nuanced networks to Oxford University which granted him, a Roman Catholic, an honorary degree when his faith would ordinarily have obstructed this process. Even with the contrast to be seen between English Newtonian and providential Freemasonry and Ramsay's embroideries of medieval chivalry, can be seen a common devotion to simplicity in the Masonic pursuit of the Name of God, perhaps best represented by comparing the economy in Webb's ritual with the embellishment of Ramsay in the Enoch legend. The essential meaningful form and content of the ritual is not blended or made so extravagant such that the lesson is lost. Rather, an emotive tension of discovery is preserved between imaginative force subjected to the strict discipline of the means used to control and express esotericism in ways comprehensible to a broader public as a foundation for policy. Before Pletho died, he founded his own Mystery School teaching

218 To Pletho, Christ Jesus would have been viewed as a plagiarized sun god (*qua* Apollo-Osiris-Mithras, etc.)

polytheism instead of monotheism with his students praying before pagan statues.

The simultaneous accepting and rejecting of rationality ordered in such a way to make of reason a *symbol* at one level and a method of thinking at another has been uniquely useful with the result that Reason was deified along lines of solar worship but extolled as a technique within craftsmanship at another. This duplicity came within Freemasonry to be an end within itself reinforcing what the late medieval political theologian John Fortescue termed a *Dominum et Tantum Regale*, an absolute monarchy in the guise of a virtuous republic through the conservative measure of a future eschatology also in the guise of restored antediluvian order. For this process the role of Enoch was aptly suited. As Zoroaster and Pythagoras redivivus Enoch and with him other patriarchs such as Melchizedek the priest king of Salem integrated sacred and secular properties in the icon of a single paragon initiate. Whilst one is tempted to see English Freemasonry as a counterpoint to Fortescue's absolutistic precept, that is as a *Dominum et Tantum Regale* both summarized in his treatise *De Laudibus Legum Angliae* (ca. 1470), it is in specific that the Chevalier Ramsay was so successful in making it clear in his 1737 articulation of the reason to create the system of higher degrees that both the English and French systems point to, albeit in different ways, to the core Masonic premise that initiatic rank and power to govern are equated. It was in fact the American amalgamation of both the English and French Masonic systems with the Continental view of the irrationality of power conferred by initiation and to a large extent its arbitrariness that linked the two national system and made it possible to create such political urban utopias as was conceived in the architecture and planning of the District of Columbia. The result was that although the process and content of the affairs managed within a purpose designed capital were *sui generis* the conduit through which the design of the legislative chambers and the monumentality surrounding them was not. Both the spatial and proportional metaphors of the architects raised up the persistent ideals not only that mystical and occult wisdom was power but that the American Constitution achieved a unique expression of this power which linked the individual to the collective with grand effectiveness and aesthetic sublimity within which was the central and core metaphor of the harmony of the heavens. In other words the architecture and design of District of Columbia itself was a premier icon of Neo-Platonic Masonic solar and astrological order, thus making the United States a Masonic Republic.

In turn, Neo-Platonic thought was understood to be the source of a profound, pagan mythology rejecting all received Abrahamic faiths and pointing to an Egyptianate rooted iconoclasm which can be traced from, as seen, from John Toland through Thomas Paine, Simon Greenleaf, a founding dean of Harvard Law School, and to the English iconoclast Richard Carlisle who was sentenced to three years imprisonment for publishing Thomas Paine's *Common Sense*. This refinement was in turn rooted in the Renaissance through the radical Enlightenment and equated through Druidic symbolism and extreme republicanism with the pure religion of Ancient Egypt. By contrast, Neo-Platonism was also associated with a very deeply apologetical mission to reconcile Christianity and through it Judaism with pagan philosophy as a means to persuade potential adherents of both faiths that the amalgam was a pious philosophy deserving of the allegiance of first rate scholars and intellects rooted in an intelligent faith. Ultimately this duplicitous capacity to appear on both sides of the theistic fence can be traced to Isaac Newton who developed his system of integrating experimental science into an alliance among and between theology, philosophy, and scientifically founded mathematical rationality without undue emphasis upon final causes. In other words Newton reconciled "science with faith" while other Neo-Platonists simply could not reconcile Paganism with Christianity and Judaism. It is likely that it was this method that appealed to J. T. Desaguliers, Newton's prime popular exponent to the ruling classes and the driving intellect bethind the revival of the Grand Lodge in 1717. Newton's ideas were easily depicted symbolically as the rise of a metaphorical sun according to Pletho's irenic solar theology and as such could be interpreted within Masonry either with the rulership of the Worshipful Master of the Lodge or of the king over his dominions depending upon the semiotic disposition of the constituency. Newton's core symbolism was therefore amenable to the Sun as the natural theological emblem for mathematics applied to science and by further explication to

God as the Great Architect of the Universe thus rendering the Masonic idea of God refined in Anderson's 1738 *Constitutions*. Anderson, a Presbyterian minister, removed Christianity as a prerequisite belief for Masonic membership (Article I, 1723, 1738). Since Ramsay's Oration was given a year before, in 1737, when nominal Christianity was still the prevailing ideology of Freemasonry, it can be argued that he was simply giving a deeper and more symbolically enriched depiction of the irenic aristocratic mission of the higher grades from Newtonian sources as interpreted by Desaguliers. By extension, since gravity was to Newton a force directly emanating from God, the same symbolic idea could be adduced by a more mystical Pythagorean Platonist that the soul according to its destiny might be lifted up or taken down by a more esoteric application of experimental science. Further, that a symbolic figure, notably Thoth Hermes Trismegistus, might be accommodated through most likely the literary achievement of Giovanni Pico della Mirandola, a student of hermeticism and Kabbalah-Cabala, of the Florentine Renaissance as his influence was felt in England at Oxford, Cambridge and elsewhere as the unfolding of mystagogical policy through various Pythagorean hermetical heroes, of which Newton was simply by 1737 the most recent. As such Newtonianism in Desaguliers' hands bridged the otherwise cavernous gap between the Christian theologian and the orally guided deist because he incorporated divine design and "miraculous" systematic order into his experimental science. The identification of kingship with providential deism, the technical term for Newton's *theology*, can be traced to Nehemiah Grew (1641-1712) whose work *Cosmologia Sacra* (1701), dedicated to William III, advocated the premise that Newton's thought documented that monarchy was inherent in the natural order and divine government of the world.[219] The Newtonian Masonic ideology inserted a further principle: that it was in effect scientific as well as divine. Thus Freemasonry found ways to express that the veracity of mathematical exactitude could be applied, as for example was gravity, to the operations of the political chain linking society to its sovereign. It is this perduring element of monarchy which survived various political and social events regardless of the philosophical underpinnings into the nineteenth century through the Masonic medium.

219 Conferring theology of Thomas Aquinas and Dionysus the Areopagite.

At the foundation of Enochian elucidation of the Newtonian concept is a principle that spirit and flesh are one which vitiates the Zoroastrian and Egyptian symbolism that Ramsay took to framing his ideology from which became the higher degrees of Masonry. This base carries forward the idea that the human soul integrates both spirit and matter in such a way that the ingredients necessary to carry the Neo-Platonic elements of Freemasonry forward into the further idea of metempsychosis are amply provided. The result is a carriage for symbolism which provided later symbolic interpreters of Freemasonry, notably George Oliver (1782-1867) and Albert Pike (1809 -1891), with the raw material through which to construct a much more mystical system from Freemasonry rooted in world religions upon which to erect a global mission for the Scottish Rite. The instrumental figure in this design was Giordano Bruno, a pre-Masonic intellect whose philosophical vision included a mystical and messianic role for Queen Elizabeth I for world order. Bruno outlined his mystical Elizabethan imperial vista in *Cena de le ceneri (The Ash Wednesday Supper,* 1584*)* wherein he bestows the Virgin Queen with the name "Astraea" or the Virgin of the Golden Age. This vista overlapped or at least ran parallel with a similar ideology developed by John Dee, but in Bruno's case extended to a genre of female deities, good and evil, that link Elizabeth to the lost imagery of the Virgin Mary. This thread of symbolism not only identified the Queen with the irenic policy of the Elizabethan settlement, it extended female mythology to a cosmic vista of a reformed British Empire advocating reconciliation amongst the various contending faiths within England to the Renaissance vision of Gloriana, a ruler whose principle aesthetic and symbolic medium was cabalistic light. The defeat of the Spanish Armada in 1588 laid open the opportunity to celebrate a new messianic element to the irenic vision of the Elizabethan Settlement and pointed a way forward to link through the imagery of kingship which ultimately came to play a critical role in the symbolism of Masonic higher degrees. Bruno derived much of his thought from the work of the Renaissance occultist Henry Cornelius Agrippa, notably a perspective which looked to ancient Egypt as a subtle metaphor through the virgin goddess Isis for Elizabeth, making her the *Virgin Queen*. Bruno shared with Puritan poet, Edmund Spenser, a reformist spirit attached to the survival and revival of chivalry as the means to affect a great moral reform in society which

Bruno envisaged in utopian terms to be effected by England and France against the reactionary Catholicism of Spain, no doubt with reference to the defeat of the Armada. As such Bruno was alleged to have founded a secret society suspected by the Vatican of being a conspiracy to overthrow the church in favor of a Hermetic-Egyptian cult supported by Protestants hostile to Rome. Bruno projected his reformism onto a cosmological scale aligned with Neo-Platonism and as such carries forward a premise taken up by Ramsay through his affinities with Persian and Egyptian symbolism through Origen's thought that evil would ultimately descend on a scale of creation toward extinction (or conversion) and good would ultimately merge with the Name of God in the Tetragrammaton. It is also possible the imagery of the Philistines[220] was understood after 1588 to be a metaphor for the defeat of Philip II (1527-1598) in his efforts to reverse the Reformation through military invasion of England by the Armada. Philip was the son of the Holy Roman Emperor, which had never formally consented to Britain's withdrawal from the Empire and, in fact, precipitated the papal bulls advocating regicide against Elizabeth I as something of a desperate and futile act. Thereafter, Spain, far from being the seat of a colossal empire, became one of many small neighboring states to the English, simply offering various Jacobite exiles sanctuary there; Spain became petty and ridiculous in European *Realpolitik.*

* * * * *

A similar principle, Enochian elucidation of Newtonianism, can be found in Renaissance style later termed the Baroque. Baroque, an artistic style dominant in Europe from the late 16th to the early 18th centuries, was highly encouraged by the Roman Catholic Church. The Council of Trent, as part of the Counter-Reformation, which essentially deemed that the arts should communicate religious themes in a direct and emotional involvement. The Council of Trent also reinforced the Catholic Mass, Transubstantiation, the Tridentine Mass mandated by Pope Pius V through the Western Church. The aristocracy also saw the dramatic style of Baroque architecture and art as a means of impressing visitors and expressing triumphant power and control.

220 Peoples who occupied the southern coast of Canaan, they were considered "sea people" or raiders. They led a series of unsuccessful incursions against the Israelites only to be defeated by King David.

Baroque palaces are built around an entrance of courts, grand staircases and reception rooms of sequentially increasing opulence. The Baroque aesthetic dogmatized ritual pomp and "the sufficiency of the flesh" and led toward the material design that strengthened Cardinal Bellarmine's (1542-1621) tract: *The Supreme Sovereignty of the Pope in Temporal Affairs* (1610). Paradoxically, John Milton (1608-1674) and the painter Peter Paul Rubens (1577-1640), both sons of Calvinists epitomized the Baroque pursuit of Tridentine[221] embroidery in literature and painting. These expressions detailed the embellishment of heavenly-celestial imagery consistent with the French high degrees (Rite of Perfection) particularly in Milton's case extended, almost breathless, celestial symbolism relating to theodicy and angelic presences in a decisively triumphant vein. In symbolism, Baroque art was sympathetic to the mission of high degree Freemasonry because of its confidence in symbolic redundancy, epitomized by the Council of Trent's enthusiasm in general rooted in Transubstantiation. It modeled its subjects in such a way that this enthusiasm extended into the elaboration of the desire of aristocracies for privilege, rank, and the embellishment attendant to investing imagery in ritual with action validated in the application of mystery to a concrete mission. It was, further, confidence in the esoteric mission of Freemasonry's elitism in the pursuit of aristocratic virtue in the identification of chivalry with the restoration of ancient ideas of union with the divine, specifically, that invested Hermeticism and Cabalism integrated with the drive to restore the Lost Word within the Enochic idiom in ways never envisaged by the *cool Newtonianism* of Dr. J. T. Desaguliers. In theological terms, high or further grades of Freemasonry integrated essence and existence such that panoply was expected aesthetically to be associated with the deepest revelation of interior truth associated with the revelation of the Name of God in ritual form.

Within the Baroque aesthetic ethic, notably in John Milton's *Paradise Lost*, is the dramatic balance between his conscience as a Puritan opposed to iconic imagery and a Baroque writer advancing the triumphant mission

221 The term "Tridentine" is derived from the Latin word *Tridentinus*, which means "related to the city of Tridentum," modern day Trent, Italy. In response to a decision of the Council of Trent Pope Pius V promulgated the 1570 Roman Missal, making it mandatory throughout the Western Church, excepting those regions and religious orders whose existing missals dated from before 1370. It is the Roman Rite Mass.

of sensual man in a battle for his own dignity. This tension contains within it the conflict at the level of theodicy between God and rebellious angels, also a thread of symbolism, in the *Book of Enoch* which seems to have inspired the Royal Arch degree based upon Enochian symbolism. Thus the Baroque idiom provided a means for mankind, as personified in Adam and Eve, to achieve through heroic ascent the burden and responsibility of their own selfhood after the Fall (in Eden) in the midst of angelic warfare against God by Satan. Milton thus presages the power of the material implicit in the Baroque imagination in such a way that the Enochic restoration of solar order, rooted in Renaissance Hermeticism, and explicated through a fresh symbolic sense of freedom which Ramsay inherited from Newtonian roots.

Further, the identification within the Baroque period of the Neo-Platonic good with a female deity in the Virgin Mary (*qua* Isis) was a Post Tridentate (Council of Trent) interpretation of the messianic view accorded to Elizabethan reform which in John Dee's moral and political universe identified utopian values with the origination of the British Empire through navigation. Within the Baroque symbolic idiom the playing out of divine imagery associated with the feminine makes the iconography in essence secular, removing it from the direct domination of the Churches, Roman Catholic and Puritan alike. It was this secularization of mysticism which, in different ways Newton, Desaguliers and through them Ramsay achieved in the creation of the high grades. Masonically, Newton's significance is that he secularized matter to be a form of power. Carrying on from Galileo, who died the year before Newton was born, 1642, the great man's achievement made it unnecessary to depict metaphysical power through references to Aristotle and by implication to Albert the Great (Albertus Magnus) and St. Thomas Aquinas' theologies, but the interplay of physical powers is akin to the movement of imagery in Baroque design. The ordering of this powerful imagery symbolically was envisaged and institutionalized by Desaguliers in his ritual celebration of Newton just as his laws in the Masonic *Constitutions* (with Anderson) sought socially to order Freemasonry's own providential mission as a parallel to Anglicanism within elite society. In other words, the introduction of heliocentrism in 1543 leading to Newton's discoveries in optics, physics, and cosmology echoed a redefinition of political and moral authority which was codified in the legislation of Grand Lodge from 1717 forward within the *Constitutions*. This device was widely emulated as Freemasonry spread from England into the Commonwealth and Empire, former colonies and abroad into various European obediences (non-territorial constitutions). These obediences in particular elucidated the fundamental Masonic mission of universal brotherhood and toleration in ways consistent with a variety of national identities and cultural affinities yet each maintained the basic premise that a gathering of Freemasons in a lodge was a metaphor for desirable social order in a manner parallel to the Christian ideal of eschatology in the Kingdom of God. Thus, just as the Church was deemed, uniquely in Augustinian terms, as the Kingdom of God on earth, the lodge was envisaged as a transformative symbol for the ideal of celestial and cosmological harmony depicted in Masonic initiation.

Like Baroque, another principle theme within Renaissance intellectual history relative to Freemasonry's received heritage of ideas was the *Ars Notoria*, the Art of Memory of Raymond Lully. This was both a mental device and a literary genre depicting how to train readers of its extensive corpus in how to search and recall ideas about the relationship between human activity and concepts about philosophical cosmology through reading items of material culture. It was a main current within the Renaissance layering of pre-official Masonic ideas and can be traced through architects such as Andrea Palladio, Inigo Jones, and ultimately to Vitruvius whose *De Architectura* was written during the Augustan imperial age in Rome and adopted through Leonardo Da Vinci and his circle. Its principle element was that sacred architecture could be derived from the dimensions of the human form through the memorization and interpretation of *memory theatres*. Its central premise was that the human form contained within it the mathematical proportions of the human form as the paragon measurements of divine structures, notably ancient temple structures and medieval cathedrals. Vitruvius writes,

> "Therefore, since nature has designed the human body
> so that its members are duly proportioned to the frame
> of the whole, it appears that the ancients had good reason for their

> rule, that in perfect buildings the different members must be in exact symmetrical relations to the whole general scheme. Hence, while transmitting to us the proper arrangements for buildings of all kinds, they were particularly careful to do so in the case of temples to the gods, buildings in which merits and faults usually last forever."[222]

This concept is reflected in the template of the Escorial (or Escurial) Palace outside Madrid, Spain for King Phillip II (1527-1598). The Escorial Palace was designed by Juan Bautista de Toleda (1515-1567) and Juan de Herrera (1530-1597). Herrera was known to be a Lullist and its overall design and ornamentation contains astrological, alchemical, magical, religious, and other Vitruvian geometric allusions.[223] Likewise numerous medieval cathedrals contain various Piscean-astrological symbols and devices. The same premise carried forward the legend that the *Ars Notoria* was derived from a winding staircase in the Middle Chamber of King Solomon's Temple the core source of Masonic lodge ritual symbolism as contained in the Fellowcraft degree. It has been suggested that the whole of Freemasonry is to remember lost experiences and knowledge, and to preserve them for the future.[224] On this Professor Curl elucidates:

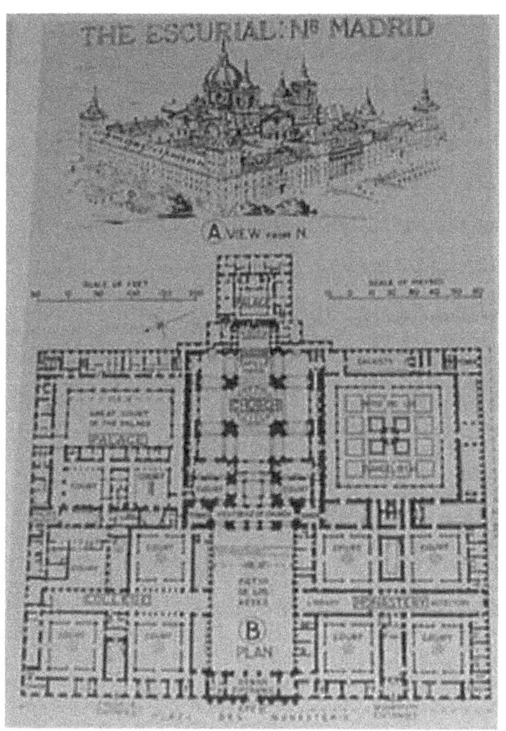

The Escorial Palace blueprint. From *The Art and Architecture of Freemasonry* by James S. Curl.

222 Vitruvius, *The Ten Books of Architecture,* Book III, Chapter i, IV
223 Curl, James S., *The Art and Architecture of Freemasonry*, page 88.
224 Stemper, William H. Jr., *Freemasonry and Force,* page 13 citing Francis A. Yates *The Art of Memory,* work also cited in *Theatre of the World*, The University of Chicago Press, 1969.

"Central to any basic understanding of Freemasonry is the role of memory, for the Lodge itself was a mnemonic of the Temple, of a lost ideal, and much else. Esoteric knowledge, too, was not safe in the hands of the ignorant or the profane, so it was safer for initiates to remember such material, possibly using emblems as aids, rather than to commit secrets to the page."[225]

The same notion was developed from the survival of knowledge engraved upon the Pillars of Enoch's within his vault with the exception that a false name for the true God was utilized as the literary and verbal device from which the engravings were drawn: J- B- O-. Years later this element drew Freemasonry into polemics of anti-Masonry because it linked the survival of pre-Noachitic evil with the pagan deity Baal combined with the pre-Christian Osiris and the Jewish God Jehovah. The result was a means for theological anti-Masonry to link the survival of evil as referenced in II Thessalonians 2:7[226] in which the so called *Mystery of Iniquity* grew through the spread of a "Great Delusion," which God sent lies and evil people (the Masons) in order to conceal the divine hand of the Deity in human affairs. The Osirian element of this evil provided a further link between the triumph of the Egyptian concept of a resurrected Sun God through an equivalency between Apollo, whose solar chariot crossed the heavens daily in the Greek religious imagination, and to Lucifer, the light bearer *qua* Venus, as a mere icon of the sunrise as eloquently described by Masonic thinker Albert Pike. Lucifer is incorrectly construed by Christians to be Satan or the Devil.

Such emblemature was at its origins both subtle and tacit. Renaissance theory of the *Ars Notoria* also achieved the identity between seals, classical statutes of gods and goddesses, namely Minerva, and rotunda, domed architecture which underscores the Masonic symbolism of a ladder leading to the Pleiades (known as the Virgin of the Spring) connecting the human moral psychology to astral and cosmic influences. This element, in turn, framed the utopian idealism which appears to be at the core of the

225 Curl, James S., *The Art and Architecture of Freemasonry,* page 44.

226 "For the mystery of iniquity doth already work: only he who now letteth [will let], until he be taken out of the way."

Frontispiece of *Splendor et Gloria Domus Joanniae* by Athanasius Kircher, features the sun ruling the cosmos with the Jesuit Tetragrammaton, I.H.S., with St. John the Evangelist and St. John the Baptist, the two Masonic "St. Johns," on either side. Minerva stands between two pillars suggestive of the Masonic Pillars of Enoch and the Pillars of Hercules the latter of which symbolizes the Spanish Monarchy. This book was written at the behest of the Spanish king's counsellor Marqques Antonio Juan de Centellas, who sent Kircher a large medal designed by Pompeio Leoni, commemorating his ancestor Honorato Juan, asking Kircher to explain its meaning.

design of the District of Columbia and which inspired the epithet against the Governor of New York DeWitt Clinton and the Clintonians that they managed a Columbian Illuminati (Chapter 10). Of the Renaissance threads in Masonic pre-history the Royal Arch of Enoch degree, one of several ceremonials dating from this period of the mid to late 18th century in various fraternal traditions, has most to do with the *Ars Notoria* motif. The specific element in the dynamic of the ritual, which is directly alluded to in Ramsay's Oration (1737), restoration of knowledge from two pillars (distinct from columns Jachin and Boaz as discussed) which contained inscribed thereupon all knowledge in the arts and science the key to which was the correct pronunciation of the ineffable Name of God, the Tetragrammaton: the four

Hebrew letters (consonants) in the Name of God. An early representation the Pillars of Enoch and Masonic symbolisms appears in an engraving by Michel Le Blon, a French mathematician of the early seventeenth century. His famed engraving as seen above contains critical elements pre-dating the first appearance of the degree in ceremonial form circa 1767.

The positioning of the individual within the Baroque concept of space and time as an initiate invested in him a sense of will and dominion regarding the infinite in Masonic thought. The Masonic use of *time and space* can be seen in the Craft Degrees,

> "Symbols of time and space are constituent parts of the ritual. They represent the word in its present state and its unfolding. The initiation and other ceremonies of the Lodge continually draw on these symbols. ....With regard to space, at least two essential symbols are always before the freemason's eye. The first is that defined by the Orient and the Occident. From the beginning of the world, it has been experienced through the movement of the sun in the sky. Recall how the Greeks represented it: in the pediments in the Parthenon that portray the birth of Athena. Moreover, this space is "drawn" by the two rows into which the brothers are divided on either side of the of the Grand Master's chair, which is located in the Orient. ....The second form of the symbol of space is that of the alternating black and white squares, which form the Mosaic Flooring positioned at the center of the Lodge."[227]

This bold concept enabled higher grade Freemasonry to imagine an infinity of worlds, a concept cultivated by Giordano Bruno, as at least a global frontier for the extension of Masonic advancement toward frontiers. As such the Newtonian influence upon English Masonic lodges symbolically gave way to an expanding vista of the world as an extended lodge. In this sense, the lodge both constrained and liberated the consciousness but

227 Henry, Jacques, *Mozart the Freemason: The Masonic Influence on His Musical Genius*, pages 34-35.

position the initiate within a field of vision which enabled him to project its values onto a broader, global, heroic stage. This capacity enabled the initiate to link his hermetical ascent to godhood through the possession of the Name of God in the Royal Arch to an expanding concept of millennial destiny whereby the Lost Word of Master Mason became an unfolding Logos through which the ritual word and the soul of the nation and world became the same. Masonry develop therefore its own piety empowering boundaries being overcome to reach the next degree and to subjugate its unique terrain to the rulership of the *parfait*, a perfected initiate as a wise Pythagorean ruler. The space created by the *haute* degrees was therefore neither nostalgic reminiscence nor Romantic longing for a golden age. It was a willful transcendence of limitation beyond the moral confines of classicism into an imperial consciousness rooted in the idiom of mystic brotherhood.

The Baroque symbolism of height, meaning elevation and exaltation, as opposed to ascent meaning hermetical initiatic *ascensio animae*, is critical to understand the dynamic power of the energy depicted in the Masonic high degrees. The display of the contending energies among and between the great forces at work within the Baroque are amplified dramatically through the warranting authority of the cabalistic array of the Tetragrammaton, a core emblem of the style. It is significant, in other words, that the heroic will Ramsay envisaged not only be achieved, as Pico della Mirandola described to reverse the inhibitions of the Fall of Adam and Eve, but also displayed in exaltation documenting its availability to other aspirants in material culture, notably in the deployment of cosmological-astrological utopias as intermediate microcosms of the unfolding of solar spirituality as a proactive moving work within society. In turn this elevation should display as a critical element the radiant unity with the Name of God, *qua* Royal Arch word of Enoch, as it ascends from the vault symbolically and plays into the formation and devolution of concrete policies extending the rule of intellectual and spiritual *Light* to the city nation and the world. The result, therefore, is the exaltation of massive materials to inspiring heights. The expansion of spatial rapture expanding under the symbolism of expanding *Light* within Baroque churches specifically underscored the implicit power made triumphant through the drama of Enoch's symbolic ascent to behold the Word of God at the supreme point of its radiance. Further, the penetration by the *Light* again symbolically provided a means in the templating of the dynamic of the ceremony for the policy explication inflames other worldliness and ennobled the elevated human form through the achievement of pomp.

Artistically, the conversion of Renaissance mannerism[228] into the Baroque replicated an earlier transition between the melancholic saturnine mindset of preoccupied meditative distraction with the subsequent achievement of a confident state of determined Pythagorean magus rulership: the pensive interiority becoming confident, radiant and triumphant. Architecturally, this idiom was symbolized by the dome comprehended as the symbolic throne room of Apollo, the sun God, presiding at once over the enclosed space of the arced circle as a vault as well as over a liberated world through which a universe is illuminated symbolically as an enlightened chamber mediating light simultaneously as incoming and outgoing. Thus, the domed chamber as an Apollonian throne room within which exalted and elevated heroic and ornamental figures became in the high grades through Enochian symbolism, an exaltation of the initiate in a full display of initiatic kingship and regal power: a spatial rapture expanding to an allusion of infinity; the methodical core of what became the essential initiatic dynamic of Masonic rooted Illuminism.

The relevancy of the firmness and clarity of the classicist artistic iconology to Freemasonry emerged as a counterpoint to the prevailing exuberance of the decorative richness of the conventional Baroque. The two elements were often intertwined, yet the balance, harmony, and symbolic purity such that a contrast between the two related styles echoed the Masonic division between English craft Freemasonry vis-a-vis the French Baroque of the Ramsay ideology. At stake was an aesthetic element of simple taste incorporated within a matrix of ideas, on either side, supporting limited, constitutional governance over and against absolutism; both of the Bourbons and Stuarts echoed in the perfection of the idealized human form as a metaphor for the political commonwealth. The Baroque

228 Mannerism is a period of European art that emerged from the later years of the Italian Renaissance around 1520. It was replaced by Baroque around 1580. Baroque in turn was a fusion of Mannerism and Rococo.

emphasis upon a female deity inspiring the movement of energy moving great masses within particular spaces and volumes was extended from design into political policy. The coordination of this visual and aesthetic effect can be seen early on in Le Blon's (page 191) Enochic imagery circa 1615 where, by implication, the Pillars of Enoch and symbolically the Tetragrammaton are associated with female as opposed to male divinity in the Baroque acquisition of the Cabala.

The Court of Louis XIV became a catalytic center for the integration of art and symbolism expressed in terms of landscape idealism. Although Nicholas Poussin (1594-1665), the master of this genre, lived most of his life in Rome, his background was the medium of courtly painting during the reign of the Sun King. Louis XIV's (1638-1715) finance minister, Jean-Baptiste Colbert (1619-1683), invited leading artists from across Europe to Versailles to articulate the greatness of France during the King's reign. As a refinement of the Baroque, classicism echoed the architecture of the District of Columbia through its resistance to the mainstream. It was not narrowly imitative or reactionary. Like Lord Herbert of Cherbourg's (the godfather of English Deism) thought; clarity, harmony and balance harnessed and defined energies of a more enthusiastic and passionate nature in ways emulative of Masonic ritual and its personal ethical and social methods. In the Greek revival architectural expression, for instance, it was the belief in the correct use of the various orders which reflected Herbert's concept of the human senses necessarily being matched with the affinities of various symbols. Similarly, color was understood to be an adjunct to form as various degrees became associated with the hues of blue (the craft lodge) and red (the capitular chapter). The result is that art during the classical epoch of painting in the 17th century came to denote an appeal to the rational faculties, that, the mind, over the senses as initiation was structured for the Freemason to subdue his passions and improve himself through initiation.

Classicism (of Poussin), as an aesthetic thread, was also related through the moral exemplarism of Venetian culture as an artistic objection to systemic approaches linking divine order to secular politics. This element underlay the political education in Venice as a republic broadcast through Europe in the late Renaissance and explains in some measure the Masonic studded artistry noted in the Cornaro villa murals. Rejection of divine system, in other words, helped to forge the creation of moral systems which did strive toward perennialism[229] through a restored sense of authority derived from modernity. In other words, pre-Christian antiquity (i.e Egypt, Babylon, Chaldea) and current non-Christian civilizations might be viewed apart from Revelation and as a reasonable approach to consensus through the virtue of primitive religion(s) upon which all men might agree. An important result of the rejection of systems for a joint clarity and simplicity within Baroque aesthetics can be seen in the enhanced state of the laity over men and morals. This premise lay at the foundation of both Anglican and Gallican (Roman Catholic Church in France from the time of the Declaration of the Clergy of France (1682) to that of the Civil Constitution of the Clergy (1790) during the French Revolution) missiology and inserted the agenda of Henry III (of England, 1207-1272) transferred to Louis XIV as a means to erect the glory of France on the virtue of the nobility as Ramsay idealized it in the high degrees, even after the Sun King's death.

The Venetian conceptual element within European classicism had much to do with the tension within the entire Masonic ethos between national patriotic aspiration and the theological doctrine of universal empire. Poussin's *The Return of the Holy Family from Egypt* circa 1627 (See Plate XI) retained elements of mathesis applied to religious iconology as a product of imperial Universalism taken up by the Jesuits, but, as part of his likely French provenance, this was subdued under the encompassing visual rhetoric of clarity in simple geometric order. The subject was conspicuously the Virgin as an icon for absolutism, but its context, on Christ familial connections, projected a more intimate and with it a more domestic approach to the French Royal Family. The vista was noticeably regal as opposed to liturgical or sacral yet the power of the pagan goddess articulated in the image of the Virgin remained. The result anticipates Franz Xaver Winterhalter's (1805-1873) family settings for portraits of Victoria and Albert two centuries later, and renders an abstracted

229 Universal philosophic insight independent of epoch or culture.

mathematically rooted social order as the object of defense through sacred geometry as a resistance to the Baroque triumphalism available in other Jesuitical examples of Marian portraiture. It is the system upheld by the royal family which took precedence over the authority vested in the Sun King himself which is projected. The Poussin portrait also underscores how the principle of harmonious balance survived within the Renaissance legacy to Freemasonry's hermetical and cabalistic elements. Such studied faculties became necessary to Italian city states, such as Florence and Venice, as a substitute for divine hierarchical order. Constitutional balance among and between the various types of powers wielded within a secular state came to rely upon the Herbertian-Deistic concept of the modification of symbolic universes at the synaptic level of the interplay between civil populations and the symbols which held them in loyal embrace to the state. In America, the result was a symbolic rendering of the whole nation as continuity from the utopian management of classical symbolic sources, and an apparent revision of Catholic Order to accommodate republican virtue.

A parallel existed between the role of Venetia as a paragon of internal peace and exemplars of all the old fashioned values with Freemasonry. This came forward through the writings of Venetian Paulo Sarpi (1552-1623) who's *History of the Council of Trent* (1619) severely criticized the extremes to which the Counter-Reformation went to insure Orthodoxy and the defeat of Protestantism. Sarpi was a lawyer and scientist who concluded the energies of the Church should be focused upon conciliation rooted in Republican virtues which anticipated George Washington in the conspicuous willingness to mute personal ambition for the public good through a readiness to descend from positions of power to the anonymity of private life. A second virtue was the capacity to invite taxation willingly through self-sacrifice in favor, again, of the common good. Both of these qualities emerged from the secularity of the Venetian state resulting even among the most affluent a core modesty in the exercise of citizenship.

Behind this tacit analogy lay a critical discernment that politics and religion, as envisaged by the Roman Catholic Church, should be separated in policy. This went counter to the Jesuit ambition to integrate the two realms but making Republican values, disingenuously, a function of monarchy and exposed millennialism as an envelope for papal ideology. The result was to hold up Venetian republicanism as not so much anti-clerical but rather a perfected society within which a harmonious balance among and between constitutionally balanced elements of monarchy, aristocracy and democracy. This concept of a perfected society was calculated to prevent tyranny and the promotion of harmonious proportion through expanded participation of citizens in government. French philosophies later transferred their admiration from Venice to England, accenting the latter's emulation of Venetian virtues, but on a nascent global scale. This important transference assisted in the movement of the Renaissance to the Enlightenment, underscoring the role of Palladian material culture and architecture through the process. In a similar way the resistance of classicism to the Baroque refined the osmosis preparing the way for English architectural ideologies to underscore the relationship between Masonic cultural forms and political order.

The coincidence of the Bramante-Raphael-Peruzzi-Michelangelo dialectic among and between Greek and Latin cross designs for St. Peter's Basilica, Rome with the outbreak of the German Reformation placed this edifice, with its core Renaissance emblemature on a collision course with the emergence of Erastian theory as applied to English, German and North American patrimonialism and architectural patronage. St. Peter's design insured that Roman Catholic triumphalism would collide with alternative views of how spirituality might relate to material culture with integral linkages to the High Renaissance emphasis upon human proportions, divine reference to issues such as dome and cupola design, and to the emergence of the Egyptianate-Baroque with the insertion of an Egyptian obelisk in St. Peter's square and within the Hudson River architectural development relative to Freemasonry in the United States (Chapter XII). The incremental influence of St. Paul's Cathedral and the success of Christopher Wren's solar dome (from the floor to the tip of the cross atop the dome measures 365 feet referencing the solar year) followed suit with its emphasis on the of the design either to Catholic or Protestant constitutional definition and symbolism depending upon James II attempt (or failure) to Catholicize

England; it cemented the inter-linkage between how policy would be connected to design and architecture in ways that were fateful to the national destiny. Similarly the dome symbolism inaugurated by Benjamin Latrobe for the U. S. Capitol and the Roman Catholic Basilica in Baltimore put forward a parallel between Apollonian dome symbolism and pregnancy: birth of the new nation and connected to Masonic ideas of solar rulership and Catholic symbolic appropriation of republicanism. Within this context, the emergence of patrons as Pythagorean and Enochic-Hermetic magi remained paramount and underscored the refinement of the expectation that post 1776 statesmen were expected to possess the qualities of Benjamin Franklin or Thomas Jefferson in the application of moral vision to the infrastructure of industrial and commercial development of the nation. After the 1626 fitting of Bernini's colonnades to the plaza of St. Peter's at the Vatican made the direct link between grand liturgical pageantry to the Square and underscored the importance of Freemasonry attempting the same objective through triumphalist pageant ritual as elucidated by the Chevalier Ramsay's ideology. The transformation of the style of Michelangelo, a bridge between the pure Renaissance form and the triumph of calculating reason attendant to Andrea Palladio's villas in the province of Vicenza in Northern Italy in their aesthetic dominance. Arguably, the Palladian ideology in architecture mirrored the formalism of class structure applied to Ramsay's high degrees in that the relationship between the workaday craftsmanship of English Freemasonry's idealization of trade guilds, twined with Newtonianism, became more rigid as chivalry transcended stonemasonry, supplanted it, as the central initiatic emblem as contained in the higher degrees.

* * * * *

The role of the Jesuits, modeled after the Knights Templar by Loyola's own admission,[230] in the origination of the Baroque style at the Church of Il Gesu (consecrated 1584) in Rome and the Society's refinement of the gaudy technique of defying Newton's laws of Gravity, classic mechanics, metaphorically speaking, in the Jesuit Church of St. Ignazio (consecrated 1722, dedicated to Ignatius of Loyola the founder of the Jesuits) in Rome underscores the association between the style, the mission of the Jesuit

230 Baigent, Michael and Richard Leigh, *The Temple and the Lodge,* page 135.

Order during the Council of Trent and afterward in the conversion of Renaissance threads of symbolism relative to Hermeticism and Cabala-Kabbalah into a comprehensive apologetical method incorporating Ancient Civilization turned toward Christian mission. Interestingly, the Church of St. Ignazio was built upon the old ruins of the Temple of Isis. Situated on the hills of Rome for maximum visual impact these and other parish Churches proclaimed the transformation between a likely Mannerist alliance with the thinking and writing of Pico della Mirandola on Hermeticism and Marsilio Ficino on Cabala. The effect was to augment the *ascensio animae* of the human spirit as a metaphor of the soul rising towards the heavens to grasp the power of the Tetragrammaton: the emblem of the Name of God, the characteristic I.H.S. (see Plate XII) symbol for the society. In this emblematic transference, the achievement was to delineate the solidity of the real above, with a heavenly array in powerful interplay with a parallel solidity of the realm below striking an equivalency through the Eucharistic Transubstantiation of two levels of created structure separating the initiated from the uninitiated. These two separate worlds joined through the parallel mysteries of the Mass and the imparting of the Royal Word to the Masonic candidate as typified in Ramsay's ideology in the 1737 Oration struck a further coincidence between the artisan order of English Freemasonry and the greatly exalted aristocratic order of the *haute* grades. Even the two principal versions of the Royal Arch, one in Britain and American without Enoch, and one in France and America with Enoch made it clear that the various Church facades in the Baroque and Rococo styles were utilizing columns and pillars distinctively to transform Renaissance secular thought into Christian apologetics. The defiance of Newtonian gravity with a science symbolically devoted to hermetical and cabalistic reversal of the curse of the Fall, in specific, utilized the imagery of solar based spiritual Eucharistic theology simultaneously to convey the premise that to eat of the holy Kabbalistic Sephirotic tree would be enough to overcome conventional social divisions as well as spiritual divisions such that the initiate-convert might know good from evil and shall not die. It is also clear that this symbolism served as an apologetical device by the Jesuit mystic Athanasius Kircher and Guillaume Postel (not a Jesuit) in their view of universal papal monarchy originating from hermetical and cabalistic roots into Counter

Reformation triumphalism through the mediumship of the eschatological occult prophecies of Joachim von Fiore. Von Fiore's idiom was adopted in America in 1818 by the Masonic writer Salem Town through an equivalency between the Royal Arch Word and the unfolding of the Christian Logos from the Docetic-Gnostic Gospel of St. John, symbolically into American policy rhetoric, architecture, and material culture. Postel himself was a religious Universalist, cabalist, professor, diplomat, French linguist and astronomer. He authored *Panthenousia* (Everywhere and Everything) and was friends with Ignatius Loyola, and although he never joined the Society of Jesus, Postel retained a lifelong affiliation with them. With regard to the United States as a "Christian" nation it should be understood in the rooted concept of *Masonic Logos*, not theological Christianity as understood by the uninitiated. Richard Crashaw (ca. 1612-1649), the noted English Baroque poet, in his *Steps to the Temple*, appears to have been one intermediary for this transition as does the set of Elizabethan writers devoted to the revival of English chivalry at the court of the Queen: Thomas Elyot, John Dee, and Edmund Spenser. But it was the overcoming of a de facto alliance between the Mannerists and hermeticism which released the full bore of Baroque instrumentality into Jesuit embroidery of the joint hermetical and cabalistic tradition as it became merged with Joachimite ideology which related to the transformation by Ramsay of the Desaguliers and Newtonian Masonic legacy into the raw material to envisage the design of a world spiritual kingdom rooted in illuministic ideas and concepts.

The Jesuit element in Masonic lore integrated dialectic interplay seeking the search for prophetic modernity in the restoration of the past. At its foundation this was pure and simple: the core Counter-Reformation strategy. Yet, to the Society, the Joachimist thread positioned the past in specific ways both as a hieroglyphical mission-method derived from Egyptianate apologetical rhetoric and from a principle of an unfolding Logos into material culture through which a sabbatarian order would be achieved as an ideal state of cultural contemplation through irenic peace. Freemasonry was, of course, ideally suited to this dual concept and explains in large part how Renaissance principles of the hermetical reversal of the Edenic myth became intertwined with cabbalistic visions of the Tetragrammaton.

The first promised eternal life and the second knowledge, restoration of lost wisdom, with apotheosis through knowing the name of God; the key to unlocking the secrets engraved, symbolically upon the vaulted pillars described in the Royal Arch ceremony of Enoch. Together, these elements elevated the Sun as an expression of Egyptianate mythology of pontifical monarchy to a dynamic prophetic symbolism of Third Age prophecy linked to the Holy Spirit.

Lastly, the role of Sir Thomas Elyot (ca. 1490-1546) in his delineation of wisdom, both divine and human as the source for the dissemination of humanism, incorporating the constitutional theory of Sir John Fortescue's *De Laudibus Legum Angliae (In Praise of English Law)* should not be underestimated as a medium for fostering the theory that ultimately defined Masonic initiation in its relationship with civil religion and utopianism as witnessed in the ideas which two centuries hence defined the iconic status of the District of Columbia. Elyot's work, *The Boke named the Governour* (1531), carved out an early modern respectability for the macrocosmic interplay with microcosmic imagery in terms of court-centered civility which made a lasting imprint upon the aesthetics of virtuosity within the legal profession as a clerisy of articulated citizens from which wise rulers might be drawn. Elyot foresaw the dynamic of wisdom effectuating itself into counsel to princes through a reworking of Christian chivalry (cf. Knight Templary) into a concept and method generating a science of virtue resulting in the perfect operation of the state. He was an older contemporary of the English humanists and Sir Thomas More, a utopian lawyer, from whose ideas he developed precepts which squarely anticipated the formulation of high degree Masonry. One, of course, scans the nineteenth-Victorian century for the parallels with the Elizabethan reconnaissance leading it to England's first empire as an extension of the enthusiasm for John Dee's ideology relating to navigation, seafaring, and the occult developed from Pletho's work on imperial design. The evidence exists mostly in the works of Charles Kingsley (1819-1875), *The Water-Babies, A Fairy Tale for a Land Baby* (1863) in which the microcosms of the sea aim to achieve a broader macrocosm or a higher cabalistic-cosmological Godhead; and in the Christ Church (Oxford) mathematician Lewis Carroll (real name Charles L.

Dodgson, 1832-1898) wherein the world of insects and animals take on human traits, forms, and qualities.

Within the sets of symbols derived from such works as *Secreta Secretorum*, the textbook of good counsel thought to have been given by Aristotle to his pupil Alexander the Great were contained a set of parallels between the symbols which positioned Tudor articulate citizens within a society which was essentially status based and depended upon a hierarchy of revelations to order the role of the individual according either to his placement within an ascending and descending order of graded society or, more organically, within a more corporeal model of the person as part of a larger organic body. Fortescue's idea carried the symbolism into a slightly more dynamic symbolism which struck and equivalency between a more "representative monarchy" within which the king's power is more augmented as he sits in council. Thus by implication, sharing power was envisaged by the Father of American Architectur, Benjamin Henry Latrobe, and would take place within his domed Apollonian chamber (domed U.S. Capitol) where the king (U.S. President) and his counselors (Senate and Congress) were bidden to engage in a more cosmic governance over an empire with astral symbolism at its core. Thus the integration of astrological order within the panoply of political imagery not only survived in purpose built arrays of connected buildings as in the District of Columbia but achieved a cosmological symmetry connecting politics through legislative and judicial process vertically to the order in the heavens and horizontally to the unfolding of Logos through the medium of Enochic symbolism of a rising magus visiting the heavens, and returning moral wisdom as a method of governance. English Freemasonry's contribution to this public sphere (cf. Preston's *Monitor*) of ethics was to position the formal process of personal counsel to the prince and by implication the same to the state or monarch, unlike the high degree Masonic ethos within the United States which positioned the Royal Arch Mason as an articulate citizen-king.

* * * * *

The inter-linkage between the writings of Masonic polemicist, London schoolmaster, and member of the Royal Society Martin Clare, to whom the first references to Ancient Egypt can be traced, in a Masonic context, called *A Perjured (sic) Free Mason Detected*[231] in 1730. Clare was a post-Renaissance Masonic scholar whose works must be discussed. Clare was a Grand Steward in 1734, Junior Grand Warden in 1735, and became Deputy Grand Master in 1741. His view was that the architect of the Pyramids was Mizraim, a descendant of Noah who carried the secrets of the antediluvian world into the architecture of the Nile region wherein the same secrets were embedded in sacred structures. These secrets were the implied core of the morality which, along with Enoch's vision of God, provided a pathway for the wisdom necessary to rule the new nation. Clare's work anticipated Ramsay's ideology but unlike Ramsay was not driven by the sociology of knowledge stemming from the Scottish Enlightenment, notably its theological rejection of Calvinism (including Puritanism) and its enthusiasm for the Stuart restoration. It is the Masonic Rite associated both with Memphis and Mizraim (the Egyptian word for Hebrews) that provided Mozart and his colleague with the raw material for the imagery of Sarastro, the wise Pythagorean ruler who opposes the Queen of the Night, in *The Magic Flute* in 1791. Sarastro's hymn to Isis and Osiris became the manifest for the new Masonic Age solar of Enlightenment and a symbolic herald of Joachim von Fiore's Third Age syncretic of the coming Age of Aquarius.

Martin Clare's description of the evolution and deployment of the Egyptian foundation for Freemasonry's antiquity reflects the projection on to a cosmographical level the otherwise historical and legendary ascent of the Art of Masonry along initiatic lines linking Adam and Eve to their descendant Enoch. This projection of a symbolic time line onto the unfolding of a path to initiation as detailed in the Hurd Plate Royal Arch certificate interlinked the Enochic vista of the heavens and the relay of heavenly secrets; a parallel to the destiny of nations that chose it as a millennial path for the development of empire. As has been seen the same entelechy or inner momentum of energy could be applied to the British empire from John Dee's interpretation of Gemistus Pletho outlined at the Council of Florence transferred to the design to preserve Tudor ideas of

231 Also called *A Defense of Masonry* written in response to Samuel Prichard's anti-Masonic rant *Masonry Dissected.*

Renaissance order carried forward to the early 18th century where in a culture of learned esoteric civility became a hedge against Puritan inroads into the mythic trajectory of imperial expansion through Egypt to Rome.

Clare lays out the template for the erection of a national capitol through his linkage betweenAntediluvian order and Egypt, tracing its origins from the Biblical cities Sidon and Tyre in Phoenicia: "Mizraim...erected a powerful nation on the Banks of the Nilus (cf Potomac) ...(thereafter) he built those inimitable Fabricks call'd the Pyramids... under these *Great Masters of Masonrya*...scattered abroad and spread the noble science into several parts of the world...taught the Grecians the First Order of Buildings...the Greeks ...built...a Great Temple of Apollo at Delphos......"[232] Clare's narrative carried on to pinpoint Rome under Trajan as the epicenter of the application of Hiram Abif's expertise from Jerusalem into Italy. Clare further thought that Masonry declined into Gothicism, a possible allusion to the early Italian epoch of Renaissance and a dig at the prevailing ideology Ramsay combated, i.e. the artisan themes of operative Masonry under Desaguliers. However, it is clear that he linked the survival of the Art of Memory (*Ars Notoria*) to the interplay of antediluvian order, Egypt, the sacrality of the Pyramids through Apollonian *Merkabah* solar symbolism into the legend of an illuminated network of Masons through whom the skills of sacred architecture were preserve and interpreted into a new framework of imperial order.

Clare's vision also underscored the manner in which the performance of ritual *qua* civil orientated ceremonial, albeit esoteric, was interlinked in the Newtonian-Desaguliers-Anderson mindset with law, envisaged as the working out of the collective will of the Pythagorean magus as this role survived from Elizabeth I and James I through the Puritan Revolution which was profoundly iconoclastic. The Egyptian-Roman nexus Clare outlines originates from antediluvian ideas of pristine order preserved within fraternalism, notably in the Friendly Societies (i.e. Odd Fellows, Foresters, Shepherds, etc.) ritual tradition, an echelon within private-public relationships enhanced by the threads of Jakob Boehme's mysticism and Emmanuel Swedenborg's correspondences, the latter with profound Masonic

232 See *A Perjured* (*sic*) *Free Mason Detected* as reprinted in certain editions of the *Constitutions*.

resonance. In turn England generated itself an array of Masonic high degrees apart from France and America, including the Royal Order of Scotland, the oldest extant ritual of this class still being worked by Freemasons. The idea of carefully graded and ranked order applied to Freemasonry's system of degrees of initiation was very close to the suppression of creativity in politics and the workings of the commonwealth at the core of Hanoverian Britain, and arguably the key to understanding Benjamin Franklin's ultimate alienation from his enthusiasm for being an imperial citizen in the run up to the American Revolution. *HIS* Freemasonry was turned against him when he was hailed before Parliament and reprimanded for advocating the single best way he understood for the colonies to remain British, an idea which surely derived from the Craft's *Constitutions* as the working out of a Newtonian regime (Desaguliers-Anderson) within the English *Constitutions*. What he did not anticipate was the intrinsic conservatism of the class system as it encouraged the Monarch toward adventurism within his own networks and how personal ethics of aristocracy,correspondences and allegory notwithstanding, made for the worst interpretation of rank and prestige in private-public affairs. The result was a signal divergence between personal and public action within a society that however it might celebrate the moral hero esoterically and symbolically did not reward the same activity socially or professionally. Clare's vision thus signaled a transition, already at work in the 17th century, whereby principles of initiatic order for the individual were transformed into a working aesthetic for the state as ritual imagery, including the Egyptian-Roman amalgam he described, became a function of national policy. Thus the Masonic underpinnings he envisaged to the dynamic of initiation in the 1730s became by the 1790s a national mission to create a secular extension of Masonic mission into federal policy as it merged Jeffersonian agrarian ideology with Federalist enthusiasms for national banking and restored foreign affairs cooperation with Britain.

What separates Martin Clare's ideology of symbolism from the application of the same mystical hierarchies at work in the surviving hermetical traditions into the nineteenth century is the transformation of the idea of order from personal inspiration into state policy and further into a national civil religion as came to be expressed in the designs of the symbolism of the United States capital the District of Columbia. This movement in another context opened the doors in May 1776 to the development of Illuminism (the occult methodology of the Bavarian Illuminati): the drive to apply sorcery[233] with statecraft as an extension of the correspondence between the political morality of the sovereign and to the individual within a conservative dialectic. It can be argued that DeWitt Clinton's motive for merging the Grand Encampment of Knights Templar ideology and ritual practice was to conceal the operations of his *public sphere* from inquiring minds who found anomalies between; for example, his enthusiasm for Catholic emancipation anticipating what massive Irish immigration might mean to a Protestant top heavy Empire State regime. It would be better to foster the development of an overlapping Catholic and Protestant fraternal unity; as for example the New York founded Elks which became, after the Civil War in which a ritual hierarchy fostered American patriotism, into a mystical fraternal ethos incorporating Roman Catholic and Protestant Masonic ritual along interfaith symbolisms. Such a concept was envisaged early by Clinton and Clintonians through the missiologies of other voluntary societies which incorporated ideas of chivalric monarchy with Republican and Jeffersonian zeal, notably in the origins of the Greek college fraternity system at Union College within Ramée's Enochic iconology (Chapter XI). This meant that to Martin Clare and to Dr. John Desaguliers and his circle that Freemasonry became a strategy in the defense of hierarchy as it made its transition into a modern oligarchic state. This idiom in time meant that monarchy and democracy understood as entitled oligarchy required the insertion of a Republic within the folds of a Monarchy in England and precisely the reverse within the United States. The Catholic element within the Masonic national imagination welcomed such symbolism, as J.J. Ramée's and Latrobe's domed symbolism (within the United States) uniquely achieved with regard to the latter as a secular national patriotic imagery of solar light became policy through state patronage of architects.

Martin Clare's Freemasonry contained within it a trace of divine cosmic order extended to the British imperial polity rooted in pre-Christian

233 Pythagorean Mysticism and the Occult combined with Kabbalah (or Cabala).

antiquity. Thus schemes of millennial and eschatological utopia derived from it where de facto conversion of political sacralities into esoteric order later elucidated into secrets outlined in the legendary history in Anderson's and Desaguliers' *Constitutions*. These esoteric concepts were to come to fruition in the United States of America, itself a Masonic Republic: America as unfolding Logos: the Grand Masonic Royal Arch Word. This in turn was twined with cosmic and astrological Masonic symbolisms associated with the emergence of Enochic solar symbolism, domes and vaults, linked to the Grand Omnificent Royal Arch word as discussed in Salem Town's 1818 treatise and reflected in the entire Clinton-Webb York Rite ritual synthesis. This ideology also complemented parallel ideas coming through Thomas Jefferson's French network of Freemasons, notably John James Beckley, a founder of Phi Beta Kappa college fraternity and member of Williamsburg Lodge No. 6, as well as from Scottish Enlightenment and French sources. These Scottish Enlightenment philosophies and French sources provided the raw material that led to the creation of the Scottish Rite in the Charleston, South Carolina in 1801. The elucidation of the Clare vision of Egyptian-Roman Masonry laid the groundwork interestingly for opposition to state power through the Enlightened Despotism of the late 18th century which equated the spread of Reason with the mission of monarchy. Freemasonry cultivated a pious thread of mystical irrationalism which intermingled with the super-rational wherever it was transmitted which invests in specific Jefferson's Masonic Unitarian circle with symbolic significance. As a result Royal Arch and Pythagorean symbolism made the symbolic designs by J.J. Ramée, Robert Mills, and Benjamin Latrobe all the more significant because it attracted English and American aristocrats, and members of learned societies who saw the Craft as a hedge against despotism. By 1751, divisions between the two interpretations of Freemasonry, pious religious or esoteric and rationalist, result in two contending English Grand Lodges, Antients vs. Moderns, the former of which celebrated the Royal Arch saga as the quintessence of all of Masonic aspiration. It was the merger of this ceremony, nurtured and expanded by Clinton, Webb and Salem Town which met up with and merged with the parallel degree which invested the design of the District of Columbia relevant to the symbolism of the millennial eschatology of the Enochic figure. The Antient metaphor triumphed in the

United States as Modern lodges eclipsed and became tainted with Toryism despite the energies of Benjamin Franklin, a Modern Freemason, who aided in keeping Pennsylvania Modern until 1785.

The divergence of Freemasonry into multiple streams of symbolism, each with its own identity and character, framed the role of the whole Fraternity near the end of the 18th century and early into the 19th century. These various rivers were impacted, in particular, by the English revulsion against Revolutionary France and its associations with secret societies. From 1793 to 1802 the English determination to rely upon constitutional law over and against revolutionary enthusiasm defined its attitude toward the Craft. As a result, by 1813-16, a consensus had been reached whereby it was arranged that there should be a single United Grand Lodge of England with a more or less uniform ritual as a de facto support for all of English civil and moral institutions. The saga is well known. However, there are specific contradictions and ironies obtained in its application. Foremost among these, is the adherence of the American Clinton-Webb synthesis to the losing side of the creation of the United Grand Lodge of England. American Freemasonry adopted the Antient tradition over the Modern for various reasons. Notable among these was that it was more amenable to adapting to the necessities of the Revolution through the adroit placement of the Royal Arch ceremony of exaltation at the apex of the initiatic ladder. This apex displaced the ideal of *the most loyal subject of the Crown* by a paragon view of *citizenship* consistent with high priesthood and monarchy as cast in Old Testament accounts of the building of the Temple of Solomon and its rebuilding through the warrant of Cyrus the Great by Zerubbabel.

Thus, high degree Freemasonry was positioned for a conceptual mission of regeneration from both Clare's (and Ramsay's) ideas about the overall mission of the Fraternity in the regeneration of both the individual and society: the United States as a Masonic, occult Republic. The Egyptian and Templar revival motifs became interwoven as the higher degrees became identified with the revenge theory of seeking the assassins of Hiram Abif and later those responsible for the murder of the last military Grand Master of the Knights Templar, Jacques DeMolay (ca. 1244-1314) in the so-called

Kadosh degrees which were further intertwined with Enochic principles associated with the recovery of the Royal Arch Vault by crusading Templars at the Dome of the Rock in Jerusalem. It was this thread in turn that engaged Masonic ideology with Counter-Reformation theologies at various levels notably a utopianism rooted in a microcosmic ideal capital as central temple unifying papal ideals of Monarchy with republican imagery those a shift of *revenge* ideology from Jacques DeMolay and Hiram Abif to Charles I and the Old Pretender in the image of the *Unknown Superiors*; the core what became known as the Rite of the Strict Observance. The development of the German based Masonic *Rite of the Strict Observance* by Freemason Carl von Hund (1722-1776) in the mid eighteenth century, came to frame the relationship between the imagery of medieval Knights Templar and deeper symbolization of Masonic antiquity rooted in Egyptian and earlier lore to the cause of the lost Stuart monarchy (Jacobitism) of Scotland and England. This thread integrated the Enochic and Pythagorean lore, the latter again rooted in Plato's *Timaeus*, to the rightful King of Scotland as a spiritual and millennial image of Restoration operating at several levels including Counter Reformation political theory, James II was an ardent Roman Catholic, to Melchizedek the priest king of Salem which became central to the Antient ceremony of the Order of High Priesthood, also known as the Order of Melchizedek. In the York Rite it is necessary for a candidate to be the presiding officer, past or present, of a Royal Arch Chapter (i.e. York Rite body) to enter the Order a Melchizedek, a chair degree (see Chapter II). Thus, within European Freemasonry a sequence of ideas developed which understood Egyptian and earlier antiquity to develop which linked Craft degrees through to legitimist political symbolism through a layering of chronology as follows: Clare's Egyptian occultism, Ramsay's Zoroastrian, Mithraic and Egyptian mutation of Greek Pythagorean mysticism integrated with the imagery of the erection of Solomon's Temple construction by Hiram Abif preserved by the suppressed Knight Templar order, the rhetoric of which was attached to the common idealized chivalry shared by Templary with Jacobite restoration. Each thread became intertwined in Charleston, South Carolina, and nearby as this region included elements in Florida integrated the Antient working of the Royal Arch ceremonials, with that of the Scottish Rite, the core of which was the degree of Mark Master Mason midwifed through Haiti and the Caribbean; therefore French and German sources, linked to Irish Freemasonry further linked to Dublin emblemature transferred in parallel form through to Boston, Massachusetts in the Hurd Plate. Both incidents document the conferral of high degrees in Craft lodges which later became separate Royal Arch lodges and merged with the erection of Rites of Perfection subsequently related to the appearance of the Henry Andrew Francken Manuscript in Albany, New York in 1767, the contents of which were summarized in Webb's *Monitor* (1797, 1802). This chronological sequence of European ceremonial appearing in Charleston, S.C., the site of the establishment of the Mother Supreme Council of the world established in 1801 documents a likely conduit impacting both the J.J. Ramée design of the Union College campus and his proposal for the Royal Arch monument of Freemason George Washington, as a Pythagorean Magus, emanating from within a vault as an extension of Enoch as illustrated from Simon Chaudron's sermon depicting this image and as engraved by J. J. Barralet in The *Apotheosis of Washington.*

J.J. Ramée's proposed design for the Washington Monument. It features Washington beneath an archway (cf Enoch) in a symbolic vault as a living Royal Arch Word. Above the statute of Washington is a rising, radiant sun. The design also featured a goddess sculpture, likely Minerva, on the keystone. Image from *Orders from France* by Roger Kennedy.

In conclusion, the identification of this Enochic anomaly, which integrated two differing European traditions becoming Masonically established simultaneously in pre-Revolutionary America, point to a symbolic linkage between the Martin Clare tradition of Masonic imagery and to the Chevalier Ramsay ideology simultaneously. The Masonic Governor of the two Florida British colonies at the time was James Grand who in turn, being Scottish, was linked to Andrew Turnbull, also from Scotland, who attempted to organize the largest British colony in North America at New Smyrna Beach, Florida, 1763-1783. This would have placed him in the highest echelon of British colonial administration with the title of Provincial Grand Master of a Provincial Grand Lodge of the Southern District of North America with units in Pensacola, Florida, and Charleston, South Carolina (later under Pennsylvania warrant and charter) and in St. Augustine Florida during the period within which Freemasonry became increasingly identified with Masonic intellectual and imperial currents throughout the empire as an extension of the cosmologic and astrologic imagery linking the expansion of Freemasonry to the symbolism of enlightened politics in the 18th century. James' Grand Lodge emanated from the Grand Lodge of Scotland. The movement of this Lodge's authorization from Scotland through into Philadelphia, where T. S. Webb was himself exalted a Royal Arch Mason, underscores symbolic and political linkages between the Jacobites and the New World because of the sentimental and symbolic links between the lore of the 1715 and 1745 revolts against England to restore the same and in turn the triumphalist ties between France and Scotland at the core of Thomas Jefferson's network linking the Scottish Enlightenment to the liberal and Universalist anti-Calvinist theories of Ramsay to French Masonic ritual ideology. It is significant, further, that this Scottish Lodge conferred the Order of the Red Cross, the theme of which depicts the symbolic linkage between the Persian emperor Cyrus the Great as an irenic pagan Prince with the Hebrew governor Zerubbabel, the central figure in Thomas Smith Webb's Royal Arch exaltation ceremony. This vignette ideologically underscored the symbolic linkage between and among Zoroastrian and Mithraic symbolism by implication from the Persian religion to Jacobite ideas of the Catholic Knights Templar Red Cross, also a reference to the Cross of St. George in legitimist imagery, through its association Knights (or Order) of the Garter (ca. 1348) and its own association with British imperial expansion propagated by Elizabethan occultist and magus Dr. John Dee. Next, the impact of Masonic ritual.

CHAPTER VI

1717 AND THE IMPACT OF RITUAL

Christ Church, Lord Herbert of Cherbury, Deism, Pythagoras, Zoroaster, Melchizedek, King David, and Scotland

"The worship of the sun was inevitable, and its deification was the source of all idolatry in every part of the world. It was the sunrise that inspired the first prayers uttered by man, calling him to acts of devotion, bidding him raise an altar and kindle sacrificial flames."
- William Tyler Olcott, *Sun Lore of All Ages*, 1914.

"The communication of this knowledge and other secrets, some of which are perhaps lost, constituted, under other names, what we now call *Masonry*, or *Free* or *Frank-Masonry*. That knowledge was, in one sense, *the Lost Word*, which was made known to the Grand Elect, Perfect, and Sublime Masons."
- Albert Pike, *Morals and Dogma of the Scottish Rite of Freemasonry*, 1871.

Masonic ritual documents the restoration of the sun (i.e. Worshipful Master ruling in the east and solar symbolism associated with the Grand Omnificent Royal Arch Word-Logos) as a dominant icon in the design of imperial administration, machinery, notably solar and stellar chronometers for navigation (cf. treatise *General and Rare Memorials pertaining to the Perfect Arte of Navigation* by Dr. John Dee), and in political metaphor. "Masonry is a march and struggle toward the Light. For the individual as well as the nation, Light is Virtue, … Intelligence, Liberty."[234] Solar symbolism, in specific, was at the core of Masonic Lodge governance as the Worshipful Master (sitting in the east) in the company with two Wardens (sitting in the south and west) who all *ruled and governed the lodge* as the sun governed and ruled the day and the planetary system. "Enthroned in the radiant East, the worshipful master is the "Light" of his lodge–the representative of the gods, one of that long line of hierophants who, through the blending of their rational powers with the reason of the ineffable, have been accepted into the great school."[235] This vernacular echoed and imitated parish governance as the Rector or Vicar worked with two Wardens to order and regulate the moral and spiritual quality and content of community affairs in resonant comity with the Sovereign, the Supreme Governor, of the Church. The French cult of personality of Louis XIV, the Sun King, presaged the more subtle English development of this idea which definitively erected solar imagery as a common denominator for the harmonious inter-working of a progressive industrial-based science and a beneficent and harmonious philanthropic social order. The integration of Elizabethan court culture and Copernican theory effectively concealed hermetical and cabalistic notions of mysticality within a revival of chivalry made fresh after the Hanoverian accession along with the Church of England that provided the liturgy that defined material culture of official piety through the Book of Common Prayer of 1549. The result was a form of modern new age Mithraism, a new cult of *Sol Invictus*, in which Masonic initiation was deemed to be a leavening device within society which integrated loyalism and its fabric with Anglican reworking of the monastic offices and Lutheran -Calvinistic approaches to soteriology (study of salvation within various religious doctrines) without rigid conformity. The Anglican mentality at the Archbishop of York Cardinal Wolsey's (ca. 1473-1530) Christ Church (1525, founded as Cardinal College), Oxford, England defines the period during the formation of Premier Grand Lodge of England which mixed legitimist Stuart and empirical Hanoverian ideologies. These seemingly opposing concepts were however reconciled by the very non-confessional nature of Matthew Parker's *Thirty-nine Articles of Religion,* 1563, defining the

234 Pike, Albert, *Morals and Dogma of the Ancient and Accepted Scottish Rite,* page 32.
235 Hall, Manly Palmer, *Lectures on Ancient Philosophy*, page 454.

Anglican doctrine which made much of uniformity of liturgical practice without insistent consistency of belief. Architecturally, the House of Convocation (1634-1637, vaulted ceiling dates from approximately 1759; see Plate XIII) in the Bodleian Library at Oxford University bore a striking resemblance to the earliest rendering of a deistic-solar Masonic lodge structure which in turn can be traced to English modifications of monastic choir hierarchy. This thread came to be modified from narrow parallel benches with directional chairs: east (Worshipful Master, rising sun), west (Senior Warden, setting sun), and south (Junior Warden, sun at high meridian) etc., as Sir Christopher Wren applied the hierarchical symbolism of academic and ecclesiastical aesthetics in the circular, semi-domed Sheldonian Theatre at Oxford (built 1664-1668) and the domed St. Paul's Cathedral, London according to Vitruvian and Palladian imagery of radiant solar light as a metaphor both for intellectual as well as spiritual enlightenment. It was this incremental imagery which Freemasonry took up in its celebration of Augustinian carryovers from Ptolemaic and Hellenistic Egypt as Roman imagery was transformed through Oxford intellectuality into a British visual vocabulary of imperial and conciliar rule. In turn Christ Church's great Tom Quadrangle would come to feature its central monument: the pagan Hermes the Philosopher or Mercury (cf. Thoth Hermes Mercurius Trismegistus) fountain, which is a copy of a sculpture by Giambologna (1529-1608), given to the college in 1928, and its perfected symmetry adjoining the medieval cathedral and its monastic cluster now converted to private residences. The seventeenth century construction pained to preserve consistent imagery of otherwise discordant elements as a seamless web of academic order.

Masonic ritual quickly moved, in the 18th century, to the two related dynamics of pansophism and the restoration of antediluvian knowledge. These threads of symbolism suffuse Masonic lawmaking through specific provisions of the *Constitutions* which deal with the regularity of authority as derived from the core symbol of King Solomon's Temple. This edifice is the defining emblem of Freemasonry and a paragon image with expressed and implied concepts relative to the application of the legendary wisdom of the monarch and his warrant to build the Temple to God. The identification of the ineffable name of God with the Ark of the Covenant in the Temple's Holy of Holies is worked ceremonially in such ways that the possession and recovery of the precise pronunciation of God's name becomes identified with solar imagery via the Royal Arch degree certificate: the Hurd Plate. Further the possession of this name becomes the warrant for the building of the Temple both as a moral teaching device as a matter of symbolic architectural practicality. Desaguliers is chiefly responsible for this equivalency. He was personally convinced that the Newtonian system of cosmography incorporated the finest elements of physical learning and mystical numinosity and worked assiduously to integrate what was fast becoming by 1717 the defining emblemature of modernity, the sun centered planetary system, as a spiritual model and intellectual template for perfection.

This quality of symbolic reference integrated core elements of imperial political policy relative to sacral kingship, construction of monumental architecture, roads, canals and the tools necessary for defense and warfare as an extension of geometric order, linking terrestrial to celestial design. As a political and literary rhetoric, the Desaguliers-Anderson traditional history leads into rules of order structured to advance empire through commerce and is consistent with the epoch of the East India Company and its associated vice regalisms for which Christ Church members became noted in the 18th and 19th centuries. The Masonic *Constitutions* therefore provided the laws necessary to manage elites through reference to Egyptianate imagery as a parallel and presumably as an alternative to canon law as the Enlightenment eroded both personal belief and religious supports for aristocracy. Yet, its multi-layered imagery and symbolic appointments made it possible to extrapolate a variety of oligarchic and even autocratic formulations within the ideology of tolerant equality uniquely in England which came to forbid religion and politics from official Masonic deliberations when other nations notably in France and its neighbors used Freemasonry as an overt form of political progressivism. Thus, as England discouraged the more mystical and resonant elements of Masonic ceremonial notably in what came to be known as the higher degrees or *haute* grades, the same degrees of rank and ritual became repositories elsewhere of deep trenches of alchemical, chivalric, hermetical and kabbalistic-cabalistic lore.

What is less evident is how this objective was accomplished within Masonic ceremonials. This is a complex yet transparent event within which all of knowledge came to be recapitulated with reference to the seven liberal arts, the medieval *Trivium* (grammar, logic, and rhetoric) and *Quadrivium* (arithmetic, astronomy, music, and geometry) in the second degree of the tri-gradual system, the Degree of Fellowcraft. This degree instructs the candidate in the meaning of the design of the Middle Chamber of the Temple, a likely allusion to the Anglican *via media* (middle ground; generally associated with Reformed Protestantism and Roman Catholicism), within which reason and mystical revelation are intertwined and consolidated. The candidate is led to a winding staircase which is structured as a mnemonic device upon which structured learning leads to a pathway to the Holy of Holies. Within the continental array of the higher degrees, the reaccession of lost wisdom is achieved through the discovery of a lost chamber of secrets which contain the key to the pronunciation of the ineffable name in the Royal Arch of Enoch degree which was likely formulated in its present form between 1737 and 1767 when it appears in Albany, New York from French Masonic sources most likely derived from Scotland through Jacobite circles and networks. Both of these ceremonies allude to the arch-martyr of Freemasonry tacitly though substantively: Hiram Abif whose refusal to betray the possession and pronunciation of the Masonic Word precipitates his death at the hands of the three ruffians. Masonic law, of which the *Constitutions* are the epicenter, guards and protects this essential concept as both a rational exposition and as a mysticated icon in the same way that canon law guards and protects the amnesias of the Eucharist as the *sin qua non* of Church experience and teaching.

* * * * *

By 1543 specific scientific discoveries were in place as a means to link the solar symbolism of Christ Church, Oxford as an imperial recreation of Cardinal's Thomas Wolsey's college as a means to interconnect the ideal of sage monarchy with the religious element of Renaissance science. This maneuver implied a substitution of Solomonic law giving for Roman

Catholic magisterium under the new Tudor Regime as noted by Oxford scholar Penry Williams whose work captured the essential premise of the Henrician Settlement (1535) as a unified religious and political paradigm. Further, the insinuation of Solomon as a metaphor and symbol for Henry himself implied specific Renaissance ideals of the so-called Oxford humanists, who migrated from England to Italy and back, investing such figures as Thomas More (1478–1535) with the technical and literary skills to address issues of the change in regimes. It is a sad irony of this era that More's Catholic triumphalism and subsequent martyrdom anticipated Thomas Cranmer's (1489-1556) death some years later just as Renaissance learning took hold of the Oxford mentality as a bridge between science and religion. Prior to Cranmer and going back to Thomas Elyot (1490-1546), through More to William Grocyn (1446?-1519), William Lilye (ca. 1468 -1522), and Hugh Latimer (ca. 1487-1555) of whom Thomas Linacre (1460-1524), was a common mentor; humanism and its followers were an isolated if influential minority at Oxford originating with the creation of Duke Humphrey's library within the Bodleian. Such minds adulated the princely ideal of a learned sovereign who possessed, as articulated in the Masonic legendary histories, an initiatic ruler who possessed divine secrets and imparted them with the help and agency of select courtiers in the application of the law as both a social and philosophical current rooted in cosmological concepts of harmony and celestial order.

The reception of the Scientific Revolution at Oxford has been well documented via rich learning, publication, and the collection of scientific instruments from medieval times to the seventeenth century at the Museum of the History of Science. Less well known is the degree to which the creation of the English Masonic orders following the establishment of the premier Grand Lodge in London June 24, 1717 parallels the development of English ecclesiastical law as an amalgam of theological vision and institutional necessity. The Lutheran Reformation, in specific, set the tone for Thomas Cranmer's approach to the governance of England through the integration of liturgy and Eucharistic mysticality through Reformed Confessionalism as a means to structure subjective inspiration as rational law giving. At Oxford, this thread became allied with the work of Christ Church Student (Fellow)

John Theophilus Desaguliers, a disciple of Isaac Newton who with English Presbyterian Minister James Anderson devised the Masonic *Constitutions* in two editions, 1723 and 1738, which sought to govern the freshly minted Craft along lines comprehensible to establishment Christians as a proto-universalistic and rational scientific ethic. This work is important as a case study in the application of quasi-mystical rationality, or numinosity to polity as an extension of millennial prophecy. In specific, Freemasonry emerging ritual integrated the Lutheran and Erastian drive for princely patronage with rational religiosity as a means to extend an ethic of solar imagery and physics. At Oxford, this amalgam was uniquely articulated symbolically by the juxtaposition of the site of Thomas Cranmer's martyrdom and Wadham College, the seedbed of the Royal Society's antecedent, the Invisible College, and more recently by Wren's Sheldonian Theatre flanked by the old University of Oxford Press building, now the Museum of the History of Science. The Invisible College included men of letters such as natural philosopher Robert Hooke (1635 - 1703), architect Christopher Wren, gardener and diarist John Evelyn (1620 - 1706), and mathematician John Wallis (1616 - 1703). The Invisible College incorporated elements of Rosicrucianism: the concept of new enlightened spiritual men ushering in a new age of enlightenment through scientific experimentation is clearly paralleled in the *Confesio Fraternitatis*. The Invisible College birthed the Royal Society which was founded 1660 with Charles II as its patron and sponsor. In turn the Lutheran concept of princely administration of the church made explicit in the Peace of Westphalia of 1648 anticipated the Masonic legal

1905 postcard of the Martyrs' Memorial, St. Giles, Oxford. The monument commemorates the Protestant Martyrs Thomas Cranmer (Archbishop of Canterbury), Nicholas Ridley (Archbishop of London), and Hugh Latimer (Bishop of Worcester) who, when Catholic Bloody Mary Tudor came to the throne, were summoned to appear before a commission in the Church of St. Mary the Virgin in Oxford to be examined for their alleged Protestant heresies. Unable to admit to a belief in transubstantiation, they were all found guilty and executed.

celebration of Solomonic monarchy and royal patronage. As such from 1737 the genealogical descent of Masonic kingship became a standard feature of the Grand Lodge of England's policy to attract princely patronage as derived from earlier legends of kingship in the *Old Charges-Gothic Manuscripts* from which the traditional histories of Masonry were traced in the *Constitutions*. After this date, when the Frederick, Prince of Wales was initiated into Masonry in 1737 by Dr. Desaguliers, an Erastian ethos emerged whereby the ritual role of King Solomon was compared to the Worshipful Master, a rising sun. This metaphor served the legal function making Masonic solar law derived from the mystical interplay of ordinances and divine rulership mediated by and through popular assemblages of the Craft dating back, according to Masonic lore, to King Athelstan the Glorious who, with the defeat of Gofraid the Norse-Gael King of Dublin at York in 927-928, unified England for the first time in 954 CE.

Like Church law, the Masonic *Constitutions* were codified in light of the end purpose of a millennial system such as Christian eschatology but accommodatingthe social and symbolic use of Isaac Newton's heliocentricity as a paragon for the ideal political commonwealth which Freemasonry claimed to advance as a band of brothers committed to universal toleration and millennial peace. Freemasonry's dynamic initiative mirrored Anglican and to a lesser extent Roman Catholic Canon Law through a substitution of secular solar based deism for evangelical and reformed catholic ecclesiology as inherited from the Act of Settlement of 1535 and its intellectual precursors notably Sir John Fortescue's *De Laudibus Legum Angliae*. The Desaguliers and Anderson's *Constitutions* make it possible to link the governance of the Tudor Commonwealth at its formal and cultural levels, notably in the recrudescence of chivalric civility, as a path to the etiquette of the law as it was introduced into the United States prior to the establishment of the faculty of jurisprudence at the Harvard Law School in 1819. The founder of this law school, arguably the premier such institution in the Western Hemisphere, Simon Greenleaf was a noted Masonic author whose works echo the Desaguliers and Anderson legacy and anticipate the thought of his later successor Roscoe Pound whose work framed the epoch of juristic and legislative activism at the outset of the 20th century.

The permeation of society through Freemasonry, of the solar rooted mechanistic model for human existence, is belied by Freemasonry's rhetoric of human liberty and toleration. These latter ideals while not absent from its legacy, and, in fact the chief evidence of its political relevancy to the French and American Revolutions, inter alia, believe the imposition of a stringent hierarchy of theophanous numinosity and rationality of a system of meaning which only gradually and incrementally came to define and shape modernity. Its impetus far predates the origin of the institution. Rather it is to pre-Masonry the concepts and ideas which made it possible, to which Masonic law owes its civilization and theological potency. No single church or government was or is capable of acting effectively to stop or curtail the power of its transformative influence precisely because of its role as a self-contained regimentation of a much broader intellectual history. It represents the most evidently self-conscious element of modernity as the distillate of deeper and broader currents of ideas which exist in archaeological layerings of symbolic strata. This quality enabled scientists, who proactively embraced the society through universities and academies, under the watchful patronal eyes of emperors and kings who were only too eager to identify their diminishing sacrality with new forms of rational magism. Therein lay the profound appeal of Freemasonry to monarchs of all sorts, from London through India to Hawaii and conspicuously to the American Presidency.

Following the precedent of canon law, Masonic law became a moral aseity: a self-authenticating plenitude within which acceptance into the Fraternity or expulsion from it assumed the parallel significance of baptism and excommunication. As the four small lodges united into the premier Grand Lodge in 1717, it became clear that like Catholicism Masonry was a theonomous institution within its moral authority was claimed in theory to be without restriction or limitation and unmediated from its god, the Great Architect of the Universe. This feature distinguished itself from the heteronymous feature of cultural and political Protestantism which from the Peace of Westphalia (1648) moved into pre-denominational status as religious allegiance in Germany was attached to the belief of the ruling prince, and therefore non-unitary in its derivation of ecclesiology and theology.

Masonic law, after 1717, was directed at the regulation of communion with legitimate and regular authority. This further feature has in part defined the history of Freemasonry through its constitutions, monitors, and obediences. These have in turn excluded others on the grounds of non-adherence to Masonry's traditional landmarks and accepted standards of common practice, such as belief in a Supreme Being. Planetary-based mechanism was mapped out symbolically within these perimeters in such specific ways that organic and existential human features were removed from the planes of idealized moral authority. It is significant that Desaguliers' son became Master of (Naval) Ordnance at Deptford since it was through the mechanization of military technology through artillery that imperialism was finally developed as an extension of regimentation of strategic bombardment. In time, Freemasonry became uniquely attached to Army regiments and as such passed into Kipling-esque legend, notably in the novella devoted to Freemasonry, *The Man Who Would Be King.*

The codification of Masonic law therefore was designed to regulate the affairs of the Fraternity as it took up the championship of a new, scientific world view with religious significance. As such, this effort was addressed to threads of symbolism within the ritual which itself developed from medieval sources into more elaborate forms in various stages moving toward a tri-gradual system within which ascribed rank was intermingled with elective and appointive office. These elements were extrapolated not only from esoteric sources but from, as has been noted, narratives of legendary history which alluded to the ritual proving a unifying thread of lore and saga establishing a warrant for the codification process. In the Desaguliers-Anderson *Constitutions*, this warrant derives from Egypt through the transmission of the Art and Science of Geometry in the hands of Ptolemy the Astronomer, Euclid, Archimedes, and Pythagoras through whom the mystery and divinity of numbers was transmitted to Greece. The core reference is to Mizraim or "Mitzraim," the Hebrew name for Egypt, and the title of an important 18th century Masonic Rite of initiatory ceremonies.

* * * * *

From its origin Freemasonry developed as an institution a set of laws, termed *Constitutions* (1723, 1738), the purpose of which was to govern the organization as well as the conduct of its members. These laws were rooted in a concept of ritual order linking tacit assumptions about the role of the individual in society and in England reflected larger issues about the significance of science in the organization of culture. The English Premiere Grand Lodge (1717) uniquely incorporated the principles relative to the politics of the Whig Party during the reign of the German Dynasty, the Hanoverians, which inherited the legitimate right through the Stuart line in the Protestant succession as provided for in the Revolution of 1688 deposing Roman Catholics from the monarchy. The English Grand Lodge further incorporated principles linking the ideas of physicist Isaac Newton to political order, Newtonianism: a pure and clean-looking empirical experimental science at one level contained within it deeper environs of symbolism and speculation rooted in English philosophical empiricism notably associated with John Locke and David Hume (1711–1776). Whilst there were earlier important elements within the framework of the socio-political synthesis reflected in the laws of the premier Grand Lodge it is clear that the position of England in world affairs in 1717, the year the Grand Lodge was instituted on June 24th, is reflected in the nature of the organization and its mission. Here it is important to understand that what the Grand Lodge said about Freemasonry and what it represented to society were not the same. From the outset, discussions of religion (i.e. confessional theology) and politics (partisan issues) were outlawed. However, there is little question that philosophical deism and liberal establishment views of social and economic organization, both dominated the Grand Lodge as it emerged as an aristocratic institution in synthesis with both the intellectual and political leadership among the national elites. It was this elitism, which further reflected associations between the Grand Lodge, the Royal Society, the premier scholarly organization of the day; and of the Royal Family, that shaped and informed the cultural context within which Freemasonry moved.

As a result Freemasonry and the Grand Lodge of 1717 became functionally a nonconfessional although ideological church within a church in countries which had established religions, such as England, Scotland, France, and Austria, exercising moral autonomy above and apart from the established liturgical forms yet allied in various ways with these forms by means of patronage patterns and intellectual activity. As the Scientific Revolution progressed it assumed the role of cultic center for solar cosmology and its concomitant Reason as Reason itself was made an icon for a universal moral initiative through which civilization might be transformed into a new millennial era of learning and peace. Important elements of theodicy were addressed in this process in the erosion of mysticality and numinosity as overt formulations as Masons came to view revealed religion as a cover for superstition. The reception of the scientific mindset within institutions such as Christ Church, Oxford, in specific provided elites with the symbolic weaponry to hold contradiction between the rational and mystical in tension and more pointedly to create hierarchies of differentiation and management for the ordering of values to accommodate tradition and innovation within the folds and confines of inherited order. It can be argued that duplicity and disingenuity were the price of such accommodations as learning was made to serve vested interests of the English monarch in its conflicts with Calvinism and empiricism. At Oxford, Christ Church played host to Charles I in refuge from Oliver Cromwell and his New Model Army; Christ Church matriculated the great John Locke whose ideas provided the seedbed for modern contractual democratic theory.

With this feature of Masonry in mind, i.e., that it attempted to *freeze* a specific view of English society circa 1717, what has been termed an end to ideology, it should be referenced that before and after 1717, currents of ideas impacted the official Masonic mission. As important as Newtonianism was to society, the intellectual period before Newton's influence was dominated by efforts to frame and support the survival of ideas relative to the survival of Renaissance ideas in the face of Jacobite intrusions to alter the national Constitution. In brief this was the major achievement by Freemasonry to contain within its circle of influence the preservation of Biblical, medieval, Renaissance itself, and Enlightenment ideas in dynamic ways such that a layering of symbolism took place to which the end of ideology premise was moved officially within Grand Lodge but with reference to much earlier public issues of policy and matters of private spiritual definition. At this point it is critical to make a differentiation between Masonry as an official institution and Masonry as a current of ideas. It is the second feature of the Fraternity and its ritual content that reflects the two great challenges to the nation before 1717: 1) the disruption of the nation by the English Civil War; and 2) the efforts by political forces associated with papal Roman Catholicism to alter the Constitution from the top (e.g. the Monarchy down). Both of these disruptive forces stemmed from the same source, the unique political nature of the English Reformation which bracketed theological controversy in its linkages with politics against two contending forces: the Puritan (Calvinist) power related to religious dissent from the established Church of England; and to continentally rooted Catholic ideas of Counter-Reformation, related to the threat of regicide and to military intervention as further threatened by the menace of the Spanish Armada when a European power attempted unsuccessfully to reverse the achievement of the English parliamentary Reformation settlement.

The immediate threat to the ideology, advocated by the premier Grand Lodge, was the threat of a second French-based invasion of Great Britain, likely again through Ireland as previously in 1690, under Jacobite auspices. This meant a consolidated force threatening de facto, as in 1588, to English minds, to reverse the political settlement of the English Reformation, restoring Roman Catholic influence to London based rule. The 1715 efforts to achieve this event just following the death of the last Stuart monarch, Queen Anne, excited traditional fears that the Catholic Church in alliance with the France of Louis XIV and XV sought to reject the internal English Constitutional settlement of 1688, the Glorious Revolution, in the name of securing independence for Scotland. Between 1715 and the next such threat in 1745 a Scots Catholic, The Chevalier Andrew Michael Ramsay, articulated a countervailing ideology for Freemasonry in Europe, with decisive French and German implications which held up Catholic triumphalism as the core mythic source for Masonic ritual through the exaltation of ritual chivalry itself telescoped retroactively into pre-Christian notably Persian and Egyptian symbolism. It seems clear that this effort was an extended effort to create a new form of Freemasonry which appeared, in a pre-critical scholarly age of sorts, as a much older version of Masonry rooted in Catholic apologetics, the sources of which are unclear; but of course need to be made more clearly so. It is therefore to Jacobite nuanced French Freemasonry to which one must turn to understand the alternatives to the English Grand Lodge's ideology specifically because it was the Scots Ramsay who lifted up, albeit for propaganda purposes, Renaissance and medieval threads as they appear in Masonic *haute* degree symbolism which led to the greatly amplified role of Freemasonry in continental European cultural affairs, notably the iconic significance of the Royal Arch of Enoch degree: the 13th in the present sequence of Scottish Rite ceremonials and 7th in the York Rite.

The result of both of these threats defined the creation of the dominant Masonic ideology of 1717, Deism. This was a current of theological ideas associated with two premier English intellects: Edward Herbert, Lord of Cherbury and John Toland. Toland advocated a cultural respite from religiously shaped political controversy through a restoration of secular pagan values apart from sectarian controversy which survived as an undercurrent within Grand Lodge ideology. This never entirely goes away but serves within official Masonry to reinforce the proscription against discussion of religion and politics in lodges. Herbert anticipated the seminal works of Hobbes, Descartes and Locke in the positioning of philosophy to merge with pre-Masonic ideas through its Enlightenment tendrils. William Preston, who invoked John Locke's name and work in his *Illustrations*, in specific borrowed into the new framework of nascent empiricism to justify the method of his own educational approach to ritual. This in effect subdued the mythological, numinous, and mystical elements of Freemasonry to lift up its pedagogical qualities in the origination of the generic class of *Monitors*. Dermott and Webb both took up this concept, Dermott before Preston, in the creation of the *Ahiman Rezon*, the Antient Monitor; as did Webb, whose book had the same name as Preston's, *Illustrations*. Herbert also developed a concept of providential continuity as available in various views of Isaac Newton theories of physics and cosmology wherein the intelligence was guided providentially from darkness into *Light*, wisdom, in harmonious ways to construct a commonwealth of irenic peace.

The Lord Herbert of Cherbury (ca. 1582-1648) thereby is instrumental to comprehending the dynamic of the symbolization process, as opposed to its precise content within this tapestry of emblematic evidence pointing to the origin of the Ramsay ideology. Parallel to John Bunyan (162 -1688) he provided the subject matter which related the higher degree formulations from the greater field of non-Christian religious observance without the complexities of having to untangle their theological import. Such de facto secularization made it possible to forge a system of morality without the necessity of ecclesiological institutions thus proving elites with the raw material necessary to achieve a moral edge within society without the risks of confessional or doctrinal conflicts. Cherbury, whose work shaped and informed a current of radical pantheistic and deistic thought which can be traced to Giordano Bruno's celebration of pre-Reformation Catholic mysticism and which influenced the writing of the *Pantheisticon* of John Toland, whom influenced a thread of deistic and pre-Christian Masonic symbolism that in turn influenced Thomas Paine and Thomas De Quincey. Each of these cultivated the principle of Druidism understood as a legacy (or comparatively) of Ancient Egypt, which thanks to Herbert, filtered into the style of Zoroastrian thought that the Chevalier Ramsay utilized to develop the ideology of the high degrees. The perimeters of this transition can in turn be drawn such that Elizabethan and Jacobean cultural resistance to the triumph of Puritanism, which Bruno insisted was responsible for the erosion of irenic mysticality which could extend the irenicism developing in the France of Henry III to create a pan Anglican-Gallican Catholicism; a policy friendly to the Reformation yet opposed to the Hispano-Papalism of ultramontane thinking in the sixteenth century. In other words Herbert's philosophies were a first cousin to Giordano Bruno's assertiveness about the pragmatism of mysticality as a bridge between pre-Reformation Catholicism and Protestantism. It offered the convenience of accommodating national icons, such as Minerva as Britannia, within the pantheon of imagery available to nation states who sought the consummation of imperial vision in opposition to the Vatican-Spanish coalition to defeat Protestantism, Nationalism, as well as Anglican and Gallican (French Catholic Church) energies to remain both Roman Catholic and irenic.

To Herbert it can be traced a legacy of irenic thinking about antiquity and its usefulness in policy issues. As such it developed a strategic conceptuality linking the English Renaissance to the unfolding of Joachimite elements in Masonry which were both co-opted through Jesuit imperial theory (as a Counter-Reformation ploy) and in turn were midwifed into American civil religion. These parameters can be demarcated generally as follows: The Humanist incursion into England from Northern Italy, notably Bologna, but including a seedbed associated with the Cornaro family and Palladian villa design in Venetia in the early 18th century. The heroization of early English Catholic humanists, notably Thomas Linacre, and his circle of Oxford Reformers Hugh Latimer, William Grocyn, William Lilye, John Colet (1467-1519), and their epigones, notably Thomas Elyot, the author of English civility found in his *Boke named the Governour*. This matrix of ideas developed further within the Anglican Settlement in the works of Richard Hooker vis-a-vis Thomas Cartwright (1535-1603), within which ecclesiastical law became a medium through which hermetical and cabalistic ideas developed as a further legacy of the English Renaissance, suppressed during the English Civil War by the Puritans, but which survived in New England and in Britain through careful efforts to insert esoteric concepts of pagan antiquity within the traditions which coalesced with pre-Masonic intellectual currents.

Freemasonry, arguably, is only possible within a context in which a universal ethic prevails. Its singular achievement in western history was to generate a body of moral ideas implemented in various ways into policy to be expressed in institutional embodiment which transcended the conventional governmental and religious institutions of the day. Herbert's essay, *De Religious Gentilium*, points not only to the hermetical foundation of his work but his anticipation of the ideological consistency between mythological secular mysticism *qua* the empiricism implicit in René Descartes and John Locke, but also laid the groundwork which documented the associations between the origins of nominalism as a unique ontology for the modern world view of experimental science. This world view, contrary to what might be conventionally expected, is neither lingering superstition nor the false numinosity sometimes associated with romantic notions of sentimentalism applied to nostalgia for a lost past. Rather, as Herbert demonstrates in a sensate and palpable way reconnects words and things through the medium of Neo-Platonism which viewed the words in ritual as a discrete epistemology and metaphysic. In this quality, he retained medievalism and laid the groundwork for carrying into Enlightenment modernity a sense of the vitality of mythologically rooted ceremonial symbolism.

Herbert's concept was that mythic words might disclose both the essence and the experience of reality, as it might have been preserved and recapitulated through Enochic *Ars Notoria* methods. In this direction, he replicates important elements of medieval writers such as Dionysius the Areopgaite, *De Divinis Nominibus*; and St. Thomas Aquinas, *De Naturae Verbi Intellectus*, *Summa Theologica Quaestio* XIII, Part I. Herbert's insight explains not only how ritual imagery drawn from mythology or comparative religion might have remained vitalistic if not pantheistic into the early modern era but also how elites and clerisies within the Masonic penumbra preserved and celebrated a confidence in their literal existence. The Masonic thread in Mozart is a case in point. Such figures as Mozart's Masonic friend and mentor, Ignaz von Born, a pansophist in 1790s Vienna took up this concept. He was widely thought to be the model and prototype for Sarastro, a Zoroastrian[236] magus from Mozart's *The Magic Flute*, and was a member of the Illuminati as master of its Vienna Lodge. Von Born's career was quintessentially anti-Jesuitical (despite being educated by them); it stood as witness against religious fanaticism; integrated within his writings are scientific treatises, satires on the clergy,[237] and essays on Egyptian symbolism. In this, he sought to midwife and cocreate a Masonic college of magi within the official lodge he was Master, *True Harmony,*[238] the object of which was to institute the performance of Masonic ritual as a restoration of the virtuality of mythology.

Herbert proceeded on the idea, as did the hermetic philosophers, that truth was law in a presumed harmony between the self and the object, a construct which deeply informed the Enlightenment notion of finding truth in symbolism. His work carried this premise from the Renaissance

236 The name "Sarastro" is derived from the word Zoroaster.
237 His work *Monachologien* published in 1783 suggested monks were a hybrid offspring of apes and men.
238 Later named New Crowned Hope.

into the 18th century. He believed that all sense perceptions ought to conform to objects as the microcosm conformed to the macrocosm. This harmoniousness between subject and symbol, it seems, came to lay the foundation for Freemasonry's conventional respectability as the "coolness" of Enlightenment and 19th century Victorian respectability domesticated the potentially fiery enthusiasm of Bruno's speculations and later of the imagination of Romanticism as Freemasonry came under Royal patronage thanks in large part to Dr. Desaguliers' strategy of development of the Grand Lodge. It also paved the way for the de facto support of Masonic rituality by the Church of England establishment as enthusiasm was truncated and the rational conscience prevailed among Masonic educators, notably William Preston and T. S. Webb. Herbert developed his view *of Truth* therefore not only as a primal consistency between the human self and its ability to reach out for symbolization through ritual mythography and mythology given the precision of the definition of the individual symbols conjoining the earth and its inhabitants, but also cultivate an interior capacity to perceive the essential harmony between the human organism fashioned as in the external world so as to create an interior lodge or court of consciousness. The Masonic ritual came to deal with the ritual expression of preparation in terms of a preparation of or in the heart as a psychological and spiritual anteroom parallel to the actual preparation chamber in the lodge within which the affinity for symbolic truth was achieved prior to seek institutional recognition. By defining truth as a certain harmony between objects and their analogous faculties Herbert not only established Masonic mysticality along more rational grounds than magic or superstition but invested the Masonic method symbolic instruction but also established a mindset in which different kinds of truth were structured and could be ceremonially arrayed in an ascending scale: truth of the thing; of appearance; of concept; and of intellect. It is not known, precisely, where and when Freemasonry came to define initiatory ceremonial into firmly assigned graded degrees. However, it seems likely that the categories of its harmonious transition came to comply with Neo-Platonism and its cognate theories of morality as a great chain of being to thinkers such as Herbert, whom, saturated with the Elizabethan world view, transferred such degrees and grades as they perceived to conform both to the structure of society and to the structure of human cognition. In Herbert's instance, he carefully differentiated such a degree system to be grounded in social and mental reality through a range of discrete categories.

Herbert's search for general principles of truth derived from mythology, which he developed in his work *De veritate, prout distinguitur a revelatione, a verisimili, a possibili, et a falso* (a/k/a *De Veritate*) was open to identification by Freemasons for the search and restoration of the Lost Word of a Master Mason. In this type of initiative, both Herbert and Sir Francis Bacon (1561 1629), sought the rejection of medieval Aristotelianism; as such were in agreement in what likely were objections on epistemological grounds to the Counter-Reformation and therefore to the Jesuit agenda. For Herbert, it is clear that natural science did not entail modern divisions between the natural world and rationality. *De Veritate*, rather, encoded an equivalency between the law of nature and the laws of God which still prevails in Masonic ritual, preserved since the eighteenth century, and likely earlier. Herbert influenced jurist and philosopher Hugo Grotius (1583-1645) and, as such, his work on war and peace called *De Jure Belli ac Pacis*, and thereby inspired Masonic legalists such as Clinton, Ephraim Kirby, Simon Greenleaf, and eventually Roscoe Pound. This quality can actually be found within Aristotelianism albeit through humanistic and stoic thought which under the influence of jurists determined European intellectual history and its direction. In this context the proliferation of lodges through the American national pioneering frontier frequently anticipated the arrival of formal governance and religion as extended into the District of Columbia, shaped by the Baroque imagination with Neoclassical Architecture, influence the interplay of moral sanctified power into the national destiny.

Thus, Herbert's work and Freemasonry came both to support the accident of an analogy between pre-established harmony; and between the subject and symbol which provided Freemasons at the level of method of viewing mythology as real without risking the charge of credulosity and intemperate intellect. Herbert's work also gave adherents of Ramsay's ideology, found in the high degrees, an opportunity to link the mind as the striving self-seeking initiation with soul, the experience of initiation itself. This dichotomy further invested Masonic intellects such as DeWitt Clinton and perhaps Dr. Benjamin Franklin. It also made it possible to define more precisely the point of initiation more aptly in terms of a vocabulary, useful to policy makers, which drew out and illustrated the faculty which comes into play as the internal active principle of symbolic apprehension. Herbert defined this event as sensus: the result of a double reciprocal action. In DeWitt Clinton's idiom Freemasonry reaches out to the citizen *qua* initiate at the same time and in the same moment the neophyte reaches out to Freemasonry to clarify morally the development of policy. This view of Freemasonry, as method subfuses Salem Town's work and his entire religiously, cast principle of millennial extension.

Within Herbert can also be seen the precursors to Scottish Common Sense Philosophy, and to American Pragmatism, as both schools of thought appear to intersect Masonic intellectuality from common Renaissance sources. These common ideas generate a fund of Deistic ideas which become identified with Masonic cosmology through Newton, Desaguliers and Anderson from hermetical and cabalistic sources which affirm the harmoniousness between subject and object at the core of his thought: 1) that a supreme Deity exists; 2) that he ought to be worshipped; 3) that worships consists of virtue and piety, conjoined; 4) that sinful man should repent and turn from evil to good; and 5) that divine judgment will follow from the goodness and justice of God. As such, Herbert conceived a common "Catholic Church" as a religion of Reason, incorporated, as will be seen, into Salem Town's esoteric synthesis drawn from DeWitt Clinton and Thomas Smith Webb. These ideals were a primitive religion before it became corroded by crafty sacerdotal order and priestcraft. As such Herbert claimed to derive the originality of his work as derived through common moral consent from the study of comparative religion. Analogously, the same study became synonymous to Freemasons with ritual initiation, as further confirmed by Preston's method assumed by Webb's Monitor. The common presumption was that antiquity and its mythologies exhibited nothing more or less than the common primitive, even pagan, Catholic Faith which Freemasonry recapitulated and summarized in the Royal Arch of Enoch template and transmitted to subsequent generations in purified form to the peoples of the earth. This *modus vivendi* conformed to Giordano Bruno's heliocentrism as the inspiration of a pre-Reformation mysticism which might come to appeal across sectarian lines to Roman Catholic and Protestant alike.

James Maxwell (b. ca. 1581) articulated a vision which linked the further Reformation of the Catholic Church to an ideology of renovation on learning and spiritual which positioned the Stuart monarchy through the triumph of its heir, Charles I, as a last world emperor who would realize a New Jerusalem of enlightened learning, evangelical truth, and universal citizenship. This vista fit aptly into the Jesuit enthusiasm for Counter-Reformation and in the realization of a new Sabbath order applied to the discovery of the new world consistent with Clare's narrative and with Ramsay's ideology. It also carried forward the John Dee principle of reformed Protestant empire derived from Pletho with the added irenical mission of vitiating the Roman Catholic magisterium with a future Reformed Joachimist order consistent with Protestant contributions to principles of religious liberty. The symbolic fulcrum was the emergence of Enoch as a paragon initiate in a variety of guises as a perfected and purified Christ, represented as the Sun of God. Presumably the District of Columbia would have been the symbolic temple-state from which such a vista might unfold consistent with jointly the Salem Town and Simon Greenleaf vision of American Masonic destiny. Maxwell's work, *Admirable and Notable Prophecies*, was commonly available to Catholic apologists for the effectiveness of the Counter-Reformation in Protestant eyes but still beckoned to Judaism and Islam to become irenic partners within a Masonic new world order. This ideology pointed to the iconology of the Jesuit Order as visually depicted by Jesuit Athanasius Kircher on the title page of his *Ars Magna Lucis et Umbrae,* Rome, 1646. This esoteric image depicts Hermes (*qua* Enoch) elevated on a white cloud, a Baroque image, supported by a doubled-headed eagle (anticipating the emblem of the Scottish Rite), between heaven and earth as a symbol of action and contemplation as a paragon formation for Freemasonry's gradual system of high degrees. The engraving depicts the Tetragrammaton emanating solar rays and light surrounded by a host of angels, Hermes (*qua* Enoch) exalted in the clouds with his caduceus, capped with an all-seeing eye,

Cabalistic title page of Athanasius Kircher's *Ars Magna Lucis et Umbrae.*

surrounded by solar fire. He looks at the zodiac which rules the sub-lunar world. Like Enoch, the Masonic high degrees carried, symbolically, celestial secrets to its activist participants as a cadre of Pythagorean initiates through whom *Arcana Coelestia* were imparted to rulers both symbolically and pragmatically to bring in a new world empire within the new world itself, to extend Maxwell's rhetoric. Arias Montanus (1527-1598), in his apologetic for the Jesuits, argued that the truthfulness in history derived in fact from a sort of Hegelian dialectic of good vs. evil which anticipated by generations Hegel's own principle as it became associated with German Masonic Templar legends and their adherents through right and left Hegelians. This dialectic played itself out symbolically in the Society of Jesus' obligation to continue in the warfare with heretics in the old world and a battle for the mission field in the Indies, the New World.

As Freemasonry developed its internal machinery to forge a broader social ethic than the moral role of the individual writ large, it became increasingly clear that Herbert's thoughts on mythology provided to its policy managers, directly and indirectly, ritual tools to correct falsehood. In general within the Ramsay ideology, this came to be expressed in a maxim,

Ordo Ab Chao or *Order Out of Chaos* in the motto of the Thirty-Third Degree of the Scottish Rite. This concept traced error to symbolic confusion between the self and the object which rationality and intellect might identify and correct. Much later, as Albert Pike reworked the legacy of Ramsay and his descendants, it held up the principle of equilibrium as depicting the desired harmoniousness among and between various grades of truth as imparted within Herbert's system, mythologically sustained and articulated. Thus, moral error was comprehended as lack of balance between the symbol and the spiritual intellect which comprehended it. The same interior energy which defined this Masonic axiom further insinuated the premise that the goal of Freemasonry resided in its presumption that all of humanity should become initiates, either directly or on their behalf by others as a means toward a balanced political economy, a natural correction. This premise also presumed that all of creation was subject, according to different levels and nuances, to some capacity within the human consciousness. As such the ground work for the concept of the global civilization to become a vast lodge was envisaged and in various ways through the prolific fertility of sociological fraternalism became a reality.

* * * * *

The purpose of Masonic Ritual is to transform the candidate into a sublime magus; that is a moral, intellectual, and freethinking being who can determine right from wrong without assistance from others. Ritual both conceals and reveals: through this revelation (and ultimate transformation) the initiate can positively affect change in the world either locally or globally. Although modern day Freemasonry, and its rituals, were the product of an amalgamation of specific currents of ideas, including, but not limited to the Ancient Mysteries, Rosicrucianism, and Enlightenment thought; from 1717 forward it is clear that its principal elements were defined through the interplay of Renaissance ideas drawn from Hermeticism, the philosophy associated with the mythic figure Thoth Hermes Mercurius Trismegistus, and cabalism through the medium of secrecy as an initiatic device derived from Neo-Platonism, the eclectic philosophy itself the product of Plato's teaching about the *Summum Bonum* or the Supreme Good. Secrecy became in fact a symbol in its own right pointing to the necessary associations between the various fields of human endeavor associated with secrets of the craft. The Masonic initiate at once came to embody a prototypical figure which is best described as a cross between Enoch, the Biblical patriarch who never died and was granted a vista of the heavens with its secrets as well as a comprehension of evil as derived from beings who were the progeny of angels and human women. The initiate was also aptly characterized as Pythagoras the quasi-mystic, philosopher and mathematician who regarded his own craft "of living" as the subject of profound secrecy to be imparted only to adept neophytes. Pythagoras further taught that man and the universe were created in God's image; and that both being made in the same image, the understanding of the heavens was the understanding of God.[239] The Pythagoreans introduced ethical and moral concepts into their teachings, and developed a highly complex system of number symbolism while interpreting mathematics in terms of geometry.[240] The generic prototype for Freemasonry in the historical and cultural sense was the Egyptian and agriculturally rooted Eleusinian Mysteries, the latter the epitome of pagan religion the eclipse of which signaled the end of mythological religion and the beginnings (not by coincidence) of Christianity. It was the impact of this cult in specific which provided the precedents within the Greco-Roman mystery religions which were taken up by Masonic ceremonials of various sorts each of which came to accommodate and to articulate particular and sometimes overlapping threads of ideas, including the concept of the dying yet resurrected sun god or solar man.

The variety of Masonic related pedagogical concepts, notably those with Biblical, medieval, occult (17th century in particular), and Enlightenment moral examples were driven at their core by the hermetic ideal of ascension and the riveting of the central symbol of the ineffable name of God, the Tetragrammaton, notably the Royal Arch Word to the process of initiation. All of Masonic initiation pinpoints and posits an essentially dualistic moral cosmos. This means that the realization within the world of the uninitiated of specific designs, notably urban utopias, was derived from a mystical

239 Hall, Manly P. *The Secret Teachings of All Ages,* page 197.

240 Hancox, Joy, *The Byrom Collection and the Globe Theatre Mystery*, pages 198-199.

source and at its core a divine origin. Within Masonic ritual this utopia was characterized by the central idiom of the building of King Solomon's Temple in I Kings, II Chronicles, and XL Ezekiel, the latter as a prophetic vision. Yet, the entire template of occult Masonic infrastructure can be traced to the ancient Iranian religion of Zoroastrianism within which the battle between good vs. evil (light vs. dark) became pragmatic and paradigmatic. The survival of moral virtue therefore became within its combat with evil and its complement disorder (chaos) the central struggle to create a "smooth ashlars" (i.e. dressed stones for construction) from "rough ashlars" to utilize Masonry's own descriptive metaphor. It is precisely the universality of this metaphor which has made Masonic ideas and institutions an endless fascination across cultures and societies.

The same parallel between the Egyptian high priest Sarastro[241] that invites comparison between the magus in Mozart's opera, *The Magic Flute* defines the symbolism and capabilities of the paragon Masonic initiate whether it be Enoch, Pythagoras or Zoroaster: the power to connect material culture to the essentially beneficent movements of the stars (astrology) and their relationship and application to human affairs positively. It is this linkage between the moral striving through initiation to possess the Name of God that drives all of Masonic ritual specifically when the supreme good, the object of ascent to divine knowledge, toward the power to rule. By further connecting this energy through political channels the image of the high priest to the presiding officer within Freemasonry, specifically, in the Royal Arch an equivalency is struck and maintained between the various elements of governance. In Andrew Michael "Chevalier" Ramsay's specific instance this equivalency is effected and managed by expanding the notion of an irenic, liberal, and philanthropic mysticism from pagan sources into the milieu of confessional Christianity (i.e. veiled paganism), such that the pagan core element is preserved and developed in such a way that the object of the search, generally articulated in terms of sun worship or solar centrality is constructed by relating the initiation of a single individual

241 Sarastro is a metaphoric stand-in for Jesuit educated Ignaz von Born who was head of the Viennese Illuminati Lodge as well as being Master of Mozart's Masonic Lodge. Adam Weishaupt, Freemason and founder of the Illuminati, and Baron Adolph Knigge who was a Freemason, Illuminist, and de facto leader of German occultism likely also served as inspiration.

to the broader vista of eschatological hope. Zoroastrianism became as a result a perfectly apt metaphor for augmenting the soul's personal struggle against evil with the ultimate combat between good and evil in the sweep of history. How this was accomplished in Ramsay's case was the erection of the higher Masonic degree system as an encompassing umbrella as a revision of English Freemasonry into a system which was understood to be hieratic and oligarchic pointing toward absolutism by opening a door, to a tyranny of virtue deemed to be necessary in order to combat a tyranny of evil.

Within Freemasonry the high degree system was constructed as a path to concentric circles of perfection within which the Sun and its concomitant, the Apollonian chariot of the *Merkabah* sun god, was developed as the thread between a utopian future realized through the geometric idealism of restored wisdom within which ordered precision and abstraction was posited as a form of monotheism. The omnipotence of the deistic Masonic God, therefore, rooted as it was in layering of pagan and pre-Christian wisdom invariably coated with Christian aesthetics and emblemature generated a form of autocracy within which democracy was secretly invested with monarchical apparatus. This irony characterized Masonic ritual of the higher degrees not only because they preached the perfection of the earth as transfiguration according to the diffusion of Light in the Zoroastrian vein but also because the world becomes the subject of a restoration as societal renovation. This is the reason why Freemasonry became associated, first, with the proliferation of *light* as knowledge perhaps epitomized by the association of the Fraternity with Pierre Bayle's (1647-1706) *Encyclopedia* and the reinvigoration of knowledge and with the mystagogues such as Pythagoras who sought to rule a Masonic like society through the application of Euclid's 47th Proposition, the emblem of the lodge's presiding officer, the Worshipful Master, a symbol of the complete man. Thereby the transition between the speculative Master Mason, symbolically, into the Master Mason as an architect (operative) anticipated the transition in Ramsay's rhetoric between the English system of understatement of the pretensions associated with Craft Masonry and the determination of the propagators of the higher grades or degrees to position the Freemason as a designer and patron of grand projects, such as the Encyclopedia, social reform, and of course of building itself. This entails the expansion of the craft of Masonry as an operative vocation from contracting into knowledge of classical and Continental styles of building derived notably from the ideas of Vitruvius, the first century Augustan imperial architect, and Andrew Palladio, the influential Italian Renaissance architect, author of *I Quattro Libri dell'Architettura, Four Books of Architecture*. Vitruvius whose work *De Architectura* provides a link between the period of Gothic Construction and the age of High Renaissance, and, in turn, whose premier Renaissance advocate Dr. John Dee is linked with the origin of speculative Freemasonry through the occult tradition of Hermeticism. The central Vitruvian idea used commonly for the construction of temple architecture was the Pythagorean Theorem: A2 + B2 = C2, the 3,4,5, triangle; it is reflective of the 47th Proposition of Euclid which in turn was the key to the Golden Ratio: the ideal that the man was the microcosm was directly related to the heavens, Deity the macrocosm. This philosophical relationship was rooted in practical geometrical tools with which, and from which, classical structures were built. The five pointed star, the pentagram, was a key Renaissance symbol for man, which when applied to structures notably the Gothic Cathedrals (as with the Cathedral of Chartres) confirmed the harmonious relationship between man and God. This concept also forges a nexus between true operative masonry and speculative masonry as both seek a higher Godhead. This idea common to Renaissance Platonic philosophy and to its architecture, was understood by Dee and his contemporaries.[242] This same theme can be seen years earlier; Leonardo Da Vinci (1452-1519) would draw (ca. 1487) the *Vitruvian Man* named after the Roman Architect; it features a man as a pentagram formed by his head two arms and legs as a symbol of the divine relationship between and man and God, a golden proportion. In other words, such geometry expresses the harmony which was traditionally perceived between human and cosmic proportions. A square containing a circle, a square contained within a circle, a square and a circle of equal perimeters, and attempts to construct a square and a circle of equal areas fascinated the geometers of ancient times and were respected as archetypes of the order in the universe.[243] Variations of these patterns seem to underlie the geometry of utopian plans, as various, for example, of Plato's ideal cities, St. John's vision of a New

242 See French, Peter J., *John Dee: The World of an Elizabethan Magus* page 140; see also Frances Yates, *Theatre of the World*.

243 Hancox, Joy, *The Byrom Collection and the Globe Theatre Mystery*, page 278.

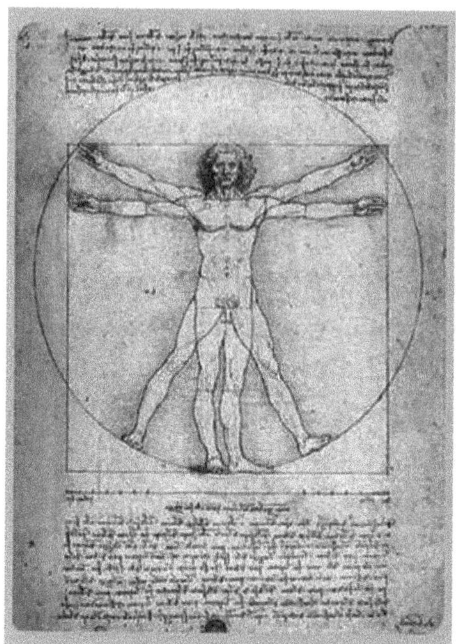

Da Vinci's *Vitruvian Man* representing man as a divine microcosm. This image influenced the work *On Divine Proportion*, published 1509, by mathematician and Franciscan Friar Luca Pacioli (1446/7-1517).

Jerusalem; and can be found incorporated into Stonehenge, the astronomical clock in Wells Cathedral, England and Shakespeare's Globe Theatre.[244] Within the streetscape of the District of Columbia a broken pentagram is formed by interlocking and connecting streets above the Executive Mansion.

In the broadest sense the introduction of an initiatic paragon into Freemasonry to operate as it were at a legal and constitutional level yet outside of and within codifications permitted Freemasonry to develop a form of apologetical method which surrogated Christianity through substituting esoteric and occult ceremonial for the imagery of the Biblical Judaic Sabbath. This device made it possible to intertwine within material culture in specific the celestial vista achieved by Enoch both in content and method with the seventh day of the week understood as ersatz eschatology. It can be argued that the ideas of the medieval mystic Joachim von Fiore, whose prophetic speculations about a Third Age of the Holy Spirit within a trinity of epochs or moral ages was envisaged by Freemasonry to be a peaceful millennial kingdom of which the architecture of the United States capital became a tacit but perduring symbol. An allusion was struck through which the U.S. Constitution was able to work itself out within Palladian and Vitruvian architecture, in specific, which modeled the operations of government as the path toward the achievement of a national peaceful destiny and indeed of an ordered global imperial empire working effortlessly to install heavenly Aquarian harmony into society. At this point the Masonic contribution was uniquely important to the origin and future destiny of the United States because it enabled and

244 Ibid.

empowered classical Greek and Renaissance political theory to operate within the trappings of medieval monarchy such that representation of the populace became integrated through the idea of a paragon initiate, itself a kind of secular savior, on behalf of the nation. Indeed, the divination of the individual human being into a de facto god was attempted by Roman politics such that idyllic concepts of the Greek polis were lifted up to absolutistic standard through Masonic ritual in the identification of the United States Presidency with a supreme initiate. Similarly, corporate power underwent the same transmutation without the support of formal constitutionality but with the agency of limitless wealth as the nation developed westward. In this instance we can look to Freemasonry as the fundamental source for extending to secular government both the method and the content.

The irenic links between Anglican imperial theory to Jesuit applications of a Third Age of the Holy Spirit derived from the eschatology of Joachim of Fiore can be seen further in common appeals to non-Christian comparative religion within a merged body of thought and symbolism linking the Egyptian mythology associated with Pythagoras and his 47th Proposition of Euclid to Zoroastrian mythology surviving in Ramsay's *Apologia* for the high degrees published in 1738. The common foundation for both concepts can be found in the essentially apologetical mindset that Anglican and Jesuit theoreticians shared about the role of reason and therefore pagan thought in their determination to advance Christian mission through politics. This extended from polemic into material culture through architecture in both traditional celebrations of the Palladian and Vitruvian elements of design which presumed correlations between the geometry of the human created form, sacred spaces, and to cosmological organization into micro cosmogonies. These micro-republics were envisaged to be the work of the MAGUS within pagan, notably Zoroastrian, mythology transformed into Egyptian priesthood, and given an equivalency in the identification of the Christian Renaissance humanist who sought to transform the essentially pagan culture of the Italian Renaissance into first loyal Catholicism and thereafter the image of the wise philosopher king working in common with medieval knightly orders, notably the Knights Templar, whose salience and lore long survived their dissolution in 1314. Ramsay's celebration through

Freemasonry of the Templar ideology as it was reworked in 18th century celebrations of chivalry pointed to the military elements of Mithraism, wherein Mithras was deemed Apollo the Sun god who was the equivalent of the Zoroastrian Phrygian sky god Bagos Papaios who appears to be a combination of both Apollo and the Phrygian sun god Attis.

It should be noted that both Zoroastrian and Egyptian mythology celebrated the equivalency between worship of the sun (later *Sol Invictis* in the Constantinian idiom), fire, and light were understood to be the tripartite material expression of the Holy Spirit as in the third age of the Joachimite division of history into three parts. This symbolism became in time the theme of both the Royal Arch of Enoch degree in the French Rite of Perfection, also termed the Knight of SOL/OMON (note the etymological coincidence between SOL, the sun, and OMON or MONO meaning one, i.e. one sun god) as well as the motto of the Order of the Red Cross, "Great is Truth (i.e. Light) and it shall prevail," *Magnus est Veritas et prevalabit*. In Ramsay's mind, the Templars represented the militant arm of religion in its Zoroastrian battle with impious *daevas*, or demons (not daemons) as well as a practical guard defending symbolically the Holy Places of Jerusalem.

Illuminism, the methodology of the Bavarian Illuminati, was the means developed within Freemasonry to transform the world into a perfected and well governed Masonic Temple. Zoroastrianism in general and Mithraism its progeny were carriers of the same idea from the illumination of light understood as a metaphor and allegory to transfigure society by means of ritual. The dualistic element preserved and reinterpreted by Ramsay in specific carried forward the dualistic warfare with evil understood also as impurity into the modern age of western civilization. Thus goodness became the pursuit of perfection which was also understood as the initiation of the whole of society and culture as a war between the forces of Light and the forces of Darkness. Unless Zoroastrian dualism is understood as a legacy through Ramsay's vision of the Masonic higher degrees, it's difficult to fathom the profundity which Masonry has worked within American society and in turn through its unique imprint upon global society. This concept not only shaped definitively the operations of the public sphere of community activity at various social levels it also positioned the United States as a world power to transfigure the world, *from darkness to light*, within a Masonic context. In Christian terminology the Masonic vision sought a perfection within society conventionally associated only with the Satanic reign of peace to come before the end of the world as presaged by John of Patmos (the Divine) in the Book of Revelation: the Holy City, Jerusalem as it were, is targeted by Babylon, the Achaemenid Empire of Cyrus the Great, symbolized by the Biblical Whore of Babylon, which both seeks to displace the Kingdom of God and which lusts after the holiness which traditionally God conferred accordingly to theological missions associated with the breaking in and furthering of his divine Kingdom. This concept was in turn furthered by American rocket scientist and co-founder of Jet Propulsion Laboratory, founded 31 October 1936, Marvel Whiteside "Jack" Parsons (1914-1952). To Parsons and his *Scarlet Woman*, Marjorie Cameron (1922-1995), the implication was clear: a new series of Masonic-Enochic occult rituals were to be devised. Known as the infamous Babylon Working, Parsons hoped to facilitate a spiritual-Babylonian new age mystical religion within the Joachimite schema. This entailed the performance of rituals and rites that would bring about the actual incarnation of the Biblical Whore of Babylon which would destroy Christianity while exalting the occultism and the Thelemic, "*Do what thou wilt*," theology of Freemason Aleister "the Great Beast 666" Crowley, the man whom Parsons called *father*. Jack Parsons was personally selected by Crowley to lead the Agape Lodge of the O.T.O., Ordo Templi Orientis or Order of the Eastern Templars, in Los Angeles, California. The O.T.O. is an androgynous secret society that was once led by Crowley that combines Freemasonry with yoga and meditations necessary to create and perform various high degree tantric sex magicks. The fourth initiatory degree of the O.T.O. is companion to the Masonic Royal Arch of Enoch; the O.T.O. also claims descent from the Bavarian Illuminati.[245] In 1972 the International Astronomical Union in France honored Jack Parsons by naming a crater on the moon after him. Parsons Crater is at 37 degrees N. latitude and 171 degrees W. longitude on the dark side of the moon.[246]

245 Crowley claimed the following personas as O.T.O. "Gnostic" Saints: Adam Weishaupt, King Arthur, Mohammed, Francis Bacon, Buddha, Pope Alexander XI (Rodrigo Borgia), John Dee, Richard Wagner, Francois Rabelais, and Friedrich Nietzsche to name a few.

246 Carter, John. *Sex and Rockets: The Occult World of Jack Parsons*, page 192.

* * * * *

Freemasonry, as the Chevalier Ramsay received it from England, first Grand Lodge was established in London June 24, 1717, developed the raw material from which Continental workings of the ritual were derived. Within these workings a common idiom developed, most likely from hermetical sources in the Renaissance Florentine academy, linking the essence of Masonic secrecy to the cultivation of solar fire and light as a central divine spark which Ramsay cultivated as the essence of the Fraternity's devotion as a cultural entity to the restoration of knowledge as a core metaphor for the spread of fire and the diffusion of light. God after all spoke to Moses and gave the ineffable name through a burning bush. From its Biblical antecedents this divinity in embryo became associated with the Masonic possession of the Lost Word of Master Mason which developed as a symbol of the proliferation of fire and light from the individual into society. As will be seen in the next chapter the Zoroastrian mythic currency accelerated this dynamic. But, its association with alterations in the way kingship was viewed in the 18th century was also critical to the proliferation of the central symbol linking the restoration of the Word through knowledge into a world concept of universal empire. Thus the division of the king's person into a complementary physical and spiritual identity, the symbolic division of Christ's Body into *two symbolic parts* by Hermes Trismegistus in his *Corpus Hermeticum*, in turn linked the medieval concept through specific Biblical and political texts into modernity as the warrant and authority ofkingship. This is time became more subtle and tacit as democratic processes began to supplant monarchy through references to education and politics merged as a developing center for the spread of progressive learning as the surest foundation of revolutionary regimes. Ramsay's origination of the idea of a panoptic *Encyclopedie* of which the Dutch author Prosper Marchand developed into a historical dictionary in 1758-59 aimed, inter alia, at a secular critique of Catholicism as an adjunct to Pierre Bayle's own *Encyclopedie*.

* * * * *

The personal Union of the kingships of Judah and Israel as a metaphor for the Stuart personal rulership of Scotland and England would not have been lost on divines and political theologians of the 17th century. This settlement in essence underscored the sanctity of the dual office as a position united by the anointment approach to sacral legitimism and made of the person of the Sovereign a de facto priest, different from Byzantine and French precedents for similar arrangements, but yet underscoring a common irenic theology linking Anglicanism to the Church of Scotland presumably along mystical lineaments recapitulating and defining at esoteric levels the status of monarchy. Both monarchies, Biblical and British, had their own legal infrastructures. The precise nature of the personal union of two separate monarchies invited further comparison with the grounds for a universal monarchy, papal or otherwise, celebrating Stuart sympathies. The result was not a unified national monarchy, as the Biblical Hebrew monarch Saul managed. The tribal elements, in other words, retained their unique cultural definitions which were, of course, a core ingredient to the celebration of the monarchy of King Cyrus in the Order of the Red Cross of Babylon in Webb's chivalric Masonic rituals.

Jacobite sensibilities came to exhibit, with the high degree ritual, ideology not only the giving of order and therefore life as it is derived from social and political civility to a renewal process within society, but also a deeper appreciation of the meaning of Scottish views of monarchy relative to the core of a national cult than was thought to be available to the Hanoverians. This enabled Enlightenment rationality and Jacobite mysticality to flourish in the whole of Britain, not the least of which was the capacity of Freemasonry and later Odd Fellowship to take up the symbolism of David and Solomonic kingship as an extension of Stuart legitimism into Victorian England as Scotland became rehabilitated during the reign of George IV to metropolitan British Imperialism. Freemasonry was instrumental to the rehabilitation of Scotland during this period, as the taint of Jacobite disloyalty faded. Sir Walter Scott (1771-1832), who learned his trade of writing romantic, historical novels from the Anglo-Irish author Maria Edgeworth (1767-1849), was an ardent Freemason; he was offered various honorific offices in Masonic Knight Templary in Scotland and was conspicuous in his adherence to the Scottish Episcopal Church.

In this context, Sir Walter Scott carried forward Jacobite sentimentality holistically as a comprehensive re-appropriation of Scottish lore. He borrowed the genre from Maria Edgeworth's invention of the historical novel dealing with Anglo-English culture. As a Freemason, Scott took up multiple affiliation with the higher degrees in essence integrating Ramsay ideology with regular English Freemasonry as validated by Thomas Dunckerley (1724-1795), the natural son of George II, who devoted his public career to the English Order of Knights Templars (formed in 1791) and its extension. Point of fact within the brief expanse of time between the death of Samuel Johnson (1709-1784) and the career of Sir Walter Scott, a range of artists and literatures commanded the English landscape, notably Samuel Taylor Coleridge (1772-1834) and Thomas De Quincy (1785-1859), who's musing brushed the skirts of Freemasonry. De Quincy's essay on its Masonry's origins dealt with the perennial issue of its Druidical and Egyptianate forebears, and Coleridge cultivated a cultish appreciation for Isis and Osiris that rivaled Mozart in its intensity. Interestingly, the coat of arms of the Episcopal Church resemble the symbols of medieval Knight Templary (see Plate XIV).

The result is a sense of personal quest linked to a direct sensuous intuition of reality in the form of social myth of relevancy to a given epoch (i.e the Middle Ages) and to a given nation (Scotland). It is, of course, significant that Walter Scott chose English Freemasonry as the arbiter of regularity, as Masons defined it at the time, and adhered to Scottish Anglicanism, as opposed to *the Kirk*, or Church of Scotland. This distanced him from Calvinism and embraced irenicism as High Churchmen viewed it in the late 18th century, slightly seditious and suspect for its Jacobite threads, but at the core loyal to the Elizabethan Religious Settlement of 1559.[247] This process further explains the appeal of Scots novels to the cult of chivalry developed in the American south following the American Revolution and celebrated notably in Virginia families devoted to antiquated ideals of gentlemanly conduct; something of an Indian Summer for American chivalry parallel to 16th century romantic ideas of knighthood in the Elizabethan era. The

247 A re-establishment of the Church of England's independence from Rome conferring upon Elizabeth the title "Supreme Governor of the Church of England" while establishing a Book of Common Prayer.

identification of a point within a circle, ⊙ a venerated Masonic solar emblem, as a symbol for the cosmos becoming incarnated in the imagery of kingship which was preserved in the higher degrees, notably as the Southern Jurisdiction of the Scottish Rite. The point represents the sun and the circle surrounding it is the belt of constellations that form the Zodiac. The Scottish Rite Southern Jurisdiction achieved fraternally what it was unable to achieve politically: the consolidation of all states south of the Ohio and East and West of the Mississippi River as a unitary Masonic sacral realm, a circle, which would take symbolic concrete esoteric form in the St. Louis' Enochic Royal Arch, the exoteric Gateway to the West.

Scottish Masonic lore incorporated not only imagery of David and Solomonic kingship through references to its monarch as Solomon but also projected a national mythology of Egyptian descendants bringing to Scotland the Stone of Scone upon which Jacob slept when he dreamed a vision of angels. A parallel military metaphor was adopted from the Jewish Maccabean Revolt[248] by Sir William Wallace. This thread has to do with Jewish immigration into Scotland after their expulsions from England by Edward I in 1290 and bears the imprint of Cabalistic (and Kabbalistic) as well as sabbatarian symbolism. The *Ars Notoria* of Raymond Lully's irenic missiology also surfaced within this ethos. The result was a singular identification of Scottish kingship with political mysticality through architectural symbolism. This implied an equivalency between practical construction and the Art of Memory built into the governance of guilds linking the process to Solomonic Temple imagery as it became related to the envisioning of the Temple as the end and mission of mysticism. It is less clear how Ramsay's ideology of the high degrees conflated with this ethos. However, his own mysticality of universalistic albeit Roman Catholic iconology appears rooted to a singular identification between monarchy and symbolism along hermetical, cabalistic, and Neo-Platonic lines.

The symbolic-ritualistic link between the Biblical scripting of Masonic symbolism to Davidic, messianic sacral kingship with its roots

248 Rebellious Jewish Army that took control of Judea at which time had been client subordinate state (like Scotland with in the English Empire) of the Seleucid Empire. The Maccabees founded the Hasmonean Empire which ruled from 164 to 63 BCE, expanding the land of Israel while reducing the influence of Hellenism.

in Melchizedek emblemature surfaced in circa 1790 with the distillation of an Order of High Priesthood with the story line relating to Melchizedek and to a related ceremonial linked to the Holy Royal Arch Knight Templar Priesthood also named The Holy Order of Wisdom or Aaron's Band which preserved mystical, medieval, and alchemical references to a scientific order of Masonry rooted in priestly symbolism associated with kingship. The relationship of this form of sacral Freemasonry surfaced uniquely in cultures within which the fear of powerlessness by the human subject took on efforts to rationalize and position it in such ways that the divine human encounter in political order was symbolized to make its management more mythically accessible. The efforts of James VI in Scotland in the 1590s in far Northern Scotland to replicate a life sized model of Solomon's Temple are a case in point. Employing the skills of his master of the works this initiative, Sterling's Chapel Royal, documented a crossover between speculative Freemasonry and the training of operative Masons as a mystical as well as practical pursuit. James VI's Solomonic pretensions carried into his anointment as King James I as he and his architects brought elements of their Masonic system into the political theology of English Monarchy through the personal union of the two realms in the person of the monarch.[249]

Such sacral kingship was realized with Scottish idiom in various ways, notably the survival of Knights Templar as presumed paladins for a restored Stewart monarch as a chief among chiefs among Scottish clans and of the reworking of Biblical precedents through Masonic ritual. One has to bear in mind that Scotland provided a safe haven for the Templars after their dissolution by Pope Clement V in 1305. Within the Bible, David's ascent to central power and core numinous awesomeness as the direct anointment of God is worked out by implication in the saga of Craft ritual, renewed by the Royal Arch degree with the rebuilding of the Temple of Zerubbabel. It is also worked out in ceremonials related to both the Orange Order and Odd Fellowship in the 1790s which pinpoint the Davidic usage of history as a work of scholarly sources as opposed to folktales while based upon purely religious beliefs, traditions of prehistorical times.

249 *See* Stevenson, David, *The Origins of Freemasonry, Scotland's Century 1590 - 1710*, pages 92 - 95. The architect of the "Solomonic" Chapel Royal was William Schaw - a likely Freemason and suspected Jesuit.

The comparison of Odd Fellow ceremonial with Masonic Craft-Royal Arch sequences of symbolism is important because there is an implied story line beginning in the relationship between Saul and David dating from the Books of Samuel (Hebrew Bible) events relating the creation of Hebrew kingship to Saul's anointment as King of Israel. This story seeminly ends in the Masonic ritual with the dedication of King Solomon's Temple depicted in celebratory form in the degree of Most Excellent Master in the T.S. Webb system (Chapter II).

David's anointment as king was therefore scripting for the Scottish Stuart monarchy in ways the Hanoverians could not easily co-opt merely through an act of parliament to insure a Protestant succession. The anointing element was in fact denigrated by rational Protestants at the time, which should shape scholarly reading of James Anderson's general labors on the genealogy of kingship and of royal patronage for the Craft. The Rite of Consecration was present in the coronal ceremonies and probably can be traced to the association of the priest king Melchizedek as Baroque composer George Frederic Handel's (1685-1759) *Zadok the Priest* is played at the coronation of the British monarch in homage to Melchizedek and his divine kingship. It is significant for Hanoverian propaganda that David was elected by the "Men of Judah" and that the "Lion's Paw of the Tribe of Judah" occupies for Freemasons a sacral symbolic place within the Third Degree. However, David's choice as a messianic monarch was a purely political act typical of rise to power as the progenitor, through Solomon of the Temple. This restricted Davidic kingship as a revision of the Jacobite theory of anointment into legitimist divine right and the basis for his power in Judah and by implication the Germanic Hanoverians right to rule as English monarchs despite being outsiders of which Masonry and its rituals –especially the high degrees–provided a bridge between the two. This action, of course, required by implication Philistine approval of vassalage kingship after their hegemony over Israel. Either they were politically comfortable with this notion at a subordinate level or it was deemed to be a divide and conquer strategy implying a stronger division between a southern and northern Judaic Kingdom. In any event the narrative scripting of Biblical re-workings in Masonic and cognate fraternal ritual is a critical subject for scholarly inquiry given the importance of such narratives as the thread from which Masonic ceremonial was woven into a wide range of tapestries. Sir Walter Scott's cultural impact on the epoch within which the English (and Welsh) Masonic Union (United Grand Lodge of England) was both formed and effected underscores this importance. The United Grand Lodge of England was formed by the union of the two English Grand Lodges known as the Moderns and the Antients in 1813 with the Duke of Sussex as Grand Master until his death in 1843. The United Grand Lodge did not approve of degrees other than the basic first three of Entered Apprentice, Fellowcraft and Master Mason. A compromise allowed the Royal Arch to continue as part of Freemasonry while other high Templar degrees were suppressed by the United Grand Lodge as being a threat of detraction from fundamental craft Masonic institutionalization. In the United States, the opposite occurred: it saw the increasing proliferation of Knight Templary as a free standing "fraternity within a fraternity" remaining unfettered.

In conclusion, the movement of David's capital from Hebron, in Judah, to Jerusalem represented the rise in messianic authority connecting his kingship to Hebrew theology. In selecting and consecrating the Ark of the Covenant as a new symbol for his elevated status just as Mount Zion became a new name in Israel's religious vocabulary. This cementing of a three way identification among and between the Ark, David's kingship, deemed to be and become more so Messianic, and the city of Jerusalem completed the saga necessary to invest Masonic ritual with a fitting end purpose, and sewed the thread of its interior coherent symbolism into a seamless whole concept. Such an investment in the restoration and recapitulation of knowledge (via the Ark of the Covenant) both echoed and anticipated the saga of the Royal Arch of Enoch ceremonial which understood the survival of learning from pre-Noahatic days of the Flood through the unfolding of all learning from the correct pronunciation of the Name of God, again understood as the restored Lost Word as an equivalency between kingly priesthood (cf. Melchizedek-David) with initiation by the investiture of the meaning of the symbolism of fire, *light*. The baroque replication of *fire* as the Name of God became clear as solar ideologies emerged to equate solar iconography with the spreading fire and light of Pentecost, with apologetical learning, and with universal enlightened kingship. To his credit, Ramsay did not conceal by implication that he received his basic understanding of Masonic ritual from the medieval association between the operative artisan stone Mason and the identification of Masons with architecture, and thus with royal patronage and its symbolic elucidation into rulership. The texts of his 1737 Oration made it clear, if only by invidious comparison, that he derived the ancient mystical mythology with reference to medieval stone Masonry and by further implication between education and the erection of King's College Chapel, Cambridge[250] and Eton College through an association among and between the symbolism of building (Lully's *Ars Notoria*), monarchy, and the preservation and dissemination of knowledge, both profane and occult. King's College Chapel, Cambridge, regarded as one of the greatest examples of late Gothic English architecture, ground-floor plan depicts a kabbalistic Tree of Life, or Wisdom, pattern reflecting Lullist philosophy.

250 King's College, Cambridge was, originally, to educate young men from Eton College exclusively.

CHAPTER VII

MEET ANDREW MICHAEL "THE CHEVALIER" RAMSAY

The Development of the Rite of Perfection
and the Scottish Rite

"The word Freemason must therefore not be taken in a literal, gross, and material sense, as if our founders had been simple workers in stone, or merely curious geniuses who wished to perfect the arts. They were not only skillful architects, desirous of consecrating their talents and goods to the construction of material temples; but also religious and warrior princes who designed to enlighten, edify, and protect the living Temples of the Most High."
- Andrew Michael "The Chevalier" Ramsay,
Discourse pronounced at the reception ofFreemasons
(a/k/a Ramsay's Oration), 1737.

"We are not to suppose that this was carried to extremity at once. But it is certain, that before 1743 it had become universal, and that the Lodges of Free Masons had become the places for making proselytes to every strange and obnoxious doctrine. *Theurgy*, *Cosmogony*, *Cabala*, and many whimsical and mythical doctrines which have been grafted on the distinguishing tenets and the pure morality of the Jews and Christians, were subjects of frequent discussion in the Lodges. The celebrated Chevalier Ramsay was a zealous apostle in this mission. Affectionately attached to the family of Stuart, and to his native country, he had cooperated heartily with those who endeavoured to employ Masonry in the service of the Pretender, and, availing himself of the pre-eminence given (at first perhaps as a courtly compliment) to Scotch Masonry, he

laboured to shew that it existed, and indeed arose, during the Crusades, and that there really was either an order of chivalry whose business it was to rebuild the Christian churches destroyed by the Saracens; or that a fraternity of Scotch Masons were thus employed in the east, under the protection of the Knights of St. John of Jerusalem. He found some facts which were thought sufficient grounds for such an opinion, such as the building of the college of these Knights in London, called the Temple, which was actually done by the public Fraternity of Masons who had been in the holy wars. It is chiefly to him that we are indebted for that rage for Masonic chivalry which distinguishes the French Free Masonry. Ramsay's singular religious opinions are well known, and his no less singular enthusiasm. His eminent learning, his elegant talents, his amiable character, and particularly his estimation at court, gave great influence to every thing he said on a subject which was merely a matter of fashion and amusement. Whoever has attended much to human affairs, knows the eagerness with which men propagate all singular opinions, and the delight which attends their favorable reception."
- John Robison, *Proofs of a Conspiracy*, 1798.

The man primarily responsible for the convergence of mythology, mysticism, and reason into the high degree and Chivalric Freemasonry, including the Royal Arch of Enoch ceremony, was Andrew Michael "The Chevalier"[251] Ramsay (1686-1743), a Scot's Catholic Universalist Freemason[252] living in Paris. He received a Doctor of Civil Law from Oxford University and was a Jacobite: a supporter of James Francis Edward Stuart a/k/a the Old Pretender; Ramsay desired to see James Stuart (as James III) and the Stuarts return to the throne of England. Ramsay in fact tutored James' sons Charles Edward and Henry in Rome; the former, of course, was Bonnie Prince Charlie or the Young Pretender, the latter the future Cardinal York. Ramsay in 1737 delivered his *Oration* which to this day has been the subject of controversy and debate. It was from this Oration that High Degree Freemasonry developed including

251 He was made a Knight of the Order of St. Lazarus from whence his title comes.
252 Horn Lodge of Westminster, 1730.

the Royal Arch degree as presumably *real* yet lost history. Ramsay stated in Oration that 1) the Masonic Order arose in Palestine during the Crusades –certain nobles and burgesses associated themselves together to restore the Christian Church to the Holy Land–this was of Knights of the Hospital of St. John and Sovereign Order of the Temple, the Knights Templar; 2) when these brethren returned to their own lands they stabled Lodges therein the purpose was architectural art and Temple building; 3) there came a time, however, when the Masonic Order was neglected in most countries, with the exception of Great Britain and especially Scotland; 4) The Scottish Nation preserved the Order in all its splendour, and in the year 1286 the illustrious Mother Kilwinning arose in the mystical shadow of Mount Heredom; and 5) from this time forward Great Britain became the seat of our sciences, the conservatrix of our laws and the depository of our secrets.[253] The linkage that Ramsay at least tried to establish between Freemasonry and the Templars must be understood to make sense of the philosophies that shaped high degree ethos. The core of Ramsay's ideology was the origination of Freemasonry during the Crusades (1095-1291), notably in the wake of the suppression of the Knights Templar (suppressed 1307-1314), which differed from Desaguliers' origination that Masonry evolved from medieval stonecutters who's skills were inherited from Biblical artisans, builders, and craftsmen. This set the stage for him to claim a Templar survival in Scotland, thus linking the chivalric layer, the Templars were drawn from nobility, of Masonic archaeology to the transmission of Judaic wisdom through the Templar Order, founded in 1118, to Scotland as a pristine conduit for its cabbalistic and hermetical wisdom. This invested Templar (and of course Solomon's Temple by default) symbolism with a deeper resonance and linked Davidic messianic kingship as analyzed in the last chapter to the movement of the Ark of the Covenant into central national significance and associating its survival, as a tradition, to the existence and presumed (at the time) writings of Thoth Hermes Mercurius Trismegistus. The premier Templar symbol is, of course, the Red Cross placed on a white background, adopted in 1146. With this device emblazoned on their mantles the knights accompanied King Louis VII of France on the Second Crusade.[254] Here

253 Waite, A.E., *A New Encyclopedia of Freemasonry, Vol. II, page* 314.

254 Baigent, Michael, Richard Leigh and Henry Lincoln, *Holy Blood, Holy Grail*, page 69.

they established their reputation for martial zeal coupled with an almost insane foolhardiness and a fierce arrogance as well.[255] On the Templars and their Masonic connection, the Chevalier Ramsay opines,

> "During the time of the holy wars in Palestine, several principal lords and citizens associated themselves together, and entered into a vow to re-establish the temples of the Christians in the Holy Land; and engaged themselves by an oath to employ their talents and their fortune in restoring architecture to its primitive institution. (?) They adopted several ancient signs and symbolic words drawn from religion by which they might distinguish themselves from the infidels and recognize each other in the midst of the Saracens. They communicated these signs and words only to those who had solemnly sworn, often at the foot of the altar, never to reveal them. This was not an oath of execration but a bond uniting men of all nations into the same confraternity. Some time after our order was united with the Knights of St. John of Jerusalem. Hence our lodges are, in all Christian countries, called Lodges of St. John.....
>
> Our Order must not, therefore, be regarded as the renewal of the Bacchanals and a source of senseless dissipation, of unbridled libertinism and of scandalous intemperance, but as a moral Order, instituted by our ancestors in the Holy Land to recall the recollection of the most sublime truths in the midst of the innocent pleasures of society."[256]

Thus the issue stemming from Ramsay's Oration, intended as an introduction to initiate in a French Lodge, can be stated: was Ramsay in attributing Templar-Masonic lineage giving voice to a parallel concept of the Lost Word which had been suppressed in earlier inhospitable times; in other words was the Templar antecedent lost history now ready to be restored within Freemasonry in a new Age of Reason? The Templar connection is important threefold; they were a quasi-monastic chivalric mystical order who spent years in the Holy Lands; they were a wealthy supra state (even after their exile from the Holy Lands in 1291) that

255 Ibid.
256 Quoted in Mackey, Albert, *Encyclopedia of Freemasonry Vol. II*, page 608.

created multinational banking; and lastly their time in the Middle East exposed them to oriental mysticism; mysticism they picked up through their encounters with the Saracens and Assassins of Hassan-i Sabbah (ca. 1050-1124). This mysticism was Sufism, a belief system imported into Blue Lodge Freemasonry. It was from the Sufis that the Templars learned banking techniques, the "note of hand" to facilitate the transfer of monies from one part of Europe to another.[257] The parallels between Blue Lodge Masonry and Sufism are so similar and obvious they do not need repeating but will be anyway; nevertheless, the principle tenet of Sufism, like Masonry, was the personal union of the soul with God: a union based on a complex system of symbols with Neo-Platonist, Buddhist, and Christian influences resulting in Islamic mysticism. Sufism appealed to educated men of letters and counted among its adherents such figures as Omar Khayyam. Khayyam was a scientist, astronomer, mathematician, poet, and philosopher who's teachings became known to Europeans circa 1700. Sufism, like craft Freemasonry features 1) teaching of morality though symbols, 2) signs and words of recognition, 3) non-solicitation of members, 4) a Hiramic martyr, Mansur al Hallaj, 5) a lost, occult, or hidden past, and 6) a tradition of building and architecture.[258] There is evidence that the same Vitruvian-Golden Mean approach used to create the Gothic Cathedrals of Europe were used by medieval Persian Architects.[259] Sufism's impact upon Blue Lodge Masonry came via one of four ways or any combination of the four: 1) the Crusades by way of the Knights Templar, 2) Moorish culture in Spain, 3) the fall of Constantinople (1453) through Byzantine cultural interaction with Europe, and 4) the works of Omar Khayyám. Ramsay's ideology also stimulated the general equivalency taken up by Sir Walter Scott and others between Masonic origins and Templar chivalry. It is likely Ramsay invented the concept of this innovation as an unmediated vision through which the grand objective of the Royal Arch of Enoch was conceived: the restoration of the Tetragrammaton and from it all knowledge and wisdom was derived from its correct pronunciation by Knights Templar within the higher degrees. Ramsay linked this Enochic element to the

257 Wallace-Murphy, Tim, *The Enigma of the Freemasons: Their History and Mystical Connections,* page 30.
258 Shah, Idries, *The Sufis* (see Introduction by Robert Graves).
259 Ardalan, Nader, and Laleh Bakhtiar, *The Sense of Unity: The Sufi Tradition in Persian Architecture*, p. 25.

composition of a universal cyclopedia or universal dictionary of the arts and sciences, a preeminent thread of the Enochic Royal Arch. The result was the perduring Masonic ritual emphasis on the recapitulation of knowledge, notably as described in the text of the Fellowcraft degree, the study of the seven liberal arts, medieval *Trivium* and *Quadrivium*, in Webb's ceremony in the 1797 *Monitor* or *Illustrations*. The purpose of this chapter is to analyze the impact of Ramsay's ideology on high degree masonry: the Rite of Perfection which became the Scottish Rite. Ramsay's ideology came not only from his 1737 Oration, but work *The Travels (or Voyages) of Cyrus to which is annexe'd a discourse upon the theology & mythology of the pagans* (Paris 1727, London 1728) which discussed Christianity as a mystical form of Zoroastrian and Egyptian theologies.

The high degree ideology took the concept of a sovereign Thoth Hermes Mercurius Trismegistus which in turn struck deep into the political theorem of two bodies of Christ conceptuality element within imperial theory and anticipates the philosophy of Samuel T. Coleridge. This entailed reworking the Christ-like aura of the Emperor in terms amenable to prevailing ideas of moral and symbolic logic useful in policy formation to different Masonic sovereigns, but preeminently linked the Enochic nexus of rulership and learned restoration of ancient wisdom (or Word) to the principle of coronation conferring special secrets paralleled in the Masonic secrets of the chair (of King Solomon). Within this sequential set of frameworks the, "Thrice Illustrious Master" (*qua* Trismegistus), uniquely in Cryptic Masonic polity was refined as an image of the Pythagorean sovereign who implemented the irenic restoration of a new reformed Catholicism to a freshly conceived ideology of a commonwealth which was, in its broadest terms, templated in Scottish Rite polity through mystical Universalism seeds of which can be found in the Jansenist controversy at the Court of Louis XIV. The metaphysics of the forms of universal mysticism which came to be aligned in Freemason Salem Town's work with Joachim von Fiore's dynamics of unfolding Logos in a new solar age of the Holy Spirit surface within the higher degrees through the movement of Pythagorean mystical numerology as a form of Pantheism: the view that the universe is in effect an organic, living mathematical-geometric entity which adept initiates can discern and manage in statecraft, as in Illuminism, but also in terms of management of the four elements: earth, air, fire, and water. At this point magic, alchemy, and sorcery touched the Masonic drive to originate polity as an incremental hierarchy of potencies conferred through higher degree initiation just as the linkages between vitalistic comparative religion as mythology, mysticism, and reason submerged. This took architecturally concrete form with the Hermetic maxim *as above, so below* as inscribed upon Trismegistus' Emerald Tablet also known as *Lapis Philosophorum*, the Philosopher's Stone. This philosophy entails the alignment of buildings, events, vistas, and various architectures of significance to certain stars, heavenly bodies, planets, and constellations to maximize their spiritual celestial Pythagorean harmonics, a theme prevalent in the District of Columbia. In *Freemasons' Book of the Royal Arch*, Bernard E. Jones further explains the importance of the Philosopher's Stone,

> "....This stone was, of course, not an actual stone, for even with the materialist type of alchemist, the 'Stone" was often a powder or a liquid. The idea of the Philosopher's Stone, ... "seems to have arisen in the early centuries of the Christian era and us in keeping with the early mystical beliefs concerning the regeneration of man." The Stone points to perfection and many of the ancient alchemists believed that they derived the Stone direct from God. The Stone had many names and was subject to many different interpretations. One old writer likened it to the Biblical stone which the builders rejected, the stone which the builders of Solomon's Temple disallowed, but believed that "if it be prepared the right way, it is a pearl without price, and, indeed, the early antitype [representation] of Christ, the heavenly Corner Stone. And here we have an idea of which much is made in some early Royal Arch rituals."[260]

What seems to be a redundant extravagance and reduplication of grandiloquent names in Masonic titles, e.g. Thrice Illustrious, Thrice Potent, and Most Illustrious, linked with vault symbolism specifically within the Cryptic Masonic degrees, association with vault ritual imagery, is very likely a replication of the ceremonial potency necessary to achieve

260 Jones, Bernard E., *Freemasons' Book of the Royal Arch*, page 228.

the symbolic movement of the content of Enoch's vault suggestive of achievement at the policy level, itself derived from the hermetical name, *Trismegistus*, thrice great. In this context, i.e. Miltonic cultural definition of the Baroque style, the very redundancy association with pillars and columns in Masonic imagery assumes a low economy as the implications, in cultural and in epistemological terms, become known and realized: columns exalt and elevate a symbolic higher Godhead. The placement of a template design for such potency by Freemasonry in the hands of decisive politiques in America at the time of George Washington's death, in particular, was itself a fateful mental design for an esoteric emblem, indeed a banner, for the development of the nation. The coupling of dense materialism with potent energy in architecture as developed along utopian and iconic lines was a decisive element enhancing the power of policy rhetoric rooted in high grades Masonic initiation while dismissing craft lodge Modern English Masonry.

In Ramsay's period, English Masonic lodges had been established in France which meant that he and others had access to the raw material contained in the digests of legendary Masonic history conflated from medieval and later texts in James Anderson's *Constitutions* of 1723 revised in 1738. The first of these would have been in his hand at the time of his Oration in 1737 which provided the foil from which he elucidated his chivalric ideology for the destiny of Freemasonry with reference to the Zoroastrian and Neo-Platonic mythology which further underlay his conception. The reference to Pythagoras via Euclid's 47th Proposition, which became the core emblem for purification through Masonic initiation in the Blue Lodge, was the central symbolic means to an end to link Ramsay's Oration to the developing Rite of Perfection and as such the high degree Masonic system. From the viewpoint of the history of ideas this reference is important because it documents in Ramsay's universe a depth of self-knowledge of the soul from the simple Homeric reference to psyche, or soul, and a deeper explication through initiatic process of how this extension of symbolism affected the politics of Masonic high grades mission from Ramsay forward. What is at stake here is the management by Ramsay of the maturation process through which he integrated Zoroastrian concepts of the nature of the soul, angelic vs. demonic, light vs. dark, and thereby struck a parallel between the human self, the political and symbolic process intertwined, and Masonic high degree initiation. This takes the creation of the higher grades system a step beyond the foppery regional message, sometimes associated with superficiality and points toward a much deeper and more dynamic sense of political symbolization consistent with the pervasive influence worked by the higher grades system which appears to have been available to polities utilizing Masonic ideology in nation building and material cultural policy. In other words one must turn to the high degrees and not the Blue Lodge to discover these esoteric concepts and principles.

It is clear that Ramsay's ideology generated a critical core of Masonic arcana which led, by 1760, to the creation of a Masonic Rite of Strict Observance by Freemason Carl von Hund. The Rite of Strict Observance was a continuation of the high degree Masonry of Ramsay; in specific this Rite was a preservation of a secret order of Knights Templar who had survived the papal suppression of 1307 by Pope Clement V.[261] This sequence of degrees celebrated the Jacobite cause by initiating the concept that it was an order ruled by an Unknown Superior thought to be the Young Pretender, Bonnie Prince Charlie. This development within the canon of the high degrees took place as the Modern Grand Lodge of England created its own Grand and Royal Arch Chapter within a Masonic milieu which was inimical to the higher degrees as a class of ceremonial and in specific to the Royal Arch itself. Such an event enjoyed the sponsorship of Cadwallader, The Ninth Lord Blayney (1720-1775), an Irish Peer and Grand Master of the Royal Arch of Jerusalem (1766), who leveraged his personal influence to achieve an objective which would have entailed some level of cooperation between the two rival English Grand Lodges, Antient and Modern. This incident underscored the persistent vitality of the Jacobite transformation of the cultural ideals associated with Freemasonry even within the bosom of Newtonian thought and pinpoints the conduit between Ireland and England which likely shaped and informed the significance of Dublin as an entrepot for the transmission of Masonic iconography into the

261 Churton, Tobias, *The Invisible History of the Rosicrucians: The World's Most Mysterious Secret Society*, page 409.

American colonies and into the new Republic. In this context, it is important to note that principle of a superior within the Elizabethan constitution as it developed into the 17th and 18th century in England denoted the great chain of being within which order in society was understood to be a metaphysical hierarchy within which the cosmos was interconnected to the person of the monarch. Even the English principle, originated in writing by Sir John Fortescue, that the monarchy was at its best when it ruled *cum politicum* that is, with the governed participating, there was no doubt that the sovereign was an ontological and immutable keystone for all of society. Further, the Unknown Superior applied to the Strict Observance ceremonial likely defined the Jacobite Pretender in the same vernacular as the Lost Word of a Master Mason, and thus made of an iconic political and cultural figure a *living Royal Arch Word*, whose restoration would become the key to a new millennial order of a pristine Logos. This concept can be seen painted on the ceiling of the Banqueting House, Whitehall, London by Baroque artist Peter Paul Rubens entitled *The Peaceful Reign of James I* (see Plate XV). King James appears triumphantly between two Enochic Pillars as a living Royal Arch Word. This equivalency was transmitted into the center of material culture as a *cultus symbolicus*, to use Lord Herbert of Cherbury's term for the resonance of solar worship, uncorrupted by priestcraft, which positioned truth as a continuum stretching from pagan antiquity into Christian revelation.

Here it should be said that the Ramsay ideology utilized the medium of Masonic legend applied in time to the creation of the various versions of the Rites of Perfection, and eventually creating the Scottish Rite, as an effort not only to integrate through dramatic ritual imagery the *as above, so below* esoteric imagery of the Renaissance epic tradition (*qua* Milton) but also to position it for application for use in material policy related culture, notably with respect to its visual capacity to integrate contained vaulted space, such as the Apollonian dome, perhaps as best developed by Latrobe with reference to Freemasonry, with the symbolism of infinity. This in turn linked the same technique to the solar theology of Giordano Bruno who envisaged an infinity of worlds to a Masonic ritual concept which rears in the monitorial literature of Thomas Smith Webb in 1797 and further in

Mormon priestly rituals. Further, this capacity to both conceal and reveal simultaneously was related to the ideational capacity of Masonic and related fraternal rituals to erect various de facto monarchies within republican ideology, a theme consistent with the Roman Vitruvian ideology implicit in Jesuit papal mission.

The high degree ideology within Freemasonry developed within the context of the Jansenist controversy (1664-1669) in France. This was an extreme form of Augustinianism emphasizing original sin, depravity, and the need for divine grace whereby an influential party within religious and socially aristocratic elites chose a path of militant piety that penetrated into most forms of thought about ethics and morality. Important figures such as Blaise Pascal (1623-1662), the mathematician, and the playwright Jean Racine (1639-1699) took upon Augustine's theory in opposition the political philosophies of the Jesuit Luis de Molina (1535-1600), who argued for a more tolerant and less rigid approach to ritual and liturgy which permeated thinkers surrounding Masonic theorists such as Ramsay in the eighteenth century. Molina died coincidentally the same year as Giordano Bruno, 1600. The core premise was that since Masonry required a desire and pursuit through the moral will for improvement through initiation, and this will has been utterly corrupted by original sin, it was not possible for Christians to seek initiation through a desire for ethical purification as the high degrees proposed. This element of Jansenism laid unique stress upon the linkage between hermeticism and its tacit Pythagorean ideal of enlightened moral rulership and the striving for nobility at the core of the chivalric, notably Knights Templar (Strict Observance) tradition within the high degree ethos. As narratives within ceremonial structure came to view Templary as the envelope within which other esoteric traditions developed, notably the 19th century view that the 18th degree of the Scottish Rite, the Rose Croix, was a subset of the Templar tradition, this stress generated a certain symbolic top heaviness within the American definition of the Scottish Rite. The works of Blaise Pascal became significant in this regard because his view, as a premier mathematician of the age, viewed reason not as a mystagogical warrant to rule through enlightenment but as the erasure of mystical inspiration which Masonry deemed to be imparted through the numinosity or secular spirituality of Pythagorean insight.

Ramsay likely inherited perduring ideas, transmitted through the Hellenistic philosopher Plotinus through 16th century French writers, about the *soul of the world* as an equivalency with the Third Age of the Holy Spirit as a depiction of the reign of universal brotherhood, a sign of the Aquarian Age, at the core of Masonic idealism. This legacy can be seen in Mozart's *Magic Flute*, in Salem Town's unfolding Logos as Royal Arch Word and in the Third Order of the Ages prevalent among followers of Joachim of Fiore in the Jesuit Order. Ramsay's own attachment to church father Origen and Neo-Platonic grandfather Plotinus points in this direction. The same element can be seen within Illuminism, both as a discrete and occult organization, and as a method of transforming the micro-universe of the lodge into the macro-universe of the world at the heart of much conspiracy theory associated with Freemasonry in the late 18th century. The consistency between Ramsay's ideology and Plotinus related to how the Renaissance passed on the doctrine of the intellect as a private soul on a path to initiation as a monadical[262] intellect. This dynamic, which can be traced in detail from Marsilio Ficino through Ralph Cudworth (1617 -1688), a Platonizing system builder who likely influenced the literary form of works by Desaguliers and Ramsay. The entire Platonic character of Masonic degree structure, whereby the initiatic ascent is implicitly echoed in the progression of the soul toward the supreme good of the Republic through a hierarchy of the intelligible world of which Masonic initiation is a symbolic replica. This concept found its fullest interpretation in the works of Albert Pike who traced Masonic structure from Plato into Ancient Egypt.

To Ramsay, the increasing interiorization of the knowledge of the human soul, which was later lionized by American Masonic thinker Albert Pike, as the imperative, *gnothi seauton,*[263] KNOW THYSELF, as the motto of the Scottish Rite and other orders touting Pythagorean ethics, underscored the initiatic route to making of "rough ashlars" or

262 In the metaphysics of Leibniz: an unextended, indivisible, and indestructible entity that is the basic or ultimate constituent of the universe and a microcosm of it. In the philosophy of Giordano Bruno: a basic and irreducible metaphysical unit that is spatially and psychically individuated.

263 Inscribed at the Forecourt of the Temple of Apollo at Delphi.

"demons" in the Zoroastrian sense into poets, prophets, physicians and princes"through utopian manipulation of material culture notably via architecture and city planning. In this context, the Enoch legend appears to be a metaphor for the imprisonment of the demonic soul within death until the Tetragrammaton revives a new life enabling the Sun, allegorized as the content of the Vault of Enoch within the Hurd Plate-Royal Arch degree certificate (replacing the Ark of the Covenant) to project the paragon initiate to be through the purifying realms leading toward scientific invention, righteous governance and direct knowledge of the divine astral order. This, of course, is a direct contradiction of the Noachite tradition of the flood wherein the evil of mankind is simply eradicated and Noah and his progeny themselves become paragon initiates, the true Noachidae also referenced in the Old Charges or Gothic *Constitutions* of Desaguliers and Anderson. As the higher grades of Masonry developed from ideology into an actual institutional system, the nature of its intended mission changed. The building of moral character within the individual Freemason as instructed in the Blue Lodge is now expanded upon to include a form of divine insight which invests him with a whole, new esoteric philosophy exclusively contained in high degree Masonry. This insight directed the *parfait* away from a moral death, understood as symbolic imprisonment, through the *Word of God* into solar fire and light provided through the reconstruction of knowledge, again emblematically, inscribed upon the two Pillars of Enoch restored through the correct pronunciation of the Tetragrammaton. Ramsay's devotion to the cause of the encyclopedia stemmed from this conviction that the knowledge he sought gave perspective both to the past history of the human soul and to its future *Apocatastasis*, the universal salvation through knowledge, i.e. light and fire, of every sentient being. This points further to the objective of Masonic initiation in the higher grades to be 1) awareness of the existence of the knowledge to rule wisely and well over ALL gradations of human pre-existence, existence, and presumably post existence; and 2) the power to achieve this status on earth as an initiatic kingly and priestly ruler.

The Jacobite contribution to Masonic mysticality involved the reversal of Catholic spirituality and its dynamic. This latter tradition was aimed at the abnegation or loss of the self, in the pursuit of a numinous event as personal experience. By contrast, Masonic mysticality took up not the abnegation of self, but the effort to enhance the self through a legacy of hermetical ascension into unity with the Name of God as realized through the possession of the Tetragrammaton. An array of degree ceremonial underscored this impulse through the proliferation of Masonic liturgies as ritual degrees along the line of an equivalency between the lore of restoring the Stuart Pretender to his rightful place on the Scottish Throne, and be implication with all of Great Britain, with the possession of the recovered word of Master Mason through the Royal Arch saga. The elements of the Ramsay ideology most relevant to the Jacobite transformation of course, involved his appropriation of mysticality involved the foundation of Quietism he derived from Archbishop of Cambrai, Francois de Selignac de la Mothe Fenelon (1651-1715). Quietism in the broadest sense is the doctrine which declares that man's highest perfection consists in a sort of psychical self-annihilation and a consequent absorption of the soul into the Divine Essence even during the present life. In the state of quietude the mind is wholly inactive; it no longer thinks or wills on its own account, but remains passive while God acts within it. This pavement supported the entire theory of Freemasonry origins from the comparative religion of Greek, Egyptian, and Phoenician antiquity, notably Mithraism, the Egyptian Mysteries, and Zoroastrianism, elements of Noachitic and Patriarchal mysteries of primitive Judaism and chivalry, each rendered in such a way that a theory of world order: a republic within which "every nation was a family and each individual a 'child.'" It is highly likely that Ramsay envisaged his friend and mentor the Archbishop Fenelon as the archetype for this Masonic kingly priest, whose novel *The Adventures of Telemachus* (1699) was the model for Ramsay's own *Voyages of Cyrus* (1727) with Cyrus the Great of Persia naturally as the protagonist. Fenelon's story recounts the travels of Telemachus, the son of Ulysses, on his educational travels accompanied by Mentor (his tutor) who turns out to be the Roman goddess of wisdom Minerva. The story completes or fills out the Homer's *The Odyssey*. Ramsay's *Cyrus* was an argument for limited monarchy addressed to a future king, possibly a Masonic priest-king such as Sarastro, the paragon for such magus priesthood. To Ramsay the mission of Telemachus and his sponsor, Fenelon, and the Masonic priest king must have overlapped and intertwined to complete the calling to complement formal ordination with arcane investiture as developed in his high grades Oration. This concept of High Grade Freemasonry would manifest itself further in the United States with the Order of the Cincinnati, a "Masonic" society exclusively for the families of Washington, his Officer Corps., and their descendants; its first President General was Federalist Alexander Hamilton (1755-1804). Hamilton dominated Washington's second term as Secretary of the Treasury (1793-1797) and, had he lived, might have realized essentially monarchical and Anglophilic concepts to develop the Society of the Cincinnati further as an extension of the aristocracy he cherished as both a personal-professional ideal. He took up values related to an idea of the Presidency which was soundly defeated by Jefferson in 1802, and, unlike Clinton, pursued military options in the Whiskey Rebellion which made him de facto Secretary of War by 1794. In an effort to secure the Presidency for himself, Aaron Burr, who killed Hamilton July 12, 1804, pursued a mission to dismember the Spanish Empire, revolutionize Mexico, and to secure Ouachita River lands in the Louisiana-Arkansas borderlands in 1805. Burr was close to Benjamin Latrobe (1764-1820) and James Wilkinson (1757-1825), both of whom were Freemasons. Latrobe was an intimate of Jefferson; and Wilkinson a friend of Joel R. Poinsett, who served under Edward Livingston as Deputy General Grand High Priest of Royal Arch Masons. Wilkinson died in Poinsett's house in Mexico City on December 28, 1825. Burr's links with the architect of the U.S. Capitol, and with three premier national Masonic presiding officers, Joel Poinsett, Ephraim Kirby, and Edward Livingston, indirectly but substantially positioned him within the network created by the Preston-Webb synthesis, between two rival public figures, either of whom might have eclipsed his mastery of inherited prestige, and applied organizational management skill. Other American elites became members of the Cincinnati. Thus Fenelon's ideology enriches our understanding of Ramsay's thought because it deems the monarch to be bound both to the prosperity of his people, and to the dynamics of law. This latter principle echoed Sir John Fortescue's *De laudibus legum Angliae*, and seems to position a *third force* between the *Dominum et Politicum Regale* of England: monarch who rules with counsel and with consent of his subjects; and *Dominum et Tantum Regale* of France:

absolute monarchy, no input from the Third Estate, with a sacral premise which does link meritocracy with heredity through the primogeniture feature linking Hamilton to Fenelon. This latter idealism in turn pervades the Scottish Rite appeal to the creation of a Masonic aristocracy or clerisy to govern the nation working through an irenic, millennial, Joachimite premise of seeking truth through the study of history, and presumably, its symbolism: Fenelon's core scholarly premise. Ramsay, therefore, understood France itself to possess millennial qualities through which its nobility might reunite all men of enlightened minds, gentle manners, and agreeable wit, not only by the love of fine arts, but much more by the grand principles of virtue, science, and religion.

* * * * *

The Chevalier Ramsay's view of apologetics, the use of non-Christian sources to advance the truthfulness of Christianity, underscored the ideology of the Masonic higher degrees not only through the identification of Cyrus the Great of Persia as a paragon Masonic king, a patriarchal Melchizedek who integrated rulership with wisdom, but also emphasized the role of the era of patriarchs in the Bible as a paragon golden age in which *true religion* was understood and transmitted. This provided Freemasons within the Jacobite circle within which Ramsay moved to link early kingship to the restoration mission of the Stuarts and thereby to the renovation of learning. This in turn linked implicitly pure patriarchal religion to the structure of the Royal Arch of Enoch ceremonial. Reliance upon good pagans as evidence for the truthfulness of Christianity understood as a universal system of salvation in opposition to Calvinist election[264] and to the Puritan political regime of Oliver Cromwell in the 17th century, lifted up in specific the thought of the Neo-Platonist in the ancestry of Masonic ceremonial through Ramsay's use of Zoroastrian mythology as the base line of his noted 1737 Oration. The core link was Origen's idea of an optimistic ascent of the initiate toward union with God, understood Masonically as the restored Lost Word of Master Mason and its further identification of this dynamic with divine kingship. To Ramsay, this link was disclosed in his work *The*

264 Calvinist teaching that before God created the world; he chose to save some people according to his own purposes and apart from any conditions related to those persons.

Voyages of Cyrus as the interplay between Persia and ancient Egypt through their adherence to authentic, true religion which itself could be emphasized as the warrant for Catholic legitimism applied to the realization of a Joachimite Third Age of millennial peacefulness as the product of the light (and fire) bearing Holy Spirit. One also looks to the impact of the thought of William Elephantine (1431-1514), the pre-Reformation Scottish Catholic priest, Bishop of Aberdeen, and humanist for the underpinnings about how the principles of the Scottish Enlightenment interlinked the ideal of a learned national mediating clerisy. The result was a profound deepening of personal philanthropy and humanistically informed Catholic devotion (*qua* Sir Thomas More) that would have penetrated Ramsay's irenic ideology which prevailed until Calvinism triumphed, and seceded the Scottish reformation as a humanistic thread with hermetical and cabbalistic pieties following its achievement. Politically, this process in England established a line of continuity between the Henrician Act of Supremacy (1534) and the Calvinism of Edward VI (1537-1553) which esteemed the latter as a naive if forgivable transgression but drew the line against the Somerset Calvinist reforms. It was the survival of this idiom which welcomed Egyptianate Catholic apologetical embroidery linking Scotland and England through the Stuarts into a vista of Reform envisaged and articulated by Edmund Spenser which drove the mythic underpinnings of Elizabethan Empire and its unique approach to lawmaking that linked the L'Enfant-Latrobe visual rhetoric to a Reformed irenic Empire with appeal to Roman Catholics through an order of mediating spiritual men, the Jesuits.

Ramsay's development of Pythagoras as an initiatic paragon for Masonic rulership rooted his ideology into a relationship based on number linking the natural world understood most likely as matter with human agency. This development was implicit not only in his relationship with Fenelon, which he idealized, but also in his use of Platonism and Origen's Neo-Platonism. Such speculations and beliefs did not reject Calvinist predestination but made it possible to link through number and mathematics, the philosophical speculation about numerology and geometry, to link the earth and the heavens through man within Freemasonry the idealization of a utopian state within which rulers would be wise, beneficent, and just. The path of Masonic initiation was thus recast to utilize the ancient mysteries and medieval chivalry in an eclectic fashion directed towards man and his surrounding through the imparting of wisdom. It is difficult not to overemphasize this point. Sage like figures[265] thus appear recurrently in 18th and 19th century fraternal ritual, notably in the United States embellishment of Masonically derived ritual in Masonic Knights Templar ceremonies: a hermit, or a retired knight; in Odd Fellowship: also a reclusive hermit; and in the Knights of Pythias as Pythagoras himself. The common reference is the introduction of an ideal, usually Greek Doric image of Sparta, as the most disciplined and purposeful Hellenic state as the model for the transformation of all of society as a global community rooted in mystical imagery. The workings of such societies, actually metaphors for lodges, were presented as solutions to the riddles of the universe as the end product of ceremonial initiation. The pursuit of Euclid's 47th proposition (Pythagorean Theorem) as a Masonic ideal pointed to the use of music and medicine as a means to purify the soul, and by extension to the purification of society and would appear architecturally in the streetscape and design of the District of Columbia. Philosophy, consequently, was envisaged as the highest form of music. In Plato's *Republic*, the preparation for the governance of the Republic the philosopher-king was given a mathematical symbol which linked the purification of the individual to the ordering and governing of society. It can be argued that Ramsay's contribution to Freemasonry was a vision that augmented and embellished triadic symbolism, such as later accommodated through the Jesuits, a third perfected age of the Holy Spirit began with his incorporation of the thought of Origen, the third century Platonist, to the idea of universal salvation applied to the ascent of man through a gradual system into Pythagorean governance.

Ramsay's affinity with the late second and third century Platonist Origen was also relevant to Freemasonry, because his exposition of higher grades theory integrated an appeal to great nobles, intellectuals and successful bourgeois in France when such an amalgam was uniquely positioned to influence the position of the development of a form of Freemasonry suited to chivalric idealism without scrupulous or effective opposition from

265 All ultimately symbolic of Thoth Hermes Mercurius Trismegistus.

the state or Church. Whilst not drawn to Freemasonry's royal patronage Louis XV did not persecute the lodges and was persuaded in effect that the mystical ceremonies were ultimately harmless if bothersome. He did not enforce papal proscriptions against Freemasonry which had the result of de facto permitting if not encouraging the tacit attacks upon Catholic and Calvinist orthodoxy through a system which encourages treating holy scripture as allegorical (Chapter III), denying predestination emphatically, advancing ideas relative to the pre-existence and survival of the soul through reincarnation (metempsychosis), and, in effect, teaching that Masons of high degree might development their divine spark of fire and light to be in effect the soul of Christ the sun. Since Origenism was condemned, 543 -553 CE, its survival within a body of Masonic thought and symbolism is significant to the history of ideas. This instance of a sound foundation for allegorical symbolism within a set of specific ceremonies made it possible for secrecy to survive both as a method and as a symbol in itself for the transmission of ideas which otherwise would have been isolated and marginalized.

Ramsay developed, in specific, Origen's idea that only the perfect initiate, the *parfait*, could navigate through the world with reference to what was concrete and corporeal on the one side and what was spiritual and mystical on the other. Ramsay's use of the Origenistic system was masterful because it enabled him to couple his Zoroastrian mythology as the latter and politics as the former, with multiple references to two types of chivalry: Knights of the Orient, the Cyrus and Zerubbabel legends, and Knights of the Occident, Knights Hospitallers and Knights Templar. Symbolically, the initiation of the latter set of ceremonies pointed to initiation by means of the Royal Arch which increasingly in the 18th century was emblematically identified with a merger between solar symbolism of radiance shining either from or into a Vault of Enoch, associated with the Royal Arch degree. This vocabulary pointed to a core dynamic within which human beings, presumably dependent upon their initiatic rank, ascended or descended along a system of degrees of creation dependent upon their participation as purified souls in the Wisdom of the Word toward deification and union with Christ, understood as it were as the the supreme initiate. The entire

Origenistic system tended toward Universalism, the *Apoctastasis*, that point at which all beings, evil as well as good, achieved salvation; in later Masonic idiom, *when order would be brought out of chaos*. The implicit, although clear, identity with ordered perfection at the union of the neophyte with the Masonic Word pervaded Ramsay's system and provided for it a niche within which the purification of society might make the leap between ceremonial, ritual into policy.

The problem of evil, or theodicy, in Ramsay's ideology is more significant. His idea of metempsychosis (transmigration of the soul) apparently transmuted through Origen from Pythagoras perhaps with reference to Giordano Bruno, a principal pre-Masonic intellect, implies a more profound rootage into cosmogony. This involved the transference of stellar symbolism into the design of material order consistent with the pervasive influence of Enochian symbolism on the development of Masonic knowledge. It will be recalled that Enoch passed through the heavens and was granted vista of human theological destiny which refined Christian and patriarchal symbolism profoundly and laid the ground work, inter alia, for the literary achievement of Dante Alighieri in *The Divine Comedy* and by implication in the eschatological significance of Dante on *De Monarchia*. In this context, the development of the ideal of the human sage as a paragon Masonic initiate *qua* Pythagoras and Enoch laid open the concept of the politician-statesman cum inventor, paradigmatically such as the sage Dr. Benjamin Franklin. In other words, the soul of this supreme Masonic initiate or *parfait* might symbolically pass through heavens, its constellations, and retrieve celestial, divine secrets which would empower scientific invention through mathematical perfection transferred into governance through virtuous irenic kingship. Within this dynamic, the ideal of the perfected utopian City as the extended solar temple which at its purest refinement directed the virtuous development of the human psyche into progressive reincarnations toward wise, princely status enriched otherwise a surface interpretation of urban idealism. In Hermetic vocabulary and context, this established a linkage through Roman Catholic and Masonic ideas about a third stage period of eschatology of the Holy Spirit through Joachimite prophecy which linked the layout of Washington D.C. to the design of

Adocentyn, the utopia created by Hermes Trismegistus to advance the deeper linkage between the symbolization of the soul as citizen to the concept of an urban city as a symbol of astral order. The Joachimite template accommodated a dialectic in theodicy wherein good was related to evil as a dramatic and apocalyptic struggle between orthodoxy and heresy. This dynamic not only anticipated Hegelian dualistic thought (action vs. reaction which leads to a synthesis of the two) as a means to harness the philosophy of history on the side of the angels, but also a means to preserve mythology as a rational element within a modern world view. The result was a system of "Catholic" higher degrees of Masonry in which two mediating orders, one aligned with the Elect One of *I Enoch* or the *Son of Man* as evangelical preaching monks, the Jesuits, and the other angels sent from the Temple of Heaven as the order of hermits: the Freemasons. These two orders, one spiritual, the other secular, mediate society both in and into a *third* or *new age* as the *Order of the Just* in keeping with the esoteric prophecies of Joachim von Fiore. This fit hand in glove within Masonic philosophy of deistic moderation and tolerance of the Blue Lodge and the Jesuit fusion of republican democratic values combined with papal monarchy as part of the Counter-Reformation as contained in the Masonic *haute* degrees. As has been seen Masonic Knight Templar ritual in specific took up this imagery through the depiction of a pilgrim warrior encountering a hermit to gain wisdom. Similarly Odd Fellowship and Pythianism (The Knights of Pythias, founded 1864, a Masonic cognate) developed subsequent imagery to install the hermit as an aged knight through whom Pythagorean wisdom was mediated to rule through a new dispensation of an in breaking irenic kingdom. The legendary histories of James Anderson reflect the vestiges of such a mindset through their linkage of royal genealogy to initiatic perfection as taken up by Ramsay and reinvested with Zoroastrian Magus symbolism and Egyptian religious resonance.

This occult schema not only repudiated Ramsay's *bete noire*, Calvinism but also the idealization and symbolism of moderation and limit in the operation of the state. The same premise rooted Ramsay's Jacobite thought on the restoration of the Stuart monarchy to a form of irenic rulership derived from Catholic ideas of the medieval *res publica Christianum* accommodated to a division within the state for those who followed, respectively: Reason; Spirit; and Gain. Pursuit in balance of these principles thus created the foundation for a neutral, in theory, form of state with a balance of three contending elements, which can perhaps be seen in Montesquieu's (1689 -1755) treatise, *The Spirit of the Laws*. One can see in modern Scottish Rite governance the blend of oligarchy and democracy as it developed from French sources during the 18th century and became applied to broader values of the application of Masonic values to American society. In searching for the parallel between Pythagorean idealism and Zoroastrianism to Ramsay it becomes clear that it exists in the transformation of Mithraic fire and therefore light as the extended initiatic metaphor linking the soul of man to matter. Ramsay, of course, was decidedly Christian in his viewpoint about Masonry as can be seen in his idealization of Christian crusading orders such as the Templars. Yet as 18th century rationalism translated soul as mind; it can be argued that revolutionary political faith aimed through secularization at organized religion both purified and refined the symbol of fire-light into a contagion generating radical change rooted in the initiatic ideal.

The Masonic concept of Reason, Spirit, Gain, therefore led not to exaltation but to an awareness of one's own imperfection and wretchedness. Ramsay's association with the French theologian Fenelon, whose biography he wrote, placed him at the edge of both conflicting traditions and thus within a context that enabled him to develop his vista as a bridge between Catholicism as a universal moral discipline and mystical chivalry as a means to provide initiatic exceptions to its inspiration. Freemasonry's high degree preoccupation with the spirit of the moral hero in the above context takes on unique significance given the *parfait* tradition in the French derived Scottish Rite. This has to do with the symbolic fact of Hiram Abif's own martyr death and the ceremonial efforts to succeed him with another worthy figure, Adonhiram. Jansenism was opposed to the moral inspiration of the hero, thus a Hiram martyr worked at odds with a chivalric exemplar. Yet, to make this ideal a mystical moral abstraction would likely have appealed to Ramsay and his colleagues because the moral weight of the individual perfected initiate would have been diffused in favor of a broader class of spiritual men of the cloth, in league with the Jesuit concept of a missionary clerisy.

*　　*　　*　　*　　*

The Chevalier Ramsay's adoption of the Zoroastrian thread for his advancement of the Jacobite cause, in specific, provided the philosophical context for the embroidery of Freemasonry's higher degrees as a means to advance the Stuart cause in conjunction with a Jesuit theology of Joachimite eschatology link with the restoration of a Stuart inspired universal monarchy. His work, *Voyages of Cyrus*, lays this out in terms of the Zoroastrian links to Mithras lifting up Cyrus the Great (as founder of the Achaemenid Dynasty) as a parallel to the paragon initiate, the *parfait*, who creates a micro-cosmogony, a utopian material and political destiny, through an amalgam of the Royal Arch of Enoch and its association with the legend of the survival of the Knights Templar. The links observable in the Royal Arch-Hurd Plate degree certificate forging lodge working through the Royal Arch incorporating the Knights Templar legend makes it clear that this central path for Cyrus as the adopted son of Mithras (the sun) is a key to understanding why Ramsay envisaged the restoration of the Stuart Monarchy in such eschatological terms and how this restoration was at the time of Freemasonry's evolution in the 18th century linked with papal monarchy. The Mithraic element of Ramsay's Zoroastrian lore forged a conceptual policy to position to integrate the recovery of the contents to the Royal Arch vault generically speaking to a rising sun within which *Light* (the sun god Mithras *qua* Apollo) was emblematized as the contents of the Ark of the Covenant as it became like Zoroaster-Mithras or Zarathustra: a divinized solar icon, God's Sun, *Dei in solis*, the risen savior.

Within Ramsay's *Voyages of Cyrus,* Cyrus thus defeated his enemies, the Medes, becomes king and founds a new Persian nation within a renovated society in which knowledge itself was renewed and restored from its antediluvian roots founding at once a new empire, dynasty and a new world order, a Third Age of the Holy Spirit, as Joachim of Fiore envisaged it through his initiation into an astral-religion implicit in the starry canopy of heaven; that is within the constellation of Orion, understood and interpreted as a Osiris risen. This sequence is detailed within the Order of the Red Cross of Babylon ritual, now the first order or degree of the modern Knights

Templar Commandery. The Red Cross ceremony was inserted by Webb as a requisite bridge ritual between the Royal Arch degree of exaltation and Knights Templary. The ritual documents Cyrus investing Zerubbabel with the star, symbolic of Sirius, Isis the sister-wife of Osiris, and sash of a chivalric order empowering him to return to Jerusalem where he discovers the contents of the Ark of the Covenant which became the inspiration for a new nation; the template of which was laid out in embryo in the design of the District of Columbia. The links between the Order of the Red Cross, which occurs in a variety of other orders in similar form: the Royal Order of Scotland, Knight Masonry of Ireland, and in elements in the modern Scottish Rite, derived from the French Rite of Perfection, and makes it clear Washington, D.C., was envisaged as a new Persepolis:[266] a sacred capital through and from which an essentially Ramsay-Roman Catholic vision of America might evolve symbolzing its New World national destiny. Ramsay's *Travels with Cyrus* became therefore an outline about how comparative religion might be brought to bear in the mission of nation building as a means to overcome within an essentially irenic Catholic ethic within a papal monarchy in such a way that at one level the nation might look like and be perceived as a democratic republic but at another remain solidly within the Jesuit fold of millennial Christian eschatology. By contrast, the Ramsay ideology, celebrating as it did the imagery of Pythagoras *qua* Zoroaster within a heliocentric affinity for utopias, borrowed deeply from pre-Reformation Catholicism which preserved a bastion against justification by faith alone as a conceptual buttress for Aristotelian pedantry in the name of reformed learning. This was made possible by the *modus vivendi* reached generally within Continental systems of Masonry. This affinity was not dogmatic or doctrinal but tended to confirm Catholic authority through parallels between high degree polity and Roman Catholic ecclesiology made explicit within Grand Orient and Supreme Council approaches to governance different from English Grand Lodge ideas of political representation. The high degrees of Masonry in its simplest explanation are Roman Catholicism, its ecclesiastical hierarchy, minus Jesus Christ in keeping with gnostic and Docetic esoteric traditions.

266 The ceremonial capital of the Achaemenid-Persian Empire, 550-330 BCE.

It should be referenced that Ramsay addressed his 1737 Oration to a unique cadre of French clergy as well as aristocratic youth. These were sons of aristocrats themselves who occupied largely non-parochial curés enabling them to devote themselves to study: literary and philosophical. Such were attracted to Masonic lodges between 1700 and 1750 in particular when, as we have seen, Jansenism, a mystical form of French Catholic piety, contested with Jesuits for the soul of the nation. So much has been written about this conflict that it is difficult to say more about it with specific regard to the Masonic idea of priesthood except that a mentality emerged linking Roman Catholic orders to Pagan Priesthood which extolled, useful for apologetical activities, the position of a clergyman learned in arcane and esoteric matters. This sacerdotal aesthetic invariably to the shape of noble clergy considering themselves, disciples of Christ or Priests of Apollo, the sun God, an aesthetic reinforced by the baroque imagery of the Palace of Versailles. As such they were expected to elucidate law and ethics for interior societies of Freemasons and others who venerated the Pythagorean doctrine of limitation and temperance and who elucidated the principle of the Golden Mean. As such, the clergy who were accommodated uniquely in various French and German rites of Masonic initiation as a special class were the archetypes of Pythagorean Magi, projecting clerical institutionalism from the outside and profane world but alternatively realizing within lodges, chapters, and councils of Freemasonry an ancient, priestly, elite status. A tradition developed of the Heptasophs, the seven sages of Apollonian law giving and ethics, of whom the Greek ruler Solon was the single historic figure. This imagery survived, interestingly, into the *Dignati Viri Septem* tradition in American collegiate fraternalism, most likely with French Masonic inspiration. Philanthropy and mysticism characterized such priests who tended toward Universalism in religious policy whilst maintaining an orthodox exterior to the world. It seems likely that the mysticism associated with the Netherlands in the late medieval and Renaissance periods shaped and informed their ethic as well. The Dutch publication by Jean Frederic Bernard (1683-1744) of the engravings of Freemason Bernard Picart (1673 -1733) in a nine volume work (began in 1723) titled, *Céremonies et coutumes religieuses de tous les peuples du monde*, is a work illustrating the ceremonial and religious costumes of the world in systematic form.

This work presaged the wide usage of liturgical and priestly vestments by Masonic orders and was noted for its appearance in the same year as the first publication of Anderson's Masonic *Constitutions*.

The Ramsay high degree ideology generated a sequence of symbols which moved through successive formulations of Knight Templar imageries. The first of these, a narrative linking the Order to the recovery of the ineffable word and its restoration was, in essence, a reworking of the Royal Arch of Zerubbabel transferred from the building of the Second Temple. The sequence invariably conflated Scottish Crusaders with Knights Templar. Eventually, the thread of revenge for the execution of the last Templar Grand Master Jacques DeMolay became intertwined with revenge for the murder of Hiram Abif in the Knights Kadosh ceremony (1741) through the Chapter of Clermont and the Council of the Emperors of East and West, leading to the creation of the Ancient and Accepted Scottish Rite from the French Rite of Perfection. The movement of Ramsay's ideology into concrete organizational expression took place between 1737 and 1767 when Masonic writers such as Etienne (Stephen) Morin and James Andrew Francken developed a system of ceremonies termed the Rite of Perfection. Francken established these in a Lodge of Perfection in Albany, New York in 1767. In turn the premier Masonic intellect of his day, Thomas Smith Webb summarized specific ceremonies from the Francken lodge and printed them in his Monitor, termed the *Illustrations of Masonry* in 1797. From the sequence of events and through parallel channels the Scottish Rite developed. Its first Supreme Council can be dated from Charleston, South Carolina in 1801 from which an Irish Supreme Council was erected. It inherited the formal structure of a systemic Masonic Rite through a conduit from Europe through the Haiti and the West Indies into New York and Philadelphia, Florida, and finally into Charleston where it was taken up by America's primary Church historian of Anglicanism and Universalist theologian Frederick Dalcho, a native of Prussia and resident of Maryland. A complex of theosophical ideas, later re-denominated philanthropy became linked to the Rite. These concepts can be traced from Jakob Boehme (1574-1624), the German mystic and original thinker within the Lutheran tradition. Boehme's hermetical and Neo-Platonic ideals influenced many anti-authoritarian and occult movements, including Rosicrucianism, Martinism, and the Religious Society of Friends.

While the national origins of the Scottish Rite have been disputed, there is little question that what is now known as the Scottish Rite was framed in France and transported in stages, largely piece meal, into North America following its origination following The Chevalier Ramsay's Oration in 1737. The structuring of actual ceremonies appears to have taken place in the College of Clermont in Paris, a Jesuit entity patronized by Catholic Scots in the service of the House of Stuart around a ceremony termed *The Scottish Master, Ecossais*. The Scotch Master, prevalent in France during Ramsay's heyday, included reference to a Vault, and probably contains one of the earliest references to what became the Royal Arch of Enoch. The Jesuit contribution to the ideology of the ritual appears to be Joachimite in its origins as a means to mediate the unalloyed Catholic truth to the masses through apologetics and was twofold: an imaged set of hermits; this icon appeared early in Knight Templar imagery as a retired knight who became a mentor to the pilgrim candidate and survived as a unifying icon within Odd Fellow initiatory degree ritual and within the first rank of the Pythian Order, likely from the imagery of the writings of Johannes Scotus Erigena (815-877) and Raymond Lully (1232-1315), both of whose methods survived from medieval origins into post Tridentate (Council of Trent) apologetics, the latter as a method to convert Muslims to Christianity. The second mean or order was a mediating clerisy integrating hermitic and activist elements from the mountain top into the lower Masonic grades as a means to reconcile action and contemplation. Specific analogues between ritual emblems and Biblical references to the Temple of Solomon seem to have been inserted within this mission such that the devolution of symbols resulted in a correlation between Joachim von Fiore's mission of the realization of a Third Age of the Holy Spirit (cf. new Age of Aquarius) through the Scottish Rite ideal mediated by a new order of spiritual men through the Rite of Perfection. Thus the pursuit of Perfection was both the pursuit of personal moral and ethical perfection but also a more programmatic approach to progress through the medium of Pythagorean logic which came to incorporate Egyptian solar ideas of kingship extrapolated from the Jacobite agenda. By 1758, the Rite was introduced into the workings of the Berlin based Grand Lodge of the Three Globes and reorganized as a Council. The antiquity of the German national character, as opposed to that of England and Spain, played into the Masonic imagination of the nation as it emerged during the reign of Frederick the Great. Uniquely, the aspiration of the Prussian King was to consolidate the dynasty, the First German Reich.

The link between the German imprint and consolidation of the whole Ramsay concept to Prussia from 16th century threads has also be referenced by R. J. W. Evans in his study of Rudolf II, *Rudolf II and His World: A Study in Intellectual History, 1576-1612* (1953), in terms of linking occult and esoteric Renaissance learning, related to the emergence of imperial theory through the Elizabethan occult magus Dr. John Dee. Dee carried forward an interior dynamism linking a mission of world reform of Hermeticism and Cabalism to world reform through a new imperial Catholicism which anticipated the Scottish Rite and its patronage by Frederick the Great by two hundred years. Lest we dismiss this coincidence as irrelevant to the political structuring of rites of national initiation out of hand, it is important to reference that various nationalities specifically developed core Masonic ceremonial to accommodate national lore and saga: notably France, America and Mexico each with the result that a national spirit merged with core ceremonial to create an identity between a deeper form of logic and national patriotism embodied in various forms of Pythagorean ideals of public sphere leadership. Arguably, this thread can be seen within the Masonic tapestry of the *Thrice Greatest* Republic and in the Webb-Preston-Clinton synthesis outlined by Masonic scholar Salem Town in his *A System of Speculative Masonry* published in 1818. The American Republic was thus triple fold because it involved various forms of alliances between 1) Masonic mysticism; 2) ideas of secular political order of an Egyptianate resonance; and 3) liberal Catholic vision.

There is, in other words, a distinctive link between the German ideal of a restored Empire of Charlemagne, within its reworking of the Ramsay ideology through various strands of Masonic imagery which shaped both the path of individual initiation and the definition of Masonic polity. That this was in place by the time Freemasonry was transmitted in the high degrees to the new world seems clear from internal evidence. The *parfait* tradition of the perfection of the candidate, the symbolism of the recovery of the Lost Word in the Royal Arch of Enoch and the Knight Templar and Teutonic Knight conflations had merged by the time what is now the Rite of Perfection: and the Scottish Rite its successor took up the double-headed imperial eagle as the emblem of its polity apparently under Frederick the Great and utilized this ritual emblem to construct a worldwide set of Rites. Other elements, notably the Rose Croix, were introduced from Rosicrucian lore giving the Scottish Rite a replete iconology of the range of eclectic ceremonials represented in its now four groupings of degrees: Lodge of Perfection; Chapter of Rose Croix, Council of Princes of Jerusalem; and Consistory of Masters (SJ) and Princes (NMJ) of the Royal Secret.

The Council of the Emperors of the East and West was the entity at the heart of the Ramsay ideology which projected into the Masonic Thirty-Third Degree the political and mystical image of a Sovereign Grand Scottish Rite Commander replete with the double-headed Habsburg eagle as its badge and as a millennial icon of a thousand year rule of the Catholic Holy Roman Empire; the Scottish Rite doubled-headed eagle looks both east and west symbolic of the Council of the Emperors of the East and West and the Catholic high degree systems.

The doubled-headed eagle is the symbol of the Scottish Rite of Freemasonry.

The eagle also appeared upon the standard of Cyrus the Great who sought to advance the Second Temple at Jerusalem as a symbol of national millennial destiny. The influence of this iconography idealized the European longing for global irenic peace, an end to religious sectarian conflict, and relief from the provincials of dynastic European princes germinated from medieval and Renaissance roots within the 18th century. The Council of the Emperors of the East and West in Paris contained within it the Thomistic principle of the achievement of perfection to wit knowledge was exalted. This was a conceptual resource for a Jesuit Masonic ploy and mission, likely developed at the College of Clermont, to subrogate through the iconization of specific emblems, Neo-Platonic gradualism, combined with Joachim von Fiore's Third Age as an equivalency between Third Order of the Ages rooted in the Holy Spirit dynamic idea, and Thomism[267] which held that God's own quiddity was his very Being, a *Summum Bonum,* which apologetically could be aptly twinned with the Masonic achievement of the *Royal Secret* as a sublime Counter-Reformation deception.

Such conceptualities underscored the critical importance of developing a theory of irenic kingship in league with Egyptian mythology. Thomism thus afforded the Jesuits an opportunity to incorporate the pursuit of Reason through an amalgam of revealed truth in creation, which enmeshed within Newton's Providentialism mediated by Dr. Desaguliers, as well as to make a leap, continuing the same initiatic path toward perfection through knowledge. John of Salisbury (ca. 1115-1176), in particular would have been a prime source for the Jesuit embroidery of perfect knighthood applied from the Ramsay ideology into the Masonic concept of Perfection, long associated with their midwifery in creating the Knight of the East ceremony depicting Zerubbabel's Order of the Red Cross conferred by Cyrus the Great within the legend of the rebuilding of the Second Temple at Jerusalem. The defense of the commonwealth by a dedicated militia thereby emerged in step with the path toward universal papal monarchy. It is significant that this embroidery took place between 1730 and 1760, a low point of Masonic ritual and literary development in England but in the flowering of the enthusiasms of the 1745 Stuart rising. It is not difficult to understand how the Baconian educational reform agenda signaling the end of the Renaissance might have been taken up in this ritualizing maelstrom which integrated knighthood as special servants of the Church

267 Theology of St. Thomas Aquinas.

with a Solomonic ideology of reformed utopian wisdom. The Baconian ideas would have been valuable because each of his monumental works, *The Proficience and the Advancement of Learning* (1605), *The New Atlantis* (1627), and *Novum Organum* (1620) successfully challenged and revised the cosmology and mysteries of orthodoxy with a fresh utopian vista derived from a new instauration of knowledge thus setting Sir Francis Bacon apart from hermits Giordano Bruno, Tommaso Campanella, and Galileo Galilei whose vistas were equally impressive but more controversial. From 1781, however, the Council of Emperors of the East and West and the Councils of Knights of the East merged within the Rite of Perfection and was alleged to be confirmed at Berlin by the Emperor Frederick the Great through the *Grand Constitutions* of 1762. This document, the authenticity of which has been contested, was followed by a further revision in 1786 in which the Prussian King resigned his Grand Commandership in favor of various national Supreme Councils, of which the Charleston, S.C. entity, became the premier and Mother Council of the World. The subsequent degree, the Scottish or Scotch Master, also emerged at this time as an extension of the Ramsay ideology and Jacobite enthusiasms. This ritual took up the Royal Arch saga of the Order of the Red Cross, Zerubbabel and Cyrus but transposed the situation to the recovery of the Royal Arch Word, the Tetragrammaton, to a party of Knights Templars rather than builders of the Second Temple. This conformed perfectly with the Jesuit Counter-Reformation as Catholic Templars, as agents of the papacy, became the recoverers of the Logos rather than operative stone masons.

The degree gradual structure of the Scottish Rite as devised between 1767 and 1804 with American Masonry exhibits features resembling the Renaissance period's structure of the *Ars Notoria* within which specific emblems, or *memory statues* at interplay with great philosophic and cosmic imagination. This interplay of the human psyche with memory images was understood to be best arrayed within circular domed structures within which specific emblems were vividly impressed upon the moral and ethical will to recall linkages between human activity and a more expansive universe of inspirational meaning. Both the Masonic tri-gradual system and the Rite of Perfection simulated this technique in two ways: the actual infrastructure of the degrees for moral narrative content; and the narrative texts themselves which detailed, uniquely in the Fellowcraft ceremony and in the Royal Arch of Enoch, the symbolic detail of the meaning of specific emblems. In the scholarly issue of the origins of Freemasonry, this line of inquiry presses the question of the content of speculative Freemasonry as intellectual history as opposed to the continuance of operative guilds which simply may have been the focus of symbolic structuring of degree ceremonies which allude to the pursuit of the Lost Word as a metaphor for sense of direct imaginative participation in a linkage between public policy and perceived celestial imagery.

It is difficult to know precisely if the Masonic degree ceremonial system, as envisaged by Ramsay from Newton's seedbed, contained within it the differentiation between being and becoming, as it related in the Renaissance crucible to the use of space symbolically, the core of the Masonic refinement to architecture and in general to material culture. What is clear, however, is that the symbolism of Geometry as a driving force, not just as a mathematical subject matter, was behind it. Geometry (almost) became a verb to Freemasons of Desaguliers rank and it was this feature of Freemasonry which surely attracted Dr. Benjamin Franklin and his contemporaries to it as it bridged the gap between the geographies and ideologies of Britain and France. This was not simply an accent on the individual versus the elite oligarchy, as Ramsay developed its chivalric ethics, but had to do more with the building of systems upon which an irenic modernity was established albeit at first in fragile and tentative terms. It is also clear that the Enochic contribution to this imagery was the creation of a new heaven and new earth, after a successful contending with evil the outlines of which were established in seminal form through the restoration of the cabalistic word as the unfolding of frontier expansion as Freemasonry envisaged consistently and without serious mythic impediment. It is clear, further, that left to its own the Renaissance was anarchistic and conservative prone to place its scholarly powers in the hands of those patrons who exercised power and violence. Left to its own without the stimulus of a driving Joachim force to instill modernity with a heliocentric energetic soul of a new age in the achievement of a new fraternity of nations it would have faltered into superficiality. It did not. Rather, the artificers of the Enochic icon avoided Erastian and simply irenic conservatism for an effective method of mustering the dynamics of elitist within which hermetical striving and ascension toward the cabalistic apotheosis of modernity.

In sum, it is beyond dispute that Ramsay's Oration "took." However Masonic historians loyal to the United Grand of England are critical of Ramsay claiming that the higher degrees are pure invention even going so far to suggest Ramsay was a fraud.[268] This is unfortunate and incorrect yet understandable due to Ramsay's own affiliations to the French, Roman Catholicism, and the Jacobite cause. Ramsay claimed in his Oration that Freemasonry descended from the Knights Templars. The premier ritualist of the Scottish Rite, Albert Pike, ran with this; he states:

"The Templars, like all other Secret Orders and Associations had two doctrines, one concealed and reserved for the Masters which was Johannism (Gnosticism/Docetism of the Fourth Gospel); the other public, which was Roman Catholic. Thus thy deceived the adversaries whom they sought to supplant. Hence Freemasonry, vulgarly imagined to have begun with the Dionysian Architects or the German Stoneworkers adopted St. John the Evangelist as one of its patrons, associating with him, in order not to arouse the suspicions of Rome, St. John the Baptist, and thus covertly proclaiming itself the child of Kabbalah and Essenism together."[269]

Was the Masonic underpinnings based on mere Templar legend, in other words, of mystical sentiment which preserved itself from the suppressions of the Templars; they were arrested on October 13, 1307, by Philip IV (*le Bel*) and his puppet, Pope Clement V, to the 17th and 18th centuries. Or was this Templar undercurrent an occult encoded relic of *real history* of esoteric Lost Word insights which, in turn, stemmed from the Templars encounters with the Assassins and Saracens, who developed their own eastern forms of Muslim mysticism, namely, as has been seen at the

268 Wallace-Murphy, Tim, *The Enigma of the Freemasons: Their History and Mystical Connections,* page 81.
269 Pike, Albert, *Moral and Dogma of the Ancient and Accepted Scottish Rite*, pp. 817-818.

beginning of this chapter, Sufism as intertwined with Blue Lodge Masonry. In turn did the Templars uncover the Vault of Enoch beneath Mount Moriah and recover some sort of divine treasure as portrayed in the Scottish Master ceremony and the high degrees in general? We will never know for sure, nevertheless the Lost Word and its recovery motif survived, both in legend and in high degree Masonic ritual from Ramsay's Oration. It should be noted that Ramsay had links to Freemason Elias Ashmole, a fellow of the Royal Society (like Ramsay) whose interest in antiquarian esoteric lore provides further link to the Masonic-Templar Lost Word or lost yet restored history nexus as preserved presumably from the Templars into Rosicrucianism and into *haute* degree Masonry. There is further concrete evidence that the Knights Templar did not just disappear from history, rather it was subsumed in some way into Scottish society under the auspices of Robert the Bruce, who was excommunicated in 1306, a year before the suppression of the Templars. Masonic organization and ritual in Scotland seems to have evolved in response to the dourness and abolition of ritual of the Calvinist Church.[270] While actual documentable evidence is lacking, it is clear, even to the most close-minded person, that visual and symbolic evidence on tombs, sculptures, and Rosslyn Chapel itself that Freemasonry owes something to the Knights Templar.[271] Rosslyn Chapel, built in the mid-fifteenth century, contains numerous references to the building of Zerubbabel's Temple with no direct reference to Solomon's Temple.[272] This symbolism encoded in stone, located in a place important to Freemasonry (Rosslyn's nave conforms to the Golden Ratio and geometric perfection), seems to be referencing the recovery of the Vault of Enoch during the building of the Second Temple and significantly underscores the importance of the Royal Arch ceremony detailing this discovery and hints towards a true yet lost part of our history. Rosslyn Chapel also includes three pillars in its east end. Their medieval names are the Earl's Pillar, the *Shekinah*, the presence of God attributed to the east end of a Christian Church where mass was celebrated *ad orientem* symbolically representing the rising sun; and the Prince's pillar. In the Hebrew Mysteries, *Shekinah* was associated with presence of

270 Curl, James Stevens, *The Art and Architecture of Freemasonry*, pp 45- 48.
271 Ibid, 48.
272 Wallace-Murphy, Tim, *The Enigma of the Freemasons: Their History and Mystical Connections*, page 64.

the Ark of the Covenant in the Holy of Holies inside Solomon's Temple; it was recovered along with the Tetragrammaton in the Royal Arch Masonic *haute* degree ceremonials. Was the naming of a pillar *Shekinah* inmedieval Rosslyn suggesting the presence of the Ark of the Covenant within its confines? Does this symbolism suggest the Knights Templar brought some hidden treasure to Rosslyn? Interestingly these three pillars were renamed in the late Georgian era (1714-1830) the Master Pillar, the Journeyman Pillar, and most famously, the Apprentice Pillar as an obvious homage to Craft Freemasonry. A further possible connection between Masonry and the Templar's symbolic rhetoric of Pythagorean-rooted ethos was through the military engineering of castles, in Freemason Henry Knox's (1750 -1806) idiom as the establishment of West Point as a modern Krak des Chevaliers, a Crusader fortress in Syria that was headquarters of the Knights Hospitallers, built ca. 1031-1150/1250 CE. Knox was a book learned artillery expert, experienced commander, second United States Secretary of War, appointed March 8, 1785, and a symbolic virtuoso whose embroidery of the Cincinnati cult and ceremonial echoed the Ramsay ideology and created a direct link through the Society from his Freemasonry into military and defense policy and practical politics. Not even the great Washington could dissuade the Society from pursuing its hereditary mission as a romantically infused sodality of elitist, cultured patriots who deemed themselves as the working elite of the nation. Thus the Templar connection, the importance of Scotland, mnemonics, Renaissance-Hermetic ideals and philosophies, the Reformation and Counter-Reformation that followed, in the history of Freemasonry, both in the development of the craft and high degrees, cannot simply be overlooked or ignored.[273]

273 Curl, James Stevens, *The Art and Architecture of Freemasonry*, page 48.

CHAPTER VIII

DEWITT CLINTON AND THE EMPIRE STATE

The Royal Arch Grand High Priest, the Knights Templar, the Order of Cincinnati, the Erie Canal, Minerva, and Illuminism

"Clinton eventually became the nation's Masonic leader, with consequences for his political career, as we shall see. In 1793 he was installed as worshipful master of the Holland Lodge, and he delivered an address in which he interpreted to the members the importance and nature of their order. Clinton was not yet twenty-five, and he felt called on to stress his unworthiness for his new office: 'Sensible I am, brethren, that neither my Age, experience, nor abilities entitle me to fill this place, to Which your partiality, not my merit, has called me.' Masonry, he said, was first and foremost a 'moral institution,' one that tried to embody the 'important truth' of the '*naturally equality of mankind.*'"
- Evan Cornog, *The Birth of Empire: DeWitt Clinton and the American Experience, 1769-1828*, 1998.

"The Templars, or *Poor Fellow Soldiery of the Holy House of the Temple* intended to be re-built, took as their models, in the Bible, the Warrior-Masons of Zorobabel, who worked, holding the sword in one hand and the trowel in the other. Therefore it was that the Sword and the Trowel were the insignia of the Templars, who subsequently, as will be seen, concealed themselves under the name of *Brethren Masons*."
- Albert Pike, *Morals and Dogma of the Scottish Rite*, 1871.

DeWitt Clinton's (b. March 2, 1769) Masonic and political career as a Jeffersonian Republican was built upon family associations which led him into Freemasonry and into membership in the Society of the Cincinnati: a premier hereditary order comprised of members of George Washington's officer corps, founded by General Henry Knox. Knox, a Freemason, rose to the rank of Major General during the American Revolution, was the nation's second Secretary of War, a bookseller and intellectual leader within military circles of Boston, and founder of West Point Military Academy. President Washington attended Clinton's commencement at King's College, founded 1754, later Columbia University. Clinton was associated with upstate private lodges, and was a Past Master of Holland Lodge No. 8 in New York City, with which George Washington was affiliated. Clinton was also Grand Master of New York, Daniel Tompkins (1774-1825) was his successor as Grand Master, who was a rival in politics and within the New York Grand Lodge. A result is that Masonic lodges in New York City were largely under the control of Tompkins who served James Monroe as Vice President (1817-1825). The city and upstate lodges formally separated in 1822.[274] Clinton was also a "brave," a member of the original Society of St. Tammany/Tammany Hall, when it functioned as a patriotic, fraternal order. He witnessed the transformation of the society into a morally defined middle class proto-Masonic order, at one level, and an opportunistic ersatz political party at another. As mayor of New York City (1803-1815), Clinton was obliged to work with the party of John Adams, the Federalists, who controlled the Council of Appointment, and remained realistic, if not entirely friendly, to British interests. The Federalists were, however, unable to control radical, Anglo-phobic factions of their own party who followed Aaron Burr –the so-called Martling Men–and later, those who followed Martin Van Buren, a non-Mason, manager of the Albany Regency[275] and an ally of Andrew Jackson. By the end of the War of 1812, Clinton had arranged political and banking interests with Federalists such that he was accused

274 Between 1822-1827, a schism occurred between upstate Masons and the Masons in New York City because "Upstate Masons" felt that Grand Lodge should be held in Albany and not in New York City, since Albany was more centrally located. In 1825, Stephen Van Rensselaer (1799-1881) was elected Grand Master to heal the wounds. "Bro. Van" became very prominent in the Ancient and Accepted Scottish Rite beginning in 1824. He became an Inspector-General of that Rite on June 17th, 1845.

275 A group of politicians who controlled the New York state government between 1822 and 1838.

by the Jeffersonian Republicans of abandoning the ideals of Jefferson and Madison, and forced out of a position of influence in New York City politics. Nevertheless his influence upon upstate New York Masonic operations, functions, and methods remained strong.

Clinton's network included the General Grand Chapter of Royal Arch Masons, founded in Boston, Massachusetts in 1797. This entity was a sovereign Masonic body at its foundation which in Masonic parlance meant that it had plenary authority to govern its affairs parallel to a craft Grand Lodge, and thus can be understood as a conceptual inheritor of Anderson's *Constitutions* of 1737, applied to a higher degree Rite. The General Grand Chapter governed four ceremonies: Mark Master Mason, Past Master (virtual), Most Excellent Master, and the Order of the Holy Royal Arch (cf. Webb's system), all of which originally were conferred in local craft Blue Lodges but were subsequently incorporated into a separate entity. As has been noted (Chapter II), its leadership were constituted as "dais" officers: High Priest, King and Scribe, reflecting the ritual narrative of the senior degree or order. Eminent Freemasons tended to occupy these offices in Clinton's era, notably Ephraim Kirby, a lawyer and judge in the Louisiana Purchase territory; Edward Livingston, of the New York dynastic family; and Joel Roberts Poinsett, the United States Minister to Mexico and South Carolina statesman. A further "worthy" to hold the position was Charles Gilman (1793-1861), a lawyer from New Hampshire, T. S. Webb's own state of residence, at a critical point in his career. Charles Gilman was the senior administrative officer of both the General Grand Chapter and the (General) Grand Encampment of Knights Templar, thus becoming the senior administrative officer of the two national bodies over which DeWitt Clinton presided.

The political context of Clinton's achievement is best defined as that of the Clintonian period in New York State politics. His public and Masonic offices were intertwined from the date of his raising, or initiation, in Holland Lodge No. 8, September 3, 1790, of which George Washington was a member, until Clinton's unexpected death on February 11, 1828 in the midst of a storm of anti-Masonic controversy brought on by the

William Morgan Affair. In brief Clinton's Masonic offices included the Mastership of Holland Lodge (1783), Grand High Priest of New York Royal Arch Masons (1798), Grand Master of Masons in New York (1806-1819), General Grand High Priest of the Royal Arch (1816-1826), General Grand Master, Knights Templar, New York State (1814-1828) and of the National Grand Encampment (1816-1828). Clinton also presided over the Cerneau Rite of Sovereign Grand Consistory of the Exalted Chiefs of Masonry, an important Scottish Rite body, intermittently, from about 1808 and until death. This was an important entity although since marginalized by two other sectional Supreme Councils. It was a source of ritual provenance including the ceremonial of the Knights Templar in New York. On its creator Joseph Cerneau and Cerneau Masonry Albert Mackey writes,

> "....This Masonic charlatan, who claimed the right to organize bodies of the Ancient and Accepted Scottish Rite, was expelled and his pretensions denounced, in 1813, by the legal Supreme Council sitting at Charleston, South Carolina. Cerneau and his adherents gave much trouble in the Scottish Rite for many years, and the bodies which he had formed were not entirely dissolved until long after the establishment of a legal supreme Council for the Northern Jurisdiction."[276]

DeWitt Clinton's principal public offices included: Lower House, State Legislature (1797 – 1805 - 1811), Upper House, or State Senate (1798 - 1802), U.S. Senate (Resigned) (1802 - 1803), Mayor of New York (1803 - 1807; 1808 - 1810; 1811 - 1815), Lieutenant Governor (1811-1813), Governor of New York State (1817-1821; 1825-1828). Clinton was also a nominee for the Presidency of the United States in the election of 1812 on the peace initiative to prevent the War of 1812. He became, however, active in the war effort, construction important fortifications for New York City. Clinton's principal public achievements were the introduction of the Twelfth Amendment to the United States Constitution, whilst U.S. Senator, construction of the Erie Canal whilst

276 Mackey, Albert, *Encyclopedia of Freemasonry, Vol. I*, page 139.

Governor of New York, and a series of civic improvements whilst Mayor of New York City, including the introduction of free public schools, effective city planning, fortifications, sanitation, and poor relief. While Mayor he dictated the nominations of two governors of the state. In state office, he removed the political restrictions on Roman Catholics, abolished slavery, and reduced punishment for debtors and misdemeanors. From 1810, he organized the construction of the Erie and Champlain-Hudson River canal but was deprived of his post on the Canal Board in 1824 by the Albany Regency. Before his 1828 death, he was instrumental in the establishment of a statewide school system, the promotion of manufactures and legal reform. DeWitt Clinton, therefore, took up, as an extension of the Washington Masonic persona the outpouring of imagery identifying Washington's commingling of official stature with initiatic resonance, utilizing the remnant networks for non-partisan political purposes, at one level, and at another, for the preferment of his partisan and civic colleagues. The result is that he exemplified the emblems and symbols of the Royal Arch degree, in specific, to establish a Masonic public sphere. This enhanced his own professional and legal career and made it possible for him to appeal to potent community leaders along moral lines. This naturally introduced the principle of mediation into higher degree Masonic theory in a parallel manner to the idea of a public sphere: Dewitt Clinton managed his networks as de facto elites of mediating members of a religious order moderating society.The idea echoed the subsequent principle of a clerisy through which Masonry emulated Anglican concepts of the deployment of the entire Erastian national Church, creating a *via media* within society through which *Christ might transform culture*, to use Helmut Richard Niebuhr's typology.

The identification of Clinton's regime makes it more possible for the Masonic scholar to identify the kerygma of Freemasonry: that is, the central core of interior ritual meaning. In the Clinton-Webb, and Town synthesis (Chapter IX) the transformative message for Masons was that the loss, recovery, preservation and interpretation of the real Word of Master Masons transcended what we now regard to be modern critical historical scholarship and averred to a previous epoch of antiquity within which the soul and the mind were undifferentiated. The allusion is, of course, to

Biblical studies wherein the kerygma was the saving work of Jesus Christ which penetrated through a variety of layers and verbiage within scripture to frame a central message for the Christian adherent. In Freemasonry, this was that the Royal Arch Word, understood to be the Name of God, the Tetragrammaton, perdured throughout the vagaries of profane (cf. secular) history to transform the life of the individual as well as community life. From the Hampton Court conference (1604) through the Long Parliament (1640) the clergy of the Church of England became simpler and more adroit at evangelicalism, framing the imperial imagery of a colonial empire in terms of Puritan mission and outreach. Through the eternal evangel of Joachimite prophecy, available through Masonic spiritual intellect this midwifed missionary zeal from the Renaissance Platonic forms of cabalistic and hermetical energies which, when integrated, transformed the new nation through the Enochic template available within the Clinton circle. The dynamic was, of course, the dissemination of esoteric ideas from circles of elites as they proliferated from county seat to county seat as lodges, chapters, and commanderies were warranted and chartered, cemented by the further elites of the Rite of Perfection, later the Scottish Rite, in its application of the Ramsay ideology.

The movement of Clinton's Masonic view of public sphere rhetoric from the Royal Arch-Knights Templar Red Cross (of Babylon) matrix of images and symbols paralleled methods devised in Europe to group cells of Freemasons together through communication by hieroglyphic-symbolic means and associations. It was this method, extrapolated from Clinton's own sense of the meaning of Freemasonry which fed conspiracy theories that his deputies, in the General Grand Chapter and Grand Encampment, the formal institutions managing the extension of the synthesis on the western and southern frontier were de facto Illumines (not Illuminati), a more theosophical element of European Masonry parallel to the Joachimite view of Jesuits as the spiritual men destined to bring form a new Masonic church and a commonwealth from 1797 (General Grand Chapter Royal Arch foundation) and 1816 (Grand Encampment of Knights Templar foundation). This involved suspicions that the careers of Edward Livingston in Louisiana and Ephraim Kirby in Mississippi were deployed in judicial and legislative capacities in frontier regions and Joel Poinsett into a parallel capacity as United States' first American Minister to Mexico, where he developed a "*Yorquino*" Royal Arch Masonic network within local Mexican politics to pursue the alleged Clintonian objective. Both the Renaissance utopian elements of *Ars Notoria* and the identification of Clinton's public sphere driven use of New York Masonry point to an objective relished during the Illuministic scare throughout Europe in the 1770s and 1780s to advance deism and cosmopolitanism to combat religious and political slavery. The alliance of the Clinton-Webb ritual synthesis with Arminian theology, notably in the person of frontier Ohio Bishop Philander Chase, pointed to specific opportunities to merge the ideal of a reformed mystical Catholicism through the agency of Knight Templary with roots in deep Renaissance imagery generating a Royal Arch take on denominational Church piety. Other senior Freemasons within the public and political arena took up Freemasonry presumably for political purposes during the Clinton era. Unlike Clinton, however, these did not seek to establish a means to amplify emblems and symbols to create a public sphere as a means to create a millennial mission from the rituals, as did Clinton and his compeers. Henry Clay (1777-1852) proposed a national Grand Lodge, organizing a meeting in the U. S. Senate chamber for this purpose; and Daniel Tompkins (1774-1825), who became Sovereign Grand Commander of the Supreme Council, 33rd degree, A.A.S.R., a rival, and more successful entity than Cerneau's rite which Clinton managed as the Grand Consistory of Exalted Chiefs of Masonry. Neither Clay, nor Tompkins, applied the same forensic intellectual skills to the development and extension of Freemasonry as an interior, symbolic source for his Solomonic figure emulating Washington and other Freemasons who held conspicuous public and Masonic office.

In Clinton's Masonic context, access to legitimate authority as conceived within Freemasonry in its various constitutions and rituals was linked to the national solar mission as pictured in the Royal Arch Hurd Plate was conceived as a substitute for kingship and an established church. By 1751, the main current of Masonic ideas in England had been altered to incorporate references to monarchy as the tacit and implicit center of the governance of the fraternity, both, as the result of the intention of its early Grand Master, John Theophilus Desaguliers, a popularizer of Newton's ideas applied to monarchical concepts extended to the movements and structure of the universe. Desaguliers, who compiled the *Old Charges*, was an academic at Christ Church, Oxford, a fellow and president of the Royal Society, and a royal chaplain. He initiated Frederick, Prince of Wales (1707-1751), son of George II, and father of George III on November 5, 1737. Two sons of George III became Freemasons and Grand Masters, the Duke of Kent of the Antients and the Duke of Sussex of the Moderns in the run-up to the Union of 1813-1814, which produced a United Grand Lodge of England.

Clinton's specific usage of Masonic ideas borrowed a principle from the Masonic mission of Dr. Benjamin Franklin, who was a provincial Grand Master of the Modern Grand Lodge in Pennsylvania, and publisher of the first American edition of Anderson's *Constitutions*. Franklin's mission: to perfect the individual through scientific knowledge and practical policy refinement as a means to regenerate society. This concept linked Franklin's persona as a scientist with seemingly magus powers to a developing oligarchic and social ideal at work in Scottish Rite Masonic approaches to governance which he obtained in Paris during Franklin's diplomatic career and within the Lodge of the Nine Sisters (or Muses) which incorporated savants and philosophers into its membership, notably Claude Adrien Helvetius (1715-1771) and Voltaire (1694-1778), as well as John Paul Jones (1747-1792) founder of the U.S. Navy. The result was a consolidation of the Newtonian principle advocated by Dr. Desaguliers with the cultural ideal of national Masonic initiation as intellectual enlightenment. The further result was a form of encoded, moral calculus designed to differentiate and integrate individuals into society as discrete morally and politically active particles of light as a metaphor for initiation. The metaphor of physical light was a Masonic ritual emblem and specifically, through Franklin, was extended to lightening and Franklin's role as a scientific mage by harnessing it. This provided both Masons and non-Masons alike within Franklin's own collegium, such as clockmaker, scientific instrument craftsman, mathematician, astronomer, and first director of the United States Mint, David Rittenhouse (1732-1796, not a Mason), with an iconography to integrate the egalitarian and enlightened mission of the Fraternity to further the *agendae* of scientific experimentation. In Franklin's instance, the parallels among Euclid's *Optics,*[277] the reference to Euclid's 47th Proposition in Masonic leadership symbolism, and the principles applying geometry to the theorem that light only travels in straight lines, can be viewed in terms of Freemasonry's mission as it changed between the colonial and revolutionary, to the early days of the new republic.

The core of Franklin's philosophy was the Newtonian principle of electrical particles constituent to color and light exhibited in Newton's *Opticks*, and the laws of motion demonstrated in the *Philosophiæ Naturalis Principia Mathematica* (1767). He was specifically interested in the *utility* of introducing electrostatics within a system of conversion which would explain the movement of charged particles in terms of positive and negative attraction. Through the study of science, Franklin, like Desaguliers, was convinced that men might learn virtue through the study of the laws of nature, a physical analogue to mysticality. One result of this study was the implication that particle electrical physics disclosed problems related to the organization of society, and that the relationship might be represented esoterically through Masonic ritual. Both Preston (Modern) and Webb (Antient) implied this through an equivalency between cosmic order and moral initiatic mission but in different ways. To Preston the matter was largely educational. To Webb it was in essence priestly. At its core this was also an agenda of the moderate European Enlightenment, which took to heart the premise that Christianity and rationality were compatible. This was the groundwork for the Masonic symbolism implicit in the Desaguliers-Anderson *Constitutions*, and was substantially transmitted into William Preston's *Illustrations* (1772). In the creation of the American Philosophical Society (1769), Franklin sought to recreate in the New World a symbolic and pragmatic analogue to the Royal Society of London, to which he was elected in 1756. Like the Royal Society, which exhibited a concerted movement of Masonic culture within Restorationist, and post-1688 English

277 *Optics* is a work on the geometry of vision written by Greek mathematician Euclid around 300BCE. The work deals almost entirely with geometry of vision, with little reference to either physical or psychological aspects of sight. *Optics* has been called one of the most important works on mathematics and geometry written before Newton.

intellectuality, Franklin's mission was to stabilize colonial society through the symbolic identification of intellect with responsible citizenship. Both organizations were voluntary, and derived members from existing Masonic structures. In Franklin's instance, this incorporated personalities such as himself who moved adroitly from religion to science without feeling the necessity to attack, formally, the sources of Christian revelation. In this sense, Franklin *was* the American Desaguliers: the practical, utilitarian sponsor of Newtonian ideas within the center of an esoteric civic initiative in America: Philadelphia.

The movement of light by wave theory and emission conflated with the Newtonian symbolic ideal comparing the monarchy with the sun as a source of initiatic light integrated during Franklin's Masonic career with principles of monarchical order. Similar ideas linked the Baroque symbolism of French monarchy during Louis XIV reign with Gallican political theology and were shared, as referenced, at a much less triumphalist, although tangible level, with Desaguliers' Newtonianism. Franklin's precedence as a statesman and scientist inspired Clinton and likely presented him with a pathway to link his pansophist activities with the extension of the Fraternity. It was also significant, that Franklin, originally an official of the Moderns, who became an Antient in the post-Revolutionary Grand Lodge of Pennsylvania. By 1751, the English Antient system of Freemasonry had accommodated ideas within a distinct tradition and in a separate Masonic authority, or Grand Lodge which linked what has been termed a subversive sociability intrinsic to English pantheism and Dutch Masonic culture as a ritual motif of restored lost glory. These threads were detailed as a replete tapestry in the two forms of the Royal Arch degree worked in North America, in the primary instance of the ritual recovery of the *Shekinah* (the Divine Presence, see Chapter I) enveloped with, in the second instance, a perduring form of Romantic chivalry through the devolution of Knight Templar ritual in the United States from the St. Andrew's Lodge Royal Arch Hurd Plate certificate. Franklin's use of Masonic ideas to advance a distinctive set of imperial research and pedagogical ideas in his popular work, *A Proposal for Promoting Useful Knowledge among the British Plantations in America* (1743), which set the tone of an indigenous American intellect, linking productive and utilitarian learning with problem solving. The same ideal can be seen in Clinton's mentality about innovation, progress, and public works. As the senior advocate of the Antient system, Clinton took up the Newtonian and Franklinian stratagem of inter-mingling the ritual symbolization of physical science with the lore of antiquity. The result of the marriage between the Modern and Antient amalgam in America, with the latter achieving and retaining the ceremonialism of its English cousin in that the leaders of the craft were able to command loyalty within the Masonic corpus of jurisprudence at both the scientific, Newtonian level, as well as through an appeal to Hebrew and earlier *mystery* antiquity and tradition.

The Chevalier Ramsay's (Chapter VII) impetus defined and shaped the Clinton's drive to achieve the studious balance among Freemasonry as an unfolding new age dawned. The Pythagorean initiatic ideal, which profoundly shaped ideals of American citizenship through developing and evolving fraternal orders and societies, notably Henry Knox's Society of the Cincinnati, and the medium of the mediating public sphere; through which the principles of the two views of the new order of spiritual men were in active interplay from the Joachimite and Jesuit trove of theologies and theories of defined millennial vision of the constitution of fraternalism as it came to impact American public order. The striking appearance of the Tetragrammaton within Joachimite literature, especially that of Petrus Alphonsi, b. unknown date 12th century, at its early stages underscore theimportance of his work to Trinitarian doctrine within the context of its application to the stages of history through the sacred name IEVE interpreted from the Hebrew יהוה applied as the Kabbalistic Pythagorean Tetractys, the Tetractys being emblem of Pythagoras' followers.

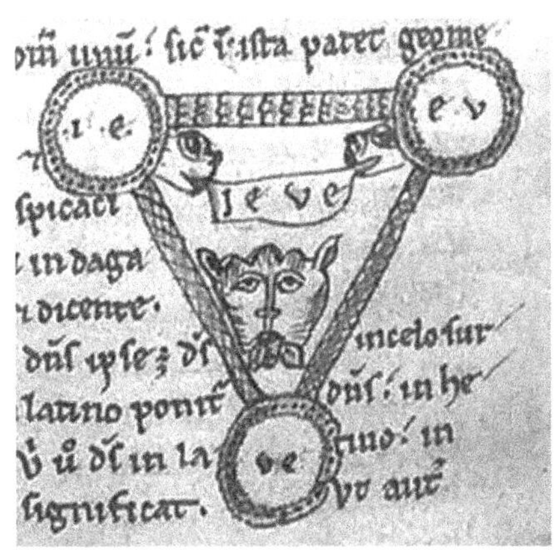

The Tetragrammaton, IEVE, as a Trinity by Petrus Alphonsi which influenced the schema of Christian mystic Joachim von Fiore's formulation of *three ages*. The triple syllable Tetragrammaton also anticipates Masonry's Grand Omnificent Royal Arch Word, itself composed of three syllables, J- B-O-.

In turn, this symbolic configuration

perdured into various rivulets into the eschatological interpretations associated with the most Christian kings of France as vehicles for the advent of a restored spiritual empire working through apostolic orders of spiritual men to bring in just kingship through the French monarchy along lines cultivated and celebrated both by Giordano Bruno and Tommaso Campanella. It should not be ignored that Fenelon, Ramsay's mentor and inspiration along Quietistic lines, was deeply engaged in the efforts to reform the monarchy of Louis XIV, the famed Sun King which strongly echo this impetus, notably in his determination to look at history in terms of a search for eschatological truth, consistent with the 1737 Oration, within which Ramsay appeals to the Cardinal Fleury (1653-1743), prime minister of France, to use Freemasonry as a stepping stone for the political theological mission of the Catholic Church. Thus, the links, from Ramsay, to Fenelon to figures such as Guillaume Postel, whose work on the reformed spiritual empire were known broadly within reformist circles during the reign of Louis XIV, forged an ethic of ecumenism with national aspiration and Universalism that really desired the brotherhood of all mankind. Thus the image of a great pacific ruler, allied with England and the papacy, emerged and was cultivated both as a means to reform the French ideal of kingship itself as well as to advance a broader vista of a mystical spiritual realm as a voluntary fraternal society crossing national lines and penetrating into universal networks cultivated by the advantage of truth provided to humanists and later philosophies as by the restoration of literature and letter. This vista was clearly energized by the discovery of the new world. This event emboldened eschatological speculations about the meaning of the discovery and made more urgent the efforts by personages such as Fenelon to pursue the reform of monarchy at home. Clinton's core mission presumed that Freemasonry was a spiritual empire that should rule the world as a philanthropic and beneficent medium through which ancient wisdom might flow. Not only did this ideal work its way into his various electoral regimes, but, as has been noted, it derived from a perduring ideal which can be traced from medieval roots of the *res publica Christianum* through Christian eschatology into Ramsay's ideology of the Masonic Catholic-Knight Templar higher degrees. At its root, utopian imagery derived from heliocentric astronomy penetrated into the core dynamism of the vision

Clinton entertained and achieved through his own management of Royal Arch Masonry and Knight Templary pivoting on the unique symbolism of the Royal Arch of Enoch emblemature of the restoration of pansophic wisdom, along Pythagorean lines, and the central Masonic illuministic impulse that lodge and chapter values ought to be projected upon the material culture and political rhetoric for the new Republic.

The Clinton Masonic culture uniquely embraced Knight Templary from the 1816 founding of the General Grand Encampment. This connoted an enthusiasm for the restoration *a general spirit or state of mind which disposes men to heroic and generous actions and keeps them conversant with all that is beautiful and sublime in the intellectual and moral world.* This chivalric thread carried forward the Ramsay ideology premise that medieval knighthood, rather than artisan craft guilds framed the roots of Freemasonry, and lifted up an equivalency between the ideal of citizenship into avenues which might shape the ethos of policy making on the grounds of common civility as opposed to partisanship. Clinton's context of activity included dealings with Alexander Hamilton, who succeeded George Washington as President General of the Society of the Cincinnati, which shared this chivalric ethos with Freemasonry; and Aaron Burr, who is not known to have been a Freemason, but utilized Masonic networks to concoct an "imperial" scheme for American Westward expansion. The executive metaphor for the interplay between the two different functions, or missiologies, of the order or active evangelists over and against, yet seamlessly cooperating with one another can be seen in the Jesuit rhetoric of the two Enochic pillars in the underground vault or crypt; on reaching into the practical world through the extension of Masonry as *geometrically rooted engineering*, the other lifting the initiate *into the celestial regions, like Enoch, from which to draw inspiration to guide the former*. In this perspective the vast iconic utility of the Royal Arch of Enoch can be seen studded through Ramsay's ideology from earlier sources, including the Joachim von Fiore's impulse within which the Logos missiology developed in the work of Salem Town from the Clinton and Webb synthesis conjointly with Franklin's aphoristic and practical approach to the evangelical militia of new scientists and science applied to nation building and into the Jefferson's imperial ideal of agrarian rusticity. It was

Clinton's contribution to see the limitation of both imageries and to identify Freemasonry on the frontier working more singularly and in an integrated fashion to transform the nation into a vast Royal Arch Chapter within which the Tetragrammaton incorporated into the Christian Logos reconciled the two viewpoints in tension into a single Masonic rite and its mission.

Within the *parfait* ethos of Ramsay's Oration and its ideology can be seen as relevant to the Clinton Masonic regime and as the precedent in Franklin's writings on moral perfection. Franklin' s intellect, as is well known, was preeminently pragmatic and utilitarian and his broad theoretical approaches to issues in policy matters and in science retained this tone and structure. He developed a set of moral injunctions which have a Masonic resonance through the presentations of the precise means and measure of obtaining virtue, which finds various conformations in the ritual, notably in reference to the twenty-four inch gauge, which was the accepted practical guide for a Mason dividing his time to achieve specific purposes. His lack of enthusiasm for organized religion followed this tone, and interestingly, one can see in his injunctions the broad outline of Benedictine spirituality from Catholic monasticism in which *laborare est orare*, *to work is to pray*. There is, in effect, something medieval about his guild-man like injunctions which did not require sainthoot, but more to the point serious earnestness. The point was not pleasing God as it was getting along in life. Franklin's Freemasonry cannot, in the end, be segregated from his attachment to French civilization and to the social concourse within which he moved, notably as a devotee to Madame Helvetius, whose late husband was, like Franklin, a brother of the Temple of the Nine Sisters (or Muses). This operated much as UNESCO[278] does today, such that it was deemed to be European wide resource for the Ramsay ideology as it came to be disseminated throughout the continent. He relished the favors of Louis XVI, accepting a small, yet symbolic portrait from him, which gave rise to thoughts that he favored some form of universal irenic monarchy as adumbrated in the Ramsay ideology. In sum, it is clear that Franklin viewed Freemasonry,

278 The United Nations Educational, Scientific and Cultural Organization. Its stated purpose is to contribute to peace and security by promoting international collaboration through education, science, and culture in order to further universal respect for justice, the rule of law, and the human rights along with fundamental freedoms proclaimed in the UN Charter.

like DeWitt Clinton, as a party for virtue: a mediating structure which blurred distinctions in society and which enabled artisans and aristocrats to mingle without self-consciousness. The Ramsay ideology extended for him this method and medium into continental networks and raised important scholarly questions about the relationship of ritual to policy which deserve deeper analysis of ramifications in American diplomatic history in the era following his 1790 death in terms of Robert Livingston (1746-1813), appointed by President Thomas Jefferson in 1801 as Minister to the Court of Napoleon I. Robert Livingston was a founding father: on the Committee of Five that drafted the Declaration of Independence; a graduate of King's College (Columbia University), first Grand Master of the Grand Lodge of New York, and during his time in France, met Robert Fulton with whom he developed the first viable steamboat. Livingston signed the Louisiana Purchase agreement with the government of Napoleon I in 1803-1804.

At its core Ramsay and Franklin overlap in their mutual confidence that the politics of learned conferencing without carefully designed sociability constituted the central building block of constitutional moral development such as the various continental congresses achieved, leading to the development, largely from France and through French influence on Scottish political Calvinism in the new nation. Given Ramsay's personal resume' of clubs and societies, Franklin's own agenda can be traced from his disaffection from the all-encompassing ideal of a renewed British Empire and commonwealth into a derivative of the Royal Society of which Desaguliers and Ramsay were noted members, as a nation writ small. In other words, Freemasonry might provide for the new nation a parallel at a more egalitarian level of the learned cell from which the sinews of the new nation might be constructed, just as the Royal Society and the Society of Arts fed the engines of imperial scientific and industrial extension into the Enlightenment Age and into what became the industrial revolution.

One need not subscribe to the various extravagant critics of high degree Freemasonry by accusing Ramsay as either a Jacobite fifth columnist or a Jesuit evangelical pawn to settle upon the core dynamic of his agenda which survived from the founding of the premier Grand Lodge of England.

The development of the Rite of Perfection (summarized in T. S. Webb's *Monitor*, 1797) and into the Clinton-Webb synthesis (Chapter IX) proves that Ramsay's high degree Masonic ethos "took." What is clear is that the various discrete threads and streams of Masonic thinking survived into concrete networks within which both Benjamin Franklin and Thomas Jefferson participated, and from which the developed purpose made vistas of their own to apply to America's purported millennial destiny in the world as a promising center for the development of a new world order. Such evidence does exist for the tangible and concrete utopian elements of these vistas can, of course, be seen in the role of Jesuit missiology, mostly of an irenic nature, in the links between the design of the District of Columbia as a Campanella heliocentric icon and the establishment of Georgetown College by the Carroll family, who held their Masonic affiliations in some sort of colloidal dispersion with the Tridentine Counter-Reformation theology. This reduces the burden of a stream in the history of Masonic ideas impacting outside culture from the weight of conspiracy theory and generates more useful and interesting terrain to study the extension of the ideology Ramsay contribution to the whole of French Freemasonry to manageable elements which promise further fertility from inquiry into specific terrains related to the civilization of Masonic culture. What should be said is that Ramsay's energies were directed at practical objectives, such as were distilled and refined in Franklin's aphorisms and within the substructure of his science of electricity, within which the idiom of physics was made to touch the vernacular of Masonic individuality within learned civic science.

* * * * *

Clinton's Masonically studded leadership at various levels in Holland Lodge; the Grand Lodge of New York, the General Grand Chapter and in the Grand Encampment of Knights Templar, avers toward the refinement of the elective leader as a Renaissance, Pythagorean Magus or Sorcerer as conferring magical power over nature and its operations. So it seemed to his lower echelon subjects as he was able to display wondrous learning as well as to affect public projects which transformed the nation, such as the Erie Canal with seeming effortlessness. The image was refined through the movement of the magus icon derived from the philosophies and theologies of Heinrich Cornelius Agrippa the Renaissance occultist, Francis Bacon who like Clinton, was an eminent lawyer. Clinton, similar to Bacon, bridged personal glorification associated with the Agrippa Magus with the leader of cooperative scientific effort as Bacon exercised in the lead up to the Royal Society, which was, in effect, a social twin to Grand Lodge. In this instance the reaction of Francis Bacon both to the ideal of the Pythagorean Magus and to the radical animism[279] of Giordano Bruno's heliocentricity, which was uniformly negative, concealed a general fear of heliocentricity, even as a modern Copernican scientific theory, because of its associations with the extreme animism of the radical Renaissance. As Bacon tends to reject the mysticality of his aura of Masonic priestliness in favor of empirical political elective power; yet it this very quality which positioned him at the cusp of Masonic legend and mythology leading into the realist pre-origins of modern Masonic history. In him and in his writing, in other words, one can see the numinous work hand in glove with the pragmatic. Clinton's awareness of Francis Bacon's *Advancement of Learning* was most likely the foundation of his pansophism.

This thread underscored the programmatic element of Webb's work which in turn was built by William Preston's *Illustrations*, which was conceived to be primarily an educational enterprise. To Preston work, Webb added Antient symbolism, with its deep hermetical, cabalistic and Enochic imprint. The difference for Clinton was that he, as did Bacon, distanced himself from the iconic principle of mathesis for experimentalism, relying not upon mystical insight as to the philosophy of Pythagorean symbolism but with the methods of measurement of observation. Clinton, like Bacon, was deeply impressed with the policy implications of Masonic emblems and strove ardently to incorporate them at once rationally and mystically into his policy program. With this, the evidence is that such images, including the use of Minerva as the seal of Union College was core. Francis Bacon's *New Atlantis*, the most commonly known Utopian text of its day, comes more nearly close to Clinton's view of how the Webb system should

279 Belief that non-human entities have souls. To Bruno, each star was a sun with orbiting planets that contained life.

be employed: the marshalling of scientific elites, as opposed to Magi, as governors of the new nation in ways Freemasonry in England. The survival of the image of the Magus as a Pythagorean symbol alluding parallel to how J. T. Desaguliers employed the Royal Society in the extension of Euclid's 47th Proposition in the Webb ritual linked Clinton ideal of rulership to qualities of mystic rational wisdom echoed in his policy method. This was enhanced by his General Grand High Priesthood, which invested him with Melchizedek's powers, through conferral of the Order of High Priesthood, detailed in the 1802 *Monitor* and by implication with various *chair* rituals linked to the Eminent Commandership of Knights Templar encampments over which Clinton came to preside nationally in 1816.

Clinton's use of mathematics as a policy function of Freemasonry remained at the iconic level of rationality applied to symbolism. This implied an emphasis upon mechanical engineering, which developed at Union College during his tenure as governor and was applied to the technical problems of the Erie Canal's construction. The legacy he inherited from Enochic symbolism by contrast was utopian as opposed to practical and carried into New York State the imperial concept likely derived from Campanella's *The City of the Sun* through which an ideal city was ruled by priests skilled in the harnessing of astral magic who knew how to keep the population in health and prosperity by means of drawing down from the heaven's beneficent astral influences. This was at its base a philanthropic activity involving the reorganization of knowledge. There were further implications of this agenda related to the Masonic involvement in the creation of the U.S. Pharmacopeia in 1820 in the chambers of Latrobe's Capitol design when the organization of pharmaceuticals was managed through Masonic networks of physicians. This configuration is important to make because it establishes the position of the District of Columbia as a utopian ideal city in relationship to the history of utopias from Sir Thomas More, through Tommaso Campanella, and Sir Francis Bacon in terms of the entelechy or interior dynamic of the occult magic or science from numinous vitalism of the hermetical Renaissance into the period of modern scientific inquiry. DeWitt Clinton's uncle resided in the District as the first Vice President to do so. Thus its empirical utility and its mythological associations with *Merkabah*-Kabbalah solar dome symbolism would have born a higher intensity of symbolic resonance than to subsequent generations.

DeWitt Clinton cultivated the Melchizedek formula of paragon prince and priest as the Royal Arch presiding officer together with the evangelical missionary idiom linked by the irenic role of Cyrus of Persia, in the Order of the Red Cross of Babylon, to his Masonic conceptual foundation within the devolution of the Royal Arch-Hurd Plate into T. S. Webb's *Monitor*. The lesson of the Chapter chair degree outlined the mission of Melchizedek as a Pythagorean and Enochian exemplar for this role, and underscored the importance of the imagery linking politics to irenic angelic order available from the Joachimite heritage further available from Ramsay's ideology through Fenelon and through Jesuit sources, likely enhanced because of Catholic involvement in the solar utopian designs of the District of Columbia. This latter thread was preserved in the theories of military engineering applied to Tommaso Campanella's concept of heliocentric urban design as a nexus between an emerging fund of ritual ideas applicable to public policy esoterica through the Society of the Cincinnati and applied to theories of public aristocracy by Alexander Hamilton who inherited George Washington's mantle of leadership, as President General, from George Washington. The significance of this society and Hamilton's role as President has been significantly underrated. It was conceived by its founder Henry Knox to be and become in effect an upper house of a permanent American clerisy to work in tandem with Freemasonry to advance the ideal of spiritual empire linking France and America through the Marquis de Lafayette (1757 -1834) among eschatological lines. Its imagery constituted a plenitude of symbolic power, as did Freemasonry under Clinton, applying monarchical reform to republic values and virtues as conceived. With Freemasonry, the Cincinnati cultivated the ideal of an angelically, warranted celestial kingship amply elucidated through iconography as in Simon Chaudron's sermon comparing Washington to Enoch and the J. J. Barralet engraving it inspired. The jewel (badge) of membership in the Order of Cincinnati over lay the sarcophagus (see Plate IX) as an authorizing talisman for his Enochic resurrection thus further underscoring the view of the Society; as its own new order of spiritual men derived from Joachim von Fiore's vision that both the evangelical and hermetical orders were, in effect, terrestrial embodiments of the angels of the apocalypse.

Lafayette became something of a national Masonic celebrity through his Royal Arch exaltation in Jerusalem Chapter No. 8, New York City, and Hamilton's other friend John Laurens (1754-1782), with whom he shared policy enthusiasms, apparently abolition of slavery among them, and an expectation that together they would work hand in hand as brothers to forge a stronger Republic union. Both Hamilton and Laurens shared a bond, which Romantic insouciance to valorous patriotic martyrdom which one associates with the early college society and fraternity movement. The symbolic threads underscored the classical friendship experienced by the Pythagoreans, Damon and Pythias[280], who risked their lives to defeat tyranny. Laurens was aware the Revolution was ending, and took what appeared to be unwarranted and unreasonable risks which led to his death in battle. Hamilton, of course, in an affair of honor was killed by Aaron Burr, not known to be a Freemason, but who was much taken by the capacities of the fraternity to inspire loyalty to ideals which in his instance were alleged to lead to the effort to establish a western frontier monarchy. This entailed a conspiracy to dismember the Spanish Empire; revolutionize Mexico which special agent Joel R. Poinsett (1779-1851) attempted through Masonic "*Yorquino*" networks whilst Minister to their Republic from 1825-1830. Poinsett sought to undermine the Spanish Empire while outwardly promoting the Monroe Doctrine of 1823. Aaron Burr was close to the architect Freemason Benjamin Latrobe (1764-1820), and to soldier and statesmen James Wilkinson (1757-1825), both of whom were Freemasons. Wilkinson was an American statesman having served in the Continental Army during the Revolution. He was appointed governor of the Louisiana Territory in1805; after his death in 1825 it was discovered he was an agent of the Spanish Crown. Joel Poinsett was in turn a Deputy General Grand Royal Arch High Priest under Edward Livingston, the latter succeeded DeWitt Clinton as Royal Arch Grand High Priest. Both Hamilton and Burr, therefore, were taken by the principle of mathematics and architecture as cognates of Freemasonry as extensions of nation building. This is, to be discussed, studded throughout the Royal Arch

280 In Greek Mythology, the legend of Damon and Pythias symbolizes trust and loyalty in a true friendship.

template and is central to the Zerubbabel and to the Templar symbolism of the two main Royal Arch ceremonies: Webb and Francken's Royal Arch of Enoch, or Solomon.

Alexander Hamilton's leadership of the Society of the Cincinnati resembled Austrian and German cameralism[281] a practical policy designed to life the pursuit of a Christian society, irenically conceived, by lifting bureaucracy into the realm of the divine right of kings, accommodating new scientific Newtonian and Cartesian cosmologies into the realm of conservative values. This movement conflated, later, with the extension of various Christian Masonic rites into German-speaking Europe linking new scientific symbolism with theology to advance and consolidate the various German princely states and the Holy Roman Empire. The interplay between Henry Knox, appointed a Major General by President Adams after Hamilton led the forces in the Whisky rebellion, was important because of Hamilton's desire to use the aristocratic features of the Society for political and presumably military purposes. A preeminent cameral was the French military architect the Marquis de Vauban (1633-1707), who served Louis XIV, but was an ardent and enthusiastic supporter of Archbishop Fenelon, in the principles advanced in his *The Examination of Conscience in the Duties of Royalty*, a generative spark in the development of the political and philosophical ideal of the Enlightenment Philosophy.

The mission of the Society of the Cincinnati can, therefore, be traced from irenic Catholic missiology through the Henry Knox foundation of the order as a de facto Masonic higher degrees within the Ramsay ideology, reunified through George Washington's iconostasis as a paragon initiate and Enoch. The thread in specific relates to the Archbishop Fenelon's apologetics for political reform within the Louis XIV culture at Versailles to which Fenelon was privy. It was also related to Fenelon's associations with Vauban, the fortifications engineer, whose work was known to Henry Knox, an autodidact on artillery, Secretary of War, and founder of West Point military academy in 1802. Roughly, the Society was an analogue to Masonic Christian Knight Templary. Fenelon was not only Ramsay's

281 German science of administration.

mentor, but also an effective advocate for spiritual and theological reform. Fenelon, in seeking to accommodate the reform of the ancient feudal constitution of France, revitalized a Quietistic theology. French soldier and diplomatist Louis de Rouvroy (1675-1755), known as Saint Simon and Fenelon both were enthusiastic to create new organic institutions of the French nobility of the sword and of the robe, as extensions of their own ideology with which Ramsay's ideology converged. Fenelon and Saint Simon's views of the French nobility as a revitalized moral force within a precarious and failing administrative state would have appealed directly, directly and indirectly, to Alexander Hamilton who saw the Cincinnati as a concrete political extension of his personal political agenda, which included a primogeniture clause underscoring the fears of Benjamin Franklin, Thomas Jefferson, John Jay, and John Adams that monarchical elements were driving the agenda of the Society toward the enlightened benevolent despotism that Fenelon envisaged and which, arguably, lay at the core of the Chevalier Ramsay's ideology. Ramsay had carefully truncated the Hebraic and Jewish cultural and theological symbolism in the official Grand Lodge of 1717 texts discerning the ideology, which, like the Cincinnati, was conspicuously missing from its emblemature given the Royal Arch *haute* ethos surrounding the Masonic element of its symbolic infrastructure. Like Masonic Templary, the ritual included the display of sacred regalia, patents and diplomas, multiple libations, and toasts to King Louis XVI included in a ceremonial liturgy. Hamilton strenuously advocated a paradoxical hereditary elite based on merit, which was misconstrued to be a secret adulation of aristocracy rooted in his own putative descent from the premier dukes of Scotland: the Hamiltons.

* * * * *

Clinton's personal style of politics was consistent with this hieratic, mystical method and involved such projects, notably the 1805 Quaker related initiative to develop a free school system through public funding for the whole of New York State. This achievement positioned his legacy for cooperation with the educational theories of John Dewey and the founding of Columbia University's Teachers College. It also made it clear to contemporaries that Clinton's personal style in public life, which contained an element of distance and aloofness from politics as opposed to the more noble calling of government contained ideas within it of importance to the nature of the nation's millennial destiny as an irenic and esoteric calling. The use of Pythagorean concepts of rulership with Egyptian notions of solar kingship provided Clinton a means to integrate charisma within organizations in unique and powerful ways. Antoine-Joseph Pernety (1716-1801) authored a Hermetic Rite which consolidated this premise and carried it into a post of librarianship at the court of Frederick the Great who invested Freemasonry with the penumbra of royal legitimacy and parenthetically with the badge of the double-headed eagle associated with the emblemature of the high degrees of the Rite of Perfection. The Egyptian thread of symbolism, which can be discerned in the origins of Mormonism upstate New York during Clinton's regime and following, established an equivalency between Masonic initiations and orders of priesthood; in Mormonism the Orders of Enoch and Melchizedek which identified comparative religion with the oligarchic polity the Masonic Fraternity placed at Clinton's disposal.

From 1721, when English Freemasonry elected its first noble Grand Master, the Duke of Montague, and 1730 when the first exposé of Masonry was published *Masonry Dissected*, a form of public Masonry emerged presupposing the Clintonian methodology. Masonry was the modish group to join in London, and as such developed in similar ways in Philadelphia, New York, and Boston. It was this era which exhibited the capability of the Fraternity to attract influentials and to appeal to learned intelligentsia, the key to its character under Clinton. A further episode defined the Clintonian ethos: the decision by the Premier Grand Lodge to change the position of the modes of recognition in 1739. For various reasons, this move generated a ritual reaction creating a more culturally Hebraic and priestly set of ritual forms which came into existence in 1751, and eventually came to dominate American Freemasonry as the Antients, and the premier loyalist and Newtonian ethos Grand Lodge, the Moderns eclipsed. The ritual definition of the Royal Arch degree, 1751-1753, signaled the capstone to the Clinton-Webb ritual system as it came to be worked as a merger of Laurence Dermott's 1756 *Ahiman Rezon* and William Preston's *Illustration of Masonry*; two text books respectively of Antient and Modern working, the former organizing craft ritual such that Royal Arch became the end point of its symbolism.

By 1819, this system was emblematically illustrated in ordered and engraved precision by Jeremy L. Cross, in *The True Masonic Chart and Hieroglyphic Monitor*, which introduced images that detailed the Clinton-Webb ritual system in terms consistent with the Royal Arch Hurd Plate of 1790, the first comprehensive visual statement of the entire York Rite. The Jeremy Cross reference to hieroglyphic was likely a coded reference to the Clintonian cognoscenti that the illuminist thread within the book of illustrations alluded to Egyptian elements in the illuministic method which was at the core of his utilizing Antient Masonry as an agent for pioneering frontier change. This element was refined in the *Templar Textbook* (1853) by Cornelius Moore, a Cincinnati bookseller, by exhibiting the radiant sun as a Mithraic *Sol Invictus* with the passion cross and the inscription to Constantine: *In Hoc Signo Vincis*. Taken together, the Cross-Moore texts documented an end point of symbolic missionary definition devolving a Masonic interpretation of the settlement and organization of the Mid-West and Mississippi River Valley as the terrain for building a heliocentric solar empire. A critical figure in this legacy can be found in Marius D'Assigny (1643-1717) whose son Fifield D'Assigny makes

THE BEAUTIFUL VIRGIN OF THE THIRD DEGREE.

The famed Beautiful or Weeping Virgin of theThird Degree engraving from Cross' *Hieroglyphic Monitor*, 1819. According to Cross it is of American origin and unknown in the York Rite as worked in England. The weeping or beautiful virgin is Isis lamenting over a broken column for the death of her solar brother-husband Osiris (cf. Hiram Abif). Isis possessed the secret name (cf. Lost Word of a Master Mason) of Amun Re/Ra enabling her raise Osiris from the dead. The Master Mason upon being raised has a substitute word whispered in his ear in low breath as the true word is lost in the Blue Lodge with the death of Hiram Abif. She holds a sprig of acacia; the acacia being sacred to the sun god Apollo. Behind her stands Kronos, Saturn, representing the sun's death or lowest demarcation in the northern hemisphere, which occurs in the sign of Capricorn which is ruled by Saturn.

the first written reference to the Royal Arch degree in 1744 in his book, *A Serious and Impartial Enquiry into the Cause of the present Decay of Free-Masonry in the Kingdom of Ireland.* Marius was an Anglican Priest in Ireland who wrote a dedicated work on, "the remarkable hieroglyphic works of Aegypt," London 1671, dedicated to the Keeper of the Great Seal, Sir Orlando Bridgeman, and various works on the *Ars Notoria*, the Art of Memory, depicted in Royal Arch mnemonics in the legendary history of the two pillars of Enoch described in the degree. The same current can be seen in Guillaume Postel's early 16th century argument that the Egyptian religion would become the irenic and latitudinarian theme of a prophetic era of heliocentrism also predicted by Giordano Bruno. To see these emblems, in consequential devolution from D'Assigny through the Royal Arch-Hurd Plate certificate (1790) into the Clinton-Webb-Salem Town ritual idiom and policy rhetoric, documents the importance of specific emblems and devices as having millennial significance as they were incorporated into lodge and chapter usage, badges and engravings.

* * * * *

To DeWitt Clinton Freemasonry would have provided an opportunity to counter New England federalist social monopoly signified in John Quincy Adam's virulent anti-Masonry to construct with the aid of European Masonic intellect new structures for the professions, notably law. Adams had been influenced by Jedidiah Morse (1761-1826) a Massachusetts geographer who in the late eighteenth century spread Illuminati conspiracy fears all over New England; Morse in turn had been influenced by the book *Proofs of a Conspiracy* by Freemason James Robison. The deep interlarding of the various layers of Masonic symbolism available through the Royal Arch of Enoch template more than afforded an opportunity to affect this conceptual and policy inroad over and against Harvard University in particular with ample reference to the emerging alliance between Columbia University and its upstate surrogate, Union College, the mother of the proto-Masonic fraternity system. This system carried Masonic ideas almost piece by piece into academia and through a variety of alumni loyalties established formulative links with the professions including honor and recognition societies with accrediting and networking associations with the academic disciplines and the professions. Clinton's cultivation of irenic policies, notably those calculated to win the influence of Irish immigrants, fed Nativist fears that he was a pawn of Roman Catholicism and that his Byzantine eschatological Masonic leadership proposed the surrender of his kingship to the papacy. One result of this fear was the development of Nativist lodges, notably the Improved Order of Red Men, which integrated Masonic infrastructure with Indian lore. A further result was the furor of the Anti-Masonic Movement which viewed Masonic ambitions and elites as proto-Catholic resulting in significant reactions within his own Jeffersonian party to proactively cultivate Irish constituencies.

In turn the relationship between Freemasonry and policy in the career of DeWitt Clinton can be best viewed in Masonic symbolic terms as a continuing pattern of association with kingship and power through the 17th and 19th centuries. Clinton inherited a Masonic system which idolized George Washington, who had been positioned as an amalgam of paragon initiate and virtuous monarch along lines identified with the Old Testament patriarch Enoch. This transformation followed along the narrative in James Anderson's legendary history. The symbolism of Washington's December 14, 1799 death was as a consequence a media event which triggered an outpouring of images identifying the Founder with Freemasonry, which, it should be said, was cultivated by the great man and his followers. Here it should be referenced that George Washington sat for a noted portrait in Masonic regalia by William Joseph Williams (1759-1823), which was utilized for defining his political role, Masonically as an icon worthy along Pythagorean

Washington lionized as a supreme Masonic initiate from *The Sentimental and Masonic Magazine*, 1795

lines (see Plate XVI). Further, in 1795 he was featured in a Dublin, Ireland publication, *The Sentimental and Masonic Magazine* (Volume VI, January-June 1795). The cover of this periodical notably exhibited an angelic cherub over which a royal crown was suspended in air over which was fixed an all-seeing eye, a direct Masonic deistic symbolic reference. The illustration itself exhibited a cameo oval portrait of Washington with three female graces super-crested with a cherub brandishing a sword tipped with a Phrygian, revolutionary cap. A military helmet crowns one grace with another blindfolded, as a Masonic initiate, holding a balanced scales and a sword, with a Masonic apron, all arrayed before a pyramid. A book with the letter "G" and a Masonic motto: *Vide, Aude, Tace* (see, hear, be silent) is positioned in front of a globe. The result is a revolutionary icon framed within the emblems of Masonic antiquity, arguably, to articulate the premise that the American Revolution was in effect a restoration of primal republican antiquity frequently associated with the works of John Toland, Thomas Paine and others. Freemasonry recapitulated within Clinton's circle through the Enoch paradigm the integration of the Renaissance concept of the artist engineer and the humanist within a pattern of public sphere patronage. A blindfolded grace as a quasi-Masonic initiate would also be incorporated into the New York State Seal of 1778 as Justice along with the goddess Libertas. The State Seal features a rising sun as its centerpiece. The classic works of Vitruvius' *De Architectura*; while *Euclidian Geometry* and *Optics* and other Archimedean and Aristotelian texts reinforced fundamental principles associated with the Masonic agenda as Clinton and his compeers conceived it. In this emphasis, Clinton carried forward Desaguliers' agenda within his own Erie Canal culture implied in Desaguliers' *A Course in Experimental Philosophy*,[282] Clinton's Masonic lawgiving predecessor.[283] Likewise the emergence of the female deity within the Clinton political and cultural context was a significant

New York State Seal

282 Volume I published 1734, Volume II published 1744.

283 In 1718 Desaguliers completed his degrees at Oxford as Bachelor and Doctor of Laws.

event within the national course of Masonic initiation depicted in the Hurd Plate of 1790. This was in essence a transpersonal, archetypical event which defined core elements of American civil religion through the Enochic solar template within which Clinton and his compeers labored. A civil religion is what Jean-Jacques Rousseau (1712-1778) described in *The Social Contract* as "...The existence of a mighty, intelligent, and beneficent Divinity, possessed of foresight and providence, the life to come, the happiness of the just, the punishment of the wicked, the sanctity of the social contract and the laws: These are its positive dogmas." which in turn could have been lifted from the tenets of Freemasonry.[284] The goddess image in Clinton's New York became material culture in the Minerva seal of Union College.

These iconic signatures and Clinton's utilization of them, spell out the infrastructure he inherited as a epigone of George Washington's mantle as a national Masonic embodiment and leader. The period of the Revolutionary War had witnessed the integration of a few colonial lodges into what could be viewed by Washington's death as a nascent, national patriotic and dynamic aristocratic network. There was national awareness of this potentiality before the War. Lodges were largely coastal, located in ports and at great distances from each other. The lodges, Irish, Scots, English, and Antient and Modern, were far removed from European Grand Lodges which were largely indifferent to their association and necessities. Through the army, largely speaking in and through the respective state militias, Masons came to know each other professionally and personally as a proposed national grand lodge was conceptualized to replicate on a larger scale the existing provincial grand lodges of Massachusetts and Pennsylvania. Military lodges were warranted, largely by the state of Pennsylvania, and this development worked with an intensification of lodge activity across the new nation. Masons in positions of national command, notably Washington and Lafayette, came to know other Freemasons from the former colonies, now states, as a network developed which was discernible but fragmented due to the various movements of military and civil administration.

284 Quoted in Kinney, Jay, *The Masonic Myth*, page 221 citing Jean-Jacques Rousseau, *The Social Contract; or, Principles of Political Right* (1762), trans. G.D.H. Cole, bk 4, chap. 8.

Seal of Columbia University designed by Samuel Johnson and approved by the Governors of King's College in 1755. The Virgin Isis, *qua* Mary, is seated beneath the Tetragrammaton contained within a solar delta appearing above Isis. Isis possessed the Tetragrammaton, the secret name of the sun deity Amun Re/Ra, which she used to obtain magic to raise Osiris from the dead in order to conceive the sun god Horus. To the lower right is a regnant Enochian rising sun referencing Malachi 4:2 that Jesus Christ *qua* Horus is "The Sun of Righteousness shall arise with healing in his wings."

At the intellectual base of Clinton's Masonic universe, as with all Freemasons following the 1717 revival were the *Old Charges* from which the legendary history were constructed. Webb rewrote this to accommodate the patriotic martyr at Bunker Hill Joseph Warren as Hiram Abif; Ramsay elucidated the chivalric figures such as Charles Martel from which he extrapolated his ideology. Odd Fellowship, which celebrated patriarchal religion's purity in its higher degrees no doubt, saw the legend of Abraham going to Egypt to teach the Egyptians *Geometry* as significant as did the authors of the Masonic rites of Memphis and Mizraim and Freemasons such as Mozart to whom Egypt became the paragon Masonic nation. Within Clinton's universe there was a Romantic Masonic impulse which sought the consolidation of Western public ritual dynamics into policy and architectural rhetoric as a transcendent political ideal. It is clear that the ideal of the Virgin Goddess developed in symbolic association with this ideal as the Virgin Mary was transformed into Columbia University's *Alma Mater* (cf. Demeter, Ceres), the mother soul of university, through Columbia University's seal featuring *Isis as Mary* goddess symbolism which would be transformed into the seal of Union College as the goddess Minerva.

The thin thread of Abraham inspiration within James Anderson's conflation of the *Old Charges* can be seen in this development as can be viewed the subsequent development of the college fraternity system in the United States where in, through the style of Nicholas Poussin, Mary is linked as Isis to the perfection of geometric order unfolding from Webb's Monitor through the extension of the design of national initiation in the St. Andrew's Royal Arch degree certificate, the solar Hurd Plate. In turn, the origins of the St. Andrew's Hurd Plate can be traced to the amalgam in Dublin associated with Maria Edgeworth's universe of historical novels within which Female Masonic orders were developed and associated with French cultural influences and with the development of Irish esotericism in the work of Thomas Moore (1779-1852) and John Banim (1749-1842); the first a popularizer of Zoroastrian imagery echoing the Chevalier Ramsay, the second author of the play *Damon and Pythias* (1821) celebrating Pythagorean secret societies as at that time were prevalent in German Romantic politics. Familiarity with this play led Justus H. Rathbone to found the fraternal order Knights of Pythias in 1864. The Edgeworth connection provided a further linkage with androgynous Masonry which came to flourish in France and America, but which was suppressed in English Masonic practices from the start. The Virgin Marianized figure of Isis as Minerva was incorporated early in the quasi-Masonic nomenclature of American higher education, both as *sigilla* of colleges and universities, notably Union College (1795), and within college fraternity rituals; just as the origination of the Order of the Eastern Star (1859) can be traced in 19th century America to Scots-Irish networks through Robert Macoy (1816-1895), an Armagh, Ireland native whose leadership made the Eastern Star a national organization. Maria Edgeworth's work also bespoke a type of embryonic feminism and linked veneration of the Virgin Mary to Baroque aesthetic appreciation for muses and goddesses. The Lodge of the Nine Sisters (Muses) in Paris, of which Franklin and Voltaire were members, and which served as a kind of international Masonic missionary cultural agency on the eve of the French Revolution, incorporated parallel imagery.

The writings of Maria Edgeworth are important in this regard because her family members, both nominally Anglican and Roman Catholic, were linked to critical figures of the period, notably Sir Walter Scott and Erasmus Darwin, and her father, a likely Freemason, devoted his energies to the application of science and education to public reform. Edgeworth's career is therefore an important indicator of the survival of Renaissance threads of *Ars Notoria* (Art of Memory) emblemature to Irish Protestantism during the period of the European Enlightenment. The ritual detail of this is redolent in the Orange Order's ceremonial, which integrated the Royal Arch idiom of exaltation with militant, Reformed Protestant mission, both of which were intrinsic to the mental landscape of the Jacobean court of Prince Henry of Wales, the son of James I, to whom was attached an ideology of Protestant reform. Orangism, essentially a form of Christian Freemasonry, articulated the principle of exaltation as a theological identity with Irish Anglicanism and Presbyterianism. It documents an indigenous flowering of symbolatry, which in Webb's system was accommodated to a more pluralistic and sectarian society. Yet it was related to the triumph of Enlightenment values, linked to Renaissance concepts, at the core of Maria Edgeworth's career, which further documents how Irish intellectuality connected to the Dublin culture of Protestant ascendancy through Masonic rivulets, specifically, as an Augustinian-nuanced idea of peace related to an ordered conception of moral unity articulating the proper and absolute relationship of all things.

Politically, a central premise of Royal Arch symbolic intellect supported the ideal of colonial autonomy, an appropriate laboratory for the origins of the Thomas Smith Webb system, loyalism to the Crown, and distance from English-Stuart Protestant plantations in Ulster. The relationship, therefore, of mystical ascent to governance emerged in a form of eccentric rationalism which sought to integrate ancient wisdom with modern initiatives to remedy social ills through patrician leadership. Within the paradoxes and ambiguities of 18th century Ireland, Masonic emblems became a means therefore to reconcile modernity with Celtic tribalism in what should be termed, for lack of a better expression, conservative radicality. This thread can be seen in the work of John Toland, an Ulster Unitarian, notably his pantheistic, solar ritualizing of Masonic symbols within advocacy of radical republican ideas linked to the Electress Sophia, mother of George I, who relied upon Gottfried Wilhelm von Leibnitz (1646-1716) for advice, and the daughter of Elizabeth of Bohemia, whose celebrated marriage to the Winter King of Bohemia, became an icon of Reformed Protestant mission on the eve of the Thirty Years War. Leibnitz, in particular, played a role in the ideas of German Freemasonry parallel to Newton in England, whose ideas shaped the Anglican nexus with Freemasonry at its core; he originated a concept of a Rosicrucian-Baconian *establishment of a secret academy dedicated to universal wisdom (theologica mystica)* at odds with the Whig Newtonianism of the premier Grand Lodge, and advocated an ideal of absolute monarchy as a means toward the preservation of Protestant unity resonant with the Irish Jewels. The marriage of Tridentine Roman Catholic and Protestant mysticality with Masonic principles of esoteric initiation became uniquely evident among Irish families governing peasantry as embattled elites. The resulting esotericized Protestantism in particular provided a means to articulate an interior symbolic irenic Irish universe within which Christianity, Enlightenment rationality, and Catholic mysticism seem to be reconciled with ceremonials, the elements of which provided secrecy and inspiration to govern without undue scrutiny, either from the Mother country, or from the uneducated masses.

The Edgeworth connection provided a further linkage with androgynous Masonry which came to flourish in France and America, but which was suppressed in English Masonic practice at the start. The Marianized figure of Isis as Minerva was incorporated early in the quasi-Masonic nomenclature of American higher education, both as *sigilla* of colleges and universities, notably Union College (1795) and within college fraternity rituals and coat of arms; just as the origination of the Order of the Eastern Star (1859) can be traced in 19th century America to Scots-Irish networks through Robert Macoy (1816-1895), an Armagh, Ireland native whose leadership made the Eastern Star a national organization. Maria Edgeworth's work also bespoke a type of embryonic feminism and linked veneration of the Virgin Mary to Baroque aesthetic appreciation for muses and goddesses. The Lodge of the Nine Sisters (Muses) in Paris, of which Franklin and Voltaire were members and which served as a kind of international Masonic missionary cultural agency on the eve of the French Revolution, incorporated parallel imagery.

* * * * *

To Clinton the republican principle created a flourishing environment for the arts but its monarchical parallel prevented the ascent of genius. At an important level this assessment whilst valuable public rhetoric was both ironical and disingenuous precisely because Freemasonry provided Clinton with ample opportunity to exercise the sovereignty of monarchy, perhaps best symbolized by his leadership in the Order of High Priesthood, the core initiatic image of which was Melchizedek, the Priest King of Salem. This template laid out important avenues for the development of a politics of philanthropy and philosophy of public leadership realized after the Civil War in the triumph of fraternalism as an expression of rising corporate leadership. In this symbolic vein, Clinton nurtured and transmitted the integrative executive image of the *last Roman Emperor* through Masonic ideology, notably the Councils of the Emperors of the East and West. The last Roman Emperor is Blessed Constantine XI Paleologos, the last Emperor of the East Roman Empire martyred by the forces of Sultan Mehmet during the assault on Constantinople on May 29, 1453. His burial remains a mystery, hence the legend of the "Sleeping Emperor," secluded by God, who would one day return to drive out the invaders and restore the Empire. Albany, New York, Clinton's policy capital, was among the first to receive and develop this ideology for American consumption, but it was not until after the Civil War that the Ancient and Accepted Scottish Rite assumed premier authority over the Masonic elites within the various state grand lodges as an extension of this symbolism. Following the Napoleonic War the deeper Enochian significance of this myth as a source of Romantic power was refreshed with the advent of popular Pre-Raphaelite medievalism celebrating ideologies of the freedom from foreign influences, national unification with the world of scholarship and historiography. The paradigmatic image of the sleeping emperor (Clinton) surrendering his kingship (mantle of York Rite elitism to the Scottish Rite) to God cuts across various Enochic, Hiramic, and mythic policy levels of the Clintonian ideology. It was the subject of a medieval *Ludus* or play depicting elements which frame an eclectic extension of the Enoch template. The antiquity and pervasiveness of this image, which was at its core eschatological, incorporated Ethiopic origins, the source of the *Book of Enoch*, but also was sufficiently extent throughout the middle ages and into the 18th century to be a common trove for various Masonic high degrees, including the imperial iconography. Clinton's own Masonic career reinforces the significance of this paradigm at various points. The result is a set of dynamic icons which link high degree Masonic imagery of monarchy. As Protestant theology came to follow Kantian devotion to reason and distanced itself from Unitarian and Universalist ideas in Boston, the Clinton system found ways to integrate the Royal Arch Hurd Plate certificate as eschatology into political theologies winding their way westward from the Erie Canal networks into powerful Masonic elites in Ohio; Indiana, the foundation sites of Eastern Star (General Grand Chapter), the Rebekahs (female version of the Independent Order of Odd Fellows) and the Pythian Sisters (female Pythagorean Knights of Pythias) which were women's sodalities idealizing the Poussin virgin Isian construct in various ritual expressions. The "Sleeping Emperor" motif, at the core of this legend can be seen at work in Barralet's engraving of George Washington as Enoch elevated to heaven and in Joseph-Jacques Ramée's design for the Washington Monument (see Chapter XII) within which Washington is depicted through emergent solar resonance as in the Union College campus template as the content of the Enochic vault, a thread carried forward in New York City into Washington Square iconography, located in Greenwich Village.

The development of a Masonic republican nobility as aristocracy ceremonialized by the high degrees took place as an autonomous clerisy. This arrangement transcended the power of the state, but as remained clear, there were and remained important linkages to academia through Columbia University andthelaw. In thisinstanceit was theeconomic power ofClinton's circle that pointed to the source of its influence and patronage of the arts and architecture. As the Erie Canal culture became more mechanistic, generating telegraph lines and railroads, architecture became defined, notably in the Gothic revival and its New York associations with the Grand Lodge Masonic Hall and the General Theological Seminary as good construction. This imparted a mechanistic resonance to Masonic elites notably as the Scottish Rite organization was defined along corporate lines where an appointee, not an elected official, governed the Rite in the various Orients or states. Critics saw the result as raising the average in cultural values and lowering the summit as the nineteenth century reconciled eastern elites with middle-western pioneer communities. The extension of order remained at the mission core of Masonic ritual, notably in linking ceremonial to fixed ratios, often best discerned in the placement of exceedingly magnifical local and regional Masonic Temples within arrays of government buildings notably county court houses often including mainline Episcopal, Presbyterian and Methodist Churches serving as recruiting grounds for membership making of Freemasonry an array of Protestant sodalities. The movement of gliding saints and angels in contending elevated, exalted array laid the groundwork for Catholic high degree Freemasonry to overcome the narrower, Mannerist Renaissance style of the encounter between the human and divine through triumphant exaltation associated with the Enochic Royal Arch ceremonies as a paragon ritual for American westward expansion. The various Methodist and Calvinist religious revivals played into such a possibility because each of these, in somewhat different ways, were alert to how Newtonianism providentialism, latent medieval mystery, and cognate ideas of secular progress were eroding the appeal and relevancy of revealed eschatological religion to the masses. Only in the United States did Freemasonry and its derivative societies constitute any real threat to evangelicalism. This was because these secret societies (Masonic or otherwise) offered an eclectic amalgam of lore and legend deriving from Biblical sources combined with esoterica that men and women both were attracted to orders and societies which purported to answer the Royal Arch divine question in different yet impactful ways.

The expansion of the frontier westward through DeWitt Clinton's Masonic network of a public sphere was a critical event in the history of the nation. Both Webb's *Monitor* and Salem Town's *A System of Speculative Masonry* made it very clear that the legacy of the higher degrees in Clintonian hands placed a vista of the cosmos and of the nation on the hands of Masonic initiates with which to envisage both the organization of urban and village life as an extension of L'Enfant's view of the District of Columbia as a projected initiatic maze along Enochian lines as well as a key to free the political imagination from parochial constraints. Ezra Ames, Grand High Priest of New York State Royal Arch Masons developed this vista symbolically into the dedicatory ceremonies for the opening of the Erie Canal featuring an actual Royal Arch, which linked New York Harbor to the Great Lakes and the Mississippi River. On the dedication of the Erie Canal in 1825,

> "Masonic officers and priests, accompanied by their own band and armed with wands and swords, bore the paraphernalia of

> their rituals - a Bible, compass and square, silver cups filled with corn, wine, oil, and an engraved copper plate. The Masons' solemn duty this day was to bless Lock 1, adorned for the occasion by a massive wooden arch adorned with evergreens. Clinton, who happened have been the country's leading Mason - the General Grand High Priest of the General Chapter of the United States - had carefully arranged the lock consecration with Albany painter Ezra Ames, Grand High Priest of the state Grand Royal Arch chapter."[285]

The Canal and specially the lock system is itself a symbol of Nilotic flooding as water rises and subsides; the Canal became itself a symbol of Masonic Royal Arch-Knight Templar westward expansion. This ceremony in turn put the J. J. Ramée solar design of Union College (Chapter XI) into ceremonial rhetorical method such that citizens began to think of the frontier in both practical and millennial terms. Clinton and his circle cultivated this vista as the origin of a culturally rich Masonic Empire State. It was elitist at its core and linked the Ramsay ideology of the *haute* degrees through Knight Templary and Royal Arch ritual categories from London and Paris into the conceptualization of the midwest, in specific, as a Nilotically managed Pythagorean Masonic regime, derived directly and indirectly from Anderson's legendary history. Masonic Kabbalah Sephirotic imagery defined Clinton's view of culture as a direct result of the application of ritual polity to political process. Clinton thought of a core unity from which emanated Enochic wisdom in the same way that a Masonic Master or Grand Master might govern his lodge. This power derived from mysticated knowledge that empowered the franchise and made the citizenry responsible to govern a symbolically infinite plurality of worlds, a term specifically referenced by Webb's *Monitor*[286] which reflects Giordano Bruno's belief that other planets potentially harbored extraterrestrial life. Columbia University came to symbolize the unity behind this conception in ways familiar to the Pierre Charles L'Enfant mentality behind the District of Columbia, as in time did Union College notably through the innovation of

285 Koeppel, Gerald T., *Bond of Union: Building the Erie Canal and the American Empire*, page 312.

286 Webb states "Numberless worlds are around us, all framed by the Divine Architect, which roll through the vast expanse, and are conducted by the same unerring law of nature."

civil engineering faculties. Clinton's core concept, in other words, was the unfolding of an elitist and esoteric Enlightenment according to high degree imagery which incorporated the entire apparatus of the various Masonic Rites of Perfection and would rely upon a vision of a spiritual intellect as the medium to engineer a *fire in the minds of men*. This meant a desire for new symbols linking the patronage of private, notably Hudson River villas to public architecture. Freemasonry provided first New York State and then the nation a ready-made indigenous mythology linking the moral purity of the local hero to the ennoblement of the population through culture. Portraiture of Republican statesmen in specific was created to articulate the image of a democratic noble of which Ramsay would have been proud, notably by Ezra Ames and his school.

The Masonic idiom was quintessentially commercial and cultural. The symbolism of work is intertwined with the unfolding of sacred wisdom and symbolically practical knowledge through the interplay of the Entered Apprentice and Fellowcraft degree. Between the simplicity of the English system and the complexity of its European analogues Clinton was able to position a unique sacral ideal that combined the two rival polities: Grand Lodge vs. Grand Orient and Supreme Council. As a result a "Clintonian chivalry" was created that extended the life of the real thing from Europe into an alliance between republican court and country through which the precise steps delineated within the St. Andrew's Hurd Plate assumed dynamic meaning. These steps provided Webb and Clinton an array of societies and academies driven by Masonic polities through which culture was extended through the cultivation of historical resources, the arts, literature and philosophy as a direct reflection of the recapitulation of knowledge and its dissemination in the Fellowcraft degree, itself a *Midrash* or spiritual expression of the Royal Arch of Enoch. Freemason Edward Livingston, later Clinton's successor as General Grand High Priest, was a highly influential statesmen and jurist who served as President of the New York Academy of the Fine Arts in 1803. The arts and the public and private policies integrating them with the creation of a public sphere afforded Clinton an Ignatian idiom of universal Catholic literature through which high degree ideology and irenic mystical vision might connect the visible

Apollo Belvedere

democratic and republican principle of the new society with a de facto Masonic monarchy over which he ruled at the state grand lodge and national Royal Arch and Knight Templar levels. The latter two entities made it possible for Clinton to dominate important elements of national Masonic mission without the convenience of a national Grand Lodge through ritual order and its process. Freemason Robert Livingston purchased a copy of the Apollo Belvedere to New York as a model for artists, which given the Apollonian symbolic intrinsic to Masonic dome symbolism was a seminal if not fateful choice through which the democratic imagery of solar light, much embroidered by Simon Greenleaf, was symbolically integrated with a divine, mythological source through which female mythic imagery began to be understood as a visual rhetoric for the new nation.

Arguably, through Freemasonry and fraternalism generally, the Ohio, Indiana (the Harrisons) and Illinois Presidents–Lincoln was a Son of Temperance–the Enochic image was developed further within American civil religion to embrace domesticity. The Rebekahs, Pythian Sisters and the Order of the Eastern Star (Masonic Order allowing both female and male membership) were organized in Indiana and with this development the image of the female fraternal initiate was positioned as a de facto co-initiate within the initiatic pantheon of the nation. As a result, the United States forged a new alliance between the sovereign monarch and the collective which transcended the personal whim of the elective kings. When the Order of the Patrons of Husbandry was developed in 1867, The Grange, an agrarian fraternal ethic emerged interlinking fertility with the imagery of the ancient mysteries such that icons of Demeter and Ceres assumed critical significance in the practical definitions of domesticity as they became related to public policy through voluntarism within which vault and cave symbolism prevailed. This preserved the Enochic dynamic of unfolding, redolent esoteric piety as an executive heliocentric icon within material culture and as a range of tacit images of authority within politics. In Masonic initiation the candidate's progress, as described in the Royal Arch Hurd Plate as an unfolding solar vista, and in Webb's Monitor, becomes an heroic figure whose success is rewarded by a vision of the Earth Goddess, Ceres, Demeter, or Cybele. The Masonic thread in *The Magic Flute* developed this chord as an archetypal saga of initiation at various levels as well. College fraternity rituals, often derived from Masonic and other orders, erected the feminine deity as an ideal within an envelope of devotion to *Alma Mater*. Initiation as a national process developed within Freemasonry as a struggle to overcome the *terrible Mother*, England, and the British Empire and to develop through new feminine imageries of uxorial and domestic partnership an iconology of androgynous leadership. Freemasonry provided this iconology as an extension of the Enochic idiom as wisdom became personified within a labyrinthine maze in a set of devolving symbols linking the core Mithraic-Zoroastrian emblemature in the Ramsay high degrees (Chapter VII) to the astral symbolism of the Order of the Eastern Star (Sirius as Isis). As Masonry expanded westward its direction demanded a revision of Christianity in favor of Mithraic styles of religiose military rooted patriotism as a new religion of state provided by DeWitt Clinton interweaving of the Knight Templar ritual idiom as emerging from the Royal Arch Hurd Plate certificate, the earliest depiction, it seems, to a single path of national initiation paralleling George Washington's use of Freemasonry as a *primus inter pares* (first among equals) presiding officer over otherwise symbiotic but autonomous entities working in coordination as the entire system developed into further replications of the Enochic ideology into non-Masonic voluntary fraternal orders and societies, notably those designed by and for women. Here we see patriotism at its most early modern expression as a defense of domestic tranquility, the core instrument of Clinton and Webb as well as Salem Town, as they paved the way for the adoption of androgynous Freemasonry as a regular ingredient of nationalistic, patriotic symbolism applied to the nation as an extension of a great family with an equivalency between initiation and matriarchal values.

* * * * *

From July 4, 1776 until the appearance of various fraternal miscellanies as a genre of literature in the 1840s and 1850s in New York State emerged from a set of three strips of semi-autonomous provinces into a consolidated empire of commerce and politics the dynamic core of which was the Erie Canal. Lodges offered the new Empire State a means to envisage itself as the cosmopolitan capital of the nation from which westward expansion would be accomplished and Freemasonry provided a template of design from which this mission would be accomplished. Masonry understood as the moral and ritual fabric of commerce projected it design symbolism onto the state and provided entrepreneurs after the destruction of loyalism an opportunity to form an elite a wide opening at the top among great merchants and holders of vast lands an opportunity to forge new links and networks through the West Indies and from Europe to establish an insurance industry and banks. The fortunes of private individuals were changed into a money market within which securities could be exchanged and capital raised. The Grand Lodge of New York provided a means for men devoted to the public interest and to a more risky and vibrant economy than before the Revolution to conceptualize the meaning of their efforts reflective of common effort within which the values of a sacred craft dominated the vocabulary of morality and ethics across sectarian and partisan confines. Notably, American Indian lore was incorporated into this vista as lodges and societies developed, generally along Nativist lines, investing the Iroquois with a type of primitive esoteric nobility in the Sons of St. Tammany and the Improved Order of Red Men. This idealization of aboriginal populations served the purpose of incorporating Indians into a servile understructure within a tiered fraternal culture which as the 19th century progressed robbed tribes of their independent status, and gave white Freemasons a means to envisage native populations as the Israelites viewed Phoenicians, Canaanites, and Samaritans ancillary populations for use in the service of erecting a supranational, new world's King Solomon's Temple.

The miscellanies documented the critical significance of the Enochic template to this progression because Clinton's system pointed through the

Royal Arch Hurd Plate engraving to the end point of his conceptual system; the convergence of Christian and irenic ecclesiastical definition within the Knight Templar iconology to the content of the vault as being an identity between denominational religionism and the Order of the Temple degree ceremony within popular domestic piety. The Odd Fellow miscellany further documented the uxorial and domestic elements of the Order's extension of fraternal culture up the Hudson River from a New York City source and elaborated upon Enochic templates as the unfolding of arcana from with a set of enclosed vaults and arches. The formality of this iconography positioned the Independent Order of Odd Fellows as an a Masonic cognate order through which parallel imagery proliferated following the end of the frontier in New York State and the extension of its fraternal cultural as a civil religion from Europe into the Great Lakes and the Canal and tributary River system westward. In one of these miscellanies, the iconography was arranged with lunar and solar emblems. The gilded cover exhibited three graces or goddesses to suggest a Marian, Isis and Minerva hagiography within a stylized Enochian vault with a radiant *all-seeing eye of Horus* as a solar emblem keystone elevated above an expanse of patriarchal tents, alluding to the patriarchal emblematic themes of the rituals of the fraternity. The three graces were likely borrowed from the Odd Fellow Manchester Unity seal; it was this first English Lodge founded in 1810 that granted the first Odd Fellow Grand Lodge in Baltimore, Maryland its charter.

Odd Fellow Manchester Unity Seal featuring Marian, Minerva, and Isian iconography and symbolism.

The Nilotic parallel to the Erie Canal played directly into the hands of policy leaders who sought ways to integrate the prosperity it generated with a reworking along Masonic lines of initiation to the movement of lodge culture westward. This provided a ready-made narrative for the role of Pythagorean magi as defined through Masonic hierarchies and as college fraternities and women's orders were developed extending the metaphor into the growing networks of female orientated improvement societies and into college fraternities developed from an extended metaphor of female deific inspiration. Odd Fellowship became uniquely significant in this culture as the earliest miscellanies were defined as extending through the organizations extensive polity of state by state representatives to a national Sovereign Grand Lodge.

By extended metaphor, the creation of the Order of the Eastern Star invested this ritual domesticity with the symbolism ofFreemasons being sons of the premier mother of the gods, widow's sons in the Isiac tradition. The identification of the Star of the Magi with an esotericized Virgin through specific defining linkages of each of the female ties to Masons, e.g. wife, sister, mother, daughter etc. positioned the sublime image of a cabalistic labyrinth with the birth, nurturing and sustenance of the individual Mason through his domestic partnerships with the symbolic role of the nativity star (Sirius) as the dynamic power behind Masonic initiation (see Chapter I, Blazing Star as Sirius-Isis). DeWitt Clinton's imagination made it possible to identify the construction of the Erie Canal with Freemasonry's westward expanding domesticity as meeting the necessities of public financial and investment support, engineering professionalism and community stability conflated into an economy and political commonwealth within which female roles had to be included in tandem with the social development of the frontier. In this regard, the Canal construction worked an integral material, social and economic transformation within the nation through New York's strategic placement along corridors of westward expansion in a parallel way to the political effects of the Revolution a generation earlier. At its origin the Erie Canal was proposed as both a symbolic and corporate financial extension of support from Washington, D. C. as Thomas Jefferson's promises of internal improvements was taken up as a national economic and political ideology. The role of religion as a moral network defining progress which came as a result of the success of the Canal was strained as denominational division increased within New York State with an emerging conflict between a conviction that the nation was Christian in its broadest mission but the nature of the precise authenticity of commitment came to be questioned in its developing pluralism. Masonry, as a result, was a useful method of approach to resolve this dilemma as Churches became another variety of de facto lodges, one affiliation among many within a prosperous family's community. For example in Mormonism, specific Royal Arch and Enochic threads became deeply embedded within the sect's cultus such that ceremonies of initiation were adopted in close parallel to Royal Arch exaltation. Within the Episcopal Church, the Knights Templar were developed as an Anglican sodality as the various encampments and commanderies were developed locally to echo the language of Episcopal services and the ethos of the liturgy of the Book of Common Prayer.

By 1856 Masonic literature extended outside of lodge walls into the culture to domesticate and frame the whole society domestically. This achieved the extension of the core design template of the ritual into the level of lore and legend through the efforts of ritualistic entrepreneurs such as Rob Morris of Kentucky who originated the Order of the Eastern Star, which its founder ascribed to French Masonic allies during the Revolution. The role of females in Freemasonry, religious persecution of Masons, and anti-Semitism were frankly addressed in such works as communities came to be touched with the Nilotic reach of Erie Canal related development and preferment within Masonry came to be equated with success within the community. Thus, the national path of initiation depicted in the St. Andrew's Hurd Plate not only pointed to the consummation of the Royal Arch saga in the finding and interpretation of the Lost Word of Master Masons, and its Christian interpretation but to its elaboration into a tapestry of lore designed literarily to encompass women into the same path within a framework which identified ritual ideals with the Marian, Minervan and Isis-orientated culture which was generated as a result.

* * * * *

The Illuminati scare of the late 1700s deeply touched American perceptions about the dangers of conspiracy about Freemasonry. DeWitt Clinton was accused as the chief designer and manager of the Columbia Illuminati, a conspiracy rooted in the Bavarian Illuminati which was thought to have engineered a de facto replacement for government bureaucracy and religion to achieve a supra state within which Masonic lodge symbolism was 1) projected on to the material culture of society; and 2) secret agendas were pursued which compromised the morality of society through making of churches and universities extensions of lodge ideals of religion as perpetrated during the French Revolution (1789-1799). It was this latter element of deepest alarm to society from the theological perspective in the United States because Masonry was thought to be part of the mission of the Antichrist. The civic ritual structure was, in this light, developed as a clone of Masonic ritual obligations where by office was transferred in the presence of a witness of an existing representative of legitimacy within sight of sacred objects, such as the Bible. The starkness and rationality of this ceremony, with Calvinistic and Enlightenment elements concealed, it was thought by conspiracists, a deeper allusion to high degree ceremonial within Masonry. In other words what appeared to be an essentially a simple event was merely an external expression of a more elaborate mystical and numinous event: an occult agenda at work. Clinton's possession of parallel Masonic offices to his elective mayoral and gubernatorial offices projected the premise that a secret high priesthood underlay responsible elective governance. In this context, the architectural context of an otherwise simple design was intended to carry the deeper subtleties of mythic and astral cosmogony alluding to the more latent authoritarian suprastructure signifying the place personal integrity and stability within the regime. Anti-Masonry and pro-Masonry factions therefore were both aware of material culture as a tacit and subtle carrier of the incremental elements constituting the creation of an adjunct clerisy through which the interstices of symbolism moved.

On the Bavarian Illuminati and the French Revolution Dr. James H. Billington elucidates:

> "The interaction of extremes affected the revolutionary tradition in two ways: dialectically and symbiotically. Dialectically, the radical, secular Illuminists on the Left developed their sense both of universal, pedagogic mission and of secret, hierarchical method from the conservative Christian Jesuit order on the Right. The Illuminist strain represented the hard, ideological core of the revolutionary faith as it developed from Bonneville through Babeuf to Buonarroti.

> Symbiotically, the broader spectrum of opportunistic revolutionary leaders and functionaries drew in the early days of the French Revolution on an equally broad range of reactionary, pseudo-chivalric higher orders of Masonry. The symbiosis became even more intimate during the Napoleonic era when monarchists and republicans borrowed repeatedly from one another while collaborating in common opposition to Bonaparte.
>
> The dialectic of Left-Right interaction began as we have seen - like so much else in the 'French' Revolution - in Germany well before 1789. Adam Weishaupt had derived his concept of hierarchical organization in pursuit of a global mission directly from the Jesuits, and Knigge had described the Illuminist program as one as using methods to combat Jesuit objectives, a 'counter-conspiracy of progressive, enlightenment forces.' Subsequent Illuminist propaganda contended that there was a secret Jesuit conspiracy, and that the nominally abolished order had established links between Bavarian Jesuits and Berlin Rosicrucians. As the conspiracy mania grew, Weishaupt himself was accused of being a secret Jesuit. The Illuminist became more revolutionary in the course of the 1780s precisely in the process of winning converts from conservative Masonic lodges of Strict Observance."[287]

Illuminism was based in part upon the art of Raymond Lully, a medieval philosopher, whose ideas about the irenic reconciliation of Christianity and Islam generated theories of the Art of Memory (*Ars Notoria*) related conceptually to the symbolism of what later became the Royal Arch of Enoch high degree ceremonial. In turn, Lully's ideas became integrated with the ideas on astrological reform and a concept of a limitless (i.e. frontierless) planet rooted in the concept of an infinite universe associated with the heliocentricity of Giordano Bruno. Clinton's Masonic vista of a public sphere developed this premise a step further by associating the esoteric side of public office with views that equated an unfolding idea of the Royal Arch Word, the Tetragrammaton with Christian cabalism in the achievement of a Sephirot, a surrogate for creation understood to be the rendering of material culture as a product of a unique Masonic spirituality and understanding. Within this idiom, the paradigm of the Enoch legend became pivotal as the

287 Billington, James H., *Fire in the Minds of Men*, pages 117-118.

central, dynamic icon of political economy alluding to the establishment of a clerisy necessary to staff the Columbian Illuminati.

Illuminism at its core was the product of cabalistic belief that all of creation was the unfolding of a emanation, Sophia, the Gnostic feminine personification of wisdom,emanating from the Name of God. Within Roman Catholic mysticism, Hildegard of Bingen (1098-1179) celebrated Sophia as a cosmic figure in both her writing and her art. Sophia, in Catholic theology, is the Wisdom of God, and is thus eternal. Illuminism incorporated Swedenborgian, Neo-Platonic and Gnostic dynamics into an initiatic sequence of Masonic degrees which exhibited a conflated dovetailing of ceremonial, the one leading to another, in more or less mythic chronological form. The dynamic of the articulation of wisdom into incarnational form from God through Sophia was therefore consonant with political objectives analogous to the devolution and sharing of mystical power, as Freemasonry conceived as emanating in turn from astral or celestial sources through the mediumship of the Word, conceived by Freemasons to be the Tetragrammaton, or the ineffable Name of God, symbolized by the Lost Word of Master Mason, mythically restored within the various Masonic degrees of the Holy Royal Arch. The Master Mason, as the moral paragon of fulfilled manhood, was charged, according to this tradition, because of his own free will and accord with the redemption of creation because he was created equidistant from heaven and hell, thus enabled and empowered to redeem the whole of creation and to restore a lost harmony and unity within the universe. Masonic high degree initiation was conceived illuministically as a pathway toward reintegration with the divine through a life time spent in expiation and successive reincarnation, that is, metempsychosis. In this context, all created matter became a mirror of the divine, and by parallel, the astral and cosmic concept of heaven with celestial correspondences confirming earthly moral activity. Masonry held up the unique elements of this process through contemplation of the moral order within the Universe, exemplified by the transposition of the values and emblems of lodge initiation onto path of human existence, and by the reenactment of death through representation by the candidate of the martyr architect of King Solomon's Temple, Hiram Abif, and his resurrected counterpart Adonhiram.[288]

The third, or Master Mason degree to Clinton, carried the metaphor still further into the employment of builder's trowel as a means to interconnect two or more ashlars into utopian and sacral construction. The metaphor was further extended through the Royal Arch degree along illuministic lines by appending the trowel with the sword, or by seeing the Mason's trowel as short sword, with which to defend the community. Along this internal symbolic logic symbols were thus deployed at a variety of levels to accentuate critical elements of theological doctrine through an amalgam of Renaissance political and philosophical imagery and Enlightenment theory of rationality projecting reason as a *sui genris* emblem around which to order human existence. Within this idiom, such doctrines as original sin and it affliction upon the human state became signified by the separation, for example , of a divorce between God's compasses, as for example in William Blake's (1757 -1827) *Ancient of Days* engraving (see Plate XVII), and the square, in the instrument of the human builder. Thus the core Masonic emblem, the square and compasses, could be understood to be a human effort through hermetical ascent and cabalistic apotheosis to restore or replicate paradisiacal or utopian existence through engineering and architecture in order to build a new nation. Neo-Platonism was an ingredient to this illuministic method as employed by Clinton and his circle because it was assumed that Masonic emblems were invested with a higher level of perennial meaning transcending their material form. This principle became intrinsic to the entire Ramsay ideological system as it developed into a range of concrete rites and degrees, but was uniquely applicable to a frontier culture seeking ways to project utopian emblems into civilizing communities. The origins of a national calendar can be seen as well within the unfolding of this pattern wherein specific events, notably presidential and memorial days, identified Freemasonry's public ritual legacy as a means to domesticate death as an alternative to apocalyptic and personal anxiety about mortality. Masonry and Odd Fellowship made much about the ritual funerality of mortality, generally along ideas framed about immortality in the Enochian tradition. This rational coolness about the terrors of death stood in stark contrast to late medieval and more existential views of the

288 Mackey, Albert, *Encyclopedia of Freemasonry, Vol. I*, page 19.

terrors of the grave arguably as a means to diminish the appeal of churches to common-folk and to replace the threat of death and eternal punishment with an ideal of celestial order which reworded moral virtue in terms of a blissful life in a celestial lodge or its symbolic equivalent.

The illuminist method adopted by the Clintonians included Freemasons who understood their affiliation to relate to international linkages connecting small town lodges to global issues. This phenomenon can be traced into the networks of Henry Shelton Sanford (1823-1891), Abraham Lincoln's Minister of Belgium, 1861-1865, who parlayed his affiliation for Union diplomatic purposes into ties with the French Grand Orient under Napoleon III (1808-1873) through the Grand Master Lucien Murat (1803-1878), the Emperor's first cousin and to Leopold I (1790-1865), King of the Belgians who became his personal friend. Henry S. Sanford is the founder of Sanford, Florida; the ritual content of Sanford, Florida's Masonic lodges at the time was very much of the Webb variety, a permutation of English Antient Masonry and not part of the more politically active European high degree Ramsay ideology. Yet, this inconsistency did not prevent him from forging networks and presumably sharing liberal ideas with the Coburgs (of Belgium) and Murats-Bonaparte's which linked him with Webb and Clinton through his association with the noted Episcopal Bishop and co-founder of Kenyon College (first called Jubilee College) Philander Chase (1775-1852), whom Thomas Smith Webb raised to both the sublime degree of Master Mason and exalted to the Holy Royal Arch degree.

Clinton's policies also entailed the calculation of marriages within social and commercial elites through the extended families ties of Holland Lodge, framing legal methods to preserve growing estates, astute business management, and extending territorial and legislative influence up the Hudson Valley. This involved displacing the earlier Dutch patroon elite, or merging interests with them, and of course the forging of a new religious ethic of irenicism which de-emphasized confessional and doctrinal conflict. It was the Dutch who primarily colonized New York as well as New Jersey. Catholicism appealed to American Clintonian aristocrats as a unitary ideal - preserved tacitly within the high degree structure where by Freemasons followed a hierarchical infrastructure of their own artifice whereby squires, looked to peers, and peers to upper Masonic nobles and monarchs.

These policies required a civilizing intent on the part of Clinton and his compeers, but would not have been achievable without the agency of voluntary institutions and organizations, notably Freemasonry. The metaphor was lifted up in rhetoric and architecture through the Enochic paradigm of the restoration of knowledge which proposed symbolism of human movement within communities which recapitulated the movement of man through life to death within a *gestalt* surrogating confessional religion. Thus the ordinary and conventional interplay of human beings was rhetorically and ritually channeled in straight lines, employing gauges, and squares through turning at right angles suggesting the moral emblematic infrastructure of urban utopian design, quintessential to the L'Enfant streetscape of Washington, D.C. and Joseph Ellicott's *solar* design of Buffalo, New York. The paragon for such movements were the principle of managing Nilotic flooding occurring during the heliac rising of Sirius in Ancient Egypt from which were extrapolated references to ancient Egyptian religion and Pythagorean learning eventually establishing an equivalency between the governance of civic polity and esoteric concepts of hermetical order. This symbolism was unfolded within the Webb-Clinton re-synthesis of William Preston's ritual as a means, symbolically, to prepare for the building of King Solomon's Temple by smoothing a rough ashlar for building. The symbolism was telling because it dealt preeminently with the preparation of the individual citizen for his responsibilities within a broader community as an extension of lodge initiation. The broader significance of this sequence has not been aptly explored, that is to what extent does the microcosm of the third degree Masonic ritual's loss point to a broader cultural sense that something in general society was also being lost? The inference is significant because it indicates a query about to what extent were precocious intellectual elites aware that the late medieval world view as midrashed, commentated upon by Renaissance thinkers, losing its numinosity and mysterious appeal to the educated populace.

In conclusion, DeWitt Clinton's use of Freemasonry may be said to have operated at two levels: a policy idiom within which the craft was deemed to be an empire of virtuous reason following generally along Jeffersonian ideals of an expended frontier governed, ultimately, by virtuous pansophics and politiques; and an elites striving through personal virtuous sanctity toward perfection. The Ramsay ideology detailed the second element in terms of sound morals derived from religious orders deemed, generally, to be the crusading orders of knighthood established to make perfect Christians, to inspire a love of true glory (cf. *Shekinah* in Royal Arch idiom, see Chapter I) and to make good citizen-subjects. This dichotomy mirrored the ideal of the Jesuits, referenced above, as an evangelical militia working with a more deeply metaphysical hermitical order within an order[289] which worked in tandem between Christian evangelical mission and the venerable antiquities integrating a philosophy of sentiment with a complete theology of the heart. Ramsay's overarching mission followed closely along this dual line: the encyclopedic reworking of a Christian humanist amalgamated ideology working through an Enochic summation of knowledge, akin to the scholarly expertise of the Jesuits, and into a deeper parallel between pre-Christian antiquity as expressed and confirmed Christian revelation. It was this latter impulse which raised up both the Zoroastrian mage *qua* Egyptianate Pythagoras moving toward perfection, notably within the French governance concepts of the *parfait* in conciliar Masonic polity and within the culture of Grand Orient initiation, the two of which conflated to influence Benjamin Franklin, and other members of the French lodge of the Nine Sisters, of which Benjamin Franklin was a member. This thread conjoined the ancient mysteries with the crusading religious orders as a single continuous secret shared by the morally perfect in each epoch of virtuous humanity. An equivalency was established, thereby, between the ancient mystery religions at Eleusis, Minerva to the Romans known as Pallas Athena to the Greeks at Athens, and Isis in Egypt with the crusading orders. Thus, the pursuit of the *Liberal Arts* was deemed by Ramsay a perfection of taste required for initiation which might lead through mathematics to the development of utopian architecture and to effective defense mechanisms through military engineering and force against those not softened by the peaceful and philanthropic maxims that are fundamental to the society of

289 See Grand Lodge text of Ramsay's oration.

Freemasons. Ramsay envisaged the movement of the center of Freemasonry out of Britain into France. This echoed Benjamin Franklin's own Masonic career as a premier Grand Lodge officer, a Modern, out of Pennsylvania through London associations of various sorts related to Masonry's influence in the Royal Society and the Society of Arts, into the Grand Orient ethos of *parfait* initiation. Just as Ramsay understood France to be the paragon Christian nation, Franklin and Jefferson invested French culture with a continuing edge in moral perfection through its celebration of the philosophy and pansophic tradition as a form of secular, profane (irreligious) virtue worthy on emulation in nation building through the creation of an Empire of Reason. The United States is not a profane Christian nation; rather its founders: Washington, Jefferson, Adams, Paca, Whipple, Paine, and Franklin to name a few, were enlightened deists promoting new world egalitarian empire where philosophy and science would rule, not superstitious belief. The core of Ramsay's ideology, applicable to America might be summarized in his dictum, "It is in future in our (French) Lodges, as it were in public schools, that Frenchmen shall learn, without traveling, the characters of all nations and that strangers shall experience that France is the home of all nations, *Patria gentis humanae*."[290] By such rhetoric, Ramsay linked the 17th century Joachimite vista of a universal irenic monarchy moving in tandem with a reformed Catholicism, the secular ramification of which Franklin and Jefferson envisaged for the United States through an extended ideal of virtuous morality, extended into statecraft and domestic and international policy making: *a New or Third Order of the Ages.*

290 *Ramsay's Oration*, 1737.

CHAPTER IX

THE CLINTON - WEBB RITUAL SYNTHESIS AND SALEM TOWN

The Cultivation of the York or American Rite
and Masonic Millennialism

"The last great and overwhelming scene will be the closing point in the grand drama of nature, when the trump of God shall awake the slumbering dead. This will be a moment, from the very nature of the event of unutterable astonishment. That period will arrive, when the curtain shall drop, and time shall be emerged with eternal duration. - Yet however great may be the the awful grandeur of this scene, however bright the ineffable displays of the Omnipotent power, and the terrible majesty of the Highest, the beauty of the moral world will arise from the ruins of nature, irradiated with the beams of immortality. The bright effulgence of the Divine glory and justice, and all the adorable perfections of the very Godhead shall fill the universe be displayed before its countless millions, while the righteous shall ascend, in transport of joy, to realms of everlasting felicity. This solemn event is faintly prefigured in the sublime degree of a royal arch Mason."

- Salem Town, *A System of Speculative Masonry,* 1818.

DeWitt Clinton defined the Masonic and public career context of Thomas Smith Webb's ritual through the practice of the ceremonial itself and, more publicly, in the policy implementation of the 1797 *Monitor*, called the *Illustrations of Masonry*. Clinton, in other words, provided the institutional means for Webb to insert the rendering of William Preston's 1772 *Illustrations*, the model for Webb's work, through his leadership in various key New York State Masonic organizations, the national General Grand Chapter of Royal Arch Masons and a Scottish Rite styled organization, Cerneau Masonry, derived from the French high degrees called the Rite of Perfection. In each of these organizations Clinton's network applied ritual definition to architectural design for public education and civic works as with the Erie Canal. He was linked intimately through George Washington to Benjamin Franklin, whose Masonic career encompassed the principal alterations of 18th century ritual style and initiation in France, England and in America. Clinton, a Jeffersonian Republican, was nevertheless in sympathy with Federalist Freemasons as well. He was part of an critical network of political and diplomatic lawyers active in the leadership of the Royal Arch degree institutions, and identified with Joseph Cerneau in the development of the American Scottish Rite system.[291]

In this vein, Clinton and the Clintonians developed 17th century liturgical elements within Anglicanism and elements from the Cambridge Platonists (Henry More (1614-1687), Ralph Cudworth (1617-1689), and Benjamin Whichcote (1609-1683) were the big three who expounded a perennial philosophy, classical philosophy applied to modern life, proposed by humanist Renaissance philosophers such as Marsilio Ficino; in opposition to the developments of Cartesian empiricism (cf. René Descartes' "knowledge is acquired by reason, and not experience"), and Puritanism (extreme Calvinism), two nominalist currents of thought into a public religious sphere which made it possible to reinvent the legal and other professions through their associations with collegiate fraternalism, derived from the Webb and Ramsay traditions through the devolution both of the Union College and Miami University of Ohio Triad of fraternities

291 Mackey, Albert, *Encyclopedia of Freemasonry*, Vol. I., page 156.

coming out of Williamsburg, Virginia with Phi Beta Kappa (Chapters X and XI). This positioned the Clinton-Webb synthesis, which it should be remembered was modeled structurally after William Preston's *Illustrations* (1772), pathed Anglican liturgy into Newtonian and Lockean liturgies creating within Freemasonry in England a public monitorial device echoing the Book of Common Prayer as a semi-public device standardizing private lodge ritual practice and enabling it to enter the public vocabulary of morality as Masonry came to enjoy royal patronage as well as the support of popularizers of science. Webb was born in Boston, Massachusetts. It would not have been lost on DeWitt Clinton or Simon Greenleaf that associating the development of the nascent American legal profession with Masonic Pythagorean symbolism as an esoteric underside to a rational pragmatic ideal would have cut into the social monopolies Federalists exercised through Harvard College and brought it more in line with the tradition of public spiritual intellect visible in the environs of Holland Lodge with its links to the Livingstons, Clinton, Pintard; the Renwicks, Hosacks, and Mitchills families who embraced his system. Edward Livingston in specific, the author of Louisiana's two legal codes, was a General Grand High Priest of all Royal Arch Masons starting in 1829 (three terms) and Minister Plenipotentiary to France (1833-1835) was an exemplary model of the success of the Clinton ideal and a link to how French and German Masonic thought penetrated Clinton's New York through the devolution of Clinton's own Cerneau system of Masonic high degrees.

Clinton's efforts made it possible for the Webb system to connect the principle of Royal Arch Masonic initiation through Enochic templates to public policy and works, such as the Erie Canal and Frederick Graff's Fairmount Water Works. Graff, a student of Benjamin H. Latrobe, designed the waterworks in 1812; it was built in-between 1812-1872 in Philadelphia. These feats of civil engineering, especially the Erie Canal, positioned Freemasonry for further growth and influence in the east and the country's westward expansion in the Presidency of Andrew Jackson, following Clinton's death in 1828. Jackson's own relationship to Masonry has been factually detailed in other works, but the relationship of his career and its impact on the concept of a *Masonic* United States Presidency has yet to be analyzed in terms of this influence. To assess Jacksonian Freemasonry, notably his links to Southern unionism through his ties with Florida governor Richard Keith Call (1792-1862) and Samuel Houston (1793-1863) were shaped by Clintonian ideas about the pansophic nature of Freemasonry and its enhancement of the utility of the order to nation building. Therefore, the purpose of this chapter is to outline the context and content of DeWitt Clinton's relationship to Masonic ritualist, Thomas Smith Webb, whose transformation of British Masonic ritual into a unique American synthesis. Webb altered and redefined Masonic initiation from the works of William Preston and Laurence Dermott, two critical English writers of the period 1751-1818. He did this with specific reference to the Royal Arch degree, a ceremony and template of ritual order at the core of Freemasonry's high degree ideology and culture. In this context, the Enochic ethos applied to the definition of public policy through material culture and its symbolism became a useful means to repudiate efforts to put forward ideas related both to traditional definitions of original sin and natural law and to hold up the positive values at hand because these recrudescent tendencies tend to reject out of hand the achievements of the Clinton-Webb synthesis and its inheritors.

Unlike Clinton, Thomas Smith Webb's profession was more modest; he held no public office. Freemasonry was his life. He was made a Freemason in Keene, New Hampshire, before 1793, when he moved to Albany, New York. There he opened a book store, and worked with an English Mason, John Hanmer, who most likely was his source for William Preston's *Illustrations of Freemasonry*. This was published in 1772 and was as a result the first quasi-public ritual oriented Masonic text book, from which Webb designed the first American Masonic *Monitor* (1797). The revised edition, 1802, augmented the earlier work, and laid out a system of appendant orders and degrees derived from the essential interior symbolism outlined previously. In 1797, he was twenty-six years of age. Most of Webb's Masonic career was conducted in Providence, Rhode Island which positioned him between the two principal centers of colonial Freemasonry, Boston which claimed the first lodge in the nation, and Philadelphia, where Webb took the Royal Arch degree himself.

Webb was initiated in Rising Sun Lodge in December 1790. This is a direct reference in the name of the lodge to the Ramée template of Union College, as will be seen, and to the pervasiveness to identify the candidate and Masonry with the contents of Ramée vault, which had extended into the symbolic culture of the whole American fraternity. He became Grand High Priest of Royal Arch Masons in Rhode Island (1803-1815), Rhode Island Grand Master (1813-1815), and likely drew amplifications of his work from St. Andrew's Royal Arch Chapter, in Boston detailed in the text. In Rhode Island he took up wall paper manufacturing, and for ten years, 1806-1816, served as General Grand King of the General Grand Chapter. In that year, without clear documentation regarding the date or place of his initiation, he organized the national Templar organization, General Grand Encampment of Knights Templar and Appendant Orders for the United States of America, and was elected to service as Deputy Grand Master under Clinton. The two Masons worked hand in glove on the joint ritual and policy development of the York Rite.

Thomas Smith Webb attended a Boston, Massachusetts convention which separated the working of the Royal Arch degree from Craft Masonry and created a Masonic organization independent of the state grand lodge system, then developing from colonial roots. This positioned the ceremonial of the Royal Arch working from prior and post craft ritual to position a unified, coherent path initiation for the individual as a sequence of degrees, of which Clinton became head in 1816. Webb declined leadership of this body at the highest level, in favor of Clinton, and worked assiduously within Clinton's official hegemony to strengthen its organization and ritual structure. By 1798, the entity had become firmly established as the Grand Royal Arch Chapter of the Northern States of America, in Hartford, Connecticut. It was changed in 1799 to the General Grand Chapter of Royal Arch Masons, and in 1806 "of the United States" was added and "Northern States" was dropped. This institution positioned the Royal Arch ceremony of exaltation as the *sine qua non* for Masonic advancement in America, both through the actual identification of the Webb Royal Arch as the summation of Masonic ritual preferment, and by implication, by the interior length and sequence of the Royal Arch of Enoch (also termed Solomon) as a desirable and companion order.

In 1815, Webb moved through Boston into Ohio, extending the Webb system through Ohio, Kentucky, and through brief visits to other states. In 1817, he took up residence in Worthington, Ohio and established linkages with other ritualists, such as John Snow[292] and Jeremy Cross, who illustrated Webb's ceremonial in pedagogical and didactic form, lending unprecedented clarity to the conferral of the degrees and orders. Before his Cleveland, Ohio death on July 6, 1819, he organized the Grand Chapter of Ohio, and individual Royal Arch Chapters in Madison and Brookville, Indiana, where he came into contact with David Wallace, the governor of the state and father to the noted soldier and author, General Lew Wallace, who subsequently devised a fraternity along Royal Arch ideological lines from the story line of his famous novel, *Ben Hur* (1880), known as the Supreme Tribe of Ben Hur. Webb further reached into the deep south to create a Knight Templar unit at Natchez, Mississippi. He was not inclined to philosophical speculation about Masonry, but directly inspired the 1818 work of Salem Town, *A System of Speculative Masonry*, which should be understood as a millennial extension of the 1802 *Monitor*.

Freemasonry, in the 18th century, developed various ontologies for managing the relationship between the ritual and public policy. In England, this was the alliance between Grand Lodge and the Royal Society which lifted up Newtonian providentialism as the paragon intellectual ethos through which various Whig prime ministers utilized the Enlightenment through royal patronage from 1737 to develop and missionize elites to serve the purposes of the Hanoverian regime. In France, the Ramsay ideology did the same with regard to placing Zoroastrian and Mithraic imagery within chivalric lore as a means to achieve an otherwise contradictory agenda: integrating nobility with egalitarianism. In Germany, the Kantian ethos of the pursuit of reason as moral law became the underpinning for various Templar oriented rites consonant with the origins of Romanticism. The foundation of such efforts was to extend Kant's argument for the existence of God through Masonic ritual concepts: that is, that the existence of a mortal law required a sovereign deity to enforce it and to provide a means to disclose its workings according

292 Snow was a prominent Royal Arch Mason, and was the First Grand Commander of the first encampment of Christian knighthood northwest of the Ohio River.

to the faculties of perception of initiates, themselves candidates for rulership by virtue of their ethical enlightenment and social-political eminence. A further ontology was the Clinton-Webb synthesis applied to American imperial expansion integrating conventional proto-Anglican imagery, which can be traced to the Elizabethan civic thread of hermetical and cabalist lore, through the role of the articulate citizen (*qua* Thomas Elyot), with French increments, to the forging of an indigenous American or York Rite.

The ontology for the Clinton-Webb synthesis involved a ritual sequence deriving from the core icon of the Royal Arch of Enoch degree. This was the Red Cross of Babylon which according to the story line sequence should be part of the capitular section of Chapter degrees as outlined by Webb in his treatment of the Royal degree. The text involved a promise to Zerubbabel, a Jewish governor in the Persian Empire to restore the holy vessels to a restored Temple in Jerusalem, and the details of an argumentation that persuaded the king to empower him to pursue this objective. In terms of the solar Royal Arch Hurd Plate, it was this empowerment through the creation of a chivalric order, *Sol Invictus,* which celebrated truth as the greatest power on earth, above wine, women and the king himself, which indicated the placement of a core icon within the Clintonian synthesis equating the movement of Masonry westward from Babylon as the third order of history coming to fulfillment within the York Rite. The same age of a truth spirit involved allusions to the rough and rugged road of the Royal Arch degree, of which the Order of the Red Cross of Babylon was a sequential cognate, and pinpointed the restoration of the Royal Arch Word as the end point of the eschatology Salem Town elucidated in his view of millennial Masonry and the role of the Logos as the true Mason's Word. The driving dynamic of the order was therefore to equip an elite militia warranted by a Babylonian prince, Cyrus the Great, as the eschatological mission of Clinton's vision of the role of Masonry in the New Republic. The rebuilding of Jerusalem and the construction of the second temple as framed in the Royal Arch of Enoch and in the Order of the Red Cross invited comparisons between the District of Columbia as a Babylonian astral *cosmopolis* from which its designers understood mythically the nation to develop as a new Babylonian kingdom. Parallel symbolism emerged in the third degree, or Priestly Order of Odd Fellowship, in the Degree of Truth; and in the Master of the Royal Secret within the Scottish Rite. On this Pike states:

> "When Truth comes into the world, the Star of Knowledge (cf. Sirius) advises the Magi of it, and they hasten to adore the Infant who creates the Future. It is by means of the Intelligence of the Hierarchy and the practice of obedience, that one obtains Initiation. If the Rulers have the Divine Right to govern, the true Initiate will cheerfully obey. ....The Heavens and the Earth were personified as Deities, Even among the Aryan Ancestors of the European nations of The Hindus, Zends, Bactrians, and Persians; and the Rig Veda Samhita contains hymns addressed to them as gods. They were deified also among the Phoenicians; and among the Greeks OURANOS and GEA, Heaven and Earth, were sung as the most ancient of the Deities, by Hesiod."[293]

In all instances, the consummation of narrative initiation was projected through illuministic methods from the path of the single initiate onto the path for the transformation of the nation as a whole.

It must be noted that Webb's weaving of Dermott's Antient textbook, the *Ahiman Rezon*, combined with Preston reflected Giovanni Pico della Mirandola's human exaltation. The hermetical and cabalistic supplanted Preston's celebration of Pythagoras. Webb's ritual synthesis also submerged Toland's *Pantheisticon* and later Thomas Paine's Celtic Druids (see Thomas Paine's *Origin of Freemasonry,* 1818) as precursors to Masonry along with Persian and Egyptian cosmology. Paine writes, "To come then at once to the point, *Masonry* (as I shall show from the customs, ceremonies, hieroglyphics, and chronology of Masonry) is derived and is the remains of the religion of the ancient Druids; who, like the magi of Persia and the priests of Heliopolis in Egypt, were priests of the sun. They paid worship to this great luminary, as the great visible agent of a great invisible first cause, whom they styled 'Time without limits.'" Webb afforded few elements of Bruno's radical pre-Masonic thinking in *Spaccio della Bestia Trionfante*, *Expulsion of the Triumphant Beast*, 1584, which glorifies the magical, astral religion of Egypt, and his popular political manipulation in *De Gli Eroici furori*, *The*

293 Pike, Albert, *Morals and Dogma of the Ancient and Accepted Scottish Rite,* pages 843-850.

Heroic Frenzies, paralleling Machiavelli's *The Prince*. The result was a ritualized historical-mystical allusion as a hermetical element of *ascensio*, linked to cabalistic apotheosis. Webb further opted for a more universal application of Royal Arch symbols. No precise relationship to Christianity, such as Orange Royal Arch ritual, indicates a secular direction away from the Vitruvian icon of a five-pointed star as the human form. To summarize,

> "My brother during these sublime rites and ceremonies, you passed under the Royal Arch, were invested with the Purple of the Fraternity (cf. *ascensio* or power to rule - purple is associated with monarchy) and received the Royal Mark of this degree (cf. Webb's keystone) the five pointed star symbolic of the five points of fellowship in which you were raised. *The shock you experienced in receiving this beautiful emblem signified the sting of the serpent or the fall of man. But this mark has still a higher meaning and alludes to the brilliant star* (cf. Sirius) *that guided the Wise Men of the East* (cf. Alnitak, Alnilam, and Mintaka in Orion's Belt), which … the shepherds saw at night while watching their flocks on the hills of Bethlehem…"

This passage, in connecting the Christian doctrine of the Fall in Eden with the *Vitruvian Man*, to the coming of Jesus Christ to the shepherds and the Magi, with the raising of the candidate to sacred power, linked apotheosis and *ascensio* to the transformation of a Royal Arch initiate into the figure of St. Michael the Archangel. Webb's Chapter officer-image of a Captain of the Hosts (cf. St. Michael) created social power as extension of *ascensio* which was eschatological, without being confessionally explicit. As a civic emblem this avoided two extremes: 1) a rational, or Biblical, justification for rejecting English politics, while 2) providing a mystical order which appeared both reasonable as well as spiritual. This effectually substituted orthodox exclusivism with an irenic equivalency between the dignification of the initiated individual, in the New Nation, with the collapse of Eden. In turn it can be argued that the recovery of the Royal Arch Tetragrammaton symbolically equates to the restoration of the Garden of Eden prior to Adam and Eve's fall.

The Clinton and Webb ritual synthesis integrated two opposing methods and viewpoints which contributed to its success: the mystical and mysterious vis-a-vis the rational and idealist. The first quality was indeed aimed at co-opting elements of denominational religion notably Episcopalian liturgical elements; the second to incorporate the traditions of secularity articulated within the threads of Egyptian links to radical republican theory in the works of John Toland, Thomas Paine, Thomas De Quincey, and in Simon Greenleaf. Together, virtuous piety and anti-prelaticism provided a means for career Freemasons to operate within a range of viewpoints transcending ordinary conduits of community and civic life. When anti-Masonry emerged in 1826 opposition to the synthesis, it became clear that it riveted upon the association perceived between monarchy on one side and infidelity on another. Such a double barreled objection emphasized the associations of Freemasonry with the universal monarchy presumed to be the result of the Antichrist, and underscored the further presumptions that Jesuitical designs to advance the papacy as such lay at the foundation of Clinton's and Webb's work. Clinton's pansophism further underscored the perception that advancement of learning was the ideology generated by Freemasonry through its devotion to the study of the natural and physical sciences, the subject of numerous lectures by Clinton to Phi Beta Kappa at Union College and elsewhere.

The Clinton-Webb synthesis also relates to the confession standoff between Puritan and Anglican circles of thought in the 17th century as the issues of the English Civil War migrated into the religious awakenings in 18th century America. It appears as if the circles surrounding Philander Chase in the Episcopal Church, which included both Clinton and Webb, which included a middle way of reconciliation through mystical and secret society culture in toleration was the order of the day, with and between stultified doctrinal difficulties. In other words, Clinton presided over a cadre of liberal and inquiring *politiques* through which some of the most profound and fertile tendencies passed from one camp to the other undiminished and safely without interference. This nexus for example tends to make common cause between the *Calvinist City on the Hill*: a holy commonwealth and utopian schema such as Campanella's *The City of the Sun* in the context of learned societies and circles. In this instance, Washington, D.C.'s design and template appeared to be progressively Puritan as an extension of the Holy Commonwealth just as the Illumines (not Illuminati), a theosophical *Elu* or Perfect Elect,[294] and Puritanism achieved a pragmatic equivalency. Such can be seen in the members of the Metaphysical Club at Cambridge mid-19th century and in the various links between Presbyterian New York, which like Clinton, was a participant in this communion.

In this context, Webb and Clinton were able to extend the pathway of national and individual initiation as a path to Babylon, imagined to be a golden age of Cyrus the Great as a paragon irenic prince, into the destiny of American through solar symbolism of the St. Andrew's Hurd Plate and the Joachimite interplay between two types of orders: one artisan and practical, the other mystical and symbolically celestial. This mechanism in effect surrogated conventional Biblical concepts of apocalyptic thought and placed eschatology in the hands of a complete conceptual system, echoing the Enochic template, as the Erie Canal opened the frontier to the West along Pythagorean interpretations of Nilotic flooding and the development of a civilization rooted in esoteric (celestial) management of practical (artisan) political economy. An important result of this maneuver was the identification of Biblical apocalyptic thought with the expanding frontier of the nation such that the unfolding of the Royal Arch Word as Logos became de facto the end point of Holy Scripture and the Biblical pursuit of Holiness as applied to national prophetic destiny.

Dr. James Anderson set the tone and the dynamic of the identification of the artisan, practical, mission of the Jesuit Order as transferred into the Thomas Webb system by identifying the *Eureka!* incident regarding the finding of the meaning of Euclid's 47th Proposition (a/k/a the Pythagoreum Theorum), the emblem of the Worshipful Master of the Craft Lodge, with the discovery of the Lost Word of Master Mason by Zerubbabel during the construction of the Second Temple under the warrant of Cyrus the Great. Thisis detailed inthe Scotch Master degree later developed atthe Jesuit College of Clermont where Catholic Knight Templars (not temple builders) discover the Lost Word in a hidden underground vault. The legendary history

294 The fourteenth degree of the Scottish Rite, the final degree of the Lodge of Perfection once one has received the Holy Royal Arch.

in the 1723 (revised 1738) *Constitutions* drew out the parallels between and among these two threads of Masonic symbolism as being the chord of continuity between the Pythagorean Order and Freemasonry. The pivotal equivalency was the secret of building which was to be understood as a result of mystically mediated initiatic insight enabling the neophyte to draw down from heaven the secrets of the chair necessary to conduct statecraft as a form of sorcery as well as to erect buildings designed as mnemonic devices in architecture to impart political esoterica to the initiated prince, sovereign, or monarch. Masonry, as legendarily conceived, preserved these pivotal unwritten secrets for imparting to worthy candidates with the aid of written ceremonial instructions, presumably including Webb's semi-esoteric public monitor, the *Illustrations*. To Anderson, these esoteric elements included four principles of Masonry: a point within a circle; a line; a superficies; and a solid, within which array the square became the proper emblem of the Divine Essence. Anderson, further, set up the Essenes as successors of the Pythagoreans and de facto as a higher representation of their order leading into the development of cabalism, understood to be a reference to the Holy Royal Arch, as it possessed the correct pronunciation of the ineffable Name of God. This also signaled the differentiation between *speculative* and *operative*, with the former being de facto the hermitical order in possession of the Royal Arch Word and the latter, the artisan-craftsmen who were deployed as evangelists, within the Jesuit-Joachimite typology. This precedent invested in Anderson's legendary history a template developed by Ramsay and by Webb as the perfecting of operative into speculative as the ascent of the neophyte from one order of evangelists, into the York Rite within which the tacit initiatic objective was the hermit to whom the Pilgrim Warrior repaired in his preparation for Jesuit styled Templar Knighthood. It also drew the heliocentric parallel between the Druids, as early British priests, as inheritors of Pythagorean teachings from Egypt as laid out in the writings of John Toland; Thomas Paine; Thomas DeQuincy; and elucidated as paragons of egalitarian public citizenship by Simon Greenleaf, in *A Brief Inquiry into the Origin and Principles of Free Masonry* (1820). The result was a simultaneous presentment within the legacy of the Clinton-Webb system of a template summarized and recapitulated by the Royal Arch of Enoch degree linking celestial hierarchy with artisan egalitarianism within one set, or array, of emblems describing a national path of initiation as an equivalency with, and alternative to, Biblical eschatology.

The Society of Jesus viewed itself and its existence of the dramatic context within which was founded as apocalyptic. It developed ritual imagery through specific pieces of stage drama to underscore that its chosen mission field was the frame within which history would be consummated, not only in a battle between good vs. evil, but did so with replete astral-solar symbolism as an equivalency between astral bodies and angelic forms. In their theological idiom, however, both the Old and New Testaments are conflate as representing a future age of peace and harmony within which evil, cast as the Antichrist would be defeated and the proto-Masonic era of millennial peace and brotherly love would be achieved under an irenic papal monarchy. This dynamic, as referenced, shows up with in the Order of the Red Cross of Babylon within which Cyrus the Great was celebrated as such a monarch: empowering the Israelites to restore its Temple from the warrant recovered from the hidden Vault of Enoch. The Cyrus reference in turn evoked the *Pax Romana* transferred from the Empire to the papacy as the earthly reign of orthodoxy within which the temporal authority of the papacy would be lifted up, as was Cyrus, as the medium through which the two mediating orders would insure peaceful compliance with orthodoxy, defeating heresy, in order that a universal irenic empire might be realized. This idiom, in terms of the Ramsay ideology of high degrees, implied that Masonic chivalry conferred by the Orders of Malta and of the Temple, together with the cognate degrees treating with chivalry in the Rite of Perfection point to the restoration of an unknown superior monarch representing the papacy's orthodoxy: the secular arm of a theocratic state. The pervasiveness of this allusion strikes anyone who reads these *haute* degree Masonic texts as concealing within them a Trojan Horse: a restored Catholic regime in the name of universal peace and harmony.

The two orders, hermits and active evangelists, point to a symbolic consolidation of the priority of Enoch within Clinton's esoteric ritual icon as a template for policy order: the two columns or pillars of the Temple. Technically, the columns on the porch of the Temple of Solomon, Jachin and Boaz, are different from the Pillars of Enoch, upon were inscribed all of knowledge derived from the correct pronunciation of the Tetragrammaton (see Chapter I). The differentiation between columns and pillars further alluded to the priority of Enoch as a template for Clintonian policy order and the energy which drove it through a separation between the "blue" craft and "red" capitular elements of rhetoric in Webb's *Illustrations*. Webb adroitly equipped Clinton with a set of vibrant and numinous symbols which linked the artisan with the hieratic elements of high degree initiation as a pathway between levels of citizenship accommodated to the two Jesuit-Joachimite classes of spiritual men, investing in the active evangelical militia a potency suggesting a progression into the contemplative and celestial orders. In other words, what the Society of Jesus considered to be a set iconology of two separate entities, Clinton and Webb established through the sequence of Masonic degrees as a mirror of the public sphere order as a progression. This dynamic squared with the principle of egalitarianism within Webb's revision of the English Rite, which replaced the Holy Royal Arch as a kingly-priestly end-point taking the place of de facto allegiance to English royalty as the tacit objective of initiation. The Prestonian English system therefore ended with the subject being a "*most loyal subject of the king*" as the ideal of initiation whilst the Webb concept was that the private citizen could become a *priest-king* himself, a *parfait* (Chapter II). This idea became, in time, the same objective of American Odd Fellowship, with its prevailing patriarchal theme, in its third degree: The Priestly Order of the Temple of Truth, which sustained the core drive of the Webb system within a more politically unified polity of governance. In the Webb-Clinton system, the system of chair degrees consolidated the base relationship between initiatic rank and polity achievement through three degrees: the actual Past Master; the Virtual Past Master and the Order of High Priesthood. These ceremonies, in the first and last instance, were reserved for Masons who had been duly elected and installed as the presiding officers of lodges and chapters. The middle degree was invented to satisfy the ancient requirement that a Royal Arch Mason must be a past master of a lodge to qualify for exaltation (initiation). The effect was to integrate egalitarian approbation with esoterica in an amalgam which made it clear that the ideal citizen integrated both styles of spiritual men at work within Freemasonry evocative of the Joachimite imprint of Jesuit missiology.

Thus, the two mediating orders, in other words, linking Joachim of Fiore's interior millennial construct of spiritual men established a dynamic which can be seen at work in various ways within the Clinton-Webb synthesis: 1) in the operative vis-a-vis speculative dichotomy with Masonry as it was developed in the Anderson legendary history; 2) in the column vis-a-vis pillar bifocality in symbolism linking the Craft lodge to the Royal Arch Chapter; and 3) to the rendering of Pythagorean vis-a-vis Egyptian *kerugmatik* (preaching) dichotomy within Freemasonry. This latter reference also entailed the interplay between Druids as British and American forerunners of egalitarian heliocentrism as the core metaphor for radical democracy which enable forensic Masonic writers, notably Simon Greenleaf, to explicate the founding of the United States as the realization of ancient British lore in the symbolism of the Druids. Quintessentially, this symbolism dealt with the dynamics of the illumination that came through mystic, solar inspiration. As a generic element of the Masonic symbolic vocabulary of initiatic advance, in this instance, progress from the rank of practical evangelism to the contemplation of Holiness to the Lord (the Royal Arch motto) the openness can be found within the entire of Masonic high culture to Illuminism as both a specific organization and as a method which suffused Freemasonry through the late 18th and 19th century. Giordano Bruno took up a parallel dichotomy between two types of men –those of transcendental faith and men of science–in a typology which struck an analogue between the Jesuit appropriation of Joachim's thought and Freemasonry. As a pre-Masonic intellect the specific elements of his configuration of solar religion substantially informed the shape of the two clerisies which framed Masonic vocabularies of operative vs. speculative views of the Fraternity and generated energies leading to the high degree mentality. Not only was this predicated upon the notion that Egyptianate lore, conspicuously in the works of John Toland (i.e. *History of the Soul's Immortality*), who was familiar with Giordano Bruno's work, and with Tommaso Campanella's *The City of the Sun*, as a paragon for the template of the District of Columbia.

The development, in specific of the Masonic Rite of Memphis (now defunct) is important in this respect because it carried forward the Egyptianate imprint within the Anderson text of an entire system of ninety six degrees devoted to the explication of Pythagoras as an Egyptian initiate. This Rite, and a cousin, the Rite of Mizraim (Hebrew for the land of Egypt) spelled out a canonical core of legends worked into discrete illuministic elements particular modalities of core Masonic ceremonies such as the Royal Arch Mason, the chivalric analogues to degrees set in the medieval era, and pre-eminently the Mark Master Mason degree. This order and degree became pivotal within the Clinton and Webb system because it set up the moral economy for paying a Master's wages according to a Biblical periscope in Matthew XX; and because it asked of the candidate to inscribe his personal Mark, or Masonic signature, within the keystone placed in an archway that led to the vault within which the Tetragrammaton was concealed and from which it was recovered. As such, the Mark Master within the Rite of Memphis distilled essential elements of the entire Rite and therefore of what was likely unwritten lore alluded to in the Pythagorean legend within Freemasonry that the secret of secrets within Freemasonry lay in the ability to merge statecraft with knowledge of the Pythagorean theorem as a result of divine inspiration of wisdom (Sophia) through the transmission of the Real Word of Master Mason (see Chapter II discussion of Mark Master Mason). The ceremony is cast in terms of the migration of a working evangelist from the quarry seeking admission to a higher order, and thus evokes the progression of a member of the world evangelical order into the contemplative order of hermitical mystics.

Comparatively, the badge of the Memphis Rite neophyte was a well-worked keystone; the neophyte was made to appear as Horus, an Egyptian solar deity, presenting himself before a representative of King Osiris, a Masonic surrogate for King Solomon. The piece of work born by the neophyte was noted for its departure from the accepted shape of oblong or square. Yet, because of its singular beauty (cf. Mark Master Mason ritual symbolism) was presented to the chair of Osiris. The Memphis Rite configured the symbolism of the Masonic ceremony to be the secrets necessary to construct a passage way between the Middle Chamber, in Webb's working, the place where all learning was recapitulated and summarized, to the Holy of Holies within which only High Priests were admitted. Because Horus was, by default, the candidate, the mythic son of Osiris and Isis, and because his piece of work was fitted to the vaulting of this chamber, he was admitted to the rank and mysteries of the degree. It was in specific the shaping of the stones to absorb continual pressure which made them serviceable according to the Rite, thus striking an equivalency between the judiciousness of a Knight of Christ: a hermit contemplative of the second order of monks consistent with the Joachimite dichotomy of esoteric, spiritual men.

In this idiom, the Vault of the Royal Arch of Enoch becomes by association a continuation of the Middle Chamber and the Holy of Holies (cf. Fellowcraft degree) an embodiment of both sets of symbols: the place where all of knowledge is recapitulated and the place where the Name of God is rediscovered. The first allusion is to the apologetical interpretation of lost wisdom; the second to its ineffable sacral significance. This earthly cosmography depicted the lost stupendous Temple of Ptah, 4000 years in the making, an analogue to the Jesuit idea that papal authority was prefigured and anticipated by the Egyptian Pharaohs as surrogates for Osiris. Jeremy Cross' work echoes the parallel principle and the opposite end of the continuum established by Anderson, itself taken up by Desaguliers and Anderson in the conflation of the *Old Charges*, or *Gothic Manuscripts*, as discussed the source of legendary histories.

Clinton and Webb were practically alert to the capacity of the image of mysteries penetrating into broader philosophical systems, such as Platonism and Pythagoreanism. This was the muscle of the core Clintonian agenda confirmed and echoed by Webb's Monitor. On the cusp of modern historical inquiry emerging from early modernity, Freemasonry provided a central means to integral the remaining elements of precritical thought about mythography, as detailed in the Anderson text, in league with the Joachimite thread from the Jacobite overlay to Jesuit ideology of the two orders extended into the Ramsay symbolic universe. In summation: they inherited a presupposition that rites of initiation were yet integrally linked to the conduct of the spiritual life, a like Jesuit element, and that the driving forces of history were guided by ancient mysteries, with which Freemasonry and religion were almost synonymous. Almost, of course, is the executive principle within this method because not even the fulsome rhetoric of Clinton and Webb, Salem Town excepted, would have cavalierly ventured a clear identity. Yet, the thrust of the whole system, to create a Christian patriotically American indigenous rite, underscores the intimate parallels between confessional Christianity in the period of the Second Great Awakening and the mission of the General Grand Chapter. Here it is crucial to see the Christian theological idea of the covenant working in tandem with the Masonic concept of Illuminism. The collective premise that God called an entire people toward holiness conflated with great effect to the nation being a Lodge of faithful Masons moving toward the reclamation of the Word of God. The nexus became the cabalistic dynamic of the empowering might of possession of the Royal Arch Word as a millennial device empowering initiatic discernment in such a way that the path of national initiation mirrored the movement of the Exodus. In the United States this Exodus represented Masonic westward expansion of the frontier.

There is no extant study on the ethical efficacy of Masonic ritual that can be found, apart from more general analyses of the dialectic between the ritual object of reverence and a confidence that this object reciprocates ritual celebration and meets the participant half way to achieve the purpose for which the ritual is performed. American Masonry has always existed within an envelope of practical piety which plays to the expectation that any morally focused prayer will be answered. This became truer as the Masonic Fraternity incorporated Christian symbols through the Knights Templar which could be deemed consistent with evangelical piety and fundamentalism. In other words, as the Clinton-Webb system moved toward the frontier and increasingly homogenized and saturated American religiosity at the crossroads among and between all mainline Churches, an executive principle emerged which Americanized its capacity to cooperate with much of organized religion. The stoical Puritanism of Clintonian Freemasonry preserved its universalistic and Arminian core as the York Rite evolved in the United States and became the preferred local idiom for pragmatic ecumenical enthusiasm working for local entrepreneurial and political cooperation. Yet, it was in fact the Lollard element within Freemasonry's suspicion of an ordained clergy which survived. This impulse did not make policy inroads into English Constitutionalism until the reign of Edward VI whose attachment to Calvinism is well known, except for a tradition of lay knights "nearish" to the king which kept alive legends of cooperation between Lollardy and Templar survivals. There was a Dutch resonance to the use of the word "Lollard" Middle-Dutch meaning "a mumbler of prayer" which possibly survived in the Dutch Reformed enthusiasm for Freemasonry in America, resulting in a division between the Reformed Church in America (pro-Masonic) and the Christian Reformed Church (anti-Masonic) within the Hudson Valley. Links between Dutch painting and the proliferation of the Hudson River school of landscape painting also survived investing in liberal Calvinism within Clinton's bailiwick an affinity for the broader naturalistic aesthetics of Calvinism within the Netherlands as its ethos survived and prospered in an alliance through Holland Lodge No. 8 in Manhattan, of which Clinton was Worshipful Master and George Washington himself an honorary member. Through this alliance between New York City and State Calvinism with local Dutch aristocracies an affinity developed between the lingering Estates concept consistent with the Dutch office of the *stadtholder* (city keeper) and the style of indirect hegemonic idealistic leadership struck between Calvinist ideas of election and the creation of a learned utopianism of oligarchy most frequently associated with the English utopian and intellect Francis Bacon whose objective of a reformation of knowledge conflated with the idea of a secret society governing a utopia through an analogue of the Rosicrucian Invisible Society or College functioning as the visible Masonically studded Royal Society under the Stuarts and Oranges (William and Mary). This idiom decisively influenced the lay leadership of Union College of Schenectady, New York, notably Scottish Rite founders in the Yates (i.e. Joseph C. and Giles Fonda) and Gourgas (i.e. John James Joseph Gourgas) families, and Clinton himself who became the Sovereign Grand Commander of the Cerneau body of the Ancient and Accepted Scottish Rite, a more Christian looking version of the Rite of Perfection with a closer and more recent linkage to France.

Given recent scholarly ideas and research linking the teachings of John Wycliffe's (ca. 1328-1384) Lollardry (14th century theological reform movement critical of the Catholic Church especially the Eucharist) and the survival of medieval Knight Templary into the early modern period, it is important to say that the elevation, consolidated by Martin Luther, elevating the secular prince to de facto rulership over the churches anticipated by Marsilius of Padua (ca. 1275-ca. 1342) in his *Defensor pacis* (1324) and Wycliffe, greatly enhanced the power of the Clintonians as they crafted society precipitated through Freemasons such as David Brearley (1745-1790), the author of the Constitution of the Protestant Episcopal Church. He was a signer of the Constitution of the United States and Grand Master of Masons in New Jersey as well as the de facto founder of the lay dominated polity of American Anglicanism as reflected in the emergence of Masonic Knights Templar as a de facto Episcopal sodality. Wycliffe, a professor of Divinity at Oxford University wanted the Bible printed in English (as opposed to Latin) so it could be read by the common people and not just the educated clergy. Although most of people in England at this time were illiterate, Wycliffe believed this would stimulate the populous into a new reformed religious revival and spark interest in learning how to read. Wycliffe formed a group called the Order of the Poor Preachers who distributed Bibles in English to anyone who could read; as such they were attacked as being *mumblers of the prayer* by reading the scripture in English, not Latin. The Order of the Poor Preachers was vehemently denounced by the Catholic Church. The Church, so enraged by Wycliffe letting the genie out of the bottle, denounced him as a heretic at the Council of Constance (4 May 1415). In 1428, Pope Martin V ordered the exhumation and destruction of his bones; his corpse was burned, along with approximately 200 hundred of his works, with the ashes thrown into the River Swift. The Lollards, like the Templars, met in secret and used a cell/counter-cell type (a fifth column) structure anticipating those used by the Jesuits and the Illuminati; this same structure would be implemented by modern espionage and security agencies such as MI5 and MI6, the CIA, the FBI, the Tonton Macoute, Stasi, and Heinrich Himmler's (1900-1945) infamous *Cult of the Black Sun*, the SS. With John

Foxe's *The Book of Martyrs*[295] (ca. 1559) praising the glorification of the godly prince lifted up above other secular rulers to reform the Church which was a central Lollard premise; this ideology was later adopted by Clinton and his ecumenical colleagues in the interplay between New York state religious communalism as it related to Roman Catholic electoral emancipation and the legal protection of the Catholic right to confidential auricular confession. There is very little concrete evidence except the pervasive consistency and survival of Templar related ideas from the suppression of the Knights Templar in 1314 and its American revival in 1816 under DeWitt Clinton.

That notwithstanding, the issue of Lollard survival is of more than passing interest to students of Masonic origins because of its identifications with Erastian principles of princely-priestly Melchizedekian threads of leadership as ritualized and typified in Royal Arch idiom whereby the secular sovereign was invested with non-sacerdotal authority over spiritual matters. In the Netherlands specifically, which bears the deepest imprint of Continental European pre-Masonry through its associations with 17th century Dutch aesthetics of *light* and the hegemonic concept of a martyred stadtholder, a cult of patriotism developed typified by a triumphalist iconology associated with the symbolism of Lions and the House of Orange as a further semiotic pointer toward a core lament of Masonic ritual having to do with the raising of the corpse of Hiram Abif by the strong grip of the Lion's Paw (for astrological symbolism see Chapter II), the Masonic proto-martyr and with the continued associations between the House of Orange with European opposition to the concept of the British Empire. Lollards were also linked to John Colet's (1467-1519) reformist sermons at St. Paul's Cathedral

Coat of Arms of the House of Orange – Nassau, Netherlands.

295 John Foxe (1517-1587) authored *The Book of* Martyrs: a history of medieval church, including histories of the Inquisition as well as Wycliffe and the Lollard movement.

and by implication to the Dean's affinity with the mystical teachings of Heinrich Cornelius Agrippa, a quantum source for the movement of occult ideology and esoteric ideas into England and further refinements relative to esotericism and Elizabethan policy of Baconian irenicism. This influence on Elizabeth was the most reasoned application of the Anglican *via media* upon her religious policy with the added increment that it insisted upon friendly policies toward Dissenters and Puritans in Parliament which *if* they had been adopted might have averted the English Civil War and blunted the impact of William Laud (1573-1645) in his determination to advance Anglican liturgy as a policy objective while opposing the radical reforms of the Puritans.

Lollardy also carried forward the opposition to Transubstantiation as the core of its theological opposition to Counter-Reformation amalgams which provided the dynamic ideology for Baroque art which was reflective of the Masonic high degree structure of turbulent and dramatic symbolism inserted by Ramsay into the provident Newtonianism associated with Desaguliers' revival of Grand Lodge in 1717. Lollardy also anticipated the Jesuit cell structure of Bavarian Illuminism which exercised influence through the application of propaganda technologies which made maximum opportunistic use of anti-clericalism to set the stage for a broader Reformation crisis in a parallel way that Illuminism set the stage for the European Revolutions of the nineteenth century (1832, 1848, etc.). The merger of Lollardy with Continental humanism of an iconoclastic variety and with Lutheran ideas of princely ecclesiastical leadership provide evidence that this movement, supported with alleged association with suppressed Templars, converged at least at the ideological level in opposition to papal overreaches in politics and Counter-Reformation strategies within ten years of the death of Henry VIII in 1547. The success of Templar and Hospitaller ritual imagery restored by Clinton and his associates revealed how residually influential remained the chivalric longing for a medieval reformed synthesis within which a new high degree Catholicism merged with Craft Newtonian Freemasonry might complement generic American Protestant through such currents as they worked their way into pansophism and epistemological reform at the beginning of the nineteenth century in the United States.

When in 1528 Sir Thomas More (1478-1535) was licensed by Bishop Tunstall (1474-1559) to read heretical books the groundwork was laid to interlink Lollardy and Lutheranism to his own utopian ideas which likely influenced Francis Bacon in his envisioning a proto-Masonic *House of Solomon* as an archetype for a Masonically driven Royal Society during the Presidency of the same by Dr. Desaguliers. The Baconian devotion to an oligarchic utopian management of a positivistic approach to the natural order presaged the realization of the Pythagorean viewpoint implicit in the *Timaeus*, the most commonly available of Plato's writings during the middle ages. This element greatly influenced Thomas Jefferson (1743-1826), whose partisan intellect incorporated DeWitt Clinton's uncle, Vice President George Clinton (1739-1812) and pointed through such panoptic intellects to DeWitt who in turn came to function as something of a clearing house between public service, patronage, and Freemasonry's growing interstate network. It was this integration of positivistic naturalism with the remnants of utopian rooted mythography which pointed to the evidence for the integration of the reality of mythology and a scientific view of mythology existing side by side within the pre-Masonic intellectual and symbolic terrain. The apparent sympathy between Lollard coalesced anti-clericalism and Lutheranism; Thomas Cranmer (1489-1556, leader of the English Reformation) was in effect a Lutheran, underscores the ripeness for the Baconian vision of the *via media* applied to epistemological reform and oligarchic elitism and oligarchy. William Tyndale's (ca. 1494-1536, Protestant Reformist) 1526 New Testament, found readership among all Protestant minded literati in London through the Coleman Street Group in London near to where the Masons Livery Company, established its livery hall circa 1356 to regulate stonemasonry, next to St. Stephen's Coleman Street which in the seventeenth century was a Puritan stronghold. The continental side of this putative cooperation can be traced to surface in Lutheran theologies of politics but also to the more esoteric reforming of epistemology associated with liberal Calvinism as it came to be installed as an adjunct to Stuart court culture after the Elizabethan Renaissance faded, notably through the Heidelberg Court of Frederick and Elizabeth Stuart. The irenicism of this thread of surviving humanism was deeply imprinted with hermeticism and cabalism and averred further to the Baconian concept of moderation rooted in the oligarchic reform of knowledge.

DeWitt Clinton's synthesis of the Thomas Smith Webb (and by default William Preston) ritual forges a link between Renaissance, animist[296] magism[297] involving Egyptian symbolism with a more empirical, rationalistic, and conventional form of scientific policy method which emerged in and around Clinton's patronage of Freemasonry and learned societies. The pinpoint of the numinous element within Masonic emblems of leadership, including the Ramée design of Union College, paved a more concrete avenue between hermetical and cabalistic elements within the thought of Giordano Bruno, Tommaso Campanella, and John Dee in their explications of utopian architecture linked to imperial extension which find expression in Clinton's use of Masonic offices and symbolism.

Within this context, the issue of the numinosity of Masonic emblems within Webb's ritual should be addressed in terms of the survival of a much more participatory element than has been previously been invested in their significance. This has to do with the survival of a sense of transcendence and potency surviving in the New World linked to utopian constructs, such as envisaged by Tommaso Campanella and Christopher Columbus (1451-1506) in their awareness of their own destiny and the urgency of bringing in a new world ideology to sustain a reformed Catholic empire. Even the word, "Catholic," bears scrutiny at this point because of the tendency to view political ethics after the Council of Trent as simply reactionary presuppositions. Rather, it seems that, for example, for Clinton to have envisaged an American Knights Templar Order directly implies a central papal monarchy of which it would be the spiritual and military arm. This falls into place with the Ramsay ideology and with the irenic philosophies of the Carroll family's approach to Jesuit theology which understood Egyptian symbolism to be an irenic, apologetical advice. This in turn points to linkages between Athanasius Kircher, Guillaume Postel and others who say a universal reformed papal imperium in Nilotic symbolic

296 Belief that non-human beings have souls

297 Transforming magic into power. Pike writes: "Magism was the Science of Abraham and Orpheus, of Confucius and Zoroaster. It was the dogmas of this Science that were engraved on the tables of stone by Hanoch and Trismegistus. *Morals and Dogma,* page 839.

terms as emerged in the resonance between Clinton's Erie Canal leadership and the references in Desaguliers and Anderson to Pythagoras as keys to the engineering necessary to build the pyramids. This issue remains one of the substantial questions relative to the vitality of Masonic emblems in the early modern period. From Samuel Charles Lee's (1625-1691) *Orbis Miraculum;* or *The Temple of Solomon*, a paragon representation of the symbolism of King Solomon's Temple through the methodical template of the District of Columbia the question has been consistent, if variously posed. Did Enlightenment Freemasons deem their semiotically tapestried ceremonials as having a *life* of their own? "Symbols consequently change their meaning according to the level of intelligence upon which their interpreter functions."[298] Are Masonic symbols and emblems a result of interest to intellectual historians because they represent a major protrusion of medieval and renaissance participation in the cosmos into modernity such that they anticipated the Romantic Movement, the Pugin Egyptianates, and the Pre-Raphaelites in that they *came alive* to the initiated adepts who created them anew in their lives and in the countless rites and degrees generated by Anderson and Desaguliers, as well as the Ramsay ideology?

The Clinton era of Masonic consolidation should be regarded not only as moving the nation toward a mission of political-theological expansion but as a meeting between gnosticism and the individual patriotic soul seeking to find itself within a new national framework of meaning. On the eve of English colonization of the New World, foreordination and the idea of divine election, derived from Christian antiquity from Augustine and Thomas Aquinas, loosed its hold upon Americans; many were beset with melancholia within their spiritual lives. The York Rite offered assurances that life might be a steady progression by degrees toward a joint national and private salvation within which Washingtonian confidence and perseverance might combine to forge a pragmatic ethic. It would not have been lost, existentially, upon the individual Freemason, and members of other cognate fraternal orders that what the world considered to be melancholia was in effect a meditative state within which the individual pilgrim warrior might enter his and her own, as adoptive Masonry developed a chamber

298 Hall, Manly Palmer, *Lectures on Ancient Philosophy*, page 343.

of reflection where the candidate ponders mortality, as the first step toward receiving the substitute word of Master Mason. Comparatively within the York Rite this Grand Word is *Immanuel*: *God with Us*, as the Knight Templar ritual work promised. This worked perfectly within the Webb System as it developed a Royal Arch-Knights Templar solar clerisy selected from the Blue Lodge to moderate the new nation: in Greek Kabbalah-Cabala the numerical value of Immanuel (Jesus) is 888 symbolizing a higher, spiritual, regenerated intellectual mind. In other words Christ is in *you*, the hope of glory in keeping with Masonic themes of *ascensio* and apotheosis.

* * * * *

No single Freemason was more enthusiastic about extending the idea of national initiation through covenantal illuminism, than the Masonic preacher and Grand Chaplain Salem Town (1779-1864). His 1818 work, *A System of Speculative Masonry,* laid out a replete theology of national Masonic initiation as his own career took him from upstate New York into the mid-west into the founding culture of Methodism and higher education. He and his descendants participated in all three of the epochs of frontier Masonry: the Clintonian succession to Founding Father's Masonic triumphalism; the Anti-Masonic Period and its furor; and the extension and consolidation of the entire Clinton and Webb system into Indiana and the mid-west. This later period witnessed his seminal significance, through theological education as well as secular higher studies, in the goodly heritage mentality of Freemasonry's transformation from post-colonial elite into the beginnings of a national fraternal culture. No less than three of the prevalent women's fraternal orders, the Rebekahs (female Odd Fellows), the Pythian Sisters, and the General Grand Chapter of the Order of the Eastern Star, were organized in Indiana. Indiana, in turn, transformed Ohio's role as the Masonic frontier cornerstone into a pioneer trajectory which took up railroads as a means of fraternal evangelism as an extension of the Erie Canal, as an extension of the imagery of Masonry's mythic role in the geometric management of Nilotic flooding, from Anderson amalgam of Gothic *Constitutions*, into the enriched landscape, Masonically, of Illinois and Iowa. The creation of the formidable Theodore Sutton Parvin library of Masonic books in Cedar Rapids, Iowa can be traced indirectly, although concretely, to Town's activities and writings, as can the founding of Mason City, Iowa and other towns and hamlets on the path toward the far west. To Town the United States was a Masonic Republic, expanding Logos recovered in the Royal Arch ritual, under a symbolic umbrella that echoes von Fiore's Third Spiritual Age.

Salem Town wrote after the repulsive excesses of the French Revolution had disaffected all but the most ardent Francophiles in Thomas Jefferson's circle and following the final triumph of Britain against Napoleon I. He also wrote before the furor of the Morgan period of anti-Masonry that wreaked substantial damage upon Clinton's broad Masonic vista both at the theological and political levels. Yet, his ardency for the symbolic content of the tradition he espoused was unalloyed in its basic premise, that is, that Jews and Egyptians, refined and articulated Masonic symbolism through a very intimate connection between the nobility of both respective countries, who visited each other's court. The allusion to nobility[299] was a telling reference to the Ramsay ideology, which Town explicated that the Masonic Order had first flourished in Egypt under the direction of Egyptian priests whose valuable secrets were imparted to Pythagoras. Town's emphasis upon the initiation of Greek intellects into Egyptian Mysteries and the transmission of their wisdom to Rome in the shape of obelisks inscribed with many hieroglyphic and Masonic emblems almost certainly was intended to underscore the significance of his work to the cosmogonic-astrological elements within District of Columbia's architecture and design.

Salem Towne's vista also relates to the premise that a purified Roman Catholicism along Egyptianate symbolic lines might be the means of restoring Unity to Christendom. He did not mention the Church in so many words, but the full scale adoption of the emblematic gear of Templary as the point of definition of the York Rite served the same function. His tone shapes the premise that emphasis upon the mystical rather than the dogmatic doctrinal side to Catholicism could influence non-Catholics to return to a Catholic union. Clinton's views of Catholic emancipation and his views that

299 Town, Salem, *A System of Speculative Masonry,* page 103

the confessional should be protected by law upheld this tone with concrete policy implications. The same principle can be put for the Knight Templar view of the ritual libations administered to the pilgrim warrior neophyte in the knighthood ceremony at a triangular delta shaped altar lit with a symbolic number of tapers. This Eucharistic, liturgical premise derived from the Renaissance roots of Masonry in hermeticism and cabalism which held that God animates all of creation, including the sacrament diverted chivalric Freemasonry from conventional Protestantism in its drives away from popish pretension and superstition perceived by Calvinists and Baptists in specific to be part of the doctrine of transubstantiation. This view, which also held that the movement of the earth was the result of a spiritual animation from God, as opposed to gravity, which was not fully described as a force, until Newton's period, was likely perceived by members of the order at the time to be an extension of the entire Royal Arch ethos: regarded during the Morgan era as the core of blasphemy within the whole Fraternity.

This element of Town's carried forward is analogous to ideas posited by Giordano Bruno who insisted that it would be possible to unite religious sectaries at war during the sixteenth century across Europe to a new rite, presumably something like Clinton-Webb Masonry which held to Copernicanism symbolically if not scientifically and afforded itself an opportunity to carry the ideas of a third irenic age into imperial definition. Such a point of view would have conflated easily with the Jesuit and Jacobite usage of Masonic networks and intellects, such as Emanuel Swedenborg, to advance the Fraternity as a type of Mithraic-Zoroastrianism redivivus, consistent with forms of cultural Anglicanism associated with Edmund Spenser (ca. 1552-1599), Philip Sidney (1554-1586) and Sir Fulke Greville (ca. 1554-1628), a noted humanist at the court of Elizabeth I. In Connecticut, specifically, Philander Chase and other clergy, tended to define Freemasonry as an Anglican sodality with much the same philanthropic and leaderly agenda as the Episcopal Church, which remained there and elsewhere an important denominational ally of the Fraternity during the Morgan era. What is remarkable about this progression is a certain hidden consistency throughout its continuity: the endurance of the hermetical thread, enhanced and augmented by cabalism which validates and enlivens the phenomenon as it achieved unique, if not monumental, expression in the structure of Masonic ideas. It forms, in other words, one of the grand layers of the interior archaeology of Freemasonry, Biblical, medieval, Renaissance and Enlightenment elements, which Salem Town inserted firmly within a Joachimite millennial dynamical base.

The oligarchic parallels between a pre-Reformation ideal of a holistic commonwealth thus appears to lay at the foundation of Town's vista constructed from the Clinton-Webb synthesis. Masonic Knight Templary, within which Salem Town was a pro-active and consummate operative, as much as said this as thousands of Royal Arch Masons marched under the beauceant of a medieval Roman Catholic fraternity as the de facto ideal of cultural Protestantism. In sum, Town's enthusiasm for pre-Reformation antiquity as preserved within the Egyptianate resonance in Roman Catholicism's preservation of the idea of universal empire. The effect was achieved in that his vista carried the Logos symbolism rhetorically and esoterically into mainstream America as the frontier expanded, not only through Freemasonry, but through numerous cognate fraternities and sororities devoted to analogous objectives.

* * * * *

Salem Town positioned the Royal Arch mission as an extension of the High Priesthood held by Egyptian hierarchs as a paragon for balancing statesmanship with sacral mission through his work. He credited the universality of the empires of Alexander and of the Romans to the integration of the mysteries held by the indigenous leadership of Israel whose High Priest in full vestments greeted Alexander the Great at the gates of Jerusalem for this purpose and to foresight of Augustus to welcome obelisks into the sacred geometry of Rome and its Athenian predecessor which he believed had been founded by an Egyptian: Cecrops. The same hand can be seen in L'Enfant's lifting up the buildings and spaces of the District over residential and commercial structures as a means to iconize architecture as the principal medium of interpreting the mysteries of the nation to its citizens, as a lodge might instructs its members and officers in Masonic ceremonial. The icons were foremost, and only after these were established to their most persuasive public effect were the streets and blocks laid down. In this vein, it should be noted that no precedent existed for L'Enfant's design, not even St. Petersburg, Russia, to achieve the desired effect except for Masonic symbolism as an extension of its Baroque components, the dramatic interplay of symbolic figures and temples to achieve dramatic and semiotic effect.

In this vernacular, Town pointed to the Druids as did Simon Greenleaf within his *A Brief Inquiry into the Origins and Principles of Freemasonry* (1820) delineated almost simultaneously as the descendants of Pythagoras as priestly instructors of the people. Town considered Pythagoras to be the founder of the Druids, who Town considered to be a Mason, thus circumstantially investing the Druids with knowledge of Masonry.[300] This idiom invested an "….Arch Druid in each nation (cf. Grand High Priest as the resident surrogate for Pythagoras) who held sufficient authority to Convene ... others at pleasure ... whenever the General good required Council (General Grand Councils were the president dais officers of the General Grand Chapter of Royal Arch Masons)."[301] Town extended the Druidical pedigree into the Anglo-Saxon development and cultivation of Freemasonry from Pythagorean roots into the creation by Augustine of Canterbury (d. May 604 CE), a Benedictine Monk who later became Archbishop of Canterbury as the first exponent of Freemasonry as a Christian sect into England through architecture. This aptly conflated his mythic narrative with King Athelstan (ca. 894-939) and the York legend of Freemasonry which came to be the name of the Clinton-Webb rite.

Town's system was distinctive in that it developed with singular clarity the relationship between the ancient pre-Masonic occult mysteries, notably Zoroastrianism and its link to Egyptianate Pythagoreanism, the great and immortal witness of George Washington, the father of his country's salvation, necessarily the beginning of America as a national lodge. Town writes:

> "The great and immortal Washington was a Free-Mason: - that father of his country's salvation was our brother. In him was combined every

300 Ibid, page 109.
301 Ibid.

excellence of character, in the field, in the cabinet, and the church. He was one of fairest, brightest, greatest ornament. - The weight of his talents and character was never withholden from Masonic support. This man could have had no motive in deceiving the world, no motive in patronizing assembles, unless, in his view, the institution *ought* to be encouraged and maintained. Suffice it to say, therefore, as Free-Masonry was countenanced and approved by this great and good man, it could be on no other ground than that of its own intrinsic worth, and consequent importance to mankind. If such men have not only honored the society with their presence, but sanctioned the institution by precept and example, who shall presume to condemn it? If the testimony of men, first in the affections of their countrymen, is valid in relation to other matters, why not equally so the case before us?"[302]

To George Washington's exemplary character, Town traced the movement of an integrated natural and moral philosophy from Persia into Egypt through Zoroaster's influence, as a mathematician and philosopher, into the work of Socrates in his effort to generate the new man; from the initiation rites of archaic societies wherein philosophy (cf. Enlightenment Reason) and wise men (theosophy) were comingled. He believed, in essence, that Masonry embraced and inculcated evangelical truth through its preservation of the Name of God. Speculative Freemasonry had the same co-eternal and unshaken foundation as the doctrines of Christianity taught to be Divine Revelation. Town worked with an organized, financially subscribing network that not only included Thomas Smith Webb (cf. *Illustrations of Masonry*), but DeWitt Clinton himself. He also worked with the noted portrait artist and Grand High Priest of New York Royal Arch Masonry, Ezra Ames, who organized the Royal Arch dedicatory ceremonial of the Erie Canal opening, but organized the leadership of an array of local lodges, chapters and commanderies/encampments defining the origin of the entire American Rite as it began to move westward and into Canada.

By establishing an identity between Masonic principles and divine revelation, Town struck an equivalency between the Masonic transference of the Tetragrammaton, J- B- O-, a syncretistic amalgam of Jahweh, Baal,

302 Ibid, pages 16-17.

and Osiris, and the Logos of the fourth gospel: claiming that Masonry's mission was to seek with diligence this pre-existent Divine Word; in every age of the World, even before Christ, seemingly anticipating *Morals and Dogma of the Ancient and Accepted Scottish Rite* by Albert Pike. The precise communication of the Logos was always therefore accompanied with moral and religious instruction consistent with the learning inscribed on the pillars of Enoch. Further, Town identified the Masonic Word to be the single element Adam carried from his sweet communion with God before the apostasy in the Garden of Eden into the creation of the new world, after the Fall through communion with nature. It was this quality of the Lost Word which became the essence and foundation of Speculative Masonry, preserved through the Craft by way of the ancient mysteries mediated by Zoroaster and Pythagoras. The specific point Town took up was that Masonry was in effect the national sacred ceremonial of American because, as in Israel, the name was known by the nation. Conceptually, this further identified the governance destiny of the nation with a Royal Arch Chapter, which invested the management of the polity of the Chapter with the capacity and political theological warrant to pronounce it.

Town's concept of governance thereby creates an alternative or parallel governance idiom in pragmatic application to the illuministic impulse through the Clinton-Webb system. The ideal polity of the nation was not simply a proto Mithraic, or heliocentric, but integrated solar Egyptianate governance with the conciliarism[303] of a three way communication, through syllables, of three sovereigns: Hiram, King of Tyre, King Solomon, and the wise architect Hiram Abif. This imagery conflated aptly with the American Constitution in its division among executive, legislative and judicial branches with Masonry being and becoming the maieutic[304] efficacy by midwifing the political and spiritual will to make the system work.[305] In this maneuver, Town in effect borrowed deeply from the energy available

303 Conciliarism was a reform movement in the 14th, 15th and 16th century Roman Catholic Church which held that final authority in spiritual matters resided with the Roman Church as a corporation of Christians, embodied by a general church council, not with the pope.

304 Pedagogical method based on the idea that the truth is latent in the mind of every human being due to innate reason but has to be "given birth" by answering intelligently proposed questions (or problems).

305 The tripartite division of government within the United States also represents the tripartite division of governance in the Masonic Lodge to be discussed in Chapter XVI.

to myth creators by harnessing the integral *elan* (eagerness) between myth and Nature, as refined and defined in the Enlightenment and subsequently developed through the Romantic Movement. As a result, the personal qualities of the sovereigns are poured out into the "springs of action" at work at the fulcrum or pivot of the constitutional system. Samuel Coleridge developed this idea into the mission and function of a national clerisy, extending from the Christianity of the governors of the state, parallel to the *kings two bodies* from Biblical and medieval precedent in political theory. In Town's idiom, Masonry channeled the Christian belief of the governor of the commonwealth to join the moral authority of pagan antiquity with the evangelical truth of Christianity in a new interior vocabulary of power. It is the abstracted essence of the Clinton-Webb system which suffused Town's Masonic political theology into codification in the framing of the organization of the professions along Masonic lines, as subsequently developed by various Masonic jurists, such as Simon Greenleaf and Roscoe Pound, drawing coherent and workable lines between the products of the system in law making from the myth conjoining of revelation and Reason as envisaged in Royal Arch polity.

Further, Town drew out the conceptual legacy between Adam's experimental, by which he meant scientific and observational capabilities to *speculative truth*, in Masonic terms. The allusion is to the promise of the serpent; that to eat of the forbidden fruit empowered the participant to know good from evil and to experience immortality; you shall not die. The latter quality of speculative Masonry, in other words, integrated speculative Masonry precisely with the Fall and the necessary surrogation to equate the sweet communion of Adam and God with the communication of the Name of God, by syllables, J- B- O-. As a result, an eclectic syncretism was inserted into Christian revelation through which Town applied the Webb ritual both as speculative Freemasonry and as pagan authority as an apologetical tool, reminiscent of the Jesuit utilization of Egypt and the warrant in antiquity for universal papal empire. The Royal Arch of Enoch polity, therefore, assumed a conceptual capacity consistent with American national destiny incorporating Counter-Reformation triumphalism under the guise of irenic toleration.

Town, further, assigned the dynamic of Adam's use of speculative Masonry, as descended through Noah, through the metaphor of the Jewish custom of pronouncing the true Name of Deity as part of the early origins of the world. It was Town's intent to demonstrate not only that the communication of the Royal Arch Logos Word was at the dynamic spring of action for the governance of the nation but to position the General Grand Chapter as the sanctum sanctorum, or supra governmental agency, through which this objective was achieved. In this aspect, it is noteworthy that Town identified DeWitt Clinton specifically as General Grand High Priest as the executive of executives as the priest-king (cf. Melchizedek, David) at the head of the nation. This capacity perdured in national Royal Arch Masonry until the General Grand Priesthood of Charles Gilman dismantled the polity sovereignty of the General Grand Chapter just prior to the American Civil War (1861-1865), apparently in league with Albert Pike, a delegate to the convention in which this objective was realized. The result was to position Pike's subsequent Sovereign Grand Commandership of the Mother Supreme Council of the Southern Jurisdiction. It is likely that Town envisaged Royal Arch Masonry taking the place of political parties in the founding of the national working constitution of the Republic. Clearly, DeWitt Clinton's management of the irenic public sphere and his principles of tolerant patronage apart from ideological and religious tests was consistent with this objective. The line of thought, if so, would have progressed from the speculative origins of divine warrant in pagan mythology invested in the proto-Masonic collegiality of the Founding Father as a lodge moving into a national elite, as confirmed and accommodated in the design of the District of Columbia as a solar utopia linking the conciliatory capacities of partisan institutions to the national Royal Arch of Enoch priesthood.

The salient issue appears to be that Town aptly targeted a consciousness and latent ideology within the nation, closely allied with Clinton's pansophic public intellect, which, whilst identified with Thomas Jefferson, was not narrowly a result of his direct personal influence. According to Town, this latency can be traced to Plato's employment of a mediating, apologetical philosophical method which became identified with Logos through which the Jews were taught to speak irenically of God as the Word, a device taken up by St. John the

Fourth Gospel; to Town this concept denominated as the Masonic economy. Town realized, uppermost, that the preexistence of the logos as the object of political worship dispensed and mediated from a central imperial capital made it possible to lift up within institutional fraternalism the craftsmanship (Masonic) and patriarchal composition, akin to Odd Fellowship, of the elites necessary to manage the subordinate and echelon-assigned capacities of governance as a populist movement aspiring individually and collectively through Amphictyonic[306] Covenantal (a/k/a Federalism, a political concept in which a group of members are bound together by covenant with a governing representative head.) as patriarchs and elders of Israel to the governance of a nascent world empire. Town's implication was that Royal Arch Word, identified with Logos, further identified with Jeffersonian enhanced Clintonian speculative Masonry as articulated in the nation's capital and Vitruvian learning in general preserved the capacity for memory necessary to recall through anamnesis the recapitulation, esoterically transmitted, from God, through Adam and Noah into the foundation of the First Temple by King Solomon as the wisdom necessary to govern the nation. Town saw that the very ubiquity of this dynamic throughout history confirmed the truthfulness of the content of speculative Masonry as embracing and incorporating the Masonic Logos as an apologetical tool.

The Masonic Millennialism of Salem Town's development of a national destiny; the United States as a Masonic Lodge-Royal Arch Chapter spreading Logos (cf. Christ as the *Sun of Righteousness* or, alternatively America as an exoteric Christian nation) by spiritual men in the Joachimite ethos; for Freemasonry can be traced to the development of comparative religion as a dynamism driving English deism. Comparative religion in the 17th and 18th century took up the use of mythology for ideological purposes and reworked it to demonstrate that antiquity could be utilized to drive moral and ideological issues. The deistic grand master in the 17th century was the Lord Herbert of Cherbury (Chapter VI). Herbert's contribution underscored the quality of Town's millennial orbitry in terms that there was an economy, precise and exact, between the mind's capacity to comprehend symbolic

306 League of Greek tribes, founded by Athenian King Amphictyon, whose leaders traditionally met at Thermopylae before the rise of the Greek polis.

truth and the existence of objects available for comprehension. This meant that Masonic millennialism, through which an irenic social and political objective might be realized, conformed to the exact spatial qualities of the frontier as new faculties developed to conform to new images. Such a microcosmic geometry and geography required dependence, actually codependence, upon astronomy and geography as mathematics generated not only the technical date for travel, by land and sea, but also a mystical confidence available through de facto Masonic "worship of the sun" through its rituals. In this sense, Clinton and Webb relied upon an internal force unfolding different modes of apprehension through the medium described in the St. Andrew's Royal Arch Hurd Plate. Transposed onto the Masonic work of converting the nation into a Masonic Lodge within the process of public policy initiation, Herbert provided the template consistent with the solar utopianism implicit and tacit within the L'Enfant-Daniel Carroll design of the District of Columbia, which might unfold into concrete material culture. This entailed political will in specific public works, such as the Erie Canal, which affirmed the existence of a singular and ubiquitous concept of TRUTH, what high degree Scottish Rite Masonry cast as The Royal Secret (32nd degree), which integrated and comprehended all of creation within the natural and fabricated man-made world. Thus to Herbert can be traced a legacy of irenic thinking about antiquity and its usefulness in policy issues. As such, it developed a strategic conceptuality linking the English Renaissance to the unfolding of Joachimite elements in Masonry which were both co-opted through Jesuit imperial theory and in turn were midwifed into a new American civil millennial religion

A useful example of the Herbert typology at work in the Clinton-Webb synthesis is the relationship to graded rituality to material culture. This was echoed, perhaps presaged, by the L'Enfant template within which squares and circles were connected by expansive avenues to the devolution of county and township planning into the frontier. The result is that Masonic lodges and temples took their place in the county seats and state capitals into the frontiers as anchor building, frequently placing a magnifical temple as a silent and in effect to the uninitiated as inscrutable icon for the moral guidance of the *oculati*: those who had eyes to see the broader esoteric web of interconnections and iconologies available to initiates. This ability, implied further. a correspondence to position the human intellect in the microcosmic position of God as the Great Architect of the Universe (GAOTU) by a mass of lesser architects, moral and speculative as well as virtual and pragmatic, with the result that the divine harmonial image might be replicated countless times and in multiple places to echo the layering of Masonic ritual order, ranging from the Persian magi into and through Egypt into the Pre-Reformation Catholic world of mysticism through Giordano Bruno and the 17th century; Herbert to Isaac Newton.

In conclusion, to Salem Town, this affinity conflated with a millennial state which Masonic logos theory carried into the whole of society in league with the pervasiveness of the moral authority conferred upon the craft by antiquity. The triumph of Protestant nominalism within Reformation pedagogy was at odds with platonic ideas of universal harmony aspiring toward the *Summum Bonum* of rational mysticality in the same way the mathematically rooted observation and scientific methods came to be opposed to the idea of a Christian commonwealth as an *a posteriori* idea of society, as Thomism (cf.Aristotle) and Catholic political theory promulgated. The pristine example of antiquity as a measure for republican utopianism had more in common, in other words, with the moral philanthropy of Catholicism than with a blind individualism sanctioned through rhetorical pedantry wedded to self-interest through private theological inspiration. At this level, Town carried the Clintonian pansophist idea into a supportive concept of a mystical clerisy consistent with Jeffersonian ideas of agrarian romanticism preserved through Vitruvian and Palladian order whereby the patronal villa tended to become the template for enlightened hegemony over pioneer, developing regions of a frontier nation. It was, after all, the affinity between the Roman republic and the Roman Empire in tandem working toward a broad philanthropic ideal which trumped the heroization of individualistic liberty at the expense of a desired global reign of peace which was at stake. With this in mind we now explore the United States as a Masonic Republic in the Salem Town millennialist concept: that the new nation was itself a de facto Masonic Temple spreading the Logos of the Royal Arch while announcing a new, astrological Solar Age.

CHAPTER X

THE UNITED STATES OF FREEMASONRY

The First Masonic Republic and John James Beckley

"Notably among these we find General John Sullivan, First Grand Master and Governor of the State of New Hampshire; Pierpont Edwards, first Grand Master of Connecticut; General James Jackson, Governor and Grand Master of Georgia; William Richardson Davies and Richard Caswell, both Governors and Grand Masters of North Carolina; General Rufus Putnam, first Grand Master of Ohio (raised in American Union Military Lodge); General Mordecai Gist, Grand Master of South Carolina; Robert R. Livingston, Chancellor of New York, who swore George Washington in as first President of the United States on a Masonic Bible, while Grand Master; DeWitt Clinton, John Marshall, afterwards Chief Justice of the United States; General David Wooster of Connecticut; Franklin and Milnor of Pennsylvania, Aaron Ogden of New Jersey; Paul Revere of Massachusetts, and innumerable others were instrumental in the establishment and promotion of the American institution of Masonry as it is to-day."
- Charles H. Callahan, *Washington: The Man and The Mason*, 1913.

"The rituals leadings to each new level of membership were not, as is sometimes suggested, childish initiations. They were awesome rites of passage into new types of association, promising access to higher truths of Nature once the blindfold was removed in the inner room of the lodge. Each novice sought to become a "free" and "perfected" Mason capable of reading the plans of the "Divine Architect" for the "rebuilding of the temple of Solomon," and reshaping secular order with moral force."
- James H. Billington, *Fire in the Minds of Men: Origins of the Revolutionary Faith*, 1980.

"As the Government of the United States of America is not, in any sense, founded on the Christian religion, …"
- language from the Treaty of Tripoli, Article XI, submitted by President John Adams to the U.S. Senate; ratified 1797.

George Washington's death on 14 December 1799, provided Freemasons with an ample opportunity to shape his image as a paragon Masonic initiate in Enochian visual terms. In a sermon delivered in January of 1800, fellow mason Jean-Simon Chaudron (1758-1846) elegized the late President as Enoch being lifted directly to heaven by angelic beings. Similarly, J. J. Barralet depicted this concept in fulsome imagery soon thereafter; within a political context it signaled the end of the Federalist period whilst heralding the beginning of the Jeffersonian era. This imagery appealed to the network surrounding DeWitt Clinton and his Jeffersonian aligned ritualists, politiques and designers as an apologetic device, at once, making it possible for Washington to be cast within a panoply of icons intended to drive hidden, rejected, and otherwise lost wisdom into a Logos definition articulated as the millennial vista for the *Masonic nation*. Chief among these was Clinton's own Masonic colleague Ezra Ames (1768-1836) a Washington portraitist, regalia manufacturer for Masonic organizations, and Grand High Priest of the Grand Chapter of Royal Arch Masons of New York. In this capacity, Ames presided over the dedicatory ceremonies for the Erie Canal, for which he designed and executed a ritual detailed to frame the ideal of the canal and its locks passing through and underneath an actual Masonically consecrated Royal Arch en route to the frontier thus linking the Empire State to the Mississippi valley via the Great Lakes anticipating the construction and dedication of the "Royal" Gateway (to the West) Arch in St. Louis, Missouri symbolizing Masonry's westward expansion.

The intellectual vitality of early American republic Freemasonry can be traced to the energies expended upon its expansion into the American frontier following the War for Independence. The evidence for this energy can be seen in the devolution of almost random orders and rites descended from the ideas which shaped and informed the Ramsay ideology of higher degrees such that a unique American or York Masonic Rite emerged from discretely differentiated emblematic sources as evidenced in the St. Andrew's Royal Arch Hurd Plate of 1790. This solar pathway documented the creation through extension of Royal Arch Chapters, Cryptic Councils of Royal and Select Masters, and Encampments and Commanderies of Knights Templar as coordinated Masonic rite of sequential chronological episodes, with some disjunctures, governed by different governance entities with a common thread or theme linking the loss, recovery, preservation and Christian interpretation of the Masonic Word, the ineffable name of God, following the pattern established in the drama of the Third Degree ritual of Master Mason.

Within the political context that emerged from Renaissance sources within the United States, it is critical to reference that Freemasonry's application of the elements contained within the Enoch template for policy design contained a latent absolutistic theory of Pythagorean rulership derived through the Neo-Platonic overlay provided by the whole infrastructure of the graded degree system, as a Platonic reflection guiding the hermetical and cabalistic energy drive toward utopian micro-cosmogony. This entailed an enthusiasm which sought to supplant humanistic scholarly virtue for both patriotism and absolutism linked with the writings of Niccolò di Bernardo dei Machiavelli (1469-1527) through an equivalency between a centralized array of architecture and symbolism *built* into a national capital district which in turn provided a design for other state capitols with Apollonian domes and radial street structure revealing the outlines of Enochic radiation of emerging solar energy as nascent federal rulership parallel with solar utopianism. Machiavelli's role for *The Prince* appears to be a channeling of classical sources reinforcing autonomous spheres of action replicative of Masonic autonomy implicit and latent in Dr. Anderson's *Constitutions of the Free-Masons* and focused as the Scottish Rite conveyed a style of symbolical oligarchy through the forming of professional etiquette in engineering, law and medicine particularly to guide the creation of a general pathway toward its achievement with spheres of autonomy characterizing an overall policy direction.

The influence of early Republican politics upon Freemasonry, in the United States, can be seen not only in the general identification of the

Fraternity with the careers of DeWitt Clinton and Edward Livingston in the creation of a *haute* degree ideology reflective of a new, paragon sense of citizenship, apart from the ideal of a loyal subjecthood to the British monarch, but also to the triumph of the Neo-Pythagorean character of Copernicanism tacitly and implicitly integral to mystical aspirations towards the infinite as it was applied to the Masonic colonization of the western frontier. Patriotic citizens following the controversies surrounding the Jay Treaty of 1794 were equally convinced that British alliances were suspect sui generis, not the least of which were the recent memories of England using American Indians to provoke armed conflict in the west but also because the idea of joining interests commercially might lead to a rejection of France as a moral ally in the success of republican government as an extension of the American Revolution. In short: the Jay Treaty averted a second war with England while establishing peaceful trade with Great Britain in the midst of the French Revolutionary Wars which began in 1792. The Jay Treaty was hotly contested by Thomas Jefferson and his republicans who supported the new French Republic.

The defeat of a major British invasion from Canada at Saratoga in 1777 in their effort to transform the Hudson Valley into the principal military and commercial conduit cementing the two core regions of British North America, coupled with the Declaration of Independence, intended to encourage European allies for the new nation; both made it clear that cultural affinities linking colonial Freemasonry with the French higher degree system and its ideology would succeed in the United States. The French were, after all, allies with the colonies in their war for independence. In turn English Masons were driven by a classist rivalry between Antients and Moderns which truncated ideological extension of the rituals to parallel concepts of citizenship. The Lodge of Reconciliation of December 1813, dominated by the Grand Lodge Modern regime of the Duke of Sussex, a son of George III, insured that the future of British Freemasonry, England, Wales, Scotland, and Ireland, would closely follow the interests of the aristocracy and ultimately merge under Royal Patronage after 1876 with the constitutional mission of the monarchy. By contrast, the Clintonians and Livingstonians were determined that American Freemasonry echo and mirror the iconology of republicanism in ways which enabled and empowered its leaders to avert partisan apparatus when the need was warranted to achieve critical policy objectives. Important differences in the methods of intellectual activity consonant with Freemasonry were at stake as well. Freemasonry was conducive to pansophist and encyclopedic approaches to learning, seek epistemological holism, as opposed to individualistic and solipsistic approaches to the dissemination of learning. This was an increasing risk to its credibility as technical research tended to follow a more Franklinian approach of individual experimentation (cf. Francis Bacon) whilst the Masonic pedagogy in so far as it can be summarized was collegial and eclectic yet tending toward a grand synthesis epitomized by the reign of liberty and reason as a universal imperium.

The aesthetic element of this design cannot be avoided precisely because it was the inspiration between ritual and policy that made the carrying out of what was an essentially illuminist agenda for normal, evolving political process. Just as this process can be traced from George Washington's Enochic penumbra into Clinton's interlocking of national Knights Templar and Royal Arch polity with his own domination of Empire State irenic ideology, the same ethos dominated his creation through Erie Canal expansion westward into the Ohio Canal system and similar avenues into Indiana with reference to the Pythagorean, and therefore Enochic, template in the legendary histories prefacing the 1723 and 1738 *Constitutions*, available to every proficient Freemason directly after Benjamin Franklin's publication of the same and the Thomas Smith Webb and Salem Town reworking of its central and core forces. Thus it can be successfully argued that as seminal for the influence of Freemasonry upon American society, there have been quintessential ceremonials which have channeled and framed its application at critical points, notably the iconic template of the Royal Arch of Enoch. This design became paradigmatic for the development of the nation in particular material ways and determinative of the methods through which policy achieved realization.

It is significant that the Jeffersonians, including Thomas Jefferson himself, collared the Federalists with a hidden and secret agenda to pursue rapprochement with Britain at the level of permanent alterations in the class structure of the nation. It was, however, those around Jefferson, namely John J. Beckley, who were members of Phi Beta Kappa, an offshoot of Williamsburg Lodge No. 6, who were proponents and in some instances, participants in the Clintonian management of Royal Arch and Knight Templar enthusiasms for a practical mystique surrounding egalitarian citizenship. Noted Federalists, such as George Washington, Rufus King, were Freemasons, of course. Yet, the strength of the General Grand Chapter can be largely traced to the line of Clintonians and friends and followers of the Livingstons, whom Clinton held in the highest regard for their aristocratic approach to statesmanship, politics and institutionalize learning. The latter element was assuredly heliocentric and cosmogonically solar in its symbolism likely originating from the Modern Masonic strain of Desaguliers' Newtonian heliocentric physics. Yet, Clinton, Webb and Town adroitly positioned their view of Freemasonry as a medieval legacy (cf. Ramsay *haute* degree ideology) in tune with Copernican theory even though the Roman Catholic Church had condemned Giordano Bruno and Galileo for advocating its veracity over and against the Church's teaching of both the magisterium and the Holy Scriptures. This eclectic approach to Masonic legendary history, nevertheless, assisted them to fabricate a mythic chronology from antiquity along the lines of Bruno and Campanella in their unitary approach to Egypt and the pre-Reformation Catholic regime, quintessentially through Knight Templary with the help of Jeremy Cross's hieroglyphic engravings and Cornelius Moore publishing mission.

Jefferson, and the Jeffersonians, including their Northern variety, personally attached to the charisma of the man, but suspicious of his Francophilia and its refusal to deal with Hamiltonian and *Adams' England*, quintessentially DeWitt Clinton, saw the author the first version of the Declaration of Independence (with its use of the Christianized words "sacred and undeniable" redacted by Freemason Benjamin Franklin and replaced with "self-evident"), the Virginia Constitution, and the manifest on religious liberty in Virginia, as a de facto pope and prophet, the sage of Monticello seeking to breathe religiosity into the secular mission of liberty. Clinton was wise to see this as needing a Knight Templar Christian imprimatur to work and fashioned fraternalism as the chivalric envelope within which to disseminate the amalgam, albeit preserving intact the Royal Arch iconology of both rites as they developed within American Masonry. The curiosity of Jefferson's idea of his country being Virginia, like *Mary*land (named after Roman Catholic Queen of England Henrietta Marie (1609-1669), wife of Charles I who signed the Charter of Maryland making it a colony), easily construed to aver Mariology, adoration of the goddess, concealed a comprehensive attachment of the heart to his own state (commonwealth) which elevated the Declaration of Independence sacerdotalism in the name of liberty to an echelon very near indeed to Jesuit missiology as it was intermingled with the ideology of tolerant secular republicanism. This concept can be seen in concrete form on the Seal of Virginia.

Top: The observe Seal of Virginia features the goddess Virtus symbolizing peace and virtue standing victorious over Tyranny. Bottom: The reverse Seal features the goddesses (left to right) Ceres from the Eleusinian Mysteries, Libertas or Liberty, and Aeternitas, the divine personification of eternity. The Virginia Seal is another source of the goddess as an emblem of sublime perfection, emerging within the Jeffersonian-Clintionian circle.

It was this devotion to eradicating heretics as those who opposed liberty associated with papal monarchy itself enveloped within global kingly vision epitomized through Egyptian ideas applied to Counter-Reformation principles.

The political culture of the nation in 1797 tends to support this concept, as Alexander Hamilton and other Federalists succeeded in their support for the Jay Treaty with Great Britain which moved France as the most favored ally out of first place in favor of renewed and fresh linkages with

England. Suspicions of French Revolutionary ideas divided the nation from 1796 through 1799, providing Federalists ample reason to exploit nascent anti-Masonry through the mediation of James Robison's exposés of Freemasonry, *Proofs of a Conspiracy* (1798), in support of an indigenous Columbian Illuminati in league with John James Beckley, the founder of Phi Beta Kappa, George Clinton, DeWitt's uncle, the Vice President ofthe United States under Jefferson, and DeWitt himself. As a result Democratic Republicanism became a safe haven for Masonic elitism even though the principles of Jeffersonianism were thought to be egalitarian and agrarian. This combination of elitism and egalitarianism generated political aspects of Vitruvianism as the material culture which sustained the concepts of both, seemingly opposite icons, producing an architectural surrogation for the constitution in the form of a public material cultural medium which might reconcile aristocracy akin to the Ramsay ideology with populism through the collegiality implied and celebrated within Royal Arch polity through the use of secular mythology as de facto speculative Craft Lodge Masonry. As such, Logos theology applied to politics became the means to identify the Royal Arch Word and the knowledge of how to transmit it as the common means, as Salem Town elucidates,

> "....That a knowledge of a divine LOGOS or WORD, should have been the object of so much religious research from time immemorial, adds not a little to the honor of Speculative Freemasonry. The same WORD which breathed the spirit of life into Adam, *which translated Enoch to heaven* (cf. George Washington depicted in the Barralet engraving as Enoch), which moved Noah to prepare the ark, which called Abram (cf. patriarchal thread in Odd Fellow ritual circa 1797), and separated him from his kindred and his father's house, which was manifested to Jacob, which appeared to Moses in the burning bush, which went before, and led the Israelites from Egyptian bondage, which filled the tabernacle with the glory of his presence, which overshadowed the mercy-seat in the temple of Solomon, and which appeared in the flesh for the salvation of man, has been peculiar to the Masonic Institution, since its organization by Solomon, and probably to the patrons of Masonic principles since the days of Enoch."[307]

307 Town, Salem *A System of Speculative Freemasonry*, page 151.

The result, in America, that the Vitruvian architectural idiom associated with Jeffersonian culture, i.e. of an empire in republican (*qua imperium romanum*) apparel, as emerged during the 1803-1804 Louisiana Purchase and through the Meriwether Lewis and William Clark explorations (1804 -1806), both Freemasons, which carried Royal Arch leaders such as Ephraim Kirby and Edward Livingston into its proconsular operations. The western frontier was also explored by masons Christopher "Kit" Carson (1809-1868), John C. Fremont (1813-1890) and Zebulon Montgomery Pike[308] (1779-1813) the latter being a relative of Albert Pike. In addition, the Louisiana Purchase would have been an active element in this increment as Jefferson's own policy led to a seemingly contradictory event to his principle of simplicity of governance adding in effect a Catholic empire named after St. Louis of France to the nation, an acquisition which was symbolized within a painting inserted by the restored Bourbon King Louis XVIII within Latrobe's Roman Catholic Basilica in Baltimore, Maryland; a building that incorporates his second Apollonian dome.

In the run-up to and the context of the Jay Treaty, Jefferson was careful to distance the mission of his followers in ways consistent with the Clinton-Webb-Town vista of national Masonic order. This was to persuade George Washington himself that Jeffersonian Demoractic-Republicans were not radical Jacobins, but devoted constitutionalists seeking simply to establish a morally warranted republican monarchy apart from Great Britain within the United States, establishing an autonomous aseity apart from the moral ontogeny of the British monarchy. Jefferson, in other words, was convinced that both Adams and Hamilton were attracted to the aesthetic and spiritual allure of the legitimacy of British kingship and were determined to set the nation on a course which would lead inevitably to recolonization. The Jay Treaty further augmented the sovereign standing of American commerce as an extension if its technical liberties secured from George III in addition to treating particular grievances. As an aspiring state within a state early post-Revolutionary Freemasonry contained within it through various concordats securing American grand lodge autonomy through eventual

308 Initiated in the mysteries of Freemasonry in Lodge #3 in Philadelphia while some sources question whether he was a Freemason.

De facto recognition from England a precedent for this impulse, which notably, by comparison, the American Episcopal Church was unable to achieve in the recognition of the validity of Episcopal consecration of United State elected by the diocese. Samuel Seabury (1729-1796), the first so elected bishop, and a Tory Freemason during the Revolution, was only able to secure legitimacy through consecration by Scottish Bishops.

* * * * *

In this context, the importance of John James Beckley (1757-1807), becomes significant both to the history of Freemasonry in America and to the broader implications of its interior symbolism following the death of George Washington in December, 1799. Beckley was both Clerk to the House of Representatives and Librarian of Congress, when the two posts were managed by one person. He was par excellence an Enochic figure both as a disseminator of thought and as a recapitulator of the relationship, mystically and pragmatically conceived, as the person most responsible for disseminating information required for informed and effective legislation. In brief, he was singularly responsible for developing the Clintonian premise that ritual and public policy intertwined both in method, public initiation, as well as content, a disseminator of political wisdom.

A staunch partisan of Thomas Jefferson (1743-1826) and therefore of DeWitt Clinton, Beckley's appointment January 29, 1802 as the first Librarian of Congress coincided with the publication year of Thomas Smith Webb's revised and expanded 1797 *Monitor* or *Illustrations*. This quasi-esoteric textbook both reorganized the system of Lodge initiation to pivot upon the objective of Royal Arch exaltation (initiation) and modified and solidified the General Grand Chapter as the first effective interstate Masonic network. Beckley presided over the creation of the linkage between a unique American style of initiation as an equivalency with paragon citizenship. His rhetorical and administrative skill enabled him to position the Royal Arch culture as a mystically-nuanced icon. This took place as George Washington, the de facto head of the Masonic Fraternity whilst President, gave way to the creation of the Jeffersonian Republican (Democratic) Party, he deployed the concept, extracted from the Royal Arch of Enoch ethos, that knowledge was of great usefulness in the creation of a public policy rhetoric and its operation. The transmission of this iconology into the foundational premises of American Freemasonry is important to consider. In other words, the mythological rendering of Masonic liturgies and ritual not only survived within the Clinton and Webb system, but the ideal of an Unknown Superior (cf. Rite of Strict Observance) did as well. This was not a literal survivorship. Rather it developed within the cultural infrastructure of the whole of the York or American Rite which defined parallels between Royal Arch rooted theories of initiation, political policy formulation, and the principle of citizenship as the Clintonians applied it to the workings of the rite and its related philosophy.

The effect of this esoteric thread made public and forensically can be traced to controversies identifying the Jay Treaty with clandestine diplomatic negotiations. Enochic imagery appealed directly to the imagination and sensibilities of Jeffersonian Republicans, the core of the future Democratic Party, the members of whom were cordial toward deism, classical architecture (cf. Palladian-Vitruvian ideology) with which Jefferson was associated (i.e. domed Monticello, domed University of Virginia Library), and suspicious of latent Puritan affinities with Federalism rooted in nascent anti-Masonry notably in public fears of conspiracy within the Francophilic culture surrounding the third presidency. The Enochic idiom made it possible, in other words, to associate the restoration of secret wisdom with divine virtue as public policy for political mission. Elements of Enochic imagery appeared in summary form in Thomas Smith Webb's 1797 (revised 1802) *Illustrations of Masonry*. This parallels the Christian resurrection inserted as an apologetical device within the Clinton-Webb system (Knight Templar membership is open only to Christian Master Masons) which conflated with Beckley's cultural context. As such, there was continuity between Jefferson's own religion of deism through a direct implication that the virtue of the initiate, rather than supernatural power of Christ, led to such a translation. A result was to insert, further, religiously nuanced secular, noetic[309] ideas and concepts of virtuous citizenship into

309 Noetic theory is an alternative metaphysical philosophy concerned with the study of mind and intuition, and its relationship with a proposed divine intellect.

the process of nation building, merging the Clintonian-Webb rituality with Jeffersonian culture. The same idiom through which the emblem of the Pythagoreans theorem became the badge of the Worshipful Master point to Beckley's determination to construct a clear leaderly path for his hero and de facto employer Jefferson and his clients to identify themselves symbolically with an *heliocentric imperium*. This is a useful analogy because Pythagoreanism was deemed a middle way between a philosophical school, which would have had Jeffersonian allusions and secular affinities, with a religion, which appealed to DeWitt Clinton's Knight Templar Christian symbolism, through an Enochian-solar template: J. J. Ramée's core contribution to the entire concept via his template of Union College.

As Jefferson's close colleague and a correspondent with Ephraim Kirby, DeWitt Clinton predecessor as the First General Grand High Priest, Beckley was a central conduit between the third President of the United States and Freemasonry. This placed him squarely between the main currents of Jeffersonian patronage of European values, notably from France, as well as the expansion of the Clintonian political order to the West relative to the populism of Andrew Jackson (1767-1845) and his effective symbolism as an image of frontier-rooted leadership in continued opposition to British interests and his loyalty to the principles of the Union. Architecturally, Jefferson was also positioned to manage the unique values associated with the Palladian style of material culture, and to integrate this Masonically resonant of cultural form in Jackson's Masonic network. Jackson served as Deputy Grand High Priest of the Royal Arch Grand Chapter of Tennessee (1826), which was an integral constituent of the General Grand Chapter and thus subordinate to the Clinton Masonic regime.

Beckley was also an initiate of Phi Beta Kappa (its name means "Philosophy, the Guide of Life"), the first college fraternity-Greek letter society founded on 5 December 1776 and was a link between William and Mary College, Williamsburg, Virginia and Union College, Schenectady, New York. The Union College chapter of Phi Beta Kappa, called "Alpha," of which DeWitt Clinton was an active, speech giving member. This tie, together with his Librarianship of Congress, positioned him as an inheritor of the Royal Arch ideal of creating a national repository of recapitulated wisdom as a mission objective if Freemasonry's general mission to celebrate ritual intellect within society. This broad program took form as a teaching device within craft ritual in the Fellowcraft degree and as the aforesaid object of rediscovery and recapitulation in the Royal Arch of Enoch degree in the Rite of Perfection, now the Ancient and Accepted Scottish Rite. Phi Beta Kappa in turn incorporated many Masonic elements including secret mottos, rituals and initiations, pledges of loyalty and secrecy, secret handshakes, signs, symbols, and jewelry in the form of badges, pins, and rings.[310] The formation of Phi Beta Kappa in Williamsburg was not without solar symbolism: the society met weekly in Raleigh Tavern's Apollo Room.[311]

Beckley underscored this linkage by choosing words in his rhetoric which anticipated the availability of translations of the Ethiopic *Book of Enoch*. This was first published in 1821 in English, with notable reference to the sun as a source of mystical inspiration. It also referred to laws of celestial physics applied to what might be termed architecture and engineering problems through imaginative vision. The first symbol became a metaphor for liberty. The second became a premise that the destiny of America lay with the unfolding of an order of geometrically-nuanced design derived from God. This was an optimistic, politically significant vision which counter-pointed elements of Christian belief in original sin –notably Calvinism–with a new vista of national progress. At its core was the presupposition that the nation, like Enoch, need not fear mortality; that wisdom for governance would be provided to the national leadership with a style of civic immortality as conferred upon George Washington as the immortal Enochian founder of the United States. David Brearley, the author of the Constitution and Canons of the American Episcopal Church, and a signer of the United States Constitution was an important subscriber to this vista, as were irenic Roman Catholics, the Carrolls, whose lands were taken up and developed by Pierre Charles L'Enfant for the District of Columbia. The result was a millennial resonance linking Anglican and Catholic liturgy to Freemasonry's medium as the Enoch-icon took on strong

310 Jeffers, H. Paul, *The Freemasons in America*, page 152.
311 Ibid.

symbolism of dynamic political order as a form of imperial monarchy within the envelope of a republic through visual, architectonic hierarchical order in the image of egalitarianism and brotherhood.

Thomas Jefferson's accession to the Presidency of the American Philosophical Society in 1797, underscored his public image as a ruler invested with ancient wisdom. The event invited comparison with Benjamin Franklin, as a jointly construed scientist and statesman, an accolade DeWitt Clinton actively cultivated. The identification of experimental science with restoration was critical, further, to Jefferson's persona and the profile of wisdom as an integration of Biblical and classical learning intermingled with Newtonian providentialism and experimentation. Franklin was depicted as a mage, with affinities with sorcery, who might draw down the magic of electricity from the heavens for human use, a parody of the role of the *prisci theological.* The usefulness of this idiom was invaluable during the aftermath of the Reign of Terror (1793-1794), given Jefferson's affinities with France, to counter epithets that Jeffersonians were de facto Jacobins. It enabled an identifer for Beckley's propaganda mission, for such was his overall brief, because it enabled him to cast progress as an essentially conservative cultural process associated, not with political radicality, but learned quasi-mystical Pythagorean intellect. This meant that both Franklin and Jefferson might assume the mantles of sages, like Enoch role as a mystagogue, in the service the creation of a national library, which was constituted largely from Jefferson's own collection of books. The effect was to merge Beckley's partisan role as clerk to the House of Representatives with his role of the keeper of the national literary and intellectual fund of wisdom.

Beckley's activities while calculated to undermine Anglo-American diplomatic ties, through its alliance with Clintonian Freemasonry actually resulted in the strengthening of the cords of alliance through a common ritual idiom with the Antient Grand Lodge of England. The Jeffersonians attempted to effect the same alliance with France through the efforts of Edward Livingston, General Grand High Priest, Minister to France, and consummate legal scholar, whose home base was New York City, of which he was Mayor, and subsequently New Orleans, but this endeavor ended only with the cementing further the core American and British resolve throughout the 19th century to cast first Spain, and then France under Louis XVIII and Charles X, as nefarious outsiders determined to wreck individualistic and capitalistic devotion to liberty and freedom. This was alloyed into a de facto henotheism in which Antient Masonic symbolism defined two national, cooperative religiosities within which the Enochian template defined both the dynamic of old world subjecthood and new world citizenship as its content. Thus, Beckley's efforts to define citizenship apart from British subjecthood ended up producing a further reconciliation of hierarchy with equality parallel to the definitions of the English Constitution but in reverse order, inserting a monarchy in the folds of a republic. This arrangement was still further cemented by Webb's reuse of William Preston's model and method of the *Illustrations of Masonry*, the core template for Webb's own text, which by 1802 Webb redefined kingship as civic priesthood with the difference that American Masonic mystical, Pythagorean initiation took the place of Anglican sacral coronation (i.e. most loyal to the monarch), the Clinton-Webb synthesis provided a numinous center for the devolution of deeper meaning into civic life. There was semiotic element to this maneuver such that the Clinton-Webb synthesis looked value free and normative whilst it pressed cabalistic-hermetical Joachimite eschatology through toward a pervasive and cooperative ethic. To Beckley, the author of the first campaign biography of Thomas Jefferson called, *Address to the People of the United States*, the President epitomized this ideal: the character of Jefferson matched private virtue with eminent public deeds. Beckley describes Jefferson as,

> "….a man of pure, ardent, and unaffected piety; of sincere and genuine virtue; of an enlightened mind and superior wisdom; the adorer of our God, the patriot of his country; and the friend and benefactor of the whole human race."[312]

The result was to lift up Jefferson as a paragon Masonic initiate whether he be Freemason in actuality or not through key concepts of piety, virtue, learning and wisdom framed with adoration of deity and philanthropy;

312 Quoted in *The Revolution of 1800: Democracy, Race, and the New Republic*, page 186.

the latter the future 19th century apologetical mission of institutional Freemasonry. This balanced, within Jefferson's person, moral aristocracy and democracy, blending into one figure the desired constitutional qualities of the Presidency, as it emerged following, yet distinct from the British crown, with the Pythagorean and Apollonian signature of Enochic millennialism.

The difference between Beckley's consummate characterization of Jefferson and the paragon image of George Washington was distinct, but perceptible. Washington was celebrated as a *Cincinnatus*, patriot citizen-soldier with a public disdain for aristocracy, although a consummate aristocrat himself. Beckley deemed Jefferson to be a more permanent and practical model for the Presidency, perhaps realizing that the founding of the nation would make of its founder an icon which did and could not invite emulation. The rhetoric of intellectual enlightenment with mystical Enochic virtue provided Beckley with the tools to drive a wedge between the inherent aristocracy advocated by Alexander Hamilton, for one instance, and thoughtful Christian evangelicals who were alarmed at Jefferson's alleged radicality and his rumored disbelief in divine revelation. The Biblical piety associated with Royal Arch symbolism would disarm religious criticism of his hero, and in effect lay the groundwork within Virginia Freemasonry through Beckley's leadership of Williamsburg Lodge No. 6 near William and Mary College for a *modus vivendi* between grass roots religious populism and revivalism and Freemasonry which has remained unraveled as Baptist Church membership overtook sedate Anglicanism in the tidewater, again thanks to the Clinton-Webb ritual synthesis.

Beckley's ties with lawyer-jurist Ephraim Kirby, General Grand High Priest from Connecticut, a Jeffersonian magistrate in the south, and an originator of case law publications, whom Beckley referenced as a correspondent, parallel usefully the fact that George Washington was initiated in Fredericksburg, Virginia lodge the first known site for the conferral of the Royal Arch ceremony of exaltation. This placed Beckley at the core conduit for the definition of capitular Masonic ceremonial, as Royal Arch ritual came to be termed, at precisely the point the Clinton-Webb synthesis developed as a national model for the York or American

Rite, as depicted in the St. Andrew's Hurd Plate. Benjamin Hurd was himself a predecessor both to Kirby and to Clinton as executive of the Royal Arch interstate network, and thus documented *in situ* a leading figure who defined the infrastructure of the 1797 Monitor as an extension of his engraving, linked ultimately to Webb's own exaltation in Philadelphia and to the Clintonian Masonic regime.

The prefiguring of Christian revelation within the Royal Arch thrust within Webb's and Hurd's concept lifted up, again, the Pythagorean ideal within Jefferson's public persona at the pinpoint when John Adams, wittingly or otherwise, made common cause with Jedidiah Morse, father of Samuel F. B. Morse (of Morse Code fame), the first clear prestigious clergyman to take up anti-Masonry. This thread, developed into a steady flood of apologetics defending Jefferson from Federalist slander was uniquely calculated to underscore private virtue over conformity to conventional orthodoxy. There were firm hints that the United States, as an inheritor of such ancient morality was in effect exempt from the Calvinist view of original sin, which was restricted, only, to the old world and not relevant to the wondrous reality of the unlimited, it seemed, realities of the American frontier. Theologically, Beckley worked this adroit argument with a parallelism to the Royal Arch of Enoch, which was itself designed to preserve ancient wisdom from Noah's flood. Beckley's view of religion might be usefully compared with that of the classical period in Greece and with the early Renaissance, as in both instances larger city states moved slowly but surely to overcome their smaller rivals. These periods called for a religiosity of confidence rather than abasement. As such it is interesting to note that Calvinism, with its call for the abasement of the individual soul because of original sin should give way to a fresh spirituality within which intellect and revelation should be reintegrated to accommodate new principle of citizenship and policy. As such he turned rhetorical guns upon Jesuits and others who sought in the old world to suppress the progress of scientific inquiry and advancement as part of this new spirituality. He fell upon the role of optimistic visionaries as a type of clerisy even secular priesthood rejecting clerical castes and inherited authority. This was in essence the Royal Arch ideology: transformation of the citizen *qua* initiate in his pursuit of mystical inspiration to carry the nation into a new era and new frontier. This ideological line of reasoning positioned an alternative to kingship as an extension of secular, civic priesthood. Mystic knowledge took the place of constitutional sacral coronation.

The Beckley embroidery of Jefferson's person was inserted within the Clinton-Webb synthesis in accord with Salem Town's vista of an unfolding Logos as the core of material culture, moving westward. This was a critical element of Jefferson's legacy, in part, to make up for this lost cause, the extension of slaveholding into the Louisiana Purchase in lieu of his own vision of an Arcadian nation of small yeoman farmers. Freemasonry forged a millennial ethic integrating monarchical values, which can be traced to the Ramsay ideology of higher degrees as an amelioration of egalitarian ideas reconciled with failed Jeffersonian vision. This reality became clear enough to its senior membership as the Mother Jurisdiction of the Scottish Rite extended its reach into the states created from the Louisiana Purchase after the Civil War and in such a way that Ramsay's esotericism saturated the Anglo-Irish Newtonian Grand Lodges with a culture of graded initiatic advancement linked with dynamic principles of citizenship. At deeper levels, the Masonry developed by the Governor of East Florida, James Grant can be seen at the core foundation of this achievement as a Lodge was erected at Pensacola in East Florida, with links to Charleston wherein the Supreme Council was founded, at almost the precise moment the Louisiana Purchase was made. The strategic placement of the city in Anglican ecclesiastical context, mediated by Frederic Dalcho and Joel Poinsett, set the tone for the eventual deconstruction of the General Grand Chapter as a sovereign entity by Charles Gilman and Albert Pike in 1859. This maneuver insured that there would be no competition for sovereignty in the purchase, and within states westward at a policy level.

Freemasonry reflects within it institutions the same, or similar principles reflective of the division of common law (case made law, judicial rulings and decisions) from civil law (codified state law). Cogently stated, the Grand Lodges derived from British roots incorporated the principles articulated by Sir John Fortescue and Richard Hooker. The Supreme Councils for the higher degrees and their craft equivalents, the Grand Orients, followed civil statutory law and Roman legal principles. In the first instance, there is in particular a striking parallel between the former and the latter with regard to English limited monarchy, wherein the people are co-determinants with the sovereign of legal order and the latter where absolutism characterizes the order in the nations where personal authority and its application dominate procedures. In the United States, Grand Lodges came early to dominate the craft degrees, and absolutism of the higher degrees. Some Grand Lodges contained elements of both ingredients, either in theory or in practice, such as Louisiana where Masonic writers on law, such as Edward Livingston, were adept at managing both institutions. The Pythagorean magus ritual element within Masonic entities tended to reinforce the latter, high degree system.

CHAPTER XI

SEALS, MOTTOS, COLLEGES AND UNIVERSITIES, THE MASONIC APRON, AND THREE OF THE SEVEN WONDERS OF THE ANCIENT WORLD

Masonic Symbolism takes Concrete Form in the United States

"But, lest these secret processes fall into
uncultured hands and be perverted, the
Great Arcanum was always concealed in symbol
or allegory; and those who can today discover its
lost keys may open with them a treasure
house of philosophic, scientific, and religious truths."
- Manly Palmer Hall, *The Secret Teachings of All Ages*, 1928.

"Then I saw in my dreams that the shining men bid them
call at the gate, the which when they did. Some from above
looked over the gate, to wit, Enoch, Moses, and Elijah, &c.
to whom it was said, "These pilgrims are come from the City
of Destruction, for the love that they bear to the King of
this place." And then the pilgrims gave in unto them each
man his certificate, which they had received in the beginning;
those therefore were carried into the King, who when he had
read them, said, "Where are the men?" To whom it was answered,
"They are standing without the gate." The King then commanded
to open the gate. "That the righteous nation," said he, "that keepeth
truth may enter in." [Isaiah 26:2]
- John Bunyan, *The Pilgrim's Progress*, 1678.

There are many concealed mysteries in the United States that need explaining. When one understands, as we have seen, that the United States of America was founded upon Renaissance and Enlightenment values that permeated Freemasonry; is it no wonder that Masonic symbolism, especially that associated with the high degrees, has embedded itself in the United States via its state seals, mottos, landmarks, and emblems? Be it a college or university seal, a state motto or logo, or an architectural design, there is, but not always, a Masonic intelligence behind it. Naturally, it should not be alarming that the Nation's Capital, the District of Columbia, has a Masonic template and its monuments, federal buildings, and its overall design contains Masonic symbolism. Although this is the specifically the subject matter of Chapter XIV, Masonic symbolism in the United States in general, for one reason or another, is neither seen and only seldom spoken of. When Masonic symbolism is seen, even by those initiated into Masonry, its true esoteric meaning appears to be lost. The observer is left with nothing or even worse: a default-profane explanation that does not satisfy, and raises more questions than it answers.

With this in mind it is this author's intent to remedy this condition. Most people in the United States, both mason and non-Mason, are not familiar or well versed in the area of esoteric Masonic symbolism. Brother George H. Steinmetz immediately addressed the issue of the mason's non-familiarity with the symbolisms of his own fraternity in the introduction to his book *The Royal Arch: Its Hidden Meaning*. Steinmetz philosophizes,

> "The modern Masonic Lodge, insofar as the secret doctrine of Freemasonry is concerned, is as a child playing "soldier" with a set of chessmen. The child senses a difference in the value of the pieces because of the variation in form and size. Perhaps the horses' head of the knights suggest cavalry, the larger, more ornate pieces, officers, and the pawns, foot-soldiers. The child, however, does not play the game of chess or which these symbols of a bygone day are intended. He is blissfully ignorant of the proper moves, or the meaning of the symbology of the various pieces."[313]

313 Steinmetz, George, *The Royal Arch: Its Hidden Meaning*, page 1.

To put it plainly, one may know that the Statue of Liberty was a gift from French masons to American masons, or that the Washington Monument is an Egyptian obelisk. This pseudo-elucidation is not good enough any longer; it simply does not provide a satisfactory answer to the mysteries from whence this symbolism comes from. It is the purpose of this chapter to unravel some of these modern Masonic mysteries in depth; to finally provide the proper symbolic explanation of some of these various pieces, which seems up until now to have been lost.

The Great Seal of the United States of America

Esoteric and Masonic philosopher, Manley Palmer Hall, states,

> "Not only were many of the founders of the United States Government Masons, but they received aid from a secret and august body existing in Europe, which helped them establish this country for a peculiar and particular purpose known only to the initiated few. The Great Seal is the signature of this exalted body - unseen and for the most part unknown - and the unfinished pyramid upon the reverse side is a trestleboard setting forth symbolically the task to the accomplishment of which the United States Government was dedicated from the day of its inception."[314]

This quote is often interpreted by conspiracy theorists that the some secret cabal, usually the Bavarian Illuminati, somehow secretly controls and manipulates the United States. Although the Great Seal of the United States contains both exoteric and esoteric symbols, any "aid" that assisted our founding fathers was guided upon Enlightenment and Renaissance ideals that can found in the doctrines and tenets of Blue Lodge Freemasonry and skirts the *haute* degrees. The Great Seal is a source of controversy; some extreme conspiracists claim that obverse and reverse seals of the United States are Satanic (a notion this author finds ridiculous), while other

314 Hall, Manly P, *The Secret Teachings of All Ages*, page 283.

apologists merely claim that the Great Seal has no symbolism, Masonic or otherwise, and as such no real meaning, hidden or obvious. The obverse is recognizable to all: it features and American bald eagle, it is the reverse seal that is the source of controversy: it is an unfinished pyramid with an all-seeing triangulated eye overhead. With regard to obverse seal, "The Eagle was the living Symbol of the Egyptian God *Mendes* or *Mentra*, whom *Sesostris-Ramses* made one with *Amun-Re*, the God of Thebes and Upper Egypt, and the representative of the Sun, the word *Re* meaning *Sun* or *King*."[315] Regarding the reverse seal, an unfinished Egyptian pyramid crowned by an all-seeing eye, the truth is found where it always is: somewhere in the middle. To begin to understand the symbolism of the Great Seal, a brief history of it is in order.

The Continental Congress created the first committee to design the Great Seal of the new nation on July 4th, 1776. It was compromised of Benjamin Franklin (a mason), John Adams, and Thomas Jefferson. Franklin's seal featured Moses parting the Red Sea thus defeating Pharaoh and his hosts. Adams' design featured Hercules, while Jefferson, who suggested a two-sided seal, obverse featured the Children of Israel in the wilderness while the reverse displayed Hengist and Horsa, two Germanic brothers who led the Anglo-Saxon and Jutish armies that conquered the first territories of Great Britain in the 5th century CE. Interestingly, Dr. Franklin's design for the seal, Moses, reflects his secret codename within British Intelligence (either as an agent or double agent) via his contact with the Hellfire Club; he was also known within the British Intelligence community as "Number 72," a reference to the Hebrew Kabbalistic Tetractys and *Shem ha-Mephorash*. *Shem ha-Mephorash* was the word that Moses used to part the Red Sea at Exodus 14:19-21. Also assigned to this first committee was portrait painter familiar with heraldry named Pierre Eugene Du Simitière's (1736? -1784). His seal featured a shield, divided into six parts representing Holland, France, Germany, England, Scotland, and Ireland; with a rustic American soldier on the right side and the goddess Libertas on the left side; Libertas' left hand rested on an anchor signifying hope. Above the shield was a deistic all-seeing eye within a triangle radiating solar light,

315 Pike, Albert, *Morals and Dogma of the Ancient and Accepted Scottish Rite*, page291.

beneath the shield was the motto, *E pluribus Unum*, or *out of many, one*. On August 20, 1776, the committee presented their report to Congress. The committee members chose Du Simitière's design, though it was changed to remove the anchor of hope and replaced the rustic soldier with the Roman goddess Justitia holding a sword and balanced scales. Surrounding the main elements was the inscription "Seal of the United States of America MDCCLXXVI." Four components from this committee, shield, all-seeing eye, Roman numerical date (1776), and motto, would be incorporated into the final design of the Great Seal; the Adams, Jefferson, and Franklin ideas for the seal were rejected outright. The all-seeing eye is a Masonic symbol representing a deistic divinity: it appears on numerous Masonic documents, degree certificates, furniture, and other regalia since Masonry's official inception in 1717. It is sometimes called the "Eye of Providence" or the "Eye of Horus," the latter referring to the benevolent, triumphal Egyptian sun god who reincarnated in the Pharaoh.

The second committee was formed in January 1777. It was chaired by John Morin Scott (1730-1784); its other members were lawyer William Churchill Houston (1746-1788), politician and teacher James Lovell (1737 -1814) who were all members of the Continental Congress. Assisting them was Francis Hopkinson (1737-1791), a signer of the Declaration of Independence and reported designer of the United States flag. Some sources claim Hopkinson was a Freemason, others reject this notion; to this author's knowledge there is no documentable evidence to suggest Hopkinson was initiated into the mysteries of Freemasonry. Hopkinson contributed to the design of the Great Seal of New Jersey; in turn he used the image of a truncated pyramid on a 1778 fifty dollar colonial note. Hopkinson's suggestions to the second committee for the Great Seal of the United States would ultimately come to fruition; his ideas included red and white stripes totaling thirteen upon a blue background for the shield, a constellation of thirteen stars, and an olive branch. The third and final committee was formed on May 4, 1782 by the Secretary of Congress Charles Thomson (1729-1824) to finalize the Great Seal of the United States. On the committee of three were Chairman Arthur Middleton, John Rutledge, and Elias Boudinot. Rutledge took no part in the committee and

The truncated or unfinished pyramid on Hopkinson's 1778 fifty dollar colonial note.

was replaced by Arthur Lee of Virginia; while Boudinot, who was familiar with coats of arms and heraldry, gave the committee his utmost attention. It was Thomson, Lee, and Boudinot enlisted artist, lawyer, and scholar William Barton (1754-1817), a member (1787) and counselor (1790-1793) of the American Philosophical Society. Barton's uncle was famed mathematician, surveyor, and astronomer David Rittenhouse who like his nephew was a member of the American Philosophical Society. Barton's contributions to the final design of the Great Seal were profound: he suggested the eagle of the American bald species for the obverse as well as the unfinished pyramid –taken likely from Hopkinson's fifty dollar note–for the reverse. Barton also contributed the Latin phrases *Annuit Coeptis* and *Novus Ordo Seclorum* –taken together "*Approving Commencement of the New Order of the Ages*." The phrase, *Novus Ordo Seclorum*, is lifted from the fourth Eclogue of Virgil (70 BCE-19 BCE). By June 1782, Thomson had gathered all the material and recommendations from all three committees and, with the help of Barton, the Great Seal of the United States was approved.

The Great Seal of the United States was cast in 1825, 1841, 1885, and 1904. It was from these casts, namely the one of 1885, that the number thirteen was incorporated into the Great Seal (see Plate XVIII). Thirteen is everywhere:

- 13 stone levels in the pyramid.
- 13 stars in the hexagram constellation over the eagle.
- 13 vertical stripes in the shield.
- 13 olive berries on the branch clutched by the eagle.
- 13 olive leaves on the branch clutched by the eagle.
- 13 arrows clutched by the eagle.
- 13 letters in *Annuit Coeptis*.
- 13 letters in *E Pluribus Unum*.
- The Roman numeral date MDCCLXXVI or 1776 refers to the country's origins of July the fourth, '76. Add the last two digits of the date 1776, 7 + 6 to get 13. The phrase, "July the Fourth," contains 13 letters; the term, *Novus Ordo Seclorum*, contains 17 letters, while the date "MDCCLXXVI" contains 9 letters; add 17 + 9 to get 26, or 13 twice.

The use of the number thirteen exoterically reflects the original thirteen colonies, of this there is no doubt. Exoterically the number thirteen seems to also refer to the original thirteenth degree in the Rite of Perfection which became the thirteenth degree, the Royal Arch of Enoch, in the Scottish Rite, Southern Jurisdiction. The recovery of the Tetragrammaton within this thirteenth degree, discussed throughout this book, and the repetition of the number 13 suggest that the seal is an emblem of high degree Masonic Logos of the Fourth Gnostic-Docetic Gospel of St. John. The concept of the "Royal Arch Word," as expanding Logos applied to the new nation of the United States was detailed in the treatise of Masonic theorist Salem Town and turned into material culture by DeWitt Clinton and his Royal Arch Grand Chapters and Christian Knight Templar Commandaries. The number thirteen symbolizing this thirteenth degree is apparently confirmed by the number of feather in the eagle's wings which highly suggest the influence of the Scottish Rite: the dexter (right) wing contains 32 feathers, the sinister (left) wing has 33 feathers which symbolizes the two highest degrees of the Ancient and Accepted Scottish Rite: the 32nd degree known as the Master (or Sublime Prince) of the Royal Secret, and honorary 33rd degree of Inspector General.

The Great Seal of the United States can be easily located: it is on the back on the one dollar bill. It was placed there with the approval of President and Freemason Franklin D. Roosevelt in 1935. Roosevelt was influenced and impressed by Freemason Henry A. Wallace (1888-1965), Secretary of Agriculture and former Vice President who saw the seal and interpreted the phrase *Novus Ordo Seclorum*, New Order of the Ages, meaning *New Deal of the Ages* symbolizing the New Deal of the Roosevelt Administration. Wallace wanted the seal, both obverse and reverse, placed on a coin, but instead Roosevelt placed it on the back of the one dollar bill. It has been suggested that Wallace was motivated by Russian artist, philosopher, theosophist, mystic, and esoteric Nicolas Roerich (1874-1947), who Wallace referred to in numerous correspondences as his "Guru." It has been argued and suggested that Roerich understood the Great Seal as an emblem of new world Masonic solar enlightenment that heralded a New Order of the Ages of which Wallace, and allegedly Roosevelt, subscribed. As such the placement of the Great Seal on the back of the one dollar bill further advanced a new Masonic order *of the ages*. Although this was denied by Wallace's daughter Leslie Douglas[316], some interesting coincidences remain that seem to confirm a higher Kabbalistic hand was at work. The seal was publicly placed on the back of the dollar in 1935, roughly 72 years prior to 2012, minus four years. It takes the sun approximately 72 years to move one degree backwards through each house of the Zodiac congruently with the Precession of the Equinoxes and the Great Platonic Year (see Chapter III). Thus the public placement of the seal in 1935, symbolically and esoterically, heralds a New Order of the Ages a *Novus Ordo Seclorum* reflective of the new solar Age of Aquarius syncretic with the Third Age of the Holy Spirit in Joachim von Fiore's lexicon which astronomically begins circa 2012. Coinciding with the public placement of the Great Seal on the United States upon the reverse of the dollar bill,[317] was the movement of the Presidential Inauguration ceremony from

316 Hieronimus, Robert, *Founding Father, Secret Societies*, page 103.

317 The obverse of the dollar bill features Freemason and first President George Washington.

March 4th to January 20th with the adoption of the 20th Amendment in 1933. Since 1793 United States Presidents were sworn in on March 4th under the sign of Pisces. The inauguration ceremony was moved in 1933, again approximately 72 years before 2012, to the cusp of Aquarius-January 20th symbolically proclaiming the new and forthcoming "Masonic" Aquarian Age and the United States Presidential Masonic leadership that presides over it. The movement of the inauguration date from the March 4th to January 20th naturally abandons the waning old age of Pisces and welcomes the new waxing Age of Aquarius. Presidents are sworn-in under the sign of Aquarius since 1933; however they are elected months earlier under the house of Scorpio, occurring on the Tuesday following the first Monday in November, because Scorpio rules power, fortune, andthe wealthy.

The Great Seal of the United States' reverse embodies components of Masonic solar sovereignty: it is essentially a Masonic sundial. The seal's reverse features a truncated Egyptian pyramid and suggest Masonry's Egyptian origins as geometry was "improved" with the Nile's flooding, as suggested by Dr. Anderson's *Constitutions* of 1723, 1738. Masonry, following the Renaissance-hermetical tradition, identified Egypt and its sacred mysteries as the source of all wisdom reaffirmed by Masonic author Martin Clare in his treatise. The Masonic triangulated solar all-seeing eye of Horus (or Providence) radiating *light* suggests Masonic foundation, protection, and oversight of the United States as it watches over; it never sleeps. The all-seeing eye symbolically declares the United States as the beacon of new world Masonic "Craft Lodge Newtonian solar enlightenment yet forever twined with concepts of monarchy and spiritual dictatorship exalted in the kabbalistic *haute* Masonic degrees reflecting astrological, hermetic order. In sum, the solar all-seeing eye emulates the idiom that the sun was raising over a new enlightened era, a theme picked up and ran with by the French Revolutionaries of 1789. As Dr. James Billington states, "....The ideal was not the balanced complexity of the new American federation, but the occult simplicity of its great seal: an all-seeing eye atop a pyramid over the words, *Novus Ordo Seclorum.*"[318]

318 Billington, James, *Fire in the Minds of Men*, page 6.

PENNSYLVANIA: THE KEYSTONE STATE

Pennsylvania is known as the Keystone State; the reason why can be found in Royal Arch Masonry. In its purest form a keystone is a symbol of strength. It supports an arch, without a keystone an arch cannot stand and is an architectural impossibility. A keystone is the strongest part of an arch, as it binds and unites the other stones together, making it whole and able to stand together against the elements.[319] Within the Mark Master Mason and Royal Arch ceremonies (and the Masonic Rite of Memphis-Mizraim, as discussed earlier) the Keystone and its symbolism is of great importance. The Keystone of Hiram Abif is first recovered in the Mark Master Mason degree, only to be discarded, as previously explained. The Keystone is later found in the Royal Arch degree as workers clear the rubble of the first temple to make way for the Temple of Zerubbabel. The Keystone is found by the workers (Templars in the Scotch Master ritual) in the northeast section of where the new temple is to be built and is symbolic of the summer solstice when the sun is at its strongest.

The Keystone is removed and an aperture or trapdoor appears where the Keystone was found. The workers take the Keystone to the Grand Council who inspect it and confirm that it is the Keystone of Grand Master Hiram Abif. The workers are sent back to investigate the aperture; through which is discovered nine arches under which lie a dark hidden vault. According to the ritual the sun shone with glorious splendor into the aperture where the keystone once sat. The sun illuminates the hidden vault below which reveals the Ark of the Covenant (York Rite) with the name of God, the Lost Word, engraved on a golden delta within a circle (it is found upon the Foundation Stone in the Scottish Rite). According to the Webb ceremony the sun's rays make the recovery of the Ark and the Tetragrammaton possible. The sun's rays illuminate the Ark upon which the name of God is located, through its pronunciation all learning is made possible. As such, a keystone is linked with the rediscovery of lost antediluvian knowledge; with the correct pronunciation of the Lost Word ancient knowledge is reborn: the keystone itself becomes a symbol of new birth. This symbolism

319 Brown, Robert Hewitt, *Stellar Theology and Masonic Astronomy*, page 87.

was analyzed in Chapter III.

On July 4th, 1776, the Second Continental Congress adopted the Declaration of Independence declaring the thirteen colonies were now independent states no longer under the yoke of Great Britain. This occurred within the sign of Cancer, the Keystone of the Masonic Northern Royal Arch. In 1776, Sirius (cf. Isis) was ten minutes, fifty-nine seconds in Cancer,[320] the symbolism would be drawn upon during the second cornerstone laying ceremony of the Washington Monument in the District of Columbia years later. On July 4th the sun rises with Sirius beginning the "Dog Days of Summer," thereby Isis the Virgin Mother becomes united with her sun god Horus, or alternatively with Amun Ra/Re, whom she possessed his sacred and holy name, the symbolic Lost Word of a Master Mason. On September 17, 1787 the 55 state delegates of the Constitutional Convention formally adopted the United States Constitution, erasing the Articles of Confederation while uniting the thirteen states (formerly colonies) forever while at the same time giving birth to a new country or new temple: The United States of America. This occurred under the sign of Virgo the Virgin (cf. Mary as Isis in the Christian Mysteries), whose astrological signs are achievement, diplomacy, worldly honor, work on behalf of others or of science, and sacrifice of everything for duty, conforming with the hermetic maxim of *as above, so below* of Hermes Trismegistus.[321] This is also in harmony with Renaissance concepts of cosmological and spiritual divine order; in other words the heavens were symbolically imbuing even blessing the deeds, actions, and as will be seen in chapter fourteen the architecture of the new nation. During the Constitutional Convention, Freemason George Washington presided over the convention in a wooden chair featuring a golden sun with a golden cap perched over it (see Plate XIX). Washington –who did not actively partake in the debates–appears to have delegated that duty to Edmund Randolph, a mason who served as Washington's aide de camp during the Revolution.[322] Randolph was the country's first Attorney General, then governor of Virginia, and later Grand Master of

320 Ovason, David, *The Secret Architecture of Our Nation's Capital,* page 138.
321 Devore, Nicholas, *Encyclopedia of Astrology,* page 367.
322 Baigent, Michael and Richard Leigh, *The Temple and the Lodge,* page 342-343.

Virginia's Grand Lodge.[323] That notwithstanding, Washington seems to have presided over the Constitutional Convention just as a Worshipful Master oversees his lodge: as a Worshipful Master sits in the in the east symbolizing the rising sun, it is only proper that President Washington's chair displayed a *rising sun.* While the members were signing the Constitution, future President James Madison noted:

> "Doctor Franklin, looking towards the President's chair,
> at the back of which a rising sun happened to be painted,
> observed to a few members near him, that painters had found
> it difficult to distinguish in their art, a rising, from a setting, sun.
> I have, said he, often and often, in the course of the session,
> and the vicissitudes of my hopes and fears as to its issue,
> looked at that behind the President,
> without being able to tell whether it was rising or setting;
> but now at length, I have the happiness to know,
> that it is a rising, and not a setting sun."[324]

The rising sun on Washington's chair symbolized new birth of a new nation just as the dawn brings the birth of a new day. The sun is of course Apollo, the cap represents the cap worn by the goddess Libertas, the goddess of Liberty. The Declaration of Independence and the United States Constitution gave birth to the new age of liberty by way of the creation of the American Republic; these documents represented total departure from old age European monarchies and Vatican spiritual dictatorship, although as noted these latter precepts can be found exemplified in the Masonic *haute* degrees. Both documents bound and united the originally thirteen colonies into one, whole country; a new nation, *E pluribus unum* or *out of many, one*. "The keystone of the Royal Arch of the great Temple of Liberty is a fundamental law, charter, or constitution; the expression of the fixed habits of thought of the people, embodied in a written instrument, …."[325] This "written instrument" became reality in both the Declaration of Independence and the U.S. Constitution, both documents are symbolic Masonic keystones. Both documents were adopted and ratified in the city of Masonic brotherly

323 Ibid.
324 Madison, James, *Notes of Debates in the Federal Convention of 1787*, page 659.
325 Pike, Albert, *Morals and Dogma of the Ancient and Accepted Scottish Rite*, page 211.

love: Philadelphia; "Philadelphia" is compounded from the Greek *philos*, loving, and *adelphos*, brother. Philadelphia, the largest city in the state of Pennsylvania, it is the state where the United States, the great Temple of Liberty, was newly born out of the ashes of revolution; it was where the *thirteen colonies were united, bound together into one*: *the United States of America*. The state of Pennsylvania appropriately becomes the Masonic Royal Arch Keystone State because the colonies (later states) became *one* in the city of Philadelphia, the thirteen colonies were bound and locked together, when Congress adopted the Declaration of Independence (1776) and later the state delegates ratified the U.S. Constitution (1787) at the Constitutional Convention. Pennsylvania as the Keystone State is also reflected in Benjamin Franklin's use of Freemasonry. Franklin, a Pennsylvanian, use of Masonry is not only instrumental to comprehending the Webb-Preston synthesis because over a long career he shifted from a Modern to Antient in a symbolic Masonic ritual context. Part of this shift was simply because Pennsylvania Masons changed their English Masonic allegiance. Yet, his Masonic experiences in Paris suggest he was also attracted to the developing systems of *haute* degrees of Freemasonry which originated in France, and later were transplanted to America. Newtonians such as Franklin, and Jacobites such as The Chevalier Ramsay, shared, therefore, an essential concept that the esoteric core of Freemasonry should not be subject to undue probing, but positioned as a general equivalency between the core of Masonic ritual and politically nuanced metaphysics, with the result that a general equivalency might be established which would allow, jointly, the peaceful consolidation of British national institutions after protracted religious controversy and Civil War (of Cromwell). Symbolically in America this meant an increasing emphasis upon the mathematically nuanced elements of mysticality, much more inclined to Ramsay than to Newton, within an emerging American idea of the learned active socio-political Royal Arch scholar who symbolically possessed the Tetragrammaton. From June 7, 1758, when the first Antient Masonic Lodge was established in Pennsylvania, until Webb was exalted (initiated) a Royal Arch Mason in Philadelphia, May 18, 1796, Pennsylvania had become the purest and most important emplacement of Antient Freemasonry in the New World. It was the Antients that held the Royal Arch to be Masonry's most sublime, exalted degree. Pennsylvania, thereby, became a great *Keystone* creating a Royal Arch, *the United States of America.*

HERMES THE PHILOSOPHER VISITS GETTYSBURG COLLEGE

Thoth Hermes Mercurius Trismegistus once visited Gettysburg College as the symbol predominately and proudly displayed on the Gettysburg College seal. The college was founded in 1832 in Adams County, Pennsylvania by a small group of Lutheran Ministers, namely Samuel Simon Schmucker (1799 -1873), and the radical republican Thaddeus Stevens (1792-1868). On its seal was Hermes the Philosopher, *qua* Mercury-Thoth, cf. Trismegistus, who as has been seen, is the sage who decodes the Enochian literary pillar giving birth to the seven liberal arts (medieval *Trivium* and *Quadrivium*) from the *Old Charges* (i.e. Cooke Manuscript, see Chapter I). As such, Hermes or Mercury, when used as an emblem of higher education, is a Masonic symbol. Stevens, a vehement anti-mason, would have been ignorant of the esoteric Masonic symbolism of Hermes Mercurius Trismegistus and would have had no understanding whatsoever of the occult nature of the symbol within Masonry. To Stevens and his anti-Masonic ilk, Hermes or Mercury was merely a messenger of the gods and would not have objected to its use. Circling Hermes-Mercury on the seal is the austere Latin phrase, *Sigillum Collegii Gettysburgensis* or "Seal of Gettysburg College," with the date of the college's founding, 1832. His placement on the Gettysburg college seal is appropriate as Gettysburg College is one of the nation's leading liberal art colleges in the vein of Union College, but how exactly Hermes got there appears to be a mystery.

The original seal of Gettysburg College featuring Hermes the Philosopher (a/k/a Hermes Mercurius Trismegistus) which parallels Christ Church's iconic Tom Quad fountain.

The Gettysburg college archives do not reveal how Trismegistus became the seal or who is ultimately responsible for his placement on it. In his book, *A Salutary Influence: Gettysburg College 1832-1985* Professor Charles Glatfelter states:

> "At long last, the battle had been won. When the trustees met a few weeks later, as their first item of business they directed that the College seal be altered, but in one respect only, by substituting *Sigillum Collegii Gettysburgensis* for the old *Sigillum Collegii Pennsylvaniensis*. Had they decided to conduct some historical research before taking action, they would presumably have found what every succeeding investigator has found: no evidence that their predecessors had ever formally adopted a seal. The charter of April 7, 1832 directed the first trustees to 'cause to be made for their use, one common seal, with such devices and inscriptions thereon, as they shall think proper, and by and with which all deeds, diplomas, certificates and acts of the said trustees, shall pass and be authenticated.' The trustees had indeed caused such a seal to be made, but the only evidences of that fact are the impressions made when it was used in the years before 1921."[326]

The trustees that met a few weeks later include, but not limited to, the Reverend Henry L. Baugher, professor of Greek Language and later of Moral Science; the Reverend J. H. Marsden, professor of Botany, the Reverend Ernest Hazelius, professor of Latin and German Literature, and Reverend Samuel Simon Schmucker, professor of Intellect and Moral Science, all Lutheran ministers. This coterie was no doubt familiar with Lutheran godfather and Christian esoteric Jakob Boehme; his writings on mysticism provided the raw material from which Hermes' relation to the seven liberal arts would have been known to this group. There can be little doubt Boehme's influence resulted on the placement of Hermes-Mercury on the Gettysburg College seal; Gettysburg College is, after all, a Lutheran College. Reverend Schmucker by all accounts was an interesting character. Schmucker was a professor at the college for its first two years (1832-1834) and was

326 Glatfelter, Charles, *A Salutary Influence: Gettysburg College 1832 - 1985, Vol. II,* page 422.

actively both in the Lutheran Seminary in Gettysburg and the College. Between the years 1838 and 1846 Schmucker published several monographs regarding Lutheranism and Evangelism, including *Fraternal Appeal to the American Churches on Christian Unity* in 1838. It was his writings that gave birth to Evangelical Alliance, a Christian charitable organization that was created at conference at Freemason's Hall in London in August, 1846. Schmucker was one of the Americans to attend this conference and his appearance at it and its venue cannot be written off as coincidence.[327]

Whether Schmucker was initiated into the mysteries of Masonry is not known, but Schmucker's motives and loyalty within the Lutheran Church had been in question. Many Lutherans believed Schmucker to be a double agent or fifth columnist actually working to destroy the American Lutheran Church on behalf of another agency. Whatever Schmucker's true motives and alliances, his place in Gettysburg College history is without question. Schmucker Hall on the southside of the campus bears his name to this day. As an interesting sidenote, Schmucker Hall does not contain the theological department as one would think. Instead, the hall that bears Schmucker's name is dedicated to the pursuit of the arts and music, the domain of Hermes Mercurius Trismegistus.

The author started this section by stating Hermes Mercurius Trismegistus *once* visited Gettysburg College. Hermes Trismegistus no longer appears on the college seal. The seal was changed in 2006 to coincide with the college's 175th anniversary in 2007. The new seal features the cupola on top of Pennsylvania Hall, an icon recognizable to every student, past and present, of Gettysburg College. The austere Latin phrase, *Sigillum Collegii Gettysburgensis*, has been removed and replaced with the equally simplistic *Gettysburg College*. The date of 1832 is all that remains from the old seal. Although Thoth Hermes Mercurius Trismegistus is gone from the Gettysburg College seal, his influence still remains: the Gettysburg College's Student Art and Literary Magazine still bears the name, *The Mercury*.

327 Wentz, Abdel Ross, *Pioneer in Christian Unity: Samuel Simon Schmucker*, page 285.

APOLLO 13

It should come as no surprise that the second man to walk on the moon, Edwin "Buzz" Aldrin, is a Freemason. When Apollo 11 set down on the moon on July 20, 1969, not only was an American Flag being carried by the astronauts; Aldrin, a 32nd degree Scottish Rite Mason, carried a special Masonic banner to the moon. The banner was embroidered for him to take on his lunar journey by the librarian of the Scottish Rite House of the Temple in Washington, D.C.[328] The double-headed eagle, the symbol for the Scottish Rite had indeed landed, symbolically, on the moon in the summer of 1969.

The third lunar mission, Apollo 13, was launched on April 11, 1970 and carried three astronauts: James Lovell, John Swigert, and Fred Haise within the module. The module never made it to the moon; an electric failure caused an explosion that caused the oxygen tanks to shutdown. The mission was aborted and all three men, using a sextant to navigate their cosmic course, safely returned to Earth on April 17.

Apollo, from whom the mission takes its name, is the principal sun god who drives his solar chariot across sky bringing life and light to the world. In its earliest rendition in the United States the sun, as engraved in the St. Andrew's Royal Arch degree certificate (Hurd Plate, 1790), is the symbol for Logos, the Tetragrammaton, in the T. S. Webb system. The Webb system was in turn based on Henry Francken's Rite of Perfection of Albany, New York which was based on its French predecessor. Francken's Rite of Perfection eventually became the thirty-three degrees of the Scottish Rite; the Holy Royal Arch was the thirteenth degree within the Rite of Perfection and remained thirteenth degree in Scottish Rite. It is within this degree that the Lost Word of a Master Mason or the name of deity is recovered paralleling the seventh degree in the York or American Rite of T. S. Webb and DeWitt Clinton. The symbol for the Apollo 13 moon mission is, no doubt, taken directly from the Scottish Rite 13th degree and incorporates solar symbolism; the sun is the source of *light*: wisdom and

328 Ovason, David, *Secret Architecture of Our Nation's Capital,* page 241.

knowledge. The emblem for Apollo 13 is the sun, Apollo, being driven across the heavens in a golden, horse drawn chariot (see Plate XX). The sun radiates thirteen sun rays symbolic of the 13th degree of the Scottish Rite: this symbolism is appropriate as the mission was Apollo *13*. It is this degree where the candidate beholds the solar delta (cf. St. Andrew's Hurd Plate) containing the Tetragrammaton, Logos, allowing restoration of divine knowledge from the Pillars of Enoch. In keeping with this theme, the mission's motto is appropriately *Ex luna, scientia* or "*From the moon, knowledge*." This simply cannot be a coincidence as none of the other Apollo missions' insignias resemble anything close to that of Apollo 13's kabbalistic-*Merkabah* solar chariot. It is another example of hidden, Masonic, solar *haute* degree symbolism.

THE MYSTERIES OF UNION COLLEGE OF SCHENECTADY, NEW YORK

As referenced, the finer points of John J. Beckley rhetoric (adherents of a "Pythagorean" Thomas Jefferson as a *heliocentric imperium*) appeared as visual representation in Joseph-Jacques "J. J." Ramée's 1813 design of the proposed campus of Union College of Schenectady, New York. The First President of the College, Dr. Eliphalet Nott, sought a *Newtonian golden mean*: *in science and nature the patterns of divine perfection* and was therefore attracted to the simple geometry yet profound symbolism of Ramée's forms and the grand order of the buildings arrangement. Ramée, a French architect and likely Freemason, used avant-garde principles encountered just before the French Revolution in Paris, integrating Neo-Classical forms and plain surfaces to create an impression of abstraction rather than conventional massiveness. As a result this medium achieved a resonance with the clean lines reviewed in legendary forms of the *Old Charges* wherein geometry was understood to be a speculative abstraction of operative; the two terms were synonymous with Masonry in the narrative text. The objective was an understanding of the college in noetic and initiatory terms: a tightly knit utopian community. The result was an optimistic outlook about the role of education within the mission of the college as it provided leadership for the nation.

Union College was originally founded in 1795 and was the first institute of higher learning in the United States to offer degrees in civil engineering or *operative masonry*. Ramée's template features a rising sun emerging as the contents from an Enochic vault (see Plate XXI). The central building representing the rising sun was a domed rotunda originally intended to be a *pantheon of enlightenment*, or library. The placement of an Apollonian dome on a library was not original to Union College. It is highly likely that Ramée was influenced by the domed Bodleian Library at Oxford University, arguably the world's greatest learning center. The Bodleian, one of Europe's oldest and largest libraries, features a dome on its Palladian styled Radcliffe Camera symbolizing it as a temple of Apollo the Sun, in this case a *temple of intellectual light*; light meaning learning, knowledge and wisdom. The Radcliffe Camera was constructed between 1737-1749. The result was that the Ramée design of the Union College campus tends toward a Christian symbolic view of Apollo, which thread can be seen in the works of noted medieval theologians. For example, the name of the great mathematician Pythagoras means *the mouth of Apollo*; itself a reference to the Delphic Oracle, which under the influence of Apollonian culture was regarded as his shrine and sacred source of solar divination and prophecy. The exclusive Masonic temple for Oxford University students is named the Apollo University Lodge, an esoteric reference to the domed Bodleian. The Apollo Lodge dates from the 1820s with Oscar Wilde being its most famous member. Dr. Nott, a clergymen yet a disciple of the Enlightenment, intended Union College's domed building to be used for religious purposes.[329] The template of Union College is emblematic of the Masonic Ritual the Royal Arch of Enoch. It would serve as the general basic design for many college and universities campuses throughout the country. It is clear that the dissolution of the monasteries by Henry VII and the iconoclasm of the Puritans during the reign of Edward VI and into the Cromwellian Commonwealth period provided an ample incentive to psychologically and spiritually interiorize such imagery. This likely fed Baconian ideas of the reorganization of learning along utopian lines generated by various utopian

329 Kennedy, Roger *Orders from France*, note on page 273.

writers, including Bacon and possibly Campanella whose works inspired French classicist architects, like Ramée, working within Masonic circles.

David Parish, a wealthy German-Scottish land speculator who was key in developing upper state New York including the Hudson Valley, was the central patron for Ramée's dome (cf. arch) iconography as instrumental to neoclassical architecture and its proliferation six years before Jefferson founded the University of Virginia in 1819. Jefferson borrowed from Ramée's occult Masonic template when planning the University of Virginia, his own college of enlightenment and illumination. The University of Virginia, like the Ramée template of Union College, features an Apollonian domed rotunda symbolizing the sun emerging from a vault or *empty space* created by two parallel series of buildings. Like Union College, the University of Virginia's domed edifice was intended to be a library; unlike Union College, it actually became a library.

Joseph-Jacques Ramée's network also included the Samuel Smiths of Baltimore, Maryland, a close link to much of the politics of Thomas Jefferson's circle. Ramée's Masonic template of Union College was executed and utilized by the college in various ways in its projection of values into utopian ideas of pedagogy. These elements, notably appear to reflect the pansophist concepts of John Amos Comenius, an educator promoting the idea of universal education, whose principles of pedagogy were aimed at the creation of a governing class through methods of instruction through a labyrinthine utopian city, which likely inspired John Bunyan's *The Pilgrim's Progress*[330] published in 1678. *The Pilgrim's Progress* no doubt drew inspiration from Comenius' *Labyrinth of the World and Paradise of the Heart* published in 1623. Bunyan's work was based upon the premise that a higher faculty of spiritual intellect might be achieved among students through pansophic striving which reflected the tradition envisaged by the Chevalier Ramsay of a universal encyclopedia of human knowledge. Comenian ideas were not only pansophist; they were in a narrow sense totalitarian and linked to chiliastic concepts of millenarian theology.

330 *The Pilgrim's Progress* is a character driven story about the protagonist's perilous journey towards salvation through the Slough of Despond and the Delectable Mountains, Vanity Fair and ultimately to the Celestial City.

Thus, education was deemed instrumental to religious salvation through conformity to a new, irenic faith distinct from either Roman Catholic or Protestant confessions, administrated by a *novus* Academy of Wisdom.

Amatrix of ideas, either paralleling Comeniantexts, or closely resembling the same is evident in Ramée's designs and in the philosophy of leadership of Union College by Eliphalet Nott. Not only was the Supreme Council conceived within the broader culture of the society but the original American college fraternities were as well. These bodies devolved from joint Phi Beta Kappa and Masonic templates erected the Pythagorean premise that *philosophy was the guide of life* each through the core concept of a belief in a universal authority and a comprehensive conception of society in revolt against outdated pedagogies, design in all, to fit the necessities of a new nation. There is, within this complex, an important tie between Comenius and Tommaso Campanella in their common search for a purified, reformed Roman Catholicism which rejected Tridentine triumphalism and Protestant scholasticism in favor of something like the pre-Reformation of a mystic Catholic vision such as lifted up by DeWitt Clinton and his enthusiasm for Knight Templary, and in the chivalric grades of the Scottish Rite.

The labyrinthine metaphor in Comenian pedagogy related to the navigation of received orthodoxy so as to find within it guideposts and landmarks to achieve a higher spiritual intellect through learning. As will be seen this element survived in Charles S. Peirce's theory (semiotics) of agapism with pragmatic philosophy and remained a core of Masonic and derivative initiation throughout the 19th century. The executive premise and dynamic was that conventional faith was truthful but that its essence could only be accessed through suprarational means. Anti-rationalism was of no use, nor was ordinary piety. Rather, inserted within such received doctrines were stepping stones through which initiates might overcome the stifling elements of homogeneity and move into a super celestial realm of divine order, characterized in Peirce's case, by pure triadic mathematics and in the professions by military and civil engineering.

The core idea was that heterogeneous objects might be conceived and utilized in terms of their unitary through labyrinthine symbolism as complete and unitary through the Lullist Art of Memory or *Ars Notoria*. This was, in effect, a Francis Bacon-like program of educational reform which carried with it an implicit promise of the relief of toil by lifting up mankind to the level of divine order, a consummate Enochic objective. The concept presumed the existence of an erudite community, which Masonically, came to resemble the Supreme Council of the Ancient and Accepted Scottish Rite cofounded by Joseph C. Yates in 1801. Joseph C. Yates (1768-1837) was a founding trustee of Union College and the seventh Governor of New York both preceded by and succeeded by DeWitt Clinton. Giles Fonda Yates, his kinsman, was born in Schenectady New York in 1796; he was an early Grand Commander of the Scottish Rite (Northern Jurisdiction), an alumnus of Union College, a student of philosophy and the occult, and with the prolific Van Rensselaer family had both patriotic and Masonic connections to link the College mission to the origination and mission of the Ancient and Accepted Scottish Rite.

The symbolic transformation of a library into a rising sun is, essentially, the conversion of Sir Isaac Newton into a symbolic Pythagoras, Euclid, and Enoch. It not only deepened the ritual metaphor for the Royal Arch of Enoch or Solomon it also underscored how the emergence of the sun as the content of the Vault of Enoch, replacing the Ark of the Covenant, as depicted in Ramée's rendering could be interpreted as providential deism rooted in experimental science within the American setting. At Union College the comparison was uniquely apt because the college was a magnet for a variety of Masonic intellects, architects of churches, and Episcopal Bishops. It was also the site of the origination of the American college fraternity from elements which appears to include Phi Beta Kappa symbolism, Freemasonry, and the teaching of engineering within Newtonian providential scientific aegis and an irenic approach to sectarian interplay with higher education all under the watchful eye of DeWitt Clinton. In this reference, Newtonian solar symbolism was also a support for superintendency of intelligent providence through policy in matters of society of politics. This deepened into an argument for a non-partisan energy creating and administrating a public sphere of policy formation and implementation accessible through a system of expanded electorates and the development of a clerisy predicated upon Freemasonry's rank and public prestige which suffused the clergy, the legal profession, and medicine in each instance managing what came to be called professional etiquette.

Union College also saw the emergence of the Union Triad, along with Miami University of Ohio, college fraternal system originating from Phi Beta Kappa at William & Mary in Williamsburg, Virginia. At Union College the fraternities filled a void in student life due, in part, to the decline of the military marching band.[331] The Union Triad consisted of Kappa Alpha Society (1825), Sigma Phi (1827) and Delta Phi (1827) all emerging toward the end of DeWitt Clinton's life. The Miami Triad consisted of Beta Theta Pi (1839), Phi Delta Theta (1848) and Sigma Chi (1855). Union College's designation of the goddess Minerva, the seal of the college, as the protective goddess Alma Mater (cf. Marian-Isis symbolism from Columbia University seal) drew an ideological line between the Illuminati degree of Minerval and the symbolic principle that the goddess Minerva was the means, or divine spark in man, seeking union with the divinity within the cosmos by means of a ritually embroidered ladder which appeared in Jeremy Cross's illustrations. The result is the equivalency of Minerva with the operation

From Jeremy Cross' 1819 *Masonic Chart or Hieroglyphic Monitor*: The Entered Apprentice Degree, Jacob's Ladder leading to the Pleiades symbolizing Enochic celestial wisdom (top); the Blue Lodge, a point within a circle representing the sun, and four goddesses (bottom, left to right) Ceres who pours the pitcher of Aquarius necessary to reap the autumnal harvest, Minerva the goddess of wisdom, Isis (Mary) as the moon who holds a mirror reflecting the sun's light, she also holds the caduceus of Hermes (cf. Thoth, i.e. Hermes Trismegistus), and Justitia.

331 Jeffers, H. Paul, *The Freemasons in America*, page 152.

of the graded degree sequence within both the craft lodge and Ramsay's ideology through adapting her as a heroic enthusiasm directed toward a religion of natural contemplation. "Thus all natures are symbolic ladders, for by ascending the concatenated orders of his own intelligence man comes proximate to his own rational and enduring part."[332] This device de facto erected symbolically a means to utilize esoteric graded teachings, as in the Rite of Perfection structure which generated the Scottish Rite, with oligarchy and a further ideal of Masonic divine monarchy. On the Astro-theological symbolism of a ladder Albert Pike further explains,

> "Celsus, as quoted by Origen, tells us that the Persians represented by symbols the two-fold motion of the stars, fixed and planetary, and the passage of the Soul through their successive spheres. They erected in their holy caves, in which the mystic rites of the Mithraic Initiations were practised, what he denominates a high *ladder*, on the Seven steps of which were Seven gates or portals, according to the number of the Seven principle heavenly bodies. Through these the aspirants passed, until they reached the summit of the whole; and this passage was styled a transmigration through the spheres."[333]

The transference of Isaac Newton's solar energy into Ramée's elucidation of the Royal Arch of Enoch imagery within the template of Union College plays out accordingly such that the sun is moved out of its vault into a massive redolence enlightening the new American nation. The template for this energy was of course provided by Ramsay in the enunciation of the ideology of the degree. Yet its association with the emergent feminine deity can be seen on the Union College Seal: it features the roman virgin goddess of reason, magic, and wisdom Minerva with the Masonic college motto: *Sous les lois de Minerve nous devenons tous freres* or "We all become brothers under the laws of Minerva." The association, again in the Ramée rendering of abundant, effulgent power with unfolding solar mass, within the design of Union College's campus, de facto makes the

332 Hall, Manly Palmer, *Lectures on Ancient Philosophy,* page 427.
333 Pike, Albert, *Morals and Dogma of the Ancient and Accepted Scottish Rite,* page 233.

United States higher educational system a profoundly symbolic but also a secular icon moving previously theological imagery into an irenic vista of the restoration of lost knowledge in a new non-denominational setting at the engineered Erie Canal frontier of the new nation at the origin of its industrial expansion. Thus the application of the artistic and architectural properties of mass into a policy driven material culture originated within the alliance between Thomas Jefferson and his Vice President's nephew, DeWitt Clinton, symbolically defined the iconography of westward expansion.

The transposition of the sun as the contents of an Enochian vault in the campus designs by J. J. Ramée, in his renderings for the design of Union College, Schenectady New York, within the context of the Masonic regime in an around the college during the governorship of DeWitt Clinton underscores an end point of definition within which the Royal Arch of Enoch template was designed for policy purposes out of the troves of Masonically laden raw material. This icon defined the environs of the first college founded in the newly independent American Republic, and points to the ambiguous nature of Platonism, with its solar imagery, played perfectly within Freemasonry in the American "new world" or Egyptian context. The survival of the medieval emphasis within spirituality on meditation on the Names of God through Cabala, has often been noted in its similarity to Royal Arch imagery. Further this dynamic, evident in the narratives of both Webb's working of the Royal Arch and the imagery surviving in Ramée's design of the Union College campus imagery of the degree ceremony confirm the primacy of Enochic iconology as an instrument depicting pansophism and Salem Town's rhetoric which invested sacral memory with the power to discern the movement of the Tetragrammaton into history within the nation building epoch of the American frontier. From 1817 to 1825, the rhetoric was modified to accommodate symbolism into western expansion through the Erie Canal system, and its parallels in Pennsylvania and Ohio. The ritual narrative describing these efforts was provided in various engraved editions of the Order of the Red Cross of Babylon, the first of three Knights Templar orders conferred in the encampments and commanderies established as an extension of the national path of initiation in the St. Andrew's Hurd Plate (1790) and T.S. Webb's 1797 Monitor.

CALIFORNIA: EUREKA (I HAVE FOUND IT)

Seal or Coat of Arms of Theta Delta Chi featuring Minerva upon its Crest.

The coat of arms of Sigma Alpha Epsilon college fraternity, its Crest feature Minerva standing next to a lion.

The Seal of California (see Plate XXII) is, ostensibly, a Masonic symbol and represents the completion of Masonic and Odd Fellow westward expansion. Its main components are the Roman goddess of wisdom and reason Minerva overlooking a landscape featuring a harbor-river, a gold miner, and a bear all which appear under the word, *Eureka*. Upon further investigation these symbols reveal an esoteric meaning adroitly concealed. The image itself took concrete form in the Minerva seal of Union College. It then moved into the sigillism of Theta Delta Chi college fraternity, founded at Union College in 1847. Theta Delta Chi no doubt lifted Minerva from the Union College Seal. From there Minerva appeared on the crest of Sigma Alpha Epsilon Fraternity founded 1856, and further westward through Odd Fellowship seemingly by Odd fellow and Masonic Grand Master of California Leland Stanford Sr., the founder of Stanford University in1891 and the eighth Governor of California serving from 1862 to 1863.

In the Union College-Schenectady area, a variety of intellectual-political currents conflated with the opening of the Erie Canal such that Freemasonry was projected westward no so much as an aggregate of individuals, although this was heroically significant and became more so as Ohio through Thomas Smith Webb developed powerful Masonic links to the United States Presidency, but as a catalyst for symbolic mythology and its

Top: The Odd Fellow Seal of California Lodge #1, Below: Seal of California Odd Fellow Grand Lodge.

penetration of public policy and material culture. Stanford's affiliation with it into California and ultimately onto the state seal comes directly from the seal of the first Odd Fellow Lodge in California: California Lodge No. 1, founded in San Francisco in 1849, the same year the California seal was adopted. This seal was in turn was used as the Grand Odd Fellows Lodge of California seal. The Seal of California is, as one can clearly see, a replication of these Odd Fellow seals.

The Seal of California was designed by Odd Fellow Robert S. Garnett who was the first general officer to be killed in the American Civil War in July 1861 during the Battle of Corrick's Ford. The California State Seal contains Royal Arch Enochian symbolism. The word "Eureka" while to an exoteric eye is merely a reference to a city in California, it is the word exclaimed by Pythagoras, *EUREKA* or *I HAVE FOUND IT*, discovering the 47th Proposition of Euclid as inscribed on the mathematical Pillar of Enoch. The 47th Proposition of Enoch or the Pythagorean Theorem is restored by the correct pronunciation of the ineffable Royal Arch name of deity, the Lost Word of the Master Mason. By pronouncing the Lost Word Pythagoras was able to decode the Enochian mathematical pillar restoring Euclid's 47th Proposition. This is confirmed by the presence of the working tools of a Royal Arch Mason: the pick axe and shovel used to both locate and recover the vault containing the Lost Word during the Royal Arch ceremonies. This is exoterically presented as a miner of the 1849 gold rush, yet esoterically symbolizes the discovery of the Hiram Abif's keystone during the construction of the Temple of Zerubbabel. Couple this symbolism with Minerva and there can be no doubt the Seal of California is representative of Royal Arch *haute* degree masonry.

As an interesting conclusion to this narrative it is worth noting that the goddess Minerva is often depicted accompanied by an owl, a symbol of wisdom and her sacred totem. An owl is a symbol of wisdom because it can *see things in the dark*, the implication being that the initiated can see things that the profane and vulgar cannot, and will never, be able to see. As such Minerva is an important icon of secret societies and why owls are repeatedly used on the seals of college fraternities and sororities. This further provides explanation why the owl, associated with Minerva's appearance on the California State Seal, is venerated yearly in July at the Bohemian Society[334] (a/k/a Bohemian Grove) located in Sonoma County, California during the Cremation of Care Ritual or Mid-Summer Fire Festival.

TEXAS: THE LONE STAR STATE

"The Ancient Astronomers saw all the great Symbols of Masonry in the Stars. Sirius glitters in our lodges as the Blazing Star, (*l'Etoile Flamboyante*). The Sun is still symbolized by the point within a Circle; and, with the Moon and Mercury or Anubis, in the three Great Lights of the Lodge."[335] So wrote 33rd degree mason Albert Pike in his tome *Morals and Dogma of the Ancient and Accepted Scottish Rite*, first published in 1871. The link between the Egyptian Dog Star Sirius and the Masonic Brotherhood can be clearly seen in the symbolism and iconography of Texas being known as the Lone Star state. When one thinks of Masonry and Texas, one is immediately drawn to the Alamo, which was originally a Catholic Mission named San Antonio de Valero. By the time of the Battle of the Alamo between February and March 1836 the brothers occupying it had all but converted it into a Masonic Temple. The Freemasons felled at the Alamo by the forces of General Antonio Lopez de Santa Anna included Davy Crockett, Colonel William B. Travis, James B. Bonham, James Bowie, and Almeron Dickerson. The fall of the Alamo led to the Battle of San Jacinto fought on April 21, 1836 and was the decisive battle of the Texas Revolution. Led by Freemason and General Sam Houston, the Texan Army engaged and defeated Santa Anna's Mexican forces, in a fight which lasted just eighteen minutes.

334 Formed in 1872, the Bohemian Society plays hosts to U.S. Presidents, industrialists, politicians - foreign and domestic, diplomats, military leaders, and heads of education and science.
335 Pike, Albert, *Morals and Dogma of the Ancient and Accepted Scottish Rite*, page 486.

The Alamo aside, many Freemasons also contributed substantially to the fight for Texan independence and are at the core of Texan history. These include, as mentioned, Sam Houston as well as David G. Burnet, Lorenzo de Zavala, Thomas Rusk, Mirabeau Buonaparte Lamar, John A. Wharton, and James W. Fannin, Stephen F. Austin (known as the Father of Texas), Edward Burleson, Benjamin Rush Milam, and Juan Seguín. Masonic historian Harry L. Haywood states "Texas is truly the daughter of Masonry."[336] It is no wonder that at the celebration of the Festival of St. John the Baptist in 1844 at Portland, Maine, Brother R. W. Teulon, a member of the Grand Lodge of Texas, in reply to a toast complimentary to the Masons of that Republic, observed "Texas is emphatically a Masonic country: all of our presidents and vice-presidents, and four-fifths of our state officers, were or are Masons; our national emblem, the Lone Star, was chosen from among the emblems selected by Freemasonry, to illustrate the moral virtues–it is a five-pointed star, and alludes to the five points offellowship."[337]

The *five points of fellowship* form a pentagram, the symbol within Masonry for the Dog Star Sirius.[338] Sirius is the brightest star in the night sky and as such it is the *lone star*, and according to Pike, a star that symbolizes fellowship. "It is the Pentalpha of Pythagoras, or Pentacle of Solomon; has five lines and five angels; and is among Masons, the outline or origin of the five pointed Star, and an emblem of Fellowship."[339] When Texas joined the union in December 1845 is was not only the largest state, but arguably the *brightest* Masonic state in the country: Texas is thus known as the Lone Star state. The iconography can be seen on the Texas Flag and its Great Seal. Regarding the flag, the dark blue background suggestive of the nighttime sky and the white pentagram is the blazing star Sirius, while on the Great Seal the pentagram is the central symbol of focus (see Plate XXIII). The admission of Texas to the Union not only paved the way westward for the inclusion of more American States but it made the United States a truly continental nation which was at the hearts of our Masonic Founding Fathers from its inception.

336 Quoted in Jeffers, H. Paul, *The Freemasons in America*, page 55.
337 Quoted in Ibid, page 64.
338 Pike, Albert, *Morals and Dogma of the Ancient and Accepted Scottish Rite*, pages 486 and 842.
339 Ibid, 634.

MASONIC APRONS AS A SYMBOL OF JOACHIMITE ESCHATOLOGY

The most central emblem of Freemasonry is the apron. This piece of leather or fabric presented to an initiate at his Entered Apprentice degree became for him the highest device of pure nobility. As a Masonic icon, therefore, the apron stylized comprehension of the celestial–terrestrial essence of divine policy arrangement among cooperative oligarchs. Each member possessed one, and until the late nineteenth century, American Masonic aprons were not regulated by size or design.

The patriotic Joachimite vision of a new world order, comprised of autonomous spiritual individuals, was articulated in the evolution of the American Masonic apron. There was a transition from a general pattern of the random placement of symbols toward a unified and cohesive allegorical scene depicting an initiatic progress through history. This represented a re-ordering of the iconographic style of the Irish jewels so that a hierarchy of levels was telescoped into a receding perspective of steps and vaults, attendant by emblems of *enchiridion*, notably Knights Templar motifs, such as in the Royal Arch Hurd Plate degree certificate of 1790. Principles of imperial republican rule were integrated within such representations, to connect Masonic ritual expression to an emerging idea of prophetic order, such as that articulated in the Order of the Red Cross. The design of Masonic aprons of the period 1800–1830 represented an increasing integration and refinement of millennial ideas at precisely the period that Webb and Clinton's system modified colonial and Revolutionary War Freemasonry. It is also the period when political individualism *emerged as a theory... capable of practical development*.

Joachimite prophecy affirmed each individual was an autonomous evangel of a new spiritual order, the nation as lodge or Royal Arch chapter, under the guidance of the Holy Spirit, the solar All-Seeing Eye of the Great Architect of the Universe (G.A.O.T.U.) as the Tetragrammaton. Each Mason was invested with an apron, as a symbol of his elevation to initiatic rank. An important nineteenth century English Masonic scholar of symbolism quotes this ritual reference as follows:

"....a badge more ancient than the Golden Fleece or Roman Eagle, and more honourable than the Star and Garter."

The apron was constructed of white lambskin, a probable reference to the purity of the Lamb of God, invested with chivalric, classical, military, and through the Garter reference, royal patronage. Esoterically the lambskin symbolizes the constellation of Aries the Ram (cf. lamb), the first house of the zodiac and the house the sun enters into after its resurrection from death-winter at the vernal equinox.

The period in which iconography of Masonic aprons achieved full expression of detail, ca. 1800–1830, inherited a French tradition of Masonic embroidery, demonstrated in an important apron owned by George Washington, as well as techniques of American artistic and folk art. Aprons of this period incorporated frequent references to arches and deltas (triangles) within more conventional craft Masonic emblem structures, which indicated a tradition of initiation consistent with Webb's Antient Scots-Irish roots. Aprons of this period were also artistically designed to complement emblematic jewels, such as the Irish set referenced. The dynamic of policy representation shifted from a vertical motif concerning the structure of the universe, with its concomitant political hierarchy, toward a horizontal motif concerning the end of time. This was managed through a process of ritual initiation in which each degree was invested with a particular structure of Masonic inaugural polity.

Compared with Preston's apron tradition, Webb's indicated greater detail of apocalyptic themes. The United Grand Lodge of England, after the Union (1813), strictly regulated the size and decoration appropriate to aprons, according to rank and office. A similar pattern developed among American Grand Lodges in the 1850s, notably in Pennsylvania, which copied the style of the English procedure. Yet, before Masonic judicatories achieved tight control after the period of anti-Masonry, the patriotic and eschatological aspects of apron design reflects three clear characteristics which illustrated the nature of Webb's and Clinton's system:

1) The use of perspective as an emblem of millennial and initiatic history;

2) The use of a vault within a vault (pillars within pillars, or the Pillars of Enoch placed in-between Jachin and Boaz with a small central vault located in the center) as an Enochic device of restored wisdom; and

3) The use of an all-seeing eye as a key to a Joachimite eschaton of celestial order on earth.

In the first instance, aprons of ca. 1800-1830 emphasized a path to initiation including steps, arches, staircases (winding or angulated), and vaults. This indicateda progression from the Irish jewels hierarchy towarda more egalitarian initiatic view of symbolic history, accessible to the Royal Arch Mason, with a view of Masonic governance consistent with Webb's and Clinton's idea of civic order. There was a strong connection between the emblems of each successive degree arranged to link ritual lessons with rulership. An implicit polity equated rulership with wisdom in the arrangement of the various emblems, as well as a more didactic expression of regality.

The Benjamin Hurd Royal Arch Plate degree certificate (1790) motifs were most clear on aprons dating from ca. 1805–1810, produced in New England. Connecticut, for example, maintained a strong tradition ofdissent and irenicism associated with Universalist theology as well as with the high churchmanship of Episcopal Bishop, Samuel Seabury (1729–1796). These aprons incorporated the three presiding officers of a Royal Arch Chapter atop three pillars, the first two of which–associated with the King and Scribe–were arranged in a foreground position to that topped by the figure of the High Priest, positioned upon two pillars, connected by an arch, which contained the Enochian vault. The policy symbolism of this pattern associated the two ancillary officers on a Royal Arch dais, the King and Scribe, with the columns found in a Lodge, J and B. These were linked to the role of the two corresponding senior officers of a Craft Lodge, Senior and Junior Warden. The implication was that the de facto Master of the Lodge was also the mitred High Priest positioned as a guardian and ruler over the contents of the Royal Arch of Zerubbabel, as well as the contents of the vault of the Royal Arch of Zerubbabel paralleling the contents of the vault of the Royal Arch of Enoch. Further policy symbolism was that the High Priest figure was superimposed over the emblems of the Knight Templar degree or order. As cited above, this order was developed by Webb and Clinton as a Christian enchiridion for the Royal Arch, which included the Order of the Red Cross. The militancy motif indicates that the designer of the Hurd Plate, and those who subsequently developed the aprons, understood the priestly figure not only to be a ruler over the Craft elements of Freemasonry, but also the Pontiff who exercised hegemony over the militant extension of Royal Arch teaching throughout the new nation. Indeed, the pontiff motif was preserved precisely because the High Priest was situated on the arch, which served as a bridge between the two outer Enochian pillars.

A still further indication of the eschatological dynamic of this arrangement was its accessibility through the use of perspective, a motif which differentiated the more hierarchical elements of both Scots-Irish and Antient Masonry, with its associations with Stuart monarchy, and proto-absolutism, and Preston's Whig kingship, from the structured egality of Webb and Clinton. Indeed, the stepped access from the Craft emblems, outside Jachin and Boaz columns, into the Enochic vault, guarded by Templar emblems, gave the firm impression that initiation, like citizenship in the new nation, was the premier dynamic. By contrast, rulership had a hegemonic or merely superintending role. The second apron characteristic was the use of a vault within a vault as the central core of the Royal Arch Hurd Plate degree certificate, and the aprons which replicate its design. This positioned finely architectured buildings within an arch, including domestic residences. The idea was that architectural proportion contained implicit references to Masonic esoterica, which also related to the domesticity of Masonic home-life in the new nation and to the role of Freemasonry as the protector of women and children.

This second characteristic also emphasized the millennial principle that the search for the New Jerusalem in the new America involved an encounter with mortality, an Adamic and saturnine iconographic element which linked emblems of death with the recovery of lost wisdom through contemplative *melancholia*. This initiatic principle was referenced in Albrecht Dürer's *Melencholia II* (1514), analyzed by Erwin Panovsky, Frances A. Yates, and Wilhelm Waetzoldt regarding hermetically informed representations of St. Jerome in his chamber, or study, contemplating a skull.

Webb incorporated emblems of mortality as a principal element of the Royal Arch Mason's initiation as a Knight Templar. The candidate, exalted, and knighted in the Order of the Red Cross, was compelled to sit alone in a darkened Chamber of Reflection with a skull, crossed bones, and bowl of water, and asked to answer specific questions, an event designed into the Knight Templar Apron, which Cornelius Moore (1806-1883) describes in his *Templar Text Book* (1853) as follows:

> "...of black velvet of a triangular form, trimmed with silver
> ...a triangle with twelve holes...in the center a cross and serpent...
> a skull and cross bones...also a star with seven points;
> in the center of each star a red cross."

Funeral emblems in Masonic initiation appeared frequently in aprons of the 1800-1830 periods, and can be traced to vault *mausolea* in France, Scotland, and Ireland. Each nation utilized important Masonic rites associated with Enochian vault motifs, notably the *Neo-classical Egyptianizing of Hellenistic ideas*. In Connecticut, where a charitable ethic of Masonic dissent survived, an esoteric tradition of scholarly inquiry connected to John Winthrop, Jr., F.R.S. (1606-1676), whose alchemical library, including John Dee's books, also survived and has been carefully studied. Winthrop's seminal role as the first Governor of Connecticut under Royal Charter resulted in the establishment of his family in Connecticut cultural and political affairs. When Connecticut anti-Masonry reached its highest pitch, a resilient, vault-like infrastructure within Craft Masonry resisted legislation to require disclosure of lodge records, and allied itself with an emerging liberal element in Episcopal parishes, eventually causing the *furore* to subside.

The third apron characteristic was the use of an all-seeing eye as

Joachimite key to a celestial order on earth. In common with hermetical principles of human proportion as a means to replicate sacred geometry on earth, Joachimism sought *plenitudo intellectus* among men obviating any necessity of clergy, sacraments, and preaching. The resulting direct knowledge of God by vision and contemplation connected Joachim with hermetical and Enochian symbolism. A pervasive device in early American Masonic aprons, this all-seeing eye represented fulsome "Logos" wisdom ascribed to the initiate's relationship with Deity ritually articulated without Christian soteriology. It was also an emblem of wise, perceptive rule consistent with American political and spiritual sovereignty, engaging all mankind perpetually in it; and in doing so attained to that blend of millennium and utopia ...(the) union of virtue and commerce ... America's global role prophesied.[340]

The all-seeing eye was also established by law as the eye in a triangle on 20 June 1782, by Congress, as discussed. By 1800, the eye's common appearance on the triangular flap of Masonic aprons often replaced the radiant sun in the same place on English aprons. The homespun rendering suggested the eye either of the initiate looking into, or an officer looking out of a small peephole, with which the entrances to Masonic lodge rooms were increasingly equipped. By linking the national seal with the symbolic principle that 1776 began a new American Order of the Ages within the definition provided by the all-seeing eye, the congress set a symbolic tone for lawmaking taken up enthusiastically by Masonic symbolists and engravers. Both Freemasonry and the United States became determined imperial harbingers of a virtuous, commercial world order of just autonomous citizens, without need of hierarchical or sacramental mediation. This was a legislated philanthropic (tax-exempt) Joachimite dynamic of toleration expressed in eschatological terms with legal implications for the developing millennial destiny of the nation. The result was the pragmatic juristic identification of a voluntary association with the power of spiritual vision and cohesion.

In sum: Joachimite elements of the Great Seal were reproduced upon countless Masonic aprons. These invested the initiate with an esoteric

340 Summarizing passages from John Locke's *Two Treatises of Government II,* 49; quoted in Pocock, J.G.A., *The Machiavellian Movement: Florentine Political Thought and the Atlantic Republican Tradition,* page 542.

warrant to be a priest and prophet in a new national religion. This implied a safely interior apocalyptic element in the dedication of each Masonic lodge to the Holy Saints John, and the role of the *Novus Dux* (new leader) referenced in the Revelation of St. John the Divine, 7:2:

> "Then I saw another angel ascend from the rising of the sun, with the *seal* of the living God and he called with a loud voice..."

Freemasons among Episcopal laity attempted to modify the canons and *Book of Common Prayer* of the new national Church to reflect similar principles, notably Rufus King (1755-1827) and David Brearley (1745-1790), a move heartily resisted by Bishop Samuel Seabury (1729-1796) who had been a Loyalist during the American Revolution.

THE HOUSE OF THE TEMPLE OF THE SCOTTISH RITE OF FREEMASONRY

Three of the Seven Wonders (manmade) of the Ancient World are replicated in the United States. The original wonders were built by ancient stone workers and craftsmen known as the Dionysian Artificers. It is these Artificers that were the progenitors of the medieval stone masons responsible for the great cathedrals of Europe and the forerunners to modern day Freemasons.[341] The first to be discussed is the House of the Temple of the Scottish Rite of Freemasonry.

The House of the Temple is located at 1733 16th St., Washington D.C., North West. It is modeled after the original seven wonder: the Mausoleum of Halicarnassus. The Mausoleum was the tomb of King Mausolus, from which comes the word *mausoleum.* It was erected by his sister and widow Artemisia, 353 BCE. The architects of the Hellenistic building were Satyrus and Pythios, while four other artificers ornamented the building: Scopas (east frieze), Bryaxis (north frieze), Leochares (west frieze) and Timotheos

341 Hall, Manly Palmer, *The Secret Teachings of all Ages*, page 188.

(south frieze).[342] Descriptions of the Mausoleum from the time, namely those of Vitruvius and Pliny, are unfortunately ambiguous at best. The site was excavated by C. T. Newton and Biliotti in 1857 and 1865.[343] In the 1950s the site was excavated by a Danish team led by Kristian Jeppesen; it is from these excavations that we have an idea of what the Mausoleum of Halicarnassus looked like.[344] Interestingly enough, the House of the Temple of the Scottish Rite is itself a mausoleum: it contains the mortal remains of Masonic author and philosopher Albert Pike.

The edifice was designed by neoclassical architect John Russell Pope (1874-1937). The cornerstone ceremony occurred on October 18, 1911; *Festival Te Deum* was sung by the Scottish Rite Choir of Saint Louis and the ritual was performed by the Grand Master of the District of Columbia Brother J. Claude Keiper who used the gavel originally used by George Washington at the cornerstone laying ceremony of the U.S. Capitol.[345] Elliott Woods, then architect of the U.S. Capitol and 32nd degree Scottish Rite Mason, acted on behalf of Pope at the ceremony because Pope was not a Freemason.[346] The House of the Temple (Mother Council of the World) features a truncated pyramid as its roof with thirteen levels or steps. The original blueprints reveals that Pope's design contained a truncated pyramid with an unspecified number of levels, but more than thirteen.[347] Who is responsible for the final inclusion of the thirteen levels is not known, but the thirteen steps symbolize the 13th Degree of the Rite of Perfection: the Royal Arch. The Royal Arch remained the 13th degree in the Scottish Rite, Southern Jurisdiction known as the Royal Arch of Enoch; it is within this ritual that the Tetragrammaton is symbolically recovered. The House of the Temple naturally sits *thirteen* blocks from the White House. This, as will be seen in Chapter XIV, is a symbol of perfected, Masonic government.

342 Curl, James S., *A Celebration of Death,* page 28.
343 Ibid, page 30.
344 Ibid.
345 Oval, David, *The Secret Architecture of Our Nation's Capital,* page 223.
346 Ibid.
347 Ibid, page 225.

THE GEORGE WASHINGTON MASONIC MEMORIAL

The second of the Seven Wonders of the Ancient World to be replicated in the United States is the Pharos Lighthouse of Alexandria, Egypt. Its modern day copy sits atop Shuter's Hill in Alexandria, Virginia overlooking the distant, but still visible, District of Columbia as the George Washington Masonic Memorial. The original lighthouse was designed and built by Sostratus of Cnidus during the reign of Ptolemy (283-247 BCE);[348] it was likely the tallest building in the world during its time. The lighthouse stood until the fourteenth century until it was destroyed by earthquake; its' remains still visible until CE 1350. The land-based George Washington Masonic Memorial obviously does not protect ships from wrecking ashore; rather it serves as a symbolic protective beacon of the District of Columbia. The concept of a mystical lighthouse protecting an inland city derives from an eleventh century Arabic grimoire (the term "grimoire" is thought to originate from the Old French word *grammaire)* that circulated medieval Europe called *Picatrix*; wherein a lighthouse sat atop a citadel protecting the city of Adocentyn from harm by way of supernatural properties.

The cornerstone of its duplicate, the George Washington Masonic Memorial, was laid in 1923; it was completed nine years later. The Memorial is dedicated to the concept of George Washington as a Freemason and houses many artifacts and relics; included among these are the apron, sash, and trowel used by Washington during the cornerstone laying ceremony of the United States Capitol in 1793. Since 1940 the memorial has been the meeting place of Alexandria-Washington Lodge #22, which was the lodge –known then as Alexandria Lodge #22–that George Washington was a member of during the waning years of his life. The hidden architectural symbolism of the George Washington Masonic Memorial lies in its height; it is 333 feet tall.

The "three threes" or "three times three" is a cryptic reference to the Royal Arch degree. "Three times three" must be formed by three companions

348 Hall, Manly P., *The Secret Teachings of All Age*, page190.

in order to communicate the ineffable Name of God, recovered during this ritual.[349] Each one of the companions takes hold with his right hand of the right wrist of his companion to his left, and with his left hand takes hold of the left wrist of the companion on his right. Each one then places his right foot forward with the hollow in front, so that the toe touches the heel of his companion on the right. This is called "three times three;" that is, three right feet forming a triangle, three left hands forming a triangle, and three hands forming a triangle, ... They then balance three times three, bringing the right hand with some violence down upon the left. The right hands are then raised above their heads, and the words "J- B- O-," the Grand Omnific Royal Arch Word, is given in a low breath.[350] Three times three equals nine (3x3=9) symbolic of a thirteenth degree Royal Arch Mason, known as a Knight or Master of the Ninth Arch within the Scottish Rite Northern Jurisdiction. It was under nine arches that Enoch (and by reference Hiram Abif) concealed the Tetragrammaton. The George Washington Masonic Memorial height, 333 feet, is symbolic of the Logos of the Royal Arch degree interposed with the Lullist *Ars Notoria* concept.

Three Times Three created by Masons to communicate the Royal Arch Word and is a reference to the three syllables of the Grand Omnific Royal Arch word. From *Duncan's Masonic Monitor*.

THE STATUE OF LIBERTY

The Statue of Liberty was a gift from French Orient Freemasons to American Freemasons to celebrate the 100th anniversary of the birth of the first Masonic Republic: the United States of America. The statue was the idea of French Mason Édouard René Lefèbvre de Laboulaye, who viewed the statue as way to symbolically restore the friendship between the United States and France that existed prior to the ratification of the Jay Treaty of 1794. The Statue of Liberty was designed by a fellow French Mason named Frédéric Auguste Bartholdi. It is the third of the Seven Ancient Wonders to reproduced, first chronologically, in the United States as the

349 Duncan, Malcolm C., *Duncan's Masonic Ritual and Monitor*, page 223.
350 Ibid and page 224.

Statue of Liberty is the modern day Colossus of Rhodes. This is confirmed by an inscription on a bronze plaque inside the statue. It reads:

The New Colossus
"Not like the brazen giant of Greek fame,
with conquering limbs astride from land to land;
here at our sea-washed, sunset gates shall stand
a mighty woman with a torch, whose flame
is the imprisoned lightning, and her name
Mother of Exiles. From her beacon-hand
glows world-wide welcome; her mild eyes command
the air-bridged harbor that twin cities frame.
Keep, ancient lands, your storied pomp!" cries she with silent lips.
"Give me your tired, your poor, your huddled masses
yearning to breathe free, the wretched refuse of your teeming shore.
Send these, the homeless, tempest-tossed to me,
I lift my lamp beside the golden door!"
- Emma Lazarus, 1883

The Colossus of Rhodes represented the solar god Helios and was made between 282 and 290 B.C by workers under the command of Chares of Lindos. The Colossus, like the Statue of Liberty, once stood in a harbor.

American Masons played their part as well. Freemasonic architect Richard Morris Hunt designed the pedestal upon which Liberty would sit. While a student at Ecole des Beaux-Arts in Paris, Hunt would begin his career renovating the Louvre for Carbonarist and member of the Supreme Council of the Ancient and Accepted Scottish Rite in France Napoleon III from 1846 to 1855; mainly working on the Pavillon de la Bibliothèque, Library Pavilion, opposite the Palais-Royal . Hunt also designed the Moorish styled tomb for the secret society Scroll and Key at Yale University in 1869-70. The cornerstone of Morris' pedestal was laid according to Masonic ritual in August 1884 organized by the lodges of New York State. The statue's actual name: Liberty Enlightening the World draws from the Masonic and Illuminist ideals of democracy, egalitarianism, and enlightenment; the statue holds aloft a torch symbolizing divine illumination. The statue itself is an

She of Seven Points, the Egyptian goddess of geometry, Seshat.

ancient wisdom goddess, most likely the Egyptian Goddess Seshat (who is the proto-type to the Roman Minerva and the Greek Pallas Athena) who is the feminine counterpart of Thoth, the Egyptian god of wisdom and scribe to Osiris. Thoth is syncretic with Hermes Mercurius Trismegistus who, as has been explained, decodes the Enochian literary pillar from which Freemasonry comes in the *Old Charges*.

Liberty's crown features seven emanating solar rays: the vulgar explanation is equated to there being seven seas and seven continents, which when investigated, does not satisfy. The esoteric explanation reveals the true symbolism: the seven solar rays symbolize the seven pointed star visible over the head of Seshat.[351] The use of an Egyptian goddess as a light bringer or bearer is not surprising, conspiratorial, nor alarming as the nineteenth century saw a great revival in Egyptology. Bartholdi in 1869, seven years prior to the 1876 centennial anniversary of the United States, suggested a statue of a robed woman holding a torch entitled, "Egypt Bringing Light to Asia" for the opening of the Suez Canal in Egypt. Seshat, being the Egyptian goddess of architecture, astronomy, and wisdom, conforms perfectly to the Masonic notion of perfection and kabbalistic syncretism. Bartholdi himself was quite familiar with Egypt

351 The seven pointed star over Seshat and the seven rays in Liberty's crown also symbolizes the lunar cycle, as the moon enters a new cycle every seventh day: First Quarter, New, Third Quarter, and Full. The moon was emblematic of the goddess in the ancient world and as such the placement of seven rays in Liberty's crown is apropos. The seven pointed star and seven rays also likely represent the seven lights known to the ancients: the sun, the moon, Venus, Mercury, Mars, Jupiter, and Saturn. It is from these seven lights that today we have seven days of the week. Hence, we have the Moon's day, or Monday. Tuesday is derived from the Scandinavian name of Mars, the name of the day in French is Mardi, derived from the Latin, meaning Mar's day (this is why the Mardi Gras festival is celebrated on a Tuesday). Wednesday is from the Scandinavian Mercury or Woden, hence Woden's day or Wednesday; Thursday is from the Scandinavian Jupiter, known to them as Thor -Thor's day or Thursday; Friday is from the Scandinavian Venus -Fria's day or Friday. The weekend belongs to Saturn's day and the day of the Sun. See *Stellar Theology & Masonic Astronomy*, page95.

Frontispiece of *Le Soleil Mystique*, 1852.

and its mythos as it was a favorite subject matter of his paintings which he created under the pseudonym "Amilcar Hasenfratz." It is also highly likely that both Laboulaye and Bartholdi drew inspiration for the physical appearance of the Statue of Liberty from the frontispiece of *Le Soleil Mystique* (*The Mystic Sun*) published in 1852: it features a goddess as the embodiment of Craft Freemasonry surrounded by cherubs holding aloft Masonic emblems such as the square and compasses. She carries a torch before the twin pillars Jachin and Boaz.

Esoterically the number *seven* is embedded in the statue. This number is significant within the Ancient Mysteries and Masonry; Albert Mackey elucidates:

> "In every system of antiquity there is a frequent reference to this number, showing that the veneration for it proceeded from some common cause. ...The Pythagoreans called it a perfect number, because it was made up of 3 and 4, the triangle and the square, which are the two perfect figures. They called it also a virgin number, and without a mother, comparing it to Minerva, who was a motherless virgin, because it cannot by multiplication produce any number within ten, as twice two does four, and three times three does nine; nor can any two numbers, by their multiplication, produce it.
>
> It is singular to observe the important part occupied by the number seven in all the ancient systems. There were, for instance, *seven* ancient planets, *seven* Pleiades, and *seven* Hyades; *seven* altars burned continually before the god Mithras; the Arabians had *seven* holy temples; the Hindus supposed the world to be enclosed within the compass of *seven* peninsulas; the Goths had seven *deities*, viz., the Sun, the Moon, Tuisco, Woden, Thor, Friga, and Seatur, from whose

> names are derived our days of the week; in the Persian mysteries were *seven* spacious caverns, through which the aspirant had to pass; in the Gothic mysteries, the candidate met with *seven* obstructions, which were called the "road of the seven stages;" and, finally, sacrifices were always considered as the most efficacious when the victims were *seven* in number.
>
> .....The Sabbath was the *seventh* day; Noah received *seven* days' notice of the commencement of the deluge, and was commanded to select clean beasts and fowls by *sevens; seven* persons accompanied him to ark; the ark rested on Mount Ararat in the *seventh* month; the intervals between dispatching the dove were, each time, *seven* days; the walls of Jericho were encompassed *seven* days by *seven* priests, bearing rams' horns; Solomon was *seven* years in building the Temple, which was dedicated in the *seventh* month, and the festival lasted *seven* days; the candlestick in the tabernacle consisted of seven branches; and, finally, the tower of Babel was said to have been elevated *seven* stories before dispersion. Seven is a sacred number in Masonic symbolism. It has always been so. In the earliest ritual of the last century it was said that a Lodge required seven to make it perfect; but the only explanation to be found in any of those rituals of the sacredness of the number is the seven liberal arts and sciences, which, according to the old 'Legend of the Craft,' were the foundation of Masonry. In modern ritualism the symbolism of seven has been transferred from the First to the Second Degree, and there it is made only to refer to the seven steps of the Winding Stairs; but symbolically seven is to be found diffused in a hundred ways over the whole Masonic system.
>
> .....Hippocrates says that the centenary number, by its occult virtue, tends to the accomplishment of all things, is the dispenser of life and the fountain of all its changes; and, like Shakespeare, he divides the life of man into seven stages."[352]

On the mysticism of the number seven Albert Pike adds,

> "....There were *seven* planets and spheres presided over by *seven* archangels. There were seven colors of the rainbow; and the Phoenician Deity was called HEPTAKIS or God of seven rays;

352 Mackey, Albert, *Encyclopedia of Freemasonry, Vol. II,* pages 682-684.

> .... John, in the Apocalypse, writes *seven* epistles to the *seven* churches.
>
> .... Enoch was the *seventh* patriarch, Adam included, and Lamech lived 777 years. .... Israel was in the hand of Midian *seven* years before Gideon delivered them. The bullock sacrificed by him was *seven* years old. Samson told Delilah to bind him with *seven* green withes; and she wove the *seven* locks of his head, and afterwards shaved them off. Balaam told Barak to build for him *seven* altars. Jacob served *seven* years for Leah and *seven* for Rachel. Job had *seven* sons and *three* daughters, making the perfect number *ten*. He had also *seven* thousand sheep and three thousand camels. His friends sat down with him *seven* days and *seven* nights. His friends were ordered to sacrifice *seven* bullocks and *seven* rams; and again, at the end, he had *seven* sons and three daughters, and twice *seven* thousand sheep, and lived an hundred and forty, or twice *seven* times *ten* years. Pharaoh saw in his dream *seven* fat and *seven* lean kine, *seven* good ears and *seven* blasted ears of wheat; and there were *seven* years of plenty, and *seven* of famine. Jericho fell, when *seven* priests, with *seven* trumpets, made the circuit of the city on *seven* successive days; once each day for six days, and *seven* times on the *seventh*. 'The *seven* eyes of the Lord,' says Zechariah, 'run to and fro through the whole earth.'. .... *Seven* angels, in the Apocalypse, pour out *seven* plagues, from *seven* vials of wrath. The scarlet-colored beast, on which the woman sits in the wilderness, has *seven* heads and ten horns. So also has the beast that rises up out of the sea. *Seven* thunders uttered their voices. *Seven* angels sounded *seven* trumpets. *Seven* lamps of fire, the *seven* spirits of God, burned before the throne; and the Lamb that was slain had *seven* horns and *seven* eyes."[353]

Liberty has seven rays emanating from her crown. On the crown is a series of twenty-five windows, add 2+5 to get 7. On the torch there are a series of raised portions or leaves that total the number 16; the pedestal has four Grecian columns on each side totaling 16 in all; add 1+6 to 7. The statue stands at 1,813 inches (151'.1") divide 1813 by 7 to get 259, add 2+5+9 to get 16; add 1+6 to get 7. The statue also reflects the Thomas Smith Webb-York Rite high degree system; the Royal Arch degree of Exaltation is

353 Pike, Albert, *Morals and Dogma of the Ancient and Accepted Scottish Rite,* pages 58-60.

naturally its *seventh* degree.

Ultimately Seshat would be intertwined by Bartholdi with Libertas, the Roman goddess of Liberty for whom the statue takes its name. Around the Statue of Liberty's feet are broken chains symbolizing freedom and liberation from the bonds of slavery. Libertas was the daughter of Jupiter and Juno according to Latin author Gaius Julius Hyginus. Libertas originally wore, or carried on a stick, a cap which itself was a symbol of liberty; in ancient Rome when a slave was liberated from bondage he shaved his head and wore a pileus or cap of liberty symbolizing his new found freedom. This is without a doubt the origin of the Phrygian cap worn by the sans-culottes during the French Revolution symbolizing their new found liberty. The Statue of Liberty would see the replacement of her cap with the seven points of Seshat. The Statue of Liberty was dedicated on October 28, 1886 by President Grover Cleveland. Seventy-nine years later, after the dedication of the Statue of Liberty, October 28, 1965 would see the placement of the keystone to the Masonic "Royal" Gateway Arch in St. Louis, Missouri, its symbolism will be detailed in the next chapter.

The use of Masonic symbolism is not limited to the items discussed in this chapter. As will be seen, the operative Masonic influence on the development of this country can be seen in the development of areas and city vistas with regard to the design and placement of buildings and architectural icons within the United States. The Masonic high degree symbolic influence on the architectural development within the Hudson Valley in New York by way of the Erie Canal and Union College, and upon the cities of Baltimore, Maryland, and St. Louis, Missouri, will now be discussed.

CHAPTER XII

THE HUDSON VALLEY AND THE VISTAS OF BALTIMORE, MARYLAND AND ST. LOUIS, MISSOURI

Masonic Design and Architecture in the New World

"Architecture consists of Order,
Arrangement, Eurythmy, Symmetry,
Propriety, and Economy."
- Vitruvius, *De Architectura* (Book I, Chapter ii, I), ca. 15 BCE.

"Great Washington, too, stands high aloft on his
towering main-mast in Baltimore, and like one of
Hercules' pillars, his column marks that point of human
grandeur beyond which few mortals will go."
- Herman Melville, *Moby Dick*, 1851.

"This effort to preserve the Mysteries in the Dark Ages
was successful because the speculative Masons adopted
as much as they could of the operative Masons' terminology,
and entrusted them with some of the secrets. The latter then
faithfully carried on the forms without comprehending
more than half of what they meant."
- Charles W. Leadbeater, *Freemasonry and its Ancient Mystic Rites* (originally published as *Glimpses of Masonic History)* 1926.

Many of the moral lessons taught within the Masonic Lodge involve using the symbolism of building tools to teach moral instruction. Without question this form of speculative Masonry was borne out of operative Masonry, the actual construction of building and edifices. It is beyond doubt that operative Masons knew and understood the mysteries of their craft. When operative

Masons began admitting speculative Masons, some of their mysteries were lost or forgotten; retained only by a select few.

As Masonic symbolism has been reflected in seals, logos, and college templates, Masonic influence can be seen on a much broader scope, within the design and layouts of cities, and in New York within the Hudson Valley which borrows from Italian Renaissance architecture. The operative Mason understood the hermetic maxim of *as above, so below*, that is the alignment of edifices to certain cosmological events, stars, and constellations in an effort to symbolically draw down the heavens onto earth. The layout of cities and communities can also reflect symbolism contained within *haute* degree Masonic ritual, as is the case with Union College.

There is little doubt that American cities and their design reflect this philosophy, the subject of which would be too lengthy to fully discuss. Evidence can be found in Pittsburgh, Pennsylvania, and Memphis, Tennessee. Rather than a broad discussion, the symbolism and vistas of two cities will be analyzed. These are the cities of Baltimore, Maryland, and St. Louis, Missouri. As will be revealed, Baltimore was influenced by the design of the District of Columbia while in turn St. Louis was informed by Baltimore. But first, the Hudson Valley must be discussed as it linked via the Erie Canal New York (the Masonic Empire State) to the Mississippi Valley and ultimately the Gulf of Mexico.

THE HUDSON VALLEY

Within the three major epochs of Italian architecture, 1480-1500; 1500-1540; and 1540-1580, integrating inventiveness associated with the Republican drives to recapture the virtues of the Latin origins; the perfection of the Renaissance style; and the early Baroque, it was the second period which inspired the designers of Hudson Valley architecture –the pinpoint of how the eclectic elements of other architectural traditions were consolidated to refine governance through a reformed American Republican vision of governance and patrimonialism in balanced harmony. The moderation of Greek revivalism and the pragmatic sobriety of Roman mass intertwined to Ramee's renderings of Union College further integrating imperial rulership with the hellenic prospect of mythological esoterica and moderation. The triumphal arch, in particular, appealed to the aesthetics of Clintonians as one was erected to consecrate the opening of the Erie Canal in 1825 and of course inserted as an Enochic-Royal Arch *rising sun* in the campus design of Ramee's Union College (1790). This style avoided the luxuriant excess of the early imaginative inventiveness of residentiary designs as well as the exaggerations of the Baroque for a Vitruvian elegance which in the hands of the recipients of the patronage of Clinton's Masonic and allied elites set the tone for the monumental styles exported Westward along the Erie Canal into Ohio and Indiana, uniquely as county court houses assumed a temple-like presidency over various fraternal, civic, and legislative levels of local policy etiquette as Nilotic threads of land granting were extended with inland navigation and Revolutionary War pensions. Masonic symbolism and the Erie Canal continues: the iconography on the 1825 ticket granting admission to the New York State Militia and Citizens Erie Canal Ball exhibited the caduceus of Hermes (cf. Thoth Hermes Trismegistus) thus linking the canal to Royal Arch legend and its related ethos while presenting the Erie Canal itself emanating solar rays (cf. rising sun); so too did the artifacts and iconology of DeWitt Clinton's own career exhibit similar esoteric, nuances.

Ticket granting admission to the Erie Canal Celebration Ball, November 7, 1825. The caduceus of Hermes can be seen on the left. The canal and its lock system is presented radiating solar light as an Enochic sun celebrating the United States' Masonic westward expansion.

In the 12th and 13th centuries Italy set the stage for students of policy in history for the amalgamation of temple (church) architecture and the same idiom applied to technical and material progress. DeWitt Clinton and his circle, notably Joel Pintard and Edward Livingston, were aware of this integrated icon and turned the feats of engineering from Manhattan up the Hudson River valley into a network of villas constructed as "Vitruvian villas" supported by riparian devices, later including the Fulton Steam engine, as well as residences echoing the villas of the Venetia within which, as at Cornaro, Masonic imagery first began to appear linking mnemonics to the *Ars Notoria.* The inspiration of these edifices by the early Italian Renaissance was clear. The unique connection was between aesthetics and practicality at the surface level, but, in depth, all elements pointed toward the evolution and development of a central Enochian icon for the imperial unfolding of a unified national vision in stone a metaphor for social policy.

The American usage of this idiom appeared more egalitarian than its Italian precursors in part because Jefferson's own Monticello style was obliged to reconcile agrarian myth with policy mission. The appearance of the esoteric rustic Temple to Apollo, such as at the domed Monticello, fitted Jefferson's mission aptly. This transference of what had been a provincial villa design emigrated well from the city states of Northern Italy but somehow was not diminished in latent impact from such a triumphal vista as St. Peter's became. In this sense the District of Columbia became the Federal supra state, a new St Peter's, Rome, for the new nation and in turn it averred to the potentiality of radial smaller temples throughout the nation which preserved the High Renaissance within edifices adaptable to formal reason. This was depicted in proto-Masonic ritual vignettes of Clinton's own system with the addition that Christian Enochic millennialism could be accommodated within Jefferson's patrimonialism while the architecture of Monticello itself made such an innovation appear strange and Francophile-Italianate. This is an important reason that the Gothic revival became more amenable to Clinton's Knight Templar ideology as Gothic Hall in New York City gave way to Masonic Hall and to the West Building and in the building of General Theological Seminary under Freemason Joel Pintard. Yet, the Hudson River villas remain as a transition point between the great continental definitions of religiosity and policy on the way to Palladian formalism. As the English Jacobite connection between Palladianism and private residency design flourished in the 18th century, notably at Mereworth Castle in Kent, England, the further evolution between the great patrimonial families along the Hudson, notably the Livingstons, with profound Masonic linkages to Holland Lodge No. 8 in New York City and to the prototype of a Masonic intellect, so also emerged a tangible interplay between France and Scotland on Masonic ritual policy definition. Masonic vault symbolism likely emerged within this interplay, as the first ceremonial degree to feature an Enochic-like vault was from which the Ark of the Covenant was derived, was associated with James I (James VI, King of Scotland) in the fourteenth degree in the French Rite of Perfection, an ancestor of the Old Pretender.

Palladian country house Mereworth Castle in Mereworth, Kent, England features a Vitruvian-Palladian dome symbolic of heliocentric rulership and design, built in the 1720s.

The Hudson Valley School of architecture also bore the imprint of Scots architect Sir William Bruce (ca. 1630-1710), whose tour of France mirrored those of his English colleagues tour of Palladian architecture in Italy. On the design of Palladian villas,

> "This in turn has led to the adoption of a triumphal arch motive on the *piano nobile* so that there is a small arch with a mezzanine above it followed by a large arch and then another small window; but the extreme complication of this façade becomes evident when one analyses it in further detail. Not only is there an A B A rhythm of the bays but there are, as it were, counterpoints introduced by the small -

and very Mannerist - pediments set above the smaller arches, which are alternatively triangular and segmental. ...Furthermore, there is a great complication introduced by the texture of columns which separate the bays on the *piano nobile*. ...The front of the building is simple, and rather austere, with a certain amount of texture in the window-surrounds and with a marked emphasis on the vertical, central, elements like a double triumphal arch. "[354]

Palladian architecture can be seen in Walter Livingston's (1740-1797) villa, Teviotdale, a key representative of Franco-Caledonian design. It features a domed central window and pillars supporting an entrance portico inspired by Palladio's Renaissance, *Villa Capra–La Rotunda*, on a smaller scale. The patronal currency of such families laid the groundwork for the migration of French Freemasonry from Hispaniola into upstate New York, notably at Albany as Scots American merchants exercised privateering rights in developing trade routes between the Caribbean, Philadelphia and the Chesapeake Bay. The conduit between high degree Freemasonry, Albany, New York, the run up by Etienne "Stephen" Morin and Henry Andrew Francken's establishment of the so called ineffable degrees of the Rite of Perfection, notably their early pervasive association with the restoration of the Name of God has yet to be fully researched. However, it is the foundation of symbolic transfers ultimately from France into upstate New York which come to balance the influence of Jefferson's Francophile circle with substantial increments before Jefferson which make of Clinton's New York such an important cradle for the embroidery of Freemasonry and architecture in Hudson Valley residencies and which likely position the Ramée intaglio of the Royal Arch of Enoch within the Union College campus design.

THE INFLUENCE OF THE DISTRICT OF COLUMBIA UPON BALTIMORE, MARYLAND

The layout and general design of Baltimore, Maryland, charted in 1797, was influenced by District of Columbia, the New World's City of the Sun; its template came to materialization in 1791-1792. The District of Columbia's vista will be discussed in the next chapter. It all begins with the linkage between

354 Murray, Peter, *The Architecture of the Italian Renaissance*, pages 185 and 238.

the Roman Catholic establishment of Maryland with refugee recusants in 1584 to the symbolization of Grand Master Andrew Jackson as a paragon initiatic President through references to his Royal Arch Masonic affiliation is dotted with initiatives to universalize Catholicism through intellectual currents of what became Freemasonry as it emerged from the refinement of Zoroastrian inspired ideology. In specific, Lord Baltimore's colony provided the seedbed for accommodating post-Tridentate Catholicism and its vision as Ramsay expounded it for a national Masonic dream of millennial expansion via his Oration. The most likely model for the microcosm envisaged by the founders of the District of Columbia can be traced through the Carroll family from Baltimore into the creation of Georgetown University as a symbol of the restoration of universal knowledge within the legend of Enoch's vault from the invocation of the Tetragrammaton, so visible in the aesthetics of Il Gesu, The Church of the Holy Name of Jesus a/k/a the Mother Church of the Jesuit Order, and the origination of the Baroque style of architecture as an evolution from Andrea Palladio and his Vitruvian inspiration (see Plate XXIV). This element featured domes as throne rooms for the Apollonian triumphal tacit within the design of Mereworth Castle in Kent, England and in Jefferson's Monticello; and positioned the Jesuit mythology as a template for the unfolding of majestic solar order as an expression of the restoration and renovation of wisdom derived from the correct pronunciation of the ineffable Name of God, *le Nom de Dieu.* Again Ramsay's vision, which derived from his devotion to Universalism over Calvinist predestination, was a theme in the world of U.S.A. Scottish Rite founder Frederick Dalcho.

The legacy of nominal religious liberty in Maryland and in Baltimore through the George Calvert family likely inspired members of the Carroll family, both Anglican and Roman Catholic to apply their *palatine powers* as Lords Proprietors to make way for a New World concept of religious pluralism in the City of Baltimore which early developed Jesuit ideas of aristocracy in England to utopian concepts through Jesuit Henry More (1586-1661), descendant of English Chancellor Sir Thomas More, and the Provincial of the English order. This element unified the principal of an English Catholic bishop, e.g. of Durham, to colonial administration mediated through James I's relaxation of the Act of Supremacy of 1534. It further

Title page of Dr. John Dee's *General and Rare Memorials pertayning to the Perfect Arte of Navigation*, 1576.

developed the ideas linking court culture at the center of Elizabethan and James I's policy toward empire and colonial expansion rooted in the theories of occultist Dr. John Dee who believed England's imperial concept was linked to its astrological destiny through the mathematics of navigation and thus introduced the same linkage anticipated by Ramsay of the cosmological relationship between the two as it related to the expansion of liberty and irenic religious toleration.

The policy of religious toleration was carried on by both the Prince of Wales, Henry Stuart and the daughter of King James I of England, the Countess Palatine of the Rhine: Elizabeth Stuart whose consort became Frederick V, the Protestant "Winter" King of Bohemia precipitating the Thirty Years War were identified with hermeticism and cabalism applied to imperial and colonial policy along utopian lines. For example, Elizabeth and Frederick patronized the kabbalistic-cabalistic garden at Heidelberg known as *Hortus Palatinus*.[355] The architect of the garden was Salomon de Caus (1576-1626); the garden featured mechanical fountains, labyrinths leading to statues of Hermes and Minerva, pyramids, and other occult and polyhedral

Engraving of *Hortus Palatinus*; a symbol of proto-enlightenment that embraced Pythagorean harmonics. It was slowly destroyed during the Thirty Years War by the same reactionary forces that burnt Bruno at the stake and stemmed the tide of inquiry in Protestant Europe.

355 Curl, *The Art and Architecture of Freemasonry*, page 42.

shapes and forms.[356] Known as the Eighth Wonder of the World, the Protestant-Renaissance-Rosicrucian garden embraced astrological order synchronized with Platonic and Pythagorean harmonics.[357] "It might as well have been a Masonic frontispiece."[358] Thus the maze would come to represent a quest for wisdom, especially occult, to those who solved its riddles and hence intellectual perfection.

Further, Elizabeth was the mother of the Electress Sophia of Hanover, mother to future King of England George I. George I was a patron of the proto-Masonic ritualist John Toland whose work *Pantheisticon* (1720) laid the utopian ground work within Freemasonry for the elaboration of higher degrees envisaged by the Chevalier Ramsay. Toland, in specific, was aware of the theories of Lord Herbert of Cherbury, the originator of English Deism who rooted his writings in an explication of comparative religion notably Zoroastrianism as the moral warrant from which a ruler might draw for moral precepts necessary for policy and nonsectarian religious policy. Toland himself was fully aware that Christianity was anything but original. Within the American context, this policy first found expression in the Toleration Act of 1649, granting religious liberty to all Christians in Maryland and establishes a working model for later adoption in 1776, the same year as the creation of the deistic Illuminati, of the religious side to political liberty referenced in the Declaration of Independence and ultimately codified in the First Amendment.

The convergence of these Renaissance attitudes in Maryland, even what one could describe as Rosicrucian, can be seen in the architecture and layout of the District of Columbia, a seemingly prototype of city of Baltimore which lies approximately 50 miles to the northeast of the Federal City on the shores of the Chesapeake Bay. The District of Columbia not surprisingly would rest on what was originally Maryland soil in an area known as Foggy Bottom. The template of the District of Columbia was first created by French architect Pierre Charles L' Enfant in 1791. Baltimore's layout borrows from it. Baltimore's early vista features a domed building

356 Ibid.
357 Ibid.
358 Ibid.

Photo of Baltimore, 1850, from the Peale Museum: Latrobe's domed Basilica overlooks Mills' Washington Monument which parallels the District of Columbia, where Latrobe's domed Capitol overlooks Mills' Washington Monument obelisk. From Mark B. Miller's *Baltimore Transitions*, 1998.

upon a hill: the Baltimore Basilica (a/k/a Basilica of the National Shrine of the Assumption of the Blessed Virgin Mary) overlooking a monument dedicated to the first Masonic President George Washington. The Basilica (see Plate XXV) was the first Roman Catholic cathedral in the United States. It was designed to be entered from the west thus during Sunday service the congregation would face eastward symbolically worshiping the rising sun. Jesuit John Carroll (1735-1815) served as ordinary of the Archdiocese of Baltimore; he was the first archbishop in the United States and lies buried beneath the dome of the Baltimore Basilica. John Carroll also founded Georgetown University in 1791, the same year the cornerstone was laid for the U.S. Capitol, syncretic of two orders of men that mediate the New Third Age within a Joachimite envelope. John Carroll was cousin to Charles Carroll of Carrollton, the only Roman Catholic signer of the Declaration of Independence from Maryland, and brother to the Daniel Carroll; he was one of five men to have signed both the Articles of Confederation and the United States Constitution. Daniel Carroll was a Freemason who chaired of the Federal Commission that designed the District of Columbia.

The architect of the Basilica was Freemason Benjamin Henry Latrobe (1764-1820), the father of American Architecture, who was responsible for another domed building, the U.S. Capitol several years before. The United States Capitol was built between 1791 and 1811, the Basilica between 1806 and 1821, completed one year after Latrobe died in 1820. The design of the Basilica and the use of a dome by Latrobe was likely inspired by the Pantheon in Rome and from Vitruvian and Palladian inspiration. The Basilica's solar dome stands behind two towers, likely inspired by an engraving of Solomon's Temple being razed in Martin van Heemskerck's *Septem Orbis Miracula* as engraved by Philip Galle in 1752. Construction of the Baltimore Basilica began in 1806 and was completed in 1821; likewise the Baltimore George Washington Monument was inspired by what would become the Washington Monument obelisk in the District of Columbia. The Baltimore Washington Monument came to fruition years before the Washington Monument in the District of Columbia but no doubt owes its origins to the L'Enfant plan which also featured a central monument dedicated to George Washington, the first Masonic President.

Solomon's Temple engraved by Philip Galle in 1752 as a domed, circular building with Jachin and Boaz displayed on its porch investing the Basilica as a New World restored Temple and a national Masonic millennial icon. Image from Curl's *The Art and Architecture of Freemasonry*.

Construction began on the Baltimore Washington Monument in 1815 and was completed in 1829, nineteen years before the cornerstone laying ceremony of the Washington Monument in the District of Columbia. The Baltimore Washington Monument was the first monument dedicated to the Virginian; it is a replication of Trajan's Column in Rome. The statue of Washington that sits atop the monument was sculpted by Enrico Causici. The monument owes its design to Masonic *Monitors* that were published and proliferated during this time, many of which with illustrations of particular elements from architectural history enmeshed with public design to reinforce levels of symbolism in meaning within public policy. Among these were the structures of Antonine Rome suggesting a sophisticated metropolis of a global empire suggested by the Rome of Trajan (d. 117 CE). Masonic and classical non-Masonic imagery intertwined to project a national imagery of absolute power, wisdom, and virtue. Trajan's Column, constructed by Apollodorus of Damascus (circa. 113 CE) developed this symbolism with specific regard to intellectual civic mission by erecting Trajan's Column between two libraries, named Trajan's Forum, one Latin, the other Greek. The column fixed at 125 feet, which inscribed a spiral visual narrative of Trajan's Dacian campaigns, linked with the libraries found its way into a succession of 18th century European designs reflective of the Enoch saga of the restoration and celebration of *lost* knowledge. As a civil religious icon, the impact of this imagery was to establish a means to articulate the patriotic mission of a people through symbolic learning which makes the District of Columbia (and Baltimore's) design more intelligible and to anticipate the extended theory of a science of order into the public policy consciousness, as developed by Freemason Roscoe Pound, arguably from the writings of Simon Greenleaf. Subsequent Roman emperors, notably the stoic Marcus Aurelius, refined this idiom in such a way that national legend and history became integrated with philosophical significance. Masonic certificates, as diplomas for personal rank, warrants and charters for organizational legitimacy, came to incorporate the same imagery, evoking the spiral inscriptions of the Trajan and Marcus Aurelius columns[359] resulting in a panoplied and variegated set of unfolding symbologies incorporating heroic deeds of initiation into supreme moral exemplarism, imperial heraldry, and the specific devices associated with the building of King Solomon's Temple. Mills' Baltimore Washington Monument was supposed to incorporate bronze reliefs and inscriptions relating the history and virtues of Washington on its shaft thereby linking the deeds of the man to the destiny of the nation.[360] The Baltimore monument was the first giant freestanding structure to be erected in the New World.[361]

359 The Column of Marcus Aurelius is a Doric column modeled after Trajan's Column celebrating the Roman Emperor. It stands in the Piazza Colonna in Rome.

360 Hayward, Mary Ellen and Frank R. Shivers, Jr., *The Architecture of Baltimore: An Illustrated History,* page 82.

361 Ibid, page 83.

Both monuments to the first Masonic president are overlooked by domed buildings: the Basilica in Baltimore and the Capitol in the District of Columbia. Both Washington Monuments were designed by FreeMasonic architect Robert Mills. His placement of monuments to a Masonic President before domed buildings is indicative of Masonic solar rulership and invested George Washington as the sublime Enochian Magus of the new Masonic Republic; it supports the conclusion, for the forgoing reasons, that the District of Columbia was a symbolic antecedent to what became modern day Baltimore, Maryland. This should not be alarming as both Latrobe and Mills were busy in both Baltimore and the District of Columbia, so too was architect Maximilian Godefroy, a chief competitor to both Latrobe and Mills. Godefroy designs are still seen in Baltimore to this day. He is responsible for the Baltimore Battle Monument on Calvert Street and the sculpture in the tympanum of the Unitarian Church on Charles Street. Godefroy was the architect of the first Masonic Hall in Baltimore. It was built in 1814 but razed in 1895; it sat on the *northeast* corner of St. Paul St. and Lexington Avenue. Godefroy's, Mills', and Latrobe's chief competitor, J. J. Ramée, also designed a building just outside of the old Baltimore City line.

J. J. Ramée, following his rendering of the Union College campus, effected an association between and among former Lt. Colonel in the Continental Army, Baltimore Mayor, and U.S. Senator Samuel Smith (1752 -1839) through the patronage of land speculator and financier David Parish. Samuel Smith was friendly with both Thomas Jefferson and Washington, D. C. architect Pierre L'Enfant. This array placed Smith in further association with the Masonic resonance of Fort Mifflin, near Philadelphia, designed by Dr. Benjamin Franklin and through his commercial privateering interests with Haiti, the source of high degree ceremony transmitted to the United States.

The Samuel Smith legacy in Maryland invested in both architecture and finance with a range of tacit energies and subtleties which placed cosmopolitanism before nationalism with a substantial ingredient of enthusiasm for French literature. Samuel Smith was among the first to envisage the construction of the Washington Monument. As Smith's friend Ramée moved his Union College rendering of the tracing board of the Royal Arch degree ceremony from the campus design, with likely reference to Simon Chaudron's *Apotheosis of Washington* as Enoch engraved by J. J. Barralet; Ramée further proposed that the Washington Monument within the District of Columbia, later erected as an obelisk, be a Royal Arch with the President himself in the place of the Union College symbolic sun, its domed library, with a windowed array of a radial sun burst pointing the way, like Enoch, rising to the heavens; Washington is depicted as the contents of the Vault of Enoch emanating solar light. Ramée's design for the Washington monument depicts Washington as the actual contents of the Vault of Enoch emanating solar resonance. This thread was carried forward in New York City into Washington Square Royal Arch symbolism. The result is a set of dynamic icons which link high degree Masonry to the image and concept ofmonarchy.

Samuel Smith was also linked to the Catholic irenicism of the Calvert legacy and Carroll tradition through his ties to Daniel Carroll. This enthusiasm remained at the aesthetic rather than level of policy, either commercial or statesmanship. It is also likely that Smith knew the Murat brothers, both of whom were Freemasons, Napoleon Lucien Charles was the Grand Master of the French Grand Orient; and Achille, a member of Andrew Jackson's Florida circle of Masonic leaders through his niece, Mrs. Jerome Bonaparte or Betsy Patterson. Patterson Park located in downtown Baltimore is named after her family. Smith also presided over a Masonic cabal linking his brother Robert, Jefferson's Secretary of the Navy, Albert Gallatin, Secretary of the Treasury, in opposition to President John Quincy Adams. It was Quincy Adams who steered the Federalists into the Anti-Masonic Party led by former Attorney General William Wirt, himself a rumored Freemason. Its first nominating convention was held in the Unitarian Church in downtown Baltimore in September 1831. President Andrew Jackson would defeat Wirt as Jackson, like Washington, was a paragon of Freemasonry and unquestioned leader of the emerging Democratic Party. Andrew Jackson (1767-1845) was made a Freemason before 1801, served as deputy Grand High Priest of Tennessee Royal Arch

Masons in 1826, and introduced the Marquis de Lafayette to the Grand Lodge of Tennessee in 1825. He was associated with Aaron Burr in the Ouachita River plan to establish a state between Arkansas and Louisiana, and embodied personal values of leadership deeply resonant with Masonic ideals of natural, aristocratic leadership (*ascensio*), and divine approbation (apotheosis). Jackson, despite pressure, never apologized nor caved in to anti-Masonic sentiments that stemmed from the Morgan Affair. President Andrew Jackson remains one of Freemasonry's staunchest guardians and is linked to Baltimore, Maryland, by defeating William Wirt and his anti-Masonic cabal.

The Samuel Smith Baltimore network also had links to Freemasons Stephen Girard, a banker instrumental in the creation of the first Federal Bank, and multi-millionaire John Jacob Astor (1763-1848), the former of whom maintained a stiff anticlericalism ingredient to his Masonic French-Swiss legacy. Although architect J.J. Ramée was known to Samuel Smith, as was no doubt Latrobe, Mills, and Godefroy; Ramée did not design Samuel Smith's Baltimore estate Montebello; but he did work for another Smith of Baltimore: Denis Smith. Denis Smith, (no relation to Samuel) was a banker involved in the 1918 Baltimore federal bank crash that led to the *McCulloch v. Maryland* Supreme Court decision.

Ramée positioned Minerva, likely in emulation of Union College's Minerva seal in his execution of Calverton (see Plate XXVI) the Denis Smith summer estate which sat 2.5 miles west outside the old Baltimore city line. The sculpture of Minerva at Calverton was created by Antonio Capellano, who created a relief entitled *Preservation of Captain Smith by Pocahontas* within the United States Capitol rotunda. Calverton was ultimately completed after Ramée left for France in 1816, the year coincidentally when DeWitt Clinton organized the Masonic Grand Encampment of Knights Templar, a national network at that time of influential patrimonial Masons who redeveloped Masonic emblemature along Christian ideological lines.

J. J. Ramée's insertion of an Isis inspired goddess of reason and wisdom he alludes to a proto-Marian image, in the estate named after Lord

Calvert, a devout Roman Catholic, commissioned by the Smith family; thus correctly investing Isis or Minerva with the iconography of the Virgin Mary, along the ideological image of absolutism within the Baroque style of late Renaissance material culture. The coupling of the Virgin Mary with Isis (via Minerva) in this way, through the Calvert-Carroll thread of irenic Catholicism within Maryland, provides important evidence that the allusion was an intentional conceit underscoring Roman Catholic mission through Egyptian occultism and apologetics to the destiny of the United States through the Chevalier Ramsay's ideology.

In turn, this appearance with Jeffersonian enthusiasm for French culture from his own Franco-Caledonian roots makes it most persuasive that his own Palladian formulations at Monticello and the use of the Ramée design at the University of Virginia were further icons linking the simplification of an agrarian rusticity with national destiny and an allusion to the Jacobite principle of a return to a new medievalism and chivalry celebrated in Ramsay's high Masonic degrees. This was in effect a cult of liberty within which universal papal monarchy as envisaged by Jesuit missiology with republican virtue as lifted from Augustan Rome and Vitruvius within which the realization of a theology of esoteric Logos was derived from Christian mystic Joachim of Fiore. It was then transmitted into the Clinton-Webb Masonic ritual *haute* degree synthesis and described in detail by Freemason Salem Town as the unfolding of the Royal Arch Word, *qua* Logos, into manifest destiny, and thus westward expansion via the Mississippi bringing liberty, nationalism, and fraternity to the expanding boundaries of the new Masonic Republic. Thus the arrangement in the St. Andrew's Hurd Plate of 1790 of specific Irish Masonic totems into a solar-Enochic path of national initiation made clear, further, that this path was a symbolic effort, again as outlined by Ramsay within his Zoroastrian theodicy as discussed in his *Voyages of Cyrus*, that autonomous mythic entities to gain power allegorically through the irenic religiosity of Cyrus the Great and utilize the Second Temple at Jerusalem as an icon of national millennial destiny. As nativist driven anti-Catholicism prospered in the wake of massive Irish immigrations in cities such as Baltimore (and New York), the period following profound anti-Masonry, allegations were made that the Whore of Babylon *lusted* to become the Holy City of Jerusalem and was attempting to do so through a restored Freemasonry dominated by higher degrees notably the Ramsay ideology of the Scottish Rite.

Not only did Baltimore emulate the design and philosophies encrusted within new Federal City, it followed suit with its own philanthropic institutions promoting New World enlightenment. Baltimore would be home to arguably the greatest hospital in the world: Johns Hopkins University which opened in 1876. It should come as no surprise that its first president was Bonesmen Daniel Coit Gilman (1831-1908) who had been instrumental in the creation of Skull and Bones (known as the Russell Trust, its members are called Bonesmen) secret society at Yale University. This society was derived from German Masonic influences associated with the range of high degrees including the Rite of Strict Observance and developed parallel to a further order called "Mystic Seven" at Wesleyan University in Middletown, Connecticut which shaped the development of one of the earliest college fraternities at the Miami University (Ohio) called Beta Theta Pi. Baltimore was also home to both the first lodge, Washington Lodge #1, and the Grand Lodge of Odd Fellows in America; the former being formed in 1819, the latter in 1821. Odd Fellowship was founded in Baltimore by an eccentric Englishman named Thomas Wildey (1782-1861). Baltimore also saw the creation of a secret society called the Knights of the Golden Eagle in 1872 emblematic of a new age chivalric Templar Order. Both Odd Fellows and the Golden Eagle, like Freemasonry, promoted humanistic and hermetical ideals through symbolic rituals intended to teach moral instruction while concealing their own respective esoteric secrets through veiled and hidden allegory.

The Basilica Cathedral of St. Louis and the "Royal" Gateway Arch to the West

The intellectual vitality of early American republic Freemasonry can be traced to the energies expended upon its expansion into the American frontier following the War of Independence. The evidence for this energy can be seen in the devolution of almost random orders and rites descended from the ideas which shaped and informed the Ramsay ideology of higher degrees such that a unique American or York Masonic Rite emerged from discretely differentiated emblematic sources as evidenced in the Royal Arch Hurd Plate of 1790. This pathway icon documented the creation through extension of Royal Arch Chapters, Cryptic Councils of Royal and Select Masters, and Encampments and Commanderies of Knights Templar as coordinated Masonic rite of sequential chronological episodes, with some disjuncture, governed by different governance entities with a common thread or theme linking the loss, recovery, preservation and Christian interpretation of the Masonic Word, the ineffable name of God, following the pattern established in the drama of the Third Degree of Master Mason.

The Jesuit Order, *Societas Iesu*, has long been associated with Freemasonry, especially the high degrees, despite various condemnations of Freemasonry by intermittent Popes, beginning in 1738 with Pope Clement XII. Clement XII believed that masterminds behind the revival of Freemasonry in 1717 were one and the same as those who brought about the Lutheran Reformation years earlier. Evidence of a conspiracy or papal paranoia? We may never know; nevertheless there is an ambiguous yet persistent thread linking the Ignatian concepts of Counter-Reformation with Masonic enthusiasms which has never been satisfactorily unraveled. Yet, the very persistence of the latent similarities between the two traditions, notably the emphasis upon Egyptianate symbolism of ancient Empire applied to papal monarchy, and to Pythagorean lore underscores the significance of the dual heritage of the two currents of ideas. It must be explained that the Jesuits of today do not resemble by in large the Jesuits that existed prior Congress of Vienna of 1814-1815. The Jesuit Order,

> "...was founded in 1534 by Ignatius Loyola, a Spaniard of ardent imagination and earnest spirit, and was confirmed by Pius III in 1540. There can be little doubt that he intended it to be a mystical and contemplative association, resembling, in many things, the colleges of Egyptian priests; . . .The Jesuits appear to have taken the Egyptian priests for their model. Like them, they were the conservators and interpreters of religion. The vows, they pronounced, bound them to their company, as indissolubly as the interest and politics of the

> Egyptian priests fixed them in the sacred college of Memphis. ...After the Order of Jesus had fallen from it high estate, and became merely a secret society of political agitators and intriguers, some ardent enthusiastic men conceived the idea of superseding it by a new Order (cf. von Fiore's Third Age of the Holy Spirit) that should retain all the good of the old, and be better adapted to the circumstances of modern times, and the wants of modern society. The Society of the Illuminati and that of the Rosicrucians were formed with this aim and purpose. The adepts of the Illuminati were governed by rules nearly identical with those of the Jesuits, and the whole machinery of the two orders was constructed after the same idea."[362]

The Jacobite influences within Freemasonry, in particularly, appear to transcend the surface contradictions between restored medieval chivalry, attached to the Jesuit zeal for Catholic triumphalism and apologetics associated with the ideal of a restored Stuart claimant to the British throne, and Enlightenment rationalism and reach into the value of Jesuit missiology as an extension of utopian concepts of Roman Catholic iconography articulated in the New World. Indeed, the entire Scottish Rite ritual cultural ethos, derived from Paris, through Bordeaux, and the West Indies was carried into Charleston and New Orleans in such a way that it suggests the appeal of a Catholic and Masonic ritual amalgam that drove unified sets of symbolism into material culture linked to the otherwise disparate currents of symbolism which Freemasonry and Counter-Reformation enthusiasms shared; notably, Renaissance thought: hermetical, cabalistic, Neo-Platonic and Joachimite; the Third Age vernacular associated with the medieval prophet and millennialist Joachim of Fiore. It was the latter influence which indeed appeared to recapitulate and define parallel and previous currents of intellectual history into a single common rhetoric of an irenic Third Age of the Holy Spirit, following upon the first *Age of the Father*; a second age, *Age of the Son*, into a vibrant millennial age midwifed into policy and imperial realization through a set of prophetic of two orders foreseen by Joachim, an order of hermits and an order of monks the former the Masonic Order with the second of the two being Jesuits. The precision of the parallel between the Jesuit ideal of a peaceful, irenic papal empire and the Masonic vista of

362 Macoy, Robert, *A Dictionary of Freemasonry*, pages 181-182.

a utopian Egyptianate reign of brotherly love, perhaps best exemplified by Mozart's vision of Sarastro's (*qua* Zoroastrian) court in *The Magic Flute* strikes a commonality of mission of purpose which historians have found difficult to ignore. In specific, the French hegemony within the Mississippi Valley appears to be linked in concrete ways through New Orleans and the city of St. Louis such that Baroque icons of the Tetragrammaton, the Name of God, can be seen within Masonically nuanced higher degree symbolism worked in Louisiana, named after the Sun King Louis XIV, and from the symbolism of Baltimore, Maryland. This symbolism takes form (prior to the Louisiana Purchase) in the architecture of the first St. Louis Cathedral of New Orleans of 1727, modeled after the baroque Il Gesu; and finally into the Cathedral Basilica of St. Louis and the St. Louis "Royal" Arch-Gateway to the West Monument memorializing the connection of the Mississippi valley to New York by way of the Erie Canal. The St. Louis Cathedral of New Orleans (rebuilt in 1850) is the seat of the Roman Catholic Archdiocese in New Orleans. It sits next to Jackson Square which features a statute of Masonic Grand Master Andrew Jackson symbolically linking Freemasonry with Catholicism, in stone. It cannot be stressed enough that Freemasonry shares with Catholic apologetics a common concern: the integration of the contemplation of esoteric or inchoate teachings through symbolism, verbal and visual, with activity. All of Masonry moves in such a way culturally that

The 1727 St. Louis Cathedral of New Orleans was modeled after *Il Gesu*, the mother church of the Jesuits.

the individual Freemason is urged to move the rough ashlar of his existence into the smooth ashlar of moral perfection. Indeed, it is shared ideal of spiritual perfection, which Calvinism denied was possible in a world after the Fall of Adam and Eve in the Garden of Eden, but which the Ramsay high degree ideology and Ignatian spirituality shared in common. The primacy of the Enochic ritual paragon underscored this concern. The two orders were parallel to the two Pillars of Enoch: one contemplative, the Freemasons; the other evangelical, the Jesuits.

The imperial network of French Monarchy was symbolized by a gift of a painting, by the restored Bourbon King Louis XVIII, within Benjamin Latrobe's second Apollonian domed building in the Roman Catholic Basilica in Baltimore, Maryland. The painting is titled, *St. Louis (Louis IX of France) Burying his Plaque-Stricken Troops Before Tunis A.D. 1270* (see Plate XXVII). The placement of King Louis IX, wearing the tunic of a Knight Templar, while combating the Egyptian Empire (Eighth Crusade) appears to represent Louis XVIII's deep interests in the mysteries of Egypt. It was King Louis XVIII who requested an obelisk for Paris from Khedive (Viceroy) Muhammad Ali Pasha of Egypt as a new symbol of his solar kingship of France.[363] The gift of the painting of Louis IX in Egypt to the Baltimore Archdiocese sent a symbolic message to the Bonapartes of Baltimore: Jerome's brother, Emperor Napoleon I, was a pretender and thus the illegitimate successor to the kingdom of Egypt. The painting also served as a possible cryptic warning to their other brother, Joseph Bonaparte, a Freemason and former King of Spain now exiled in New Jersey. The warning was simple: the Catholic Church and the Bourbon Monarchy in specific will not forget that it was *you* who ended the Spanish Inquisition as it was King Louis IX who drastically expanded the Inquisition within France. As such the imagery of Baltimore, *Mary*land (cf. Marian-Isian symbolism) became linked to a triumphant concept of expanding irenic looking Catholic missiology just prior to massive Roman Catholic immigration into the United States. This positioned the Louisiana Purchase of 1804 as an added province within which to unfold Masonic jurisprudence and with its integration of legendary esoteric symbolism and

363 Habachi, Labib, *The Obelisks of Egypt*, page 156.

mathematically precise Pythagorean Nilotic order of the Mississippi River via New Orleans and the Erie Canal achieved through Scottish Rite (cf. Stuart imagery via Ramsay's Oration), Clinton's York Rite (cf. Knights Templar) and Blue Lodge Masonic solar imperial and cosmological order. This imagery can be seen in the architecture of the city of St. Louis, named after King of France Louis IX, the only canonized King of France.

Louis IX (1214-1270) was a devout Catholic and emblematic of Christian piety and rulership of France. His membership in the medieval Templar Order has been debated, nevertheless he led the Seventh Crusade featuring a contingent of Knights Templar led by Templar Robert of Artois, against the Egyptians , 1248-1254. The Crusade was a failure and resulted in the capture of Louis; a ransom was paid for his release from Egyptian ruler Ayyubid Sultan Turanshah. Louis IX was also responsible for collecting *alleged* relics relating to Jesus Christ. He acquired a piece of the True Cross and the Crown of Thorns worn by Christ during the Passion. The nexus linking St. Louis, Missouri to Maryland can be seen in the symbolism and design of The Cathedral Basilica of St. Louis in the city of St. Louis: it is a replication of the Baltimore Basilica partially informed, no doubt, by the painting of Louis IX within the Latrobe's domed Baltimore Basilica. The Cathedral Basilica of St. Louis features two towers emblematic of the Enochian Pillars before an Apollonian dome indicative of Masonic solar symbolism and expansion of Masonic values westward. The Cathedral Basilica of St. Louis was completed in 1912 and was the Archdiocesan replacement for the original Basilica of Saint Louis, King of France, the first cathedral west of Mississippi. The first Basilica of St. Louis today is dwarfed by the Gateway Arch to the West, an actual Masonic Arch symbolic of the Templar Order (Knight of the Ninth Arch). The Gateway Arch also encodes Masonic-astrological alignments.

The cornerstone to the Gateway Arch was laid on February 12, 1963. Instead of an actual cornerstone being laid the first of the 142 steel sections as part of its foundation was set in place. The keystone was set in place on October 28, 1965, coinciding with the anniversary of the dedication of the Masonic Statue of Liberty in New York Harbor kabbalistically linking the Mississippi valley forever to the Clinton's York Rite Knight Templary nuanced Empire State. The halfway point between February 12, 1963 and October 28, 1965 is *June 21, 1964.* June 21 is the date of the summer solstice when the sun reaches the keystone, its apex, within the house of Cancer as the sun travels along the northern "Royal Arch" of the Zodiac. The Gateway Arch to the West is, in actuality, a monument symbolic of the both the Royal Arch of Enoch, and the Royal Arch of the Zodiac. The Arch dominates the skyline of the city of St. Louis, which is named after Catholic King and Saint, Louis IX, conforming with the concept of divine, papal monarchy in Ramsay's *haute* degree ideology and mythology. It is a sublime example of hidden Masonic solar symbolism in the United States and echoes the iconography of the modern day Adocentyn: the District of Columbia, the Masonic *City of the Sun*. But to fully understand the symbolism in Washington, D.C., one must first comprehend the impact of Masonic law.

CHAPTER XIII

MASONIC LAW AND SEMIOTICS

Simon Greenleaf, Charles Sanders Peirce,
and Emanuel Swedenborg

"The ethical value of Masonic law and counsel
in those matters which belong to the
conduct of life in the value of moral law -
written or unwritten - as recognised - *mutatis mutandis* -
by civilised conscience at all times everywhere.
Masonry, by its proper hypothesis, is 'a system
of morality, veiled in allegory and illustrated by symbols.'"
-Arthur Edward Waite, *A New Encyclopedia of
Freemasonry*, 1970.

The founding Dean of Harvard Law School, Freemason Simon Greenleaf (1783-1853) published *A Brief Inquiry into the Origin and Principles of Freemasonry* in 1820. Greenleaf claimed Freemasonry descended from the Pythagorean and Druidic Mystery Schools.Attorneys to Greenleaf were New World Pythagorean Magi who interpreted and exercised great care and prudence in the promulgation of the law. As founding father John Adams stated, the New World was to be governed by "laws, not men." Greenleaf also authored *Treatise on the Law of Evidence* (III vols., 1842-1853), *A Full Collection of Cases Overruled, Denied, Doubted, or Limited in their Application, taken from American and English Reports* (1821), *Reports of Cases Argued and Determined by the Supreme Judicial Court of the State of Maine* (1820-1832), and a biography of his colleague Joseph Story *A Discourse Commemorative of the Life and Character of the Hon. Joseph Story* (1845). Greenleaf's *Lectures* were contemporary with Salem Town's *A System of Speculative Masonry* (1818) and constitute a companion piece to this work designed by an early pre-eminent legal educator. As such, again contemporaneous with Samuel T. Coleridge, who cultivated the idea of chivalric literati within the envelopes of Romanticism; Greenleaf's objective was to develop a Masonic clerisy as an ideal for the educated Harvard lawyer which he envisaged as the Clerk Templars chivalric Egyptian priest. The Clerks of Strict Observance –founded in 1767– was led by Johann Auguste Starck who stated that the order was a descendant of the clerical or legal arm of the Templars and that it wished to reunite with what it saw as the descendants of the military arm of the Templars as exemplified by von Hund's Rite of Strict Observance. Greenleaf's premise was simple: to lift up the deeper meaning of the basic Masonic obligation as the foundation for the patrons of L'Enfant's utopian city and Latrobe's domed Apollonian chambers. Greenleaf also wrote at a time when the legendary history of the Craft was still perceived to be empirical narrative. Thus his treatise on the origin of Freemasonry details what his contemporaries thought about the deeper meanings of the Fraternity. In this capacity, he constructed his own intelligentsia of Masonic lawyers as an extended clerisy, including articulate non-lawyers whose circles were shaped and informed by initiate attorneys as they assumed leaderly careers pointing toward Washington, D. C. Greenleaf was careful to pinpoint the sources for his treatise, notably its Scottish linkages which proposed the core Ramsay ideology through the works of Elias Ashmole, since lost, and a *History of Free Masonry* (1804) by Alexander Lawrie which linked Freemasonry to ancient mystery religions through Scottish Masonry to England.

Simon Greenleaf's Masonic work documents the relationship between defining the Patriarch Enoch as a Pythagorean figure, while linking the Druidical priestly presence through Phoenician exploration of Egyptian sources. Thus Enoch brought the content of Masonic knowledge to a greater mystical perfection as he was deemed to have caused the emergence of the restoration of learning from the vault into solar Apollonian radiance through the application of Pythagorean learning to the inspiration of the new Republic through mathematics and the laws derived from it. The result was for Greenleaf a precritical logic of unfolding of the Logos envisaged by Salem Town along lines delineated in the L'Enfant-Latrobe District of Columbia template from the national capital into districts of Masonic Grand Lodge administration was devolved into districts, paralleling judicial and congressional districts, symbolically as an extension of the Latrobe-L'Enfant template just after the moral and political defeat of Jedidiah Morse and the Federalists in 1800[364] and theological attacks on Masonry and before the onset of the Morgan fervor in 1826. This period enables the historian to see a sequence of Masonic and mythic legal unfolding from legendary history which linked the emergence of Enochic design to civil religion through monumental architecture which also links the dynamism of a Third Age of Masonic millennialism rooted in Third Age eschatology within its Tudor derivative of an articulate citizen (cf. Elyot's The *Boke named the Governour*) applied to the patronage of architecture into republican administration which *lines up* Enoch, Pythagoras, Phoenicia-Egypt through the evangelical fervor of Celtic and Druidical lore into Scottish Masonic environs which made of the latter a purified sect of solar inspired fervent priestly republicans. The same template gives the premier likely conduit for Jesuit penetration of the Masonic agenda through various reservoirs of Masonic-Egyptian symbolism and makes of the Druids a likely metaphor for the Society of Jesus just as Joachim of Fiore's ideal of a new order of spiritual men was used for this purpose under the principle of a *Novus Dux*; a further likely image for the Unknown Superior of Strict Observance ritual positioned Counter-Reformation apologetically theory for application to the United States.

Greenleaf, in specific, envisaged the Pythagorean metaphor, which arguably was taken and developed in various ways by Salem Town in his elucidation of the Clintonian concept of a public sphere as a positivistic pursuit of perfection as a policy through the state's administration ofpublic works. These were rendered as the result of a mediating order mission to *contemplate* as Enoch heavenly secrets as divine and spiritual objects, namely arithmetic, music, geometry and astronomy understood as problems respective to the meaning of numbers and magnitude. The same subject matter was unfolded from the Masonic meaning of the Middle Chamber lecture in the Webb ritual, and in both versions of the Royal Arch degree with which both Webb and Greenleaf worked. This construct enabled

364 Thomas Jefferson and the Jeffersonian Republican-Democrats defeated John Adams and the Federalists in the 1800 Presidential elections.

Greenleaf to develop Freemasonry as a means to explicate Jeffersonian principles with a kind of secular mysticism through which numbers and implicitly intelligent forms in the divine mind were set to play to explain, through Masonic ritual, how nature through reason developed from a socio-political unity comprehended as a core metaphysic into the whole culture assuming new properties through a collective pursuit of progress in the rhetoric of national initiation, as illustrated in the arrangement of the solar St. Andrew's Royal Arch Hurd Plate (1790). The raw material of this progress could be measured from the ideas depicted by Desaguliers and Anderson in the principles and symbolism of geometry applied to the political organization of the nation through surveying and organization of transportation, notably the engineering of bridges and canals as symbolically emanating from a first being and progressing through various orders, the mediating clerisy itself which thereafter ordered respective emanations into a coherent symbolization of an extended utopian political economy. This was understood to be ineffable because it linked heliocentric Hermeticism to the possession of the Name of God through Masonic ritual illustrated through symbols and resemblances to numbers. The imagery of Egypt pervaded this application of Masonic ritual to social engineering and policy, and eventually through American philosophical pragmatism to the social engineering of legislation and judicial administration.

Simon Greenleaf was careful to point out how both Copernican and Newtonian models for utopian thought could be traced to Pythagoras and in turn to Egypt. This concept meant that the initiate into Freemasonry was both a candidate to become a philosopher-king, and through this office a further candidate, like Enoch, by means of contemplation to be assimilated into an assembly of the gods, a celestial, heavenly lodge as a pantheon of adepts. This status was conferred through Masonic initiation by integrating through private Masonic prayer and public virtues, symbolized through linking education to legislation by means of friendships and reverence for the dead in the Chamber of Reflection. Such would be an apt summary for Clinton's public sphere, created and maintained through Freemasonry, as a means to imitate God, and through such contemplation *to become like a priest of Egypt, the Jesuit ideal.*

Greenleaf directly anticipated the proliferation of voluntary fraternalism in the United States as an agency to disseminate moral and mathematically nuanced Pythagorean ideologies through cadres of white robed priests. This pointed through Freemasonry to Odd Fellowship, the Knights of Pythias, Mechanics, Red Men; to Elks, Moose, and the Fraternal Order of the Eagles leading toward the Knights of Columbus as extended sodalities each of which articulated a role for a legally trained cadre of magi or officers skilled in metaphorical wisdom and in philanthropic mission. Odd Fellowship in specific dated from 1819 and was the first fraternal order within the country to consolidate a national grand lodge with concomitant laws rooted in Antediluvian order which symbolically devolved into hermetically inspired Kabbalism through a Royal Arch motif, the Royal Arch of Titus. It followed the railroads and became identified with important politicians such as Schuyler Colfax and industrialists such as Leland Stanford, Sr. both of whom applied the network to the expansion of the railroads, Colfax as an attorney, Stanford as a capitalist. Colfax invented the Rebekahs, the Odd Fellow female degree, anticipating the opening of the fraternal tradition to women and an alliance between esotericism and domesticity carried into localities by the Eastern Star and the Daughters of the American Revolution, the emblem of which alluded to the female Masonic grade of Heroines of Jericho, a Royal Arch auxiliary. This nexus followed from Greenleaf's ideology to reconcile the teachings of the ancient mysteries with Biblical references as an extension of the Desaguliers and Anderson legendary history and to see analogues, and parallels between Masonic hagiography and the Biblical, confessional witness, epitomized in the Knight Templar orders.

Greenleaf was also careful to delineate that his Druids were skilled in rhetoric to fabricate two sets of material and political symbols; a likely allusion to Jesuit duplicity, one open only to initiates and concealed to others; another for public consumption. The former included the secret doctrine of the one God understood in Royal Arch terms of the Tetragrammaton, J-B- O-, the syncretistic revision of JHVH at the core of the Clinton Webb system and pointed to the latter's insistence that so long as the Royal Word was itself eclectic, incorporating Jewish, Babylonian and Egyptian elements of symbolism, the civil religion of the nation as implemented by Clinton's regime would be irenically safe. The result points to a thread of Universalist irenicism witnessed in Clinton's own anticipation of Irish immigration to the American electorate and its merger with French Catholic legal infrastructure in Louisiana aptly linked through Scottish Enlightenment Masonic ideology of applied Pythagoreanism seeking a perfected moral and civil order in pursuit of a just imperial order.

Greenleaf was at pains to reconcile lodge going Masons with critical meanings of the administration of his Enochic-Pythagorean vision as an extension of the core iconology achieved in the District of Columbia template. This involved, inter alia, a careful emphasis upon the necessity for opening the lodge and conducting its affairs carefully as a means to achieve the eschatological solar symbolisms implicit in the L'Enfant-Latrobe Apollonianism and in specific to establish, notably through a Christian interpretation the importance of preserving astral imagery through the Blazing Star motif in Lodge ritual as a star of Sirius, the Eastern Star identified with the Virgin mother Isis *qua* Mary, and the coming of Christ, *Sol Invictus*. This latter emblem married Masonic symbolism with Marian-Isis imagery translatable into Minerva, and her Greek equivalent Pallas Athena, symbolism later incorporated into the seal of Union College, Schenectady, New York and the Greek-letter fraternity system founded there from Phi Beta Kappa, William and Mary, Williamsburg, Virginia, from Masonic roots, and establishing the significance of retain the *as above, so below* metaphors from Hermeticism and Kabbalism-Cabalism within District of Columbia millennial imagery. The latter was specifically significant in retaining the infrastructure of American legal links to the role of the articulate citizen in the English Renaissance which relied conceptually on a working model for a spiritual monarchy linked to Constitutional mission through relics of medieval stately symbolism. This further implied the importance of incorporating Anglicanism, as a political theory, within a broader mission to reform Catholicism to accommodate American mission as a descendant of English Common Law theory extrapolated by Sir John Fortescue in *The Governance of England.*

To Greenleaf the reach between Astronomy, Astrology, and Geometry was necessary to preserve through public architecture a symbolization for the construction of a new *res publica Christianum* within which a secularized spirituality linked legislative and judicial process to an expanding coherent physical universe. Greenleaf viewed Freemasonry as a handmaiden to Christianity shorn of its sectarian and confessional exclusivism and as a joint enterprise in the pursuit of a gospel of peace with what became mainline Christian denominationalism. This represented a de facto marginalization of American Christianity such that local churches developed as adjuncts and vice versa to lodges of various sorts integrating a *Christianate esoterica* within which Masonic ideas of civil religion flourished and framed material culture, symbolically, as an unfolding template of political and material order. Greenleaf lived through the Morgan anti-Masonic furor and presumably was involved in the reconstruction of the fraternity following this setback.

* * * * *

Freemasonry's impact upon the legal profession can also be traced to the role of mythography through ritual imagery in the construction of networks which integrated secularized principles of a mystically shaped initiatic cadre of lawyers moving toward the refutation of the positive symbols of myth in a rising pragmatism and instrumentalism in the legislative mission of the law. This meant that even though specific Masons were eminent Freemasons, it was not the esoteric elements which came to the surface, as for example the panoply of the monarchy suffused English legal symbolism, through the House of Lords and the purpose of the Law Lords: the most senior members of the judiciary of England. Rather, it was through a decided mission of Simon Greenleaf through his *Treatise on the Laws of Evidence*; DeWitt Clinton on the use of the law in the framing of patterns of patronage for reform; and later Roscoe Pound, an eminent Masonic scholar and Dean of the Harvard Law School who insisted upon the role of judges within the legislative process and upon the law as a quintessentially rational process *apart* from the law as deduction from divinely ordained principles of ethics. In this instance, Masonic jurists such as David Brearley, Chief Justice of New Jersey, Grand Master of New Jersey, and the author of the constitution of the Protestant Episcopal Church (USA) applied his secular skill to creating a bicameral legislature within American Anglicanism without complicating references to numinosity or its *via media* mysticism or the occult. Similarly, members of Giles Fonda Yates' family were active within researching and writing on the mystical symbols of the Scottish Rite (NMJ), as was Albert Pike a generation later, but were careful to separate their Masonic mission from their legal theorizing about the role of law. This did not mean that substantial contributions were not made to the concrete infrastructure of the court system districts and to the town by town, county by county, selection of Masonic affiliated judges and legal educators, but that the law as a Masonic sodality came to operate separately from its mythic origins, such as can be seen in Greenleaf's writings and in Pound's linking through parallels between Freemasonry and the legal workings of the medieval Church, as he did for example, in Masonic Jurisprudence an address given at Harvard in 1917. Pound thus spoke,

> "If the law of the medieval Church became for a time the law of the world and gave idcas and doctrines to the law of the state which are valuable for all time, it is not at all impossible that our universal organization, coming much later to the work of lawmaking, may in its turn develop legal ideas of universal value which contributing directly thereto in its ordinary work."[365]

In the case, for example, of Oliver Wendell Holmes, Jr., a member of Pound's circle, this involved an unpretentious elucidation on the role of historical explanation attendant to his dissenting opinions, which became a personal mark of his distinction in viewing the law as an adjunct of political process. The result was, in Holmes' case, a perduring philosophical interest in the law as a social science which evokes French essayist and poet Charles Peguy's (1873-1914) noted dictum: *everything begins in mysticism and ends in politics*. This development, it should be said, paralleled the movement of theological ethics within the Churches toward post-Kantian emphasis upon reason, as opposed to revelation, the structuring of ethical

365 Pound, Roscoe, *Lectures on Masonic Jurisprudence*, page 21.

and moral discourse as it was applied, through the Social Gospel and Progressive movements, for example, into public policy. Toward the end of the 19th century, the issues facing Freemasons about the law tended to pivot on two points; 1) the separation between values and obligation from the movement of symbolism within the law; and 2) a secular (Masons often used the word profane in a similar instance) which denied the inevitability that insistence upon the forms of Druidical-Pythagoreanism detailed by Greenleaf must lead toward totalitarianism, wherein judicial review and legislation become de facto the same process. Rather, Masonic legal educators such as Pound, deeply steeped in Masonic symbolism as well as in the training of Harvard lawyers, were determined to be as precise as possible about applying scientific philosophy to the law whilst rendering its methods as an obstacle to the symbolic logic arguably at the center of linking mathematical mysticism to the prevailing civil religion of the nation. In short, they became determined opponents to undue cooperation between Church and State within the Scottish Rite (SJ) via a massive educational commitment involving lobbying and publication.

Just as the Judicial Act of 1789, creating the U.S. federal judiciary, opened great wells of power over the states and even over the great man himself, George Washington, it constructed subdivisions within the nation within which that power was concentrated and from which it emanated. It was inevitable that esoteric symbolism would come to be associated with the Court through such Freemasons as DeWitt Clinton, as discussed an eminent city mayor and state governor and through Greenleaf as the jurisdictions came to resemble districts of the Grand Lodges and as other eminent Freemasons were appointed to the Bench. Even the institution of the Court at the Royal Exchange in New York City took on the symbolism of an exchange of a monarchy for a republic as the decision was addressed whether or not the United States was (simply) a League of Sovereign States or a new nation. Masonically, the Court resembled a Masonic Supreme Council of the higher degrees. Such bodies contained ceremonials relevant pointedly to the judgment of Craftsmen, including the assassins of Hiram Abif, with titles such as "Provost and Judge." Cosmic symbolism was also present. A judge dresses in the black robes[366] of the father of the gods representing Saturn-Kronos, who instructs and informs twelve jurors in the box of the law and their duties; the twelve jurors symbolize the twelve houses of the zodiac. The Scottish Rite Supreme Councils, one in the South in 1801 another in the North in 1813, were an aseity and did not depend, as did Grand Lodges that governed local craft lodges, upon constituent lodges for their existence, but upon the rank and standing of its members. The paramountcy and hegemonics of the Supreme Court entailed a de facto presidency over an entire learned profession as well which came to constitute a legal de facto priesthood rooted in self-regulation and canons of practical wisdom affected by peers. As the Supreme Court came to represent the potentially conflicting interests of popular sovereignty vs. fundamental law and as the United States Constitution achieved symbolic, if not sacral status, responsibility evolved upon the legal profession to act as a mediating priesthood on behalf of the nation. As a result, elements of subjectivity entered both into the profession as a secular clerisy and into the operations of the etiquette of the law which left to individual lawyers broad interpretation with regard to how laws were to be adjudicated. This variety and variegation altered the dynamic, even the majesty of the law from state to state and by differing federal districts with the result that the large regions outside of statutory enactments were left to the discretion of specific attorneys whose training was not at all standardized and well into the 19th century. As a result both the Churches and lodges came to be training grounds for these subjective elements with the result that official position in one arena would and could often be interpreted as proficiency in the other.

The Masonic author Roscoe Pound[367] (1870-1964), has written persuasively of the overlap and interplay between Freemasonry and law making since the revival of Freemasonry in 1717 to invest in both the Latrobe and L'Enfant symbolism in the District of Columbia a concurrence and resonance of design linking material culture to philosophy in general,notably

366 Saturn-Kronos rules the sign of Capricorn in which the sun is "at death" as it is in its lowest demarcation in the Northern Hemisphere. Saturn thus associates itself with death and the color black.

367 Lancaster Lodge No. 54 AF & AM Lincoln, Nebraska of which he served as Worshipful Master. {Pound was also a 33rd degree, P.D.G.M. (HON.) of Massachusetts.

American pragmatism as a cognate of the writings of Emmanuel Kant and their influence upon Charles S. Peirce and his network and the development of a science of Masonic law behind the legislation of various state and national grand lodges. This interplay underscores the critical significance of classical and derivative forms of architecture in the construction of the United States Capital which make clear the Fraternity's influence upon the nation through the cultivation of specific iconologies of meaning mediated through the collective design of buildings and streetscapes. Within Germany, in specific, these iconologies developed simultaneously applications of the higher degrees, notably through such philosophers as Johann Gottlieb Fichte (1762-1814) a systematic philosophical presentation related to pan-German nationalism and its links to the core Rite of Perfection derived from French sources that a parallel developed within German society whereby the machinations of Freemasonry as a voluntary society exercised significant influence upon national and international affairs.

Pound further detailed the process of the unfolding of Masonic law into the national civil religion as a form of secular eschatology. This process incorporates what resembles the element of the thought of Joachim of Fiore contained within Salem Town's work as an unfolding Logos or Royal Arch word, and conflates with his predecessor Simon Greenleaf's detailing of Druidical and Pythagorean lore. In summary, it involves three dynamic steps: 1) the movement of ritual process through a prescriptive and unwritten constitution as a small but not clearly defined body of fundamentals beyond change; 2) a universal, attested Masonic common law that denominates and characterizes all, or most Masonic institutions, applied to the United States. Otherwise traditions, seminal treatises, Grand Master's decisions and Grand Lodge committee reports point to the actual legislation of state Grand Lodges as they carried the resonance and numinosity of the ritual into broad national practice in alliance with parallel and replicative bodies of other fraternal orders derived from Freemasonry or in other ways imitative of its ritual methods of the devolution of symbols and emblems into material culture. In these instances, Freemasonry benefited from realizing its influence in both written and unwritten ways. To Pound, the interplay of these methods generated a unique American Masonic science of jurisprudence. At the core of this

Science, as symbolically designated by Greenleaf, is a Pythagorean complex of millennial and eschatological imageries, again derived from the ritual and expressive of them in material culture, notably the Gothic or Old Manuscript Charges; notices of the lodges from the early modern and Enlightenment periods, including the formation of the higher degrees, lodge records contemporaneous with the earliest organizational activity, and Grand Lodge records. Of these, Anderson's *Constitutions*, William Preston's *Illustrations of Freemasonry*, revised by Thomas Smith Webb, and Laurence Dermott's *Ahiman Rezon* also incorporated by Webb. From such the infrastructure of Masonic ritual symbolism has shaped material culture not as has been said because it is empirically true but because it is authoritative.

* * * * *

Along the higher degree polity model, Harvard mathematician Benjamin Peirce (1809-1880) structured institutional control of American science as an elitist monopoly making of two organizations the official arbiters of government interplay with mathematical morality: The American Academy for the Advancement of Science and the National Academy of Sciences. This was clearly an extension of DeWitt Clinton's own proto-Masonic method of structuring intellectual and scholarly societies in a tiered array of initiatic accessibility consummating in an oligarchic elite governing through public sphere rank, apart from partisan egalitarianism. Both the Peirces, father Benjamin and son Charles Sanders, approached mathematics with an amalgam of social superiority and obscurantism. This method echoed Greenleaf's Pythagoreanism and placed both father and son within a pedagogical vortex where in mathematics was deemed critical to career success and sorting the practical differences between theory and practice in policy matters. This positioned their ventures into the public realm within Cambridge and Boston society through the Metaphysical Club in a manner originated in New York by Clinton's patronage of private societies within which important intellectual was accomplished apart from the more formal university settings. Its high degree Masonic Rites looking to further the ethos echoed the symbolism of Euclid's 47th Proposition as the power to rule set the Peirce's up in opposition to sentimental egalitarianism, and positioned mathematics as not only the key to scientific thought, but to the moral ingredient in all thought. This was a clear parallel to the Pythagorean mission within Freemasonry established a primary linkage between the Geometry detailed in Anderson's legendary history and through to the significance of mathematics in the formation of the professions in the United States later so substantially informed by pragmatism and John Dewey's educational theory.

John Dewey (1859-1952), not a Freemason, but intellectually connected to Daniel Coit Gilman and William Howard Taft, both proactive members of Yale's Masonically nuanced and resonant Skull and Bones[368] society, with links to the Illuminati, Hegelian, and Strict Observance German traditions, became the oracle of this viewpoint, working with others in Harvard's own Metaphysical Club, which set out to both forge links between Pragmatism in the social sciences as well as to assess its comport and significance, addressed himself specifically to the issue of social engineering. In DeWitt Clinton's era, this operation of Masonic networks was taken as a given as lodges and their members were openly deployed to engineer projects such as the Erie Canal; which profoundly transformed both the economy and the frontier expansion of the northern states and their economy. Dewey added a specific approach to reorganizing beliefs and behavior worthy of Greenleaf's mythologies, applying Pythagoreanism to the development through public education as an extension of law making as the scientific element in social science. The result is that both Dewey and Oliver Wendell Holmes were divided within themselves about how the law might envelop a political technology of social engineering derived from Pythagorean Masonic rhetoric available in the works of Greenleaf, Pound, and extravagantly, in Pike, as well as guard against dogmatisms which would generate excess in setting up inalienable rights and self-evident principles for moral and political action, the seeds of which can be traced back to the Anderson and Desaguliers application of Newtonian providentialism to lawmaking. It should be emphasized that Dewey, Holmes and Pound were theorizing, as it were, upon a full century within which Masonic based fraternalism had saturated the nation

368 Skulls & Bones was founded in 1832 and has produced three United States Presidents, William Howard Taft, George Herbert Walker Bush, and George W. Bush.; not to mention numerous Senators, Congressmen, captains of industry and lawgivers.

as a massive social movement. This is clear from even casual glances at how small town and Washington, D.C. networks were dominated by a voluntaristic initiatic ethic which was able to trace Presidential enthusiasm for joining from Andrew Jackson, through anti-Masonry, through James Buchanan, and an array of post civil chief executives who were conspicuously reliant upon lodges and their members for political purposes, regardless of the increasing parodies offered by such social critics as Samuel Clemens (1835-1910, a/k/a Mark Twain, himself a Mason), Ambrose Bierce (1842-1913), and the "Sage of Baltimore," H. L. Mencken (1880-1956). This network became noticeably corporate during the U. S. Grant and Rutherford B. Hayes Presidencies through the Odd Fellowship affiliations of Schyuler Colfax and Henry Shelton Sanford, America's senior internationally trained diplomat and link through Leopold II to the colonial reorganization of Africa. Both in their own ways were adroit at managing fraternal networks within legal corporate professionalism which established a major connection to the nation's first corporations, the railroads which inserted ceremonial and rhetorical ethics into commonplaces such that the Dewey generation was well equipped to pursue the theorizing lay out for them through Freemasonry, Odd Fellowship and specifically the Knights of Pythias, a remarkable fraternal order rooted specifically in legal and Pythagorean private and public ritual rhetoric.

Charles S. Peirce's (1839-1914) development of a theory of *Semiosis* or the interpretation of the meaning of signs as cognates of groups of three, called *Triads,* owes much to elements within the Clinton-Webb system represented in Boston by Simon Greenleaf and his roots in the Royal Arch Hurd Plate if not through direct inspiration then through the activities of Harvard's own Metaphysical Club. This organization operated as a de facto Masonic lodge in the continental sense in the interplay among its members and their patrons and associates with the geometrically and mathematically laden universe seeking to extend scientific precision into the professions. The Metaphysical Club also explored the nature of scholarship, notably through the interplay of John Dewey, with religion and public education into political policy of the public sphere anticipated by DeWitt Clinton in his educational reforms and their links to Freemasonry. This was seemingly carried forth through the Lancastrian Method. The Lancastrian Method was an education system popular in the late nineteenth century where abler students assisted teachers by passing on information and knowledge to other students. Semiosis was C. S. Peirce's eschatological Freemasonry in the same way that Greenleaf deemed Geometry, Anderson's synonym for Masonry in its legendary history, the equivalent of Pythagorean logic as the realization of a triadic ordering of the moral and eschatological meaning of history through the interplay of *sign, object,* and *interpretant.* Such thought erected a bridge between the mission of Kantian Reason, envisaged mythically as the inspiration of a Virgin Goddess *qua* Isis and Minerva, who inspired mathematically rooted learning, making of Philosophy (Sophia, wisdom) as the guide of life as articulated in the Phi Beta Kappa motto, the link between Freemasonry and the college fraternity system. Peirce's attachment to private clubs and societies, the Episcopal liturgy, and to the idea of the feminine within the third person of the Trinity, expressed in an intellectual aesthetic of triadism, places his devotion to logic structurally both as an inheritor of high degree Masonic motifs and Joachism. His melancholic personality epitomized Renaissance saturnine elements thought to generate mathematical ingenuity.

Charles Sanders Peirce's association with Freemasonry can only be conjecture but Pierce links to the Freemasonry of Simon Greenleaf's world into legal Pragmatism was likely through the extended network of the Cambridge, Massachusetts. The chief of these was his affiliation with the Metaphysical Club (formed 1872), a proto Masonic society preoccupied with "reading the cosmos right … as a living symbol." The second was his association through the United States Geodetic Survey with the publication of the *Atlas* (1875) of T. Ellwood Zell, a noted Freemason and founder of the Loyal Legion of the United States (1865) which incorporated Society of the Cincinnati symbolism. Cartography applied to railroad structure and timetables bore a deep consonance with the Masonic alliance with post-Civil War industrialism. Zell also published an American edition of Edmund Spenser's *The Faerie Queene* (originally published between 1590-1596); the symbolism of which deals directly with the survival of the Counter-Reformation in Renaissance England and contributed to the revivalism of chivalry in American fraternalism through the foundation of the Order of the Knights of Pythias, with which Zell's colleague, Samuel Brown Wylie Mitchell, M.D., the founder of Phi Kappa Sigma Fraternity (a/k/a the Skullhouse) in 1850, was associated. In turn the Pythian Order was deeply interlinked to the symbolism of Peirce's core symbolism through Pythagorean related ritual and the emblem of the *Tetractys*, the symbol of the followers of Pythagoras. To Peirce, the mathematical and scientific methods pointed inexorably to divinity in an evolutionary plan applied to the unfolding the nation as an exercise in the realization of perfection. Peirce also attached to Skull and Bones (the Russell Trust) co-founder, Daniel Coit Gilman, President of Johns Hopkins while employed by the United States Coast and Geodetic Survey. The result was that his unique stripe of metaphysics became intertwined through a Washington, D.C. nexus both to the expanding clerisies of national government and to the lineages between Gilman and the pragmatism in educational theory generated by John Dewey. He was, further, a member of the Century Association in New York, a noted community of moralist intellects which came to permeate under the pansophic leadership of Episcopal Bishop Henry Codman Potter, an alumnus of Union College, associated with the J.J. Ramée template –as described in Chapter XI. Potter was chaplain to the industrialist of the day, and related to Peirce as a noted communicant of the Episcopal Church. One finds, therefore, in Peirce a pansophic and Pythagorean magus intellect with both the drive and the creative capacity to generate a system with ample identification with major contributors to esoterically nuanced elites of proto-Freemasons; in Potter's instance to an officer of the Grand Lodge of New York in the finest tradition of DeWitt Clinton. Reference is made to Peirce because the networked context of his associates, notably the families of Gifford Pinchot (1865-1946) and the William James (1842 -1910) point to the maze-like symbolism of his own work, quintessentially, in working out of the foundation for American civil religion. This teleology of perfection implied within the early material culture of the capital but also a recapitulation of the end point of a distinctive metaphysic stemming from divine measurement. To him classification was an act of piety to replicate the order of creation and intention of God. Pinchot was a member of Skull and Bones, the first chief of the United States Forrest Service, and

28th Governor of Pennsylvania; James was pioneering psychologist and philosopher writing on both the subjects of mysticism and pragmatism. Shorn of the mythic vocabulary of Greenleaf and Clinton, he was able to extend into a quest for meaningful signs and symbolism: Semiotics.

The interplay of Pythagorean mythology with the universe of Masonic ritual generated a field of thought which integrated the principle of *parfait* or initiatic perfection into non-Masonic revolutionary thought. This element was central to the J. J. Ramée Enochic template at Union College as the labyrinth and maze concept unfolded through symbolism within policy rhetoric. Thus the Masonic Pythagorean thread unfolded into Peirce's use of logic as the ethics of the intellect through which self-control was achieved to serve human happiness in the same way that the Webb system lifted up the purpose of Masonic initiation to be to learn to subdue passions and to improve oneself in Masonry, again what Desaguliers and Anderson understood to be *Geometry*. DeWitt Clinton's pursuit of the Presidency through Masonic networks and the non-partisan public sphere involved a parallel and earlier form of the pursuit of perfection as a cognate of Pythagorean political office of which the central emblem became Euclid's 47th proposition and its association with mystical, Enochic leadership. Peirce shared with Clinton a conviction that progress in society through science and technology would generate truth and justice, an application at the core of the Clinton-Webb system, evidenced in Erie Canal the symbolic integration of politics, westward Masonic expansion via symbolic Nilotic flooding, and engineering.

The interplay through mathematics between the moral and the physical within Peirce's thought was rooted in the Peirce's (both father and son) approach to cosmology: that the universe was a de facto book to be read and that thought and matter were emanations of the ideas present in the mind of the creator. This quality of symbolic cosmology was related to issues of institutional imperial navigation when Peirce and colleagues created a nautical almanac for navigation purposes in the style of John Dee's Renaissance expostulations on the relationship among navigation, cosmology, and warfare. Peirce positioned nautical mathematics to amplify the original relationship between American territorial expansion and geodetic surveying, thus insuring an institutional link between Pythagorean imagery and the establishment of an American empire uniquely envisaged in the view of Royal Arch Enochic mission through the leadership of the General Grand Chapter under Ephraim Kirby, DeWitt Clinton, Edward Livingston; and related to the diplomatic career of Joel Poinset, a South Carolina Freemason with ties to the environment surrounding the creation of the Scottish Rite Supreme Council in Charleston. As such the movement of such figures as Ephraim Kirby, Edward Livingston and Joel Poinsett into proconsular administrative (Chapter VIII) and juridical positions in Alabama-Mississippi, New Orleans, and Mexico further suggests that Royal Arch Masonry combined within it a trove of dynamic ideas associated with the spread of a Jeffersonian inspired network as outlined in Greenleaf's work into the developing frontier of the nation. This proposes an extended allegorical metaphor for imperial republican expansion at the core of Jefferson's vista for the nation in competition with England and a developing mission agenda for fraternalism as it was staged and implemented as a local oriented public sphere policy by DeWitt Clinton and his circle, again notably Thomas Smith Webb and Salem Town.

Peirce's rhetoric pointed to the essential integration of religion and politics within the Clinton system expressed within Egyptian ritual emblems of solar hegemonics. This idiom was as referenced at the core of lodge practice throughout the nation and underscored an official disingenuity through which religion and politics could not be discussed officially within the lodge but were in fact treated in various ways under the rubrics of philanthropy and community service as an elite mission. This symbolic device removed the European view of a royal family as a family tree and treated each Masonic initiate as a ruler directly descended from the sun as a Worshipful Master. Family, therefore, except within the precincts of the Society of the Cincinnati, became a trivial connection within the Clinton-Webb theory of rulership. The symbol of the obelisk in specific was taken up within Odd Fellowship's initiatory degree wherein the candidate through the person of a hermit encounters a human skeleton as the object lesson of the purpose of the fraternity; that mortality, being common to all mankind, undercuts hereditary as the warrant to rule. This was replaced by Truth as a function of solar regality as the Sun God inspired the workings, both of Hermetical and Cabalistic initiatic elements: the first through striving toward ascent, the second through the possession of the Name of God as warrant to rule.

The likely sources of Peirce's concepts therefore relate to Greenleaf's method of interpolating mythologies, notably the Pythagorean Egyptian and Druidical ideas in his Masonic writing through intermediate sources - notably within German metaphysical writing also descended through Friedrich Wilhelm Joseph Schelling (1775-1854) and his compeers into logical and mathematical formulations in the same way that the imagery of Nilotic flooding shaped and informed the public liturgies and net-workers defining the construction of the Erie Canal. The common denominator was a Joachmite Third Age of eschatology linking Egypt to Greenleaf and Clinton-Webb to Peirce's determinative system of triads applied to the interpretation of signs, a quintessential moral mission of Freemasonry. Schelling's thought recapitulated the rituals of Freemasonry in terms of his own understanding of three universal ages of the Church: St. Peter (Roman Catholic), St. Paul (Protestantism) and St. John the Evangelist (Masonic or tolerant and irenic). One immediately sees a parallel between Schelling's *ages* and the Three Ages of Joachim von Fiore. Mozart's ideal of initiation at the hands of Sarastro in *The Magic Flute* indicated this method, mythic to rational, as did the dynamic of the Ramsay ideology which formed the foundation of the German Masonic Rites, notably those of Masonic writers and reformers Ignaz Aurelius Fessler (1756-1839) and Friedrich Ludwig Schroeder (1744-1816) current in Germany in the early nineteenth century. Fessler and Schroeder sought to reconcile the high degrees with craft masonry. The result was a linkage between post-Kantian devotion to metaphysics and reason. Peirce's treatment of logic as the property of signs can therefore be traced to the Clintonian-Webb-Greenleaf method of managing Pythagorean symbolism in Egyptian mythic formulation as the seed bed for making a new metaphysics out of Geometry in step with the development of philosophical pragmatism. In this context, Schelling's influence was instrumental through his own association with a Third Age of the Church of the St. John the

Evangelist, a Masonic saint as a model for the ideal of Egyptian initiation contained in *The Magic Flute* and, further, the equivalency between this concept and the Transcendentalist ideal. Thus the imperial nautical thread in the Peirce's and American Romanticism conflated into a developing premise that morality through mathematics was the foundation of strategic and commercial navigation, territorial expansion and its management after the Louisiana Purchase and the mounting sense of destiny to be achieved in the alliance Pragmatism made possible between Democracy and Education.

Thus, the celebration of Mozart's Pythagorean magus, Sarastro, incorporated qualities and virtues of the composer's Masonic mentor and contemporary Ignaz von Born (as well as Freemasons and Illuminists Adam Weishaupt and Adolph Knigge), after whom he was modeled and from whose work on Egyptian symbolism the opera was designed. Within the cusp between the German Enlightenment and the emergence of Romanticism, again associated with Schelling, can be seen impinging onto the Transcendentalist Movement in Boston which owed much to German Masonic ideas associated with the high degrees, notably the institutionalization of esoteric imperial theory of a new in breaking age of mathematically nuanced reform. Whilst practical and tending toward anti-intellectualism, Romanticism incorporated in Boston a core conviction consistent with the Clintonian system, that each individual possessed a spark of divinity which properly cultivated might achieve the type of higher inspiration envisage by Peirce's pragmatism despite its opposition to industrialism and technology. The Egypt metaphor in Greenleaf therefore was calculated to appeal to Transcendentalist inspiration to democratic self-government and to an aesthetic of reaching for the stars contained within nascent Pragmatism.

Charles Sanders Peirce has been assessed as moving backward toward the maternal as a means to retrieve a perduring icon which might express his efforts to address the sense of loss detailed in Masonic ritual. This description underscored why such figures as DeWitt Clinton, Greenleaf and later Roscoe Pound riveted upon the salience of the core Masonic martyrdom as a national moral paradigm, but more to the point why femininity as a function of this loss and of an ideal restoration should come to dominate such important intellects. Peirce had a microcosmic relationship with the general societal problem of melancholic loss which linked him to the tradition of Renaissance Saturnity and inspiration and to the broader question of why Enochian theory became so substantially significant within the Clinton-Webb impact on culture. This may be said to have dealt with a desire for a new ritual language within Pythagorean symbolism as it addressed as an ethic of logic the urgency of representation in policy from a mathematical foundation. The same can be said of the philanthropic theosophy within the higher degrees identified by Emanuel Swedenborg, Schelling and in later more eccentric efforts by ritualists such as Albert Pike to bridge the gulf between modernity and mythic symbolism through a universal rite of global initiation.

Emanuel Swedenborg (1688-1772) was a Swedish philosopher, Jacobite emissary, scientist and theologian. He wrote several works trying to reform Christianity which were based upon dreams and visions delivered to him by the Lord starting on Easter weekend 1744. There was a Masonic Rite bearing his name, of Swedenborg, developed by Abbe Pernetty circa 1760.[369] Pernetty himself was an esoteric and disciple of mystic Jakob Boehme. The Rite of Swedenborg consisted of the degrees of 1) Apprentice, 2) Fellowcraft, 3) Master Neophyte, 4) Illuminated Theosophite, 5) Blue Brother, and 6) Red Brother.[370] To Albert Pike, the Swedenborg Rite was nothing but Kabbalah minus the principles of Hierarchy.[371] The Rite, now extinct, nevertheless influenced the rituals and design of occult organizations such as the Hermetic Order of the Golden Dawn and the Ordo Templi Orientis (Order of the Eastern Templars); both societies, unlike Freemasonry, admitted women into their ranks. The former was founded in the late nineteenth or early twentieth century by mystical Freemasons S. L. MacGregor Mathers (1854-1918), William Robert Woodman (1828-1891), and William Wynn Wescott (1848 -1925) and combined Rosicrucianism, Alchemy, Tarot, Masonry, magic, astrology, and mysticism. The O.T.O., founded in the early twentieth

369 Mackey, Albert, *Encyclopedia of Freemasonry*, Vol. II, page 746.
370 Ibid, page 747.
371 Pike, Albert, *Morals and Dogma of the Ancient and Accepted Scottish Rite,* page 823.

century, incorporated all the components of the Golden Dawn[372] while adding the element of sexual mysticism. The O.T.O. was primarily led by English occultist and Freemason Aleister Crowley (1875-1947); both orders still exist to this day. Shorn of Victorian accretions of respectability, like the philosophies and theologies of the "Great Beast" Crowley, Swedenborgian thought within the Anglo-American community emerges as one source for the commonality between the Clinton-Webb system and Peirce's symbolic universe. A further commonality was Swedenborgianism's own integration of science and angelology derived from the Masonic interplay of a an *Illumine* clerisy working from Jacobite and Masonic ritual troves which became the core of the German rites linked to Templar and Strict Observance lore and to the various circles around the works of William Blake, widely thought to be a Swedenborgian. This trove became allied with the Antient system of masonry, in America pro-Revolutionary style of Royal Arch and priestly Freemasonry, opposed to the more loyalists Newtonian providentialists Moderns which in turn came to link Clintonian orbits with the symbolism stemming from the St. Andrew's Hurd Plate, Webb, Greenleaf and Town's millennial vista. The association within Scottish Rite Freemasonry between Cabala and Enochic initiation whereby society became perfected through the realization of hieroglyphic secrets association with the emergent Sun were outlined in seminal summary form by Webb and refined through the creation of the Rite of Perfection as two separate Scottish Rite Supreme Council in the United States (Northern and Southern), with DeWitt Clinton leading a third Cerneau group. Lingering Jacobite sympathies within the Swedish "Hat Party" linked to the Christian Swedish Masonic rite provided Emanuel Swedenborg with espionage related funding, expertise in mining engineering and its symbolism relative to caverns and vaults, to mystical Masonic rites integrating Pythagorean leadership with the Strict Observance (of von Hund) principle of Unknown Superiors in possession of the secrets necessary to confer esoteric and occult leadership.

Swedenborg's career anticipated a Masonic style of intellect as his writings were translated and proliferated in the late 18th and throughout the

372 Other members of the Golden Dawn included *Dracula* author Bram Stoker, poet W. B. Yeats, Freemason A.E. Waite; Kabbalist Israel Regardie, and mystic Dion Fortune.

19th centuries. This was, at its core, the interlinkage of esoteric statecraft with mining engineering and science considered its unitary capacity to organize all of learning with what was sometime known as theological theosophy. To Clinton this was evident in the Erie Canal and Union College designs as they echoed the Pythagorean principles of Nilotic Flooding and solar radiance as the source of all learning. To Peirce, it was triadism and its ultimate achievements: agapism, the rendering of creation into a blissful realm of mathematical precision shaped and informed by Swedenborgian idealism.

In conclusion, Peirce's thought underscored the application of scientific method to Freemasons in the public order the perduring significance of an evolutionary cosmogonic-astrologic ontology and metaphysic related to the working of signs and semiotics, a perennial Masonic enthusiasm. Masonic pursuers of the ideal of the expansive intellect as an ingredient to the public sphere such, as DeWitt Clinton anticipated, his concept of a working fellowship of truth seekers across party lines developing the nation. Later, Henry Codman Potter (1835-1908), a bishop of the Episcopal Church, developed a further expansive, progressive policy driven network through Masonic conduities from Union College which resulted in an extension of Clinton's irenic and public sphere within religion and in cooperation with J. P. Morgan and Viscount James Bryce, historian and author of *The American Commonwealth* (1888) an effective approach to Anglo-American policy in the run up to World War II. Metaphorically and symbolically, the common link was the Masonic concept of squaring the circle: a rhetorical device derived from both the Pythagorean references in the ritual of the Clinton-Webb system and from medieval Masonic lore. At its core, this dynamic connected republic Pharaonic leadership emblems through the Pythagorean maze to the end purpose of the perfection of society as the object of social engineering. The Webb ritual further traces this process to the central design drawn upon "the threshing floor of Ornan the Jebusite" rendered in medieval lore as the *Vesica Piscis*, from which the Temple of Solomon was constructed. As the nation was compared rhetorically increasingly during the 19th century as a broader Temple the method of perfecting its citizens took on scientific features adverse both to lingering ideas of original sin

Frontispiece of Rosicrucian Johann Valentin Andrae's *Mythologiae Christianae sive virtuous et vitiorum vitae humanae imaginum libri tres*,1619. The book is a collection of allegories and stories; its frontispiece displays the Pillars of Enoch with a central sun incorporating the Jesuit Tetragrammaton of I.H.S. symbolizing Christ as God's Sun beneath the question, *Quid si sic*? or "What if thus?"

and natural law with the result that the vision within Freemasonry in general and the higher degrees in particular found expression in the extended symbolism of the Latrobe Capitol building and the L'Enfant urban design within the District of Columbia –the Masonic, utopian *City of the Sun*. Such irenic movements can be seen in the crossing of dogmatic frontier by Utopianists and Christian millenarians as the works of Thomas More (1478 - 1535), Tommaso Campanella (1568 - 1639), Francis Bacon (1561 - 1629), and Johann Valentinus Andreae (1586-1654), a Rosicrucian, worked through conceptual interplay all to the benefit of a Masonic metaphor of building a restored Temple of Zerubbabel. Andreae authored the utopian work *Description of the Republic of Christianopolis* in 1619; it is a Platonized metropolis governed by the wise, enriched by the arts and sciences, where no citizen lives in poverty. On Andreae's Rosicrucian influence upon Masonry, Tobias Churton explains:

> "Every scrap of ideology or philosophic principle that be diligently extracted from James Anderson's two books of Masonic Constitutions (1723 and 1738), save Anderson's weak handling of the principle of reason, could have been taken from the writings and influence of the

greatest unsung hero of European thought, Johann Valentinus Andreae, a giant among men who preferred to keep out of the limelight."[373]

On the Rosicrucian-Masonic nexus, Manly Palmer Hall philosophizes,

> ... "In the meantime a group of men in England, under the leadership of such mystics as Ashmole and Fludd, had resolved upon repopularizing the ancient learning and reclassifying philosophy in a accordance with Bacon's plan for a world encyclopedia. These men had undertaken to reconstruct ancient Platonic and Gnostic mysticism, but were unable to attain their objective for lack of information. Elias Ashmole may have been a member of the European order of Rosicrucians, and as such evidently knew that in various parts of Europe there were isolated individuals who were in possession of the secret doctrine handed down in unbroken from the ancient Greeks and Egyptians through Boethius, the early Christian Church, and the Arabians.
>
> The efforts of the English group to contact such individuals were evidently successful. Several initiated Rosicrucians were brought from the mainland to England, where they remained for a considerable time designing the symbolism of Freemasonry and incorporating into the rituals of the order the same divine principles and philosophy that had formed the inner doctrine of all great secret societies from the time of the Eleusinia in Greece. In fact, the Eleusinian Mysteries themselves continued in the custody of the Arabians, as attested by the presence of Masonic symbols and figures upon early Mohammedan monuments. The adepts who were brought over from the Continent to sit in council with the English philosophers were initiates of the Arabian rites, and through them the Mysteries were ultimately returned to Christendom. Upon completion of the bylaws of the new fraternity the initiates retired again to Central Europe, leaving a group of disciples to develop the outer organization which was to function as a sort of screen to conceal the activities of the esoteric order.
>
> Such, in brief, is the story to be pieced together from the fragmentary bits of evidence available. The whole structure of Freemasonry is founded upon the activities of this secret society of Central European

373 Churton, Tobias, The Invisible History of the Rosicrucians, page 365.

adepts; whom the studious Mason will find to be the definite "link" between the modern Craft and the ancient wisdom. The outer body of Masonic philosophy was merely the veil of this cabalistic order whose members were the custodians of the true Arcanum. Does this inner and secret brotherhood of initiates still exist independent of the Freemasonic order? Evidence points to the fact that it does, for these august adepts are the actual preservers of those secret operative processes of the Greeks whereby the illumination and completion of the individual is effected. They are the veritable guardians of the "Lost Word"–the Keepers of the Inner Mystery–and the Mason who searches for and discovers them is rewarded beyond all mortal estimation."[374]

374 Hall, Manly Palmer, *Lectures on Ancient Philosophy*, pages 449-450.

CHAPTER XIV

THE DISTRICT OF COLUMBIA - THE CITY OF THE SUN

The Masonic Utopian Template

"The temple is built in the form of a circle; it is not girt with walls, but stands upon thick columns, beautifully grouped. A very large dome, built with great care, in the centre or pole, contains another small vault as it were rising out of it, and in this is a spiracle, which is right over the altar."
- Tommaso Campanella, *The City of the Sun: A Poetic Dialogue between a Grand Master of the Knights Hospitallers and a Genoese Sea Captain, his guest*, 1623.

"Nothing was more capable of seducing men than the Heavenly Bodies, and the sun especially. His beauty, the bright splendour of his beams, the rapidity of his course, *exultavit ut Gigus ad currendam viam*, his regularity in enlightening the whole earth by turns, and in diffusing Light and Fertility all around, essential characters of the Divinity who is Himself the light and source of everything that exists, all these were but too capable of impressing the gross minds of men with a belief that there was no other God but the sun, and that this splendid luminary was the throne of the Divinity. God had fixed his habitation in the heavens, and they saw nothing that bore more marks of Divinity than the sun."
- Abbe Antoine Banier, *The Mythology and Fables Of the Ancients,* 1711.

"The analemma is a basis for calculation deduced from the course of the sun, and found by observation of the shadow as it increases until the winter solstice. By means

of this, through architectural principles and the employment of the compasses, we find out the operation of the sun in the universe."
- Vitruvius, *De Archtectura, (*Book IX, Chapter i, I), ca. 15 BCE.

The relationship between theemergence of the District of Columbia as an icon for national civil religion can be traced through Freemasonry to the relationship between the development of the legal profession as an extension of the chivalric symbolism attached to the articulate citizen in the Elizabethan Renaissance, notably to the concept of the lawyer implied in The *Boke named the Governour* by Sir Thomas Elyot and to utopian ideas of epicentral cities as the temples to civic virtue as typified by ideal of the Pythagorean Magus as attorney. The core principle relates to the lifting up of Roman Catholicism as the form of Christianity most loyal to its pagan origins, *Sol Invictus*, as detailed by the likes of Athanasius Kircher, John Toland, and Simon Greenleaf and by further association to Tapping Reeve's Law School in Litchfield, Connecticut of which General Grand Royal Arch High Priest Ephraim Kirby was a graduate. Kirby helped create this interstate structure as an arbiter of moral civility and etiquette which attracted eminent jurists such as DeWitt Clinton, Edward Livingston, and Joel Poinsett. These Royal Arch presiding officers together with Simon Greenleaf forged an echelon of Knights Templar within Masonry through the Royal Arch degree which interconnected Christian variations of solar symbolism to a modern, secular form of priesthood. The priesthood, in turn, had deep Renaissance links to treatises such as *The Strange Deaths of Hermes and the Sibyls*,[375] which celebrated the collapse of Egypt as the paragon lawgiving nation of antiquity as it related to the utopian ideology refined by architects Pierre L'Enfant, J.J. Ramée, and their patrons as the individual gave way to the state as the prime mediator of classical form into the architecture of law giving. In time, this current shaped the relationship between Masonic Temples and county court houses in countless mid-western localities and implied an intimacy between the law and Freemasonry which perdured into

375 The twelve Sibyls were not goddesses, but legendary prophetesses revered in Roman lore: the Sibylline Books were a source of divination in ancient Roman history and religion. See *Athanasius Kircher's Theatre of the World*, page 268.

the modern writings of Roscoe Pound and Earl Warren through Masonic influences upon American pragmatism. The introduction in Germany of a clerical order in 1767 lifted up the priest chaplains within the survival of the Templar Order which laid claims to powers over natural processes as an extension of Egyptian numinosity through an order of Clerks of Strict Observance or Clerks Templar. The *Clerici Ordinis Templarii*, also known as the Spiritual Branch of the Templars, claimed preeminence not only over the Rite of Strict Observance (who claimed the Young Pretender, Bonnie Prince Charlie, as its Grand Master) but overall Lodges of Ordinary Masonry as well. Founded by theologian Johann August von Starck (1741-1816), it consisted of seven degrees that required the candidate be a Roman Catholic as a prerequisite for admission; to many von Starck was an emissary of the Jesuits having instituted this Rite at their behest. The Templar linkage to Freemasonry was also a subject of an international Masonic Congress at Wiesbaden, Germany 1776. It was enclosed within a huge international envelope of fantasy which increased the Egyptian-Templar appeal to lawyers who studied in Germany from both England and America and who like Samuel T. Coleridge (author of *The Rime of the Ancient Marnier*, 1798) knew German and began to work on the idea of an ideal heliocentric clerisy which should manage the preservation of civility as a chivalric ideal into what became the origins of the Romantic period. The specific associations between European elites of grandees and nobles with deep Egyptianate symbolism and nomenclature became allied with architect Augustus Welby Northmore Pugin's innovation of the Gothic Revival which in turn gave way to the Neoclassical and Egyptian revivals. The effect of Germanic ritual innovations in the high degrees was to bring Masonic theorizing into mainline intellectual currents into contact with a lineage of Scottish, Strict Observance, and Egyptian rivers and rivulets of symbolism which were invited into the Romantic inter-threading of professional aspirations, notably in the United States as a new republic, in order to satisfy the longing or deeper pedigrees for the role of the articulate citizen relative to the survival of a respectable ideal of cosmic order, itself a legacy from the Renaissance in Italy and in England. Within this maze, the idea developed that Freemasonry was itself a calculated enterprise of the Jesuits to restore the Stuart pretenders as universal sovereigns, which was taken up uniquely and effectively in the composition of Swedish Freemasonry in the creation of a civil order, the Order of Charles XIII in 1811. This order constituted the top echelon where Swedish aristocracy attached to the monarchy as attached to the emerging professions during the Bernadotte period when French Freemasonry and Swedish counterparts developed a unique dynastic and conceptual intimacy. A Protestant suspicion of *crypto Catholicism* was also at work in driving underground the more zealous appeals by Masonically informed identities between Egyptian symbolism and public architecture such that the Neoclassical more formalist threads of the interior emblemature of the Clerks of Strict Observance was obliged to give way to a purism best anticipated by classical painters such as Nicholas Poussin who's work included critical symbolic threads between Mariology, Virgoian, and Isis imagery rooted in geometric mathesis applied to classical forms thereby muting more overt expressions of the turbulent drama of the Baroque and masking symbolism related to the Tetragrammaton, a noted Jesuit (cf. I.H.S.) and Masonic icon.

The specific utopian model which bears the most salient reference to the District of Columbia can be found in Tommaso Campanella's *The City of the Sun* (1602). Campanella (1568-1639) was a Dominican Friar, alleged black magician, and astrologer who attempted to fuse his cosmological views and interpretations with those of Joachim von Fiore's New or Third Age of the Holy Spirit prophecies. This ideal urban imagery had been insinuated by its author within a set of Catholic missionary vistas linking policy design through astral mythology to political policy to heliocentrism. It distilled the Enochic imagery contained within Freemasonry into a type of Pythagorean Christ. *The City of the Sun* therefore should be deemed an earlier parallel effort in Christian apologetics to utilize the Copernican and Keplerian discoveries in astronomy in the same way that Dr. Desaguliers made use of the Newtonian constructs in physics as a means to preserve the Renaissance linkage between the hermetical dicta of as *above, so below*. If Pierre Charles L'Enfant and Benjamin Henry Latrobe were not aware of Campanella's vista directly, it is highly likely that Daniel Carroll (1730-1796), a convinced Roman Catholic and Freemason was cognizant of its core idea: to reconcile Catholic missiology with American, New World patriotic order.

In any event, the design and premises directly anticipate the core idea of Washington's design: a national capital with its symbolism linking occult astrological symbolism with geographic resonance underscoring the mission of the nation. While Blue Lodge Masonic symbolism is apparent, one must turn to the esoterica found in the Royal Arch ceremonies for a proper symbolic analysis of the District of Columbia. The overall template of the District of Columbia, namely the Federal Triangle, is given to the Egyptian goddess Isis; astrologically, her star Sirius, as it is Isis who secretly possessed the sacred name of God, Amun Re or Ra, thereby linking Isis to the possession of the name of Deity, the Lost Word of a Master Mason, a theme that predominates the Royal Arch ritual within both the York and Scottish Rites of Masonry and the third degree of the Blue Lodge as analyzed. Therefore the link between the Royal Arch vista of the District of Columbia and the star Sirius as Isis and her antecedent, the Christian Mary, the constellation Virgo, is an easy one to forge. The identification of an ideal utopian city as an Egyptian temple extended from sacred buildings from which to govern the nation was lifted up by Daniel Carroll and his contemporaries through the establishment of the District of Columbia as a *spiritual* yet *Masonically secular* place from which Enochic and Pythagorean Magi might rule the nation. The core idea of course stems from the creation of Jerusalem as capital of the Holy Nation of Israel within the Temple of God (Solomon's Temple) was established with high priests and kings situated for this purpose; but the further imperial and republic iconology of Rome became clear as the District of Columbia took shape as a successor to Philadelphia, New York, and even Annapolis. The secular equivalent of the vision of God was critical to the entire strategy because the policy of a new nation required a utopian and millennial setting for the symbolic purity of the new nation. Thus, for a "Christian"[376] nation, the Biblical precedents of seeing God became uppermost in the range of hidden symbolism available to the designers of the streetscapes and vistas notably the trance missions from which Isaiah and Ezekiel initiated their vision of a just and holy nation.

376 The word Christian appears in quotations because the United States is not a Christian Nation; the separation of Church and State as contained within the First Amendment bears this out. The United States should be thought of as a Masonic Republic trying to promote, as does the Masonic Lodge, Judaic-Christian values (such as faith, hope, charity) while distancing itself from the theology of religion(s).

The attachment of Catholic irenicism through the Carroll family in the design of the District of Columbia, the establishment of Georgetown University by John Carroll within the District, and the patronage extended to Benjamin Latrobe in the domed Roman Catholic Baltimore Basilica and Capitol Building underscore the significance of understanding the linkage between Counter-Reformation ideology and Masonic symbolism. The two threads are related in various ways through the Chevalier Ramsay's ideology of the high degrees and within the interior symbolism of the restored king[377] associated with the restoration of mystic wisdom: the restoration of the Lost Word of a Master Mason. Thus Jacobite ideals became associated with the Stuart monarchy through important Masonic rites, notably the Rite of Strict Observance of Carl von Hund related also to the *Chevaliers Bienfaisant de la Cite Sainte*, a Swiss fraternity with strong symbolical links to the ideology of a reformed universal monarchy to a world spiritual order. This thread incorporated a vista of ritual interiority linking the Jesuit enthusiasm for apostolic piety with the purity of antediluvian religiosity which came to be an encoded reference to Hermeticism and Cabalism, within which Renaissance ideas implicit in the symbolic linkage between the promise to Eve in the Garden of Eden promised that to eat of the Tree, a Sephirotic-Hebrew-Kabbalistic allusion, meant that she and Adam 1) would not die; and 2) would know the difference between good and evil. The survival of this thread was also twinned with the Enochian legend through the survival of this wisdom as an alternative to Noah's Flood, thus positioning a means through the Tetragrammaton and its precise pronunciation to the survival of wisdom necessary to rule a universal empire as a papal monarchy to the restoration of all knowledge. The projection of this myth onto Joachim von Fiore's concept of a Third Age of the Holy Spirit through a new order of spiritual men, in turn, can be traced into various Masonic ceremonies designed to celebrate the symbolic role of Egypt, its Mysteries, as a triumphant apologetical metaphor into modernity through the writings of Athanasius Kircher and Guillaume Postel. The silence of a perfected contemplation was envisaged as the eradication of imperfection, notably heresy, on a new world empire which Jesuits were quick to see in the transformation of the British empire into a papal agency through Masonic

377 To Ramsay this would have been the Old Pretender.

irenicism envisaged, again, by Andrew Michael Ramsay's concept of a reformed, universalistic and irenic idiom of *national Masonic initiation* to take fruition in the District of Columbia.

Tommaso Campanella's *City* as the influence of the new Federal City was not exclusive. The Masonic layering of symbolism in the District of Columbia also made it possible to identify the founding of the American legal profession with the symbolism of the higher degrees, as seen in the previous chapter. As the Supreme Court and related judicial environs were associated with the District of Columbia, the founding Dean of the Harvard Law School, Freemason Simon Greenleaf, penned a manifesto linking the practice of the law in the new capital city symbolically to Freemasonry in *A Brief Inquiry into the Origin and Principles of Freemasonry* in 1820, tracing Freemasonry origins from the Eleusinian, Druidic, and Pythagorean Mystery Schools. The title page of this work incorporated solar radiance with the cross and crown of Clinton's Knight Templar order, a polemical statement that both Greenleaf and DeWitt Clinton identify with a common rhetorical vocabulary through chivalric symbolism. To Simon Greenleaf this was an investigation of the primary principles of Nature to seek the knowledge of God through the subtleties and tacitry of obscure images and symbols which would take physical form within the District of Columbia, namely the Pythagorean Federal Triangle as contained within the original L'Enfant street plan (see Plate XXVIII).

The title page (or frontispiece) of Simon Greenleaf's *A Brief Inquiry into the Origin and Principles of Freemasonry,* 1820, features a solar cross and crown representative of the DeWitt Clinton's Knights Templar.

The coincidence of the opening of the New World with the establishment of a *The City of the Sun* ruled by a universal monarch through a mediating order of new spiritual men continued Campanella's utopian concept which reflected directly the iconology of the

District of Columbia, solar universal harmony. The core principle can be traced to the uniquely English enthusiasm to integrate a quasi-chivalric *militia of Christ* to English enthusiasms for integrating microcosmic with macrocosmic order in turn traceable to the hermetical enthusiasm for Egypt. The same principle was worked out in the libretto, written by Freemason Emanuel Schikaneder, of *The Magic Flute*, Mozart's 1791 opera rooted in a tradition of a Masonic Rite of Mizraim-Memphis depicted in the sumptuous imagery of Sarastro's Castle, a model of and for initiation in Egyptian Freemasonry and the Illuminati. A concept is developed wherein a Temple of Wisdom is utilized to project through the panoply of initiation and integration of reason and nature allusive to the Jeffersonian precept that the former might be interpreted and mediated by a class and style of American *Politiques* functioning as Pythagoreans through a structured clerisy. In this sense Thomas Jefferson, who helped design the District of Columbia, viewed philosophy as a science of nature fathomed through reason applied to pragmatic social design and engineering.

In Jefferson's *Notes on the State of Virginia* (1780), this element is developed as a kind of initiatic consciousness with which positivism appears as an extension of heliocentric utopianism akin to Mozart's idiom and reflective of the Campanella precedent in *The City of the Sun.* Jefferson is in a way operating de facto as a *Pythagorean Philosophe.* To the Jeffersonians this meant a high deistic ideal of spiritualized metaphysical positivism linked to an unfolding of benevolence symbolized through heliocentric material culture in imagery of architecture as a public metaphor. Thus essential Christianity shorn of extraneous revelation linked to advanced scientific and social thought was inserted within utopian designs consistent with the Egyptian ritual metaphors that can be traced to Martin Clare and eventually through Jesuits apologetics to Campanella. In turn Jefferson's plans for the development of the University of Virginia provided an Enochian educational foundation to benevolent positivism consistent with Greenleaf's depiction of the Pythagorean ideal of Masonic initiation: an interplay of private (esoteric) and public (exoteric) mathematically (positivistic) mysteries mediated through a benevolent secular-Christian clerisy effected with a Homage to the Sun, as the design of the University of Virginia was influenced by the

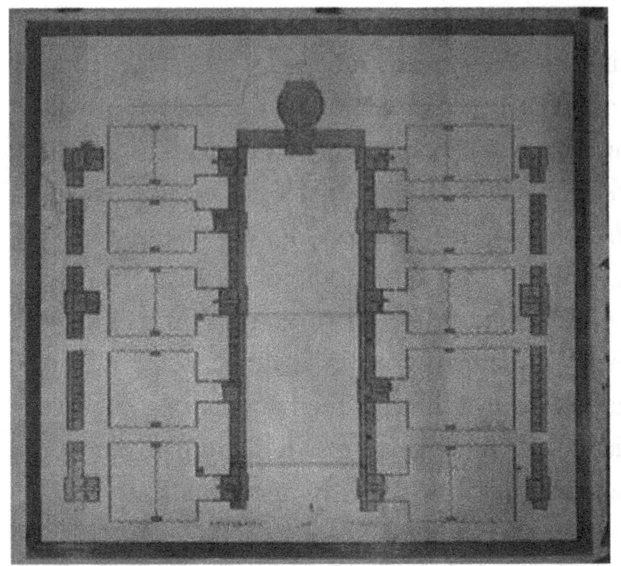

Jefferson's template, engraved by Peter Maverick, for the University of Virginia features a domed-solar rotunda, a library or a temple of intellectual light, emerging from a vaulted area created by parallel buildings on either side mirroring Ramée's design for Union College.

Ramée Union College design, as a core principle integral to its architecture. Jefferson, a deist, naturally forbade the teaching of theology at the University of Virginia. The seal of the University of Virginia proudly displays the Apollonian domed rotunda as its central solar icon.

The seal of Jefferson's University of Virginia.

The center of *The City of the Sun* was a perfectly round dome within which was represented, symbolically, a replica of the solar system and imagery of the world with particular reference to world religious leaders understood as occult Magi. The temple included references to Pythagorean rulership through Euclid's 47th Proposition and to Osiris as the premier Egyptian Deity and by reference to his virgin sister-wife Isis; yet positioned such that Christ and his twelve apostles took exoteric places of honor within its design. The purpose of the architectural appointments of the domed circle, represented by the Masonic emblem of the point within the circle was to develop an intellectual race dependent upon linking human conception along Neo-Platonic lines to astral arrangements. The point within a circle is a symbol "...of great interest, and brings us into close connection with early symbolism of the solar orb and the universe, which was predominate in the ancient sun-worship."[378] As a result, the imagery was more astrological than commonly appears in Jesuit apologetics yet is precisely designed such that the Enochian principle was preserved: to interpret heavenly secrets to a priestly mediating order for implementation of enlightened policy. This feature of *The City of the Sun*, with its detail about a quasi-Druidical (cf. Greenleaf) styled executive imagery, underscores the eschatological premise between the author's utopian mission and his determination to represent on earth a Copernican heliocentrism in a Catholic-Christian esoteric, occult framework.

The Campanella and Greenleaf Masonic concept of iconology, together give maximum credibility to Catholic utopianism as a point of origin for thinkingaboutthemythos designofthe DistrictofColumbia. ToCampanella's three fundamental interrelated concepts were key: 1) a universal mystical empire akin to Rome; 2) Plato's Republic ruled by philosophers, and 3) a priestly Egyptian state; Simon Greenleaf inserted Pythagorean symbolism derived from his view of Druids as the mediating order necessary to achieve this objective. The consolidated icon of philosopher, priest and king governing a state through the interpretation of science understood as celestial mystical wisdom defined the power of the state as a theocracy within which the appearance of representation was maintained through heliocentric imagery. This was an effort to frame a reformed Roman Catholicism of nature in ways hospitable to British concepts of a Reformed Protestant Empire as well through court Anglicanism associated with Edmund Spenser whose work *The Faerie Queene* (1590, 1596) put forward a vast poetically articulated concept of the Church of England as a hermetical and cabalistic mystical body. John Dee's occult philosophy lies behind Spenser's work; one of the Rosicrucian manifestos contains a tract which is closely based on Dee's *Monas Hieroglyphica* (1564), a treatise on symbolic language.[379] As such Spenser's *The Faerie Queene* has a character called "The Red Cross Knight" which symbolically represents Dr. Dee and transforms him into a proto Christian Rosenkreutz[380] which means in English *Christian Rose Cross*. The white magic of *The Faerie Queene* also serves to balance out

378 Mackey, Albert, *An Encyclopedia of Freemasonry* Vol. II, p. 573.
379 Yates, Frances, *The Occult Philosophy in the Elizabethan Age*, page 170.
380 Ibid.

the darker, Egyptian sorcery of Dominican friar Giordano Bruno. Bruno, like Spenser, lionized good Queen Bess as a universal monarch who would usher in a new, reformed, Egypto-Judaic-Christianity for the New World.

The City of the Sun became deeply linked both to the papacy and to Cardinal Richelieu's (1585-1642) ambitions for the French Monarchy.[381] Its author was convinced that its emphasis upon angelic hierarchies and mediate celestial secrets was in turn related to the reform of Catholicism to incorporate heliocentrism with utopian missiology, underscoring a critical Jesuit premise of *back to the future*. This meant that the key to perfection with a future Catholic state should entail a restoration of antediluvian order as a symbol for restoring the Fall. The restoration of the antediluvian order was spear headed by the Red Eminence: he was a protector of Campanella who linked solar rulership to the Bourbon Monarchs. The symbolism can be traced to the throne room within the Palace of Versailles, it was called the Solon de Apollo, its ceiling featured a painting of Apollo driving his solar chariot across the sky (see Plate XXIX) investing Louis XIV, the first Monarch to rule within Versailles, as the *Sun King*. Richelieu established the premiere learning center *L'Académie Française* in 1635; its centerpiece the L'Institut de France building features a dome symbolically radiating intellectual light and knowledge; in America this is paralleled with the founding of the Catholic University of Notre Dame in South Bend, Indiana in 1842. Notre Dame's main building features its most iconic symbol which is, of course, an Apollonian solar golden dome. Further solar symbolism would take concrete form in France years later under the reign of Napoleon I as the *Arc de Triomphe* (1806). The *Arc de Triomphe* (representing the solar path of the sun in the Vitruvian-Palladian idiom) is a replication of the Royal Arch of Titus which details the fall of the Second Temple of Zerubbabel on its friezes, where according to Masonic lore, the Vault of Enoch containing the Lost Word was recovered. It symbolically invests Paris as Campanella's *Solar City*: the Arc correctly sits in a circular road with radial streets emanating from it as sun rays, solar light, a symbolic point within a circle and was most likely influenced by the L'Enfant radial street plane of the District of Columbia. A parallel can be seen in Sir Christopher

381 Yates, Frances, *Giordano Bruno and the Hermetic Tradition*, page 374.

Wren's design for London after the Great Fire of 1666. Wren, a Freemason and member of the Royal Society, designed a giant triumphal arch dedicated to Charles II as a symbol of his solar rulership but it was never executed.[382] The Arch as a symbol of solar rulership would eventually come to fruition: a replication of the Arc de Triomphe would be placed in Washington Square in New York City in 1892. The Arch in Washington Square originated from a makeshift wooden arch that was made just north of the square in 1889 on Fifth Avenue to commemorate the centennial of Washington's inauguration symbolizing the beginning of his Masonic solar rulership of the country. The permanent marble arch in Washington Square was designed by architect Stanford White (1853-1906); in 1972 New York University's Bobst Library opened across the street from the Washington Square Arch itself a symbolic temple of light or wisdom in keeping with the Royal Arch Masonic ideology and philosophy of the restoration of knowledge.

*   *   *   *   *

The roots of Campanella's Solar City and the District of Columbia can be found in deeper occult parallels within the literature formulated by hermetical philosophers Giovanni Pico della Mirandola and Marsilio Ficino in Renaissance Florence; both prophetically predicting the restoration of the Egyptian solar religion as the correct political theology of the planet and itself the model for a New World civil religion. In other words they believed the Abrahamic solar faiths of Christianity, Judaism, and Islam would ultimately be exposed as substituted forms of Egyptian sun worship with in New World–what became the United States. It would be this New World that would midwife civilization from the waning Piscean Age into the "Masonic" Aquarian Age, *a New Age of the Holy Spirit*. Simon Greenleaf's Druids and Campanella's Solarians are the de facto mediating Joachimite order through which heavenly signs are mediated by a Sun Priest, an executive (cf. Arch Druid iconography) or President, who frames policy based upon his knowledge of the correspondences between science (i.e. Egyptian natural religion), grades of being, and heavenly correspondences. This polity was replicated from 1797 within the General

382 Hutchinson, Harold, *Sir Christopher Wren, A Biography*, page 65.

Grand Chapter of Royal Arch Masons with reference both to Enoch (cf. Webb's 1797 *Monitor*) and the priest king Melchizedek of which the Grand Master DeWitt Clinton became the symbolic presiding executive. To reiterate, again, from Chapter 8: this configuration is important to make because it establishes the position of the District of Columbia as a utopian ideal city in relationship to the history of mystical utopias of Sir Thomas More (Utopia, 1516), through Tommaso Campanella, and Sir Francis Bacon (The New Atlantis, 1626) in terms of the entelechy or interior dynamic of the occult magic or science from numinous vitalism of the hermetical Renaissance into the period of modern scientific inquiry. DeWitt Clinton's uncle George Clinton (1739-1812) resided in the District as the first Vice President to do so. *Thus its empirical utility and its mythological associations with Merkabah-Kabbalah in arch and dome symbolism would have born a higher intensity of symbolic resonance than to subsequent generations* (see pages 316-317).

The parallel is with the Masonic Royal Arch high priest, symbolically the United States President, as an Enochian figure himself but as a distillate of Hebrew elements from King Solomon's Temple, Platonism with a restored Egyptian utopian hermetical faith. As such, the District of Columbia would come to symbolize and embody philosophically and architecturally the religion of Egypt as describe in the *Corpus Hermiticum* text *Asclepius* or *The Perfect Sermon*, a dialog between Hermes Trismegistus and Asclepius (with Tat and Hammon as listeners), wherein they discuss the resurgence of pagan Egyptian power and sorcery. This was combined with the magical and astrological elements contained within the *Picatrix*, namely the ideal occult city of Adocentyn: a city allegedly built by Hermes Trismegistus in East Egypt. Hermes placed around the circumference of Adocentyn engraved images and ordered them in such a way that by their virtue the inhabitants were made virtuous and withdrawn from all wickedness and harm. *Asclepius* not only documents that the Sun, or Light, is a second god whose divinity governs all earthly, living things, it provides an actual description of magical practices that the Egyptians used to make gods. As a result the District of Columbia can be kabbalistically linked through references to Isaiah 19:18: "In that day five of Egypt's cities will follow the Lord of Heaven's Armies. They will even begin to speak Hebrew, the language of Canaan. *One of these cities will be Heliopolis, the City of the Sun.*" to the realization of Joachim von Fiore's Third Age of the Holy Spirit, the coming solar Aquarian Age, as unfolding Logos. In effect, Campanella actually foresees the creation of the York Rite of Freemasonry as depicted in the solar path of initiation of the St. Andrew's Royal Arch Hurd Plate degree certificate of 1790 through the introduction of an irenic Christianity ritualized within the libations alluded to at the Knights Templar triangular altar within the design, as transferred from the Irish Jewels. Interestingly, *Picatrix* also contains reference to a hidden underground vault, perhaps a reference to the Enochic vault discovered in the Royal Arch degree and the vaulted space under the Apollonian dome as described by Campanella. The metaphor thus continues within the ideology of *The City of the Sun* to accommodate Apollo as a presiding deity within whose kabbalistic sun chariot imagery epitomizes all of the good and philanthropic qualities of pagan mythology are arrayed as doing worship to Jesus Christ as a *Supreme Magus* or *God's Sun* with the affect that virtuous ethics are directed at the achievement of good will through social efficiency. On this British historian Frances A. Yates explains:

> "Bruno's exposition of the Hermetic reform in the *Spaccio della Bestia Trionfante* can be illuminatingly compared with the *Citta'del Sole*. In the *Spaccio*, too, Christ remains in heaven, revered as a Magus. The reform of the heavens is also centred on the sun; the good planetary influences, Venus, Jupiter, Mercury, unite under Apollo to bring about universal good will. In the gods who reform the constellations a beneficent relationship between the planets and the zodiac and other constellations of the heaven is established, typified in the City of the Sun by the relationship between the star images on the dome of the temple and the altar with its planetary lamps. Virtue triumphs over vice in the *Spaccio* as the good sides of astral influence rises as virtues, and the bad sides are thrown out, as vices. So in the City of the Sun, the inhabitants are maintained in virtue and vices are expelled. The nature of the reform too is similar with, in both cases, a direction of ethics towards social utility. In spite of the extremely different literary form of the two works there is concordance between them at a deeper level."[383]

383 Yates, Frances A., *Giordano Bruno and the Hermetic Tradition*, page 373.

This symbolism was no doubt carried over from France by Pierre Charles L'Enfant and into Benjamin Latrobe's domed Capitol building. In turn, Freemason Benjamin French (1800-1870) oversaw the completion of the Capitol and its dome in the nineteenth century. From the basement of the Capitol from the top of the dome is a staircase containing 365 steps symbolic of the solar year. Campanella's solar, cosmological, and magical city was ruled by a Sun Priest further anticipating Masonry's Worshipful Master, a Royal Arch High Priest, Christianized York Rite Knight Templary, and arguable the United States Presidency.

From 1791, the City of Washington came to embody stability amidst the chaos of Revolution and sea changes in political representation which defined the Jeffersonian agenda in terms of material culture. With the defeat of absolutism, cities ceased to be feudal fortresses and became creatures of a more representative, if oligarchic state, which might give or withdraw political favors as a result of the loyalty of the metropolis to centralized power. L'Enfant's design therefore integrated the grand idea of American patriotism with a Baroque imagery of despotism, with the exception of 16th century fortifications. It was this alloy which similarly defined the Freemasonry of Jefferson's period through Clinton and his compeers as the celebration of centralized authority within the folds of equality through patriotism. Notably, the squares and rectangles superimposed with circles of the streetscape were devoted to the *Ars Notoria* concept of linking classical memory to public policy through inspiration. L'Enfant believed such statuary would convey the meaning of Egyptianate and other classical cultures to the youth of the nation through the imagery that the avenues of the district progressed toward and supported the purpose of a broad irenic, patriotic mnemonic. This concept had also been used across the Atlantic to convey similar patriotic notions within the symbol of the French Revolution, the Guillotine. It would come to epitomize the equality, liberty, and fraternity of the New French Republic as it did away with, quite horrifically, the Bourbon Monarchy and the *ancien regime*. The egalitarian-democratic device[384] would execute noble and peasant; it

384 The Guillotine of April 1792 does not resemble its Scottish, German, or Italian predecessors. The design of the French model can be attributed to Dr. Guillotin directly who was apparently not aware of the earlier devices. See Gerould, Daniel, *Guillotine: Its Legend and Lore,* page 13-22.

featured a slightly raised rectangular plank for the body with a "....square plate with a circle for the head and the triangular blade certainly suggest Masonic allegories: in the climate of the 1780s, when Masonic motifs would have been familiar to many, the connection might not have been as tenuous as we might think today."[385] The shape of the French guillotine is a Pythagorean right triangle, a symbol of Masonic rulership (cf. Worshipful Master) and social purification, albeit in this case of the French Revolution it was used in a nefarious manner. Its advocator and designer, Dr. Joseph-Ignace Guillotin (1738-1814), was a Freemason.

* * * * *

Arguably, the vista achieved by Pierre L'Enfant in 1791 benefited from this analogy in the design of the District of Columbia as a utopian exercise in political economy applied to nation building. Like Nicolas Poussin, he rendered imagery as a pictorial language unprecedented since Athenian cooption of classical virtue, as articulated by Herbert, and lifted in various ways by Andrea Palladio in the Venetian Republic resulting in clarity and intellectual precision. In this idiom, ideal landscapes of classicism were conjoined with utopian ideals in architectural achievements such as the District of Columbia design. Actual vistas, to Poussin, the countryside outside of Rome was integrated with pictorial convention to achieve balance and harmony between human forms, drawn from Biblical or classical sources. Both Herbert and Poussin viewed classical mythology

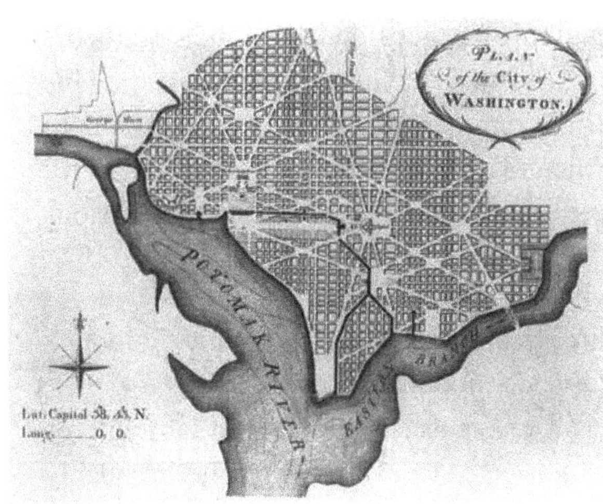

The Pierre Charles L'Enfant template of the District of Columbia, revised by Andrew Ellicott, features circles with streets symbolically radiating solar rays. The Federal Triangle forms the Pythagorean Theorem (47th Proposition of Euclid) indicative of Masonic rulership.

385 Curl, James S., *The Art and Architecture of Freemasonry,* page 140.

as a textbook from which to refine symbolic forms through which each gesture and expression would point to a consolidated integrated whole as came to be expressed in high ceremonial through which the initiate became simultaneously an observer and a participant. In specific, each gesture and movement was restrained and restricted to mathematically exact and precise lines capable of depiction in a path of initiation, individual and social. These vistas were enveloped with solar imagery, *light* as a symbol of all pervasive meaning and providence, the central key of the design. The result was to transform conventional geographics into the imagery of a pure, golden age with elements of landscapes: trees, rising ground, classical remains of buildings, or expanding foliage in relationship to the clarity and order derived from the pristine human form. Such symbolic vistas were capable –in the hands of Poussin and importantly by Herbert–capable of infinite variety emulating the Giordano Bruno ideal of infinite worlds as transferred into, for example, Webb's rituals and the architecture and template of the District of Columbia. The result reflected the Masonic dictum to bring *order out of chaos* (confusion) in material culture. There is, of course, a parallel between Giordano Bruno's purity of Egyptianate heliocentricity through the study and representation of statues and bas-relief. Herbert's work, in specific, parallels Poussin's effort in this regard because of his saturation in the morality and visible remains of the ancient world as both Andrew Michael Ramsay and Salem Town were able to lift them up for fraternal celebration through Freemasonry as it devolved into multifarious forms and institutions.

Pierre L'Enfant's design of the streetscape of the District of Columbia carries this public metaphor into broader application by designing avenues, circles, squares, and rectangles as a transposed inscription in labyrinth or maze form that articulated the devolution of local Masonic unites, arguably lodges, rectangles or oblongs, and chapters of higher degrees (*squared circles*) as devolved centers of light devolved from the doomed Apollonian chariot throne room of the United States Capitol by Benjamin Latrobe in the vein of the Solon of Apollo within Versailles. The District of Columbia's streetscape as a labyrinth is another solar allegory; on the symbolism of a labyrinth Albert Pike explains,

> "The celebrated Labyrinth was built in honor of the Sun; and its twelve places, like the twelve superb columns of the Temple at Hieropolis, covered with symbols relating to the twelve signs and the occult qualities of the elements, were consecratedto the twelve gods or tutelary genii of the signs of the Zodiac. The figure of the pyramid and that of the obelisk, resembling the shape of a flame, caused these monuments to be consecrated to the Sun and to Fire. And Timaeus of Locria says: 'The equilateral triangle enters in the composition of the pyramid, which has four equal faces and equal angles, and which in this is like fire, the most subtle and mobile of the elements.' They and the obelisks were erected in honor of the Sun, termed in an inscription upon one of the latter, translated by the Egyptian Hermapion, and to be found in Ammianus Marcellinus, "Apollo the strong, Son of God, He who made the world, true Lord of the diadems, who possesses Egypt and fills it with His glory."[386]

The shape of a lodge, a rectangle (oblong), and its cosmological symbolism is explained in the Entered Apprentice Degree:

> "The form of a lodge is oblong, in length from east to west,
> in breadth between north and south, as high as *Heaven* and as
> deep as from the surface to the center. It is said to be thus
> extensive to denote the universality of Freemasonry, and it
> teaches that a Mason charity (or care) should be equally extensive."[387]

Latrobe's neoclassical Capitol naturally features an Apollonian dome symbolic of a chamber of light: this invests the U.S. Capitol as a Temple of Light; *solar light* in this instance defined as new world democracy ruled by the elected Senate and House of Representatives. The Capitol and the Executive Mansion (White House) cornerstones were laid according to Masonic ritual; George Washington presided over the laying of the Capitol's cornerstone on September 18, 1793 under the sign of Virgo whose hallmarks mirror Masonic ethos-philosophy (see Chapter XI). Virgo is Mary in the Christian Mysteries; Mary is Isis who is the Magna Mater of the Masonic Mysteries. As the nation was compared, rhetorically and

386 Pike, Albert, *Morals and Dogma of the Ancient and Accepted Scottish Rite,* pages 459-460.
387 Quoted in Stemper, William H. Jr., *Freemasonry and the Force,* page 33.

increasingly during the 19th century as a broader Temple, the method of perfecting its citizens took on scientific features adverse both to lingering ideas of original sin and natural law with the result that the vision within Freemasonry in general and the higher degrees in particular found expression in the extended symbolism of the Latrobe Capitol and the L'Enfant urban design. The result can be seen in the proliferation of state capital domes deriving from the Latrobe design each ultimately shaped and informed by the influence of the Pantheon through, most likely, the Florentine Cathedral dome by Filippo Brunelleschi (1377-1446) and, perhaps, the Maryland State House in Annapolis constructed between 1772-1779. Brunelleschi articulated the Christian usage of architectural symbol, and the Renaissance view of man, which informed the evolution of Masonic ritual. The nexus has been the Church's determination to construct housing for worship to glorify God and man's place within the created order in the divine human relationship. Described best in terms of indicative sign, rather than subjective symbol, it detailed Christian revelation in medieval society as normatively conventional, rather than as pointing to a reality beyond itself. In the more self-consciously philosophical era of Grand Lodge (*c.* 1717), imagery was viewed as ideas dwelling in God's Mind made known to man through human design. The Capitol sits on a hill circled by a road with streets radiating from it denoting solar divine light: a point within a circle as a new world temple of democratic, Masonic light. The United States Capitol also draws from Roman sources: Capitol Hill is named after Capitoline Hill of Ancient Rome. Capitoline Hill was one of the Seven Hills of Rome; the Seven Hills represent the sun, moon, Mars, Venus, Saturn, Mercury, and Jupiter, the King of Gods. The Temple of Jupiter once sat on Capitoline Hill; the Capitol building conforms with the hermetic maxim of *as above, so below* symbolically aligning governance with the supreme godly rulership of Jupiter, known as Zeus to the Greeks. On the apex of the Apollonian dome, since 1863, stands the Statue of Freedom designed by Freemason Thomas Crawford; she faces east greeting the rising sun.[388]

Thus the interplay of reason both as a method for political policy formation and as an icon within which a layering of symbolisms were carried

388 Wasserman, James, *The Secrets of Masonic Washington*, page 83.

into the same policy mission as visual rhetoric, was not only identified as a means to frame laws as a means to achieve the rulership of a learned clerisy through Freemasonry it provided an instrument to defeat lingering enthusiasms for original sin and natural law including Thomism and Aristotelian *a posteriori* politics as the foundation of the American nation. This double barreled rejection of Calvinism and Thomism resulted in Platonic Pythagoreanism becoming the principle intellectual medium through which symbolic labyrinths and mazes were architecturally configured integrating material culture with policy as a means to extend the dynamic of initiation into public spheres of influence and order. L'Enfant's vision of the District of Columbia street plan as a labyrinthine maze which might be navigated through the mastery of legal studies emerged as the principle extension of Benjamin Latrobe's dome design for the Capitol building and provided a means to approach the central temple of the nation through specific references to other lesser centers of bureaucratic power and influence. The Chevalier Ramsay's ideology and Martin Clare's narrative pointed the way conceptually through this maze because, both taken together were de facto refutations through an appeal to syncretistic application of ancient Egyptian symbolism defined to defeat orthodoxies associated in France with Fenelon's controversy with Bossiet over Augustianism (Jansenist controversy) and against, in Ramsay's case, Calvinism and in Clare's case against anti-Masonry itself. The interplay of the concept that the urban utopian labyrinthine maze was, in effect, the projection by L'Enfant of the inscriptions drawn symbolically from the two Enochic pillars, one discovered by Hermes Trismegistus the other by Pythagoras, according to myth and the Masonic Cooke Manuscript circa 1450, underscores the attachment by Latrobe and L'Enfant to the *Mysterion* concept as an *occult descriptive key* to American civil religion as an alternative, both to Catholic and Reformed intellectual infrastructure. The metaphorical and metaphysical guide to navigating this Enochic maze was to be found in inspiration by the Goddess of Reason, typified within a barrel vault at Calverton outside Baltimore by Ramée: as Minerva representing Pallas Athena, Isis, and the Virgin Mary as the ideal inspiration as the spiritual intellect along lines developed by Greenleaf's Druidical Pythagoreanism and as an imperial icon integrating Elizabethan and Counter-Reformation enthusiasms for the Virgin Mary,

Isis, the constellation Virgo in the Christian Mysterion.

Pharaonic associations between the architecture and layout of D.C. defined further the Egyptian monarch as the core icon with power over the regenerative energies of the nation. Thus this image, uniquely ascribed esoterically to George Washington in his Enochian solar ideography beneath the Capitol Dome in the *Apotheosis of Washington* by Constantino Brumidi (see Plate XXX) and in Robert Mills' rendering for the Baltimore Washington Monument, placed the Founder of the Nation as symbolically the subject of an Enochian pillar frieze designed but never fully executed, within which, similar to Trajan's Column,[389] the founding of the nation and the city that bears his name to the man were *intertwined* as conceptually applicable to the L'Enfant street design as a *symbolic labyrinthine* or *Pythagorean occult maze*, in the vein of the Rosicrucian *Hortus Palatinus*. This result further carries forward the solar symbolism linking George Washington to an emergent Apollonian sun god Horus, the child of Osiris and Isis, and to Isis as a proto-Virgin Mary rendering by implication Horus with the birth of Jesus Christ, the Sun of God. The ultimate result was to align the cityscape of the District of Columbia according to the Tudor concept of order as a hermetical, astrological, and kabbalistic reference. This astral reference was anticipated by Dr. Rob Morris years later with the origination of the Order of the Eastern Star in 1850 which contained reference to the Magi from the East as Persian rulers come to worship the Star in the East, presumably thought by Morris to be Sirius. The cabalistic Lost Word remains a reference to the secret, esoteric reference to the Eastern Star, Sirius, worshipped as Isis, who possessed the secret name of Amun Re/Ra and to the *Five Points of Fellowship* necessary to communicate

The pentacle emblem of the Order of the Eastern Star.

389 The Baltimore Washington Monument, like Trajan's Column, was intended to have bronze reliefs on its shaft detailing Washington's life, thereby linking the "deeds of the Man to the destiny of the Nation" through the medium of Neoclassical architecture. See Chapter XII.

the substitute word of Master Mason at the raising to the degree of Master Mason after the Real Word, recovered in the various Royal ceremonials was lost. The symbol for the Order of the Eastern Star is a pentagram representative of Sirius.

Thus the effect achieved, symbolically, a depiction of both the content and the method by which the American civil religion would be disseminated and incorporated particular esoteric images as emblems which made this dynamic persuasive and desirable, as we have seen within the hidden symbolism of Baltimore, Maryland. Other cities, such as Buffalo, New York developed parallel streetscapes. Not surprising as it was the Joseph Ellicott, brother of Andrew Ellicott, who planned the template of Buffalo.

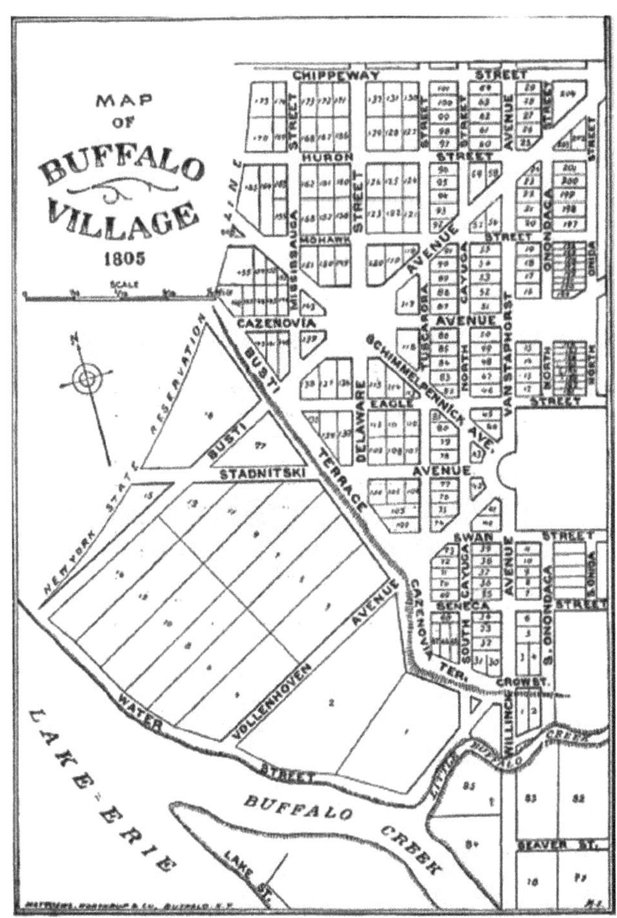

The Joseph Ellicott template for Buffalo, New York.

The Buffalo plan mirrors the District of Columbia plan because of the Royal Arch symbolism syncretic within the opening of the Erie Canal. It too features its city center with radiating streets emanating solar divine Masonic light. This was, of course, achieved at the level of civil piety and not intended to be a key to geometric order except that, Masonically, George Washington was widely regarded by Freemasons to be the quintessential Magus and Worshipful Master of the nation as a symbolic Craft Lodge, a ritual element routinely referenced in the opening rituals of private lodges. This entailed a widened variety of aspects of kingship found nowhere else in the ancient world and made a deep imprint upon Freemasons who say the rulership of Egypt as a paragon for the integration of republican and imperial virtues within the national destiny. Freemasonry's use of the Logos concept both to epitomize and consolidate the significance of the Royal Arch Word in a manner parallel to Logos theory in the Gospel of St. John and the interplay of this method with allegory underscore the manner in which Neo-Platonism and Docetic gnosticism projected the ideal of the paragon initiate onto the public sphere of political order through the Presidency. The series of presidents, from George Washington's transformation as Enoch, through Andrew Jackson, in specific, lifted up the office as device to transform the nation into semi-divinity in the same way that Zoroaster transformed the Persian Kingdom into a Mazdean[390] regime rooted in *imitatio dei*, the imitation of God. It is this symbol that the Presidency is deific, or God-like, that legitimates and authorizes the immense experiment in temple building that framed the District of Columbia as an exercise in a solar utopia and magnified its principal architects as Zoroastrian-Pythagorean Magi through which dwellings, monuments, and governmental buildings in general were structured to bring into material form creating stellar, celestial harmony. In this instance, both the Hermetical and Cabalistic Neo-Platonic roots of Freemasonry's impact upon American civil religion are more significant historically than has been assessed.

As Freemasonry moved within the United States into a broader European cultural and philosophical medium of expression, notably in philosophy and in music, the various aggregates of emblems, such as can be viewed in W. A. Mozart's *Magic Flute*, links the emblemature of domes with vaults and columns in extended visual metaphors within which mythic deities, such as Isis, Horus, and Osiris, preside over the dissemination of classical virtues such as Wisdom, Reason, and Nature. This theme, as well as the hermetic dictum of *as above, so below* can be seen in the architectural template of Washington, D.C. But, unlike Campanella's *City of the Sun*, Christ and his Twelve Apostles would obviously be removed and replaced with their

390 Pertaining to Ahura-Mazda: the beneficial deity within Zoroastrianism.

correct astrological antecedents. Not only does this marry the District of Columbia with the hermetic maxim, but exoterically it conforms to the Masonic concept of separation of church and state.

The District of Columbia was a square of ten miles exactly on each side. As discussed the number ten within Pythagorean Mysteries is the number of perfection. Thus the shape and size District of Columbia was symbolically invested with perfection. In addition, the square refers to moral integrity: equality, fair dealing and honesty.[391] The square is also a symbol of physical existence as defined by the interplay of the four elements: Fire, Air, Earth, and Water.[392] These elements are not considered to be the literal qualities of their physical representatives but the ideal components of God's creation.[393] Within the District, the L'Enfant street plan of 1791 took form as circles placed or twinned overtop rectangles or oblongs: the former symbolic of the sun and higher degree Masonic Rituals and the latter a symbol of the Masonic Lodge. This plan was no doubt heavily influenced by Freemasons George Washington and Daniel Carroll; but was also informed by Thomas Jefferson, astrologer and astronomer Benjamin Banneker, and Andrew Ellicott, who, like Washington, was a land surveyor.

The Capital City is architecturally enveloped with the Egyptian hieroglyph for Sirius, which in Egyptian Mythology is the star associated with the virgin mother of the sun, Isis. The hieroglyph includes a dome, or *benben*, the sacred stone of Heliopolis where first rays of the rising sun fell. The *benben* is the Capitol Dome represents the sun god Apollo, and as a cabalistic New World Temple of Light, or democracy. The glyph also features an obelisk which took concrete form in the Washington Monument and a pentagram that would take shape as a broken pentagram, created by geometric roundabouts, with the Executive Mansion or White House located at its bottom point.

Egyptian hieroglyph for the Dog Star Sirius.

The Washington Monument is not only associated with the hieroglyph

391 Wasserman, James, *The Secrets of Masonic Washington*, 46.
392 Ibid.
393 Ibid.

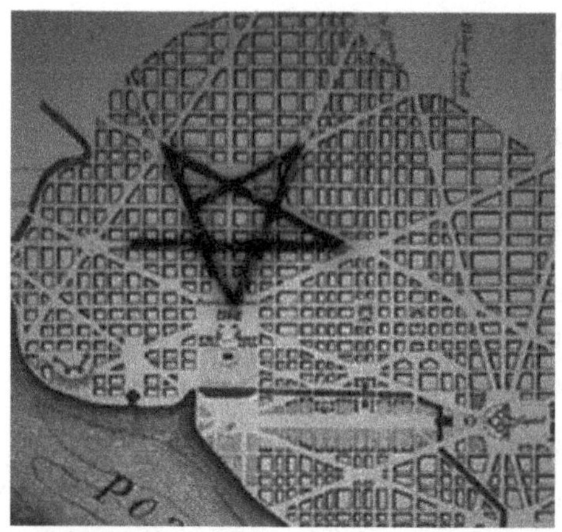

The broken pentagram formed by streets connecting circles including Logan Circle and Mt. Vernon Square over the White House.

of Sirius; the monument contains other hidden astrological symbolism. An obelisk is a symbol of Amun-Ra/ Re, the foremost Egyptian sun god, thus further linking George Washington himself, and the Federal City with solar Egyptian symbolism. This symbolism would again change as under the rule of the Pharaoh Akhenaten (Amenhotep IV) of the 18th Dynasty the obelisk would come to symbolize the sun god Aten, the physical embodiment of the sun; the name Akhenaten means, "the spirit of Aten." The cornerstone was laid on July 4th, 1848; it is on this date the sun passes over Sirius thus uniting Isis with Amun Ra/Re or, alternatively, her solar son Horus, the heir of Osiris. Construction was halted on the obelisk due to funding and the outbreak of Civil War in 1861. Construction would begin again; a second cornerstone was laid on Saturday, August 7, 1880, *at one minute to 11 o'clock.*[394] The time 10:59 am, is a concealed, esoteric reference to the location of Sirius on July 4, 1776, because Sirius *qua* Isis was *ten minutes, fifty-nine seconds* in Cancer.[395]

The symbolism of the Capitol building, having already been discussed; the symbolism of the home of the Executive, the White House, will now be analyzed: it too is an emblem of Freemasonry. It was designed by a Freemason, James Hoban (ca. 1758-1831), and is modeled after Leinster Palace in Dublin Ireland. Leinster Palace was originally the home of the 20th Earl of Kildare, James Fitzgerald, who also founded the Grand Master of the Grand Lodge of Ireland. The cornerstone was laid according to Masonic Ritual on October 13, 1792, coinciding with the arrest of the Knights Templars by King Phillip IV (a/k/a Phillip the Fair) of France on October 13, 1307. The cornerstone of the White House was laid 485 years later. The date of October 13, 1932 would

394 Ovason, David, *The Secret Architecture of Our Nation's Capital,* page 129.
395 Ibid, page 138.

also see the cornerstone laying of the Supreme Court building. Exoterically it is the 140th anniversary of the White House ceremony; esoterically the cornerstone spiritually aligns the Supreme Court building to the House of Libra as the sun is fully in Libra on October 13th. The Supreme Court building is symbolically ruled by the stellar balancing scales emblematic of justice and equilibrium; *as above, so below*.

The streets above the White House complete the hieroglyph of Sirius as the five pointed star is created by various roundabouts. The Executive Mansion sits at the bottom point. The pentagram is broken, as Rhode Island Avenue does not connect to Pennsylvania Avenue at Washington Circle Park. The use of a broken pentagram can be seen in the work of Freemason and Illuminist Johann Wolfgang von Goethe's (1749-1832) *Faust*, Part I of which was published in 1806, but was based on a partial printing entitled *Faust* of 1791, the same year of the L'Enfant template. Goethe's play was in turn based on *The Tragical History of Doctor Faustus* by Christopher Marlowe (1564-1593) published in 1604 eleven years after Marlow's death. In Goethe's play Dr. Faust summons Mephistopheles in order to make a pact to gain more occult knowledge and magical power. Mephistopheles appears within his study (Scene 6), then, after conversing, Faust bids Mephistopheles to leave. The following dialog occurs:

Mephistopheles:
Let me own up! I cannot go away;
a little hinderance bids me stay,
the witch's foot upon your sill I see.
Faust:
The pentagram? That's in your way?
You son of Hell explain to me,
if that stays you, how came you in today?
Mephistopheles:
Observe it closely! It is not well made;
one angle, on the outer side of it,
is just a little open, as you see.

On this symbolism, Masonic scholar Manly Palmer Hall opines,

> "The pentagram is used extensively in black magic,
> but when so used its form always differs
> in one of three ways: The star may be broken at one
> point not permitting the converging lines to touch;
> it may be inverted by having one
> point down and two up; or it may be distorted
> by having points of varying lengths."[396]

There is a deeper symbolism at work here. The character of Dr. Faust (or Faustus) represents the Elizabethan sage Dr. John Dee. Dee, who was aided by a fellow mystic named Edward Kelly (1555-1597), formulated a highly complex system of conjury called Enochian Magic. The Enochian system of Dee and Kelly (or Kelley) had its own language; the language was allegedly spoken between God and Adam in the Garden and between Enoch and God when he was exalted into the heavens. Enochian Magic was developed from the *Corpus Hermeticum* which in turn rehabilitated the occult Egyptianate magic as discussed by Thoth Hermes Mercurius Trismegistus in the book *Asclepius*; it approved of both natural and demonic magic in order to communicate with supernatural entities.[397] This was not necessarily demonism or Satanism, rather a way for man to understand nature, the world, and the universe via interactions with these beings. In other words, the Renaissance Magus, as articulated by Giovanni Pico della Mirandola combining magic with Cabala, fused with the natural and hermetic magic of Ficino and the darker, Egyptian magic of Bruno and the sorcery of Agrippa, brought the Magus in contact with angelic (and perhaps demonic) hierarchies. Through the practice of Enochian Magic, Dee and Kelly communicated with angels; they discovered,

- That Jesus Christ was not divine.
- That no prayer ought to be made to Christ Jesus.
- There is no sin.
- Man's soul goes from one body to another (i.e. reincarnation).
- That as many men and woman are now, there have always been.

396 Hall, Manly Palmer, *Secret Teachings of All Ages*, page 327.
397 French, Peter, *John Dee: The World of an Elizabethan Magus*, pages 86-89.

- That the generation of mankind from Adam and Eve is not historical but allegorical.

Despite condemnation from Biblical scripture, St. Augustine, The Inquisition and Catholic Church in general against idolatry and demonism, Renaissance magi such as Dee, Bruno, Ficino, and Campanella simply ignored such warnings; Dr. Dee's system was named after the Biblical patriarch Enoch, whom, as we have seen, is of utmost importance within Masonry and the Royal Arch degree. Dee, like Origen, seemingly had access to a copy of *I Enoch* as Dee's knowledge of demons and angels was extensive; could this have been the same volume that inspired the Royal Arch ceremony born out of Ramsay's Oration? The practice of Enochian Magic was allegedly suppose to allow the practitioner communication with both angelic and demonic entities to gain divine wisdom, represented by Mephistopheles in *Faust*, just as Enoch himself conversed with angels, both divine and demonic, and was taught mystical knowledge by them. Enoch was also an intermediary for these demonic angels known as the Watchers, a race of fallen angels or evil beings who fathered offspring known as the Nephilim through sexual congress with human women. Within Goethe's *Faust* the personification of Mephistopheles, as a stoic aloof academic, symbolizes the bringer of wisdom, *light*, in this case infinite knowledge, both scientific and religious, that Faust, like Dee so eagerly craved. This parallels Enoch's serving as an intermediary on behalf demons who possess forbidden knowledge as described in *I Enoch*. This same theme would be developed years later by Masonic ritualist Albert Pike who correctly baptized Lucifer as the bringer of light, esoteric knowledge, in his *Morals and Dogma of the Ancient and Accepted Scottish Rite of Freemasonry* published in 1871. Just as Mephistopheles is the bringer of *light* (or wisdom) by way of a broken pentagram within Goethe's Faustian Universe, Lucifer to Pike was the planet Venus, the *Light-bearer*, the Son of the Morning, as Venus is often visible in the east before sunrise when the sun (not Venus) rises bringing light and salvation to the world. As Venus appeared in the east before sunrise it was referred to as the false light, hence the association with Lucifer, the fallen angel (cf. the Watchers element from *I Enoch*, see Chapters I and IV). Venus, a feminine planet, due to its close proximity to the sun (Christ Jesus) took on the female persona of Mary Magdalene within the Christian Mysterion; the Gnostics often referred to Magdalene as *Mary Lucifera* hence her later demonization by the Christian Church. Mephistopheles embodies one of Dee's Enochian Principalities who brings *light* or knowledge to Faust, just as Venus or Lucifer symbolizes the coming of true *light*, the sun representing knowledge and wisdom, within Masonry.[398] The broken pentagram thus becomes an Enochic symbol within the context of the District's street plan: the nexus formed by its use by Goethe's Dr. Faust *qua* Dr. John Dee, and his practice of hermetical Enochian cabalistic magic as identified by the Biblical patriarch Enoch from his mediations with a host of evil angels: the Watchers. The placement of a pentagram within its streets above the White House also completes the hieroglyph of Sirius within the Mysteries of Isis. Just as the virgin goddess Isis, whose star is Sirius (*Sothis*), aligns with Orion or Osiris via the Three Kings (Orion's Belt) to birth the sun, Horus, at the winter solstice; Washington, D.C. becomes cabalistically synchronized to Egyptian occult-theology-astrology of Sirius as the true mother of the sun; the sun being the ultimate symbol of Masonic *light* or wisdom which is alternatively brought before sunrise by Venus, *the Son of the Morning*, or Lucifer. The Egyptian Trinity of Osiris, Isis, and Horus can be further seen in the template of the District of Columbia, *est civitas Solis*, by way of its Pythagorean Federal Triangle.

*   *   *   *   *

The Capitol (the *benben*), the Washington Monument (the obelisk), and the White House (the pentagram) form the geomantic Pythagorean Federal Triangle[399] which was part of the original L'Enfant. The three edifices form a Pythagorean triangle with the hypotenuse connecting both

398 Pike, Albert, *Morals and Dogma of the Ancient and Accepted Scottish Rite,* page 321. Venus or Lucifer itself has no actual or symbolic importance within Freemasonry. Venus was the Roman goddess of beauty and love who was accepted by the Greeks as Aphrodite. Venus is an inferior planet and is merely an icon of the coming sunrise; the sun being *the symbol* for Deity and sublime wisdom within Masonry.

399 The Washington Monument is not aligned properly to the White House due to the instability of the land within the National Mall as it could not hold the weight of such a heavy monument. As such the proper east/west-north/south alignment is marked by the Jefferson Pier Stone; it forms the corner of the 90 degree angle opposite the hypotenuse, Pennsylvania Avenue. The Jefferson Pier Stone rests 390 feet northwest of the Washington Monument. See Ovason, David, *The Secret Architecture of Our Nation's Capital,* page 126; and Wasserman, James, *The Secrets of Masonic Washington,* 134-135.

the White House and the U.S. Capitol: the executive and the legislature, representatives of which are duly elected by the people. The Pythagorean Theorem is also known as the 47th Proposition (or Problem) of Euclid, which all Master Masons are instructed to meditate upon after being raised to that sublime degree. "The *Forty-seventh proposition of Euclid* was invented and explained by Pythagoras, and is so extensively useful that it has been adopted in all Lodges as a significant symbol of Freemasonry."[400] The Pythagorean Theorem is represented by the jewel worn by the presiding Worshipful Master of a Masonic Temple and thus represents Masonic leadership and rulership. The hypotenuse of the Federal triangle is formed by Pennsylvania Avenue, an occult reference to the Keystone state, itself a symbol of strength and new birth within the Royal Arch degree as analyzed. The executive and legislative branches, connected by Pennsylvania Avenue, are Masonically consecrated with Royal Arch symbolism of Logos drawing upon the symbolism of Hiram Abif's keystone that was discovered in the Mark Master Mason degree and rediscovered within the Royal Arch ceremonies. Pennsylvania Avenue was originally intended as a grand thoroughfare: an unobstructed view between the Capitol building and the Executive Mansion for nearly a mile. The Pythagorean Federal Triangle within the District of Columbia also embodies the Egyptian Triad. The perpendicular side is formed from the White House to the Washington Monument, the base is from the Washington Monument to the U.S. Capitol, and the hypotenuse from the Capitol to the White House by way of Pennsylvania Avenue; "....the perpendicular is designed by them to represent the masculine nature, the base the feminine, and that the hypotenuse is to be looked upon as the offspring of both; and accordingly the first of them will aptly enough represent Osiris, or the prime cause, the second, Isis, or the receptive capacity, the last, Horus, or the common effect of the other two."[401] Triads of the same kind are found in the Kabbalah.[402] Pennsylvania Avenue, the hypotenuse, contains Masonic astrological symbolisms as well.

---

400 Macoy, Robert, *A Dictionary of Freemasonry,* pages 311-312.
401 Pike, Albert, *Morals and Dogma of the Scottish Rite,* pages 87-88, quoting Plutarch.
402 Ibid, page 87.

Within Masonry the symbolism of the Setting Sun conforms with "… the duty of the Senior Wardens to pay and dismiss the Craft at the close of the day, when the sun sinks in the West, so now the Senior Warden is said in the Lodge to represent the setting sun."[403] Author David Ovason, in his book *The Secret Architecture of Our Nation's Capital: The Masons and the Building of Washington, D.C.*, adroitly notes the setting sun on the date of August 10th forms a astrological equilateral triangle in the sky. The star Regulus within the constellation Leo rests over the White House on the horizon if one looks westward down Pennsylvania Avenue towards the setting sun on August 10th. Regulus is the brightest star in constellation Leo; Leo being ruled by the sun thereby ordaining the Executive Branch with Masonic solar symbolism; the nexus formed by the raising of a Master Mason from his symbolic death by the strong grip of the *Lion's Paw*, a reference to the constellation Leo. Hanging in the nighttime sky above Regulus are the stars Spica within the constellation Virgo and Arcturus within the constellation Bootes: these three stars frame the Constellation Virgo within a triangle over the capital city[404] thus investing it with Isis-Marian as the symbolic Virgin mother of the *City of the Sun* (cf. Horus, Mithras, Apollo, Amun Re/Ra, Osiris, and Christ Jesus). Masonic ritualist and scholar Albert Pike traced stellar triangles: he articulated that the stars Regulus, Arcturus, and Spica actually form an equilateral triangle: a astrological Past Master's Jewel which itself is a symbol of Masonic perfection on the spiritual plane.[405] Albert Mackey states,

> "The equilateral triangle appears to have been adopted by nearly all the nations of antiquity as a symbol of Deity, in some of his forms and emanations, and hence, probably, the prevailing influence of this symbol was carried into the Jewish system, where the yod within the triangle was made to represent the Tetragrammaton, or sacred name of God."[406]

403 Mackey, Albert, *An Encyclopedia of Freemasonry,* Vol. II, page 682.
404 Ovason, David, *The Secret Architecture of Our Nation's Capital: The Masons and the Building of Washington D.C.*, pages 345-350.
405 Quoted in Ibid, page 258.
406 Mackey, Albert, *Encyclopedia of Freemasonry, Vol. II,* page 800.

The District of Columbia also comes to symbolize Solomon's Temple, a new Jerusalem, becoming an actual city of *perfection,* of Logos: a beacon of solar and cosmological order so that the New World's City of the Sun will bring Masonic order out of chaos. On this Albert Pike writes:

> "The Temple of Solomon, re-built and consecrated to the Catholic worship would become, in effect, the Metropolis of the Universe; the East would prevail over the West, and the Patriarchs of Constantinople would possess themselves of the Papal Power."[407]

The House of the Temple: the Headquarters of The Supreme Council, 33°, Ancient & Accepted Scottish Rite of Freemasonry, Southern Jurisdiction would come to rest thirteen blocks from the White House. The thirteen blocks represent the 13th degree of Rite of Perfection and the Scottish Rite Masonry: The Royal Arch of Enoch,[408] thereby masking the United States Presidency as a Masonic symbol of Logos and investing the Presidency as a de facto Masonic leader of the United States millennial Masonic Republic with the President akin to a Joachimite *Novus Dux.*

In *Disclosure on Architecture*, Masonic architect Sir Christopher Wren argued that the buildings in a city should inspire their people to love their country, and that their architecture should "aim at Eternity;" he drew upon his knowledge of the ancient world and Masonic Legend as he discusses Cain's City of Enos, the Tower of Babel, the Pillar of Absalom, the Pyramids of Egypt, the Temple of Solomon, Noah's Ark and the Two Pillars of Enoch. It is apparent that Enochian, astrological, and a general theme of Masonic-Egyptian solar rulership permeates the District of Columbia as a city for all Eternity. The minds behind the District of Columbia, both its design and actual construction, were, like Sir Christopher Wren, all Masons including George Washington, Daniel Carroll, Benjamin Henry Latrobe, Robert Mills, and James Hoban; all familiar with the esoteric lore of Masonry, its charges and histories, and in particular the Royal Arch ceremonies. Benjamin Banneker (1731-1806), not a Freemason, was also instrumental in the development of the template of the nation's capital;

407 Pike, Albert, *Morals and Dogma of the Ancient and Accepted Scottish Rite,* page 816.
408 Knight of the Ninth Arch in the Northern Jurisdiction.

he was a free African American surveyor well versed in mathematics and astronomy. Banneker wrote several almanacs accurately tracking lunar and solar eclipses while predicting various weather forecasts upon the United States eastern seaboard.

Pierre Charles L'Enfant was ultimately removed from his duties regarding the design of the District of Columbia by George Washington in January 1792, for his hardheadedness and arrogance. Thomas Jefferson also had input on the architectural design and layout of the new Federal City. Jefferson was not a Freemason, but was familiar with Masonic and Illuministic philosophies and principles from his time in Paris as ambassador from 1785 to 1789. Paris and France in general, was at that time a hotbed of the Illuminati as well as occultism; Jefferson was an ardent supporter, some would argue quasi-instigator, of the Illuminati-styled or propogated French Revolution. The Marquis de Lafayette often consulted Jefferson on the drafting of the *Declaration of the Rights of Man and of the Citizen*, the cornerstone of the French Revolution, which Jefferson willingly obliged; it was approved by the National Assembly of France 26 August 1789. Nevertheless, it is unlikely that Jefferson realized the comport of how the French Revolution and the Illuminati might have served latent Jesuit and Catholic apologetic principles by eradicating, during The Terror, the very precipitators of the Revolution, nor would he have believed it if the evidence had been presented to him. The founder of the Illuminati Adam Weishaupt, was after all, educated by the Jesuits and was accused of Jesuitism and being a Jesuit in disguise by fellow Freemason and Illuminist Adolph Knigge (1752-1796). The Illuminati was modeled after the Society of Jesus; the adepts of the Illuminati were governed by rules nearly identical with those of the Jesuits: both their constructs so similar (such as cells and the implementation of counter-cells) they can barely be separated.[409] It should be pointed out that the Illuminati (of 1776) *appears* to be a Jesuit sponsored program; at its root base was the retaliation against Rome for the suppression of the Jesuits by Pope Clement XIV in 1773 due to their political meddling in Spain, Portugal, and France not to mention their seemingly unfettered interest in Egyptian occult iconography. Pope Clement XIV's *Dominus ac Redemptor* was ignored in non-Catholic

409 Macoy, Robert, *A Dictionary of Freemasonry* 182.

countries including Prussia allowing the Jesuits freedom to plot, scheme, and remain generally at large. It should come as no surprise that the birthplace of the anti-Catholic Illuminati was Bavaria, Prussia, a mere three years after Clement's papal brief. The Illuminati would be held responsible for the anti-religious pogroms during the early days of the French Revolution. The occult ideology behind these pogroms ultimately it turned against itself leading to The Terror (1793-1794) of Maximilien Robespierre (1758-1794) where no one was spared, not even Robespierre himself. Such conspiracies would have made no sense to Thomas Jefferson even if they had been rooted in concrete politics of Jesuit participation (in this case as a fifth column) in nation building and as a force in general within European politics.[410] What would have been persuasive to Jefferson was the survival of architectural form as de facto ideology through the clientage of elites devoted to special interests and to provincial compartmentalized interests within which Freemasonry very successfully inserted its polemical symbolism through the veneration it drew on behalf of George Washington, Benjamin Franklin, and his own Vice President George Clinton. This de facto ideology would take concrete form within architecture and street design of the District of Columbia. Jefferson was also influenced years earlier by egalitarian Masonic ideals which flourished in Masonic Lodges both in the New and Old World that took form in his deistic and humanistic Declaration of Independence of July 1776, drafted a two months after the founding of the Illuminati (as the Perfectibilists) in Bavaria on May 1, 1776. It should come as no surprise that several of the signers of the Declaration of Independence were Freemasons. Included among these are, but not limited to, John Hancock (1737-1793) and Robert Treat Paine (1731-1814) of Massachusetts, William Whipple (1730 -1785) of New Hampshire, Joseph Hewes (1730-1799) of North Carolina, and Richard Stockton (1730-1781) of New Jersey. Likewise many of the ratifiers of United States Constitution in 1789 were Freemasons. The United States Constitution is, one could successfully argue, a Masonic document because it incorporates several important elements of the *Constitutions of the Free-Masons* of Anderson such as a separation of *church and state*

410 Despite the apparent downfall of the Catholic Church due to the execution of its clergy, the loss of the Papal States, and the closure of the Inquisition under the reign of Napoleon I, the Concordat of 1801 restored the Catholic Church within France. The end game was achieved after the Napoleonic Wars at the Congress of Vienna (1814-1815) where the Papal States, the Inquisition, and the Jesuits were fully restored.

(Article I, 1723, 1738). The three branches: the executive, legislative, and judicial correspond to the triple division of government within a lodge by its three officers: the Worshipful Master, the Senior and Junior Wardens representative of the sun in its three manifestations in the east, west, and south.[411] Supreme power was, in the ancient world, always associated with three-fold division.[412] As discussed in earlier chapter it is easy to forge the nexus that the United States is, by and large, a Masonic Republic based on Masonic principles of liberty and egalitarianism. Is it not common sense that Freemasonry and its high degrees should influence, if not dictate, the architectural design and layout of the first Masonic Republic's Capital City as a vista that embodied these New World-Hermetical-Enlightenment-Qabalistic concepts? *Doubt it not!* With the end result being the successful symbolic architectural transformation of George Washington into an Enochic sun god, and the District of Columbia into a perfected solar Masonic Temple.

411 Mackey, Albert, *Encyclopedia of Freemasonry,* page 736.
412 Ibid.

CHAPTER XV

SO DARK THE CON OF MAN: MASONIC AND ENOCHIC SYMBOLISM IN CINEMA

Being There, National Treasures, the Dan Brown Universe, *Excalibur* and *The Ninth Gate*

"The Templars and the Freemasons believed
that the treasure was too great for
any one man to have, not even a king.
That's why they went to such lengths to keep it hidden."
- Special Agent Sadusky, *National Treasure,* 2004.

"Yes. In the garden, growth has it seasons.
First comes spring and summer, but then we have
fall and winter. And then we get spring and summer again."
- Chance the Gardener, *Being There*, 1979.

Freemasonry has often been a favorite subject of Hollywood. Many motion pictures deal with the subject of Masonry in a variety of ways portraying it in both positive and negative lights. While *The Man who Would be King*[413] (1975) and *Tombstone* (1993) would be an example of the former, *From Hell* (2001) and *Murder by Decree* (1979) would exemplify the latter. In the movie *The Man who Would be King* renegade soldiers convince African tribesmen they are Gods by the wearing of Masonic emblems. In *Tombstone* many of the lawmen who battle the villainous Cowboys wear Masonic medals and medallions. On the other hand, films like *From Hell* and *Murder by Decree* portray Freemasons as being above the law, who murderously enforce their mandates. *From Hell* and *Murder by Decree* are loosely based on the 1976 book *Jack the Ripper:*

413 Based on the novella of the same name by Freemason Rudyard Kipling.

The Final Solution by Stephen Knight; the former is also based on a comic book series bearing the same name. Knight's book hypothesizes that the Jack the Ripper serial murders of 1888 in Whitechapel, London, England were part of a sinister Masonic conspiracy to eliminate witnesses privy to the fact that there was a Roman Catholic heir to the English throne. According to the films (and the book) the Ripper murders are re-enactments of Masonic penalties while the placement of certain tokens around each of the victims reveal Masonic symbolism and hence their involvement. Despite there being very little, if any, evidence to suggest any Masonic influence in the Ripper murders, the conspiracy persists and does not seem to be going away any time soon. Masonry in cinema is an interesting subject, but it is not this author's intent to list out all movies that include Masonic symbolism which would be a daunting task. Rather this chapter analyzes a few examples of hidden Masonic, Enochian, solar, and kabbalistic symbolism contained within movies that may not noticed by the viewer at first glance.

Being There

Many Masonic references occur in films where the imagery is subtle and concealed. This is generally because the movies themselves are not directly about Masonry. For example, in the film *Being There*[414] (1979) the viewer is able to view Masonic insinuation at the conclusion of the film. The movie details the adventures of a savant named Chance portrayed by Peter Sellers, himself a Freemason of Chelsea Lodge #3098, and his interaction with the Washington, D.C. aristocracy. Chance is a gardener who becomes incorrectly known as "Chauncey Gardner." Chance himself is, symbolically, a solar hero who endlessly drones on and on about the solstices, the equinoxes and the changes to the weather and vegetation, that they bring. Chance becomes friends, albeit accidentally, with a D.C. billionaire named Benjamin Turnbull Rand. Rand is an influential member of the D.C. ruling elite who is consulted frequently by industrialists and political elites including the President of the United States played by Jack Warden (1920-2006). Throughout the film, the President seeks economic advice and leadership that Rand willingly provides; it becomes clear that

414 The movie is based on the 1971 novel of the same name by Jerzy Kosinski.

the President is a mere puppet of Rand and will implement whatever policy or strategy Rand advises. Rand's advice to the President becomes more and more heavily influenced by the cryptic seasonal metaphoric musings of Chauncey Gardner.

Rand's involvement with this ruling elite and a secret cabal who "pull the strings," of the United States government is confirmed at the film's conclusion. Benjamin Rand dies and the movie concludes with his coffin being placed into a Masonic styled crypt. Rand's crypt is the reverse seal of the United States of America only with the capstone in place symbolizing completion: the temple is now finished; as such the life is complete or finished. As the President reads his eulogy, and as the coffin approaches the tomb, Rand's pallbearers, described by the President as Rand's "close friends," can be heard discussing whom they should *select* to be the next President of the United States regardless of the sentiments of the American people. If they do not select the right person, they worry they will lose the Presidency. Their likely candidate is none other than Chauncey Gardner; at the movie's conclusion Gardner, like the sun god Christ, walks on water.

National Treasure and National Treasure: Book of Secrets

Some movies are overtly Masonic and none comes to mind more than the *National Treasure* movies. The first *National Treasure* movie, released in 2004, was truly the first movie to explore the Masonic if not occult or hidden history of the United States of America. The film details the adventures of treasure hunter Benjamin Franklin Gates portrayed by Nicholas Cage. Gates and his coterie are searching for the lost treasure of the Knights Templar which, according to the film, was moved from Europe and hidden in America around the time of the U.S. Revolution by the Freemasons. Gates deciphers clues left behind by famous masons including Dr. Benjamin Franklin and Charles Carroll of Carrollton[415] to finally locate the Templar Treasure hidden in a vault under the grounds of a New York

415 Charles Carol of Carrollton was not a Freemason contrary to what the movie states.

City church. The sequel *National Treasure: Book of Secrets* involves the search for El Dorado or the Lost City of Gold. What is not noticed at first is that both the *National Treasure* movies conceal hidden Enochian-Masonic symbolism.

For Example, the first *National Treasure* is the Royal Arch of Enoch ritual revealed. Like the Scotch Master Degree, the hidden vault containing the treasure is discovered by a group of Knights Templars and not workers building the Second Temple. At the beginning of the movie the audience is told by John Adams Gates (Christopher Plummer) that the Templars originally found the treasure in secret vaults under Solomon's Temple. This is in complete harmony with the Royal Arch-Scotch Master ceremony –at *National Treasure's* conclusion the characters are descending into a vault to discover the treasure of the Knights Templar; it is symbolic of the treasure of Freemasonry which is the recovery of the Lost Word: the Name of God concealed within the vault below. The first *National Treasure* movie is the quest for this. The vault lies beneath Trinity Church located in New York City. Trinity Church symbolizes Solomon's Temple where the vault containing the treasure (cf. Lost Word) was originally discovered under Mount Moriah by the Templars (cf. Scotch Master's degree). Trinity Church is in *New York*, a clear reference to Royal Arch Grand High Priest DeWitt Clinton and his Knights Templary founded 1814. Earlier in the film when Ben Gates is stealing the Declaration of Independence, he steps into the Nation Archives' gift shop to hide from Abigail Chase. Abigail Chase's name is an amalgamation of Abigail Adams (1744-1818) and Samuel Chase (1741-1811); the former the first second lady and second first lady of the United States, the latter a signatory of the Declaration of Independence from Maryland. In the gift shop one will see three copies of David Ovason's book *The Secret Architecture of our Nation's Capital: The Masons and the Building of Washington D.C.* sitting next to the cash register. The three books naturally represent the first three degrees of Masonry: Entered Apprentice, Fellowcraft, and Master Mason and anticipates the final location of the treasure under Trinity Church as quasi-Masonic Solomon's Temple. The National Archives building overlooks Pennsylvania Avenue; Pennsylvania is the *Keystone State*; the Keystone is initially recovered during the Mark Master degree and rediscovered during the Royal Arch ceremonies. Pennsylvania Avenue is the hypotenuse of a Pythagorean right triangle that forms the Federal Triangle (Chapter XIV) and which Ovason's book claims is symbolic of the astrological sign of Virgo (cf. Marian-Isis symbolism); it also represents the 47th Proposition of Euclid.

Its sequel also contains Masonic symbolism. Albert Pike is referred to quite a bit in *National Treasure: Book of Secrets* (2007), namely by the character of Mitch Wilkinson played by Ed Harris. Pike was a 33rd degree Scottish Rite Mason credited for re-editing the Scottish Rite rituals. Pike was also author of the book *Morals and Dogma of the Ancient and Accepted Scottish Rite of Freemasonry* published in 1871. People who watch the film hear the reference, but most people seem to miss that Pike himself is in the movie, Pike can be seen interacting with John Wilkes Booth during the opening sequence when they approach Thomas Gates to solve the Playfair cipher in Booth's diary. Pike wears a Knights of the Golden Circle watch fob which reveals Pike as a Copperhead[416], according to the movie. It is Pike who retrieves the scorched page from Booth's diary when Thomas Gates throws it into the fire in order to prevent Pike and his ilk from solving the cipher. The burnt page is passed down to Mitch Wilkinson who claims descent from Albert Pike.

Further Masonic and esoteric symbolism appear in *National Treasure: Book of Secrets*. When Riley Poole is entering the five letter code at the beginning to solve the Playfair Cipher, the first word he enters is "bacon." This is a reference to Sir Francis Bacon, author of proto enlightenment works including *The New Atlantis* published in Latin in 1624, in English 1627, who often embedded codes and numerological riddles in his works. In Riley Poole's book *The Templar Treasure,* the information about the President's Secret Book is contained in Chapter 13. This refers to the 13th Degree of Scottish Rite Masonry (cf. Rite of Perfection) the Royal Arch of Enoch. As explained the 13th degree reveals wisdom by beholding the delta containing the sacred named of God. In turn the President's Secret Book imparts the final clue or piece of knowledge which reveals the location of El Dorado

416 Northerners who during the American Civil War supported the Confederacy.

which is located beneath Mount Rushmore. Mount Rushmore features two Masonic Presidents: George Washington and Theodore Roosevelt and was sculpted by Freemason Gutzon Borglum, a brother of Howard Lodge #35 in New York City. Finally, in *National Treasure: Book of Secrets* the President instructs Ben Gates to "take a look" at page forty-seven of his Secret Book to solve some great mystery. Page *forty-seven* is a reference to the 47th Proposition of Euclid, which all Master Masons are told to meditate upon after being raised to that degree, and the emblem of a Worshipful Master. According to Josephus, in his *Antiquities of the Jews*, Solomon's Temple stood for *four hundred and seventy years* before being destroyed by Persian King Nebuchandezzar II (ca. 634-562 BCE). in 587 BCE.[417] The construction of Solomon's Temple and the *word* necessary to build it, its recovery in Masonic ritual, dominates Masonry and its rituals as analyzed in this book.

THE DAN BROWN UNIVERSE: THE DA VINCI CODE AND ANGELS AND DEMONS[418]

Thirteenth Degree-Enochian symbolism is also replete in the Ron Howard directed film, *The Da Vinci Code* (film 2006, book 2003), while *Angels & Demons* (film 2009, book 2000) displays one example of Astro-theology. Both movies deal with secret societies and their conflicts with the Roman Catholic Church, the Vatican. *The Da Vinci Code* is heavily based upon the book *Holy Blood, Holy Grail* (1983) by Michael Baigent, Richard Leigh, and Henry Lincoln. When viewing *The Da Vinci Code*, pay close attention to when Professor Robert Langdon and Captain Bezu Fache are in the elevator descending in the Louvre, right after Langdon sees the Opus Dei pin on Fache's jacket, one will immediately see on the elevator keypad that the Mona Lisa is kept in Room *13* (*Salle 13*). Again, this is symbolically referring to the 13th degree of both the Rite of Perfection and the Ancient and Accepted Scottish Rite, the Royal Arch of Enoch. Here,

417 Steinmetz, George, *The Royal Arch: Its Hidden Meaning*, page 70.

418 The Blu-ray extended director cuts were viewed for this analysis.

the Mona Lisa has the phrase "*So Dark The Con Of Man*," written on it which imparts the clue that leads to Langdon and Sophie Neveu[419] to discover the key to the vault located at Haxo 24. An arch is held together a by Keystone (cf. Mark Master Mason-Royal Arch symbolism); in the *Da Vinci Code*, the Keystone is the Cryptex housed at Haxo 24. The Cryptex contains a map locating treasure, the Holy Grail.

Haxo 24 is the street address where the Cryptex (or Keystone) is located. The 24 seems to refer to the 24th degree of Scottish Rite Masonry (Southern Jurisdiction), or the Prince of the Tabernacle. The Jewel for this degree is the Phoenician letter Aleph in gold. The Aleph alludes to and refers to the pentagram and is synchronized with Saunière (the owner of the Cryptex) as he dies forming Da Vinci's *Vitruvian Man* symbolizing a divine microcosm as represented by the pentagram. As the movie progresses more thirteenth Enochian Royal Arch degree symbolism keeps appearing. When the albino monk Silas discovers the stone tablet, which he initially thinks is the Keystone, under the floor of the Parisian Church Saint-Sulpice, it is reads Job 38:11[420]. When one adds 3+8+1+1 one gets *13*: again a symbolic reference to the thirteenth degree, the Royal Arch of Enoch, where the Keystone of Hiram Abif is recovered by temple builders. It is the Keystone a/k/a the Cryptex that contains a map revealing the location of the Holy Grail that Silas seeks. This addition also works if one adds 38 + 11 to get 49; add 4+9 to get 13. When Sister Sandrine attempts to call Jacques Saunière to warn him that Silas is on the prowl, observe his phone number. The last three digits are 333; add 3 + 3 + 3 to get nine, a reference to the thirteenth degree called "Knight of the *Ninth* Arch" in the Scottish Rite Northern Jurisdiction, their Royal Arch ceremonial. This also refers to the nine arches under which the Tetragrammaton is recovered in the various Royal Arch ceremonies. When Andre Vernet, the bank manager, is escaping with Langdon and Neveu from the Swiss Bank, located at Haxo 24, he is stopped by an agent of Bezu Fache and asked about his Rolex watch. Vernet is driving the armored car with Langdon and Neveu in the back having successfully recovered the Keystone from the Swiss Bank. They

419 The name Sophie Neveu refers to the Gnostic goddess Sophia. Sophia or "Divine Wisdom" represents the feminine aspect in all things which is a main theme in both The Da Vinci movie and book.
420 "And said, Hitherto shalt thou come, but no further: and here shall thy proud waves be stayed?

are attempting to decode it. Vernet, in an effort to dissuade the agent from investigating further, tries to sell the agent his Rolex; the time on it reads 1:12 a.m. Add 1+12 to get 13 once again, because the Masonic Royal Arch *Keystone* is in close proximity to Vernet–it is in the back of the armored van which Vernet drives.[421]

The film *Angels and Demons* includes only one real hidden symbol in the form of a coat of arms. Albeit, more Astrotheologic than Masonic, it is still worth mentioning. When Robert Langdon (Hanks) and Vittoria Vetra (Ayelet Zurer) enter the Pantheon looking for the first marker, Vetra asks Langdon why the graves are at an angle. He responds they are facing east to worship the rising sun; that new religions adopt the customs of the pagan religions to make the transition easier. He states that December 25, the birth of Christ, is really the celebration of the birthday of the unconquered sun, *Sol Invictus*. What Langdon fails to mention is that Christianity is not original, rather, it is the pagan mystery religion(s) under a new name.

This is confirmed when Langdon and Vetra realize the Pantheon is not the location of the first marker, rather it is in the Chigi Chapel in the Church of Santa Maria del Popolo. Entering the chapel, they see the cover to a demon hole on the floor. The mosaic on the cover features a coat of arms[422] above the motto, *Mors Ad Caelos* (*Death opens the way to Heaven*), with two images on the shield. There are two *Fleurs de Lis* and two images of the sun placed on a cross, *crucified*, symbolizing that Christ is the sun as referred to by Langdon in the Pantheon minutes earlier. The *Fleur de Lis* more than likely represents a bee, or lily of France. Within the Greek mysteries the nine muses (patron goddesses of the arts) could transform into the form of bees[423], and is likely the reason the Temple of the Nine Muses (or Sisters) is the premier Masonic Lodge within the Grand Orient deFrance.

421 Many movies and television shows incorporate Qabalistic Numerology on clock faces and other numeric icons often to convey occult-esoteric messages. For example, the number 8 when turned sideways symbolizes infinity or the continuality of time and space. One can see the infinity symbol in the telephone booth keypad in both *Bill & Ted's Excellent Adventure* (1989) and *Bill & Ted's Bogus Journey* (1991) that must be pressed to initiate time travel. In the *Back to the Future* trilogy (1985, 1989, 1990) the DeLorean must reach *88* miles per hour to activate the "Masonic" triangular Flux Capacitor in order to break the space-time continuum. The inventor of the time machine, "Doc" Emmett Brown, represents Pythagoras, who rises from the grave at the end of the first film in keeping with theme of the third degree Master Mason ritual.
422 This is not the actual floor mosaic in the real Chigi Chapel in Rome, Italy.
423 Hall, Manly P., *The Secret Teaching of all Ages,* page 269.

EXCALIBUR

To understand the symbolism of the film *Excalibur* (1981) one must first understand the legend of King Arthur and the Grail Mysteries. First, King Arthur, like Apollo, Dionysus, Jesus Christ, Bacchus, Mithras, Osiris, Amun Ra/Re, and Horus, is a metaphor-avatar-stand-in for the sun and its annual travels among the Houses of the Zodiac based on the Earth's orbit around it. It has been claimed by certain authors that the character of King Arthur is based upon real life Christian Emperor Charlemagne, or even his grandfather Charles Martel. Some historians suggest that the story of King Arthur is the same as Jesus Christ: i.e. that Jesus Christ and King Arthur are one and the same person. It is further argued that the story of Christ was brought to England by Joseph of Arimathaea in the first century and was somehow transformed into the Arthurian legend. In fact, some claim that like Enoch before him, Joseph of Arimathaea, after he imported the Christ legend to England, was transported to the Heavens in corporeal form. Some more lurid claims hold that Joseph of Arimathaea was buried with the Holy Grail in Glastonbury Tor in a currently undiscovered burial vault. The characters in Arthurian Legend, like those within the Christian Mysteries, are the planets and their corresponding Zodiac; vestiges of the Egyptian-Mediterranean Mystery Schools. As has been discussed, the passing of the sun through these houses, either by way of the Precessionof the Equinoxes or earth's orbit around the sun, is the basis for many religions; it is also the basis for many folktales, nursery rhymes,[424] legends, and myths. King Arthur and the Knights of the Round Table is one of these.

King Arthur takes him name from the star Arcturus, the brightest star in the constellation Bootes and third brightest star in the nighttime sky. The constellation Bootes represents Arthur's father Uther Pendragon (*of the Dragon*) who takes his name from the nearby constellation Draco which means dragon. King Arthur's mother Igraine is the zodiac constellation Virgo,[425] represented by the star Spica, which sits close to the constellation Bootes (Joseph, Christ's earthly father in the Mysterion) and the star

424 For example in the nursery rhyme "Jack & Jill;" Jack is the sun, Jill is the moon, and the pail of water they are after is Aquarius' water pitcher.
425 The virgin birth is absent from the Arthurian legend.

Arcturus. King Arthur is a metaphoric stand-in for the sun and its travels through the zodiac based upon the Earth's orbit around it. The twelve Knights of the Round Table are the twelve houses of the Zodiac. There are sometimes twenty-four Knights of the Round Table representing the diurnal and nocturnal phases of the twelve houses.[426] Mordred, who is Arthur' son and the Knight that betrays him, symbolizes the sign of Scorpio–Typhon in the Egyptian Mysteries–while Merlin the Magician represents the sage Thoth Hermes Mercurius Trismegistus. Queen Guinevere, King Arthur's wife, while not a Knight of the Round Table, represents the House of Cancer: the "White Queen" who is ruled by the moon, representing Isis, whose star Sirius rises when the sun is in Cancer (summer solstice); Cancer is ruled by the moon. Sir Lancelot is the House of Leo, who is the best and bravest of Arthur's Knights, is Leo, the sole house of the sun. King Arthur and his Knights search for the Holy Grail, signifying divine esoteric secrets or knowledge, in which Albert G. Mackey saw as a parallel to the Lost Word sought by Freemasons of the Blue Lodge. Arthurian astronomical-astrological symbolism is on full display in John Boorman's *Excalibur*, which is based upon *Le Morte d'Arthur* (*The Death of Arthur*) by Sir Thomas Malory published 1485. *Le Morte d'Arthur* appears to be a conglomeration of all the Arthurian Mysteries and borrows from Wolfram von Eschenbach's thirteenth century poem *Perzival.* Nineteenth century composer Richard Wagner likewise based his opera *Parsifel* upon Malory's and von Eschenbach's works. While King Arthur's legend is not necessarily Masonic, it is still a solar allegory and an interesting one at that.

Accordingly, within the movie *Excalibur,* Merlin the Magician, portrayed by Nicol Williamson, is the messenger of wisdom and light and is a metaphoric stand-in for Thoth Hermes Mercurius Trismegistus. When *Excalibur* opens, Merlin, the great wizard, is first seen rising over the horizon personifying a "rising sun" as the messenger of divine solar light. Mercury is closest to the sun, as such Mercury (Hermes to the Greeks) was the symbolic messenger of its light, so too is Merlin the keeper of "the light" or divine esoteric magical wisdom that both Uther Pendragon and King Arthur seek and rely on. The tip of Merlin's staff displays two serpents

426 Hall, Manly Palmer, *The Secret Teachings of All Ages*, page 590.

symbolic of Hermes' caduceus. King Arthur, portrayed by Nigel Terry, is the sun, and he is first seen during as a young adult during a drawing of the sword from the stone festival which occurs on Easter Sunday. Arthur successfully draws the sword and begins his reign as King. Arthur naturally starts his journey as King on Easter Sunday, which is a celebration of the vernal equinox when the Sun begins its solar journey through the northern arch of the zodiac on its way to the summer solstice in June. The sword of power Excalibur represents the brilliance of the sun's rays, which is why it can only be drawn from the stone and wielded by one person: King Arthur –the sun. Arthur draws Excalibur on Easter Sunday symbolic of the Vernal Equinox. Arthur thus begins his youthful solar rulership as King as the sun emerges from the tomb of winter. The sun, having been dead for three months (21 December to 21 March), begins its journey to the summer solstice as the stone of winter is rolled away. The sun emerges from its symbolic tomb as it is once again resurrected or *born again* on Easter. Just as Christ's tomb is opened by a stone, so too does Arthur begin his Kingship by drawing Excalibur from a *stone*. Thus, allegorically, the freeing of Excalibur from the stone equates to the removal of the stone from Christ's tomb: the rebirth of the sun, solar light, at the vernal equinox.

Through the film the audience is introduced to the various warlords that will become the Knights of the Round Table, yet within *Excalibur* it is not clear how many knights consist of the Round Table. Nevertheless the round table is eventually formed; it is the wheel of the zodiac forged by Merlin's (Hermes) wisdom. Arthur is seen ruling in peace until his half-sister, the sorceress Morgana le Fay, played by Helen Mirren, reappears. Morgana le Fay is the house of Libra which is ruled by the planet Venus. The first day of the autumnal equinox occurs in Libra thereby the sun begins to enter death foreshadowing the winter months. When a feminine character represents Libra she often appears as a trickster or charlatan as the sun is deceived by this character and sent heading into death or the winter months. Within the Arthurian Legend Morgana le Fay often controls Mordred who is trying to replace Arthur as King. In *Excalibur*, she has an incestuous relationship with Arthur and conceives Mordred, who is the traitor, a murderer of the sun, the house of Scorpio, which follows Libra or le Fay.

When Mordred enters the picture, he is always seen wearing golden armor symbolic of the sun golden rays in the house of Scorpio. Mordred does not carry a sword, rather his weapon is a golden spear signifying Scorpio's stinger. King Arthur now appears as a weak old man because the sun *qua* Mordred is exalted in the House of Scorpio; King Arthur is now dying because the sun is descending to the winter months of December, January, and February. This is a parallel of the Egyptian Mysteries when Scorpio *qua* Typhon was exalted, and Orion *qua* Osiris, the sun, waned and died.

King Arthur sends his Knights out to locate the "Holy Grail" which can only restore life. The great Grail Mystery, at least within the Arthurian context, is this: the grail is the cup that the constellation Aquarius pours his water out of in-between January 21 and February 19. It is missing; until the chalice is reunited with the water bearer, the sun is trapped in winter. Sir Percival represents the sign of Aquarius; it is only Percival that can find and locate the grail. This is why, earlier in the film, Percival is drawn to Sir Lancelot who is the House of Leo, *the opposite house of Aquarius*.

Percival sets out to find his lost cup when he encounters Morgana le Fay. She tells him that he has "crossed the great wasteland" and has searched for "ten years and a day," meaning that sun has been trapped in winter for that long. When the water bearer is finally reunited with his grail only then can the land be reborn because only then can Aquarius symbolically pour his water out onto the northern hemisphere of the Earth. This symbolizes the coming spring rains when the sun is *born again* at the vernal equinox: the days become longer, spring is now here, and winter is over with. The knight that recovers the chalice is Sir Percival who represents the water bearer and ultimately the constellation of Aquarius. By finding the "Holy Grail," the water bearer is reunited with his lost water pitcher: Percival is now the sign of Aquarius. By drinking from the cup of Aquarius, the sun symbolically exits death or winter and moves towards the vernal equinox where it, and the earth, will be born again.

Throughout the movie *Excalibur*, King Arthur and Merlin contemplate the conundrum: "*you* (Arthur) *and the land* (Earth) *are one*" which is the riddle that Percival solves near the end of the film. Arthur (the sun) and the land (Earth) *are indeed one*: when the sun dies in the winter months so too does the Earth die: crops stop growing and the land becomes a frozen wasteland. As Percival hands the grail to Arthur he states "You and the land are one… (drink and) you will be reborn and the land with you." Percival, discovering the Grail, is Aquarius pouring Spring rain unto the Earth. The sun now is able to leave winter behind, and move towards the vernal equinox where it will be "born again," so too is the Earth, the land, reborn. Plant life springs anew, the weather becomes warm (life), the cold (death) is gone, and the sun begins its triumphal march back along the northern arch to the summer solstice. One can view this symbolism *as plain as day* within this film: when Arthur drinks from the Grail he immediately springs to life. The drawbridge is lowered at Camelot; the vernal equinox is now here: the stone of winter is rolled always and King Arthur and his Knights ride forth to Carl Orff's "O' Fortuna" as plant life, foliage, and Spring returns all around him signifying the end of winter. The sun, King Arthur, is indeed *born again and the land with it*!

THE NINTH GATE

Examples of occult Freemasonry, Kabbalah, Gematria, and astrological symbolisms are on display in the 1999 movie *The Ninth Gate* starring Johnny Depp, Lena Olin, and Frank Langella. The movie, based on the book *The Club Dumas* (1993) by Arturo Perez-Reverte, is about a book dealer named Dean Corso (Depp) who is hired to research a satanic grimoire for an eccentric book collector, publisher, and occultist named Boris Balkan (Langella). The tome is called the *The Nine Gates (or Doors) to the Kingdom of Shadows* and was written by Aristide Torchia. According to the movie, Aristide Torchia wrote, *The Nine Gates to the Kingdom of Shadows* in league with the Devil in Venice, 1666, and was burned at the stake by the Inquisition as a result. The character of Aristide Torchia conjures Italian mystic Giordano Bruno, who was burned at the stake by the Inquisition in 1600. Boris Balkan is a veiled rendering of English author, occultist and Freemason, Aleister Crowley. The grimoire, *The Nine Gates to the Kingdom of Shadows*, signifies Hebrew Kabbalah. *The Nine*

Gates is based on a book called the *Dalomelanicon*, a mysterious book written by Satan himself. The *Dalomelanicon* is based upon early twentieth century gothic writer H.P. Lovecraft's invented grimoire, *The Necronomicon*, which, according to Lovecraft, was composed by the "Mad Arab" Abdul Alhazred.

The Kabbalah is Hebrew mysticism and is heavily based on the *Zohar*, a set of books that contain mystical and esoteric beliefs about Torah; the *Zohar* assigns allegorical interpretations to Holy Scripture. The Kabbalah forms the Tree of Life or Wisdom, containing ten circular centers called of the Sephiroth. Nine of the Sephiroth symbolizes different levels of human consciousness, intellect, and emotion (Nine Gates) while the tenth, Kether or Crown, represents above consciousness. The light of human consciousness is transformed in each of the nine Sephirot, both positively and negatively. Many Kabbalists believe that when the nine gates (or portals), or Sephiroth are unlocked it grants the candidate access to separate universe, Kether, containing spiritual divine enlightenment. The eternal Godhead, *Ain Soph*, or divine enlightenment is now accessible. The ten Sephiroth are arranged in three columns and are connected by twenty-two paths corresponding to the twenty-two cards of the Major Arcana of the Tarot and the twenty-two letters of the Hebrew alphabet. The twenty-two paths combined with the ten Sephiroth equal 32, a reference to the thirty-two degrees of Scottish Rite Masonry.

The Nine Gates book signifies the nine Sephiroth of human consciousness.[427] Within Kabbalah, the 22 letters of the Hebrew alphabet can be converted to numerical equivalents. This could be called "Pythagorean-Kabbalism" giving rise to the concept of Gematria: the study of letters, words, and their occult numerological values and meanings. Gematria was studied and practiced by the Victorian based secret society the Hermetic Order of the Golden Dawn and later the Ordo Templi Orientis. A copycat Golden Dawn-O.T.O. secret society appears in *The Ninth Gate* as the Order of the Silver Serpent presided over by Liana de St. Martin-Telfer portrayed by Lena Olin. Liana de St. Martin, a devote Satanist and occultist, originally owned the copy of *The Nine Gates* which

427 The frontispiece engraving for the Nine Gates is a serpent in a tree symbolizing the Kabbalistic Tree of Life.

Corso is investigating; it was sold to Boris Balkan by her husband shortly before he killed himself without her knowing he disposed of it. Liana de St. Martin-Telfer is named after Louis de St. Martin (1743-1803), who was a French teacher of mysticism that he based on Cabala. Louis de St. Martin endeavored to found a secret cult with magical or theurgical rites. Louis de St. Martin was influenced by Christian mystic Jakob Boehme; St. Martin was the first to translate Boehme's work from German to French. Louis de St. Martin's published letters show that he was interested in spiritualism, magical evocation, and the works of Emanuel Swedenborg. Martinism is a form of mystical Christianity is often thought to be named after him.[428] In turn a Martinist Order was founded in 1886 by Augustin Chaboseau (1868 -1946) and Gerard Encausse (1865-1916, a/k/a Papus); the latter being a disciple of Freemason, magician, and occultist Eliphas Levi. The Martinist Order was influential in the creation of the Hermetic Order of the Golden Dawn in the late nineteenth-early twentieth century. The Order of the Silver Serpent meets yearly at the estate of Liana de St. Martin in France, to read and perform rites from *The Nine Gates*, which is a homage to occultist Louis de St. Martin.

The movie features two book sellers and restorers, Pablo and Pedro Ceniza, who personify Gemini the Twins. They are twin brothers who are consulted early in the movie by Corso as they once owned the copy of the Nine Gates that Corso is now investigating. When Corso questions them about the engravings contained in the book, they immediately turn to the third gate (or chapter) and its corresponding engraving which, as it turns out, is no coincidence. This engraving features an archer in the clouds about to fire down an arrow upon a gated bridge below as a traveler approaches. The traveler symbolizes the Fool card of the major arcane of the tarot. They explain to Corso this symbolizes that if one travels too far, terror and even death may descend from above. They further inform Corso that books of this nature always contain occult riddles and conundrums. The face of the archer in the clouds is the face of the Ceniza Brothers, or Gemini. It is the third engraving in the book because Gemini is the third house of the

428 Some sources suggest "Martinism" was named after Jacques de Livron Joachim de la Tour de la Casa Martinez de Pasqually (1727?-1774) who was an esoteric, theurgist, and theosophist and tutor and teacher of both Louis de St. Martin and Jean-Baptiste Willermoz.

Zodiac. Gemini is ruled by the planet Mercury who was known to the Greeks as Hermes and to the Egyptians as the god Thoth, as discussed in earlier chapters. Thoth was the Egyptian god of wisdom who was fused with the Greek Hermes and the Roman Mercury to create the wise Hellenistic sage Hermes Mercurius Trismegistus who, as has been explained, restores the liberal arts as inscribed on the Enochic literary pillar according to Masonic legend (cf. *Old Charges* of Dr. J. T. Desaguliers). It is from this pillar that all leaning is made possible; as such Gemini the Twins, the Ceniza Brothers, are found in a bookshop that specializes in esoteric, lost wisdom. The Latin phrase under the engraving of the third gate reads VERB. D.SUM C.S.T. ARCAN or VERBUM DIMISSUM CUSTODIAT ARCANUM: "The Lost Word Keeps the Secret." The Lost Word is the Tetragrammaton recovered during the Royal Arch ceremonies, and parallels Royal Arch Masonic-Enochian ideology.

Esoteric engraving that reveals the Third Gate to the Kingdom of Shadows, and its diabolical mystery.

According to the movie, once all nine engravings signed "LCF" or Lucifer are collected, they form a Satanic puzzle which, when solved, will make the Devil appear in person.[429] The engravings within *The Nine Gates*

429 All of the nine engravings within the Nine Gates contain numerous Hebrew letters. When the engravings are properly numerically arranged along with their Hebrew letters they solve the Satanic Riddle of the Nine Gates, which is: "To travel in silence by a long and circuitous route, to brave the arrows of misfortune and to fear neither noose nor fire. To play the greatest of all games and win! Foregoing no expense is to mock the vicissitudes of Fate and gain at last the key that will unlock the Ninth Gate." It should be remembered that

are influenced by the engravings of German goldsmith and engraver Michel Le Blon; many of his engravings contain Rosicrucian, hermetic, and Kabbalah-Qabalah (and its Christian equivalent, Cabala) symbolism while incorporating occult riddles. *The Nine Gates'* engravings bear a striking resemblance to engravings contained in the Luther Bible of 1533-34. Pablo and Pedro Ceniza are the keepers and watchmen of the Ninth Gate and appear to only allow those whom they feel worthy entry. As Corso leaves their occult bookshop, a cryptic warning unfolds. Terror suddenly descends from above: a scaffold collapses, nearly killing Corso. The Ceniza Brothers are the gatekeepers because they possess the original Ninth Gate engraving. Without this original, Lucifer cannot be summoned. Terror and death once again descends on those who are ill prepared: Balkan, unbeknownst to him, uses an incomplete set of the engravings to solve the satanic mystery. Balkan pays for his mistake: he is burned alive while trying to gain entry into the ninth portal. Although eight of the nine engravings were originals, the ninth engraving that Balkan used was a forgery, hence he was deemed unworthy to gain admittance. In search of the original ninth plate, Corso returns to the Ceniza's Bookshop only to find it has closed permanently. Two unassuming workmen are cleaning out its contents. The original ninth engraving is found resting on top a dust covered wood bookcase. It falls to the ground, and is discovered by Corso when the two workmen pull the bookshelf from the wall to the ground. Corso, now with all nine original engravings is granted entrance into the Ninth Gate. The two workmen are, in fact, the Ceniza Brothers (cf. Gemini) from earlier in the film.

These are some examples of Masonic and Enochian symbolism found in cinema. These are obviously not all, but some that the reader may want to keep an eye out for when viewing these films. Other movies that contain Masonic symbolism but would be too lengthy to discuss include, but are not limited to the films *The Matrix* (1999), the Star Wars Movies (Episodes I -VI, 1977-2005), and *The Lord of the Rings* (2001-2003). George Lucas has stated, in many interviews, that he was influenced by mythologist Joseph Campbell; *The Matrix* and Tolkien's *The Lord of the Rings* contain

Lucifer is not the true light but is the Light Bringer because the planet Venus, Lucifer - often rises as false light in the morning hours before the rising of the true light: *the sun*. This film clearly confuses Lucifer with the concept of the Christian Satan or Devil.

Gnostic and pagan overtones. It is no surprise that Freemasonry has worked its way into Hollywood as many actors and directors from its Golden Age were masons. On that list would be Clark Gable, Cecil B. DeMille, Joe E. Brown, Tom Mix, William "Bud" Abbott, Audie Murphy, Douglass Fairbanks Sr., W.C. Fields, Elmo Lincoln, Ernest Borgnine, Oliver Hardy, Al Jolson, "Red" Skelton, Roy Rogers, Gene Autry, Will Rogers, Louis B. Mayer, and John Wayne to name a few. Modern Hollywood Masons include Richard Pryor, Michael Richards, Telly Savalas, and Bronson Pinchot.

CONCLUSION

"Posterity may know we have not loosely through silence permitted things to pass away as in a dream."
- Richard Hooker, *Laws of Ecclesiastical Polity*, 1593.

"Speaking of the Temple of Minerva, or of that of Isis who was styled the Mother of the Sun God, and whose Mysteries were termed *Isiac*, at Sais, he (Herodotus) speaks of a Tomb in the Temple, in the rear of the Chapel and against the wall; and says, "It is the tomb of a man, whose name respect requires me to conceal. Within the Temple were great obelisks of stone [phalli], and in a circular lake paved with stones and revetted with a parapet. It seemed to me as large as that at Delos" [where the Mysteries of Apollo were celebrated]."
- Albert Pike, *Morals and Dogma of the Ancient and Accepted Scottish Rite*, 1871.

"In the opening years of that momentous seventeenth century, every kind of magic and occultism was rampant."
- Frances A. Yates, *Giordano Bruno and the Hermetic Tradition,* 1964.

Freemasonry teaches moral and social perfection; in Masonry's own terms the initiate is instructed to, "improve himself in Masonry." Whatever that "improvement" is, the individual mason is left to decipher and figure out for himself. *The Royal Arch of Enoch* could never have been written if the author was not a member of the Masonic Lodge and exposed to its teachings. As stated in Chapter II, I do not believe that I have violated any oaths or obligations that owe to the Masonic fraternity. Being a Mason, I would never do anything to discredit the fraternity that I proudly claim membership. Rather, this author believes this work is a celebration of Masonry that endeavors to explain Masonry's importance on the development of society and its influence on material culture. Even more so, this book demonstrates that the United States of America's creation was based on Masonic ideology and philosophy; as such the incorporation of Masonic symbols in its emblems and insignia of the new nation, the solar template of its Nation's Capital, should not be viewed as evidence of a vast conspiracy, rather a ceremonialization of Masonic patriotism, egalitarianism, liberty, and enlightenment.

Learned Masonic scholar Albert Mackey addresses symbols and their significance. Mackey writes:

> "A symbol is defined to be a visible sign with which a spiritual feeling, emotion, or idea is connected. . . . . At a still earlier period, the Egyptians communicated the knowledge of their esoteric philosophy is mystic symbols. In fact, man's earliest instruction was by means of symbols.
>
> 'The first learning of the world,' says Stukely, 'consisted chiefly of symbols. The wisdom of the Chaldeans, Phoenicians, Egyptians, Jews, of Zoroaster, Sanchoniathon, Pherecydes, Syrus, Pythagoras, Socrates, Plato, of all the ancients that is come to our hands, is symbolic.' . . . . 'Symbolical representations of things sacred,' says Dr. Barlow (*Essays on Symbolism,* I., page 1), 'were coeval with religion itself as a system of doctrine appealing to sense, and have accompanied its transmission to ourselves from the earliest known period of monumental history.'
>
> . . . . The Hebrews borrowed much of their early religious symbolism from the Egyptians, then later from the Babylonians, and through them this symbolic imagery, both verbal and objective, has descended to ourselves.
>
> The Egyptian priests were greatly proficient in symbolism, and so were the Chaldeans, and so were Moses and the Prophets, and the Jewish doctors generally - and so were many of the early fathers of the Church, especially the Greek fathers.
>
> Philo of Alexandria was very learned in symbolism, and Evangelist St. John has made use of it.
>
> The early Christian architects, sculptors, and painters drank deep of symbolic lore, and reproduced it in their works.'

> . . . .In Freemasonry, all the instructions in its mysteries are communicated in the form of symbols. Founded, as a speculative science, on an operative art, it has taken the working-tools of the profession which it spiritualizes, the terms of architecture, the Temple of Solomon, and everything that is connected with its traditional history, and adopting them as symbols, it teaches its great moral and philosophical lessons by this system of symbolism. But its symbols are not confined to material objects as were the hieroglyphics of the Egyptians. Its myths and legends are also, for the most part, symbolic. Often a legend, unauthenticated by history, distorted by anachronisms, and possibly absurd in its pretensions, if viewed historically or as a narrative of actual occurrences, when interpreted as a symbol, is found to impress the mind with some great spiritual and philosophical truth. The legends of Masonry are parables, and a parable is only a spoken symbol. By its utterance, says Adam Clarke, 'spiritual things are better understood, and make a deeper impression on the attentive mind.'"[430]

Once the symbol is properly understood, the motivation behind it becomes more conspicuous. This was discussed in the magnum opus of Canadian esoteric Manly Palmer Hall, titled *The Secret Teachings of All Ages*, first published in 1928. Hall, who was initiated into the mysteries of Freemasonry in Jewel Lodge #374 in San Francisco in 1954, states:

> 'Symbolism is the language of the Mysteries; in it is the language not only of mysticism and philosophy but of all Nature, for every law and power active in universal procedure is manifested to the limited sense perceptions of man through the medium of symbol. Every form existing in the diversified sphere of being is symbolic of the divine activity by which it is produced. By symbols men have ever sought to communicate to each other those thoughts which transcend the limitations of language. Rejecting man-conceived dialects as inadequate and unworthy to perpetuate divine ideas, the Mysteries thus chose symbolism as a far more ingenious and ideal method of preserving their transcendental knowledge. In a single figure a symbol may both reveal and conceal, for to the wise the subject of the symbol is obvious, while to the ignorant the figure remains inscrutable. He who seeks to unveil the secret doctrine of antiquity must search for that doctrine not upon the

430 Mackey, Albert, *Encyclopedia of Freemasonry, Vol. II*, pages 751-752.

open pages of books which might fall into the hands of the unworthy but in the place where it was originally concealed."[431]

With Masonry, it seems that there are genuine secrets contained in its rituals and emblems, but it is up to the individual mason to discover, unlock, their deeper esoteric meanings. Hall also explains that modern masons are in general opposed to occultism, "The average Masonic scholar is fundamentally opposed to a mystical interpretation of his symbols, for he shares the attitude of the modern mind in its general antipathy towards transcendentalism. A most significant fact, however, is that those Masons who have won signal honors for their contribution to the craft have been transcendentalists almost without exception."[432] In other words, Masonry has genuine secrets but is up to the Freemason to discern and discover what they are; the mason must start the journey, no one will start it for him. This is especially true when trying to decipher the high degrees.

Masonry has endeavored to preserve the secrets of the Ancient Mysteries such as the ritual of the dying yet resurrected sun god or man. The candidate undergoes a symbolic death, and like the sun, is born again from the tomb of winter, darkness-ignorance and is now able to receive the *light* as a new being. The candidate reborn is now able to *craft* society in a positive manner as the lessons of the mysteries are now his to behold. These mysteries faiths and the aastrological secrets they taught influenced Judaism, incorporated into Christianity and thus suppressed, and twined with Islam to become Sufism. The solar allegory was originally preserved in the third degree Master Mason degree, the Kabbalistic and astrological secrets were placed in the higher degrees of Masonry exemplified by the Holy Royal Arch. One must ask the question: is the Royal Arch of Enoch ritual allegory or occult, hidden, lost yet real history? Was the Vault of Enoch discovered beneath Mount Moriah? If so who discovered it? What did the vault contain? Are the contents of this vault the lost treasure of the Knights Templar? Was this treasure sequestered at Rosslyn Chapel at some point after the suppression of the Templars? Or was this Royal Arch Rite and the high degrees in general a Counter-Reformation deception, works of

431 Hall, Manly Palmer, *The Secret Teachings of All Ages*, page 37.
432 Hall, Manly Palmer, *Lectures on Ancient Philosophy*, page 451.

the imagination, to covertly lure Protestants out of the Craft Lodge and into the Catholic *haute* degrees thus confusing and even dividing their loyalties?

While we may never know the answer to these questions; what is beyond dispute is the Masonic High Degree of the Royal Arch of Enoch takes priority. This book documents its influence upon policy, rhetoric, and material culture. Masonic knowledge about the *Book of Enoch* far surpasses what was generally known about Enoch in the mid-eighteenth to the early nineteenth century. Evidence of this can be found in the Masonic *Constitutions* (1723, 1738), the Masonic Monitor of Thomas Smith Webb, and of course the Holy Royal Arch degree which incorporates *I Enoch* into its ritual prior to its discovery in 1773 and translation to English in 1821. This was cultivated in the Oration of Ramsay of 1737, imported into America, and served as the template that defined the United States as a Masonic Republic, *a New Order of the Ages*, expanding the Third Joachimite Age and Royal Arch Logos as propounded by Salem Town. These esoteric concepts can be found in Sir Francis Bacon's *The New Atlantis* (1627) that depicts the creation of a utopian land where generosity and enlightenment, dignity and splendour, piety and public spirit are the commonly held qualities of the inhabitants of Bensalem. Bensalem's state sponsored scientific college, Salomon's House (Solomon's House), is the very eye of this kingdom. *New Atlantis* clearly echoes the philosophy of three Rosicrucian manifestos (Chapter IV). This idiom, as analyzed and discussed, was taken up by American Masons such as Benjamin Franklin, George Washington, Simon Greenleaf, John James Beckley, and of course DeWitt Clinton. It was codified in both the York and Scottish Rites. From the country's federal beginnings in 1789 Masonry was omnipresent: Freemason George Washington was sworn in as President by Freemason and Grand Master Robert Livingston on a Bible borrowed from a New York Masonic Temple (St. John's Lodge #1, Ancient York Masons). This Bible was in time used to swear-in Presidents Warren Harding (1921, a Freemason), Dwight D. Eisenhower (1953), Jimmy Carter (1977), and George H. W. Bush (1989, a Bonesmen, not a mason). Masonry influence upon the new nation, its guidance, and its oversight, symbolized by an all-seeing eye depicted on the reverse seal of the Nation, came to an end with the Morgan Affair of 1826 (see Chapter I). Public perception of

Masonry was transformed; Freemasonry, all but overnight, was accused of being a conspiratorial organization embracing skullduggery and subterfuge; a drastic shift from 1776 where Masonry was deemed by the public as a patriotic organization and a benevolent fraternal order that contained all the tools for democratic nation building. Masonry survived the Morgan Affair, forever changed. The Royal Arch degree, once the pinnacle of Masonic initiation, became seemingly de-emphasized exoterically nevertheless its esoteric theology and philosophy remained strong.

Nevertheless, a historical conundrum is presented that demands further investigation: how is it that Masonry contained elements of *I Enoch* which was not known to western history at the time? Clearly someone had access to a copy in Europe, with regard to the cultivation of the higher degrees of Masonry this person was likely the Chevalier Ramsay. Was this copy part of the treasure brought back by Knights Templar from the Holy Land? Did some secret Rosicrucian or Vatican library house it and if so who exactly had access to it? This author cannot say, but hopefully *The Royal Arch of Enoch* has raised questions that will one day be answered. I stated in the Introduction that I was going to present new information, I believe I have succeeded. On that this tome concludes as it began, with a quote, that opens *I Enoch*:

> "And he began his story saying: Enoch a righteous man,
> whose eyes were opened by God, saw the vision of
> the Holy One in heaven, which the angels showed me,
> and I heard everything from them, and I saw and
> understood, but it was not for this generation, but
> for a remote one which is to come."[433]

The generation that Enoch describes is no longer remote; it is the living present. The past is the past–*the future is now*–it is up to this current generation, like Enoch, to understand these divine secrets and mysteries as the new age approaches. The time has come; your eyes have been opened: *see the vision.*

433 *I Enoch*, 1:2

G

PLATES

Plate I: The Priestess Card (#2) of the Major Arcana of the Tarot from the Rider-Waite deck. The card depicts The Virgin Isis (immaculate conceiver of the sun) in-between the two pillars of Freemasonry: Jachin and Boaz. This symbolizes that nature attains productivity by means of polarity. As wisdom personified (cf. Sophia), Isis stands between the pillars of opposites demonstrating that understanding is always found at the point of equilibrium (hypothetical point equidistant from all extremes) and that truth dies or is "crucified" between two thieves of apparent contraction; thus the truth is found, "somewhere in the middle." Christ Jesus, symbolizing the truth, light, and the way, *Logos*, dies at Golgotha or the "place of the skull," because all truth dies in the human mind. The two thieves depicted on either side of Christ at his crucifixion symbolize the two thieves of human life: fear of the future and regret of the past. Christ symbolically dies at age 33 because there are 33 vertebrae in humans on top of which sits the skull, identified as Golgotha, the place where truth, *light, Logos* dies within the New Testament. Isis' dress turns into water at her feet symbolizing the tears that she cries as she laments her fallen brother-husband Osiris. Her tears turn to rain with the rising of her star Sirius at the summer solstice, causing the Nile to flood and the land of Egypt to be reborn, At her feet is the moon which rules the sign of Cancer under which the summer solstice (June 20-22) occurs. Isis appears in the Book of Revelation at 12:1 where she is clothed with the sun with the moon at her feet crowned with twelve stars symbolizing the twelve houses of the zodiac.

Plate II: Top: Painting of an Interior of a Viennese Masonic Lodge, likely Crowned Hope (f/k/a True Harmony), ca. 1790. The Lodge features statues of the two decoders of the Enochic Pillars: Thoth Hermes Mercurius Trismegistus (the Philosopher, right) and Pythagoras (left) within the wall recesses. The Philosopher Hermes, by decoding the first Enochic Pillar restores knowledge of the seven liberal arts and sciences. According to various Masonic monitors it is from the seven liberal arts that Freemasonry comes from making Hermes Trismegistus the Godfather of Freemasonry. Pythagoras restores mathematics by the decoding of the other pillar on which is inscribed Euclid's 47th Proposition. Middle: The Seven Liberal Arts by Cornelis de Vos, 1590. Hermes or Mercury is seen protecting the seven liberal arts, while (bottom) Hermes or Mercury (the Philosopher-Trismegistus) is prominently displayed atop a fountain in the geometric epicenter of the commanding Tom Quad leading to and from the cathedral of Christ Church of Oxford University as a symbol of higher learning and symmetric academic perfection. As Isis was taught geometry by Thoth (cf. Trismegistus), Christ Church rests on the banks of the *Isis River* (portion of the Thames renamed) as an homage to the immaculate conceiver of *God's Sun*, the sun being the source of all en*light*enment.

Plate III Top: *Moses* by Michelangelo Buonarroti ca. 1513-1515 depicts Moses with the Ram's horns of Aries identifying Judaism as an Arian Age religion. The sculpture was commissioned in 1505 by Pope Julius II for his tomb. Bottom: *The Adoration of the Golden Calf* by Nicholas Poussin, ca. 1634. The Hebrews attempt to restore the worship of the Egyptian Apis Bull, the symbol of the old age of Taurus, which angers Moses *qua* Aries in the background (left) who smashes the bull with the stone tablets upon which is inscribed the Ten Commandments, the laws for the new Arian Age.

Plate IV: Mithras slaying the bull symbolizing the end of the Age of Taurus. This fresco from the mithraeum at Marino, Italy (third century) shows the tauroctony and the celestial lining of Mithras' cape. To the right and left can be seen a ladder of ascension anticipating Masonry's use of Jacob's Ladder, or the Ladder of Minerva, in its iconography.

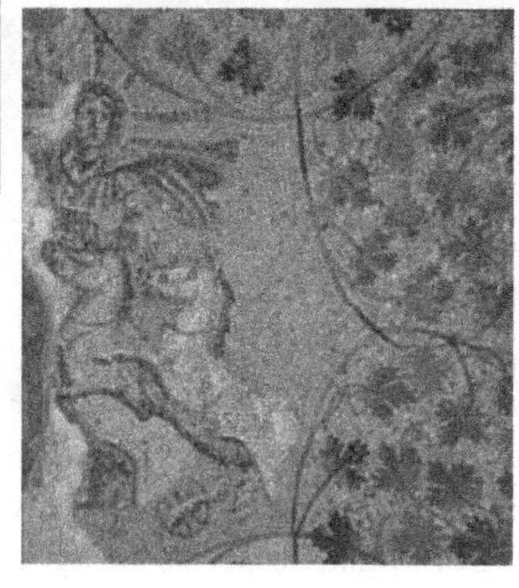

Plate V: (Left) Image contained within the *Codex Bruchsal* (ca. 1220) depicting Jesus Christ in the *Vesica Piscis* or the, "bladder or measure of the fish," denoting Piscean Age sun worship. The sun can clearly be seen behind Christ's head with a cross on it. The cross is created by the four Royal Stars in each of the fixed houses of the Zodiac: Aquarius (air) the man and its opposite house Leo (fire) the lion; Taurus (earth) the ox and its opposite sign of Scorpio (water) as an eagle. These astrological symbols (as seen in each corner) represent the Four Gospels which the preserve the astrological story of Christ as the sun. (Top Right) Mosaic of Pisces the Fish discovered on the floor of a third-fourth century Christian Church in Megiddo northern Israel denoting Christianity as a new age Piscean solar religion. (Right Center) The former leader of the Catholic Church Pope John Paul II (born Karol Józef Wojtyla, 1920-2005) with the sun as the supreme emblem of Christianity. (Lower Right) Pre-fourth century floor mosaic, near the tomb of Pope Julius I (as Pope 337-353 CE), in the Vatican grottos features Jesus Christ as *Sol Invictus* in the triumphal solar chariot of the sun god Apollo.

Plate VI: *The Last Supper* by Leonardo Da Vinci, ca. 1498. Da Vinci brings order out of chaos by symbolically communicating the heliocentric nature our solar system which would be revealed by Nicolaus Copernicus in 1543 and confirmed by Galileo Galilei in 1610; yet Da Vinci appears to have already been aware of this. The painting features Jesus Christ surrounded by the 12 Apostles. Jesus Christ is the sun; the 12 Apostles are the 12 Houses of the Zodiac that Jesus, being the sun, travels around with annually. Jesus, the sun of God, is in the center of the painting because the sun is the center of our *solar* system. Above the center, back window, is a Vitruvian arch representing the majestic sunrise. The 12 Apostles *qua* 12 Houses of the Zodiac, sit in four groups of three also representing the 12 months of the calendar year. The four group-sets signify the two solstices (winter and summer) and two equinoxes (vernal and autumnal). As such, two groups of three sit at each side of Jesus Christ the *sun of god* signifying his annual passage. Within each group of four are three Apostles, who epitomize the three months that compose each the four seasons.

Plate VII: The twelve houses of the zodiac are divided into separate houses, or keystones, each of 30 degrees, symbolizing the 30 days (with cusps) it takes the earth to orbit the sun and pass through each house. With this the sun is born again as its rays enter a new house due to the earth's elliptical orbit around it. This 5th to 7th century zodiac wheel mosaic discovered in the Beit Alpha Synagogue in 1929 in Israel features a sun god, Apollo-Helios, in the center emanating sun rays about his head (transformed into a "Crown of Thorns" in the Christian Mysterion) driving a solar chariot. At each corner are the four seasons with their Hebrew names: *Nisan* (Spring); *Tamusz* (Summer); *Tishri* (Autumn) and *Tevet* (Winter), emblematic of the solstices and equinoxes.

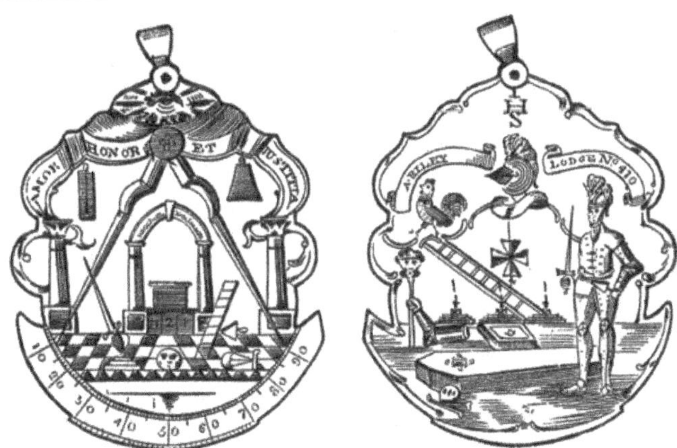

An Early Irish Jewel carrying Emblems of Many Degrees and showing Sojourner with Sword and Trowel

Plate VIII: (Top) Late eighteenth century Irish Past Master Jewel featuring the Ark of the Covenant deposited between the Pillars of Enoch with a sun overhead; by contrast American Past Master Jewels display the sun in the center. (Bottom) Two Irish Royal Arch Jewels circa 1780-1790. The one on the left features the Foundation Stone as a Templar-styled altar between the Pillars of Enoch with an arch overhead. The sun, featured in a triangular styled trapezoid, can be seen rising beneath the altar-Foundation Stone with the solar all-seeing eye overhead. The one to the right features a warrior-Templar styled monk with the Jesuit I.H.S. overhead.

Plate VIII continued: The St. Andrews Royal Arch degree certificate of 1790, the Hurd Plate, awarded to those exalted into the Holy Royal Arch. It displays a vault with a rising sun as its contents replacing the Ark of the Covenant as depicted in Masonic Monitors and the ritual degree work. Above is a triangular Templar styled altar with a skull and cross bones; leading to the vault are seven steps anticipating the first seven degrees of the York Rite, its seventh is the Royal Arch of Zerubbabel, that form a symbolic solar pathway of initiation creating a Masonic irenic clerisy which moderates the New World, the United States, and its nineteenth century westward expansion. Irish Jewels from B.E. Jones' *Freemasons' Book of the Royal Arch*, Hurd Plate courtesy the Grand Lodge of Massachusetts.

Plate IX: The *Apotheosis of Washington* (also known as the *Commemoration of Washington*) engraving by J. J. Barralet ca. 1800. This engraving is based on a sermon delivered by Simon Chaudron shortly after Washington's death equating Washington to Enoch (cf. Thoth Hermes Mercurius Trismegistus). Washington is being raised from the grave in corporeal form (wearing grave clothes) assisted by Kronos (Saturn, death) and an angel as Libertas laments at the base of the tomb. George Washington represents Enoch, like the Prophet Elijah, one of two people in the Bible to have never died. The two jewels draped over the edge of Washington's sarcophagus are the insignia of the Society of the Cincinnati (right) along with a Masonic Past Master's Jewel (left). The former, an eagle, was designed by Pierre Charles L'Enfant who also provided the street plan for the District of Columbia; the latter features compasses opened to an angel of 60 degrees symbolizing the perfected man and rebirth to the spiritual plane. In the center of the jewel is the sun, the supreme icon of Masonry.

Plate X: Portrait of Elizabethan Magus Dr. John Dee (1527-1608/09) formerly in the possession of Elias Ashmole, now kept in the Ashmolean Museum, Oxford England. Dee was a mathematician, occultist, scientist, navigator, and spymaster (he was friends with Francis Walsingham and William Cecil), whose imperialistic philosophy was heavily influenced by Georgius Gemistus Pletho, a Byzantine scholar of Neo-Platonic philosophy and attendee of the Council of Florence (1438-1439). Dee was also Queen Elizabeth I's court astrologer who, along with Irish medium Edward Kelley (1555-1597), developed a system of magic called Enochian Magic that allowed one to communicate with their Guardian Angel via angelic and demonic intervention. Insert lower right, Dee's autograph 007 sigil: Dee was, like Giordano Bruno, one of Sir Francis Walsingham's spies; 007 was Dr. Dee's cabalistic signature on intelligence correspondences to Queen Bess and is the source of Ian Fleming's MI6 agent James Bond's codename "Double-O Seven." The actual signature is eyeglasses, symbolizing that the correspondence was for "her eyes only" and that he was her "eyes in the field." This symbolism explains the term "for your eyes only," which is still used in modern day espionage. (007 material see Deacon, Richard, *A History of the British Secret Service*, New York: Taplinger, 1969, pages 12-13, 27-30; see also Spence, Richard, *Secret Agent 666*, page 20.)

Plate XI: *The Return of the Holy Family from Egypt* by Nicholas Poussin circa 1627. It features the Holy Family symbolically returning (or at least Christianized) from their true Egyptian roots. The centerpiece of the painting is Mary *qua* Isis (left) who presents her solar messiah who is, in turn, adored by celestial angels.

Plate XII: Seal of the Society of Jesus a/k/a the Jesuits explained. The cross symbolizes either the terrestrial cross formed by the two equinoxes (winter and summer) and solstices (vernal and autumnal) or the celestial cross formed by the constellations Aquarius, Leo, Scorpio and Taurus. Alternatively the cross is formed by the two solstices and two equinoxes. I.H.S., the Jesuit Tetragrammaton, within the Christianity it is derived from the first three Greek letters of the name of Jesus: *Iota* (I), *Eta* (H), *Sigma* (S). However, with the Mysterion it's emblematic of the Pagan Mysteries; "I.H.S." symbolized the Greco-Roman solar god Dionysus-Bacchus. The three nails are in fact the Hebrew letter *Vav* or *Vau.* In Hebrew Gematria, Vav equals the number 6 and literally means nail. The three of them, when added, equals 666. Add 6 + 6 + 6 to get the number 18. Then add 1 + 8 to get the number 9, an inverted 6. Within Pythagorean Numerology, 9 is the number of man (10 is the number of God) because nine represents the 9 months of his embryonic life. Taken altogether, the Jesuit Seal decoded means, "Man (or men) who worship Dionysus or Bacchus the Sun." This is confirmed by the fact that all these symbols rest on a solar disk indicative of sun adoration.

Plate XIII: The House of Convocation (1634-1637) occupies the lower floor of the Bodleian Library and Divinity School, Oxford University, Oxford England. It anticipates the overall rectangular design of Masonic craft lodges and was a likely template for Masonic Lodge meeting rooms.

Plate XIV: Left: the symbol of seal of the Knights Templar: their premiere emblem is the red cross placed on a white background as seen on their shields. Right: the arms of the Episcopal Church, the mainland Anglican Church in the United States, features a Templar-esque red cross on a white shield. The red cross on white background is also known as the Cross of St. George. In addition the nine stars appear to symbolizes the nine French Knights who founded the Templar Order. The Episcopal Church remained amicable to Masonry during the anti-Masonic William Morgan era due in part to the influence of Philander Chase.

Plate XV: *The Peaceful Reign of James I* (ca. 1632-1634), by Peter Paul Rubens Banqueting House, Whitehall, London. Masonic sovereign King James I is symbolically deposited between the two Pillars of Enoch as the contents of the Vault of Enoch, a living Royal Arch Word. Above James can be seen a *royal arch* while Hermes the Philosopher appears in the lower left of the painting. Hermes decodes one of the Enochic Pillars' within Masonic philosophy and legend as stated in the *Old Charges* of Dr. John T. Desaguliers. Also appearing in the painting is Minerva the virgin goddess of wisdom (middle right) representing the encoded divine wisdom inscribed on the two pillars. Fire, in keeping with Zoroastrianism, is extolled by a Mithraic Roman soldier as the supreme source of solar *light* (center).

Plate XVI: Pastel on paper of Freemason George Washington in Masonic regalia, 1794, by William J. Williams of Philadelphia. Washington wears the solar jewel of a Past Master. The Past Master Jewel in specific was derived from legendary Masonic history and linked the concept of Masonic rulership both with the restoration of Egyptian values integrated with Biblical legitimacy as the template or ideal virtuous exemplification of moral order and leadership.

Plate XVII: Watercolor: *The Ancient of Days* by William Blake, 1794. Urizen kneels within a solar disk using compasses as a tool of geometric, spiritual perfection. The term, "Ancient of Days," is used by T. S. Webb in the "Most Excellent Master" song:

"Fulfilled is the promise
by the Ancient of Days,
to bring forth the cap stone
with shouting and praise."

Plate XVIII: The Great Seal of the United States of America. Harvard professor Charles Eliot Norton (1827-1908) called the Great Seal a, "dull emblem of the Masonic fraternity." On the left is the obverse; it features an American bald eagle while the reverse (right) features an unfinished pyramid with an all-seeing solar eye overhead. In turn the thirteen stars over the eagle's head form the Magen David symbolizing divine and cosmic influence and protection. The Latin phrase *Annuit Coeptis Novus Ordo Seclorum,* or *Approving Commencement of the New Order of the Ages,* heralds a new solar age syncretic of Joachim von Fiore's Third Age of the Holy Spirit. The number thirteen is omnipresent and esoterically suggests the *thirteenth degree* of the Rite of Perfection (known as the Royal Arch of Enoch in the Scottish Rite, Southern Jurisdiction) and the recovery of the Tetragrammaton thus investing the seal with God's divine presence or *Shekinah* associated with the Hebrew Ark of the Covenant. It is upon the Ark that God's name is engraved upon a golden delta and recovered in the Royal Arch Masonic ceremonies. The eagle's nine tail feathers represent the nine arches under which Enoch concealed the Tetragrammaton. The Great Seal of the United States thus becomes an emblem of Royal Arch millennialism in the Salem Town idiom of expanding Logos. The Roman numeral date at the bottom of the pyramid MDCCLXXVI is 1776; it refers to the birth of the United States when the Second Continental Congress declared independence from Great Britain on July 4th of that year. The Great Seal was placed on the back of the one dollar bill in 1935.

Plate XIX: The chair that George Washington sat in during the Constitutional Convention of 1787-1789 featured a rising sun symbolic the Worshipful Masters who sits in the east while presiding over a Masonic Lodge. There are thirteen sun rays radiating from the sun representing the thirteen colonies, now one United States of America. The golden cap represents the cap of Libertas, the goddess of Liberty.

Plate XX: The Symbol for NASA's (National Aeronautics and Space Administration) Apollo 13 Moon mission draws upon high degree Masonic Symbolism. The sun is the symbol of the Tetragrammaton, Logos, on the St. Andrew's Royal Arch degree certificate (Hurd Plate). Within the Royal Arch ceremonies the recovery of the word (the sun) symbolically restores knowledge hence motto, *From the moon, knowledge.* The Royal Arch degree is the thirteenth in the Scottish Rite from whence Apollo 13's insignia symbolism originates.

Plate XXI: Left: Masonic architect J. J. Ramée's template for Union College of Schenectady, New York is a rising sun, radiating *light*, emerging from an enclosed vaulted quadrangle symbolic of the Royal Arch ceremonies and its associated solar imagery. The quadrangle or "quad" would hereafter become an architectural staple on American college campuses across the nation. Union College was the first college in the United States to offer degrees in Civil Engineering, Operative Masonry, and is the birth place of the Union Triad or the College Fraternal system. Its seal is appropriately Minerva, the goddess of wisdom and reason (right below). Its Masonic motto in English is, "We all become brothers under the laws of Minerva," forever investing American college students, both male and female, as quasi-Masonic initiates who receive *degrees* accompanied with a certificates as symbols of their intellectual accomplishments. The Union College library has a domed, temple of enlightenment, which was influenced by the domed Radcliffe Camera of the Bodleian Library of Oxford University (middle right). Ramée's domed library would ultimately become the Nott Memorial constructed between 1858-1879 (top right).

Plate XXII: The Seal of California. It features Minerva with a miner digging towards a hidden vault or crypt (gold to the profane) suggestive of high degree masonry.

Plate XXIII: Postcard displaying the Flag and Seal of Texas both of which feature the pentagram, its primary Masonic symbol.

Plate XXIV: Top: The solar nave-vault in Il Gesu, the Mother Church of the Jesuits also called the Church of the *Most Holy Name of Jesus* (cf. "I.H.S." as a substitute for the Hebrew Tetragrammaton). The vault features a name of God, I.H.S., symbolized by the sun as the Christianized Tetragrammaton. The nave-vault symbolically defies gravity while exalting godly Enochian Baroque into a levitational ethos; a religious theme that predominates the architecture and art of the Counter-Reformation. Il Gesu features a fresco of St. Ignatius of Loyola being exalted into heaven, like Enoch, which anticipates *The Apotheosis of George Washington* inside Brumidi's Capitol dome. Bottom: Il Gesu serves as a model for numerous Jesuit and Catholic churches around the world; the original 1727 St. Louis Cathedral of New Orleans being one of them.

Plate XXV: (six images): Top Left: The Baltimore Basilica of Benjamin Henry Latrobe, the first basilica in the United States. Top Center: The first Basilica west of the Mississippi dedicated to St. Louis (Louis IX) King of France in St. Louis, Missouri seen beneath the triumphal Gateway to the West arch. Top Right: The Archdiocese of St. Louis was moved to the Cathedral Basilica of St. Louis which is a replication of the Baltimore Basilica. Left Center: The Baltimore-Washington Monument by Robert Mills. The Baltimore Washington Monument is a replica of Trajan's Column located in Rome, Italy (bottom right). It is located on Charles Street in the heart of downtown Baltimore, Maryland on land once owned by Freemason and Revolutionary War Lt. Colonel John Eager Howard. Bottom Left: The Washington Monument obelisk in the District of Columbia also by Robert Mills. Mills' original design featured a pantheon at the monument's base which was never constructed.

Plate XXVI: Dennis Smith's Calverton (photo ca. 1873) estate, located a short distance westward of the Baltimore City line, by French architect J. J. Ramée. Calverton was completed after Ramée departed for Europe in 1816 by a Baltimore architect named Robert Long, who was also the director of Smith's bank. The barrel vault over the entrance features the Roman virgin goddess of reason Minerva created by Antonio Capellano. Shortly after its completion, Denis Smith went bankrupt and Calverton was turned into an alms house and eventually a Hebrew orphanage. It burnt down in 1874. Photo courtesy of the Maryland Historical Society.

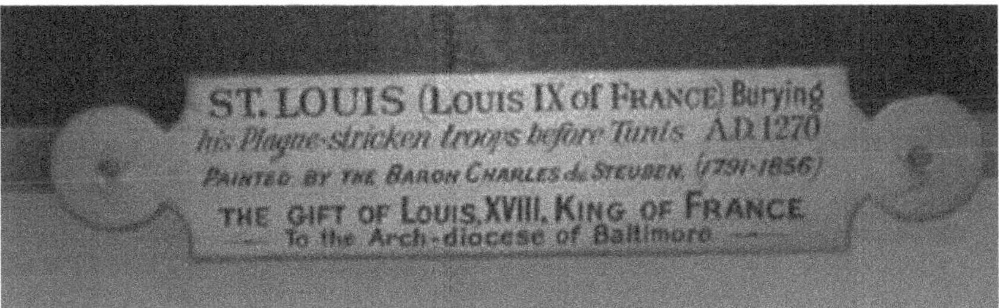

Plate XXVII: Oil painting titled, *St. Louis - Louis IX of France - Burying his Plague-Stricken Troops before Tunis A.D. 1270*, by Charles de Steuben (no relation to Baron von Steuben of the Revolutionary War). Louis IX is dressed as a Knight Templar; he wears a white tunic featuring a Templar red cross. The painting was a gift to the Archdiocese of Baltimore from King Louis XVIII.

Plate XXVIII: The Federal Triangle: The 47th Proposition of Euclid, the Pythagorean Theorem, is represented in Washington, D.C., by way of the Federal Triangle. The Federal Triangle is formed by the Capitol (the vantage point of this photo), White House, and the Washington Monument obelisk. The hypotenuse is Pennsylvania Avenue which is an esoteric reference to the Royal Arch-Masonically nuanced Keystone State. The 47th Proposition of Euclid is the symbol of the Worshipful Master and denotes Masonic rulership.

Plate XXIX: The ceiling of the Solon of Apollo features Apollo in his solar chariot; the Solon of Apollo served as the throne room in the Palace of Versailles thus investing the first monarch to rule within it, Louis XIV, as the Sun King.

Plate XXX: *The Apotheosis of Washington* by Constantino Brumidi beneath the United States Capitol dome, 1865. It features Washington, like Enoch, exalted in the heavens as a divine monarch. George Washington sits above a rainbow suggesting Royal Arch symbolism. To the top, Hermes the Philosopher *qua* Trismegistus can be seen advising and providing money to Robert Morris Jr., who served as the Superintendent of Finance from 1781-1784, managing the economy of the fledgling United States during the American Revolution. To lower left, Minerva counsels Dr. Benjamin Franklin, while in the lower right, Ceres of the Eleusinian Mysteries bestows her blessings on the new nation by giving Libertas, wearing a red Phrygian cap, a cornucopia. The seventy-two stars surrounding the fresco refer to the seventy-two years it takes the sun to move one degree backwards through each house of the zodiac based upon the astronomical Precession of the Equinoxes.

BIBLIOGRAPHY

Agrippa, Heinrich Cornelius. *Three Books of Occult Philosophy*. 1651. Reprint, translated by James Freake and edited and annotated by Donald Tyson, Woodbury, Minnesota: Llewellyn, 2009.

Alighieri, Dante. *The Divine Comedy*. 1555. Reprint, translation by C.H. Sisson, Oxford: Oxford University Press, 1993.

Allen, J.W. *A History of Political Thought in the Sixteenth Century*. New York: Barnes and Noble Inc., 1960.

Anderson, James and John T. Desaguliers. *The Constitutions of the Free-Masons*. 1723. Reprinted by Benjamin Franklin, Philadelphia, 1734.

Anderson, James and John T. Desaguliers. *The (New) Constitutions of the Free-Masons*. 1723. Revised, 1738.

Anderson, Karl. *Astrology of the Old Testament or the Lost Word Regained*. 1892. Reprint, Pomeroy, Washington: Health Research, 1970.

Apocalyptic Spirituality. Translated and introduction by Bernard McGinn, Mahwah, New Jersey: Paulist Press, 1979.

Ardalan, Nader and Laleh Bakhtiar. *The Sense of Unity: The Sufi Tradition in Persian Architecture*. Chicago and London: The University of Chicago Press, 1973.

Athanasius Kircher: The Last Man Who Knew Everything. Edited by Paula Findlen. New York: Routledge, 2004.

Baigent, Michael, Richard Leigh and Henry Lincoln. *Holy Blood, Holy Grail*. New York: Dell Publishing Group., 1983.

Baigent, Michael and Richard Leigh. *The Temple and the Lodge*. London: Corgi Books, 1990.

Baird, Robert. *Religion in America or an Account of the Origin, Relation to the State, and Present Condition of the Evangelical Churches in the*

United States. New York: Harper & Brothers, 1844.

Baker, Paul. *Richard Morris Hunt*. Boston: MIT Press, 1980.

Barber, Richard. *The Knight and Chivalry*. New York: Harper and Row, 1974.

Barbiero, Flavio. *The Secret Society of Moses: The Mosaic Bloodline and a Conspiracy Spanning Three Millennia*. Rochester, Vermont: Inner Traditions, 2010.

Barker, Margaret. *The Gate of Heaven: The History and Symbolism of the Temple in Jerusalem*. Sheffield, England: Sheffield Phoenix Press, 2008.

Barker, Margaret. *The Lost Prophet: The Book of Enoch and its Influence on Christianity*. Sheffield, England: Sheffield Phoenix Press, 2005.

Beckley, John James. *Justifying Jefferson: The Political Writings of John James Beckley*. Edited by Gerald W. Gawalt, Washington, D.C.: Library of Congress, 1995.

Bedini, Silvio A. *The Life of Benjamin Banneker: The First African-American Man of Science*. New York: Scribner, 1972.

Benichou, Paul. *Man and Ethics: Studies in French Classicism*. Translated by Elizabeth Hughs, Garden City, New York: Doubleday Anchor, 1971.

Bernstein, Richard B. *Are We to Be a Nation? The Making of the Constitution*. Boston: Harvard University Press, 1987.

Berry, Gerald. *Religions of the World*. New York: Barnes and Noble Inc., 1955.

Birch, Una. *Secret Societies: Illuminati, Freemasons and the French Revolution*. 1911. Reprint and edited by James Wasserman, Newburyport, Massachusetts: Red Wheel/Weiser, LLC, 2007.

Billington, James H. *Fire in the Minds of Men: Origins of the Revolutionary Faith*. New York: Basic Books, Inc., Publishers, 1980.

Blavatsky, Helena P. *Isis Unveiled, Volumes I & II*. 1877. Reprint, Pasadena, California: Theosophical University Press, 1999.

Bonwick, James. *Egyptian Belief and Modern Thought.* 1878. Reprint, Indian Hills, Colorado: Falcon's Wing Press, 1956.

Book of Enoch. Translated by R.H. Charles, London: Society for Promoting Christian Knowledge, 1917.

Borneman, Henry S. *Early Freemasonry in Pennsylvania*. 1931. Reprint, Philadelphia: Grand Lodge of Pennsylvania, 1981.

Bossy, John. *Giordano Bruno and the Embassy Affair*. New Haven, Connecticut: Yale University Press, 1991.

Bowen, Catherine Drinker. *Francis Bacon: The Temper of a Man*. Boston: Little Brown and Company, 1963.

Bowling, Kenneth R. *Peter Charles L'Enfant: Vision, Honor, and Male Friendship in the Early American Republic*. Washington, D.C.: George Washington University, 2002.

Brodie, Fawn M. *Thomas Jefferson: An Intimate History*. New York: W.W. Norton & Company, 1974.

Brands, H.W. *The First American: The Life and Times of Benjamin Franklin*. New York: Doubleday, 2000.

Brown, Robert Hewitt. *Stellar Theology and Masonic Astronomy or the Origin and Meaning of Ancient and Modern Mysteries Explained*. 1882. Reprint, Breinigsville, Pennsylvania: Merchant Books, 2009.

Brownlie, Ian. *Principles of Public International Law*. Oxford, England: Clarendon Press, 1990-1995.

Buckley, Terry. *Aspects of Greek History, 750-323 BC: A Source-Based Approach.* London: Routledge, 1996.

Bullock, Steven C. *Revolutionary Brotherhood: Freemasonry and the Transformation of the American Social Order, 1730-1840*. Chapel Hill, North Carolina: The University of North Carolina Press, 1996.

Bunyan, John. *The Pilgrim's Progress*. 1678. Reprint, New York and

Scarborough, Ontario: New American Library, 1964.

Burman, Edward. *The Assassins: Holy Killers of Islam*. Wellingborough, England: Aquarian Press, 1987.

Burtt, E.A. *The Metaphysical Foundations of Modern Science*. Garden City, New York: Doubleday and Company, 1954.

Busenbark, Ernest. *Symbols, Sex, and the Stars in Popular Beliefs: An Outline of Moon and Sun Worship, Astrology, Sex Symbolism, Mystic Meaning of Numbers, the Cabala, and Many Popular Customs, Myths, Superstitions and Religious Beliefs*. 1949. Reprint, San Diego: The Book Tree, 2003.

Callahan, Charles H. *Washington: The Man and the Mason*. Washington, D.C.: Press of W.F. Roberts Co., 1913.

Campanella, Tommaso. *The City of the Sun: A Poetical Dialogue between a Grandmaster of the Knights Hospitallers and a Genoese Sea-Captain, his guest*. 1623. Reprint, Radford, Virginia: Wilder Publications, LLC., 2008.

Campbell, Joseph. *The Hero with a Thousand Faces*. Princeton, New Jersey: Princeton University Press, 1973.

Carter, John. *Sex and Rockets: The Occult World of Jack Parsons*. Los Angeles: Feral House, 2004.

Cavendish, Richard. *The Tarot*. New York: Harper & Row, Publishers, Inc., 1975.

Charles, Joseph. *The Origins of the American Party System*. New York: Harper & Row, Publishers, Inc., 1961.

Chernow, Ron. *Alexander Hamilton*. New York: Penguin Press, 2004.

Chernow, Ron. *Washington: A Life*. New York: Penguin Press, 2010.

Churchward, Albert. *The Arcana of Freemasonry: A History of Masonic Signs and Symbols*. 1915. Reprint, San Francisco: Weiser Books LLC, 2005.

Churton, Tobias. *The Golden Builders: Alchemists, Rosicrucians, and the*

First Freemasons. York Beach, Maine: Red Wheel/Weiser, LLC, 2005.

Churton, Tobias. *The Invisible History of the Rosicrucians: The World's Most Mysterious Secret Society*. Rochester, Vermont: Inner Traditions, 2009.

Churton, Tobias. *The Magus of Freemasonry: The Mysterious Life of Elias Ashmole - Scientist, Alchemist, and Founder of the Royal Society*. Rochester, Vermont: Inner Traditions, 2006.

Clauss, Manfred. *The Roman Cult of Mithras: The God and his Mysteries*. 1990. Reprint and translated by Richard Gorden, New York: Routledge, 2000.

Coil, Henry W. and Allen E. Roberts. *Coil's Masonic Encyclopedia*. Revised edition, Richmond, Virginia: Macoy Publication & Masonic Supply Company, 1996.

Comenius, John Amos. *The Labyrinth of the World and the Paradise of the Heart*. 1631. Reprint and translated by Matthew Spinka, Ann Arbor: The University of Michigan Press, 1972.

Commager, Henry Steele. *The Empire of Reason: How Europe Imagined and America Realized the Enlightenment*. Garden City, New York: Anchor Doubleday 1978.

Cornog, Evan. *The Birth of Empire: DeWitt Clinton and the American Experience, 1769-1828*. Oxford: Oxford University Press, 1998.

Coward, Barry. *The Stuart Age: England, 1603-1714*. London: Longmans, 1994.

Cropper, Elizabeth and Charles Dempsey. *Nicolas Poussin: Friendship and the Love of Painting*. Princeton, New Jersey: Princeton University Press, 2000.

Cross, Jeremy. *Cross' Masonic Chart*. 1819. Revised by Will. M. Cunningham, New York: Clark & Maynard Publishers, 1869.

Crowley, Aleister. *The Book of Thoth*. 1944. Reprint, San Francisco: Weiser Books, 2010.

Crowley, Aleister. *The Confessions of Aleister Crowley*. 1969. Reprint and edited by John Symonds and Kenneth Grant. London: Penguin/Arkana Books, 1989.

Crowley, Aleister. *Magick*. 1973. Reprint and edited by John Symonds and Kenneth Grant, London: Routledge & Kegan Paul, 1981.

Crowley, Aleister. *Magick Without Tears*. Edited and introduction by Israel Regardie, Tempe, Arizona: New Falcon Publications, 1991.

Crowley, Aleister. *777 and other Qabalistic Writings of Aleister Crowley*. 1912. 1955. Reprint and edited by Israel Regardie, Boston: Red Wheel/ Weiser LLC, 1986.

Curl, James Stevens. *A Celebration of Death: An introduction to some of the buildings, monuments, and settings of funerary architecture in Western European Tradition*. 1980. Reprint, London: B.T. Batsford Ltd., 1993.

Curl, James Stevens. *The Art and Architecture of Freemasonry*. London: B.T. Batsford Ltd., 1991.

Currey, Cecil B. *Code Number 72 Benjamin Franklin: Patriot or Spy?* Englewood Cliffs, New Jersey: Prentice-Hall, Inc., 1972.

Davies, Howard and David Holdcroft. *Jurisprudence: Texts and Commentary*. London: Butterworths & Co Ltd. 1991-1994.

Denslow, Ray V. *Freemasonry and the Presidency*. Trenton, Missouri: Missouri Lodge of Research, 1952.

d'Esclapon, Pierre F. de Ravel. *The Masonic Career of Major Pierre Charles L'Enfant*. Scottish Rite Journal of Freemasonry, Southern Jurisdiction, Vol. CXIX Number 2, March-April 2011, pages 10-12.

Devore, Nicholas. *Encyclopedia of Astrology*. New York: Bonanza Books, a Division of Crown Publishers, Inc., n.d.

Dobree, Bonamy. *English Literature in the Early Eighteenth Century, 1700-1740*. New York: Oxford University Press, 1959.

Donnelly, Ignatius. *Atlantis: The Antediluvian World*. 1882. Reprint, New York: Dover Publications, Inc., 1976.

Doren, Carl Van. *Benjamin Franklin*. New York: The Viking Press, 1938.

Duncan, Malcolm C. *Duncan's Masonic Ritual and Monitor; or, Guide to the Three Symbolic Degrees of the Ancient York Rite and to the Degrees of Mark Master, Past Master, Most Excellent Master, and the Royal Arch*. New York: Fitzgerald Publishing Corporation, n.d.

Dujardin, Edouard. *Ancient History of the God Jesus*. 1938. Reprint, Pomeroy, Washington: Health Research, 1993.

Eschenbach, Wolfram von. *Parzival*. ca 1197- 1215. Translated with introduction by Helen M. Mustard and Charles E. Passage, New York: Vintage Books, 1966.

Eusebius. *The History of the Church from Christ to Constantine*. Translated by G.A. Williamson, New York: Dorset Press, 1984.

Evans, G. R. *The University of Oxford: A New History*. New York: I.B. Tauris & Co Limited, 2010.

Evans, Robert J. Weston. *Rudolf II and his World: A Study in Intellectual History, 1576-1612*. Oxford: Oxford University Press, 1973.

Fay, Bernard. *Revolution and Masonry, 1680 - 1800*. Boston: Little, Brown and Company, 1935.

Fazio, Michael W. and Patrick A. Snadon. *The Domestic Architecture of Benjamin Henry Latrobe*. Baltimore: The Johns Hopkins University Press, 2006.

Ferguson, Arthur B. *The Articulate Citizen and the English Renaissance*. Durham, North Carolina: Duke University Press, 1965.

Ferguson, Arthur B. *The Indian Summer of English Chivalry: Studies in the Decline and Transformation of Chivalric Idealism*. Durham, North Carolina: Duke University Press, 1960.

Ficino, Marsilio. *The Book of the Sun (De Sole)*. 1494. Reprint and Translated by Geoffrey Cornelius, Darby Costello, Graeme Tobyn, Angela Voss and Vernon Wells. Sphinx 6: A Journal for Archetypal Psychology and the Arts, London, 1994.

Formwalt, Lee W. *Benjamin Henry Latrobe & the Development of Internal Improvements in the New Republic, 1796-1820*. Washington, D.C.: Ayer Publishing/Catholic University of America, 1979.

Fox, William L. *Lodge of the Double-Headed Eagle: Two Centuries of Scottish Rite of Freemasonry in America's Southern Jurisdiction.* Fayetteville, Arkansas: The University of Arkansas Press, 1997.

Francken, Henry Andrew. *Francken Manuscript*. 1783. Reprint, Whitefish, Montana: Kessinger Publishing, LLC, 1993.

Franklin, J.H. *The Rebuilding of King Solomon's Temple*. Omaha, Nebraska: Press of the Douglas Printing Co., 1910.

Frazer, J.G. *The Golden Bough: A Study in Magic and Religion*. 1922. Reprint, London: Papermac, 1994.

Friedrich, Carl Joachim. *The Philosophy of Law in Historical Perspective*. Chicago: The University of Chicago Press, 1969.

Freke, Timothy and Peter Gandy. *The Jesus Mysteries: Was the "Original Jesus" a Pagan God?* New York: Three Rivers Press, 2001.

French, Peter. *John Dee: The World of an Elizabethan Magus*. 1972. Reprint, London: Ark Paperbacks, 1987.

Garin, Eugenio. *Astrology in the Renaissance: The Zodiac of Life*. 1983. Reprint and translated by Carolyn Jackson and June Allen, New York: Penguin/Arkana Books, 1988.

Gerould, Daniel. *Guillotine: Its Legend and Lore*. New York: Blast Books, 1992.

Gilbert, R.A. *The Golden Dawn Companion*. Boston: Red Wheel Weiser, 1986.

Gill, Joseph S. J. *Personalities of the Council Florence and Other Essays*. New York: Barnes and Noble Inc., 1964.

Glatfelter, Charles H. *A Salutary Influence: Gettysburg College 1832-1985, Volumes I & II*. Gettysburg: Gettysburg College, 1987.

Godwin, Joscelyn. *Athanasius Kircher's Theatre of the World: The Life and Work of the Last Man to Search for Universal Knowledge.* Rochester, Vermont: Inner Traditions, 2009. Goethe, Johann Wolfgang von. *Goethe's Faust*. 1808. 1963. Reprint, Translated and Introduction by Walter Kaufmann, New York: Anchor Books Editions, 1990.

Goodman, Paul. *Anti-Masonry and the Great Transition in America, 1826-1836*. New York: Oxford University Press, 1988.

Goubert, Pierre. *Louis XIV and Twenty Million Frenchmen.* New York: Random House, 1970.

Grant, Michael. *The Emperor Constantine*. London: Weidenfeld and Nicolson, 1993.

Greenleaf, Simon. *A Brief Inquiry into the Origin and Principles of Freemasonry*. Portland, Maine: Arthur Shirley, 1820.

Greer, John Michael. *The New Encyclopedia of the Occult*. St. Paul, Minnesota: Llewellyn Publications, 2004.

Habachi, Labib. *The Obelisks of Egypt: Skyscrapers of the Past*. New York: Charles Scribner's Sons, 1977.

Hall, Manly Palmer. *Lectures on Ancient Philosophy*. New York: Jeremy P. Tarcher/Penguin, 2005.

Hall, Manly Palmer. *The Lost Keys of Freemasonry*. 1923. 1937. 1950. Reprint, New York: Jeremy P. Tarcher/Penguin, 2006.

Hall, Manly Palmer. *The Secret Destiny of America*. 1944. 1951. Reprint, New York: Jeremy P. Tarcher/Penguin, 2008.

Hall, Manly Palmer. *The Secret Teachings of All Ages: An Encyclopedic Outline of Masonic, Hermetic, Qabbalistic and Rosicrucian Symbolic Philosophy*. 1928. Reprint, New York: Jeremy P. Tarcher/Penguin, 2003.

Halliday, W.R. *The Pagan Background of Early Christianity*. Liverpool, England: University of Liverpool, 1925.

Hancox, Joy. *The Byrom Collection and the Globe Theatre Mystery*. London: Jonathan Cape, 1992.

Harris, Ray Baker and James D. Carter. *History of the Supreme Council 33rd degree (Mother Council of the World), Ancient and Accepted Scottish Rite of Freemasonry, Southern Jurisdiction, U.S.A. 1801-1861.* Washington, D.C.: The Supreme Council, 1967.

Hayward, Mary Ellen and Frank R. Shivers, Jr. *The Architecture of Baltimore: An Illustrated History*. Baltimore: The Johns Hopkins University Press, 2004.

Heaton, Ronald E. *The Masonic Membership of our Founding Fathers*. Silver Spring, Maryland: Masonic Service Association, 1965.

Henry, Jacques. *Mozart the Freemason: The Masonic Influence on his Musical Genius*. 1991. Reprint and translated by Jack Cain, Rochester, Vermont: Inner Traditions, 2006.

Hieronimus, Robert. *Founding Fathers, Secret Societies: Freemasons, Illuminati, Rosicrucians, and the Decoding of the Great Seal*. Rochester, Vermont: Destiny Books, 2006.

Higgins, Godfrey. *Anacalypsis: An Attempt to Draw Aside the Veil of the Saitic Isis or an Inquiry into the Origin of Languages, Nations and Religions, Volumes I & II*. 1833. Reprint, New York: A&B Book Distributors, Inc., 1992.

Higgins, Godfrey. *The Celtic Druids*. 1827-1829. Reprint, New York, Cosimo, Inc., 2007.

Hinman, Eugene E., Ray V. Denslow and Charles C. Hunt. *A History of the Cryptic Rite, Volumes I & II*. Tacoma, Washington: General Grand Council, 1931.

Hollister, C. Warren and Judith M. Bennett. *Medieval Europe: A Short History*. 1964. Reprint, Boston: McGraw-Hill, 2002.

The Holy Bible containing all of the books of the Old and New Testament, King James version.

Horne, Alex. *Sources of Masonic Symbolism*. Trenton, Missouri: The Missouri Lodge of Research, 1981.

Hornung, Erik. *Conceptions of God in Ancient Egypt: The One and the*

Many. Ithaca: Cornell University Press, 1996.

Hornung Erik, *The Secret Lore of Egypt: Its Impact on the West*. Ithaca: Cornell University Press, 2001.

Hutchinson, Harold F. *Sir Christopher Wren, a Biography.* Newton Abbot, Devon, England: Readers Union, 1976.

Iamblichus. *On the Mysteries of the Egyptians, Chaldeans and Assyrians*. Translated by Thomas Taylor, 1821. Reprint, London: Stuart and Watkins, 1968.

Israel, Jonathan I, *The Radical Enlightenment: Philosophy and the Making of Modernity, 1650-1750*. Oxford: Oxford University Press, 2001.

Jeffers, H. Paul. *The Freemasons in America: Inside the Secret Society*. New York: Citadel Press, 2007.

Jones, Bernard E. *Freemasons' Book of the Royal Arch*. 1957. Reprint, London: George G. Harrap & Company LTD., 1970.

Jones, Bernard E. *Freemasons' Guide and Compendium*. 1950. Reprint, Nashville: Cumberland House, 2006.

Jones, Carlton. *Lost Baltimore Landmarks: A Portfolio of Vanished Buildings*. Baltimore: Maclay & Associates, Inc., 1982.

Jones, W.T. *Kant and the Nineteenth Century*. New York: Harcourt, Brace, and Jovanovich, 1975.

Kant, Immanuel. *Critique of Pure Reason*. 1781. 1787. Reprint, Translation, Edited, and Introduction by Marcus Weigelt. London: Penguin Classics, 2008.

Kennedy, Roger G. *Mr. Jefferson's Lost Cause: Land, Farmers, Slavery and the Louisiana Purchase*. New York: Oxford University Press, 2003.

Kennedy, Roger G. *Orders from France: The Americans and the French in a Revolutionary World 1780-1820*. New York: Alfred A. Knopf, 1989.

Kerenyi, Carl. *Dionysus: Archetypal Image of Indestructible Life*. 1976. Reprint and Translated by Ralph Manheim, Princeton, New Jersey:

Princeton University Press, 1996.

Khan, Yasmin Sabina. *Enlightening the World: The Creation of the Statue of Liberty*. Ithaca, New York: Cornell University Press, 2010.

Kinney, Jay. *The Masonic Myth: Unlocking the Truth about the Symbols, The Secret Rites, and the History of Freemasonry*. New York: HarperCollins Publishers, 2009.

Klein, Milton M., *The Empire State: A History of New York*. Ithaca and London: Cornell University Press, 2001.

Knight, Stephen. *Jack the Ripper: The Final Solution*. New York: David McKay Company, Inc., 1976.

Koeppel, Gerald T. *Bond of Union: Building the Erie Canal and the American Empire*. Cambridge, Massachusetts: Da Capo Press, 2009.

Landon, H.C. Robbins. *Mozart and the Masons: New Light on the Lodge "Crowned Hope."* London: Thames and Hudson, 1982.

Lang, Andrew. *Oxford: Brief Historical and Descriptive Notes*. London: Seeley and Co., Limited, 1890.

Leadbeater, Charles Webster. *Freemasonry and its Ancient Mystic Rites*. 1926. Reprint, New York: Gramercy Books, 1998.

Levi, Eliphas. *The History of Magic*. 1860. Translated by Arthur Edward Waite, 1913. Reprint, London: Rider and Company, 1951.

Lewis, W.H. *The Splendid Century: Life in the France of Louis XIV*. New York, Garden City: Doubleday and Company, 1953.

Little, David. *Religion, Order and Law: A Study in Pre-Revolutionary England*. New York: Harper & Row, Publishers, Inc.,1969.

Livingstone, David. *The Dying God: The Hidden History of Western Civilization*. New York: Writers Club Press, 2002.

Lovell, Jim and Jeffrey Kluger. *Lost Moon: The Perilous Voyage of Apollo*

13. Boston: Houghton Mifflin,1994.

Lumpkin, Joseph B. *The Books of Enoch: A Complete Volume Containing 1 Enoch (The Ethiopic Book of Enoch), 2 Enoch (The Slavonic Secrets of Enoch), 3 Enoch (The Hebrew Book of Enoch)*. Blountsville, Alabama: Fifth Estate, 2010.

Lundy, John P. *Monumental Christianity: The Art and Symbolism of the Primitive Church.* London: Swan Sonnenschein & Co., 1889.

Machiavelli, Niccolo. *The Prince*. 1513. Reprint, translated and edited by Daniel Donno, New York: Bantam Books, 1981.

Mackey, Albert Gallatin. *An Encyclopedia of Freemasonry and its Kindred Sciences, Volumes I & II.* New York and London: The Masonic History Company, 1921.

Mackey, Albert Gallatin. *The History of Freemasonry, Volumes I - VII.* Addenda: William James Hughan, New York and London: The Masonic History Company, 1906.

Macoy, Robert. *A Dictionary of Freemasonry: A Compendium of Masonic History, Symbolism, Rituals, Literature, and Myth*. 1870. Reprint, New York: Bell Publishing Company, 1989.

Madison, James, *Notes of Debates in the Federal Convention of 1787,* Introduction by Adrienne Koch, New York: W.W. Norton & Co. Inc, 1987.

Maier, Bernard. *Dictionary of Celtic Religion and Culture*. Rochester, New York: Boydell Press, 1997.

Malory, Thomas. *Le Morte Darthur: The Winchester Manuscript.* 1470. Reprint and edited by Helen Cooper, New York: Oxford University Press, 2008.

Marshall, Peter. *The Magic Circle of Rudolf II: Alchemy and Astrology in Renaissance Prague*. New York: Walker & Company, 2006.

Mathers, Samuel Liddell MacGregor. *The Kabbalah Unveiled.* 1970. Reprint, York Beach, Maine: Samuel Weiser, 1997.

Maxwell, Jordan, Paul Tice and Gerald Snow. *That Old-Time Religion:*

The Story of Religious Foundations. Escondido, California: The Book Tree, 2000.

Melanson, Terry. *Perfectibilists: The 18th Century Bavarian Order of the Illuminati*. Walterville, Oregon: Trine Day, 2009.

Melville, Herman. *Moby Dick*. 1851. Reprint, New York: Pocket Books, 1999.

Menand, Louis. *The Metaphysical Club: A Story of Ideas in America*. New York: Farrar, Straus, and Giroux, 2001.

Michael, Prince of Greece. *Louis XIV: The Other Side of the Sun*. Translated by Alan Sheridan, New York: Harper & Row, Publishers, Inc., 1983.

Miller, Mark B. *Baltimore Transitions: Views of an American City in Flux*. Baltimore: Pridemark Press, 1998.

More, Thomas, Francis Bacon and Henry Neville. *Three Early Modern Utopias: Utopia, New Atlantis, and The Isle of Pines*. New York: Oxford University Press, 2009.

Morgan, Giles. *Freemasonry: Its History and Myths Revealed*. New York: Fall River Press, 2009.

Mumford, Lewis. *The City in History*. New York: Harcourt, Brace and World, 1961.

Murray, Peter. *The Architecture of the Italian Renaissance*. New York: Schocken Books Inc., 1974.

Odd Fellows' Offering for 1848. Edited by James L. Ridgely and Paschal Donaldson, New York: Edward Walker, 1848.

Odd Fellows' Offering for 1850. New York: Edward Walker, 1850.

Olcott, William Tyler. *Star Lore of All Ages*. 1911. Reprint, New York: G.P. Putnam's Sons, 1937.

Olcott, William Tyler. *Sun Lore of All Ages: A Collection of Myths and*

Legends. 1914. Reprint, Mineola, New York: Dover Publications, Inc., 2005.

Osman, Ahmed. *Christianity: An Ancient Egyptian Religion*. Rochester, Vermont: Bear & Company, 2005.

Ovason, David. *The Secret Architecture of Our Nation's Capital: The Masons and the Building of Washington, D.C.* New York: Perennial/ HarperCollins Publishers, 2002.

Painter, Sidney. *French Chivalry: Chivalric Ideas and Practices in Medieval France*. Ithaca: Cornell University Press, 1957.

Palladio, Andrea. *The Four Books of Architecture*. 1570. Reprint, New York: Dover Publications, Inc., 1965.

Partner, Peter. *The Murdered Magicians: The Templars and Their Myth*. Oxford: Oxford University Press, 1981.

Pauwels, Louis, and Jacques Berger. *The Morning of the Magicians: Secret Societies, Conspiracies, and Vanished Civilizations*. 1960. Reprint, Rochester, Vermont: Destiny Books, 2009.

Pendle, George. *Strange Angel: The Otherworldly Life of Rocket Scientist John Whiteside Parsons*.
Orlando, Florida: Harcourt, Inc., 2006.

Perry, Frederick. *Saint Louis (Louis IX of France) the most Christian King*. New York: G.P. Putnam's Sons, 1901.

Pike, Albert. *Morals and Dogma of the Ancient and Accepted Scottish Rite of Freemasonry*. 1871. Reprint, Richmond, Virginia: L.H. Jenkins, Inc., 1960.

Pinnell, Patrick. *The Campus Guide: Yale University, an Architectural Tour*. Princeton, New Jersey: Princeton Architectural Press, 1999.

Plato. *The Works of Plato*. Translated by B. Jowett. New York: Tudor

Publishing Company, n.d.

Pocock, J.G.A. *The Machiavellian Movement: Florentine Political Thought and the Atlantic Republican Tradition*. Princeton, New Jersey, Princeton University Press, 1975.

Pound, Roscoe. *Lectures on the Philosophy of Freemasonry*. Anamosa, Iowa: The National Masonic Research Society, 1915.

Origen: An Exhortation to Martyrdom, Prayer, and Selected Works. Translated by Rowan A. Greer, Mahwah, New Jersey: Paulist Press, 1988.

Preston, William. *Illustrations of Freemasonry*. 1772. London: G & T Wilkie, 1795.

Primm, James Neal. *Lion of the Valley: Saint Louis, Missouri, 1764-1980.* Boulder, Colorado: Pruett Publishing Company, 1981.

Quinn, Michael. *Early Mormonism and the Magic World View*. Salt Lake City: Signature Books, 1998.

Ralls, Karen. *Knights Templar Encyclopedia: The Essential Guide to the People, Places, Events, and Symbols of the Order of the Temple*. Franklin Lakes, New Jersey: New Page Books, 2007.

Ramsay, Andrew Michael. *Ramsay's Oration*. 1737. Translated by De la Tierce in Gould, Robert Freke, *History of Freemasonry Throughout the World, Volumes I-III*. 1883-1887. Revised by Dudley Wright in VI Volumes, Volume III, pages 10-15, New York: Charles Scribner's Sons, 1936.

Ramsay, Andrew Michael. *The Travels of Cyrus, to Which is Annexed a Discourse upon the Theology and Mythology of the Pagans: Volumes I & II*. 1727. 1728. 1802. Reprint, Chestnut Hill, Massachusetts: Adamant Media Corp., 2005.

Reade, W. Winwood. *The Veil of Isis; or The Mystery of the Druids*. London: Charles J. Skeet, Publisher, 1861.

Regardie, Israel. *The Complete Golden Dawn System of Magic*. Tempe, Arizona: New Falcon Publications, 1994.

Remes, Pauliina. *Neoplatonism: Ancient Philosophies*. Berkeley, California: University of California Press, 2008.

The Revolution of 1800: Democracy, Race, and the New Republic. Edited by James Horn, Jan Ellen Lewis, and Peter S. Onuf, Charlottesville, Virginia: University of Virginia Press, 2002.

Robison, James. *Proofs of a Conspiracy Against all the Religions and Governments of Europe Carried on in the Secret Meetings of the Freemasons, Illuminati, and Reading Societies*. 1798. Reprint, Boston: Western Islands, 1967.

Russell, Jeffrey Burton. *Lucifer: The Devil in the Middle Ages*. Ithaca, New York: Cornell University Press, 1992.

Russell, Jeffrey Burton. *Mephistopheles: The Devil in the Modern World.* Ithaca, New York: Cornell University Press, 1992.

S, Acharya. *The Christ Conspiracy: The Greatest Story Ever Sold.* Kempton, Illinois: Adventures Unlimited Press, 1999.

S, Acharya. *Suns of God: Krishna, Buddha and Christ Unveiled*. Kempton, Illinois: Adventures Unlimited Press, 2004.

Shah, Idries. *The Sufis*. Garden City, New York: Doubleday, 1971.

Siculus, Diodorus, *The Antiquities of Egypt*. Translated by Edwin Murphy, Brunswick, New Jersey: Transaction Publishers, 1980.

Spence, Lewis. *Ancient Egyptian Myths and Legends*. 1915. Reprint, New York: Dover Publications, 1990.

Spence, Richard B. *Secret Agent 666: Aleister Crowley, British Intelligence and the Occult*. Port Townsend, Washington: Feral House, 2008.

St. Clair, Marisa. *Sun & Moon Signs: An Astrological Guide to Love, Career, & Destiny*. New York: Smithmark Publishers, 1999.

Steinmetz, George H. *The Royal Arch: Its Hidden Meaning.* New York: Macoy Publishing and Masonic Supply Company, 1946.

Stemper, William H. Jr. *Crafted Links: The Transformation of Masonic*

Ritual Order, 1772-1802: An Intellectual History of the Preston-Webb Synthesis. Oxford University D-Phil. Thesis, 2001.

Stemper, William H. Jr. *Freemasonry and the Force*. Ames, Iowa: Research Lodge No. 2, 1984.

Stevenson, David. *The First Freemasons: Scotland's Early Lodges and Their Members*. Aberdeen: Aberdeen University Press, 1988.

Stevenson, David. *The Origins of Freemasonry: Scotland's Century, 1590-1710*. Cambridge: Cambridge University Press, 1988.

Sutton, Anthony C. *America's Secret Establishment: An Introduction to the Order of the Skull and Bones*. Walterville, Oregon: Trine Day, 2002.

Sypher, Wylie. *Four Stages of Renaissance Style: Transformations in Art and Literature, 1400-1700*. Garden City, New York: Doubleday, 1955.

Tawfik, Younis. *Islam*. New York: Konecky & Konecky, 1998.

Thomas Jefferson's Notes on the State of Virginia. Edited by William Peden, Chapel Hill, North Carolina: University of North Carolina Press, 1955.

Thomson, David. *Europe Since Napoleon*. 1957. Reprint, London: Penguin Books, 1990.

Thomson, Katharine. *The Masonic Thread in Mozart*. London: Lawrence and Wishart, 1977.

Town, Salem. *A System of Speculative Masonry, in its Origin, Patronage, Disseminations, Principles, Duties, and Ultimate Design, Laid Open for the Examination of the Serious and Candid.* 1818. Salem, New York: H. Dodd & Co., 1822.

Tsarion, Michael. *Astro-Theology and Sidereal Mythology*. Seattle: Taroscopes, 2008.

Turner, Paul V. *Joseph Ramée: International Architect of the Revolutionary Era*. Cambridge: Cambridge University Press, 1996.

Tutorow, Norman E. *Leland Stanford: Man of Many Careers.* Menlo Park, California: Pacific Coast Publishers, 1971.

Vitruvius. *The Ten Books of Architecture (De Architectura)*. Translated by Morris H. Morgan, Ph.D., New York: Dover Publications, Inc., 1960.

Waite, Arthur Edward. *A New Encyclopedia of Freemasonry and of Cognate Instituted Mysteries: Their Rites, Literature, and History*. 1970. Reprint, New York: Wings Books, 1994.

Walker, Barbara. *The Woman's Dictionary of Sacred Symbols and Objects*. San Francisco: Harper & Row, Publishers, Inc., 1988.

Walker, Barbara. *The Woman's Encyclopedia of Myths and Secrets*. San Francisco: Harper & Row, Publishers, Inc., 1983.

Walker, D. P. *The Ancient Theology: Studies in Christian Platonism from the Fifteenth to the Eighteenth Century*. London: Gerald Duckworth and Company Ltd., 1972.

Wallace-Murphy, Tim. *The Enigma of the Freemasons: Their History and Mystical Connections*. New York: The Ivy Press Limited, 2006.

Wasserman, James. *The Secrets of Masonic Washington: A Guidebook to Signs, Symbols, and Ceremonies at the Origin of America's Capital*. Rochester, Vermont: Inner Traditions, 2008.

Wasserman, James. *The Templars and the Assassins: The Militia of Heaven*. Rochester, Vermont: Inner Traditions, 2001.

Webb, Thomas Smith. *Freemasons' Monitor or Illustrations of Freemasonry*. 1797. 1802. Parts I and II in one volume, Salem, Massachusetts: Cushing and Appleton, 1808.

Webster, Nesta H. *Secret Societies and Subversive Movements*. 1924. Reprint, Hawthorne, California: Christian Book Club, n.d.

Weinbren, Daniel. *The Oddfellows 1810-2010: 200 years of making friends and helping people*. Lancaster, England: Carnegie Publication Ltd., 2010.

Weil, Simone. *Intimations of Christianity Among the Ancient Greeks*. London: Ark Paperbacks, 1987.

Weir, Alison. *Henry VIII: The King and His Court*. New York: Ballantine Books, 2008.

Wentz, Abdel Ross. *Pioneer in Christian Unity: Samuel Simon Schmucker*. Philadelphia: Fortress Press, 1967.

Wiebe, Robert H. *The Search for Order: 1877-1920*. New York: Hill and Wang, 1967.

Willey, Basil. *The Eighteenth Century Background: Studies in the Idea of Nature in the Thought of the Period*. London: Chatto and Windus, 1940.

Williams, Penry. *The Late Tudors: England 1547-1603*. Oxford: Oxford University Press, 1998.

Wilson, Colin. *The Occult: A History*. New York: Random House, 1971.

Wilson, John F. *Public Religion in American Culture*. Philadelphia: Temple University Press, 1979.

Wolf, John B. *The Emergence of the Great Powers, 1685-1715*. New York: Harper and Row, Publishers, Inc., 1951.

Wood, Gordon S. *The Americanization of Benjamin Franklin*. New York: Penguin Press, 2004.

Wright, Jonathan. *God's Soldiers: Adventure, Politics, Intrigue, and Power - A History of the Jesuits*. New York: Doubleday, 2004.

Wright, Louis B. *The First Gentlemen of Virginia: Intellectual Qualities of the Early Colonial Ruling Class*. Charlottesville: Dominion Books, 1964.

Yates, Frances A. *The Art of Memory*, London: Routledge & Kegan Paul. 1966.

Yates, Frances A. *Giordano Bruno and the Hermetic Tradition*. London: Routledge & Kegan Paul, 1964.

Yates, Frances A. *The Occult Philosophy of the Elizabethan Age*. London: Routledge & Kegan Paul, 1979.

Yates, Frances A. *The Rosicrucian Enlightenment*. London: Routledge & Kegan Paul, 1972.

Yates, Frances A. *Theatre of the World*, Chicago: The University of Chicago Press, 1969.

INDEX

Note: Terms that are common to this book and repeat often such as (but not limited to) "Enoch," "Freemasonry," "DeWitt Clinton," "Royal Arch," "Masonry," "Scottish Rite," "Solomon," "York Rite," "Thomas Smith Webb," and "William Preston," etc., do not appear in the Index. Some of these terms are the specific content of chapters.

Printed in August 2023
by Rotomail Italia S.p.A., Vignate (MI) - Italy